Literary Lives

This classic and longstanding series has established itself making a major contribution to literary biography. The books in the series are thoroughly researched and comprehensive, covering the writer's complete oeuvre. The latest volumes trace the literary, professional, publishing, and social contexts that shaped influential authors—exploring the "why" behind writers' greatest works. In its thirtieth year, the series aims to publish on a diverse set of writers—both canonical and rediscovered—in an accessible and engaging way.

More information about this series at
http://www.palgrave.com/gp/series/14010

Adam Roberts

H G Wells

A Literary Life

palgrave
macmillan

Adam Roberts
Department of English
Royal Holloway, University of London
Egham, Surrey, UK

Literary Lives
ISBN 978-3-030-26420-8   ISBN 978-3-030-26421-5   (eBook)
https://doi.org/10.1007/978-3-030-26421-5

Cover illustration: Lebrecht Music & Arts / Alamy Stock Photo

This Palgrave Macmillan imprint is published by the registered company Springer Nature Switzerland AG.
The registered company address is: Gewerbestrasse 11, 6330 Cham, Switzerland

Preface

This is a literary biography of the English writer Herbert George Wells, and its emphasis is, by design, more on the literary than the biographical. The latter forms the spine of the book, and what follows provides, I hope, a reasonably thorough-going account of Wells's life. But my focus is on what Wells wrote, in both fiction and non-fiction. I make no claims to have uncovered any new material about Wells's actual life. Indeed, I'm not convinced there *are* any new biographical discoveries lurking in the archives: the 'secret' elements of Wells biography—his many extramarital affairs, his two illegitimate children—have long been known. Not only did he often fictionalise these adventures in his novels, he wrote a lengthy and detailed account of that side of his life for posthumous publication (it finally appeared under the title *H. G. Wells in Love* in 1984 and is often quoted in what follows). Wells was an individual constitutionally disinclined to secrecy. He was also, as it happens, an extraordinary and powerful writer, much of whose immense oeuvre has fallen into public neglect. The purpose of the present volume is to try and address that latter neglect and to come to some conclusions about the brilliance.

Wells described himself, in his own *Experiment in Autobiography* (1934) as an 'originative intellectual worker', describing the type as 'not a normal human being': 'he does not lead nor desire to lead a normal human life. He wants to lead a supernormal life.' Much of Wells's life was indeed supernormal, not least the sheer sustained quantity of good writing he produced across six decades. I have tried, in this book, to neglect nothing important in that output, but the constraints of space have proved continually pinching. It can't be helped, but it leads to some compression. Conventional biographies of Wells all follow the *Experiment in Autobiography* in giving a good deal of space to their accounts of Wells's childhood: the lower-middle-class milieu into which he was born, his mother a housekeeper at Uppark (sometimes called 'Up Park') in West Sussex, his more indigent shopkeeper father, the attempts to confine Wells in the bonds of various trade apprenticeships. It is a compelling story and important to an understanding of Wells as a writer, not least because Wells himself returned to it often in his fiction. But for my purposes, and considering the limited space available to me, I do not indulge my fascination with that period at the expense of Wells's later decades. Indeed, one of my main purposes in writing this book has been to open up awareness of the novels Wells wrote in the 1920s and after. The consensus is that *Mr Britling Sees It Through* (1916) is the last notable novel of Wells's career, and even that title is little read today—his science fiction and (perhaps) *Ann Veronica, Kipps* and *Mr Polly* aside, pretty much his entire corpus has fallen into desuetude. That's not only surprising, it's an injustice; and many—though I concede, not all—of the later novels are fascinating and brilliant.

Wells's reputation today is a curious thing. During his own life he was, arguably, the most famous writer in the world: a novelist, short-story writer, journalist, social critic and (handling the word with the sugar-tongs of scare-quotes) 'prophet' with genuinely international reach, the personal friend of Presidents and press magnates, of film-stars and writers and philosophers, from America to Russia, from Europe to Australia. He sold extraordinary quantities of his books, commanded immense fees for his journalism, more-or-less single-handedly defined (if he didn't quite invent) British science fiction and left his mark indelibly on the novel of lower-middle-class aspiration. But his reputation was already waning by the 1940s, and in the aftermath of his death much of his brilliance has become eclipsed—his social prophecy proved inaccurate, new generations of socialists discarded his influence as a political thinker and people stopped reading his many novels. The exception in this latter case is his science fiction, works largely the product of his first decade of concerted literary production, and a mode he himself pretty much disavowed in later life as he moved into different literary genres, but nonetheless work that has been kept vigorously alive by generations of science fiction fans. In five novels in particular, Wells created more-or-less from whole cloth the premises for what became some of the most important SF modes of the twentieth and twenty-first centuries: *The Time Machine* (1895) the first notable description of technologically facilitated time travel; *The Island of Doctor Moreau* (1896) which stands at the head of a SF tradition of stories about 'uplifted' or scientifically enhanced animals; *The Invisible Man* (1897) the first SF treatment of invisibility; his nonpareil alien invasion narrative *War of the Worlds* (1898) and *When The Sleeper Wakes* (1899) which Leon Stover describes as 'the one single source inspiring all the great dystopian novels of the twentieth century, from *We* to *Brave New World* to *Nineteen Eighty-Four*' [Stover, 12]. SF fans are, in the main, passionate about their genre and have done more to keep Wells's name and writing alive than any other body of readers. And since SF has grown from a congeries of small-scale local fandoms in the 1960s and 1970s through an increasing domination of blockbuster cinema by SF in the period after *Star Wars* (1977) to the situation today, when SF and superhero movies dominate global culture, the significance and fame of these earlier Wells's titles prevail.

This preface is as good a place as any for a personal note, and something at least approaching full disclosure. It was through his SF that I first read and fell in love with H.G. Wells, and it is only subsequently that I came to read and admire his other kinds of writing. I am now Professor of Nineteenth-Century Literature at Royal Holloway, University of London. I am also a science fiction writer, and in all of my 20 published novels can be discerned the manifest influence of Wells's SF. It is was one of the great honours of my life to have been elected, as I was in 2018, Vice President of the H.G. Wells Society.

Whilst I'm touching on personal matters, and on the principle that (absolute neutrality in a biographer being a chimera) the reader deserves to know in what ways I am positioned with respect to my subject, I'll add a few more prefatory notes. My love for SF, and Wells's SF in particular, is something of which I am unashamed, and inflects my sense of his larger achievement as a writer. I note that my political affiliations—although of course I aim for an ideologically neutral tone in what follows—are what you might call left-wing, and find much common ground with Wells's political views. Wells was as important an advocate for socialism as any of his generation (although I cannot share his enthusiasm for a putative World State, and I find his flirtations with eugenics and anti-Semitism repellent). It is common enough, I understand, for biographers to come to identify with their subjects, as dogs grow to resemble their owners, and the longer I have worked on Wells the more I have been struck by intervital parallels. Like Wells, I publish prolifically, dividing my time between fiction, especially science fiction, and non-fiction. Wells was born in the summer of 1866 and grew up in Bromley, south-east London. I was born in the summer of 1965—exactly 99 years later—and grew up in Sydenham, close-by (just on the far side of the Beckenham cricket pitch where Wells's father sometimes played). My background is more middle-class than was Wells's, but only because of the advances in social welfare in twentieth-century Britain which, in a small but definite way, his proselytising for socialism brought about. My parents were, in Neil Kinnock's resonant phrase, the first in their families for a thousand generations to go to University, and I am accordingly only one step away from the *echt* Wellsian servant's parlour and shop counter. Like Wells I was a sickly, bookish youth. Like him I was moved away from London for my teenage years (in his case to Sussex, in mine to East Kent) into boredom and misery, which existence was eventually relieved by the possibilities opened-up by further education. Wells won a scholarship to the Normal School of Science in South Kensington, now part of Imperial College, itself part of University of London, at which university I presently work—in 1890 Wells earned his BSc from the University of London's external programme. Wells worked as a (school) teacher in the 1890s, living in a number of places to the west and south-west of London whilst simultaneously pulling together the beginnings of his writing career. I worked as a (university) teacher in the 1990s, living in a number of places to the west and south-west of London whilst simultaneously pulling together the beginnings of my writing career. And here I have stuck: for the last quarter-century my home has been variously Windsor, Egham, Putney, Staines and Ascot, and this whole territory—over which Wells's Martian tripods march in their devastating triumph—is intensely familiar to me. Wells lived in Woking, a few miles south-east of where I am writing these words, and then in Kingston (my daughter was born in Kingston hospital) before moving to Sandgate in 1901 to construct his own house.

And at this point I'll stop, in case my listing of these distant parallels really does begin to sound too absurdly hubristic. Wells's writing quickly made him both a literary star and a wealthy man. Through the 1900s Wells consolidated his position as one of the most prominent thinkers, journalists and writers of his generation. During the 2000s I very much didn't do anything of the kind. By 1919, 100 years before the writing of this present work, Wells was globally admired and influential, living a life of expansive sexual licence and world travel, working on a book (the *Outline of History*) that was to become one of the bestselling and most influential works of history ever written. None of this has even the remotest parallel in my dully conventional and unremarkable life. Indeed, the starkness of the difference between Wells's life and mine would be comical if it weren't so ordinary. But that ordinariness is precisely the point. The heart of Wells's achievement is that he was able to parlay his ordinariness into something *extra*ordinary, in his life as much as in his art. My lived experience of the former gives, once we factor in a century's changes in day-to-day life in south-east England, enough of an insight to be able, I think, to say something about that ordinariness, even if much of my perspective on that extraordinariness must perforce assume a kind of starstruck astonishment at just how much he achieved, and just how good he was. The purpose, in other words, of these last two paragraphs has been to establish that this present text has been written out of a position of genuine admiration for Wells the writer, and an equally genuine, if more conflicted, love for Wells the man.

A brief note on the format of what follows. With the exception of the very first, the chapters of this literary biography accrete around particular Wellsian books. In many cases these works are no longer in print, and most are little read. I have accordingly included summaries of plot and examples of style, that my analyses might be grounded in more than mere assertion. These summaries necessarily include spoilers for the stories concerned, and if you wish to avoid such you are advised to read the novels themselves first. In the absence of a uniform edition of Wells's books I have consulted first editions, noting textual variants rarely and only if relevant. To avoid any excession of footnotes references are incorporated into the main body of my text, and in the case of Wells's writing are identified by short-title followed by book, part, chapter (references to secondary criticism are tagged to page numbers).

I note two more things before proceeding. The remit of the present study includes both Wells's fiction and his non-fiction, and I attempt to give as full an account of both sides of Wells's writerly career as I can in the space permitted me. As far as the fiction goes I am interested in the literary and aesthetic calibre of Wells achievement and remain determined to challenge the widespread but erroneous belief that Wells's novels are formless or baggy, expressions of a naïve naturalistic desire to express the bagginess and shapelessness of life. It is my belief, as a literary critic, that Wells's novels are nothing whatsoever of the sort. Critics have been rather misled by Wells's own statements in this regard. Such a literary-critical claim can only be substantiated with a large quantity of evidence from the works themselves. Mindful of the constraints of space I have 'read' a few indicative novels at the sort of length needful to illustrate the extraordinary care Wells took into creating a high degree of artistry in his fiction—my accounts of *Love and Mr Lewisham*, *Kipps* and *William Clissold* are longer than some of his other novels to this end.

On the question of Wells's non-fiction it seems to me a critic has two duties. One is to try to summarise, and understand, Wells's various views in a way that situates them in the context of the era that produced them. I hope I have done that here. But another, equally important, though more often overlooked, duty is to engage with those ideas as living quantities, to pay Wells the compliment of taking them seriously *as* ideas, rather than as quaint artefacts of a bygone age. The beginning of the twenty-first century is, in some ways, very different to the beginning of the 20th; but then again, during the writing of the present volume, questions of resurgence nationalism and nativism, of anti-Semitism and 'race purity', of the viability of socialism and the pressures of fascism, have at no point been out of the news. Since engaging these ideas was core to Wells's career as a writer of non-fiction, I sometimes discuss the ideas in Wells's non-fiction in modern-day as well as contemporary contexts. In other regards this literary biography can, I trust, speak for itself.

Bibliography

Leon Stover (ed), *When the Sleeper Wakes: a Critical Text of the 1899 New York and London First Edition* (McFarland, 2000).

Contents

List of Figures

1

Childhood

Herbert George Wells was born upstairs at 'Atlas House', a crockery and glassware shop run by his parents at 162 High Street Bromley in what was then Kent but is now Greater London. The massive expansion of the metropolis, inexorably swallowing land from its surrounding counties, stands as objective correlative to the changes of the intervening century-and-a-half, a tide of increasing urbanisation and technological development that Wells in his writing, of course, anticipated.

Bertie, as he was known in the family, was the fourth and last child of Joseph Wells, formerly a domestic gardener, by this time a shopkeeper and professional cricketer, and his wife, Sarah Wells née Neal, who had worked in domestic service. Both were relatively old when Bertie was born. Sarah, born in 1822, was approaching her 44th birthday when she went into labour, a parlous age to give birth, even today. Joseph was a few years younger: born in 1828, the son of the head gardener at Penshurst Place in West Kent. In his son's words, Joseph 'grew up to gardening and cricket, and remained an out-of-doors, open-air man to the day of his death'. He could read and do rudimentary sums, but this was the limit of his book-learning. He was, however, a remarkably talented cricketer. At this time, the sport was divided into upper-class 'gentlemen' and lower-class 'players', and payment for the latter was ex gratia, which made it hard to make a living at the game. But Joseph Wells still has a place in the cricketing history books as the first bowler ever to take four wickets in four consecutive balls in a first-class match—a fantastically rare bowling achievement. This feat occurred when Kent played Sussex at Brighton in 1862, and one of the four wickets Wells took was Spencer Austen-Leigh's—Jane

© The Author(s) 2019
A. Roberts, *H G Wells*, Literary Lives, https://doi.org/10.1007/978-3-030-26421-5_1

Austen's great-nephew—which provides a connection, howsoever tenuous, between *Pride and Prejudice* and *War of the Worlds*. Cricketing is a seasonal sport and income from it in the nineteenth century much too precarious to live upon, so Joseph Wells also undertook manual work. It was whilst working in the gardens at Uppark, a stately home in West Sussex near the Hampshire border that he met and courted Sarah Neal, then a lady's maid.

Sarah, though also lower-middle-class, was a notch or two socially superior to her future husband. Her father, a Chichester innkeeper, had found the money for more extensive schooling than was usually the case for women of her class in the mid-nineteenth century, which meant she was more literate and refined than Joe and also more religious. Indeed, friction between Sarah's devout low church Anglicanism and Joseph's freethinking agnosticism made the marriage troublesome, as did the fundamental mismatch of their personalities. Their first child, a girl called Frances, was born in 1856. After a period in which Joe proved unable to settle at a variety of country-house gardening jobs, the two moved to Bromley. Joe had inherited a £100 on the death of his father and the two of them used this money to acquire Atlas House from Joe's cousin George Wells and furnish it with china crockery and glassware. Neither had any experience as shopkeepers and though Sarah was less feckless than Joseph, the shop, ill-situated and unprepossessing, did not prosper. Joseph's cricket occasionally supplemented the family income and, hoping to improve matters, Joseph began to stock cricket bats, balls and gear alongside the crockery; a strange combination of saleables that did little to attract customers.

After their daughter two boys were born to the couple—Frank in 1857 and Fred in 1862—before their first-born, little Frances, died in 1864. H.G. Wells later said that 'deep down in my mother's heart something was broken when my sister died two years and more before I was born. Her simple faith was cracked then and its reality spilled away' [*Experiment in Autobiography*, 44]. Sarah's anxiety at being able to support the family, and her increasing estrangement from her husband, were compounded by her proneness to what we would nowadays call depression. Joseph was often away, and after Herbert George's birth in 1866, his parents took to sleeping in separate rooms: the back bedroom for Sarah and a front room for Joe. Wells later wrote that 'this separation was, I think, their form of birth control'.

A broken leg marked a turning point in young H.G.'s life. In the summer of 1874, when he was seven and playing outside, one of his father's friends, a man called Sutton, picked him up and tossed him in the air, accidentally dropping him. Wells landed across a tent peg and broke his tibia. Weeks of convalescence followed—the bone, badly set, had to be re-broken and reset. It was time which Wells spent in bed reading. His father brought him books home from the Bromley Institute. 'I cannot recall now many of the titles of the books I read, I devoured them so fast' he later noted. Amongst the ones he could remember were books of imperial adventure, Wood's *Natural History*, histories of the Duke of Wellington and the American Civil War, the works of Washington Irving and Fenimore Cooper as well as 'the bound volumes of *Punch*':

> The bound periodicals with their political cartoons and their quaint details played a curious part in developing my imaginative framework. My ideas of political and international relations were moulded very greatly by the big figures of John Bull and Uncle Sam… And across the political scene also marched tall and lovely feminine figures, Britannia, Erin, Columbia, La France, bare armed, bare necked, showing beautiful bare bosoms, revealing shining thighs, wearing garments that were a revelation in an age of flounces and crinolines. My first consciousness of women, my first stirrings of desire were roused by these heroic divinities. I became woman-conscious from those days onward. [*Experiment in Autobiography*, 55]

Wells received his first formal education 1874–80 at Thomas Morley's Commercial Academy, a private school only a few doors down Bromley High Street from Atlas House. Wells's two older brothers were apprenticed into the draper's trade. Then, in 1877, Joseph Wells fell from a garden trellis and broke *his* leg so badly it put an end to his career as a cricketer. The subsequent reduction in family income took a toll on the family. Sarah could rarely afford to buy meat; bills went unpaid. When Frank finished his apprenticeship and took his first proper job as a draper's assistant (at a meagre 10 shillings a week) he gave Sarah money to buy young Bertie boots and she wept with relief. Joseph's accident left him sullen and withdrawn, and it was this emotional breakdown of the marriage, as much as Sarah's need to earn money, that led to their final separation. Sarah was still fondly remembered by the family at Uppark and in 1880 was offered the job of housekeeper, which she took, leaving Atlas House for good and moving to West Sussex.

Bertie, 14 now, was apprenticed to a draper's shop as his brothers had been before him: an upmarket establishment in Windsor called Rodgers and Denyer. Apprentices lived in, worked from 7:30 am until 8:30 pm 6 days a week and received sixpence pocket-money. Wells's portrait of this life in *Kipps* is a vivid account of the boredom and drudgery involved. Constitutionally unsuited to the life, he soon lost this position and for a time he worked as a pupil-teacher in Wookey, in Somerset, a school run by a distant relative called Alfred Williams—a larger-than-life character with a hook for a hand and the booming jollity of a natural confidence-man. But Uncle Williams's educational credentials were forgeries and Government Inspectors deprived him of the school in 1880. Wells returned to his mother at Uppark. He spent the winter of 1880–81 expanding his reading. Sir Harry Fetherstonhaugh, the house's quondam owner, 'had been a free-thinker, and the rooms downstairs abounded in bold and enlightening books'.

> I was allowed to borrow volumes and carry them off to my room. Then or later, I cannot now recall when, I improved my halting French with Voltaire's lucid prose, I read such books as *Vathek* and *Rasselas*, I nibbled at Tom Paine, I devoured an unexpurgated *Gulliver's Travels* and I found Plato's *Republic*. That last was a very releasing book indeed for my mind, I had learnt the trick of mocking at law and custom from Uncle Williams… Here was the amazing and heartening suggestion that the whole fabric of law, custom and worship, which seemed so invincibly established, might be cast into the melting pot and made anew. [*Experiment in Autobiography*, 106–7]

This is Wells looking back in 1934, and his stress on Swift and Plato reflects a desire to dignify his intellectual pedigree in the light of the non-fictional and utopian work he had done in the twentieth century. What is not mentioned here, because he was so ubiquitous a figure that he went without saying, was Dickens, whom Wells read often and intently. He went on to be much more of a Dickensian writer of fiction than he was a Swiftian or Platonic one.

Young Wells, however, could not be allowed to rest idle. His mother arranged for a new apprenticeship, this time at a chemist's shop in Midhurst, a West Sussex village a few miles from Uppark: Samuel Cowap's emporium in Church Hill. Wells started for a trial period of 1 month, during which his deficiency in Latin—considered a necessity for a dispensing chemist—was addressed by lessons in Midhurst Grammar School under the tutelage of Horace Byatt. The apprenticeship at the chemist's was never articled, but after his trial month in the shop came to an end the young Wells stayed on at Byatt's school. He hurried through the curriculum, eager to learn, but his mother was set upon his learning a trade as his older brothers had before him. She arranged a second draper's apprenticeship, at Edwin Hyde's shop on the King's Road at Southsea, on the Hampshire coastline. Wells protested but had no choice in the matter and took up his position in May 1881—more 13-hour days, more being constantly harassed and chivvied by superiors, more rounds of mind-dulling drudge work. Wells endured this labour for 2 years—a remarkable stretch of time, in retrospect—experiencing bouts of depression and suicidal ideation. He dreamt of leaving, but his mother had paid Hyde a bond of £40, a large sum, and he did not feel he could.

It is worth pausing for a moment on this development. We are likely to read Wells's life teleologically, as it were—with, that is, a sense of where it was going. From that perspective, these adolescent experiences of Wells's, though clearly detours from the true path his life would take, at least provided valuable raw material from which some of his best, and most influential, writing would later be crafted. We might even take this fact as providing a redemption of and therefore justification for the existential misery entailed. But life is not lived retrospectively, and for Wells's 2 years of misery, at this key early stage in his life, meant that a consciousness of existential *frustration* became constitutive of his larger being-in-the-world. This is evident in various practical senses. He was always afterwards motivated to work both hard and tirelessly, to avoid falling back into any such state of powerlessness, and it left him with a lifelong sympathy for the disempowered underclasses of the world. But it is also evident psycho-sexually. Frustration is, after all, the plastic idiom of desire, and Wells's desiring appetites were on a scale to dwarf those of many people. The contrast with Dickens, aforementioned, is instructive: two hugely successful novelists, both from lower-middle-class backgrounds, both driven by a ferocious work ethic and social conscience, and both marked by a sense of having been banished, at a young age, into a work environment as demeaning as it was exhausting. For Dickens, this was his experience working in a Blacking Factory in the 1820s, something he fictionalised in *David Copperfield*. But the differences, as well as the similarities, are interesting: Dickens resented his experience bitterly and felt so acute a shame about the episode that he kept it secret from everybody (including his wife) with the one exception of his best friend John Forster. More, he blamed his mother: the abortive autobiographical fragment Dickens drafted, and which Forster published for the first time in his *Life of Dickens* (1872), ends: 'my father said I should go back no more, and should go to school. I do not write resentfully or angrily: for I know how all these things have worked together to make me what I am: but I never afterwards forgot, I never shall forget, I never can forget, that my mother was warm for my being sent back.' Wells, though the experience of apprenticeship made him miserable, never resented it in this fashion, and certainly never felt it to be intrinsically shameful. Nor did he blame his mother, with whom he was extremely close all through his life. He did not feel as catastrophically aban-doned as Dickens had done, and when he fictionalises the experience in *Kipps* and elsewhere, the tone is neither resentful nor shamed.

At any rate, the draper's life proved increasingly intolerable. Two years in, with 2 years of his apprenticeship still remaining, matters finally came to a crisis. Sixteen-year-old Wells screwed his courage up and left. By mid-1883 his indentures at Hyde's had been cancelled and Bertie began a new life as a student-teacher at Midhurst School.

Wells was much certainly better suited to teaching than he had been to drapery. He worked hard at Midhurst, cramming the school's older boys for examinations attached to a governmental scheme to train science teachers. The school received money for pupils who passed the government's exams—£4 for an advanced pass, less for a bare pass—and Wells successfully guided several pupils to the highest marks. Indeed he did so well in this line that in 1884 the 18-year-old Wells was himself offered a government-funded scholarship to attend the Normal School in South Kensington to study science. 'Normal Schools', based on the model of the French *Écoles Normales*, were so called because they sought to instil and reinforce certain norms in their students—most were in fact what we now call 'teacher-training colleges'. Thomas Henry Huxley, the famous scientist and evolutionary theorist, known as 'Darwin's bulldog', had established the South Kensington school and Wells, when he took up his place, was taught biology and chemistry by Huxley himself, as well as by various other teachers and laboratory demonstrators. Wells never got to know Huxley beyond saying 'good morning' to him whilst holding open the door for him to pass through, but he later declared him 'the greatest man' he ever met. 'I was under the shadow of Huxley, the acutest observer, the ablest generalizer, the great teacher, the most lucid and valiant of controversialists,' Wells recalled in his *Autobiography*. 'I had been assigned to his course in Elementary Biology and afterwards I was to go on with Zoology under him' adding 'that year I spent in Huxley's class, was beyond all question, the most educational year of my life'. After 3 years of false starts, he began to believe he had finally settled into the proper groove of his life.

He hadn't, though. At the beginning, taught by Huxley, Wells worked hard and passed his first-year examinations with first-class honours. He spent a happy summer visiting his father in Bromley and going down to his mother in Uppark. But his second year went less well: lectures no longer delivered by the inspiring Huxley, but instead by the dull Professor Guthrie. Wells's dedication slackened. He did poorly on his second-year exams and lost focus further in his third and final year. He had hoped the Normal School would prepare him for a career as a research scientist, but after graduating he had instead to ready himself for the life of a schoolteacher.

One of the distractions during his third year had been his own writing, something he had dabbled at for several years and which he now attempted in a more systematic way. He and friends from the South Kensington Debating Society established a magazine, which they called the *Science Schools Journal*.

Wells edited this until the school registrar reprimanded him for neglecting his studies, and he passed the job over to a friend. Though the *Journal* was in effect a school magazine it provided an outlet for Wells's first creative work. A couple of whimsical science-fiction shorts appeared, under the pseudonym 'Septimus Browne': 'A Talk with Gryllotalpa' (February 1887), on the enormousness of cosmic perspectives, and 'A Tale of the Twentieth Century' (May 1887), a jollier piece about a perpetual motion machine causing ructions on the London Underground. Much more importantly for the writer Wells was to become it was the *Science Schools Journal* that published 'The Chronic Argonauts' (across three issues, April, May and June 1888), the first version of what would later become *The Time Machine*.

Part of the responsibility for Wells's academic underachievement can be laid at the door of his distractibility: reading Carlyle and looking at Blake's engravings in the Art Room rather than buckling down to his studies. Part of it was indigence: a guinea a week (3 shillings a day, most of which went on rent) was not much to live on, and Wells often missed meals. One pen-portrait from his *Autobiography* has him sitting in his rented room, reading by candlelight with his topcoat on and his feet wrapped in his underwear for warmth resting in the bottom drawer of his clothes-chest. But a third, more enduring distraction was sex, or the lack of sex. Wells, though malnourished, underweight and prone to illness, was a highly sexed individual, something for which life as yet provided him no outlets. As is often the case with this sort of erotic frustration Wells reacted by retreating into a quasi-priggish coolness. His few youthful clinches with girls struck him as 'hot, uncomfortable, shamefaced stuff'. A more straightforward individual might simply have sublimated his erotic desire into his studies, but Wells was never a straightforward individual. He walked the streets, unable to afford and in any case rather repelled by, the city's many prostitutes. At his first London lodgings, 'my landlady came into my room to change the pillowcase while I was there and provoked me into a quasi-amorous struggle. She was wearing a print dress carelessly or carefully unhooked at the neck.' When the young Bertie did not respond 'she became reproachful.' The thought of sex, he later recalled, 'excited me considerably, bothered me with contradictory impulses, disgusted me' and most of all 'interfered vexatiously with the proper copying out of my notes of Professor Huxley's lectures'.

In 1886 Wells moved to new lodgings in 181 Euston Road run by his Aunt Mary—she had been married to Wells's father's brother, a man who had himself failed as a draper and died in the workhouse. His widow, though, had prospered as a landlady. Wells recalled Aunt Mary as a 'lovable' woman and

Wells lived with her for nearly 2 years. Here he met Mary's daughter, his own cousin, Isabel:

> A dark-eyed girl of my own age, in the simple and pretty 'art' dress that then prevailed came shyly into the room and stood looking at us. She had a grave and lovely face, very firmly modelled, broad brows and a particularly beautiful mouth and chin and neck. [*Experiment in Autobiography*, 227]

Isabel and Wells were poorly matched. She had no interest in books or learning, was reserved to the point to shyness and if we are to believe Wells's own account, was moved by no great sexual urgency. He, however, fell desperately in both love and lust with her, a state of affairs the prim restraint of their courtship—walking around London, 'whispering in a darkened staircase, hugging in furtive silence on a landing'—naturally inflamed. She was, presumably, flattered by the attention of her clever and eloquent cousin, and though he was skinny, unprepossessing and often ill photographs of the young Bertie show a sweet face and attractive eyes. More, he was charismatic, clever and funny. In Isabel, Wells had found a person passive enough not to interfere with the fantasies he projected upon her, respectable enough not to trigger his sexual aversion (throughout his life Wells made something of a sexual fetish of 'cleanness') and pretty and pliable enough to engage his erotic yearning.

Leaving the Normal School with neither a strong degree nor enthusiastic references, Wells took such work as was available to him, leaving his incipient relationship with Isabel hanging fire. His first job took him far from London, to work as a teacher at the Holt Academy, a private school near Wrexham on the border between North Wales and England. The school was remote and ill-run, and Wells struggled to teach the classes of recalcitrant and resentful boys. During this time he wrote a number of short stories. One he worked on for a while had the wince-inducing title 'The Death of Miss Peggy Picksersgill's Cat' (since Wells later burnt it, its contents remain a mystery). He flirted with the minister's daughter Annie Meredith, seemingly forgetting, at least temporarily, his passion for his London cousin. Annie rejected his advances on the grounds (as she later recalled) 'he told me he was an atheist and a socialist' [Mackenzies, 71]. Frustration remained the dominant mode of Wells's young life.

As is the case at many private schools in Britain, then as now, there was at Holt more emphasis on sport than book-learning, and although he was a weakling Wells had enough youthful bravado to attempt the life athletic. In the autumn of 1887 he played football with the boys:

I had a rough time on the field because that was where the bigger louts got back upon me for my English accent and my irritating assumption of superior erudition. One bony youngster fouled me. He stooped, put his shoulders under my ribs, lifted me, and sent me sprawling. [*Experiment in Autobiography*, 242–43]

It proved a serious injury: 'there was a vast pain in my side. In the house, I was violently sick. I went to lie down. Then I was moved to urinate and found myself staring at a chamber-pot half full of scarlet blood. That was the most dismaying moment in my life. I did not know what to do.' A doctor diagnosed a crushed kidney, which can certainly cause haematuria, but which, though Wells accepted the diagnosis, seems unlikely. The fact that the pain soon diminished and that he passed no more blood suggests something else had transpired (perhaps temporary laceration in the bladder or urethra). Wells wanted to return to his mother and convalesce but leaving the school would have meant forfeiting the £20 half-year's salary due to him at Christmas, so he returned, unwell, to work. Within a week he was coughing up blood, something he connected with the footballing injury ('my lungs were imitating my kidney') although there was surely no physiological link between the two things. A second doctor at the time diagnosed tuberculosis, which would probably have been a death-sentence had it been an accurate assessment of his health—it's more likely Wells had some severe inflammation of the lungs, perhaps pleurisy. He was nauseous. He himself later speculated that he had appendicitis, but since his appendix was never removed, and appendicitis is not a condition that simply disappears, this cannot have been the case. Still, there's no question that Wells's health was chronically poor throughout his life. He suffered from an ongoing, if imprecise, pulmonary condition, anxiety concerning which tended to make worse. In later life he was diagnosed as a diabetic. Working in an unheated classroom during a Welsh winter, eating too little and suffering various physical shocks certainly did his health no good. At any rate, he proved physically incapable of continuing at Holt Academy despite his best intentions. In December 1887 Wells forfeited his salary, took the train from Wrexham down to London and from there travelled to his mother at Uppark.

Joseph, his father, had given up the hopeless Bromley shop some years earlier and had come down to Sussex to live in a little cottage near Uppark, the rent for which was paid by his estranged wife. Wells's brothers also came to the house for Christmas 1887, by which time Bertie reported that he was feeling a little better. He beguiled the time by writing a 35,000-word novel of love and romance, later destroyed, called *Lady Frankland's Companion*. A friend from South Kensington, William Burton, had taken a job as an industrial chemist for the Wedgwood company in the Potteries and in April 1888 Wells travelled up to stay with him in Stoke-on-Trent. The journey wore Wells out, and there was blood in his sputum when he arrived. Indeed, with his illness and the other demands he made upon them, Burton and his wife found Wells to be a trying guest. But the new industrialised surroundings, quite unlike anything Wells had seen before, had a salutary effect on his imagination: 'I found the Burtons and their books and their talk, and the strange landscape of the Five Towns with its blazing iron foundries, its steaming canals, its clay whitened pot-banks and the marvellous effects of its dust and smoke-laden atmosphere, very stimulating.' [*Experiment in Autobiography*, 251] He resolved to write a 'vast melodrama' of life in the potteries, 'a sort of Staffordshire *Mysteries of Paris*'. We don't know how much of this novel he actually drafted, although we know how much of it survives: none. The fact that he was planning such a project speaks as much to an uncertainty of writerly focus on Wells's part as it does to his youthful ambition.

By summer his health had improved further and he returned to lodgings in London. He met up again with his cousin Isabel and recommenced his courtship of her, this time in earnest, waiting only for a proper employment opportunity to propose marriage. In January 1889 he took up a new post as a schoolteacher at the Henley House School, in Kilburn, North London: a considerably more respectable and professional establishment than Holt. Its owner, John Vine Milne (father of A.A. Milne, the *Winnie-the-Pooh* author) had enlightened pedagogic attitudes, and Wells seems to have enjoyed the work. He also picked up the threads of his own education. In July 1889 he passed the Intermediate examination for his BSc at London University and continued studying in zoology, geology, mental and moral science. In 1890 he finally took his BSc degree, passing with first-class honours in zoology. Wells left Henley House and looked for other teaching work in London.

Again, the temptation to discern some manner of quasi-novelistic or providential shape in Wells life up to this point is probably worth resisting. He was a man in his early twenties with a variegated body of mostly unedifying life experiences behind him, some false starts in retail, some others in pedagogy. Our focus here, his writing, was developing awkwardly in fits and starts. Strictly speaking, the first book Wells published was the drily titled *Text-Book of Biology* (1893), which he jerry-rigged out of the teaching notes and set-pieces of a certain Dr William Briggs. Briggs ran a financially successful tutoring company, employing 'over forty first-class honours men' (as Wells recalled it), a team Wells joined in 1891, working out of a building off the Strand. The business involved cramming applicants 'to the widely sought-after London University Matriculation'. Briggs had gone through all the previous University matriculation examination papers, filleted the questions that tended to be repeated from year to year and prepared 'a hundred or so model answers' with which his teachers then drilled their students: a more-or-less cynical but undeniably effective approach. Briggs hired Wells to run the biology component: 'I took over and revised a course of thirty correspondence instruction papers,' Wells later recalled, 'and I developed an efficient drilling in the practical work to cover about forty hours or so of intensive laboratory work.' After Wells became famous the *Text-Book* was reprinted in 1909, revised by J.T. Cunningham; and it was reprinted yet again in 1932, when Wells was even more famous, with further revisions by W.H. Leigh-Sharpe. But though these editions present the book as being by Wells, in both cases almost all of his writing, and every last one of his original drawings, have been taken out, and the whole book rewritten and re-illustrated. Which gives some sense of the scientific merit of the original edition.

As he was plugging away at this teaching, Wells was trying to start a career as a writer of short magazines articles and stories. He also collaborated with his old fellow student R.A. Gregory from the Normal School: the two men co-wrote a small 'cram-book' called *Honours Physiography* (1893). Wells later remembered 'we sold [this] outright to a publisher for £20—which we shared, fifty-fifty'. *Honours Physiography* is, like the *Text-Book of Biology*, stodgy stuff, although the final chapter, 'General Facts of the Distribution of Life in Time and Space', kindles a small spark in the breast of the reader who knows what Wells will go on to write: 'it is difficult at first to realize how extremely localized and temporary a thing the whole career of life is, compared with the play of lifeless forces… From the point of view of the stellar astronomer, life is an entirely local thing, an eddy in one small corner of the immense scheme of Being' [*Honours Physiography*, 174–75].

Wells was also making his first serious attempts to write his own original material. He sent an article entitled 'The Rediscovery of the Unique', worked up from a paper he had read at the Debating Society in South Kensington, to the prestigious *Fortnightly Review*. He did this without expectation that they would accept it, but uncertain what else to do with it. To his astonishment, they published it in their July 1891 issue. Excited by this development, Wells sent another article (now lost) called 'The Universe Rigid'. Harris, with an access of trust in his writer unusual in editors, accepted this without reading it and sent it straight to the printers. He 'only read when he got it in proof', Wells later recalled. 'He found it incomprehensible and his immediate staff found it incomprehensible. This is not surprising, since it was a laboured and ill-written description of a four-dimensional space-time universe, and that sort of thing was still far away from the monthly reviews in 1891.' Harris summoned Wells to his office. It's worth quoting Wells's description of this encounter at length:

I found his summons disconcerting. My below-stairs training reinforced the spirit of the times on me, and insisted that I should visit him in proper formal costume. I imagined I must wear a morning coat and a silk hat and carry an umbrella. It was impossible I should enter the presence of a Great Editor in any other guise. My aunt Mary and I inspected these vitally important articles. The umbrella, tightly rolled and with a new elastic band, was not so bad, provided it had not to be opened; but the silk hat was extremely discouraging. It was very fluffy and defaced and, as I now perceived for the first time, a little brownish in places. The summons was urgent and there was no time to get it ironed. We brushed it with a hard brush and then with a soft one and wiped it round again and again with a silk handkerchief. The nap remained unsubdued. Then, against the remonstrances of my aunt Mary, I wetted it with a sponge and then brushed. That seemed to do the trick. My aunt's attempt to restrain me had ruffled and delayed me a little, but I hurried out, damply glossy, to the great encounter, my début in the world of letters.

I was shown up to a room that seemed to me enormous, in the midst of which was a long table at which the great man was sitting. At the ends were a young man, whom I was afterwards to know as Blanchamp, and a very refined looking old gentleman named Silk who was Harris's private secretary. Harris silently motioned me to a chair opposite himself ....

I got across to the table somehow, sat down and disposed myself for a conversation. I was depleted and breathless. I placed my umbrella and hat on the table before me and realized then for the first time that my aunt Mary had been right about that wetting. It had become a disgraceful hat, an insult. The damp gloss had gone. The nap was drying irregularly and standing up in little tufts all over. It was not simply a shabby top hat; it was an improper top hat. I stared at it. Harris stared at it. Blanchamp and Silk had evidently never seen such a hat. With an effort we came to the business in hand.

"You sent me this Universe Gur-R-R-Rigid," said Harris, picking up his cue after the pause.

He caught up a proof beside him and tossed it across the table. "Dear Gahd! I can't understand six words of it. What do you *mean* by it? For Gahd's sake tell me what it is all *about*? What's the sense of it? What are you trying to *say*?"

I couldn't stand up to him—and my hat. I couldn't for a moment adopt the tone and style of a bright young man of science. There was my hat tacitly revealing the sort of chap I was. I couldn't find words. Blanchamp and Silk with their chins resting on their hands, turned back from the hat to me, in gloomy silent accusation.

"Tell me what you *think* it's about?" roared Harris, growing more merciless with my embarrassment, and rapping the proof with the back of his considerable hand. He was enjoying himself.

"Well, you see——" I said.

"I *don't* see," said Harris. "That's just what I don't do."

"The idea," I said, "the idea——"

Harris became menacingly silent, patiently attentive.

"If you consider time is space like, then—I mean if you treat it like a fourth dimension like, well then you see...."

"*Gahd* the way I've been let in!" injected Harris in an aside to Gahd.

"I can't use it," said Harris at the culmination of the interview. "We'll have to disperse the type again,"—and the vision I had had of a series of profound but brilliant articles about fundamental ideas, that would make a reputation for me, vanished. My departure from that room has been mercifully obliterated from my memory. [*Experiment in Autobiography*, 294–96]

Wells still had his day-job to fall back on. Indeed, working for Briggs was rather more lucrative than a conventional teaching job. At Holt, his salary had been £40 p.a. With Briggs, and depending on the hours he taught, he could earn up to £300 a year. He also continued writing and submitting to magazines, not discouraged by the *Fortnightly* debacle, and by the early 1890s, he was generating a consistent revenue stream through this work. It all meant he was finally in a position to marry Isabel. In October 1891 he rented a house in Wandsworth, in south London, on an annual rent of £30, and on the last day of that month, he and Isabel were married in Wandsworth Parish Church.

The honeymoon period—to deploy a cliché that happens in this case actually to be germane—did not last long. At some point prior to the marriage Wells's 'secret shame' at his virginity 'became insupportable': 'I went furtively and discreetly with a prostitute. She was just an unimaginative prostitute. That deepened my wary apprehension that round about the hidden garden of desire was a jungle of very squalid and stupid lairs.' He anticipated his married sexual life would be 'flame meeting flame' and it was not. Isabel was content, it seems, to keep house for Wells whilst he caught his daily train into Central London to work at Briggs's. The two of them might have settled into conventional domesticity. But Wells's sense of sexual incompatibility between himself and his wife made him miserable.

It was a profound mortification to me, a vast disappointment, that she did not immediately respond to my ardours. She submitted. I had waited so long for this poor climax. "She does not love me," I said in my heart. I put as brave a face as I could upon the business, I dried her tears, blamed my roughness, but it was a secretly very embittered young husband who went on catching trains, correcting correspondence answer books, eviscerating rabbits and frogs and hurrying through the crowded business of every day. [*Experiment in Autobiography*, 351–52]

Matters did not improve. Wells fell prey to 'the gloomy apprehensions' that 'lovemaking was nothing more than an outrage inflicted upon reluctant womankind'. Then he had a brief affair with one of Isabel's associates, which sex proved much more satisfying. After this, Wells reports, 'my eye and fancy wandered'. He wanted 'to escape from the pit of disappointment into which I had fallen with' Isabel, whilst at the same time remaining sexually fixated upon her unresponsiveness. That might have the appearance of paradox; but actually it is, of course, common sense that the very incompletion of this sexual connection threw a glamour of erotic intensity over Isabel in Wells's imagination—the fantasy of perfect sex that, as he later put it, 'failed to embody herself in Isabel and yet had become so inseparable from her'. Within 18 months the marriage was dead, and by January 1895 they had divorced. Isabel married again some years later, to a man called Fowler-Smith, and had a child.

It is likely young Wells was unfaithful to his wife with various women, but it's certain he was with one woman in particular: Amy Catherine Robbins, one of his pupils at Briggs's academy, who was studying science with a view to becoming a schoolteacher. Amy Catherine was 6 years younger than Wells and came from a more respectable family than did he. Wells was immediately attracted to her although, given how important the articulation of sexual connection was to him, it's remarkable how little sex was to figure in this relationship as it developed. Wells and Catherine had a number of shared interests—science, socialism, writing—and were comfortable and happy in one another's company. More, both were desperate to escape a confining personal situation: for Wells his unsatisfactory marriage; for Catherine an unhappy home life. Her mother was a formidable, pious and intensely respectable widow. Her father had died after being hit by a train at Putney station—the coroner reported 'there was no sufficient evidence to show in what way he came upon the line' but suicide seems likely. We are on safe grounds hypothesising an emotionally oppressive family atmosphere for Catherine both before and after the death. Depressives certainly suffer, but those that love them certainly suffer more, and the aftermath of a suicide is always ghastly for the remaining family.

Wells wrote to his mother on 8 February 1894 that he and Isabel had separated. He rented a domicile in Hampstead for her to live in, and after their divorce paid her £100 a year in alimony for many years, even after she had remarried. Wells and Catherine eloped, much to the disgust of the latter's family, and moved into an apartment at 7 Mornington Place in North London near Camden Town. The rent, a guinea a week, was rather more than he had been paying for the Wandsworth house. Wells's financial prospects were improving.

Wells writerly productivity began to pay dividends, and he supplemented his income with reviews and articles. He wrote a weekly book review column for the *Saturday Review*, sometimes reviewed plays, and was increasingly writing comic articles and short stories. Harry Cust, editor of the *Pall Mall Gazette*, decided Wells was not being made best use of. Rather than occasional one-guinea commissions, he asked him to write regular pieces for the magazine. Lewis Hind, editor of the *Gazette*'s weekly digest and supplement *The Pall Mall Budget*, told Wells 'he was looking for single sitting shorts with a scientific flavour and would pay five guineas for anything in that line that was printable' (West, 213). Wells worked tirelessly, and later boasted of the rapidity with which his earning power increased:

In 1893 I had made £380 13s. 7d. and it had been extremely difficult to keep things going. I seem to have carried off Catherine Robbins on a gross capital of less than £100. In 1894 I earned £583 17s. 7d.; in 1895 £792 2s. 5d. and in 1896 £1,056 7s. 9d. Every year for a number of years my income went on expanding in this fashion. I was able to pay off all the costs of my divorce, pay a punctual alimony to Isabel, indulge comfortably in such diminishing bouts of ill health as still lay ahead of me, accumulate a growing surplus and presently build a home and beget children. I was able to move my father and mother and brother from Nyewoods to a better house at Liss, Roseneath, in 1896 and afterwards buy it for them. [*Experiment in Autobiography*, 310–11]

This new productivity indexes a newfound domestic contentment with Catherine. 'She was reading and making notes for her B.Sc. degree and we scribbled side by side in our front room on the ground floor, prowled about London in search of stuff for articles and had a very happy time together.' Wells wrote in pencil, Jane typed up his copy, they posted it or delivered by hand, and more often than not received proofs by return. Soon enough they had enough money to plan their wedding, and to buy their first house—not in London but 30 miles south-west of the metropolis in Woking, Surrey. 'Lynton' was a semi-detached house on Maybury Road, opposite the London railway line (the house still stands, now numbered 141 and sporting a blue plaque recording Wells's domicile). Wells and Jane took a little time to settle in: they returned to their lodgings in Mornington Road for most of October 1895, and that was the address they entered in the marriage register on 27th of that month. But they returned to Woking in November and lived happily there for a year and a half. At the end of their first year together Wells wrote to his mother with a 'picshua' (his twee term for the little doodles that are scattered promiscuously through his letters and notes) of himself writing

Fig. 1.1 Wells 'writing away for dear life', 1896

furiously at his writing desk, with the legend: 'Little Bertie writing away for dear life' and sending his love to 'Little Clock Man Little Daddy Little Mother' (Fig. 1.1).

These pet-names are a recurring feature of Wells's correspondence, and of his life too, and they lead us to one of the puzzles of his personal arrangements. He certainly loved Catherine as a person, but he had some odd animus against the *name* Catherine. In their first letters to one another they signed off as 'Bins' and 'Bits' respectively—Bins, though it looks like it is abbreviated from Catherine's maiden name, Robbins, was actually Wells, and Bits (though it *looks* a filed-down version of 'Herbert') was Catherine. Conceivably, this mode of swapping-around of identities was part of the point of the game. After their marriage Wells took to calling her 'Euphemia', and it was under that name that she appears in the short pieces collected as *Certain Personal Matters* (1897). That pet-name, however, did not stick, and by the end of the 1890s, he was calling her 'Jane', the name by which she came to be universally known. What was wrong with 'Amy' and 'Catherine', and what so appealing about 'Jane', are matters of mere conjecture, as is 'Jane's state of mind when she acceded to losing not only her maiden surname but her first names too. Conceivably she was blithe, or even actively happy, with the change; perhaps she resented it but was overborne—in this as other matters—by Wells's sheer energy and will. Jane, she had not been christened. Jane, however, she became.

Bertie and Jane's marriage lasted until the latter's death in 1927 and was, by most measures of the term, happy. Indeed we can go further and say that his second marriage provided Wells with the domestic-practical and emotional bedrock without which he would not have been able to erect the edifice of his literary career. But Wells had not found in Jane the sexual partner he desired. They enjoyed one another's company, they worked together on ideas for articles and stories, they existed 'in close association and sympathy'. Autobiographical Wells, however, adds a statement whose simplicity of statement rather belies its emotionally crushing inexorability: 'there arose no such sexual fixation between us, as still lingered in my mind towards my cousin'. One incident, recorded in the *Autobiography*, is particularly telling. In 1899 the now-divorced Isabel (and her mother) were trying to make a go of a poultry farm in Twyford, a little way west of Maidenhead. Wells cycled over to see his ex-wife, perhaps with the thought that he might invest in their concern, or otherwise provide financial support.

We spent a day together at Virginia Water, a day without tension, with an easy friendliness we had never known before. We used our old intimate names for each other. Suddenly I found myself overcome by the sense of our separation. I wanted fantastically to recover her. I implored her for the last time in vain. Before dawn the house had become unendurable for me. I got up and dressed and went down to find my bicycle and depart. She heard me moving about, perhaps she too had not slept, and she came down, kindly and invincible as ever, and as amazed as ever at my strangeness.

Because you see it was all so unreasonable.

"But you cannot go out at this hour without something to eat," she said, and set about lighting a fire and boiling a kettle.

All our old mingling of intense attraction and baffling reservation was there unchanged. "But how can things like that be, now?" she asked. I gave way to a wild storm of weeping. I wept in her arms like a disappointed child, and then suddenly pulled myself together and went out into the summer dawn and mounted my bicycle and wandered off southward into a sunlit intensity of perplexity and frustration, unable to understand the peculiar keenness of my unhappiness. I felt like an automaton, I felt as though all purpose had been drained out of me and nothing remained worthwhile. The world was dead and I was dead and I had only just discovered it. [*Experiment in Autobiography*, 359]

Wells had desired Isabel and got her. Then he had wanted to be rid of her and had desired another woman, and he got both things. This snapshot from his emotional life from the end of the decade is of a creative artist coming, painfully, to the realisation that fulfilling our desires displaces rather than satiates desire as such. It's an important, if rather plaintive, human insight and one that Wells, as he matured as a writer, would go on to explore with great imaginative richness.

Bibliography

MacKenzie, Norman and Jeanne (1973). *The Time Traveller: the life of H.G. Wells*. London: Weidenfeld and Nicholson.
West, Anthony (1984). *H G Wells: Aspects of a Life*. London: Hutchinson.

2

Short Fiction

The Stolen Bacillus and Other Incidents (1895); Certain Personal Matters (1897); The Plattner Story and Others (1897); Tales of Space and Time (1899)

When Wells stopped teaching biology for Briggs in 1894 he gave up teaching as a career altogether, instead cultivating his writing career with remarkable energy and assiduity. The foundation of this new career was the writing of comic shorts for the many journals and magazines that flourished after the roll-out of universal education that began with the 1870 Education Act created a huge new audience of literate people looking for something to read. Wells explains how he came to this lucrative mode of writing in his *Autobiography*. 'When I had been at Eastbourne [holidaying, in 1891] for two or three days, I hit quite by accident upon the true path to successful freelance journalism. I found the hidden secret in a book by J. M. Barrie, called *When a Man's Single* [1888]' That secret was to write short, comical meditations on quotidiana: pipes, umbrellas, flower-pots, cheese, that sort of thing. Wells abandoned his pretentions to high-intellectual journalism, 'rare and precious topics. Rediscovery of the Unique! Universe Rigid! The more I was rejected the higher my shots had flown. All the time I had been shooting over the target. All I had to do was to lower my aim—and hit.'

In Eastbourne, he scribbled 'an article *On Staying at the Seaside* on the back of a letter'. This he sent to his cousin Bertha Williams at Windsor 'for her to typewrite'. He posted the result to the *Pall Mall Gazette* and received a proof almost by return. 'I was already busy on a second article,' Wells recalls, 'which was also accepted.' Norman and Jean Mackenzie comment:

Wells had found the knack, at the moment when a whole new market was opening for just this kind of sketch. Even an incomplete list of his output in

© The Author(s) 2019
A. Roberts, *H G Wells*, Literary Lives, https://doi.org/10.1007/978-3-030-26421-5_2

1893 shows how quickly he learned to exploit the new situation. At least thirty articles are traceable. Their titles range from 'Out Banstead Way', 'Angels', 'The Coal Scuttle' and 'Noises of Animals' to 'The Art of Being Photographed' and 'The Theory of the Perpetual Discomfort of Humanity'. [Mackenzies, 95]

These are, really, ephemera: pieces, in David Smith's words, 'which can be read in half a dozen minutes but which will pique a reader's attention and ultimately allow him to think, "How true. I have done that myself", or to make some similar remark'. Smith speculates that the essays Wells later collected in volume form are only the iceberg's tip:

> Most of Wells's occasional pieces have not been collected, and many have not even been identified as his. Wells did not automatically receive the byline his reputation demanded until after 1896 or so … As a result, many of his early pieces are unknown. It obvious that many early Wells items have been lost. [Smith, 35]

This raises the intriguing possibility that there are some, conceivably even many, early original Wells works sitting unidentified in the back issues of the *Pall Mall Gazette* and other such magazines. Wells himself suggests as much in his *Autobiography* 'I do not now recall the order of the various sketches, dialogues and essays I produced in that opening year of journalism. They came pouring out. Some of the best of them are to be found collected in two books, still to be bought, *Certain Personal Matters* (1897) and *Select Conversations with an Uncle* (1895).' Wells certainly took pains to reprint what he could, and so extract the maximum income from his labour; but a great many pieces were never reprinted in his lifetime (scholars have latterly published several collections of this material: see, for instance, Philmus and Hughes; Hammond).

The first volume Wells mentions, *Certain Personal Matters* (1897), collected 39 pieces varying in length from a few hundred to 2000 words—whimsical bulletins from the life of an idle writer, a fictionalised version of Wells: his habits, his likes and dislikes, his wife 'Euphemia', his domestic situation and his misadventures. It would be egregious to call these pieces dated. Of course, they are dated. The mode of living, the small establishment with servants and all the paraphernalia of 1890s life has fallen into the backward and abysm of time. Then again, plenty of comic writing from this epoch still works in ways these pieces don't. Jerome K. Jerome, the enormous success of whose *Idle Thoughts of an Idle Fellow* (1886) helped create the vogue for the sort of book Wells had here published, remains hilarious, and his comic prose is still widely read today. The bald fact is that Wells, at this point in his career, simply was not as accomplished a writer of comic prose as was Jerome. A large proportion of *Certain Personal Matters* adopts a more-or-less wincing, bumptious jollity of tone. 'The Coal-Scuttle: A Study in Domestic Aesthetics' describes the shifts to which 'Euphemia' is put to hide from visitors the fact that she supplies her fire with coal:

> At first she would feign there was no such thing as coal. It was too horrible. Only a Zola would admit it. It was the epoch of concealment. The thing purchased was like a little cupboard on four legs; it might have held any convenient trifle; and there was a shelf upon the top and a book of poetry and a piece of crackled Satsuma. You took a little brass handle and pulled it down, and the front of the little cupboard came forward, and there you found your coal. But this cabinet became demoralised with amazing quickness; it became incontinent with its corruptions, a hinge got twisted, and after a time it acquired the habit of suddenly, and with an unpleasant oscillatory laughing noise, opening of its own accord and proclaiming its horrid secret to Euphemia's best visitors. ['The Coal Skuttle' *Certain Personal Matters*]

Wells presses persistently upon the 'comic paradox' pedal: 'I dislike most people; in London they get in one's way in the street and fill up railway carriages, and in the country they stare at you—but I *hate* my friends' ['The Trouble of Life']; polite conversation 'is the very degradation of speech' ['Of Conversation: An Apology'] and so on. It's an interesting question, actually, as to why Wilde's paradoxical epigrams still shine, and Chesterton's still provoke thought, where Wells's just clang dully (Wilde would never be so dull as to write: 'unless it is the face of a fashionable beauty, I know of nothing more absolutely uninteresting than a morning paper'). The problem is not only that Wilde's wit is sharper. It's that Wilde's paradoxes speak to something genuinely significant. Both Wilde and Wells, we might say, lived lives of public sexual clandestineness; but Wilde's wit repeatedly reveals his homosexuality, as a function of his love for the *unexpectedness* of beauty, where the wit in *Certain Personal Matters* repeatedly reverts back upon Wells's cover-story—bourgeois domestic conventionality—rather than upon his hidden life of polyamorous sexual incontinence. *The Importance of Being Earnest* hides its gayness, brilliantly, in plain view. *Certain Personal Matters* is a volume that only pretends to be personal. The fact is that the central paradox of Wilde, that levity is the way to apprehend the most serious matters of life, love and death, doesn't really interest Wells. The truth always seemed obvious to Wells, where it always seemed beautifully perverse to Wilde.

This truly is an unfair comparison (who is so witty as Wilde, after all?) But the essays in *Certain Personal Matter* that still work are the ones that do more than merely comically rib the platitudes of bourgeois living; the ones that engage, rather, the ideational or metaphorical resonances of science fiction. The account of the odd little creatures visible under magnification in 'Through a Microscope' closes on a splendid note, anticipatory of the opening image from the following year's *War of the Worlds*:

> And all the time these creatures are living their vigorous, fussy little lives; in this drop of water they are being watched by a creature of whose presence they do not dream, who can wipe them all out of existence with a stroke of his thumb, and who is withal as finite, and sometimes as fussy and unreasonably energetic, as themselves. ['Through a Microscope', *Certain Personal Matters*]

Better still is 'Of a Book Unwritten', another anticipation of *War of the Worlds* in which Wells drolly speculates about the direction evolution might take:

> The reader may presently conjure up a dim, strange vision of the latter-day face: "eyes large, lustrous, beautiful, soulful; above them, no longer separated by rugged brow ridges, is the top of the head, a glistening, hairless dome, terete and beautiful; no craggy nose rises to disturb by its unmeaning shadows the symmetry of that calm face, no vestigial ears project; the mouth is a small, perfectly round aperture, toothless and gumless, jawless, unanimal, no futile emotions disturbing its roundness as it lies, like the harvest moon or the evening star, in the wide firmament of face." ... man [is] destined for a similar change; imagine him no longer dining, with unwieldy paraphernalia of servants and plates, upon food queerly dyed and distorted, but nourishing himself in elegant simplicity by immersion in a tub of nutritive fluid.

Much more important for his development as a writer than his occasional pieces were Wells's short stories. His first collection of these *The Stolen Bacillus and Other Incidents* (1895) is a representative, which is to say variable, selection of Wells's early craft in this form. In the title story, an anarchist tricks his way into the lab of a prominent chemist to steal a vial of cholera to dump into London's water supply, but ends up accidentally dying himself purple. It's too random to be good SF, and too mannered and forced to be funny—as when the chemist, chasing the anarchist down the street, passes some central-casting Cockneys: '"Hullo!" said poor old Tommy Byles; "here's another bloomin' loonatic. Blowed if there aint." "What a bloomin' lark it is!" said the ostler boy.' Better is 'The Flowering of the Strange Orchid' about a timid suburban man whose hobby is growing hothouse orchids. He buys a strange bulb, it flowers suddenly and its strong scent anaesthetises him. It puts out tendrils to suck his blood but his housekeeper rescues him. 'In the Avu Observatory' concerns Woodhouse, an astronomer in Borneo who, at his telescope one night, is attacked by a man-sized bat. 'The Triumphs of a Taxidermist' and 'A Deal in Ostriches' are two shorts about an unscrupulous taxidermist boasting of the things he has stuffed—he once faked a legendary bird supposedly from New Zealand which a collector insisted upon obtaining: 'I made it out of the skeletons of a stork and a toucan and a job lot of feathers.' The humour of these two pieces has aged catastrophically: 'I stuffed a nigger once. There is no law against it. I made him with all his fingers out and used him as a hat-rack.' In 'Through a Window' Bailey, recovering from two broken legs in his home counties home, sits looking out of his window as a Malay bargeman goes on a killing spree outside. The reason for the bargeman's violence is not disclosed but pursued by the authorities, he sees that he has been being observed by Bailey:

> In another moment a hairy brown hand had appeared and clutched the balcony railings, and in another the face of the Malay was peering through these at the man on the couch. His expression was an unpleasant grin, by reason of the krees he held between his teeth, and he was bleeding from an ugly wound in his cheek. His hair wet to drying stuck out like horns from his head. ['Through a Window', *Stolen Bacillus*]

The police shoot the intruder through the open window, and Bailey finishes him off by smashing a bottle on his head. It makes for a tense narrative but the racist demonisation of the Malay is as clumsily done as it is offensive and the story lacks larger point. 'The Temptation of Harringay' is a five-finger Faustian exercise: a mediocre painter called Harringay inadvertently paints a devil, that comes to life on the canvas. The devils tempt him with greatness ('two indubitable masterpieces for a Chelsea artist's soul. It's a bargain?') but Harringay is having none of it and paints over the whole canvas with a thick layer of green. In 'The Flying Man' an Ethnologist discovers the truth behind stories of a flying man of the gullible natives of some unspecified corner of the British empire in a British lieutenant's daring escape when under attack by a native army, jerry-rigging a parachute out of an old tent. 'Æpyornis Island' is a Robinson Crusoe story with the added wrinkle that the castaway, Butcher, happens to be in possession of a gigantic egg from which hatches a chick of the titular gigantic prehistoric breed of bird. Butcher raises this bird until it is bigger than he is, but when it turns on him he has to kill it. 'The Moth' is a story about two entomologists who spend decades in scholarly battle over various species of moth with such passion that when one dies, the other is driven mad, thinking himself haunted by the ghost of his rival in the form of a moth. The story is less silly than this summary makes it sound, although only *slightly* less silly. In 'The Treasure in the Forest' two men travel to a tropical island in search of buried Spanish ingots and die, poisoned by the local vegetation.

Most of the writing here is disposable but in three of these stories, we get a sense of Wells's larger imaginative capabilities. The narrator of 'The Diamond Maker', out for a night-time stroll, meets a shabby, desperate man who offers him a gigantic diamond for £100. He has, he says, devoted his life to discovering how to manufacture artificial diamonds but, aware that the window of opportunity for capitalising upon his discovery is short, now finds that nobody believes him. The police think he's an anarchist; jewellers assume he's a thief or a fence and even the narrator is wary of him. He ends up starving on the street. It is a story about the ironies of unexpected consequence, and Wells was to write many such in his career. 'The Remarkable Case of Davidson's Eyes' concerns a laboratory accident—'something about electrometers', is Wells's narrator's commendably vague explanation—that first blinds Davidson, and then enables him to see what is happening on the exact opposite point of the globe. He looks out upon a desert island instead of his lab; when he wanders downhill into London it seems to him he is sinking under the sea, walking past shipwrecks and so on. It is a simple yet surprisingly potent conceit because the metaphorical valence of the central idea is so expressive. It works as a trope for writing itself, the imaginative dilation and the power of bringing the hidden into view. Perhaps the best story in the collection is the torrid techno-melodrama of 'The Lord of the Dynamos', set in a Camberwell electricity-generating sub-station, where three large dynamos operate under the care of Holroyd, a drunken Yorkshireman. Holroyd's assistant is a Burmese called Azuma-zi, who barely speaks English, is beaten and mocked by boss. He comes to believe that the largest of the three dynamos is a god and electrocutes Holroyd against the terminals by way of sacrificing him to this deity. When he tries to do the same to Holroyd's successor the new manager fights back, and Azuma-zi is killed. 'So ended prematurely the Worship of the Dynamo Deity', the narrator comments, sardonically; 'perhaps the most short-lived of all religions. Yet withal it could at least boast a Martyrdom and a Human Sacrifice':

Azuma-zi would sit and watch the big machine. Now and then the brushes would sparkle and spit blue flashes, at which Holroyd would swear, but all the rest was as smooth and rhythmic as breathing. The band ran shouting over the shaft, and ever behind one as one watched was the complacent thud of the piston. So it lived all day in this big airy shed, with him and Holroyd to wait upon it; not prisoned up and slaving to drive a ship as the other engines he knew—mere captive devils of the British Solomon—had been, but a machine enthroned. ... The great black coils spun, spun, spun, the rings ran round under the brushes, and the deep note of its coil steadied the whole. It affected Azuma-zi queerly. ['The Lord of the Dynamos', *Stolen Bacillus*]

I won't try to pretend the affect of this story can be neatly separated out from its racism; but I would suggest that that affect is notable, the iteration of something new in literature: a specifically technological sublime. Wells is particularly good on the trance-state evoked by the noises the dynamo makes:

A steady stream of din, from which the ear picked out first one thread and then another; there was the intermittent snorting, panting, and seething of the steam engines, the suck and thud of their pistons, the dull beat on the air as the spokes of the great driving-wheels came round, a note the leather straps made as they ran tighter and looser, and a fretful tumult from the dynamos. ['The Lord of the Dynamos', *Stolen Bacillus*]

Sound shamanically destabilises rational consciousness, and the central irony of the tale—that this atavistic numinous mind-state has been created by the very embodiment of electric modernity—is a resonant and eloquent one.

Indeed, and despite the perhaps dismissive tone of some of these previous paragraphs, it is worth stressing both how extraordinary prolific of short stories Wells was through the 1890s, and how exceptional and enduring his best work in this mode has been. The salient in any short story is, of course, brevity; and the dangers of brevity are triviality and evanescence. One way of avoiding those consequences is to structure your story around a central trope or metaphor that stays with the reader after the events and characters have dissolved in the memory. Science fiction is, simply, better at doing that than other modes of writing, because SF is a fundamentally metaphorical form of art. It is so because it aims at representing the world without reproducing it. This is another reason why Wells's science-fictional (SF) stories have proved so much more enduring than his other sorts of tales, and why his second published collection, *The Plattner Story and Others* (1897) works less well overall that his first, weighted away as it is from what we might call science fiction towards two main sorts of tale: mundane *morceaux de comédie* on the one hand and stories of ghosts, haunting and obsession on the other. On the mundane side is the perfectly disposable 'The Jilting of Jane', an offcut from the material later collected in *Certain Personal Matters*, about Wells and his fictional wife Euphemia (Jane, their servant girl, is jilted by her boyfriend; she attends his wedding and throws a boot at him). Then there's 'In the Modern Vein', a strange little misfire about an *affaire du coeur* between a married poet called Aubrey Vair and a mixed-race Indian woman called Miss Smith. 'A Catastrophe' is a vignette of lower-middle-class life: a draper whose shop is failing, saved by an unexpected inheritance. 'The Purple Pileus' concerns a henpecked lower-middle-class husband who eats the mushroom of the story's title and thereby discovers his manliness, able now to overbear his wife. 'A Slip Under the Microscope' concerns the unmasking of a cheating science student and 'The Lost Inheritance' is a shaggy dog story about a mix-up over an inheritance. 'The Sad Story of a Dramatic Critic' is an odd tale about a shy fellow who becomes drama critic for a London newspaper and finds himself increasingly imitating the much more floridly extrovert mannerisms of the actors upon whom he reports, until he reaches such a point of thespian excess that his fiancée leaves him.

There are nice touches in all these mundane tales, but none are very memorable. Much better are the stories of the uncanny. In 'The Apple' Mr Hinchcliff meets a stranger on a train and receives from him an apple. The stranger claims this is the actual apple from the Edenic Tree of Knowledge of Good and Evil, and indeed seems to regret his gift ('"No!" shouted the stranger and made a snatch at it as if to take it back') but Hinchcliff has alighted and the train is already moving on. 'He would have eaten the thing, and attained omniscience there and then, but it would seem so silly to go into the town sucking a juicy fruit—and it certainly felt juicy.' On a whim, he throws it over a wall into an orchard. The story ends:

> But in the darkness of the night Mr. Hinchcliff had a dream, and saw the valley, and the flaming swords, and the contorted trees, and knew that it really was the Apple of the Tree of Knowledge that he had thrown regardlessly away. And he awoke very unhappy.
>
> In the morning his regret had passed, but afterwards it returned and troubled him; never, however, when he was happy or busily occupied. At last, one moonlight night ... he slipped out of the house and over the playground wall, went through the silent town to Station Lane, and climbed into the orchard where he had thrown the fruit. But nothing was to be found of it there among the dewy grass and the faint intangible globes of dandelion down. ['The Apple', *Plattner Story*]

This short piece is wonderfully plangent, although being, as it is, about the things that elude us in life, it doesn't quite avoid the dangers of obliquity intrinsic to its own elusion. 'The Story of the Late Mr. Elvesham' is a Jekyll-and-Hyde retread in which an old man tricks a young one into swapping souls, leaving our protagonist trapped in the other's decaying old body. There are two marine stories, presumably indicative of a writer who holidayed a lot in English coastal resorts. In 'The Sea Raiders' intelligent cephalopods come out of the water and make war on the south coast of England, and 'In The Abyss' submarine explorer Elstead descends 5 miles in a pressurised steel sphere to the ocean bed, where he glimpses an entire civilisation of vaguely humanoid fish-people. This story lingers in the mind because it only hints at, rather than tediously elaborating, this undiscovered country. 'The Cone' is set in the Jeddah Company blast furnace: it parlays memories of Wells's time in Stoke into fiction, and is conceivably an offcut from the giant novel he planned to write at that time. Horrocks, the furnace manager, shows Raut, an artist, round his factory. Raut has been having an affair with Horrocks's wife; Horrocks knowing this, pushes him off a gangway into the furnace's mouth. There's a splendid if gnashing final scene, with Raut hanging desperately to a chain as Horrocks hurls coal at him from above to dislodge him: 'Fizzle, you fool! Fizzle, you hunter of women! You hot-blooded hound! Boil! boil! boil!' Raut ends a charred corpse. It is a fair guess that Wells sublimated some of his own sense of adulterous moral conflict into this piece.

One other story in this collection looks forward to technology that subsequently became commonplace, although unfortunately, it's one of Wells's weakest. Monson, the millionaire, protagonist of 'The Argonauts of the Air', has wasted his entire fortune trying to build heavier-than-air flying machine. Goaded by the polite mockery of attractive society women he insists he and his engineer take their prototype machine out for a spin. They do, but the plane crashes in South Kensington killing them both. This story is built around a strange failure of imaginative extrapolation: for Wells has the idea stuck in his head that a heavier-than-air plane would be completely at the mercy of eddies in the airy medium through which it passed. Most of Monson's money has gone on building 'huge scaffoldings ... which limited the flight of the apparatus', running 2 miles from Wimbledon to Worcester Park 'a massive alley of interlacing iron and timber, and an enormous web of ropes and tackle, extending the best part of two miles'. It's leaving the safety of these guide-ropes that causes the story's disaster. But the whole thing strikes the oddest note, for we cannot but note that Monson has not built a plane at all. He has built an elaborate zip-wire gondola.

Better are the collection's various stories of haunting. In 'The Red Room' a scoffer agrees to spend the night in a room reputedly haunted but despite his best efforts to remain rational, he is properly terrified and flees. The room, it seems, is haunted by fear itself. The narrator of 'Under the Knife' 'dies' on the operating table and experiences millennia of post-mortem spirit-travel only to wake up to discover the operation has in fact been successful and that his vision was an anaesthetic dream. The title piece, 'The Plattner Story' concerns Gottfried Plattner, a teacher at Sussexville Proprietary School who, experimenting with a certain green powder, becomes invisible to the people around him. He finds himself in a strange alternate dimension superposed upon our own. During Earthly daylight, Sussexville is plainly visible to him, whilst this Other World is shadowy and dim but during Earth's night Sussexville fades from view and a weird green sun illuminates the Other World. He spends 9 days in this place, and observes its inhabitants—they appear to have houses and even churches in their realm and spend their time watching the Earthly living. The story ends when Plattner sees into a room, in our world, where an old man lies on his deathbed, ignored by his much younger wife 'because she was busy turning out papers from an old-fashioned bureau in the opposite corner of the room'. Watchers from the Other World crowd around, distressed. She burns his will. At the man's death an Other World bell sounds, 'cutting through the unexpected stillness like a keen, thin blade'; 'a breath of wind, icy cold, blew through the host of watchers' and a long black arm reaches over Plattner to seize the man. Terrified, Plattner flees, falls and is returned to our world—to discover that his internal organs have swapped, left-to-right and right-to-left, inside his torso. Though 'The Plattner Story' does not escape the problems of conceptual extravagance and melodrama, Wells manages to evoke a genuinely eerie mood here.

Then there is 'Pollock and the Porroh Man' which is, simply, one of the best things Wells ever wrote. It is a straightforward matter summarising this tale, although summary does nothing to convey its distinctive and haunting quality. Pollock is a wastrel who has ended up, like many young Englishman with squandered youths and reputations, working in the nether reaches of the Empire: in this case in Sierra Leone. A local attempts to kill Pollock because Pollock has been sleeping with the man's wife: 'the Porroh man stabbed the woman to the heart as though he had been a mere low-class Italian, and very narrowly missed Pollock. But Pollock, using his revolver to parry the lightning stab which was aimed at his deltoid muscle, sent the iron dagger flying, and, firing, hit the man in the hand.' This passage from Anglican missionary C.F. Schlenker, who had worked in West Africa, and whom perhaps Wells read, explains the significance of *porroh*:

> The Porro Association is a secret society called: *am-porro*, and a member of it is called: *o-ko-porro*. It is for men only, and exists chiefly on the Rokel. All the

members of it are tattooed on their nape. It is chiefly of a political nature, and they assume a great deal of power, and are very violent, especially when offended by one not initiated into their society, upon whom they look as unclean, calling him: *o-gborka*, which signifies "any one not initiated into the great institutions of the country," or "one ceremoniously unclean." The Porros will demand satisfaction for all what they may call an offence done to them. [Schlenker, xiii]

This brings out one of the most important features of the story: for 'Pollock' and 'O-ko-poro' sound very much like variants of the same name.

The story's first stroke of genius, I think, is in this account of the last time Pollock sees the Porroh man alive:

The Porroh man stooped in the doorway, glancing under his arm at Pollock. Pollock caught a glimpse of his inverted face in the sunlight, and then the Englishman was alone, sick and trembling with the excitement of the affair, in the twilight of the place. It had all happened in less time than it takes to read about it. ['Pollock and the Porroh Man' *Plattner Story*]

The strangeness of this posture, and the flashbulb (as we now say) nature of the sight work brilliantly. Fearing the Porroh man's continued animus Pollock pays a bounty hunter to assassinate the fellow, a commission proved by delivering to Pollock the Porroh man's severed head. From this point onward Pollock is unrelentingly haunted by the head, always appearing to him inverted. He buries it, but the dog digs it up again: 'the nose was grievously battered. Ants and flies swarmed over it. By an odd coincidence, it was still upside down, and with the same diabolical expression in the inverted eyes'. He throws it in the sea, but it finds its way back to him. He decides he must leave Sierra Leone to escape the curse, and throws the head on a fire before he goes. But, taking passage on a ship for England, he finds that the captain of the ship has bought the head ('"pickled'ed", said the captain. "—smoked. 'Ed of one of these Porroh chaps, all ornamented with knife-cuts"') as a 'rummy curio' and that it is on the ship with him. Back in England Pollock hallucinates the upside-down head everywhere he goes. He's perfectly aware that the balance of his mind is disturbed, and asks his bank manager to 'recommend me a physician for mind troubles. I've got a little—what is it?—hallucination.' But it is no good. It doesn't matter what he tries or where he goes: Pollock cannot escape the head. The story ends with him cutting his own throat with a straight razor.

Stories of this kind—I mean, stories that set out to chill, or scare, to trail tendrils of dread over the tender member of the reader's mind—are aiming at something really quite personal. Like jokes, of which they are perhaps the alarming mirror-image, two people may react very differently to the same material. All I can say is that, for me, 'Pollock and the Porroh Man' generates a very powerful and unsettling affect indeed. This has, I suppose, something to do with the architecture of my own subconscious, concerning which speculation would in this context, of course, prove unilluminating. We can at least say that what links the effectiveness of this story to the still memorable (if far inferior) 'The Plattner Story' is the way they both premise haunting in terms of *inversion*. 'Plattner' inverts the convention of the ghost story by sending a living person over to as-it-were haunt the dead. 'Pollock and the Porroh Man' is more conventionally structured and owes something to the granddaddy of all such tales, Poe's 'The Tell-Tale Heart' (1843). But by making Pollock's guilt much less personal than is the case in Poe's tale Wells achieves something much more memorable. Not that Pollock is an innocent party; indeed, far from it. One effect of his experiences is to force Pollock to confront his own past:

> His wretched home, his still more wretched schooldays, the years of vicious life he had led since then, one act of selfish dishonour leading to another; it was all clear and pitiless now, all its squalid folly, in the cold light of the dawn. He came to the hut, to the fight with the Porroh man, to the retreat down the river to Sulyma, to the Mendi assassin and his red parcel, to his frantic endeavours to destroy the head, to the growth of his hallucination. ['Pollock and the Porroh Man', *Plattner Story*]

His guilt is larger than the killing of one man. It is, in a nutshell, *imperial* guilt; which brings home how far Wells has come even in the 2 years since the clumsy racism and imperial complacency of the stories in *The Stolen Bacillus* collection. The story's implication is that Pollock is haunted by the Porroh man because the two of them are versions of one another: one head-upright, one head-upside-down; white man and black man; imperialised and colonial subject; scientific rationalist and witch-doctor trader in curses. In both cases, as the passage from Schlenker's book quoted above makes clear, the real issue of power is less magical or sexual than it is *political*—which is to say, it *is* magical and sexual, and to do with possession and power, but that all these things are subsumed under the main imperial category of 'politics'. 'It is chiefly of a political nature', Schlenker reports, of the Porroh; 'and they assume a great deal of power, and are very violent'. He could be talking about the British Empire. No wonder Pollock cannot escape the curse by returning to London. As Wells's friend Conrad was to point out, 4 years after this story was first published, London is the very heart of the imperial darkness. Wells's tale is saying: strip away all the surface epiphenomena of such things and we discover this uncomfortable truth: it is we supposedly civilised and civilising men who haunt ourselves. The hanged man who pursues the upright man and they are the same man.

That *Tales of Space and Time* (1899) was Wells's third collection of short fiction in under 4 years, indicates just how productive Wells was in this mode through the 1890s. That his third collection contains five stories, two of them ('A Story of the Stone Age' and 'A Story of the Days To Come') 25,000-word novellas, shows that he is increasingly growing dissatisfied, as a writer, with the restrictions of brevity. Of those two novellas, the former is manifestly the better, a small masterpiece of prehistoric speculation set in Wells's favoured Surrey stamping grounds. The story concerns a tribe of cave-people lead by 'Uya the Cunning', strong, old and ugly. Uya takes a fancy to attractive young cavegirl Eudena, who avoids his advances by running off into the forest. Handsome young Ugh-lomi goes after her, thereby provoking Uya's ire. Rather than be killed Ugh-lomi and Eudena hide from the tribe, and Ugh-lomi accidentally invents the axe when playing about with a holey flint and a stick. He uses this new weapon to kill Uya, bringing back the chief's wife's necklace as a prize for Eudena. After fighting a monstrous lion he becomes the tribe's new leader. Wells did not invent the 'caveman story' genre of fiction (Edward Bulwer Lytton had published his caveman story 'The Fallen Star, or the History of a False Religion' all the way back in 1834) although the success of 'A Story of the Stone Age' gave life to the mode, and directly influenced the whole subsequent *Clan of the Cave Bear*-school of writing. Ugh-lomi's cleverness and skill mean that he goes from being tribal nobody to chief, which is a novel reformulation of the core narrative of social mobility that informs so much of Wells's writing, as it had done his life. And there's a nicely hidden-in-plain-sight coding of Wells into his protagonist's name: trimming down the double-u with which 'Wells' starts to a single u, reversing HGU(U) because we're going back in time, and capping it off with a reference to this portrait's simpler and less clever persona, a 'low me' instead of the evolutionarily elevated 'high me' who's doing the actual writing. The way the story ends is wittily deflating, too:

Cat's-skin had a trout. It was rare men caught fish in those days, but Cat's-skin would stand silently in the water for hours and catch them with his hand. And the fourth day Ugh-lomi suffered these three to come to the squatting-place in peace, with the food they had with them. Ugh-lomi ate the trout. Thereafter for many moons Ugh-lomi was master and had his will in peace. And on the fulness of time he was killed and eaten even as Uya had been slain. ['Story of the Stone Age', *Tales of Space and Time*]

It is certainly a much better work than its companion piece 'A Story of the Days to Come'. This starts in Wells's now: 'The excellent Mr. Morris was an Englishman, and he lived in the days of Queen Victoria the Good. He was a prosperous and very sensible man; he read the *Times* and went to church, and as he grew towards middle age an expression of quiet contented contempt for all who were not as himself settled on his face.' Then Wells skips directly forward to one of Morris's descendants:

> He had just the same stout, short frame as that ancient man of the nineteenth century, from whom his name of Morris—he spelt it Mwres—came; he had the same half-contemptuous expression of face. He did not read the *Times*: indeed, he did not know there ever had been a *Times*—that institution had foundered somewhere in the intervening gulf of years; but the phonograph machine, that talked to him as he made his toilet of a morning, dealt with the world's affairs. ['A Story of the Days To Come', *Tales of Space and Time*]

Wells sketches the future world not all that different to that portrayed in *When the Sleeper Wakes* (to which 'A Story of the Days to Come' is actually prior); but there's something small-c conservative, almost smugly so, about the humorous conceit that this future differs in merely superficial ways from our present. The tale implies that the present exerts so profound a gravitational pull that the future becomes drawn back into it. The future, according to this story, is just the present in fancy dress. The meat of the story is a Romeo-and-Juliet dilemma; Mwres's daughter has fallen in love with a lower-class lad ('"He is"—and his voice sank with shame—"a mere attendant upon the stage on which the flying-machines from Paris alight."') and the obstacles of parental disapproval include such things as brainwashing-by-hypnosis. The premise, that love is timeless or at least is transhistorical, vitiates the effective future-estrangement of the story, and for all its intriguing details it falls flat.

'The Man Who Could Work Miracles' is a little fantasy about fantasy. Fotheringay, an unimaginative small-town clerk, acquires the ability to per-form miracles. In the company of a local preacher, Mr. Maydig, he goes about at night doing good: draining swamps, reforming drunkards and the like, until Fotheringay decides, at Maydig's prompting, to extend the amount of time available for their night-time sallies by stopping the rotation of the Earth. This turns out to be a poor idea: 'when Mr. Fotheringay had arrested the rota-tion of the solid globe, he had made no stipulation concerning the trifling movables upon its surface … so that the village and Mr. Maydig, and Mr. Fotheringay, and everybody and everything had been jerked violently forward at about nine miles per second—that is to say, much more violently than if they had been fired out of a cannon. And every human being, every living creature, every house, and every tree—all the world as we know it—had been so jerked and smashed and utterly destroyed.' Fotheringay saves his own life with a wish. Now the last human alive, and fed-up with his powers, he wills himself back in time to a point before the gift came. It's all wittily and charmingly written, and as a thought experiment about the limitations of fantasy, it is even, in a small way, profound.

'The Crystal Egg' stands as a sort of pendant to The *War of the Worlds*. An antique dealer in Seven Dials called Mr. Cave offers for sale the titular egg—when a ray of light strikes it from the correct angle, it provides a real-time, moving view of a strange landscape. We are seeing what we would nowadays call a 'live feed' of Mars, including alien Martians, some hopping along on their tentacles, others wearing wing-prostheses that enable them to fly.

> Once or twice one would come to peer, and go away very shortly to some other mast, as though the vision was unsatisfactory. … He several times saw certain clumsy bipeds, dimly suggestive of apes, white and partially translucent, feeding among certain of the lichenous trees, and once some of these fled before one of the hopping, round-headed Martians. The latter caught one in its tentacles, and then the picture faded suddenly and left Mr. Cave most tantalisingly in the dark. ['The Crystal Egg', *Tales of Space and Time*]

Presumably (though this is not specified in the story) the Martians have somehow seeded these eggs onto the earth to reconnoitre their future invasion ground. What both 'The Crystal Egg' and 'The Man Who Could Work Miracles' have in common is the utilisation of a *self-reflexive* conceit. Wells's stories speak to their various imagined worlds, but also to the ground of their own imagining. Cave's egg *is* science fiction, that (n)ovum that gifts us glimpses of a compelling, exotic alienness (calling his character 'Cave' is presumably Wells's little Plato joke). Fotheringay's sudden ability to fulfil any wish projects the inside of his *imaginarium* onto the exterior world. The comic tone of the latter is saved from smugness by the fact that such projection leads to the death of literally everyone in the world and the potency of the former is in the way it grasps that the science fiction channel to alienness is also a channel by which alienness can surveil us.

Then there is 'The Star', one of Wells's very best stories, short and sense-of-wonderful. Astronomers notice a new star approaching the solar system. They observe it colliding with Neptune such that the two bodies become locked together as a flaming mass that hurtles towards the Sun. Wells deftly sketches reactions to this news: some in denial, some despairing, others indifferent:

'the star grew—it grew with a terrible steadiness hour after hour.' It passes so close to Earth that the two bodies swing about one another, causing earthquakes and floods and disaster. After this catastrophe the world occupies a closer orbit about the sun, the moon is much further away, and the shattered land is so much hotter that the few survivors are compelled to migrate to the poles. But the real touch of genius in this story is its final two paragraphs, a masterful focus-pull:

> Of the new brotherhood that grew presently among men, of the saving of laws and books and machines, of the strange change that had come over Iceland and Greenland and the shores of Baffin's Bay, so that the sailors coming there presently found them green and gracious, and could scarce believe their eyes, this story does not tell. Nor of the movement of mankind now that the earth was hotter, northward and southward towards the poles of the earth. It concerns itself only with the coming and the passing of the Star.
>
> The Martian astronomers—for there are astronomers on Mars, although they are very different beings from men—were naturally profoundly interested by these things. They saw them from their own standpoint of course. 'Considering the mass and temperature of the missile that was flung through our solar system into the sun,' one wrote, 'it is astonishing what a little damage the earth, which it missed so narrowly, has sustained. All the familiar continental markings and the masses of the seas remain intact, and indeed the only difference seems to be a shrinkage of the white discolouration (supposed to be frozen water) round either pole.' Which only shows how small the vastest of human catastrophes may seem, at a distance of a few million miles. ['The Star', *Tales of Space and Time*]

This is a strong slug of the strong black coffee of science-fiction's 'sense-of-wonder'. It does something that, really, only SF can do, describing an event that is 'sublime' in Burkean or Kantian terms—the terrifying tempest, the earthquake and catastrophic inundation—only in order to step back from it and reveal it, in all its terror and excitement, to be trivial compared with the ultra-sublimity of the cosmic frame (this, indeed, is one of the things Kant meant by his distinction between the mathematical and the dynamic sublime). It is something Wells achieves several times in his career.

After the extraordinary fertility of his 1890s, Wells moved away from writing short stories. Volumes of his short fiction continued to be issued and continued to sell well, but these were overwhelmingly reprint collections. There are some new stories in *Twelve Stories and a Dream* (1903), but the majority had appeared before; and *The Country of the Blind and Other Stories* (1911) includes, according to its own preface, 'all the short stories by me that I care for anyone to read again'. Only a handful of the 33 tales in this latter collection were previously unpublished, although two of those—'The Door in the Wall' (which first appeared the *Daily Chronicle*, 14 July 1906) and 'The Country of the Blind' (*Strand Magazine* April 1904)—are among Wells's very best, and merit a little more discussion.

The premise of the former could hardly be simpler: a conventional Edwardian man, Lionel Wallace, recalls an incident from his childhood. He saw a door in a grubby West Kensington wall and went through it into a paradisical garden: 'it was very difficult for Wallace to give me his full sense of that garden into which he came. There was something in the very air of it that exhilarated, that gave one a sense of lightness and good happening and well-being; there was something in the sight of it that made all its colour clean and perfect and subtly luminous.' In the garden are manicured flowerbeds, two panthers, marble colonnades, playmates for the young Lionel ('filling me with gladness by their gestures, by the touch of their hands, by the welcome and love in their eyes') and a welcoming woman. Lionel returns through the door in the wall to 'a long grey street in West Kensington, in that chill hour of afternoon before the lamps are lit'. The remaining three-quarters of this story are its point: the dying fall of Wallace growing to manhood, seeing the magic door in the wall at various locations but never, for reasons of mundane distraction, going through it again. The tone of this piece is exquisitely handled, and its remains one of the most affecting portraits of that palpable but indefinable sense of loss entailed by growing up—Wordsworth's Immortality Ode in science-fictional form—the way the petty business of living repeatedly get in the way of recovering that childhood numinosity. And although it is a sad story (it is, indeed, one of the saddest I know) it is not a depressing story, because Wells understands that life *is* the myriad gettings-in-the-way that define our days, and the desire to get past that is actually the desire to stop living. It is a story of wry mournfulness that leaves a sunset glow in the mind, a story that grasps how life is a necessary process of losing something. 'My depression', said Julia Kristeva in a moment of acute self-understanding, 'points to my *not* knowing how to lose.' Perhaps we don't associate Wells with the level of emotional wisdom displayed in this short piece. We should, though.

Arguably even better is 'The Country of the Blind', perhaps Wells's single greatest short story. Nuñez, attempting the ascent of the hitherto unconquered (fictional) Mount Parascotopetl in Ecuador, falls down the far side into an inaccessible though fertile valley entirely populated by blind people. Wells provides backstory rationalisation as to how this blind community came to be, although he really doesn't need to. The fable runs beautifully along its lines without such scaffolding. Nuñez is at first delighted, reciting to himself the old Erasmian proverb 'In the Country of the Blind, the One-Eyed

Man Is King'—assuming, in other words, that he will rule this place. But the locals not only refuse to acknowledge his sensory superiority, they have no concept of sight at all, and when he tries to explain his visual capacity to them they assume he is mad. Nuñez, though frustrated, realises he has to make the best of his situation since the surrounding mountains render escape impossible. He falls in love with a girl, Medina-Saroté, but the village elders disapprove of his marriage because they consider his obsession with sight idiotic and delusional. The village doctor proposes removing Nuñez's eyes, reasoning they are diseased in a manner that is affecting his brain, and, because he loves Medina-Saroté, Nuñez agrees; but on the morning of the operation he sneaks off, hoping to find a way over the impassable mountains to the outside world.

Wells published two versions of his ending: in the original (as printed in the 1911 volume) Wells leaves his protagonist high in the mountains at nightfall, his fate uncertain, but probably dying. A revised and augmented 1939 version of the story alters this: Nuñez sees an impending rock slide, cannot convince the villagers of the danger they are in and flees the valley together with Medina-Saroté just before the avalanche destroys everything. They make it to the outside world, marry and have four children, all sighted, but Medina-Saroté refuses the medical attention that might restore her vision. She now believes her husband's insistence on 'sight', and that the world around her is wonderful to behold but insists that it would be terrible for her to see it.

It's one of Wells's best known, and best, stories, all spun out of a premise both simple to the point of obviousness and elegantly wonderful in its novelty: in the country of the blind would the one-eyed man *really* be king? Wouldn't an entire country of blind people have adapted to their blindness such that sight would be superfluous? It's not flawless work: the ending's ambiguity speaks to a degree of uncertainty about the dramatic conception (Patrick Parrinder's analysis of the MS reveals a buried third ending, where Nuñez simply returns to the valley, which points to a writer barely able to make up his mind: Parrinder 1990) and the world-building of the story is unlikely to strike us as watertight. So for instance: the inhabitants of the valley think the birds are angels, since they can hear them flying about but can't touch them—although surely they'd get their hands on dead and injured birds from time to time, or trap them in their homes and realise they were just another sort of animal? But, of course, the mode here isn't realism. This is a fictional version of Plato's allegory of the cave and as such, it works brilliantly. Indeed, which of the two endings Wells came up with for this story you prefer will tell us something about your attitude to Plato's famous myth. What I mean is the way Plato tells it, the prisoner who escapes the cave and returns to tell his other encaved captives *has* seen something real and manifestly superior to everybody else. And in real life, it sometimes is true that the person who insists she has seen truth and is shunned by the mass consensus for her pains has indeed seen truth. But 99 times out of a 100 that person is not a visionary who has pierced the veil of maya but is rather delusional or a lunatic, somebody the balance of whose mind is disturbed. The population of Blind Country are surely right to shun Nuñez's tyrannical ambitions and certainly, are better suited to their niche living than he is. The original version of the story implies as much. But the avalanche conclusion steps back to the original Platonic notion: in the later version of the story Nuñez *does* have something the Blind Country people lack—a true vision—and Wells bends the story to prove his point. For myself, I prefer the latter of my two readings of Plato's allegory, and therefore the earlier ending. Perhaps you disagree.

In the preface to the 1911 *Country of the Blind and Other Stories* collection, Wells notes that 'the task of selection and revision' entailed by this volume brought home to him 'with something of the effect of discovery' that

> I was once an industrious writer of short stories, and that I am no longer anything of the kind. I have not written one now for quite a long time, and in the past five or six years I have made scarcely one a year. The bulk of the fifty or sixty tales from which this present three-and-thirty have been chosen dates from the last century. In the presence of so conclusive an ebb and cessation an almost obituary manner seems justifiable.

He goes on to speculate as to why he, in effect, stopped writing short stories. 'There was a time when life bubbled with short stories; they were always coming to the surface of my mind.' The 1890s, he argues, were 'a good and stimulating period for a short-story writer' with great work being produced almost continually by a whole tribe of short-story writers, all led by Kipling: 'Mr. Kipling had made his astonishing advent with a series of little blue-grey books, whose covers opened like window-shutters to reveal the dusty sun-glare and blazing colours of the East.' But Wells thinks the short story's golden age has passed:

> I do not think the present decade can produce any parallel to this list, or what is more remarkable, that the later achievements in this field of any of the survivors from that time, with the sole exception of Joseph Conrad, can compare with the work they did before 1900.

There's an interesting discussion to be had as to whether Wells is right in his larger literary-historical diagnosis, but his account of his own falling away can't be denied. Despite being one of the true masters of the form, the inspiration of Borges and generations of SF authors, and despite the fact that some of his most enduring literary achievements are to be found amongst his shorts, he effectively stopped writing them after the 1890s. Why?

It's not, of course, a question that admits of straightforward answer. Wells himself blames a figure he calls 'the à priori critic':

> Anyone could say of any short story, "A mere anecdote," just as anyone can say "Incoherent!" of any novel or of any sonata that isn't studiously monotonous. The recession of enthusiasm for this compact, amusing form is closely associated in my mind with that discouraging imputation. One felt hopelessly open to a paralysing and unanswerable charge, and one's ease and happiness in the garden of one's fancies was more and more marred by the dread of it. It crept into one's mind, a distress as vague and inexpugnable as a sea fog on a spring morning.

We're entitled to think that fog, however much Wells deplores it, may actually be part of the unique strength of the short story as a distinct form. In saying so I'm drawing on Timothy Clark's 2004 essay 'Not Seeing the Short Story: A Blind Phenomenology of Reading', which makes the case for the short story as a specifically *blind* mode of art. Clark argues that 'what I propose to call, non-pejoratively, the "blindness" of the short-story revisits the issue of the form's relation to realism'. He quotes *Middlemarch* to demonstrate George Eliot's novelistic commitment to as whole a sight as possible. The short story, by contrast, is necessarily determined by its pseudo-poetic brevity:

> The short story, as they say, is more 'poetic'. Eliot's effect of subtlety seems to escape this merely self-validating quality through its integration into earlier and later passages of the text. Without that, the kinship between the general 'human truths' of such a realist text and the kind of effects of 'truth' at work in a horoscope would be clearer. This lack of the trompe-l'oeil effects of a lengthy context constitutes what may be called the relative blindness of the short story. [Clark, 8]

Metaphors of *seeing*, according to Clark, pervade the critical theory related to the short story as a form. He finds a remarkable 'predominance of countervailing metaphors of sight, of the striving to "see" a text whole, the flash of revelation' in the way critics write about the short story form.

Blindness either as a total state, as in 'The Country of the Blind' (or in the short novel *The Invisible Man*), or else as a partial restriction or limitation of vision is a recurring theme in Wells's short stories: 'The Remarkable Case of Davidson's Eyes', 'The Plattner Story', 'The Crystal Egg' and many others. Conceivably Wells's increasing dissatisfaction with the short story mode correlated to a belief, which increasingly gripped him as the twentieth century progressed, that he ought as a writer to be aiming at a kind of whole sight. The novel that followed this 1911 anthology of his best short fiction—*Marriage* (1912)—is a thoroughly Eliotian exercise in comprehensive vision, in concretizing context and sheer length—600 pages in the first edition (1918's *Joan and Peter* is nearly 800 pages; both are discussed below). But Wells blindness was prodigiously more eloquent and resonant than his attempts as clear-sightedness. *He* didn't think so, but it's true. The short story form is the enclosed valley of 'The Country of the Blind'; it is the idiom of those sightless but blessed inhabitants. And the nature of Wells's later career is that he could not rest content in that place, but had to engineer a gigantic rock-fall and the opening of a new breach in the surrounding mountains to be able to scramble back to Realism.

Bibliography

Allen, Walter (1981). *The Short Story in English*. Oxford, Clarendon.

Clark, Timothy (2004). 'Not Seeing the Short Story' *Oxford Literary Review* 26:8, pp. 5–30.

Hammond, John R. (1984) *The Man With a Nose and the Other Uncollected Short Stories of H G Wells*. London: Athlone Press.

Mackenzie, Norman and Jean Mackenzie (1973). *The Time Traveller: the Life of H G Wells*. London: Weidenfeld.

Parrinder, Patrick (1990). 'Wells's Cancelled Endings for "The Country of the Blind"', *Science Fiction Studies* 17:1, pp. 71–76.

Philmus, Robert and David Hughes (1975) *H. G. Wells: Early Writings in Science and Science Fiction*. University of California Press.

Roberts, Adam (2016), *The Palgrave History of Science Fiction*. 2nd edition. Palgrave.

Schlenker, Charles F. (1861) *A Collection of Temne Traditions, Fables and Proverbs*. London, Church Missionary Society.

Smith, David C (1986). *H.G. Wells: Desperately Mortal: A Biography*. New Haven: Yale University Press.

3

Science Fiction

The Time Machine (1895); *The Wonderful Visit* (1895); *The Island of Doctor Moreau* (1896)

Looking back in the twentieth century to his beginnings as a writer Wells told his friend Edmund Haynes: 'earning a living by writing is a frightful gamble. It depends neither on knowledge nor literary quality but upon secondary considerations of timeliness, mental fashion & so forth almost beyond control. I have been lucky but it took me eight years, while I was teaching & then doing anxious journalism, to get established upon a comfortably paying footing' [Mackenzies 103]. By the middle of the 1890s his marriage to Jane had steadied his life, and increasing commercial and critical success gave him the writerly confidence to transition from journalism to fiction, and more particularly to more ambitious creative writing. The letters of 1894–95 are full of excited anticipation that rewriting his old 1888 time-traveller story 'The Chronic Argonauts' as *The Time Machine* would result in a hit. At the same time as working on this project he was writing something wholly new: a comic fantasy about an angel who falls to Earth which, under the title *The Wonderful Visit*, became in 1895 Wells's second published novel.

The Time Machine is, of course, the more famous of Wells's first two novels, and for good reason. It is, quite simply, a masterpiece. Henley paid £100 to serialise it *The New Review* over Christmas and New Year 1894–95; and a strange sort of Christmas story it must have made. William Heinemann advanced Wells £50 for book publication rights, and Wells's first book-length fiction emerged into the world in May 1895. Despite being only 152 pages long (some scenes from the serialised version were cut for the one-volume edition), Heinemann nonetheless had enough confidence in the book commit to an initial print-run of 10,000 and a 15% royalty—generous, given that Wells

© The Author(s) 2019
A. Roberts, *H G Wells*, Literary Lives, https://doi.org/10.1007/978-3-030-26421-5_3

at this time was a relatively unknown writer. Just how unknown is reinforced by the American first edition of *The Time Machine*, which was published by Holt & Co in New York as by 'H.S. Wells'.

Some critics see *The Time Machine* as Wells's single greatest novel. It has certainly had extraordinary influence on later science fiction. As fiction it benefits from its concision—Wells's years honing his art as a short-story writer pay dividends here—as well as the potent and eloquent conceit on which it is based. But it is also strikingly original in conception and execution. There had been journeys into the past and the future before: way back in 1844 Dickens's third *Christmas Carol* ghost had wafted his Scrooge into the future; and (though it's unlikely Wells knew of it) in 1887 Spanish writer Enrique Gaspar published the short novel *El anachronópete*, in which characters inside a house-sized machine go backwards in time. But in both these cases 'time travel' is revealed to be actually a sort of dream. Wells's innovation was to bring the conceit within the pseudo-scientific realm of technological possibility and to imagine a specific machine to facilitate it. He was also the first to imagine the far-future as a theatre of species decay, evolution as devolution and human dignity reduced to vacuous Eloi and bestial Morlocks. In this Wells was channelling the mood of his decade: Austro-Hungarian writer Max Nordau had mordantly defined the fin-de-siècle in a book-length attack on contemporary symbolism, mysticism, Wagnerism, aestheticism and *naturalisme* ('neurotics' 'the worst kind of enemies of society' 'a serious intellectual epidemic, some kind of Black Death of degeneration and hysteria') under the catch-all title *Degeneration* in 1892. Decadence was the decade's watchword, and not only for reactionaries like Nordau. Wells extrapolated out of cultural into existential critique and saw decadence as the logic not of art but of the cosmos as a whole. Indeed, so familiar has *The Time Machine* become that our difficulty, as readers and critics, is finding fresh eyes with which to encounter its radical strangeness.

On the one hand, Wells was living in materially and emotionally the most comfortable situation of his life; he was productive, ambitious and hopeful for the future. On the other, his health was often poor and his sexual life still defined largely by frustration. Both the future-oriented senses of possibility and the darker motivations of thwarted libido are patent in *The Time Machine*, although critics rarely talk about the latter. So: Wells's Time Traveller mounts his machine and zooms into futurity:

> I pressed the lever over to its extreme position. The night came like the turning out of a lamp, and in another moment came to-morrow. The laboratory grew faint and hazy, then fainter and ever fainter. … As I put on pace, night followed

day like the flapping of a black wing. The dim suggestion of the laboratory seemed presently to fall away from me, and I saw the sun hopping swiftly across the sky, leaping it every minute, and every minute marking a day. I supposed the laboratory had been destroyed and I had come into the open air. I had a dim impression of scaffolding, but I was already going too fast to be conscious of any moving things. The twinkling succession of darkness and light was excessively painful to the eye. Then, in the intermittent darknesses, I saw the moon spinning swiftly through her quarters from new to full, and had a faint glimpse of the circling stars. Presently, as I went on, still gaining velocity, the palpitation of night and day merged into one continuous greyness; the sky took on a wonderful deepness of blue, a splendid luminous colour like that of early twilight; the jerking sun became a streak of fire, a brilliant arch, in space. [*Time Machine*, 4]

Wells, wondering what time travel would look like from the point of view of the traveller has concluded it would seem as things appear to us now but *sped up*, rather as ciné-film can be sped up. In effect, he imagines the eye of the traveller as an aperture, like a camera, such that as information arrives more rapidly it creates the effect of film being run more rapidly through the projector gate: a modishly contemporary touch. In the mid-1890s motion pictures were still a nascent phenomenon, and marginal to the musical hall and traditional theatre—so, for example, the Alhambra Theatre created a sensation when they showed movie footage of the 1896 Derby only a day after the race was run. As Wells revised his story for publication as a novel film was very much the coming mode: by 1895 there were a few cinemas in England; by 1915 there were 4000.

This 'cinematic' account of time travel *feels* right, as description, in part because Wells's innovation has been many times specifically adapted for the screen: a thousand movie time travellers' journeys, rendered in precisely these terms. But light is both streams of particles and waves. Light with shorter wavelengths appears bluer to our eyes, light with longer wavelengths redder. Since any wavelength is inversely proportional to the frequency of the wave (waves with higher frequencies have shorter wavelengths, and lower frequencies have longer wavelengths) as the traveller speeds up in time, the frequency of the light waves striking his retina will increase, and accordingly, things will appear bluer. As he accelerates the familiar wavelengths of light will slip into ultraviolet, and he will stop seeing anything at all. To be clear: it is, of course, meaningless in a strict sense to speculate about what a 'real' time traveller would see, since there is no such thing as 'real' time travel; and I know that specialist scientists would disagree with my description here. Nonetheless, I hypothesise the visible world speeding, turning blue and then vanishing into the ultraviolet whilst objects that emit far infrared, microwaves and radio-waves come into view until these become the only things the traveller can see. I do so as a specific, speculative counterpoint to Wells's description in the passage above. The moral is that we need to come at Wells twice. Things that strike us as plain-as-daylight common-sense may, with a little temporal motion, shift into the invisible and things omnipresent but invisible may come looming up into view of our hitherto obscure infrared depths.

What *is* visible in the century-and-more of critical writings about this novel? The story, for one thing: the 'time traveller' has invented a machine that enables him to move backwards or forwards in time. He travels to the year 802,701 and discovers that mankind has evolved, or more exactly 'devolved', into two separate species: the beautiful but mindless Eloi who live hedonistic lives above ground, and the technologically advanced but ugly Morlocks who live below the ground, and who (the tale reveals) come out at night to devour the Eloi. The traveller then travels even further into the future, and sees further 'devolution': mankind becoming first rabbit-like creatures (an episode cut from the 1895 volume) and finally—in a scene of marvellously desolating vision—crab-like monsters scuttling about a terminal beach under a dying sun.

Critics tend to read *The Time Machine* as a satirical exaggeration of the class structure of fin-de-siècle Britain. The Eloi live in a neo-Hellenic communistic paradise above ground—the Greek plural form of their name points to their imaginative provenance, as does their obviously Greek costume, 'clad in a purple tunic, girdled at the waist with a leather belt. Sandals or buskins, legs bare to the knee'. It is conventional to treat the Eloi as the aristocrats; the Morlocks are identified in the tale as a Darwinian extension of the industrial proletariat: 'even now, does not an East-end worker live in such artificial conditions as practically to be cut off from the natural surface of the earth?' [*Time Machine*, 8]. The temptation is to read these cannibalistic monsters literally eating the imbecilic and beautiful Eloi as a Swiftian satire or reverse-satire, on the inherent violence of class in late nineteenth-century Britain. In Leon Stover's words, 'Wells's hated Morlocks are those antisocial elements of the working poor organised for mischief by trade unionists of Marxist persuasion' [Stover, xi]. But to think about this situation for a moment is to realise it's a misprision so fundamental it's rather amazing nobody talks about it.

Put it this way: the nature of class relations in the nineteenth century to a socialist like Wells is that the rich feed on the poor. That is to say, the rich exploit the poor, expropriating their labour to their own enrichment and thereby immiserating them. This is exactly the situation in 802,701: except that it is the Eloi who are exploited, the Morlocks who exploit them. These latter are clearly a technologically advanced population, and use their industry to supply the physical needs of the Eloi in terms of food, clothing, shelter and so on, something the Eloi are perfectly incapable of doing for themselves, as the Traveller realises early on:

> The several big palaces I had explored were mere living places, great dining-halls and sleeping apartments. I could find no machinery, no appliances of any kind. Yet these people were clothed in pleasant fabrics that must at times need renewal, and their sandals, though undecorated, were fairly complex specimens of metalwork. Somehow such things must be made. And the little people displayed no vestige of a creative tendency. There were no shops, no workshops, no sign of importations among them. They spent all their time in playing gently, in bathing in the river, in making love in a half-playful fashion, in eating fruit and sleeping. [*Time Machine*, 8]

The Morlocks are keeping the Eloi as something between pets and livestock. It is, and despite the so-often-mistaken Time Traveller's speculations to the contrary, the *Morlocks* who are the aristocrats, exploiting the proletarian Eloi as a resource. Automation, we presume, having done away with the need to exploit workers for their labour, what remains is to literalise the predatory nature of all class exploitation by literally devouring their underclass.

That readers tend to agree with the Traveller and think of the Eloi as the aristocrats, has to do with two features of the way Wells styles them: they are freed from the need to work, and they are beautiful (that is, sexually desirable). But on the former count, there's nothing stopping us reading this as a commentary upon the exigencies of full mechanic automation—a far-future society in which all physical needs are supplied by technology. And as for the latter: the person who assumes the vector of sexual desire inevitably runs from the working class to the aristocracy has presumably never heard of Arthur Munby or indeed had much experience of life more generally. That the Morlocks devour the Eloi is represented in the novella as a disgusting thing and the Morlocks themselves are physically repulsive: 'pallid bodies ... just the half-bleached colour of the worms and things one sees preserved in spirit in a zoological museum ... filthily cold to the touch' [51]. But we have little reason to trust the narrator's perspective on these beings. It would not be hard to construct a more considered portrait of these technologically advanced people: to imagine a world below characterised by advanced science, sophisticated culture and social richness. The whole novel then becomes a satire not on nineteenth-century class relations so much as on our habits of judging by appearances, our assumption that evil must coordinate with our sense of ugliness and virtue with our apprehension of pulchritude. Morlocks eat people, true; and, in the words of the song, eating people is wrong. Then again, the comparative luxury in which the Eloi are kept reflect, if anything, rather more credit upon the Morlocks than the filthy confinement in which we twenty-first-century humans keep our livestock; and if we are disgusted at the Morlocks eating their cattle and not disgusted at our own carnivorous ways we lay ourselves open to the charge of hypocrisy. The book is quite clear that however, pretty the Eloi are, they are not fully intelligent or self-aware. And if we're going to apply a twenty-first-century ethical frame to the novel we should probably aim at consistency. In other words: as our knee-jerk disgust at the Morlocks (because they are so physically unprepossessing; because they are dark-adapted; because they eat monkey-meat rather than cow- and pig-meat) disappears into the rapidly cycling ultraviolet of our ethical spectrum, a different frequency of ethical concern glooms into visibility from the infrared. Take, for example, the novella's representation of sex.

The Eloi are pseudo-Hellenic throwbacks to the dawn of history (watched over by a classical sphinx), representing the childhood of mankind, something literalised in their childlike stature and very limited mental capacity. Wells takes their name from the Greek ἧλὸς (ēlos; the plural form is ēloi), a word which originally (in Homer) meant 'deranged' or 'insane', but which came in later usage to mean: 'vain, useless, worthless'—a very appropriate title for this decorative but useless people. The first thing that strikes the Time Traveller is how very like children they are. They are 'slight creatures—perhaps four feet high'. He calls them 'exquisite creatures', 'a pretty little people … a certain childlike ease'. After he rescues drowning Weena from the indifference of her fellow Eloi the Traveller records that her gratitude and friendliness 'affected me exactly as a child's might have done'. There is, however, something precocious about this girl-child. A few lines later:

> I had not, I said to myself, come into the future to carry on a miniature flirtation. Yet her distress when I left her was very great, her expostulations at the parting were sometimes frantic, and I think, altogether, I had as much trouble as comfort from her devotion. Nevertheless she was, somehow, a very great comfort. [*Time Machine*, 8]

If we have any doubts as to what sort of euphemism *comfort* is in this context, Wells goes as far towards spelling it out as mainstream Victorian fiction permitted: 'in the end her odd affection for me triumphed, and for five of the nights of our acquaintance, including the last night of all, she slept with her head pillowed on my arm. But my story slips away from me as I speak of her.'

In short: the Time Traveller's impulse, on having travelled to 802,701 and discovered a species of intellectually vacuous, pretty-faced child-humans, is to have sex with them. But where disgust at the Morlock's cannibalism seems baked into the way *The Time Machine* has been received by readers and critics, disgust at the Traveller's paedophilia seems wholly absent. There are myriad sequels by other hands, and in some of these the Traveller and Weena have children together—that is to say: Wells's 'love story' between a full-grown man and a fair-faced, 4 ft., very-low-IQ child-girl has been unproblematically assimilated into the larger fan-reception of this novel. More, for this assimilation to happen, the original has to be reconfigured, for in that original Weena dies. The Traveller and Weena are pursued through dark woods by the Morlocks, and the Traveller, trying to scare them off by throwing fiery lumps of camphor at them, inadvertently sets the trees alight. Weena faints, is snatched by the Morlocks, and is then burned to death when the whole Morlock party is incinerated: 'I searched again for traces of Weena, but there were none,' says the Traveller, later. 'It was plain that they had left her poor little body in the forest. I cannot describe how it relieved me to think that it had escaped the awful fate to which it seemed destined.' Better burned alive than raped by Morlocks, it seems.

The Traveller repeatedly refers to the Eloi as children: 'I felt like a schoolmaster amidst children … like children, but like children they would soon stop examining me and wander away after some other toy'. Whose children are they? His of course (at one point he calls them 'my graceful children') and yours, and mine. Like the Morlocks, the Eloi are *our* descendants. Breaking off a metal lever with which to defend himself and Weena against Morlock attack, the Traveller notes:

> I longed very much to kill a Morlock or so. Very inhuman, you may think, to want to go killing one's own descendants! But it was impossible, somehow, to feel any humanity in the things. [*Time Machine*, 11]

In strict terms Morlocks and Eloi both can be male or female, but in terms of the symbolic logic of the story the Eloi are feminised and the Morlocks masculinized:—the former all share 'the same soft hairless visage, and the same girlish rotundity of limb'; the latter are more aggressive, physically stronger, more of a threat. The Traveller's adventure, in other words, is to hop over time, encounter his own children, sleep with his daughter and murder his sons. Very inhuman, you may think, to want to go killing one's own descendants! It's a deliberate and deliberately unsettling, inversion of the myth of Oedipus. Not for nothing does a sphinx preside over the whole narrative: 'Above me towered the sphinx, upon the bronze pedestal, white, shining, leprous, in the light of the rising moon. It seemed to smile in mockery of my dismay.'

I'm liable to be misunderstood in calling *The Time Machine* oedipal; so permit me to dilate upon the point a little. Oedipus, in the myth, solves two riddles. First, he meets the Sphinx, and solves her riddle: 'What is that which in the morning goes upon four feet; upon two feet in the afternoon; and in the evening upon three?' It's a very famous story, and a very famous riddle, although that very fame should give us pause: Oedipus's answer is 'man', who crawls on all fours in his infancy, strides on two legs in his maturity, and walks with a stick in his dotage. It is the trajectory of this as much as its cogency as answer here that is relevant to Wells's sphingian novella: the passage from our collective infancy, through maturity, and into the *decay* of the species: Eloi and Morlocks, rabbits and crabs, into something even less definite and so to terminal nothingness. It may not be too fanciful to see the pick-a-number,-drop-down,-come-back-up-to-one-less-than-the-original-number *shape* of the sphinx riddle's '4, 2, 3' pattern in Wells's famous future-date, 802,701.

This riddle is also posed by *The Time Machine* in a more straightforward manner. In the original myth, the sphinx describes a strange monster, but the answer reveals that this monster is not so strange—that, in fact, the monster is us. Wells, in effect, does the same, asking: what are these vacuous, diminutive infantile beings, unable to care for themselves? And what are these other monsters? These pale troglodytes that feed on human flesh? These gigantic crabs? This blob of darkness? And once again the solution to the riddle is: they are man. Which is to say: they are you, they are us. It is in this answer that inheres the buried force of the original oedipal riddle, the enduring power of that myth. The sphinx says: 'I shall describe to you a bizarre-sounding monster. Can you say what it is?' And Oedipus replies: '*Le monstre, c'est moi.*' We can speculate that all the previous challengers to the sphinx's puzzle failed not because the riddle is hard—we can be honest, as riddles go it really isn't very hard—but rather because they were unwilling to take that last step and understand that the terrible beast being described is they, themselves. Rather than accept their essential monstrosity many people would rather die. That's one of the things this myth is saying, I think.

But there's a second riddle in the Oedipus story, and it is posed not by a sphinx but by the land itself. The fields sicken, the crops die, a curse is on Thebes. Oedipus sets out to solve this riddle too, unaware that it has the same answer as the first one. What is the source of the curse? Oedipus himself—by marrying his own mother he has, unwittingly, polluted the land of which he is king. This second riddle both reveals and embodies the short-circuit of existence: man comes from sex, from the mother, into selfhood and along that temporal trajectory sketched by the first riddle towards death, and the mirroring of these two riddles reveals a profound and upsetting truth that all these things are the same thing. Sex is incest, birth is death, existence is a curse, all folded into all.

Wells's is riffing on the story-logic of this Oedipal riddle. We walk on the two legs of conventional one-second-per-second time travel, but Wells's ingenious device gives is a third option: *to leap over time altogether*. He would return to this bizarre world-leaping figure, the tripod, in *The War of the Worlds* a few years later. We could put it this way: conventional time is a single road, but Wells's machine gives us a new-branching path, a short-cut, and turns the road into a tripartite crossroad; and if that recalls us to the site of Oedipus's fatal encounter with the man he did not recognise as his own father, then maybe it is supposed to. Perhaps this seems an abstruse and remote way of engaging with Wells's novella, but it touches on something central to the way that work has disseminated itself and continues to disseminate itself, into the world, the stroke of intuitive genius Wells's imparted to his story. He invents a machine that offers a kind of ultimate freedom, escape from the 'now', the whole of the past and the future our playground. It is, when you boil it down, the fantasy of escaping mortality as such—for what is death but the formal structure of our various individual timelines? Wells's skill was to understand that the escape-route from death leads directly back *to* death: the death of the individual becomes the death of the species. There's a reason Wells's terminal beach has proved so iconic for science fiction writers. The ultimate destination of humankind's evolutionary journey through time, according to the first, serialised version of *The Time Machine*, is a strange globular creature, at first mistaken for inanimation, as black as blindness, round like one of Oedipus's plucked-out eyeballs, subsisting at the very end of time that is death:

> A shallow sandbank had appeared in the sea and the water had receded from the beach. I fancied I saw some black object flopping about upon this bank … the darkness grew apace; a cold wind began to blow in freshening gusts from the east, and the showering white flakes in the air increased in number. I saw the black central shadow of the eclipse sweeping towards me. In another moment the pale stars alone were visible. All else was rayless obscurity. The sky was absolutely black.
>
> As I stood sick and confused I saw again the moving thing upon the shoal—there was no mistake now that it was a moving thing—against the red water of the sea. It was a round thing, the size of a football perhaps, or, it may be, bigger, and tentacles trailed down from it; it seemed black against the weltering blood-red water, and it was hopping fitfully about. [*Time Machine*, 14]

This rayless obscurity is Oedipus's blindness; the black, flopping blob is all of humanity resolved into its ultimate form, death as such, mortality as such.

And the only escape from this terminus is to return, to come back in time, to go back to where you originally came from. The secret Oedipus discovers is that sex does not lead into new life and new possibilities, as the conventional wisdom claims that it does, but rather reverts back upon itself, returns to its source, the mother, folding procreation and incest and death into one monstrous taboo-violating unity.

The sphingian riddle superposes sex and death, something *The Time Machine* understands perfectly. This is why it's worth recovering the original perversity and monstrous transgression of the 'romance' between the Traveller and Weena, howsoever normalised it has become by readers and critics. It's the incestuous mirror-image of Oedipus and Jocasta, and just like the original myth, it leads into the auto-involutions of death. It is no coincidence that, having invented this extraordinary device, a machine for travelling in time, Wells never re-used it in his very many subsequent fictions—a fact that stands in the starkest contrast with all the SF writers who followed him, myself included, who have all used and re-used time machines in their work all the time. On the one hand, Wells's refusal simply to rehash his earlier ideas is a testament to his impressive ingenuity and innovation. But on the other, it is a tacit acknowledgement that there's nowhere else for the machine to go except *back to its own source*, and death. We might think that this device, and science fiction itself, will speed us through possibilities in ways that make appear dazzling new wonders transforming the everyday into the rich and strange: the sun hopping swiftly across the sky; the palpitation of night and day merging and the sky taking on a wonderful deepness, a splendid luminous colour of blue, the jerking sun becoming a streak of fire, a brilliant arch, in space. Wonderful! But although this novel shows us these things, and the technicolour far-future, and the pretty-faced young elven descendants of humankind with whom we can eat and take our ease and with whom we can even have sex, it only gives us a surface glimpse of the colour and excitement. The longer we sit on the saddle, the more these superficial excitements blue-shift into invisibility; the more alarming and disgusting truths begin to emerge from the infra-realms of reality; things that have always been true and always before us, but unnoticed, hidden in the lower-depths. Humans are monsters that devour themselves, literally as cannibals and erotically as oedipal figures. Futurity and the past are the same, inescapable path, and it leads only to death and blindness. The curse cannot be escaped-from, because the curse is us, we are the monster. Wells's *Time Machine* is a wonderfully riddling text that invites us to try and unriddle it. And generations of SF fans and writers have accepted that invitation. We should be careful, though. We're no more likely than was Oedipus to like the answer it gives us.

Wells's second full-length novel, *The Wonderful Visit* (also published 1895), inverts not only the premise of *The Time Machine* but its mood. Instead of an ordinary traveller from the 1890s exploring the exotic and strange communities of the far future, this novel describes a traveller from an exotic and strange world—an angel, from the 'Angelic Dimension'—exploring an ordinary 1890s English community. And instead of a sublime and dream haunting chill, the affect of this short novel is cosy to the point of tweeness. The Angel, like the Time Traveller, has no name (although the residents of Siddermorton, the village he visits, end up calling him 'Thomas Angel'); and like the Time Traveller he is forced to interrupt his travels because his machine is damaged, the 'machine' in this case being his wings. The Vicar of Siddermorton, Mr Hilyer, hears reports of a 'strange bird' flying about; he goes out to see for himself, taking his rifle with him, since one of his hobbies is collecting, stuffing and displaying rare birds. He doesn't mean to shoot the angel, and yet somehow he does: 'the Vicar stood aghast, with his smoking gun in his hand. It was no bird at all, but a youth with an extremely beautiful face, clad in a robe of saffron and with iridescent wings' [*Wonderful Visit*, 5]. The angel turns out to be an ingenuous, unflaggingly polite individual. He encounters all the business of our ordinary existence with astonished delight and bafflement. The novel plays with that moment in Lewis Carroll's *Through the Looking Glass* where the unicorn is amazed to see a little girl, a creature he had previously thought merely mythical. The Angel regards the Vicar, and all his fellows, as creatures out of legend—'"Dear me!" said the Angel; "There's deer and a stag! Just as they draw them on the coats of arms. How grotesque it all seems!"'—since our realm is a sort of dream dimension to the Angels, just as theirs is to us (populated as it is with 'Griffins and Dragons—and Jabberwocks—and Cherubim—and Sphinxes—and the Hippogriff—and Mermaids—and Satyrs').

The Vicar takes the Angel home, binds up his wound and dresses him in conventional clothes. Hilyer's curate and others think at first that Hilyer has installed a mistress in the vicarage ('"This comes," he heard the Curate's wife say, "of having an unmarried vicar—"'). When they realise the Angel is male the rumour goes about that he is the Vicar's illegitimate son, which gossip causes the pious, celibate old fellow much distress. The Angel himself, never having experienced pain before, and being wholly innocent of death, is horrified at the existence we mortals endure. He wanders the village, gets mocked and pelted by urchins, is shunned by the elderly matrons of the village, meets a tramp who regales him with stories of the wickedness of the local aristocrat, Sir John Gotch. All this time he is losing his natural iridescence and colour as he becomes increasingly corrupted. Only the vicar's pretty servant girl, Delia

Hardy, keeps the faith where Mr Angel is concerned, and he, in turn, develops tender feelings for Delia, which outrages the stiff sense of class-probity that obtains in the village. The novel then hurries through its denouement: the Vicar accidentally sets fire to his own vicarage. Delia rushes into the burning building to rescue the Angel's violin, the Angel goes in after her and both are burned to death. Or more precisely:

> Suddenly the flames spurted out in a blinding glare that shot upward to an immense height, a blinding brilliance broken by a thousand flickering gleams like the waving of swords.... Little Hetty Penzance had a pretty fancy of two figures with wings, that flashed up and vanished among the flames. [*Wonderful Visit*, 52]

There is charm in this novel, and some of the humorous touches work—though it has to be said that many of them don't. The comedy of manners feels often dated and plodding, and the satire is diffuse. Some of it is targeted at the restrictive idiocies of social convention, which generates one kind of affect and some at broader exigencies of day-to-day living ("'the chair,' said the Vicar, "to tell you the truth, has always puzzled me. It dates, I think, from the days when the floors were cold and very dirty. I suppose we have kept up the habit") which generates another. A third flavour of satire is aimed at existential universals like pain, dying and the like, which is yet another thing. The three targets don't coalesce very well, which blurs the book's focus. The Angel is designedly a mild and pleasant character, but that doesn't mean Wells is able to lift him out of mere blandness, and his tender passion for Delia strikes a false note. We can, of course, imagine Wells himself wanting to have sex with a pretty serving maid, but the Angel comes from a realm where there is neither marriage nor giving in marriage, and for him to become besotted with a human woman would surely be like you or I falling for a jabberwocky. Nonetheless, Wells can't let go of the notion. Having previously only encountered a selection of the village's *grande dames*, the Angel is struck when Delia waits on table for him.

> 'Was that a lady, too?'
> 'Well,' said the Vicar. 'No—she is not a lady. She is a servant.'
> 'Yes,' said the Angel; 'she had rather a nicer shape.'
> 'You mustn't tell Mrs Mendham that,' said the Vicar, covertly satisfied. [*Wonderful Visit*, 18]

The novel needs much more textual friction between the angel's world and ours but too often the novel prefers whimsy to estrangement. *The Time*

Machine builds not a detailed world so much as a compelling timescape, touching on the actual chill of sublimity in its grasp of cosmic decay; but *The Wonderful Visit* fails to situate what it describes on any fully realised foundation of estrangement. Satirising pomposity, disliking pain or lusting after pretty serving girls, are none of them strange activities and do not estrange in Wells's telling here; and the glimpses of the Angelic Dimension, though rather lovely, are too strenuously (to use an anachronistic term) *psychedelic* to work on that score. In a nutshell, *The Wonderful Visit* is not *science-fictional* enough.

These, then, were Wells's first two novel-length publications. *The Time Machine* was an immediate success, and its enduring fame has done much to consolidate Wells's position as a major literary figure. *The Wonderful Visit* has fallen into obscurity. It did well enough in its day (Wells wrote to his mother, 27 October 1895, boasting 'my last book seems a hit—everybody has heard of it—and all kinds of people seem disposed to make much of me') and Wells went so far as to stage a public reading of it at the Gaiety Theatre, Hastings, in April 1896, the purpose of which was to establish dramatic copyright preliminary to a full stage adaptation—a sign that Wells was thinking of diversifying his output into drama. In the event, the theatrical version of *The Wonderful Visit* didn't materialise (a version adapted by Wells and St John Ervine was eventually staged in London in 1921 but was not a hit).

Nonetheless, Wells felt confident enough of his earning power to resign his position on the *Pall Mall Gazette*, and to buy his first house in Woking. He had, indeed, achieved remarkable success, personal, critical and financial, in a relatively short time. Wells's *Autobiography* looks back on this whole time as 'a fairly cheerful adventure', and the inserted qualifier is something of a giveaway. His friends thought him content, and he was certainly productive but he felt the pinch of sexual frustration. Nor was he entirely hale. On the plus side, he and Jane learned to cycle. In the Surrey countryside, he and Jane 'could restore our broken contact with the open air. There I planned and wrote the *War of the Worlds*, the *Wheels of Chance* and *The Invisible Man*' [*Autobiography*, 458]. 'The bicycle was the swiftest thing upon the roads in those days,' Wells notes. 'There were as yet no automobiles and the cyclist had a lordliness, a sense of masterful adventure, that has gone from him altogether now.'

Wells was also enlarging his circle of literary friendships. Through his theatrical reviewing, he had met George Bernard Shaw, a friendship cemented by a mutual interest in socialism, although their relationship remained prickly and was sometimes actively hostile in the decades to come. On 20 November 1896 Wells met George Gissing at a literary dinner held in an Oxford Street restaurant, and the two immediately hit it off. Gissing was 9 years older than

Wells and had published 17 books, but none had earned much money or settled his fame, not even his masterpiece *New Grub Street* (1891)—an enduringly heart-rending account of a writer's subsistence-level financial precarity based on Gissing's own experience. In that novel, Edwin Reardon struggles to support his wife Amy with ceaseless, underpaid and underappreciated literary labour. Reardon is eventually abandoned by his wife, his health gives out and he sinks to death whilst his friend Jasper Milvain, less talented but with a keener eye for the main chance, marries money, rents fashionable rooms on Mornington Street and becomes a literary success. Wells was very struck by the novel: 'he rushed up to Gissing after dinner and said that when he first read New Grub Street he had been poor and ill, with a wife named Amy and living on Mornington Street.' 'I rather liked Wells's wild face and naïve manner,' Gissing jotted in his diary. 'Not at all the man I had expected' [Delany, 256]. The two men went on to forge a particular bond. Wells became friendly, over the course of his life, with a great many writers and other famous people, but he never again had the particular connection he experienced with Gissing. Though he wrote a completely different sort of fiction, was socialist where Gissing was small-c conservative, and though Wells enjoyed all the success Gissing did not, the two became very close. Wells assisted Gissing through his complicated (indeed bigamous) love life and at 1903 was present at his deathbed in the Pyrénées-Atlantique village of Saint-Jean-Pied-de-Port.

During this period Wells travelled up from Woking to London often, to meet editors and other writers, and he later told his friend St John Ervine that it was whilst 'walking in the Tottenham Court Road on a Bank Holiday when he was in a mood of discontent' that he 'thought of the plot of that clever, devilish story *The Island of Doctor Moreau*' [Ervine, 253]. This story of a cruel scientist vivisecting animals to modify them into quasi-human forms was to prove his second masterpiece. He wrote it quickly and Heinemann published it in March 1896—in light brown cloth with a rather handsome design of a tropical island embossed on the cover. It was an immediate hit and, better than mere sales it generated some sparks of actual controversy, something which would increasingly act as yeast to Wells's expanding fame. In this case, a stern review in the *Times* (17 June 1896) called its topic 'loathsome and repulsive' and advised: 'the book should be kept out of the way of young people and avoided by all who have good taste, good feeling or feeble nerves. It is simply sacrilege to steep fair nature in the blood and antiseptic of the vivisecting anatomical theatre.' Wells himself pondered adding 'A Satirical Grotesque' as the novel's subtitle, but decided against anything so obvious. Satire, after all, loses its properly Swiftian sting if diluted by too much explanation or mitigation.

Moreau appeared between *The Time Machine* (in which humans devolve into bestial forms) and 1898's *The War of the Worlds* (in which bestial aliens smash civilisation). Something was on Wells's mind: a Darwinian something. Before Darwin humans had believed themselves unique, god-formed, fundamentally different to animals. Darwin said: not so. Humans are merely animals mutated by evolution. *The Island of Doctor Moreau* is the first great novel of that revolution in thought.

A well-bred Englishman, Edward Prendick, becomes marooned upon a Pacific island inhabited only by the vivisectionist Dr Moreau, his assistant Montgomery and the various half-men Moreau has fashioned by surgical interventions upon animal life—surgery undertaken without the benefit of anaesthesia. These beast-beings have developed a rudimentary religion, with Moreau himself as a combined God of Mercy and Pain ('His is the Hand that wounds,' is their chant, 'His is the Hand that heals'). The novel's Scientific Eden also includes a version of the Biblical command not to eat from the 'Tree of the Knowledge of Good and Evil': Moreau has ordered his beast-men not to taste blood. In the course of the story, this command is transgressed and Pendrick watches, a horrified bystander, as the creatures revert to their murderously bestial origins. Wells later cheerily called the book 'an exercise in youthful blasphemy' and 'theological grotesque'. Filmed many times, adapted and continued by other writers, the bad Doctor's name has become a shorthand for vivisectionist sadism and creative bestiality.

It's worth dwelling on that name for a moment. Less than halfway through his story the narrator suddenly exclaims: 'Moreau! … I know that name.' Critics have certainly made much of the naming in this novel. *Moreau* in French means 'brown-skinned, like a Moor', and whilst the Moreau Wells portrays is exaggeratedly white, with a long white beard (a parody God-the-Father) he is also the novel's locus for its anxieties about race, miscegenation and pollution—very much part of the cultural context of imperial Britain in the 1890s. Other critics have suggested that the first syllable of Moreau's name hints at *mors*, *morte*, death; just as the second (*eau* of course means water) points to his islander isolation, or perhaps the fluidity with which he treats flesh, or conceivably the blasphemous 'baptism' he performs upon his animals. But we can go further, and treat 'Moreau' as an elongated version of the name 'More', the man who wrote the world's first Utopia—another fable set upon a distant island where human nature was reworked and refined. Moreau's island is actually named 'Noble's Island' on the map, a name which gestures ironically at nobility whilst also including an echo of More's original tale in its first syllable; for the name 'utopia' is a learned pun that means both 'good-place' and 'bad-place'. 'No-bles', Wells's 'No-' island, is a place distinctly unblessed, twisting More's happy utopian paradigm into monstrous, dystopian shapes.

The Island of Doctor Moreau is a novel whose symbolic meanings are so richly layered that, as with this discussion of naming, it is easy to get carried away. Margaret Atwood wrote a brief introduction to the novel in which she offered, in quick succession, ten different readings: Moreau as evolutionary thought experiment, as 1890s imperial adventure yarn, as scientific romance, as a rewriting of *The Tempest*, or the Bible or Coleridge's *Rime of the Ancient Mariner* and various others. There's fun to be had in such ludic hermeneutics, although we're also entitled to wonder if such prodigality of interpretation rather misses the point of Wells's novel. Because, actually, *The Island of Doctor Moreau* is simple. In fact, its brute clarity is the ground for its enduring appeal. It is simple because animals are simple, relatively speaking. We keep pets *because* they are simple. Some people even prefer pets to people, because pets give us crucial things—companionship, loyalty, love—without all the complications entailed by adult human relationships. The simplicity of animals is not an *innocence*, of course. It would be more than naïve of us to think so; it would be a category error. Yet simplicity is a central part of the way the beast signifies to humanity.

Wells is superb on the ramifications of this simplicity: not only its potential for violence—its, to use a loaded term, 'barbarism'—but also its eerie glamour, compounded of charm and strangeness. All genuinely simple beings partake of this glamour, I think because the intrinsic richness and complexity of human existence throws the truly simple into a starkly lovely but inhuman contrast. Hence, for example, the elvish quality of the first dog-, puma-, pig- and monkey-men Prendick encounters: 'they wore turbans too, and thereunder peered out their elfin faces at me, faces with protruding lower jaws and bright eyes' [*Moreau*, 6]. Hence, too, the faerie 'pointed ears and luminous eyes' of Montgomery's assistant. Freud went on to map this territory expertly in his *Civilisation and its Discontents* (1930), but Wells got there first. *The Island of Doctor Moreau* understands completely that violence is simple where civilisation (negotiation, compromise, repression) is complicated. Moreau holds his beast-men in check with a Law that is a nominalisation of Pain, his medium for creating them: a simple, if precarious, strategy. The trace of the novel is the disintegration or degeneration of this imposed structure.

If we think about it for a moment, the pain Moreau inflicts upon his creatures ought to bother us a great deal. I don't mean in an ethical sense (of course that) but *practically* speaking. Why does he not use anaesthetics? The tale was written in the 1890s, and set in 1887. Ether and chloroform had been widely used in surgery since the 1840s. But no: Moreau refuses to anaesthetise his victims because pain is as much a part of his surgical tool-kit as blades or suture-thread. In his own terrifying words: 'each time I dip a living creatures into the bath of burning pain, I say: this time I will burn out all the animal, this time I will make a rational creature' [*Moreau*, 14]. There's a name for that, too: sadism. One of the things Wells is doing in this novel is dramatising a sort of apotheosis of sadism. Pain as a metaphysical horizon of being. There's more to this, though, novel than can covered by the description 'sadism'. Prendick asks Moreau why 'he has taken the human form as his model'. 'There seemed to me then,' he adds, 'and seems to me now, a strange wickedness in that choice.' Moreau's answer ('he had chosen that form by chance') is very evidently not the truth of the matter. Prendick perhaps takes the 'strange wickedness' that makes him queasy to be blasphemy, but I think the novel is saying something else, leading us towards a rather different sort of name: love. *The Island of Doctor Moreau* is populated with variform Moreauian beast-men, but there is only one female in the novel, painstakingly (literally) created out of an altered puma. Several critics have noticed a sexual subtext here. 'Cat' was Victorian slang of prostitute. Wells adopted the pet-name 'Jaguar' when he was with his lover Rebecca West, just as she was 'Panther'. It certainly looks as though Moreau is in the business of making a mate for himself.

But this is also his downfall. Though it is the taste for blood that encourages the beast-men to revolt, it is the escape of the puma-woman that spells Moreau's individual doom. It is quite appropriate to Wells's fable that unleashed female potency is the force to destroy Moreau's garden Eden. The novel is saying: beasts are simple, and pain is simple. But it is also saying: love is not simple, and it is love that collapses Moreau's brutal idyll. Which brings me back to names, one again. For this fate also is buried in his name, too as if Wells has excavated Moreau's name from the Tarot card that could predict his doom, LAMOUREAUX, the lovers. Even so late as 1896 Wells had not yet come to an existential accommodation where his own sexual desires were concerned.

Bibliography

Delany, Paul (2008). *George Gissing: a Life*. London: Weidenfeld and Nicholson.

Ervine, St John G. (1923). *Some Impressions of my Elders*. London, Allen & Unwin.

MacKenzie, Norman and Jeanne (1973). *The Time Traveller: the life of H.G. Wells*. London: Weidenfeld and Nicholson.

Stover, Leo ed. (1996), *The Time Machine: A Critical Text of the 1895 London First Edition, with an Introduction and Appendices*. McFarland.

4

Bicycles and Tripods

The Wheels of Chance (1896); *The Invisible Man* (1897); *The War of the Worlds* (1898)

Bertie and Jane lived in Woking for 18 months; it was there that Wells planned and wrote the *War of the Worlds*, the *Wheels of Chance* and *The Invisible Man*. He and Jane would cycle round the Surrey countryside, and sometimes undertake longer journeys—down to the south coast, and once, in April 1897, all the way to Devonshire, where Jane and H.G. stayed with George Gissing. That westward journey took them 5 days, as, presumably, did the journey back.

The textual product of all this cycling was the short comic novel *The Wheels of Chance* (1896), a work that deserves to be restored to public attention not only on its own merits and as a portrait of a particular Edwardian moment, but as Wells's first novel-length excursion into what, for want of a better word, we might as well call 'realist' fiction. It is common among critics to note that almost all Wells's 'mimetic' work fictionalises some aspect of his autobiographical experience. That's, of course, of interest to his biographer; but what is more interesting is the degree to which, and the lenses *through* which, the raw illumination of life experience is refracted by the writerly imagination. In the three novels, and many of the short stories he wrote in the last years of the 1890s Wells is coming at a particular theme or topic. In a word, that theme is freedom. The richness of these books is in how they inflect that concept as social freedom, sexual freedom and existential freedom by balancing them with (on the other) licence, chaos and destruction.

In *The Wheels of Chance* Hoopdriver, a Putney draper's assistant takes a cycling holiday to the south coast and back. On the way, he meets another cyclist, the beautiful young Jessie Milton. She has run away from her Surbiton stepmother and believes a man called Bechamel will help her set up as an

© The Author(s) 2019
A. Roberts, *H G Wells*, Literary Lives, https://doi.org/10.1007/978-3-030-26421-5_4

independent woman. In fact, Bechamel has no such intentions and hopes only to seduce and ruin the toothsome Jessie. Hoopdriver helps her escape this fate. Smitten himself and hoping to impress her, Hoopdriver subsequently pretends to aristocracy and spins tales of his enormous South African wealth. He comes clean eventually, and they end the story friends—not, interestingly, married or lovers, since Jessie decides, commendably, that 'she was going to Live her Own Life, with emphasis'. Wells might be fantasising about sexual possibility as he cycled around, but it seems his imagination did not yet license even the fantastical consummation of such desires.

Wells later talked of how his erotic dissatisfaction and yearning found no outlet during his Woking years: 'so long indeed as Jane and I were in a desperate and immediate struggle with the world there was no scope for any wanderings of my desires, and we managed to carry on with the limited caresses and restricted intimacies her relative fragility and her relative lack of nervous and imaginative energy imposed upon us' [*H. G. Wells in Love*, 40]. Not until he built his own house in Sandgate in the new century did 'an ampler life and more vigorous health' facilitate Wells's extramarital affairs. It's tempting to read the 1890s furious work pace and the passion for pedalling about the countryside as indicative of a physical redirection of desire. Wells's cycling enthusiasm was, as Jeremy Withers notes, unusually intense, lasting long after the general craze fell away (Withers dates the 'bike boom' to 1895–96 and suggests it was followed by a crash 1897–98 [Withers, 8]). The point is that social freedom and sexual freedom are strongly correlated in Wells's sensibility.

Wheels of Chance is a work of unfeigned and rather exhilarating energy: brisk, lively, comic in tone rather than incident. The book gleams with youth: fresh in its descriptions, hopeful and forward-looking and a tonic to read: 'it was fine, full of a promise of glorious days, a deep blue sky with dazzling piles of white cloud … He wheeled his machine up Putney Hill, and his heart sang within him. He would not have changed places with a soul in any one of them for a hundred pounds' [*Wheels of Chance*, 4]. This is what the bicycle means: freedom, in a literal but also in a metaphorical sense. Social historians of the machine have demonstrated how important the mobility provided by this new technology was in terms of freeing up access for middle-, lower-middle- and working-class people who couldn't afford horses and carriages; and this freeing up is one of the main themes of Wells's fiction, as it was of his own life. Travel mobility literalises social mobility, the ability to make more of your life than being (for example) a mere draper's assistant. The story at the heart of *The Wheels of Chance* is one which Wells would retell several times in his later career: a love-match between an energetic young Wellsian clerk and a beautiful young woman of a different class. Indeed, the pleasure Hoopdriver derives from his freedom could not be more clearly signposted as quasi-sexual:

Hoopdriver mounted, and began his great Cycling Tour along the Southern Coast. There is only one phrase to describe his course at this stage, and that is—*voluptuous curves*. He did not ride fast, he did not ride straight, an exacting critic might say he did not ride well—but he rode generously, opulently, using the whole road. [*Wheels of Chance* 4]

These voluptuous curves direct Hoopdriver into his first encounter with Jessie on the road to Esher involves a collision eroticised so completely it reads like a bicycle premonition of Ballard's *Crash*:

The Young Lady in Grey was also riding a bicycle. Hoopdriver was dimly aware that she was young, rather slender, dark, and with a bright colour and bright eyes. Strange doubts possessed him as to the nature of her nether costume.... Her handles glittered; a jet of sunlight splashed off her bell blindingly ... the roads converged. She was looking at him. She was flushed, and had very bright eyes. Her red lips fell apart. [*Wheels of Chance*, 5]

Hoopdriver keeps bumping into Jessie all the way to the south coast. Sex doesn't happen, and yet sex is immanent in everything Hoopdriver does and wants, which is a pretty good description of 'adolescence', I'd say (at least if my own adolescence was anything to go by). Of course, in another sense. it quite mischaracterises Wells's vision to call it, as I do above, Ballardian. Ballard finds something grotesque and nihilistic in his eroticised car-crashes. Wells finds bicycle-crashes erotic in a much happier sense: a blame-free occasion for physical propinquity in a culture that otherwise prevents men and women getting too close to one another.

Sexual desire, in this novel, is a male thing. Both Hoopdriver and Bechamel desire Jessie, but Jessie reciprocates with neither. And, of course, the mobility enabled by these new 'bicycle' machines was strongly gendered. Social historians note that the figure of the 1890s 'New Woman' was both characterised and satirised as achieving a socially destabilising empowerment by virtue of this new mode of transport. 'Woman, until recently, was for ages regarded as a dependent being in the family,' noted *The Lady Cyclist* in 1896; 'in social, educational, religious and political matters, and in most outdoor exercises, she was looked upon as almost helpless.' The pushbike changed all that. 'The tens of thousands of wheelwomen of the country who have demonstrated that their sex are not an inferior portion of the human family in this wonderful form of outdoor sport have rendered untold aid to the cause of equal suffrage,

THE AWFUL EFFECTS OF VELOCIPEDING.

Fig. 4.1 1890 cartoon: A 'Rational woman' on a bicycle

by dispelling the mistaken idea of women's dependence and helplessness.' Much of this era's comedy mediated genuine anxieties about the empowerment of women and the diminution of male stature occasioned by the bike (Fig. 4.1).

Wells's narrative several times refers to Jessie's dress and manner as 'rational', 1890s code for what we nowadays might call 'feminist'; but although the narrative toys with our readerly expectations as to the mode of rationality she espouses, in the event she does not go the full Ann Veronica, and have sex with either of the men who pursue her. She is a fast woman in the literal cycle-assisted sense, but not in the sexual sense.

Running alongside the real-life plausibilities and frustrations of the mimetic in this novel are a series of more properly SF fantasias predicated, I would argue, on the cyborg potentialities of the bicycle, that ur-man-machine combination. *Wheels of Chance* is a novel with a manifest connection with the coming of the Wellsian Martians, those part organic, part machinic invaders. Chapter 16 opens with this whimsical digression:

> Some jester, enlarging upon the increase of bald heads and purblind people, has deduced a wonderful future for the children of men. Man, he said, was nowadays a hairless creature by forty or fifty, and for hair we gave him a wig; shrivelled, and we padded him; toothless, and lo! false teeth set in gold. Did he lose a limb, and a fine, new, artificial one was at his disposal; get indigestion, and to hand was artificial digestive fluid or bile or pancreatine, as the case might be. So he went over our anatomies, until, at last, he had conjured up a weird thing of shreds and patches, a simulacrum, an artificial body of a man, with but a doubtful germ of living flesh lurking somewhere in his recesses. To that, he held, we were coming. [*Wheels of Chance*, 16]

Cyborg metatextuality, this; since the 'jester' is Wells himself (the reference is to one of his *Pall Mall Gazette* essays: 'Thoughts on a Bald Head' (1895), later collected in *Certain Personal Matters*). After his first day's cycling, Hoopdriver goes exhausted to bed in a Guildford Inn and has a vivid dream:

> After your first day of cycling one dream is inevitable. A memory of motion lingers in the muscles of your legs, and round and round they seem to go. You ride through Dreamland on wonderful dream bicycles that change and grow; you ride down steeples and staircases and over precipices. ... and in another moment the houses were cracking like nuts and the blood of the inhabitants squirting this way and that. The streets were black with people running. Right under his wheels he saw the Young Lady in Grey. A feeling of horror came upon Mr. Hoopdriver; he flung himself sideways to descend, forgetting how high he was, and forthwith he began falling; falling, falling. [*Wheels of Chance*, 12]

This Juggernaut fantasia is another striking anticipation of the way the Martians will treat this corner of Surrey. It is often remarked that Wells's *Time Machine* is actually a sort of bicycle (it has, after all, a 'saddle'); it is not remarked enough that Wells's invading cyborg Martians are also, in effect, cyclists, albeit cyclists from a planet where the wheel was never invented.

Freedom is, among other things, a function of money; and one thing the successes of his early books did was give Wells the leverage to pursue his own financial interests with a hard-headed vigour. This became, indeed, his lifelong *modus negotiandi*—haggling with editors and publishers to extract as much money as possible for his writing. Norman and Jeanne Mackenzie note how, from the mid-1890s, 'he began an extraordinary process of bargaining and badgering with publishers that lasted until his death', something based on the belief that 'if a publisher was forced to pay excessively favourable terms, he would then be driven to excessively energetic efforts to recoup his investment' [Mackenzies, 111]. In January 1896 Wells signed James Brand Pinker as his literary agent to maximise his bargaining power. This strategy only worked because Wells proved able to write books that sold well, but it certainly *did* work. By the end of 1896 he was in a position to move house. The Woking house was small and lacked a study (Wells used the dining table as his writing desk). When Mrs Robbins, Wells's mother-in-law, came to live with the young couple, the lack of space proved pinching. Accordingly, Wells bought a considerably larger property, 'Heatherlea', in Worcester Park, one of the leafier suburbs of south-west London.

He continued his prolific production of short novels. Next was *The Invisible Man*, serialised in *Pearson's Magazine* in the early months of 1897 and published as a single volume later that year. Wells science fiction fable concerns a scientist called Giffin who discovers a means of making himself invisible. The story is a pseudo-scientific retelling of the 'Ring of Gyges' story from Plato's *Republic* (380 BC)—Gyges was a humble shepherd in the ancient kingdom of Lydia who chanced upon a ring that granted him invisibility, which he used to infiltrate the Court of King Candaules, seduce Candaules's queen, kill the king and to seize the throne for himself. Plato uses the story to make a point about ethics. We act in morally virtuous ways, he argues, only because we do not wish to face the disapproval and punishment of our fellow men. If we were sure we would never be found out we would act in a totally disinhibited manner morally speaking. Virtue, in other words, consists in *being seen*. In his *Experiment in Autobiography* Wells describes Plato's influence upon him as 'like the hand of a strong brother taking hold of me and raising me up', and *The Invisible Man*'s Platonic reworking keeps the moral focus in exactly the same place. As the old sailor, reading a newspaper account of the invisible man notes 'suppose he wants to rob—who can prevent him? He can trespass, he can burgle, he could walk through a cordon of policemen as easy as me or you could give the slip to a blind man!' Of course, Wells's scientist, like Gyges, has larger ambitions than mere theft. He explains to Kemp in Chap. 24 that he plans to use murder as a path to power: 'not wanton killing, but a judicious slaying… A Reign of Terror'. He informs the town of his plans:

> Port Burdock is no longer under the Queen, tell your Colonel of Police, and the rest of them; it is under me—the Terror! This is day one of year one of the new epoch,—the Epoch of the Invisible Man. I am Invisible Man the First. [*Invisible Man*, 27]

This, however, is (to quote one of the novel's chapter titles) 'The Plan That Failed'—the grand, Gyges-like ambition announced in Griffin's proclamation comes to nothing. Griffin's problem is not ambition or ruthlessness, but a more human level of incompetence, aggravated by the practical problems of his invisibility. Wells's interest here and throughout his career is in the obstacles to desire rather than the desire itself: the specific frustrations and friction of everyday life. This is the story not of a royal usurper but a petty man. For Wells, even the most startling developments in science cannot change the medium of obstruction and discontent that characterises day-to-day existence. Men are not kings. In this sense, not even kings are kings. Invisibility gives Griffin Gyges-like advantages over ordinary, visible humanity; but these advantages are bought at a price. Griffin can render himself, but not his clothes, invisible, and so must go naked, whatever the weather or temperature. Neither can he eat ('"Bear in mind," said Kemp, "his food shows. After eating, his food shows until it is assimilated. So that he has to hide after eating"') nor disguise his smell from bloodhounds. The bandages Griffin wears when he wishes to be seen are an additional part of this. To go clothed, the invisible man has to wrap his whole face and hands in bandages in a way that ordinarily would signal extreme burns or disease. His invisibility is a visible injury to himself.

Wells's satire on heartless scientific vision turns, as it always does in Wells's fiction, into a meditation upon the way scientific advance precisely does *not* vault over the practical problems of ordinary life. There is, as many critics have noted, one flaw in the Wells's quasi-scientific extrapolation of Griffin's invisibility. Wells's invisible man ought to be blind, of course (an invisible retina would stop no photons). Wells knew this fact but chose to ignore it, as have the many writers and filmmakers of the twentieth and twenty-first centuries who have followed Wells's lead in making stories about invisible men, invisible women and invisible hobbits. Or perhaps it would be better to say, Wells doesn't so much *ignore* the question of Griffin's blindness as transfer it from a physical to an ethical realm. As a portrait of a scientist (irascible, egotistical, at once petty-minded and grandiose) Griffin is not designed to flatter the profession, but this is a specific rather than a general point. Griffin *is* blind; he's just not physically blind. Glorying in his invisibility he sees himself as tyrant of the world; he is blind to the practical obstacles that will prevent that eventuality. Since *Frankenstein*, SF has been fascinated by the unintended consequences of scientific or technological advance; and 'unintended consequence' is just another way of saying 'the invisible future'. And insofar as 'the future' is the realm of science fiction, this novel is saying: SF is blind.

The last of the Woking-written books was *The War of the Worlds*, which appeared in *Pearson's Magazine* between April and December 1897. Serialisation began before Wells had even finished writing the novel, and before agreeing to it Pearson demanded to know what the ending was. Satisfied with the answer he got, Pearson paid Wells a handsome £200 for serialisation rights. Heinemann issued the story in book form in 1898.

The story concerns a giant metal cylinder that crash-lands near Woking. Out of it emerge tentacled Martians to make war upon humanity from towering mechanical tripods, laying waste to South East England before eventually succumbing to Earthly bacteria against which they have no natural defence. But you already know the story. *The War of the Worlds* is, surely, Wells's most famous novel. It has had a greater influence on the development of twentieth-century SF than any other Wells title, and possibly than any other novel (save, perhaps, *Frankenstein*). And there is a reason for that. This novel is Wells at his most vivid and economical, his most thought-provoking and chilling and mind-expanding and exciting. Its success was immediate and has proved enduring—it has never been out of print. Indices of the immediate impact it made are provided by how extensively it was pirated: two unauthorised serialisations of the novel were published in the USA before the whole book was even published: both were called *Fighters from Mars, or the War of the Worlds*, one serialised in the *New York Evening Journal* December 1897– January 1898, the other in the *Boston Post* in 1898, altering the story's location from England to New York and Boston respectively. Over the book's 12 decades of life there have been innumerable adaptations, radio, film and TV versions, sequels and comic-books adaptations.

It's worth stressing how organically this novel grows out of the writing Wells was doing earlier in the 1890s. Earlier I mentioned the various continuities between *Wheels of Chance* and *War of the Worlds*, and that Wells's essay 'Man of the Year Million' (reprinted in *Certain Personal Matters*) is directly behind passages such as this:

> The Martians may be descended from beings not unlike ourselves, by a gradual development of brain and hands (the latter giving rise to the two bunches of delicate tentacles at last) at the expense of the rest of the body. Without the body the brain would, of course, become a mere selfish intelligence, without any of the emotional substratum of the human being. [*War of the Worlds*, 2.2]

And the novel's famous opening paragraph, in which the Martians scrutinise humanity 'as narrowly as a man with a microscope might scrutinise the transient creatures that swarm and multiply in a drop of water' riffs directly from his essay 'Through a Microscope' from the same volume. More than this *War of the Worlds* draws on a crowded late-nineteenth-century sub-genre, 'future invasion of Britain' tales. The vogue for this kind of story was ignited by Chesney's *Battle of Dorking* (1871), a novelette in which a small but efficient German army enters Britain, rapidly defeating poorly organised British troops. The intrinsic interest of Chesney's tale is small: a thinly written first-person narrative into which are kneaded quantities of hectoring Tory militarism. But there's no denying the tremendous contemporary popularity it enjoyed, and the chord of British Imperial anxiety it touched. *Blackwood's Magazine*, where the story was first published, reprinted six times to meet demand. Issued as a pamphlet it sold 110,000 copies in 2 months. Dozens of similar tales appeared over the following years, imagining future invasions of Britain by Europeans, Chinese, Americans and others. Wells certainly deserves credit for the brilliant idea of replacing human adversaries with alien ones; but in other respects, *The War of the Worlds* follows the template established by these kinds of stories. The narrative centres on the life of an ordinary Englishman, and then dramatises the extraordinary erupting into it, including scenes of national military inadequacy and civilian panic; but instead of the Germans or the Chinese it is Martians that invade:

> Those who have never seen a living Martian can scarcely imagine the strange horror of their appearance. The peculiar V-shaped mouth with its pointed upper lip, the absence of brow ridges, the absence of a chin beneath the wedge-like lower lip, the incessant quivering of this mouth, the Gorgon groups of tentacles. [*War of the Worlds*, 1:4]

Lacking digestive tracts of their own, Wells's Martians directly ingest the oxygenated and nutrient-rich blood of others. This vividly visualised icon of monstrous and horrific alienness represents one of those odd synchronicities of literary culture—for Wells started publishing his tales of Martian-alien vampires mere weeks before Bram Stoker published his famous novel of aristocratic-foreigner vampires, *Dracula* (1897). This new myth, a way of representing the sense of something simultaneously other and superior, coming here to feed on our ordinary blood evidently responded to something in the air (the two men weren't friends, and didn't swap story ideas). The difference is that Stoker's predator emblematises the crushing power of the *past*, of class privilege bolstered by all that is old and traditional and deep-rooted. Wells's predators represent the future and actualise a wider sense that technology, especially the connected technologies of motility and warfare, are going to sweep away all that old class-historical inertia. It is not hard to see which of the two was the more prophetic.

Signs of Wells's growing maturity as a writer are present in the control and expressiveness of *The War of the Worlds'* prose, as with the desolate beauty he evokes in a London emptied by the Martian threat and overrun with the red weed they have brought across space. At this point in the book the last Martian is ceasing its weird cry and dying.

> Abruptly as I crossed the bridge, the sound of 'Ulla, ulla, ulla, ulla' ceased. It was, as it were, cut off. The silence came like a thunder-clap. The dusky houses about me stood faint and tall and dim; the trees towards the park were growing black. All about me the red weed clambered among the ruins, writhing to get above me in the dimness. Night, the mother of fear and mystery, was coming upon me. But while that voice sounded the solitude, the desolation, had been endurable; by virtue of it, London had still seemed alive, and the sense of life about me had upheld me. Then suddenly a change, the passing of something—I knew not what—and then a stillness that could be felt. [*War of the Worlds*, 2:8]

This quasi-Islamic cry of 'ulla ulla', the call from an alien muezzin out of a metallic minaret, is an interestingly suggestive touch when it comes to 'othering' the Martians, adding the flavour of exoticised orientalism (it has always struck me as a kind of sound it would be extremely hard to make with a beak-shaped mouth). *The War of the Worlds*, like the other invasion-fantasy books of the 1880s and 1890s, taps-in to a fundamentally xenophobic fear of foreign-ness. Are the Martians merely ciphers for racial and national otherness? Darko Suvin thinks so:

> The Martians from *The War of the Worlds* are described in Goebbelsian terms of repugnantly slimy and horrible 'racial' otherness and given the sole function of bloodthirsty predators, a function that fuses genocidal fire-power—itself described as an echo of the treatment meted out by the imperialist powers to colonized peoples—with the bloodsucking vampirism of horror fantasies. [Suvin, 78]

Wells's novel symbolically distilled the concerns of its age. His Martians are imperialists, using their superior technology to invade a nation (England) which had been accumulating its own Empire throughout the century largely because of a superior technological sophistication. In other words, the arrival of the Martians and their mechanised brutalities are the symbolic forms Wells chose to explore a deeper set of concerns about the violence of Empire-building, and about the anxieties of otherness and the encounter with otherness that Empire imposes on the Imperial peoples. But it misses the power of this book to reduce it to message-fiction. What works so well here is the minuteness of Wells's grasp upon the detail of his imagined drama. There are features of this novel that look, in hindsight, extraordinarily prescient: the alien's heat-ray anticipates laser technology; the lethal 'black smoke' they use looks forward to the use of mustard gas in World War I; and most remarkable of all Wells looks forward to that distinctively modern iteration of war as less soldiers on a battlefield and more massed tides of civilian refugees—non-combatants terrorised and massacred, living under bombardment and gas attack. The final chapter of the novel's first book (16: 'the Exodus from London') is not only one of the first but also one of the most powerful representations in fiction of the way war would come to figure in the twentieth century: huge crowds flooding away from the combat in fear of their lives. War in *The War of the Worlds* is no longer a horizontal interaction between two armies. It now has a terrible vertical vector—something the twentieth-century world would come to know only too bitterly, from shells and bombs to V2s, cruise missiles and drones plummeting down from on-high. When the narrator says 'suddenly, like a thing falling upon me from without, came fear' [*War of the Worlds*, 1:4] he is describing the Martians as externalisations of a state of mind. Indeed that, in a crucial sense, is what *The War of the Worlds* is about.

Related to this is the brilliant twist at the novel's end: the inverted fable of Western colonial aggression defeated not by military force but by microbes. It was not until many decades later that historians of the European empires made plain the extent to which it was precisely such agents that made colonisation possible in the first place: Jared Diamond's celebrated study *Guns, Germs and Steel* (1997) argues that it was European resistance to certain diseases, and the lack of those same microbes in the rest of the world, that laid the grounds for Europe conquering America and Africa rather than, as might have happened, the other way around. There's a version of Wells in the critical literature that reads him as the prophet of social as well as individual hygiene, broadly contemptuous of components of humanity he thought feeble, delinquent or decadent. When he tells us in this novel that 'Martian sanitary science eliminated illness ages ago. A hundred diseases, all the contagions and fevers of human life, consumption, cancers, tumours and such morbidities, never enter into the scheme of their life' [*War of the Worlds*, 2:2] we might even read his tone as one of admiration. But the end of *The War of the Worlds* makes plain that too ruthless a pursuit of social cleanliness is a weakening rather than a strengthening thing. Disease, like empire, is a more complex matter, and Wells's genius in his fiction (if, perhaps, not in his non-fiction) was always with the messy complexities rather than the clean simplicities.

One of the most powerful portions of this short novel is its subtle and allu-sive representation of post-invasion England. From the hints Wells drops, we can intuit a Britain profoundly changed. Some of these changes are obvious: the red weed the invaders brought with them from Mars which has now spread across the mundane landscape, the 'almost complete specimen' of a dead Martian 'in spirits in the Natural History Museum'. More haunting, though, are the artfully throwaway references in the novel's early chapters:

I was at home at that hour and writing in my study; and although my French windows face towards Ottershaw and the blind was up (for I loved in those days to look up at the night sky), I saw nothing of it. [*War of the Worlds*, 1:2]

'In those days…' Presumably, as at the point of writing this narrative, those days are long past: the night sky now a venue of fear instead of wonder. A few pages later the narrator notes that 'few of the common people in England had anything but the vaguest astronomical ideas in those days': *in those days* again pointing to a now in which everybody knows about the solar system and the dangers it poses.

People in these latter times scarcely realize the abundance and enterprise of our 19th-century papers. [*War of the Worlds*, 1:1]

Why has the aftermath of the Martian invasion so reduced the provision of news? Perhaps the implication is that a shattered infrastructure cannot support such things: but I read a different significance into this reference—that the disasters have cured humanity of its passion for news. The news is a way in which we tell stories about ourselves to ourselves, and one of the more radical things about *The War of the Worlds* is precisely its suspicion of storytelling. Wells's narrator falls in with a curate, whose narrative of the invasion (that the Martians are agents of God's judgement against a sinful world) is shown to be inadequate to events. Later he meets an artilleryman who spins a utopian future narrative with humanity creating a new high-tech subterranean civilisation. But he is shown to be an ineffectual dreamer, his storytelling irrelevant to the grim reality. The irony of this repeated suspicion with narrative is that *The War of the Worlds* is itself, of course, a story, a narrative we are invited to distrust. The narrator more-or-less says so:

Perhaps I am a man of exceptional moods. I do not know how far my experience is common. At times I suffer from the strangest sense of detachment from myself and the world about me. [*War of the Worlds*, 30]

The narrator's quixotic mood is integral to the story: sometimes he is rationally dedicated to self-preservation, at other times strangely suicidal moods overcome him ('an insane resolve possessed me. I would die and end it'). Sometimes he travels over the landscape of the novel with purpose—to investigate the cylinder, to find his wife. At other times he moves passively or even randomly. He is enough of an everyman to convey Wells's point: that the human species is inconstant, passive and easily overcome.

Part 2 of the novel is called 'Earth Under the Martians', and although the invaders die of disease before they can conquer the whole world, it is worth consider how the situation that title hints at might have developed. The global population in the 1890s was somewhere between 1.6 billion and 1.8 billion people. This was what the invaders would have needed to subdue. In Wells's novel, ten Martian cylinders land at seven English locations. Each cylinder contains five Martians, a similar number of the bipedal creatures upon which the Martians feed, the component parts for five Tripods ready for assembly, as well as a smaller number of Handling Machines. As to why no more than ten are sent, Wells's narrator isn't sure:

> Why the shots ceased after the tenth no one on earth has attempted to explain. It may be the gases of the firing caused the Martians inconvenience. Dense clouds of smoke or dust, visible through a powerful telescope on earth as little grey, fluctuating patches, spread through the clearness of the planet's atmosphere and obscured its more familiar features. [*War of the Worlds*, 1:1]

It's not clear whether this is the entire expeditionary force, or the vanguard of a larger army that never materialised or perhaps only a preliminary group sent to reconnoitre. Maybe the Martians planned to send scores or hundreds, of cylinders straight away, but as Wells's narrator speculates, the exhaust from the guns stopped them doing so. Maybe they only ever planned a small force to begin with and intended sending more when this advance guard had subdued the territory. At any rate, there's no doubt this is war and that the Martians are invading. So what is their longer-term plan? It cannot be genocide of the human population, since we are their food, and if they kill us all they will starve. It's hardly conceivable the Martians mean to ship over a breeding stock of the biped species on which they feed, an impractically laborious enterprise rendered redundant by our eminent edibility. Of course, what holds for food also holds for colonists. At five travellers per cylinder we might ask: how many craft do the Martians envisage sending, overall? Say the advance guard were to be followed by more cylinders, once the territory is subdued: how many? Hundreds? That would result in a Martian population of Earth in the multiples of hundreds. To rule a planet of over a billion souls.

Now it is, of course, true that a small force can subdue a much larger population: that was how the British ruled their empire, after all. In India, a few thousand officials and some tens of thousands of British troops ruled and policed a population of over 200 million people. It's true that they managed this, in part, through their superiority in the technology of war. The British Empire went through a particularly precarious period in the 1880s, with the imperial army suffering serious military setbacks in Africa at the Battle of Isandlwana (1879) and in Afghanistan at the Battle of Maiwand (1880); two defeats that caused sensation in the British media. That neither proved the start of massed uprisings against British rule can be explained with reference to one exigency: better guns. The Gatling gun was first used in the early 1880s and the old single-charge rifles were replaced with Maxims, the first fully automatic weapon, in 1884. These were used over and over against Zulus, Mahdists, Matabele, Afghans and Indians, and never failed. Wells, a citizen of this very imperial power, knew that much. His Martians are certainly armed with vastly superior ordnance than the Earthlings.

But guns are not enough, on their own, to hold down an empire. The British fought two costly wars in Afghanistan in the nineteenth century, both aimed at securing the northern border of British possessions in India against Russian expansion. But this aim was actually achieved by soft rather than hard power. Diplomacy and targeted financial inducements paid dividends: in 1857, £220,000 helped ensure that Afghanistan remained neutral while the British crushed the mutiny. Divide and rule, paying off some local Indian rulers and warring down others, the judicious use of bribery, flattery, treaties of mutual advantage and the like was much more important than brute force in controlling the huge populations of empire. We have to assume the Martians longer-term plans include something like this. Even a steady fleet of cylinders, fired from the red planet, each bringing only a handful (or a tentacle-clutch) of new individuals, would only very slowly build a population of colonists. A tiny elite to govern billions. Wells's novel, of course, concerns the initial stages of the invasion, when shock and awe is the strategy. But, had they not succumbed to their microbe nemesis we have to assume the Martians would not have continued on a strategy of mere destruction and massacre. The invasion, having cowed the earthlings, would have had to set up imperial structures: client rulers to keep the rest of the population in check, to ensure that the Martians were kept supplied with food (our blood) and left in peace to build whatever structures and technologies they desired.

We must remember one thing above all about the Martians: though they are horrific and monstrous to human eyes, and though Wells's novel draws on the literary conventions of Gothic horror to represent them thus for our excitement, the Martians themselves are super-rational beings, highly intelligent and quite removed from the bestial substrate of mere emotion. For them, the invasion is a rational and intellectual project. Perhaps they do view us as cattle and surely they aim to exploit us. But, having observed us so minutely for so long, they would know that we are clever cattle, capable of impressive feats of farming, engineering and urbanisation. Though they would inevitably consider us inferiors, they would nonetheless plan to talk to us, to negotiate a settlement, on terms of rationally conceived mutual interest, under the aegis of their overwhelming advantages in military might and technology.

Which brings me to one final speculation. To talk to us, they must know our language. It would make sense to gather as much information as possible before the military landing. What if the Martians had sent a lone cylinder at some earlier point in human history, to scout the territory? (Wells's 1897 story 'The Crystal Egg' suggests that the Martians had, at some point, deployed surveillance technology on our world). For a species millions of years ahead of us, evolutionarily speaking, and functionally immortal, this first contact might have been many centuries ago. Let us say they observed human life starting to build great cities, like Rome; long walls like Hadrian's wall, clearing forests for farming. Say they sent a scout to investigate, and that this individual stayed long enough to learn something of human society, luckily escaping human illness. Say this Martian returned to his homeworld with reports of the structures under which human life is organised and something too of its dominant language. The Martians are a pinnacle civilisation who have remained effectively the same for hundreds of thousands, perhaps millions, of years. They would not expect the passage of a couple of 2000 years on Earth to alter such things as the language in which earthlings communicate with one another. We tend to assume the invader's cry of 'ulla ulla' is one Martian trying to communicate with another:

> "Ulla, ulla, ulla, ulla," wailed that superhuman note—great waves of sound sweeping down the broad, sunlit roadway … "Ulla, ulla, ulla, ulla," cried the voice, coming, as it seemed to me, from the district about Regent's Park. [*War of the Worlds*, 2:8]

But what if it's not? What if it is the Martians trying to open channels of communication with us, using their best guess as to our language, Latin? Are they saying *ullus?* 'any?', 'anyone?': but the vocative plural, since they are addressing all of us, and neuter since the Martians have no gender?—'*ulla?*'. Which is to say: could it be the Martians are striding about England calling to us: 'anyone? anyone?' And being puzzled, in their emotionless and rational manner, that nobody is answering them? Wells was proud of his hard-won Latin, after all.

This is a fanciful interpretation, I concede. But if the Martians are calling out in an attempt at communication, then their story becomes more pointedly one of separation, loneliness and death. The freedom to travel, extrapolated from bicycle rides from Surrey to Devonshire all the way up to journeys from Mars to Earth captures, in this powerful and enduring novel, the mixture of exhilaration and dread that the prospect of social and sexual freedom elicited in Wells. He might be free to escape the constraints of class and sexual propriety; but by the same token, his ambition to escape social convention might render him socially invisible, like Griffin—an outcast, a fabulous beast. Perhaps, to take the wider perspective, the invisible heat of illicit passion will burn like a Martian ray and bring ruin to the world. Whatever else it is, *The War of the Worlds* is a story about how a man is separated from his wife by forces beyond his control, how he fights through chaos to return to her. The novel ends on the moment husband and wife are reunited; and very touching it is, too.

Bibliography

Smethurst, Paul (2015). *The Bicycle: Towards a Global History*. Palgrave Macmillan.

Suvin, Darko (1979). *Metamorphoses of Science Fiction: On the Poetics and History of a Literary Genre*. New Haven: Yale University Press.

Withers, Jeremy (2017). *The War of the Wheels, H. G. Wells and the Bicycle*, Syracuse University Press.

5

A New Century

When the Sleeper Wakes (1899), Love and Mr Lewisham (1900), The First Men in the Moon (1901)

With appositeness of the sort with which Providence sometimes supplies us, the calendrical turnover from one century to another marked a substantive change in Wells's life. The 1890s were one kind of living for Wells and the 1900s another. Before 1900, and despite increasing success as a writer, Wells's health was poor and he was still living a life defined largely by sexual frustration. What he called his 'compromise with Jane'—her complaisance with his sexual infidelity—was not finalised between them until after 1900. He was occasionally unfaithful to her nonetheless, but these were more-or-less secretive and more-or-less abortive affairs and neither of those qualities suited Wells as a person. The writer Dorothy Richardson, with whom Wells enjoyed a brief affair, wrote a version of him into her semi-autobiographical novel-sequence *Pilgrimage* (1915–38), 'Hypo G. Wilson', who gives us a glimpse of how masculinist and thrusting Wells appeared to the women he courted. 'There was nothing *but* man,' Hypo tells Miriam (the novels' version of Dorothy). 'Men had discovered science, science was the only enlightenment, science would put everything right; scientific imagination, scientific invention. Man. Women were there, cleverly devised by nature to ensnare man for a moment and produce more men to bring scientific order out of primeval chaos' [Richardson, 2:122]. There's a degree of parody in this, of course; still, parody tends to relate, as smoke does to fire, some mode of truth about its subject. Wells's rather grumpy reaction ('Dorothy's precision and innate truthfulness have deserted her in her account of her love affair with "Hypo"' [*H. G. Wells in Love*, 64]) surely inclines us further towards believing the veracity of Richardson's account. It is, after all, likely that that Wells looking to seduce

© The Author(s) 2019
A. Roberts, *H G Wells*, Literary Lives, https://doi.org/10.1007/978-3-030-26421-5_5

any given woman would over-compensate for his stature, class and inexperience with masculine grandiosity of speech. It doesn't reflect particularly well on him, but it is probably no more shabby than most male strategies of seduction.

This degree of cartoon assertiveness did not characterise Wells's relations with Jane. Indeed, the logic of their human intercourse goes to the other extreme, into manifest infantilisation. In his *Autobiography* Wells provides many examples of the pet-name baby-talk whimsy that, to a large extent, defined the relationship between husband and wife. There are lisping mispronunciations, *finks* for thinks, *umbler-pop* for umbrella and so on, the kind of thing that can only retain its charm within the magic space of the relationship that contains it and which inevitably seems demeaning and irritating to all those who look-in from outside. The *Autobiography* reproduces dozens of his doodled 'picshuas' as well as samples of the comic verse Wells composed for the amusement of his wife. Many of these latter, marred by baby-talk spellings and a deliberate disposability, also record a less conscious aggression. Here, for instance, is one from the end of 1898:

> It was called names
> Miss Furry Boots and Nicketty and Bits,
> And P.C.B., and Snitterlings and Snits,
> It was called names.
> Such names as no one but a perfect 'Orror
> Could ever fink or find or beg or borror
> Names out of books or names made up to fit it
> In wild array
> It never knew when some new name might hit it
> From day to day
> Some names it's written down and some it 'as forgotten'
> Some names was nice and some was simply ROTTEN.
> Sometimes they made it smile, sometimes they seemed to flatter
> Sometimes they made it weep—it really did not matter.
> Some made it pine quite fin, but fin or fat or fatter
> It was called names. [*Autobiography*, 370]

To those not 'in' on the joke, *it* seems a depressingly objectifying way to refer to one's spouse. This is a poem that rather grimaces its jollity, from its promise that Jane can never know when she will be 'hit', through its delight in her tears to, in its penultimate line, goading her over her weight. In the *Autobiography* Wells concedes that this strenuous mutual whimsy was, in its way, the sublimation of resentment and physical incompatibility: something 'that we two contrived in the absence of a real passionate sexual fixation'.

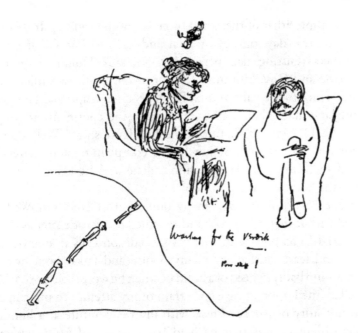

Fig. 5.1 One of Wells's doodled 'picshuas': his wife readies herself to pass judgement on his work

Many will think a rigmarole of infantilising jollity a poor substitute for sexual compatibility, but H.G. and Jane both drew other emotional and practical strengths from the relationship. Here is a 'picshua' of Wells waiting anxiously for Jane to give a judgement on the manuscript of *Love and Mr Lewisham* (Fig. 5.1).

'What the little figures rocketing across the left hand corner of the picture intimate,' Wells says, 'I do not know. They are, I think, just a decorative freak.' Perhaps so, but they are also manifestly an image of a man blasting off and flying away—a rebus of freedom that collides, significantly, with the downward curve of the frame of Wells's anxious life and Wells's sternly unsexily grandmamma-ish wife.

Through 1897 and 1898 Wells, as well as continuing his Stakhanovite production of short fiction and journalism, was working on two novels concurrently: the autobiographical *Love and Mr Lewisham* and a new science-fictional novel called *When The Sleeper Wakes*. Work was not going well. His friend Gissing had relocated to Italy and on 1 January 1898 Wells wrote to him that the books had been 'reshaped, rewritten and retyped time after time'. This weariness of tone reflected writerly frustration exacerbated by a downturn in his health. A desire to address the exhaustion and the sickness both together prompted Wells and Jane to visit Gissing in Rome—their first foreign holiday and the first time either of them had been out of the country. In March 1898 they took the two-day journey by boat and train to join Gissing and meet various others (Gissing had befriended Sherlock Holmes author Arthur Conan Doyle and E.W. Hornung, creator of the gentleman thief Raffles, in Siena). For a month the party toured Rome, Naples, Capri and Pompei before H.G. and Jane made their way back through the continent, arriving home again on the 11 May 1898. But if the holiday restored Wells's spirits the restoration did not last long. By July he was complaining in his letters both of illness and of feelings of claustrophobia. Jane and he agreed on a cycling holiday to the South Coast.

When *The Sleeper Wakes* was finally published in 1899 but Wells was so dissatisfied with it that he rewrote and re-issued it a decade later as *The Sleeper Awakes* (1910). His preface to that revised edition calls it 'one of the most ambitious and least satisfactory of my books' and talks about how he was 'overworked and badly in need of a holiday' when he wrote it. The *Autobiography* later recalled 'the impotent rage and strain of my attempt to put some sort of finish to my story of *Mr Lewisham* with my temperature at a hundred and two'. The difference was that he held back *Love and Mr Lewisham* for a comprehensive rewrite during his convalescence, whereas fiduciary necessity compelled him to publish *When the Sleeper Wakes* in its original and unsatisfactory form.

Wells's autobiography gives us some puzzling details about the 1898 illness itself: 'a sort of break-up,' he calls it, 'of the scars and old clotted accumulations about my crushed kidney', the one he'd damaged playing football when working as a schoolmaster in the 1880s:

> Nothing could have been worse for me than to start, as we did, upon a cycling journey to the south coast. I was ashamed of my bodily discomfort—until I was over forty the sense of physical inferiority was a constant acute distress to me which no philosophy could mitigate—and I plugged along with a head that seemed filled with wool and a skin that felt like a misfit. Somewhere on the road I caught a cold. We struggled to Lewes and then on to Seaford. [*Autobiography*, 494]

Jane took the feverish and agonised Wells by train to a New Romney doctor ('I was now in considerable pain, the jolting carriages seemed malignantly uncomfortable, I suffered from intense thirst, I could get nothing to drink and the journey was interminable'). The doctor insisted on the immediate removal of the injured kidney and a surgeon was called down from London to perform this operation; but when he arrived by train it was discovered 'that the offending kidney had practically taken itself off and that there was nothing left to remove'. I consulted medical professionals during the writing of the present volume, and they were unanimous in insisting kidneys never dissolve away harmlessly or otherwise teleport out of the body. Clearly *something* happened to Wells on this cycling holiday. There's no doubting Bertie's physical distress, nor the fact that after this episode his health improved not just in the short, but in the long, term. He claims he was never again bothered with the kidney. It is difficult to know what, though.

Marked by this sickness and not finished to Wells's satisfaction, *When the Sleeper Wakes* was serialised in *The Graphic* 1898–99—Wells simply could not afford to turn-down the magazine's £700 offer, nor the £500 from Harpers for the book edition and the £300 American advance. The resulting novel catches something of the quality of fever-dream out of which it was produced. The story itself starts with a man called Isbister, walking the Cornish cliffs and chancing upon our hero, Graham, driven to suicidal despair by his chronic insomnia. Isbister persuades him not to jump, but instead to come back to his hotel with him. There, for reasons unspecified in the text, Graham falls into a kind of coma. He sleeps for two centuries, during which time his money accrues hefty interest within the banking system. When Graham finally does awake he discovers that his (now) vast wealth has rendered him nominal master of the world. His sleeping form, held in a crystal cabinet, has become the centre of a kind of cult, on the basis of which the 'White Council', a small group of men who have inherited trustee status for his estate, rule the globe. Since their power depends on the endless deferral of his waking, this Council now plan on killing him, but before they can he is rescued by followers of a revolutionary leader called Ostrog (we later discover that it was Ostrog who woke Graham, by injecting him with stimulants). During the course of his flight from the Council Graham sees that London is now a huge domed urban space: 'Titanic buildings, curving spaciously in either direction. Overhead mighty cantilevers sprang together across the huge width of the place and a tracery of translucent material shut out the sky' [*Sleeper*, 5].

Ostrog stages a revolution and overthrows the Council. He pretends to instal Graham as ruler, but in fact wants power for himself and manipulates Graham as his puppet. For a while Graham is duped and beguiles his time exploring the high-tech future world: Britain now a land of huge automated farmlands, with the entire population living inside four great domed cities, each powered by giant wind-vanes. He learns to fly one of the future's 'aeropiles', discovering in the process a natural aeronautical talent. He also develops tender feelings for Ostrog's attractive niece, Helen Wotton: 'her beauty came compellingly between him and certain immediate temptations of ignoble passion' [*Sleeper*, 17]. It is Helen who reveals the truth to Graham: far from being the future utopia Ostrog claims, the world of 2100 is a place of misery for the masses who toil in factories, paid in food rather than money, suffering high rates of industrial disease and mortality, alienated from family life (children are raised not familially but in institutions) and controlled via fake-news-spewing 'babble machines'. Other systems of control include 'kine-tele-photography' and rationed visits to 'pleasure cities'. Graham confronts Ostrog, who defends the status quo on eugenic grounds: 'Aristocracy, the prevalence of the best—the suffering and extinction of the unfit, and so to better things … convenient Euthanasia … that is the way to improve the race!' [*Sleeper*, 19].

Graham leads a counter-revolution against Ostrog and expels him from London; but Ostrog recruits a police force from Africa, flying them over to act as his enforcers. A battle ensues between Ostrog's followers and Graham's for control of the runways, the 'stages' as Wells calls them, that would enable this force to land. Graham himself goes up in an aeropile to hold the Africans back until the stages are destroyed. Ostrog is also airborn and Graham attempts to engage him in air-to-air combat, although without success. It seems his side is winning, shooting down Ostrog's aeropiles with anti-aircraft guns. "'They win," Graham shouted to the empty air; "the people win!'" He doesn't have long to enjoy his triumph, though:—his craft is caught by the edge of an explosion and the novel ends with him plummeting to his death. The suicide leap averted at the novel's beginning comes true at its end.

Wells's jumping-off point for this novel was the remarkable success of Edward Bellamy's utopian bestseller *Looking Backward: 2000–1887* (1886). In that novel which a young man called Julian West falls asleep in the 1880s USA, waking 113 years later into a socialist utopia North America. Bellamy's book, dramatically inert and tediously preachy though it is, enjoyed astonishing success: over a million copies were sold, 160 Nationalist Clubs formed to propagate the book's ideas, and a Nationalist political party was established that looked, for a while, as if it might have a real shot at contesting the US Presidency. Indeed, it's hard to think of any novel, SF or otherwise, that has had such widespread and immediate an impact. A swarm of unofficial sequels and rebuttals appeared in the decades that followed, all inhabiting the same Rip Van Winkle 'sleeper-wakes-to-future-utopia' trope (over 150 of these have been identified by scholars; see Roemer, 186–207) most notably William Morris's *News From Nowhere* (1890), in which a character called William Guest falls asleep and wakes in a future utopia modelled on labouring-agrarian, rather than Bellamy's technological-urban, lines. Wells's novel exists in explicit dialogue with *Looking Backward*—early on Isbister discusses Graham's coma with his friend Warming: "'It's Rip Van Winkle come real.'"

"It's Bellamy," said Warming' [*Sleeper*, 2]. The thing that makes Wells's intervention into this crowded genre new is, in a word, its *pessimism*. Instead of wandering the gleaming world amazed at its myriad wonders, Wells's protagonist discovers the grim truth beneath the veneer of technological advance: exploitation and oppression.

The 1910 revised version, retitled *The Sleeper Awakes*, is essentially the 1899 book slimmed down: some 6000 words are cut from the first edition and various smaller adjustments made—for instance, Wells changes 'aeropile' to 'monoplane' throughout. Two more substantive changes were effected. One is that, by 1910, Wells had come to regret what he called 'the obvious vulgarity' of 'making a "love interest" out of Helen and Graham'. In the revision's preface Wells points out that, technically, Graham is 200 years older than the girl: 'not the slightest intimation of any sexual interest could in truth have arisen between these two. They loved and kissed one another, but as a girl and her heroic grandfather might love.' The other major revision is an elimination of the earlier book's political-revolutionary optimism: 'I have also, with a few strokes of the pen, eliminated certain dishonest and regrettable suggestions that the People beat Ostrog. My Graham dies, as all his kind must die, with no certainty of either victory or defeat.'

Despite Wells's dissatisfaction with this novel, critics have made great claims for it, at least in terms of its influence. According to Leon Stover, Sleeper 'is the one single source inspiring all the great dystopian novels of the twentieth century, from *We* to *Brave New World* to *Nineteen Eighty-Four*' [Stover, 12]. In this he follows Mark Hillegas, who argues that *Sleeper* provides the basic template for all subsequent iterations of this kind of story, with all the now-familiar story-props, conceits and settings: 'the enclosed super-city, the disappearance of the family, the elimination of privacy, the degradation of the working class, the use of "kine-tele-photography" and "babble machines" for propaganda, pleasure cities, euthanasia and mental surgery' [Hillegas, 123]. Wells's most obvious comparator in terms of dystopian imagining—*Brave New World*—necessarily suffers in terms of its belatedness. And yet Huxley's novel, though chronologically epigone, is manifestly the superior piece of fiction. Wells hoists a melodramatic plot of political machination, burgeoning love and aerial jousting upon his dystopian speculation which, however fun it is to read, strikes a more puerile note than Huxley's more considered explorations of the fascistic logic of regimented social pleasure. We might put it this way: *Brave New World* adopts the form of a mature philosophical novel (all that earnest dialogue between the Savage and Mustapha Mond) to dramatise the fundamental infantilisation of society, where Wells uses the infantile form of the adventure story to attempt a more serious critique of encroaching fascism. His 1910 darkening of the story's political moral, stressing the impotence of individuals like Graham against the oppressive political logic of figures like Ostrog, marks his belated understanding of this as problematic. There's an enduring bias in our culture that dystopias, from Airstrip One to Westeros, are more 'serious' than utopias. I can't for the life of me think why, but there we are. Of course it's unfair to judge Wells by a novel that was, as he published his, three decades away from even being written. We could say that both Wells and Huxley recognised fascism for the socially functional puerility it is, even if Huxley found a better fictional form for expressing that core ideological truth than did Wells—better because *Brave New World* as novel is able to distance itself from the juvenile satisfactions of sex and soma, where *Sleeper* gets rather caught up in all the surface thrills and spills, the running around and aerial dogfights. Adorno in 1951, in characteristically gloomy mood, predicted 'the coming extinction of art', something he saw 'prefigured in the increasing impossibility of representing historical events':

> That there is no adequate drama about Fascism is not due to lack of talent; talent is withering through the insolubility of the writer's most urgent task. He has to choose between two principles, both equally inappropriate to the subject: psychology and infantilism. [Adorno, 143]

Stripping out the sex for the 1910 revision makes Wells's story even more the young-person's adventure yarn. And though the book is certainly full of ingenious extrapolation about modes of social control, its power-politics is curiously flat and abstract: the 'people' mob facelessly for, or against, Ostrog; the final battle is a toy-soldiers contest between undifferentiated Londoners treated *en masse* and an entirely abstracted corps of black African 'policeman' flying-in, all viewed from a distancing godlike altitude. Not that this is exactly a failing in the novel. It speaks to the fascistic logic of this mode of absolutism, the reduction of the complexities and intersectional individualities of real history to heroic representative figures and abstracted quantities. 'It is the essential abstractness of what really happens which rebuts the aesthetic image,' laments Adorno. 'To make this abstractness expressible at all, the writer is forced to translate it into a kind of children's language, into archetypes, and so a second time to "bring it home"....' Ostrog is not a character; he is the embodiment of Wellsian pessimism about the likelihood of future history diverting into purely authoritarian forms—sleepwalking, we might say, into disaster. Hence the appositeness of Wells's 'sleeper' conceit, however clumsy Bellamy's narrative device is liable to strike us now. ('It is hard to escape the sense,' John Clute and David Langford rightly note, 'that the sleeper-awakes structure betrayed, even before the beginning of the twentieth century, an undue fastidiousness of imagination and that some straightforward magic, like a time machine, might always have been a more elegant option' [Clute and Langford]). Dystopia measures the gap between the present actuality and utopian possibilities. For Wells the body politic dozes and mutters on its uncomfortable bed, when it should awake and seize the future. In a nutshell the novelistic limitations of *Sleeper* devolve upon the aesthetic blankness of the very object of its representation. To quote Adorno once final time:

> The impossibility of portraying Fascism springs from the fact that in it, as in its contemplation, subjective freedom no longer exists. Total unfreedom can be recognised, but not represented. [Adorno, 144]

Wells was too canny a writer not to recognise the extent to which *Sleeper* butts its head awkwardly against this limit. He could see it didn't really work as a novel, although its problems are closely intertwined with the grounds of its success—success measured, if in no other way, and as already noted, in terms of influence. In 1910 Wells tried reworking it, without really solving the problems. By 1934, as he wrote his *Autobiography*, he seems to have decided that the problem was that his mode of extrapolation itself had been too flat:

> The future depicted in the *Time Machine* was a mere fantasy based on the idea of the human species developing about divergent lines, but the future in *When the Sleeper Awakes* was essentially an exaggeration of contemporary tendencies: higher buildings, bigger towns, wickeder capitalists and labour more down-trodden than ever and more desperate. Everything was bigger, quicker and more crowded; there was more and more flying and the wildest financial speculation. It was our contemporary world in a state of highly inflamed distension... I suppose that is the natural line for an imaginative writer to take, in an age of material progress and political sterility. Until he thinks better of it.

Thinking better means imagining qualitative, rather than just quantitative, change. But this does not negate the possibility that the future was indeed going to be a fascistic-authoritarian 'highly inflamed distension' of contemporary logics of commercialisation, authoritarianism and so on. And with 'highly inflamed distension' we seem to have returned to Wells's malfunctioning kidney, or whatever it was that incapacitated him, back in 1898.

Whilst on that holiday, and after the miraculous improvement to his health, Wells found himself enjoying the south coast to such a degree he began serious plans to move from London to the Sussex seaside. Searching for suitable houses to rent and finding only 'servant-murdering basements, sanitary insanitaries and not a decent bathroom anywhere' he decided to design his own domicile on progressive lines. Pursuant to this aim Jane and he sold Worcester Park and rented a cottage overlooking the beach a few miles west of Folkestone, in the tiny Kentish village of Sandgate. There they spent the winter of 1898 and liked it enough to commit to permanent habitation. On 28 March 1899 H.G. and Jane moved into Arnold House (now 20 Castle Road), a pleasant semi-detached beachside house in a sheltered spot on the Sussex coast. Wells was now rich enough to build himself a spacious and modern house from scratch.

During this time Wells worked on revising *Love and Mr Lewisham* and although not wholly happy (he complained that he had 'saved no more than one straight plank from the vast scaffold originally designed') he still considered it the best thing he had yet written. This is a judgement inevitably influenced by the fact that Lewisham is, as Wells had been, a clever, driven, lower-middle-class man working as a teacher in a provincial school. Wells draws on memories of his time under Mr Byatt, the headmaster of Midhurst Grammar School and then of his time at the Normal School and out of these experiences creates a vivid picture of what it meant to be young in the 1880s. But the novel is not straightforward autobiographical reportage. Wells is tricksier than that. He calls his alter ego 'Lewisham' because it is so nicely suburban, a comical and small-beer sort of name. But we can also note how 'Lewis' reverses and shuffles 'Wel-(l)s' to make a sort of 'sham' Wells. This novel fictionalises Wells's life in a playful and often inverted way. *Love and Mr Lewisham* is to Wells, as autobiographical fiction reworking youthful struggle and trauma, what *David Copperfield* was to Dickens half a century earlier, but Wells here puts Dickens through intriguing transformations.

Lewisham is a short novel—65,000 words—disposed into three dramatic acts. The first seven chapters (of 32) deal with 18-year-old Lewisham's time as 'assistant master in the Whortley Proprietary School, Whortley, Sussex'. At this stage in the story he is putting all his energies into self-advancement, writing out a pretentiously titled 'Schema' to timetable his work and pinning it to his bedroom wall. Raymond Williams later recorded that 'I felt strongly with Lewisham many years ago making schedules for exams', adding that he was 'the first character in fiction I ever fully identified with' [Williams, 250]. In one sense *Love and Mr Lewisham* is as its best, as a novel, in these early chapters; for it's here that Wells is able to write about his protagonist with forgiveness for his sheer ingenuousness. The book treats his yearning immaturity and inchoate sexuality with a gentleness of ridicule, leavened by its awareness of the lad's talent and energy. Lewisham meets Ethel Henderson, who lives with her mother and step-father in Clapham and is only staying in Whortley for a short time. The two go on what Chap. 6 calls 'The Scandalous Ramble' together: a long countryside walk which, though nothing improper happens upon it, nonetheless shocks the village. Lewisham ends up losing his job. Ethel returns to Clapham and, though Lewisham writes to her, she does not reply. They lose touch.

Chapter 8 opens two years later: Lewisham, now 21, is living in 'the grey spaciousness of West London', on a scholarship from the Education Department to study at Normal School of Science. He is a star student, and it looks as though his Schema is coming true. The romantic interest in this portion of the novel is pitched at a cooler level, concentrating on fellow student Miss Heydinger, who reads Browning and Rossetti and with whom he discusses politics, science and philosophy. Having established this new world and set-up the likelihood of Lewisham eventually marrying the bookish but unsexy Heydinger, Wells introduces an unexpected element: fraudulent spirit mediums.

It's a knight's-move in narrative terms, but it works. Lewisham and a friend attend a séance presided over by the elderly Mr Chaffery. They go intending, as students of science, to debunk him; and this they do, turning on the lights at the crucial moment to reveal his charlatanry. But Lewisham sees that the Medium's young assistant is none other than Ethel Henderson. Chaffery, it turns out, is her step-father. Lewisham attempts to persuade Ethel to give up her dishonest work and they take to promenading the evening streets together, Lewisham notionally walking Ethel home but in fact the two taking deliberately circuitous routes to extend their time together. Lewisham neglects his studies, sinks down the class list and when he and Ethel marry and move-in together he abandons his larger 'Schema' ambitions altogether. He also is forced to meet the pompous, unscrupulous Chaffery on something like an equal footing, since they are now family. Indeed, Wells does something very clever with this character, allowing him monologues justifying his sharp practices that work upon the reader's preconceptions by the very reasonableness of their amorality. 'You haven't said anything,' Lewisham insists, 'to show that spiritualistic cheating is Right.'

"I am prepared to maintain," said Chaffery, "that Honesty is essentially an anarchistic and disintegrating force in society, that communities are held together and the progress of civilisation made possible only by vigorous and sometimes even, violent Lying; that the Social Contract is nothing more or less than a vast conspiracy of human beings to lie to and humbug themselves and one another for the general Good. Lies are the mortar that bind the savage Individual man into the social masonry. There is the general thesis upon which I base my justification. My mediumship, I can assure you, is a particular instance of the general assertion ..."

"But how are you going to prove it?"

"Prove It! It simply needs pointing out. ... Let us look at the fabric of society, let us compare the savage. You will discover the only essential difference between savage and civilised is this: the former hasn't learnt to shirk the truth of things, and the latter has. The pure savage has no money. To him a lump of metal is a lump of metal—possibly ornamental—no more. That's right. To any lucid-minded man it's the same or different only through the gross folly of his fellows. But to the common civilised man the universal exchangeability of this gold is a sacred and fundamental fact. Think of it! Why should it be? There isn't a why! I live in perpetual amazement at the gullibility of my fellow-creatures. Of a morning sometimes, I can assure you, I lie in bed fancying that people may have found out this swindle in the night, expect to hear a tumult downstairs and see your mother-in-law come rushing into the room with a rejected shilling from the milkman. 'What's this?' says he. 'This Muck for milk?' But it never happens. Never!" [*Lewisham*, 23]

Lewisham's priggish ethical certainty (at this point in the story he has become a red-tie-wearing socialist) is shaken by the sheer, indolent self-confidence of Chaffrey's venal selfishness.

The novel moves into its final act, and Wells narrates Lewisham's sinking back down with real poignancy. He struggles to make his marriage work, fritters away his savings and ends up working at crummy tutoring jobs barely scraping a living. Chaffery absconds to the Continent with £500 stolen from a gullible client, and Lewisham moves into the Clapham house resolving to look after his wife and abandoned mother-in-law. In the last chapter we discover that Ethel is pregnant. Lewisham rips up his old 'Schema' and commits to a new guiding principle: 'it is all the Child. The future is the Child. The Future. What are we—any of us—but servants or traitors to that?' [*Lewisham*, 32]. And that's where we leave Lewisham: in a shabby, rented house in unfashionable Clapham, financially precarious, stuck in an ill-matched marriage, saddled with dependents, his huge potential unfulfilled. You can see why Wells's old friend Richard Gregory wrote to him on finishing the novel: 'I cannot get that poor devil Lewisham out of my head, and I wish I had an address, for I would go to him and rescue him from the miserable life in which you leave him.'

This is not to suggest there's anything dour about *Love and Mr Lewisham*. On the contrary, the book has a wonderfully elastic feel to it, a palpable youthful energy: the comedy is sprightly and winning, the pathos genuinely touching. And the book was a hit: as Wells wrote jubilantly to his mother soon after publication (7 June 1900): 'I am sending you a first review of *Love and Mr. Lewisham*. They have sold 1600 copies in England and 2500 in the colonies before publication, and I think the book is almost certain to beat any previous book I have written in the matter of sales.' He was right, too.

A question over which critics have disagreed is whether *Love and Mr Lewisham* is anything more than a loosely gathered series of vignettes drawn from Wells's own life, unified by the appeal of the central character—whether, in other words, it is a work of literary art, or something closer to fictionalised reportage, loose and baggy and inartistic. This is an important question with respect to the whole of Wells's career as a writer, not just this novel, and merits a little more discussion. Wells's friendship with Henry James, to whom no self-respecting academic literary critic would deny the title 'artist', is one of the ways criticism tends to frame this debate. Some take Wells at his word when he denied that he created 'art', in the self-conscious Jamesian mode, at all. 'Wells himself professed to despise art, maintaining that his ideas were more important than the vehicles that contained them', J.B. Batchelor notes, adding the pointed qualifier: 'but he was an inveterate liar' [Batchelor, 407]. Batchelor thinks Wells worked hard at his artistry, and some other critics have tried to make the case for deliberate aesthetic structure and form beneath the surface-seeming charming bagginess of these Wellsian narrative [see, e.g., Newell 1968]. Most, however, have not. Nonetheless there are three manifest ways that Wells works to impose 'form' on the content of this novel, which we might shorthand as: *intertextuality*, *class* and *metaphor*.

To be a little more precise the first of these is less intertextuality and more a kind of intertextual *reaction*. It is an obvious thing to note about *Love and Mr Lewisham* that it is an exploration of how the classic Dickensian 'social mobility' plotline would go without benefactors. What would Oliver Twist have become without the assistance of benevolent and wealthy old Mr Brownlow? How would Nicholas Nickleby have fared without the Cheeryble brothers? Later Dickens relies less exclusively on this particular deus ex machina than earlier Dickens but even in his non-benefactor novels, it's remarkable just how many people around, for example, David Copperfield are invested in the protagonist doing well in the world—that is, how often Dickens's protagonists are surrounded by a network of friends and helpers. In *Love and Mr Lewisham* Wells plots the path a Dickensian Promising Young Man might follow without such a support network. The only person motivated to help adult Lewisham is Alice Heydinger, because she is in love with him; but she is not in a position to do him material good, and her assistance is ruled out by the jealousy of Lewisham's wife. Otherwise Lewisham has no parents, no wealthy friends, no patron. He has to go it alone, without resources and without assistance, and that means he doesn't 'go it' very far.

There's another aspect of the anti-*David-Copperfield* about *Love and Mr Lewisham*, and it has to do with the sex narrative. Boil it down and Dickens's novel is about David's relationship with two women: one hopeless, infantalised but sexually alluring; the other accomplished, spiritually mature, a proper helpmeet and partner—but not a woman to whom David is especially sexually attracted. This is a rather stark way of putting it, I know; but it brings out what has always seemed to me the fundamental psychological mendacity of the novel—because the deal Dickens strikes with his subconscious in writing *Copperfield* is that he will kill-off the sexually alluring wife in order to clear away all obstacles to marriage with the sexually unappealing wife. Of course it's a fool's bargain. Sexual desire is not amenable to being killed off, and the repressed always returns. Catherine Dickens, retroactively written into being a real-life Agnes by this very novel, wasn't able actually to be a real-life Agnes because Dickens's subconscious would not agree to the deal Dickens's superego had struck with his ego. And so it was, less than a decade after publishing *Copperfield*, Dickens had put his wife away and returned, in secret, to the sexually alluring younger woman in his affair with Nelly Ternan. His life simply failed to follow his own *Copperfield* script. As for Wells: we have seen that, though marriage to Jane provided Wells with the stability he needed to make a real success of his life his *eros* remained fixated on Isabel, his first wife. For Wells marrying Jane was very much a 'swapping Agnes for Dora' move: for though Wells and Jane had two children together, Wells recalls their sex life as characterised by 'immense secret disillusionments'.

This poses, I think, a particular problem for Wells's writing. In *H. G. Wells in Love*, Wells declared that 'quite the most interesting fact' about his early married life was the way he replaced 'simple honesty of sexual purpose' with 'duplicity'. Insofar as his early mundane novels like *Lewisham* and *Kipps* are satirical, they aim their barbs at the varying hypocrisies of modern living. In social-prophet mode Wells looks to a future when all such petty duplicities could be swept away and simple honesty inform life, labour and sex. This idea has polemical clarity on its side, but that's not to say that it has been able to recruit Wells's own subconscious to the cause. Because one of the things that comes with unmistakeable, if unintended, force from *Love and Mr Lewisham* is that though Wells's daylight imagination sets itself again hypocrisy, his *night-time* imagination is in love with it. Hypocrisy, we could say, is his kink. Duplicity excites him. Wells was certainly neither the first nor the last man to separate out companionship from sex and to have fetishised the latter as a necessary function of extramarital secrecy, transgression and illicitness.

This dialectical engagement with the assumptions of Dickens's narrative of lower-class protagonists making good in the world is one of the ways Wells shapes *Love and Mr Lewisham*. Related to this is the way the novel's engagement with class itself mediates the way aesthetic form maps onto the messiness of lived experience. To put it in a nutshell: there is simply less *mess* and more inherent formal harmony and balance, in the wealthy life (in, we could say: the life of a Jamesian or Proustian protagonist) than there is in the life of lower-middle-class respectable poverty. The latter just is baggier and messier, more impinged upon by derailing contingency, more liable to abrupt stops and unfulfillments. This might explain why the socialist component of Lewisham's life is so underplayed in this novel: apart from buying a red necktie and attending a few clubbish discussions, Wells's own actual evolving socialist sympathies are downplayed. Marx insists that proletarian existence, though materially denuded, embodies a rather beautiful formal structure, a material dialectic by which History itself comes to knowledge of itself. There's a tradition of radical art going back at least to the Romantics and manifest in writers from Zola to John Berger that finds an aesthetically harmonising authenticity in the sufferings of working-class life: force, reality, anger and therefore hope. But it's interesting how little Wells buys into this idea. Compare, once more, Dickens's writing. The one time (we might say) when Dickens imagined what would happen to a talented working-class character whose upwards social mobility was *not* smoothed by benefactors, friends and providence is found in *Our Mutual Friend*: Bradley Headstone is Nickleby without the Cheerybles, someone who has had to make his own way on his own merits, unaided by friends or supporters. And the remarkable thing about this portrait is how ghastly a figure he is, driven by barely suppressed, murderous rage to wreak disaster on the world of the novel and smite his own ruin upon the lockside. Headstone is the closest Dickens comes to himself answering the question Wells later poses: what would happen to a lower-class man of talents who was *not* helped to advance by a benefactor? And the answer Dickens gives us is: he would advance a little way, but he would be thwarted and furious and ultimately doomed.

Wells's lower-middle-class protagonists are, all of them, much milder and more reasonable than this. The palpable injustice of their situation does not punch through to some substrate of pure affect, like Headstone-ish rage or Tolstoyan sainthood, but rather only further complexifies the already complex spread of human emotions. In a fine essay, 'Feeling Like a Clerk in H.G. Wells', Richard Higgins notes how much novels like *Love and Mr Lewisham*, *Kipps*, *Mr Polly* and *Tono-Bungay* elaborate a 'close examination of the relationship between class and the emotions'.

These emotions have much to add to conventional class analysis. Many of these emotions are more prosaic than we have been accustomed to observe—more passive frustration, for example, than class rage … these new feelings she describes were (and continue to be) a profound part of the lower-middle-class experience, making members of this class exemplary vehicles for exploring the significance of the emotions for an analysis of what it means to experience oneself as a member of a particular class. [Higgins, 457]

This is an important insight, I think: for the aesthetic pattern of *Love and Mr Lewisham* is in large part an *affective* pattern, and the emotions that interest Wells are lower-key and therefore more easily overlooked than the grand passions of Victorian melodrama or Marxist revolutionary anger. Lewisham is sometimes annoyed, and sometimes despairing, but he is also sometimes hopeful, sometimes amused, aroused, curious, bored, skittish. Dickens's Headstone, as character, hasn't room for such a spread of ordinariness: he's at the pitch of thwarted fury all the time.

Indeed, since one of Wells's main themes in this novel is the way impecuniousness and the pinching nature of social convention continually interfere with the stories we would *like* to plot-out for ourselves, it could almost be objected to that the patterning in *Love and Mr Lewisham* is if anything too neat. It's a three-part narrative pattern where parts one and three mirror one another, and both reflect forward and backward onto the central section. At the end of Chap. 29, a ferocious argument between the newlyweds leads to passionate make-up sex, in a room heavy with the scent of rose petals. It is a moment of affective intensity designedly placed to balance out the flower-scented affective intensity of Lewisham and Ethel's 'scandalous ramble' in Chap. 6. The final six chapters of the novel, with this erotic consummation at their heart, balance the first six chapters, something Wells underlines with various specific echoes:—for instance, young Mr Lewisham reaches down a spray of wild hawthorn for Ethel in Chap. 6 and scratches his hand; older Mr Lewisham retrieves the roses from where Ethel has hidden them in Chap. 29 and scratches his hand. The problem with this is that it—almost—tempts Wells into the same kind of psychological mendacity to which Dickens fell prey. This whole scene implies that Lewisham and Ethel's sex life will be just fine, when the autobiographical provenance tells us something very different, and the peroration with which the novel ends to 'The Child' as a kind of transcendental signifier bound to bring a new unity and order to the fundamentally broken marriage and worn-down shabbiness of the life strikes a false note. There are other misshapes, too, in the larger structure. Wells needs to keep Alice Heydinger 'in play', as it were, to give dramatic flesh to his larger triadic patterning, but for much of the novel he can't quite work out how to do this, which leads to rather egregious interpolations such as Chap. 16, 'Miss Heydinger's Private Thoughts'. But that larger pattern does, I think, hold: a three-act drama, carefully built around various triadic scenes, forms and images, that is made in order to articulate on a formal level as well as on the level of story-content the novel's core insight that there is always something disruptively extraneous that interferes with the romantic ideal of the twosome—that a corrosive supplement called 'Life', or 'Poverty', or 'extra-marital desire', or maybe 'sex as such', is always poking itself in to the potential self-contained neatness of the man-and-woman dyad.

Which brings me to the third way I think this novel works 'art' into its lump of life: by refracting its narrative (the metonymic progression of events in the life of young Lewisham) through a central governing expressive metaphor. That metaphor is, broadly, 'deceit'; or, since a metaphor needs to be concrete, it is the wonderful central episode of the fake séance and the subsequent ways Mr Chaffery attempts to justify his fakery. By juxtaposing these two things, Lewisham's love life and Chaffery's fake séance, the novel invites us to consider their points of comparison. The mediating point is the unexpected presence at the séance of the object of Lewisham's sexual desire. 'Lewisham looked across and met the eyes of the girl next that gentleman. It was Ethel! … Immediately she looked away. At first his only emotion was surprise. He would have spoken, but a little thing robbed him of speech' [11]. This encounter means that the manufactured eeriness of the actual spirit-rapping is interpenetrated, for Lewisham, with an abrupt renewal of erotic yearning. 'He sat in the breathing darkness, staring at the dim elusive shape that had presented that remembered face,' says Wells. 'His mind was astonishment mingled with annoyance. He had settled that this girl was lost to him for ever.' The event continues:

> A swift percussive sound, tap, rap, dap, under the table, under the chair, in the air, round the cornices. The Medium groaned again and shuddered, and his nervous agitation passed sympathetically round the circle. The music seemed to fade to the vanishing point and grew louder again. [Lewisham, 11]

This whole episode plays upon a kind of conceptual pun: the dark room, the physical proximity of men and women, the gasping, the shuddering—it is at once describing a séance and sex. The centrepiece of Chaffrey's performance is a disembodied, luminous hand: 'ghostly—unaccountable—marvellous'. It touches Lewisham, which makes him shudder; 'almost simultaneously, Miss Heydinger cried out that something was smoothing her hair.' The sensuality of this, and its thrillingly unconventional nature, does interesting things in terms of balancing off the material and immaterial. Sex is pre-eminently a physical act, after all. The spirit realm is famously non-physical. Yet this sort of spiritualist performance is all about the physical manifestation of the immaterial. And this in turn returns us to questions of sex, the broader appeal of which is grounded in that romantic ideal that while it *is* physical it is *not just* physical—that (for instance) it expresses an immaterial love, linking two spirits and, as at the novel's end, engendering into the world a new immortal soul. Wells is understandably suspicious of such grandiose romantic sentimentalism. For him sex is bodies interacting, howsoever pleasurably, with other bodies. And Chaffrey's séance *is* pleasurable, in a spooky sort of way, even for those who come to debunk it. More, it is this that figures the reconnection between Lewisham and Ethel. But it is also a sham, a deceit. The climax of the show is when the lights come on suddenly, and Chaffery is revealed mid-faking. As the old adage reminds us, *triste est omne animalium post coitum*; and Lewisham goes from elation at uncovering the cheat to 'an extraordinary moodiness' on the way home. The spectral hand, that had so excitingly and bafflingly caressed both him and Alice, is revealed in the bright lights of afterwards to be a prop, a kind of glove held in Chaffrey's mouth and inflated by his breath. There it sprawls at the chapter's end like a used prophylactic: 'a thing of shrivelled membrane, a pneumatic glove, lying on the table'. Disappointment hurries hard behind our erotic satisfactions.

This is what is so canny about Wells's choice of this particular metaphor to talk about sex in this novel—to reveal, we could say, the spurting, ectoplasmic story *Sex and Mr Lewisham* that lies discretely veiled behind the decent *Love and Mr Lewisham*. Chaffrey's self-justification, quoted at some length above, attempts to make a cosmic virtue of anti-hypocrisy. *Love and Mr Lewisham* works on just such a canvas. Sex itself, this novel suggests, is a kind of deceiving performance in which two parties agree to fool themselves that the variously mechanical or bestial physical actions they undertake upon one another's bodies are 'actually' transporting magical mysteries freighted with significance and accompanied by the powerful scent of rose petals. Or to put it more broadly, it is a novel that says the pleasure of sex, though real, depends upon a kind of benign mutual fakery. Revealing the 'truth' of sex, by (for instance) studying physiology and evolutionary science at the Normal School in Kensington, does not undermine our attachment to this mediumistic rigmarole, just as wealthy, foolish Lagune, having been shown that Chaffery is cheating him, continues to believe in Chaffery. Lagune scoffs 'I told Chaffery you were beginners. He treated you as beginners—arranged a demonstration' [14], like a University professor. 'If it had not been for your interruptions…'

Lagune insists adding, 'I still believe the man has powers.' We might describe this as pride, or a foolish obstinacy, on Lagune's part; but then we ought to be prepared to have the same language used to describe our own stubborn attachment to the various performances of sexual life. After all, we all know that that whole business is a mere evolutionary drive, designed to enable DNA to make more DNA. Right?

Sex is the kind of fun that feels like is more than just fun: the kind that puts us in touch, however hazily, with something beyond ourselves. It doesn't stretch the truth to say that the barebones evolutionary 'truth' of sex is actually the means by which we beat back against death as such. And in that sense Wells's spiritualist metaphor, in all its glorious, ingenious fakeness, is an eloquent one for the concerns of his whole novel. Sex, says *Love and Mr Lewisham*, is a snare, a distraction, a mere shadow compared to the grand ambition outlined in Lewisham's Schema. And at the same time this novel says: of course, sex is actually much more important than any of that stuff.

As Wells's health slowly improved, and as he enjoyed his consolidating fame (and wealth) as a writer, he declared him infinitely more at home in Sandgate than he had been in London. One of the reasons for that was the group of literary friendships he consolidated there. After briefly returning to London in 1901 Gissing was now living in Paris with his French common-law wife; but Joseph Conrad, with whom Wells had been in correspondence for some years, had moved with his family to Pent Farm, a redbrick Farmhouse in the Kent Downs only half an hour's bicycle ride from Sandgate. Wells and Conrad became good friends and through Conrad Wells came to know Ford Madox Ford who was living then in the village of Aldington, 5 miles or so west of Sandgate (he, at this point, had not yet changed his surname from Heuffer to Ford, but he is here referred to by his later name for convenience). Conrad was 9 years older than Wells and Ford 7 years younger. Neither had enjoyed his prodigious literary success, and both deferred to him on that ground. Ford called him 'the Dean of our profession', a writer 'having innumerable things, retainers, immense sales and influence and the gift of leadership. So, in some mystic way, Mr Wells might have put Literature on the map. That was how it seemed' [Ford, 115]. The three men fell into the habit of visiting one another, playing chess, discussing literature. The other key literary friendship that was formed on the south coast was between Wells and Henry James—an unlikely pairing of two men radically different in almost every respect that nonetheless lasted for many years.

Wells was building a new life in a literal as well as a metaphorical sense. On 12 February 1900 he contracted with William Dunk, a Folkestone builder and with the architect C.F.A. Voysey, to build him a house from scratch on the coast at Sandgate. Wells was intimately involved in the designs and insisted upon it being light, spacious and airy, comprising such modern amenities as electric lights and central heating, as well as being accessible to wheelchair users (Wells was still unsure enough of his health to believe that he might end up confined to such a chair). The name Wells chose was: Spade House. Honesty about the state of things—calling a spade a spade, in the British proverb—was important to him, as a man and as a writer.

Whilst the house was being built, Wells and Jane lived nearby in a rented property, and it was there that Wells wrote his next novel—the journey-to-the-moon romp *The First Men in the Moon*. This was serialised in the *Strand Magazine* from December 1900 to August 1901 and published as a single volume by George Newnes in 1901. The narrator is Bedford, a failed London businessman who has sequestered himself at Lympne—just up the coast from Sandgate—in order to write a play that, he hopes, will make him rich. He meets his neighbour, the eccentric scientist Cavor, who is developing an anti-gravitational material he calls 'Cavorite'. With Bedford's help, Cavor builds a large sphere out of this material in which both men fly to the moon where they find a complex lunar society of 'Selenites', man-sized but insectile, living under the moon's surface in caves and tunnels, ruled by the 'Grand Lunar' ('his brain case must have measured many yards in diameter'). Bedford and Cavor are captured and restrained with gold chains, a metal which happens to be plentiful on the moon. They escape but become separated. Bedford, believing Cavor lost, pilots the capsule back to the Earth, landing, improbably enough, on the same stretch of Kentish coastline from which they had departed. Back home he has difficulty persuading people of the reality of his adventure, in large part because he loses the Cavorite spacecraft when a curious boy named Tommy Simmons climbs into the unattended sphere and shoots off into space. But he still has some of the gold he brought back from the moon, and he enjoys literary success when, with a Wellsian metafictional touch, he publishes his story in the *Strand Magazine*.

In the final portion of the novel, fragmentary radio communications from the moon are picked-up on Earth—Cavor has befriended the Selenites and persuaded them to allow him to call home. His messages are receive-only, but they flesh-out the details of Selenite society: individual Selenites exist in thousands of forms and find fulfilment in carrying out the specific social function for which they have been brought up: specialisation is the essence of Selenite society, and all is under the control of the superintelligent Grand Lunar. The broadcasts stop abruptly, apparently because Cavor has guilelessly revealed to the Grand Lunar humankind's alarmingly warlike propensities. Bedford ends his narrative by imagining the Selenites overpowering the poor fellow:

I see, almost as plainly as though I had seen it in actual fact, a blue-lit shadowy dishevelled Cavor struggling in the grip of these insect Selenites, struggling ever more desperately and hopelessly as they press upon him, shouting, expostulating, perhaps even at last fighting, and being forced backwards step by step out of all speech or sign of his fellows, for evermore into the Unknown—into the dark, into that silence that has no end…. [*First Men*, 26]

On that open-ended ellipsis the story closes.

If we want to talk to the originality of Wells's *The First Men in the Moon* we need to lay our emphasis on the fourth, not the last, word in its title. Stories of reckless private individuals jollying off to the moon are in very plentiful supply, going back at least to Lucian (from whose second-century AD *Icaromenippus* Wells quotes the epigraph to *First Men*'s first edition) and positively thronging the bookshelves throughout the eighteenth and nineteenth centuries. Nor was antigravity Wells's original notion. On the contrary, it was such an old idea by 1900 it had become hackneyed. Joseph Atterley's *A Voyage to the Moon* (1827) is probably the earliest novel to utilise anti-gravitational propulsion to move its vessel from the Earth to the moon; and by the time Wells was writing *First Men* the idea of anti-gravitationally powered interplanetary flight had become enough of a cliché to find itself the butt of the SF joke: C.C. Dail's *Willmoth the Wanderer, or The Man from Saturn* (1890) features an antigravity ointment, to be smeared onto whatever thing or person you want to fly. What is conceptually original in Wells's novel, aside from various specifics to do with Selenite society, is the notion that lunar inhabitants live *inside* their world, rather than on its surface. And this, in turn, identifies what is most interesting about this novel: not its linear extrapolation of (for example) the possibilities of alien life so much as something more thematically robust:—an articulation of the difference between *inside* and *outside*.

First Men is a novel that, designedly, I think, can be read in two very different ways. We can of course read it as 'straight' science fiction, an exciting adventure in interplanetary exploration, meeting aliens and learning the world, all tinged with some lovely touches of sense-of-wonder in the tradition of such nineteenth-century interplanetary voyages as Verne's *De la Terre à la Lune* (1865) and Lasswitz's *Auf Zwei Planeten* (1897). This, I would say, is how the novel is generally read, particularly in the SF and SF-scholarship communities. But it's possible to read *First Men* quite differently: as a joke, trick, or blague, as a novel about narratorial unreliability. I'm proposing, appropriately enough, an inside-outside binary of reading, a question of whether we're in, or out, of the joke. The second kind of reading would see it as sharing a pedigree with Poe's great story, 'The Unparalleled Adventure of

One Hans Pfaall' (1835). Pfaall narrates his journey to the moon by balloon, launched on 1 April from the Netherlands: 19 days flying through the attenuated interplanetary atmosphere, before tumbling 'headlong into the very heart of a fantastical looking city, and into the middle of a vast crowd of ugly little people' [Poe 'Hans Pfaall', 993]. Pfaall claims to have returned to the Earth accompanied by one of these lunar aliens. He ends his narration with the promise of more interesting revelations to come if the burghers of Rotterdam are only prepared to give him the money necessary to pay off his creditors. In a page-long coda Poe relates 'astonishment and admiration' of the people of Rotterdam and then immediately undercuts the veracity of the narration by itemising certain salient facts: that 'an odd little dwarf and bottle conjurer, both of whose ears, for some misdemeanour, have been cut off close to the head, has been missing for several days from the neighbouring city of Bruges' and that Pfaall himself 'the drunken villain' has been seen drinking 'in a tippling house in the suburbs' with the 'three very idle gentlemen styled his creditors' ['Hans Pfaall', 996]. Harold Beaver plots out the various fooleries in the text, notes that Pfaall lifts-off on April Fool's Day, that his balloon is shaped like a 'fool's cap', and that the burgermeisters all have ridiculous names (Professor Rubadub, Mynheer Superbus Von Underduk and so on), and concludes that his hoax inverts normal expectations and turns the logical world upside down. 'Invert "phaal"', Beaver notes (referring to one of Poe's variants of the name 'Pfaall'), 'what sound do you hear but "laugh"?' [Beaver, 339].

Returning to Wells: the first thing we learn of Bedford, our narrator, is that he fled to Lympne having 'come an ugly cropper in certain business enterprises', on the run from 'cantankerous creditors'. His initial plan at Lympne was to live in an out-of-the-way place, on credit, and then abscond without paying his debts:

> I laid in an eighteen-gallon cask of beer on credit, and a trustful baker came each day. It was not, perhaps, in the style of Sybaris, but I have had worse times. I was a little sorry for the baker, who was a very decent man indeed. [*First Men*, 1]

In other words, the novel opens with the narrator saying: do not trust me. He then offers us two contradictory episodes. In the first a single sheet of newly forged Cavorite, cooling in its frame, reaches the temperature where its anti-gravitational effect comes into play, renders the entire column of air above it weightless, 'squirting' the whole lot into space and sucking in new air in a whirlwind that blows Bedford and Cavour off their feet. This disaster only ends when the tempest rips the sheet from its apparatus and sucks it away, exploding the house in the process. It makes a kind of sense, given the premise. But then, a few pages later, Bedford narrates the exact opposite circumstance: Cavor has constructed an entire spaceship lined on every side with Cavorite, such that when the metal is curled up into window-blind rollers it has no effect, but when all the blinds are rolled down *except one* the sphere will gently move in the direction of the open window. Of course we may want to explain this discrepancy in terms of what SF Fans call 'hand waving', and that's a perfectly fine way to read the novel, if the inconsistency doesn't bother us. Alternatively we might speculate that Wells knows exactly what he is doing that this is a deliberate giveaway.

Which brings us to the final act, the section most specifically reminiscent of 'Hans Pfaall'. Bedford concedes, in Chap. 21, that he has no evidence that he went on his adventures at all: no Cavor, no sphere, no Selenites, only two bars of gold (for which we have to take his word) and the adventures themselves. Then he reports that 'Mr. Julius Wendigee, a Dutch electrician, who has been experimenting with certain apparatus akin to the apparatus used by Mr. Tesla in America' has intercepted communications 'emanating from Mr. Cavor in the moon'. These communications appear to provide third-party corroboration of the whole adventure, making the publication in volume form, which we are now reading, all the more saleable. Wendigee may not strike us as so obviously a joke Dutch name as Poe's Professor Rubadub or Mynheer Superbus Von Underduk, but, when we remind ourselves that *wendige* is the Dutch for 'superfluous', 'extraneous' or 'unrelated' it may strike as joke-ish enough, especially when the content of these bulletins reveal that Cavor has befriended Selenites with names like 'Phi-oo' and 'Tsi-puff' (Φ-ω, or *pho*, is a Greek term 'expressive of dismissive contempt'; and we can take 'tsi-puff' as a version of 'tch!') who report that the entire lunar economy depends upon farming 'mooncalves', a mooncalf of course being 'a dreamer, a fool or simpleton'. Wells is having fun with us, and there's no reason why we can't join in the fun. It does not, after all, prevent us from taking the book seriously at the same time. A novel is a house in which are many rooms. We can position ourselves 'in' the joke, or if we prefer we can stand outside it.

My larger point is that this novel is doing something quite interesting with interiors and exteriors, a complex play of insides as against outsides. Wells the author was building himself a brand new house as he writes his novel; and a house, before it is anything else, is a machine for dividing the world into inside and outside. Insofar as science fiction is a literature of extraterrestrial *voyages extraordinaires* then it is a literature that houses the world—that is to say, turns the whole globe into a house in which we, who live on its surface, are 'inside', and to which the whole dark and vacuous immensity of interstellar space is 'outside'. So Wells, in need of money, goes fishing in the moon for more gold. To that end he gets his imagination to design a new kind of dwelling. This is a house that can fly, but its primary function is as any house must be, to separate inside from outside by way of keeping those inside whole and keeping the outside out. The inside, with its zero-gravity, is dreamy:

> … floating thus loosely in space [is] exceeding restful; indeed, the nearest thing in earthly experience to it that I know is lying on a very thick, soft feather bed. But the quality of utter detachment and independence! I had not reckoned on things like this. I had expected a violent jerk at starting, a giddy sense of speed. Instead I felt—as if I were disembodied. It was not like the beginning of a journey; it was like the beginning of a dream. [*First Men*, 4]

The Cavorite house not only keeps the killing vacuum and cold of space outside, it also creates a womblike suspension of time, or at least of the somatic rhythms that mark time, like eating and breathing:

> It is a curious thing, that while we were in the sphere we felt not the slightest desire for food, nor did we feel the want of it when we abstained. At first we forced our appetites, but afterwards we fasted completely. Altogether we did not consume one-hundredth part of the compressed provisions we had brought with us. The amount of carbonic acid we breathed was also unnaturally low, but why this was, I am quite unable to explain. [*First Men*, 5]

When the travellers reach their destination it is disclosed as a mode of hypertrophic *interiority*—interiority on the largest scale. The moon's inside is illuminated: 'a region of continually increasing phosphorescence … light due to the streams and cascades of water that flowed ever more abundantly downward towards the Central Sea'. 'This Lunar Sea', says Cavor, in a later passage 'is not a stagnant ocean; a solar tide sends it in a perpetual flow around the lunar axis, and strange storms and boilings and rushings of its waters occur, and at times cold winds and thunderings that ascend out of it into the busy ways of the great ant-hill above. It is only when the water is in motion that it gives out light; in its rare seasons of calm it is black. The Selenites navigate its cavernous straits and lagoons in little shallow boats of a canoe-like shape... The caverns and passages are naturally very tortuous. A large proportion of these ways are known only to expert pilots among the fishermen, and not infrequently Selenites are lost for ever in their labyrinths. In their remoter recesses, I am told, strange creatures lurk, some of them terrible and dangerous creatures that all the science of the moon has been unable to exterminate' (*First Men*, 23). Like a sort of proto-TARDIS, Wells's moon seems to have considerably more interiority than it has exteriority.

Discombobulated by their downward journey as prisoners of the Selenites, Bedford tried to cling to the default model of Earthly house: 'think of a wet roof at sunset, Cavor! Think of the windows of a westward house!' When Cavor does not answer he grows angry

> "Here we are burrowing in this beastly world that isn't a world, with its inky ocean hidden in some abominable blackness below, and outside that torrid day and that death stillness of night. And all these things that are chasing us now, beastly men of leather—insect men, that come out of a nightmare!"…
>
> "It was your fault," said Cavor.
>
> "My fault!" I shouted. "Good Lord!"
>
> "I had an idea!"
>
> "Curse your ideas!" [*First Men*, 16]

Idea is the key, of course. It was by *having ideas* that H.G. Wells was able to move in the space of a decade from literally not being able to afford enough food to eat, to being able to spend £3000 on a brand new house. And it is Cavor, the ideas man, who remains in the inside-moon, after Bedford cracks, flees, staggers over the increasingly inhospitable exterior of the moon back to the Cavorite capsule and flies home alone.

It is this that underlies one of the book's strangest and most powerful episodes. Alone in the capsule, heading homeward again, Bedford makes manifest in himself the larger outside-inside dynamic of the book and undergoes a profound existential crisis:

> Incredible as it will seem, this interval of time that I spent in space has no sort of proportion to any other interval of time in my life. Sometimes it seemed as though I sat through immeasurable eternities like some god upon a lotus leaf, and again as though there was a momentary pause as I leapt from moon to earth…. I was no more Bedford than I was anyone else, but only a mind floating in the still serenity of space. Why should I be disturbed about this Bedford's shortcomings? I was not responsible for him or them.
>
> I saw Bedford rushing down Chancery Lane, hat on the back of his head, coat tails flying out, *en route* for his public examination. I saw him dodging and bumping against, and even saluting, other similar little creatures in that swarming gutter of people. Me? I saw Bedford that same evening in the sitting-room of a certain lady, and his hat was on the table beside him, and it wanted brushing badly, and he was in tears. Me? I saw him with that lady in various attitudes and emotions—I never felt so detached before. [*First Men*, 20]

As if anticipating the weirdness of fractal geometry. Bedford goes 'inside' Bedford to discover that he is observing Bedford from an immensity of 'outsideness', and that with this profoundly unhousing, *unheimlich* erasure of inside and outside he loses all sense of himself as a self. The whole chapter, 'Mr Bedford in Infinite Space' is a fascinating high-point in *First Men*, and that's because it takes the large-scale SF metaphor that the novel literalises—the moon as hollow object of desire and destination—and reverts it back from outside metaphor to inside metaphor. It invites us to read the whole crazy outside adventure as actually being about the inside of this one person. This is the point when the 'straight' SFnal reading of *First Men* connects with the 'hoax' Poe's *Hans Pfaall* reading. Outer space and inner space are, as New Wave SF fabulists liked to argue in the 1960s, iterations of one another. This is a story about following Wyndham's 'outward urge' all the way to the moon and discovering that your hugely hollow destination slides your own subjectivity along the Möbius strip we call 'science fiction' far enough to discover that the hollowness is your own, and all of external reality a kind of illusion. This is why Wells's ingénieur figure, his ideas-man, the person who enables the entire fantastic voyage, is called Cavor. It's another iteration of Wells's hard-won Latin, an accomplishment that saw him into the Normal School and of which he was rather proud. *Cavor* is the first-person singular present passive indicative of *cavō* ('I make hollow, hollow out, excavate'). The Latin passive voice makes the subject the receiver of the action of the verb. English needs to use expanded locutions to convey this idea: 'Spade House has been constructed'; 'Bedford was flown to the moon'. So if we wanted to English *cavor* we could say either 'I am being hollowed', or perhaps just 'I am hollowed'. Cavor, we might say, is the means by which Bedford is hollowed as he journeys through infinite space, just as Bedford is the means by which Cavour's absent-minded abstractness is grounded—we might almost say, bedded—in reality. In a sense the two men are versions of one another. Inside out and outside in. *First Men in the Moon* indulges a kind of satirical levity, but does so in a strikingly profound, conceptually innovative and striking way. That's exactly Wells's peculiar genius.

Bibliography

Adorno, Theodor (1951), *Minima Moralia*. Translated by E F N Jephcott; Verso, 1974.
Batchelor, J. B. (1972), 'Kenneth B. Newell, Structure in Four Novels by H. G. Wells', *Modern Language Review* 67:2, 407–408.
Clute, John and David Langford (2015). 'Sleeper Awakes', *The Encyclopedia of Science Fiction*, 3rd edition. http://www.sf-encyclopedia.com/entry/sleeper_awakes.

Ford, Ford Madox (1937), *Portraits from Life: Memories and Criticism of Henry James, Joseph Conrad, Thomas Hardy, H.G. Wells, Stephen Crane, D.H. Lawrence, John Galsworthy, Ivan Turgenev, W.H. Hudson, Theodore Dreiser, A.C. Swinburne.* Boston: Houghton Mifflin Company.

Higgins, Richard (2008) 'Feeling like a Clerk in H. G. Wells', *Victorian Studies* 50: 3, pp. 457–475.

Hillegas, Mark (1967). *The Future as Nightmare: H. G. Wells and the Anti-Utopians.* Oxford: Oxford University Press.

Mackenzie, Norman and Jeanne Mackenzie (1973) *The Time Traveller: the Life of H G Wells.* London: Weidenfeld and Nicholson.

McLean, Stephen (2009). *Early Fiction of H G Wells: Fantasies of Science.* Houndmills: Palgrave.

Newell, Kenneth B. (1968). *Structure in Four Novels by H. G. Wells.* Mouton.

Richardson, Dorothy (1919). *The Tunnel*, London: Duckworth.

Roemer, Kenneth M. (1976). *The Obsolete Necessity: America in Utopian Writings, 1888–1900.* Kent, OH, Kent State University Press.

Stover, Leon (2000) *When the Sleeper Wakes: a Critical Text of the 1899 New York and London First Edition.* McFarland.

Williams, Raymond (1970) *The English Novel from Dickens to Lawrence.* London: Hogarth Press.

6

Anticipations

Anticipations (1901); Mankind in the Making (1903)

Wells's next book marked an important new departure for him, one that would in time radically redefine the kind of writer he was. *Anticipations* began as nine separate articles, commissioned by the *Fortnightly Review* and appearing in that magazine April–December 1901. These were republished in book form later that year as *Anticipations of the Reaction of Mechanical and Scientific Progress upon Human Life and Thought*. Although Wells's publisher, Chapman and Hall, initially thought sales would be modest, in fact they had to reprint almost straight away (seven further reprints quickly followed). 'Macmillan, my English publishers,' Wells says in the *Experiment in Autobiography*, misremembering whom actually published the work, 'were caught unawares by the demand and had sold out the first edition before they reprinted. It sold as well as a novel.'

Here the problems begin. Or, to be a little more precise, since the problems don't so much 'begin' in this book as become for the first time ineludible, let's say: this is the hinge text, the surprise success of which saw Wells move away from developing visionary futures as fiction towards extrapolating possible futures as ideological fact. Not actual fact, of course, since Wells can only ever be best-guessing what will happen. But from this point onwards Wells writes more and more in 'Prophet and Politician' mode and produces far fewer masterpieces of the science-fictional imagination. The free play of imaginative speculation is now replaced with a more rigid extrapolation from what are, inevitably, ideological bases. Bernard Bergonzi argues that what happened to Wells around this time was that 'his acceptance of a collectivist ideology destroyed the autonomy of his imagination' [Bergonzi, 171]. Since this was also the time

© The Author(s) 2019
A. Roberts, *H G Wells*, Literary Lives, https://doi.org/10.1007/978-3-030-26421-5_6

that Wells became properly active as a Fabian socialist, Bergonzi is in effect arguing that socialism destroyed Wells as an artist. That's not right, I think; but it is by way of asking the right sort of question, or at least of gesturing towards the question that needs addressing. And by 'problem' I mean: fascism. It is anachronistic to use that term discussing a book published in 1901 of course, but not wholly anachronistic; since *Anticipations* is one of the books that contributed directly to the larger sociopolitical debate that in turn lead to the rise of fascist movements in the 1920s and 1930s. It was one of many, of course; and I'm certainly not laying the blame for this latter development at Wells's door. But the politically authoritarian, eugenicist and racist elements in this work can't simply be wished-away. Looking back from the vantage-point of 1934's *Experiment in Autobiography* Wells talks rather grandly of *Anticipations* as 'the keystone to the main arch of my work', said arch being 'the structural frame of my life' and therefore 'of supreme importance to me'. Which is a very long way indeed from disowning it.

The book is structured to ease the reader in: moving from more neutral speculations about transportation and urban technologies through to more ideologically freighted speculation concerning political organisation and what we might as well call 'social hygiene'. As Wells wrote to Elizabeth Healey (2 July 1901): 'one has to go quietly in the earlier papers, but the last will be a buster.' Buster it proved: widely read and discussed, influential and effective, *Anticipations* was the book that made people start to treat Wells seriously as an intellectual heavyweight. Wells's friend Arnold Bennett—who poked the mildest kind of fun at the book by calling it *Uncle's-dissipations*—wrote to him to say either he had mastered the journalist's trick of appearing omniscient, or else perhaps he just was 'one of the most remarkable men alive'. Wells was only half-joking when he replied: 'there is no illusion. I *am* great.' He also insisted that picking-and-choosing among the individual essays would give a reader 'no inkling of the massive culminating effect of the book as a whole'. All this gives us a reason to resist the natural but fundamentally trivial desire to use our twenty-first-century hindsight to 'score' Wells for accuracy. The point of *Anticipations* is not, as it were, its prophetic epiphenomena; it is, to swap metaphors, the threads that bind together its various *fasces*. At what point in this book does bland supposition about technology morph into something more sinister?

Let's walk through. Chapter 1, 'Locomotion in the Twentieth Century' predicts a shift from collective mass-transit, such as is provided by railway companies, towards individual motility: 'there will, first of all, be the motor truck for heavy traffic … there will develop the hired or privately owned motor carriage … And thirdly there will be the motor omnibus' [*Anticipations*,

14–16]. These new cars will supersede horse traffic and require a whole new network of roads to be built ('the road surface may be made a very different thing from what it is at present, better drained and admirably adapted for the soft-tired hackney vehicles and the torrent of cyclists'). All accurate prophecy, of course, although it was clear to most people, even by 1901, that this was the direction things were heading. Magazines like *The Motor Car Journal* (est. 1898) and *Car Illustrated* often ran articles imagining similar futures. And in one key respect Wells got it quite wrong:

I do not think it at all probable that aeronautics will ever come into play as a serious modification of transport and communication. Man is not, for example, an albatross, but a land biped, with a considerable disposition towards being made sick and giddy by unusual motions. [*Anticipations*, 1]

I return, below, to this curious limitation in Wells's anticipatory vision. Chapter 2, 'The Probable Diffusion of Great Cities', develops the principle that 'the general distribution of population in a country must always be directly dependent on transport facilities'. From the predicate that human beings will tolerate no more than a 2-hour commute ('a maximum limit of two hours, one hour each way from sleeping place to council chamber, counter, workroom or office stool') Wells suggests that cities will grow as large as future technologies of transportation permit travellers to traverse from periphery to centre in an hour. Since he thinks this future tech will be very rapid, he predicts vast suburban spread, 'town' and 'country' will become obsolete terms and a new kind of 'urban region' (Wells's coinage) will come into being: 'the London citizen of the year 2000 AD may have a choice of nearly all England and Wales south of Nottingham and east of Exeter as his suburb'. Which has turned out to be, pretty much, the case.

These two alterations, in transportation and urban topography, set the scene for the following three chapters: 3, 'Developing Social Elements', 4, 'Certain Social Reactions' and 5, 'The Life-History of Democracy'. The two-class social system of a small aristocracy ruling a large commons derived, Wells thinks, from the fact that the only property, before the eighteenth century, was land, 'real estate', together with 'live-stock, serfs and the furnishings of real estate' like houses. This had to be 'held' in person by the landowner, which, except in special circumstances like war, limited the aristocrat to how far he could travel easily in a day on horseback. What Wells calls 'the Semitic invention of money' changed all that; and this new mobility of wealth will, Wells predicts, result in a new system of four classes: first 'the shareholding class'; secondly 'the abyss', at 'the opposite pole of the social scale': people 'without either property or any evident function in the social organism'; thirdly a productive middle-class of capable professionals, built around 'a nucleus of engineers and skilled mechanics': individuals defined by their education ('a revolution in the common schools of the community will be a necessary part of the process') who oversee the efficient production of food from automated farms, manage war-making, advance science and generally deploy invincible know-how actually to get things done. Finally there will be a class of social parasites: 'a great number of non-productive persons living in and by the social confusion'. Wells lists a few of these latter types: 'business managers, public and private, the political organizers, brokers, commission agents, the varying grades of financier down to the mere greedy camp followers of finance, the gamblers pure and simple, and the great body of their dependent clerks, typewriters, and assistants'. Chapter 3 ends with a smack at Parliamentary democracy ('The House of Commons is the seat of a party conflict' and has 'long ceased to bear any real relation to current social processes'). Wells believes only the 'capable men' have any business governing. Chapter 4 explores how these different classes might live their lives, and Chap. 5 returns to the, as Wells sees it, inadequacies of democracy. All extant democracies, Wells says, are 'based not on classes but upon a confusion; they are *governments of the grey*'. Not 'the people' but rather 'a scientifically trained middle-class of an unprecedented sort', says Wells, 'will become, I believe, at last consciously the State' [*Anticipations*, 5].

Chapter 6, 'War', speculates about the impact of new technologies of weaponry and efficiencies of organisation on human conflict. Wells thinks developments in the gun and cannon will completely change war, giving snipers new powers of dominating the battlefield and making battle itself a matter of 'rapid movements of guns and men'. He speculates about an air force, although thinks this will be more a matter of observation and intelligence gathering than actual fighting. He thinks future warships will become smaller and quicker, although he refuses to believe in submarines:

> I must confess that my imagination, in spite even of spurring, refuses to see any sort of submarine doing anything but suffocate its crew and founder at sea. It must involve physical inconvenience of the most demoralizing sort simply to be in one for any length of time. [*Anticipations*, 200]

These, though, are all technical speculations. The last three chapters return us to society: Chap. 7 'The Conflict of Language', imagines a future in which English and Chinese are the two global languages, with perhaps either French or German as a third. Then in Chap. 8, 'The Larger Synthesis', Wells finally names what is being anticipated: a 'new Republic', the 'reorganization which it is the main object of these *Anticipations* to display'.

> I have sought to show that in peace and war alike a process has been and is at work, a process with all the inevitableness and all the patience of a natural force, whereby the great swollen, shapeless, hypertrophied social mass of to-day must give birth at last to a naturally and informally organized, educated class, an unprecedented sort of people, a New Republic dominating the world. [*Anticipations*, 262]

Chapter 9, 'The Faith, Morals and Public Policy of the New Republic' concludes the book. The first problem the New Republic must solve involves that group 'which I have called the People of the Abyss':

> To the multiplying rejected of the white and yellow civilizations there will have been added a vast proportion of the black and brown races, and collectively those masses will propound the general question, "What will you do with us, we hundreds of millions, who cannot keep pace with you?" If the New Republic emerges at all it will emerge by grappling with this riddle. [*Anticipations*, 9]

The warning note chimes when Wells perpetrates what Gramsci somewhere calls the defining conceptual misprision of fascism as such, the deliberate confusion of political and aesthetic categories. The future rulers of the world 'will all be artists in reality, with a passion for simplicity and directness and an impatience of confusion and inefficiency'. As such they will be ruthless where 'the ugly' is concerned:

> The ethical system of these men of the New Republic, the ethical system which will dominate the world state, will be shaped primarily to favour the procreation of what is fine and efficient and beautiful in humanity—beautiful and strong bodies, clear and powerful minds, and a growing body of knowledge—and to check the procreation of base and servile types, of fear-driven and cowardly souls, of all that is mean and ugly and bestial in the souls, bodies, or habits of men. To do the latter is to do the former; the two things are inseparable. And the method that nature has followed hitherto in the shaping of the world, whereby weakness was prevented from propagating weakness, and cowardice and feebleness were saved from the accomplishment of their desires, the method that has only one alternative, the method that must in some cases still be called in to the help of man, is death. In the new vision death is no inexplicable horror, no pointless terminal terror to the miseries of life, it is the end of all the pain of life, the end of the bitterness of failure, the merciful obliteration of weak and silly and pointless things.

For a multitude of contemptible and silly creatures, fear-driven and helpless and useless, unhappy or hatefully happy in the midst of squalid dishonour, feeble, ugly, inefficient, born of unrestrained lusts, and increasing and multiplying through sheer incontinence and stupidity, the men of the New Republic will have little pity and less benevolence. The men of the New Republic will hold that the procreation of children who, by the circumstances of their parentage, must be diseased bodily or mentally is absolutely the most loathsome of all conceivable sins...

The men of the New Republic will not be squeamish, either, in facing or inflicting death, because they will have a fuller sense of the possibilities of life than we possess. They will have an ideal that will make killing worth the while … The idea that only those who are fit to live freely in an orderly world-state should be permitted to live, is entirely against the use of deterrent punishments at all … People who cannot live happily and freely in the world without spoiling the lives of others are better out of it. That is a current sentiment even to-day, but the men of the New Republic will have the courage of their opinions. [*Anticipations*, 9]

I've quoted this at some length, because it seems to me important not to distort Wells's argument with selective citation. No topic in the whole range of Wellsian study is more fractiously argued-over than this one, and it's not hard to see why. Nonetheless, what Wells is saying is clear enough. The ugly, the disabled and the inadequate will have no place in his New Republic. Where they exist they will do so on a sufferance that may very well be withdrawn; 'withdrawal' in this case meaning extermination. Parallel to this ruthless social 'cleansing', Wells says, will be a full-throated eugenicist programme to punish those who breed inferior humanity and to encourage the 'best' to breed ever stronger, more beautiful folk.

One final question remains: how does all this relate to questions of race? 'And how', Wells asks, breezily, 'will the New Republic treat the inferior races? How will it deal with the black? how will it deal with the yellow man? how will it tackle that alleged termite in the civilized woodwork, the Jew?' And his answer is: by ruthlessly applying the yardstick of beautiful efficiency:

[The New Republic] will tolerate no dark corners where the people of the Abyss may fester, no vast diffused slums of peasant proprietors, no stagnant plague-preserves. Whatever men may come into its efficient citizenship it will let come—white, black, red, or brown; the efficiency will be the test. And the Jew also it will treat as any other man. It is said that the Jew is incurably a parasite on the apparatus of credit. If there are parasites on the apparatus of credit, that is a reason for the legislative cleaning of the apparatus of credit, but it is no reason for the special treatment of the Jew. If the Jew has a certain incurable tendency to social parasitism, and we make social parasitism impossible, we shall abolish the Jew, and if he has not, there is no need to abolish the Jew. [*Anticipations*, 9]

It's the 'we' here that is so queasy. The 'Jew' is already defined as outsider even as Wells clubbishly promises that he is not going to exterminate him willy-nilly. *Only should the need arise* will that heart-sinking phrase 'we shall abolish the Jew' be actualised. The remainder of the twentieth century proved how very low the bar was set for such a criterion. 'And for the rest', Wells concludes, 'those swarms of black, and brown, and dirty-white [*i.e., mixed race*], and yellow people, who do not come into the new needs of efficiency?'

Well, the world is a world, not a charitable institution, and I take it they will have to go. The whole tenor and meaning of the world, as I see it, is that they have to go. So far as they fail to develop sane, vigorous, and distinctive personalities for the great world of the future, it is their portion to die out and disappear.

They will have to go: a century of genocide summed up in one devastatingly offhand phrase. We have gone from patting Wells on the back for anticipating the dominance of private automobiles and motorway service stations to wincing at the enthusiasm of his endorsement of eugenicist authoritarianism and genocide. What happened?

The soft response would be to suggest that after a decade of remarkable popular success as a writer Wells had come to view not just society but the entire world with a writer's sensibility. It is easy to make the people in your stories do what you want them to do, and even easy, if you have an ambitious enough imagination, to reconfigure the whole of society and culture, as Wells had done with the world of *Sleeper Wakes* and the Selenite social harmony of *First Men in the Moon*. The passage from messy, unsatisfactory Now to the gleaming, callisthenic efficiencies of *Anticipations*' Future is *actually* only the wave of the authorial pen, after all. This might, just conceivably, excuse the murderous coldness of the book's final chapter. All writers kill-off characters, and few are in any way morally troubled about doing so. We don't, after all, put Agatha Christie and Harold Shipman in the same ethical basket. So perhaps it's a sort of category error to react to Wells's moral myopia, in this book, with outrage.

This, however, is a pretty thin defence. *Anticipations* specifically does not sheathe itself in the decent prophylaxis of fiction. Wells meant for people to take him seriously, and was gratified (as well as rewarded, both financially and in terms of reputation and status) when they did. And if we take it seriously, then what is unmistakable about this book, and immanent in every chapter of it, is the way it not only looks forward to, but actively *yearns* for, the supersession of one mode of political authority ('aristocracy', or 'tradition') with another, more total one. It is a book that exemplifies, to a truly remarkable degree, everything Hannah Arendt lays out in her great study *The Origins of Totalitarianism* (1951). Arendt summarises the history of expansionist capitalism—Imperialism—as grounded in 'scientific racism' (in order to justify the subjugation of other races) and therefore in the European prototype for such racism, anti-Semitism. She describes the emergence of 'movements' that propose themselves as the solution to corrupt political parties: movements that are hostile to the state, radically anti-democratic and anti-parliamentarian, just as Wells's is. Arendt diagnoses the transformation of classes into masses, the role of propaganda and the use of terror, as essential to this form of government, and, crucially, she makes the distinction between the new totalitarianisms and the earlier, merely autocratic or tyrannical regimes. Autocracy seeks only to gain political power and to outlaw opposition; totalitarian regimes seek to dominate every aspect of everyone's life in the service of global domination. Arendt is talking about Hitler and Stalin, not about Wells (whom she doesn't discuss), but her book still figures as a remarkably *en pointe* account of *Anticipations*, with this one difference: that everything Arendt deplores, Wells valorises. In her preface to the first, 1951 edition of the book Arendt says, mordantly enough:

> It is as though mankind had divided itself between those who believe in human omnipotence (who think that everything is possible if one knows how to organise masses for it) and those for whom powerlessness has become the major experience of their lives.

It's striking that Wells, who remained emotionally and artistically so in touch with what it felt like to have been defined by being young and powerlessness, came so wholeheartedly to identify with the believers in human omnipotence in his political thinking. If we wished to be charitable we might say that he was at least genuine in believing that the latter course was the way to solve the injustice that had put him, as a child and young man, in the former camp. Still, it is chilling to read *Anticipations* through an Arendtian lens.

We might consider Wells's summary of *Anticipations*, in his letter Elizabeth Healey (2 July 1901) to be mere jocularity: a book 'designed to undermine and destroy the monarch monogamy and respectability—and the British Empire, all under the guise of a speculation about motor cars and electrical heating'. But it's worth taking that statement at face value. Wells doesn't deploy the term 'totalitarian' or its cognates, and also true that he makes occasional argumentative sallies to insist that his New Republic will keep a place for all the idiosyncrasies and individualities of life. So, yes, sexual reproduction *will* be legislated to ensure the increasing eugenic strength and beauty of the human species; but people (like Wells himself) for whom a non-generative amorist lifestyle is a pleasant hobby will still be able to pursue their sexual dalliances: 'the question of sexual relationships', he says, 'would be entirely on all fours with, and probably very analogous to, the question of golf' [*Anticipations*, 304]—in effect gifting himself a philanderer's get-out-of-jail-free-card from his own earnestly purely-procreative future. Of the future mega-cities Wells insists that they will be 'far less monotonous than our present English world':

> In many cases the houses may very probably be personal homes, built for themselves as much as the Tudor manor-houses were, and even, in some cases, as æsthetically right. As one travels through the urban region, one will traverse open, breezy, "horsey" suburbs, smart white gates and palings everywhere, good turf, a Grand Stand shining pleasantly; gardening districts all set with gables and roses, holly hedges, and emerald lawns; pleasant homes among heathery moorlands and golf links, and river districts with gaily painted boat-houses peeping from the osiers. ... Through the varied country the new wide roads will run, here cutting through a crest and there running like some colossal aqueduct across a valley, swarming always with a multitudinous traffic of bright, swift (and not necessarily ugly) mechanisms. [*Anticipations*, 61–62]

Golf again, you notice. It's all rather ... *bourgeois*, isn't it? Rather at odds with the ideological mantra of systematic efficiency. Of course, Hitler's personal aesthetic taste was deeply middle-class and conventional: in public he endorsed Wagner, but in private he preferred Franz Lehár's whimsical operettas and his Berchtesgaden Kehlsteinhaus was decorated with every detail and freak of bourgeois platitude. Maybe there is some truth after all in that old Sartre line about the rebel being the one who works hardest to preserve the abuses from which he suffers so that he can go on rebelling against them. Or, to put it another way, maybe there's a more profound Žižekian thesis here about bourgeois banality being the secret perverse truth of radical totalitarianism. Perhaps the core argument of *Anticipations* is best taken as a kind of creative paradox. Wells wants to preserve all these little features of bourgeois respectable pleasure even as he proposes a system that will extirpate the entire social system out of which they grow. We might say that this shows up Wells's 'New Republic' as lacking depth, except that lacking depth is a feature, rather than a bug, of his vision. I recall the earlier observation about Wells's refusal to believe that aeroplanes might contribute to future transportation, or add anything to war-making except surveillance, or his denial that submarines might have a place in his future-navy. A pair of symptomatic blind spots, perhaps. *Anticipations* forecasts the giganticism of the state, but limits that expansion to a *horizontal* topography: wider and wider are the borders of London set, faster transport systems linking everything into one flattened network, English and Chinese spreading over the entire surface of the world. All, to use the jargon, rhizomatic, not arboreal. His four-part class system is similarly flattened, with, of course, the exception of the *en bas* 'people of the abyss', whom the New Republic will exterminate. But those aside, the three 'classes' don't exist in a traditional hierarchical relationship, one over the other, the way actual class systems do.

Wells's implicit boast is that he has uncovered the underlying laws that determine historical change: and that therefore his forecasts are not merely adventitious guesses but rigorous extrapolations of ongoing underlying tendencies. In the *Experiment in Autobiography* he boasts that he was the first to grasp the law of 'the reciprocal relationship between facilities of locomotion and community-size, and so a realization of what was happening to the world'. History is not at the whim of 'Great Men'. It follows laws Wells is revealing to us. 'In 1900', is his boast, 'I had already grasped the inevitability of a World State.' *Inevitability* is a pretty unambiguous word.

But here's the rub: if the New Republic is inevitable (arriving, as the book says, with 'all the inevitableness and all the patience of a natural force') then why do we need to do anything to make it happen? Asking this question casts a particular light over the exhortations to, or stern-faced celebrations of, the ruthlessness with which New Republicans will pursue eugenics, sterilisation and the extermination of the people of the Abyss. To say, as a Hitler might, 'these *Untermenschen* are what stand between us and the coming of the Thousand Year Reich! We must remove this impediment, kill them all, in order to make the birth of that world possible' is to say one kind of thing, cruel and evil but logical after its own lights. But if Wells's New Republic is inevitable, then it must be inevitable whether we gas all the People of the Abyss or not. Nonetheless, Wells copestones his vision with exhortations to be firm, to dispose of all these incapables, these abyssal black, brown and yellow people, to abolish the Jew and purge the disabled and unfit. If doing so is obligatory despite the fact that such action is not necessary to the creation of the New Republic then might we be nudged towards the rather uncomfortable conclusion that, just maybe, such action is *the secret truth* of the New

Republic itself? Maybe genocide is not a painful duty needful to bring about utopia, but rather the reason we are looking forward to utopia in the first place. The syllogism 'if the story of Winston Smith is a dystopia, then a utopia must be the story of O'Brien' is misleading in obvious ways, but it at least shines the light on one crucial thing: that these are fantasies, in the first instance as well as in the last, of *power*.

An essay by Adam Phillips called 'On Not Making It Up' parallels two dichotomous models of scientific and creative work: on the one hand that the scientist or artist *discovers* truths that were there all along, and on the other that that the scientist, or artist *invents* or *creates* the truths with which they deal. Does *Anticipations* reveal the underlying truth of history, or invent a compelling (or horrifying) possible future? Do creative types disclose or concoct? This question sometimes gets caught up in the debates about the differences between disciplines of 'science' and 'art' themselves, debates peculiarly relevant to a writer (like Wells) who is so strongly associated with that mode-straddling discourse 'science fiction'. 'Gravity was always there but the *Mona Lisa* wasn't', is how Phillips puts it. 'And yet of course we think of both so-called artists and scientists as creative. Are we making additions to the world as we find it, or are we revealing more and more of what's already there?' [Phillips, 79]. He goes on to discuss utopian writing (he doesn't mention Wells):

> In his recent Gifford lectures about utopian socialists, [Jerry Cohen] suggested that they "prescribe a new form to reality. Contrast midwives, who deliver the form that develops within reality." The familiar thing is once again at stake. Prescription of something new, or facilitation of something there already, and ready to happen. "The artist," Adrian Stokes writes, "has seized upon a pose and almost painted the object out." Whereas the artist as midwife allows the object its own shape. As in all such contrasts, the differences blur in the middle ... There is the imperial (and imperious) self colonizing the world, or replacing the world with a world of his own: the artist who makes the world in his own image. And then there is the self as midwife, creating the optimal conditions for something other than the self to come to life; the artist as servant of a process. For the imperial self, the world needs to be improved. For the midwife self the world needs to be seen as it is. [Phillips, 83]

There's no question, when we put it like this, but that Wells was an Imperial Self. To much the same end Phillips quotes Denis Donoghue's distinction between the sculptor who addresses a block of stone with her chisel because she believes the statue is in there, somewhere, waiting to be delivered, and the modeller who starts with raw clay and builds what her imagination prompts her to build from nothing.

> "In craving," he writes, "the artist assumes that the block of stone contains within itself the form invented for it by nature; the artist's desire is merely to liberate that form, to disclose its hidden face. In modelling, on the other hand, the artist gives the stone his own truth, or what he insists is his own truth; the truth of the stone as a different truth is not acknowledged." [Phillips, 84]

Phillips adds that 'the great American critic R. P. Blackmur makes, in a similar spirit, a distinction between the erotic and the sacramental poet who, respectively, foist themselves upon their objects in an act of virtual ravishment or cannibalism, or reveal and reverence an object by definition other than themselves.' And this brings us back, forcefully enough, to Wells again. He was, clearly, an erotic rather than a sacramental sort of writer, as he was an erotic rather than a sacramental sort of man. And *Anticipations* is an erotic sort of book, one in which little islets of philandering pleasure are preserved, like golf links, in amongst a future-Britain transformed by prodigious mobility—immensely fast cars, hurtling down purpose-built freeways; vast reserves of capital made liquid to flow into the building of amazing infrastructure, or dazzling weapons of war. It's all thoroughly sensual, a major key restatement of a theme we've seen before in Wells whereby actual mobility (as, for example, on a bicycle) elides in his imagination with social mobility, and social freedom with sexual freedom. He was a modeller, not a sculptor, and *Anticipations* is a modular society, not a real one, not even the blueprint of a real one. How striking, then, that, as time chipped away the exterior of that monumental marble block called 'the Twentieth Century' it revealed the lineaments of a nightmare sculpture that so very closely resembled Wells's clay model. One might almost call it 'synchronicity'.

The commercial and reputational success of *Anticipations* imparted a new momentum to Wells's career that was to pull him, as the century went on, away from the merely fictional. This period in his life coincided with his time as a Fabian, which group he joined in 1903, and from which he resigned in 1908. A short period, perhaps, but very important to Wells in lots of ways. He was, at first, enthusiastic: attended meetings and delivered papers on what we would nowadays call collectivisation, the consolidation of private smallholdings into larger nationalised farms and factories. This research, he says, was behind *The Food of the Gods* (serialised in 1903 and published as a book in 1904), 'which began with a wild burlesque of the change of scale produced by scientific men and ended in the heroic struggle of the rare new big-scale way of living against the teeming small-scale life of the earth'. He adds that 'nobody saw the significance of it' and 'it left some of its readers faintly puzzled'. Conceivably fiction was too distracting a mode for these 'researches'.

> The more formal research for the realization of the New Republic was pursued in *Mankind in the Making*. I was realizing that the correlative of a new republic was a new education and this book is a discursive examination, an all too discursive examination of the formative elements in the social magma. [*Experiment in Autobiography*, 559]

Mankind in the Making (1903) presents itself as a development of the arguments in *Anticipations*, although it had markedly less impact than the earlier book, largely because it is simply not as good. It is prolix where the first book was tight, underpowered and diffusely distracted by the minutiae of its own argument. Wells's *Experiment in Autobiography*, with impressive honesty, characterises this as 'my style at its worst and my matter at its thinnest, and quoting it makes me feel very sympathetic with those critics who, to put it mildly, restrain their admiration for me'. It's hard to disagree. But since this book is sometimes taken as evidence that Wells abandoned eugenics almost as soon as he took it up, it's worth looking into that topic in the book in more detail.

Through the Fabians Wells had met and befriended Graham Wallas, and it was in part through discussion and correspondence with him that Wells wrote the individual papers that make up *Mankind in the Making*. Very broadly, Wallas argued that reformers' efforts needed to be directed towards nurture rather than nature: towards education and re-education rather than eugenics and selective breeding. The slackness of *Mankind in the Making* is in part explicable by the slowness with which Wells integrated these new ideas into his worldview, or perhaps indexes his reluctance fully to accept the case. Although he had himself been a teacher, and although his own career had grown out of education, Wells didn't really have the patience properly to embrace the slowly-slowly gradualist model of social improvement. His writing prefers sudden lightning-strikes that instantly dispose of all the clotted backstory of inequality and squalor, as happens magically in *In the Days of the Comet* (1906). And whilst Wallas's influence means that *Mankind in the Making* does downplay *Anticipations*'s more nakedly eugenic line, this is not because Wells has turned against the concept. Rather it's because he doesn't think we at present know enough to be able to apply it effectively. 'Chapter 2: The Problem of the Birth Supply' begins by asking: 'how much may we hope, now or at a later time, to improve the supply of that raw material which is perpetually dumped upon our hands?' *Raw material*, *dumped*, frankly, dehumanising terminology to apply to human beings; but *Mankind in the Making* is a book that takes it as axiomatic that population is a burden rather than a resource. Wells simply does not take the force of Ruskin's core insight that the only wealth is life. For Wells wealth is productivity, money and efficiency. For the purposes of his argument in this book humanity is a mere dead weight to be manipulated, with only the best portions capable of being 'made' into something worthwhile.

Mankind in the Making's question is not whether but *how best* can eugenics manage the transition from *Homo sapiens* to the Wellsian *homo utopiens*. Far from repudiating eugenics Wells insists that if we could be 'clear what points to breed for and what points to breed out' we would be entirely justified in doing so; and he endorses the notion that certain hereditary diseases should be 'bred out' from the population right now—for example, he reports disapprovingly that two deaf people were married in Saffron Walden in September 1902, and insists that the New Republic ought not to allow such things. But, he worries that there are just too many variables to mean that we can be sure selective breeding will definitely improve the race.

The book breaks the topic down into: the positive traits beauty, health, capacity, genius and what he calls '"energy" or "go"' on the one hand; and the negative traits criminality and alcoholism on the other. None of these, he argues, are simple: a criminal may exhibit positive traits such as daring and ingenuity alongside the negative ones of amorality and social delinquency, and to breed out the latter may breed out the former. Not that Wells is advancing a more socially progressive agenda. On the contrary.

> The "perfect" health of a negro may be a quite dissimilar system of reactions to the "perfect health" of a vigorous white; you may blend them only to create an ailing mass of physiological discords. [*Mankind*, 2]

In some ways this is more racist than anything in *Anticipations*, since it both assumes that 'race' embodies a kind of biological fixity and that miscegenation must degrade the species. 'The problems of the foreign immigrant and of racial intermarriage loom upon us' Wells says a little later, sounding every inch the reactionary. He adds that the lack of 'certainty' means 'there is nothing for it' but 'to leave these things to individual experiment' for the time being, although 'prompt and vigorous research' must perforce be undertaken into these questions. As for eugenics, *Mankind in the Making* calls, reluctantly enough, for its postponement until such time as science can work out how to prosecute it effectively.

This missing science of heredity, this unworked mine of knowledge on the borderland of biology and anthropology, which for all practical purposes is as unworked now as it was in the days of Plato, is, in simple truth, ten times more important to humanity than all the chemistry and physics, all the technical and industrial science that ever has been or ever will be discovered. [*Mankind*, 2]

In the meantime, Wells turns his attention to educating the stock we have. He thinks should teach the basics of reading and writing, instil *esprit de corps* and allow pupils to explore extensive libraries to uncover science for themselves: all reasonable suggestions. Elsewhere, though, reasonableness becomes scarce, as with this attack on the state of national education in the early 1900s.

There grows a fine crop of Quack Schools; schools organized on lines of fantastic extravagance, in which bee-keeping takes the place of Latin, and gardening supersedes mathematics, in which boys play tennis naked to be cured of False Shame … The subjects of study in these schools come and go like the ravings of a disordered mind; "Greek History" (in an hour or so a week for a term) is followed by "Italian Literature," and this gives place to the production of a Shakespearian play that ultimately overpowers and disorganizes the whole curriculum. [*Mankind*, 6]

You really do have to think Wells could have found worthier targets for his scorn than nude tennis, surely not a pastime that ever amounted to a national problem; and describing a curriculum that follows a history lesson with two lessons on literature as 'the ravings of a disordered mind' is, surely, *de trop*. In Chap. 9 'The Organization of Higher Education' Wells proposes 15 as an age at which inferior children should be syphoned-off 'into employment suited to their capacity, employment which should not carry with it any considerable possibility of prolific marriage'. The cleverer ones should go into university, and so develop (in Chap. 10) into citizens of the New Republic. *Mankind in the Making* ends with a peroration to Youth ('without the high resolve of youth, without the constant accession of youth, without recuperative power, no sustained forward movement is possible in the world. It is to youth, therefore, that this book is finally addressed, to the adolescents, to the students…'). Nonetheless this superstructure of specific educational proposals, confected in equal parts of Wells's own experiences growing up (that, for example, clever kids should be allowed free run of the library), as a teacher himself and from the reading he was doing—everything rests upon an implacable meritocratic-elitist foundation. This reformed pedagogy is not for all, and if there comes a future in which all the citizens of the New Republic do get to play with thousands of wooden math blocks and play decently clothed tennis, it will be because the 'people of the Abyss' have been written out of the equation. Immanent throughout the book is the question about how to handle what Wells calls 'birth waste'—a repellently dismissive phrase to describe what, by Wells's own calculations, amounts to nearly a third of the entire population.

Wells's answer to this problem is certainly not to establish a comprehensive welfare state that can bring everybody up to the necessary level. 'Philanthropic people', says Wells, '[strive] to meet the birth waste by the very obvious expedients of lying-in hospitals, orphanages and foundling institutions, waifs' homes, Barnardo institutions and the like.' But this merely serves 'to encourage and stimulate births in just those strata of society where it would seem to be highly reasonable to believe they are least desirable'. Wells's own estimate is that 30% of the UK population belong to this category, and must be either discouraged or actively prevented from having kids, though on the latter score he notes regretfully that 'these people are fiercely defensive in such matters as this' and that attempting to intervene is like trying to 'handle the litter of a she-wolf'. He argues that a minimum standard of housing, nutrition, education and nurture is required if any given child is going to be able to fulfil their potential, but rather than propose (say) that the state guarantee these standards for all he proposes a range of laws to punish delinquent and poverty-stricken parents ('these will converge to convince these people that to bear children into such an unfavourable atmosphere is an extremely inconvenient and undesirable thing') and brushes aside the suggestion that this would be in any sense unfair:

> It will be urged that these things are likely to bear rather severely on the very poor parent. To which a growing number of people will reply that the parent should not be a parent under circumstances that do not offer a fair prospect of sound child-birth and nurture. It is no good trying to eat our cake and have it; if the parent does not suffer the child will. [*Mankind*, 3]

Hand-in-hand with this is the proposal, important enough in Wells's view to merit italicisation, that '*it is better in the long run that people whose character and capacity will not render it worthwhile to employ them at the Minimum Wage should not be employed at all*'. Let them starve, it seems. This class

> arrests the development of labour-saving machinery, replaces and throws out of employment superior and socially more valuable labour, enables these half-capables to establish base families of inadequately fed and tended children (which presently collapse upon public and private charity), and so lowers and keeps down the national standard of life. [*Mankind*, 107]

Tough love indeed. And it is in this way that Wells brings eugenics into his argument by, as it were, the back door. Such legislation will persuade 'an increasing section of the Abyss' to 'contrive to live childless', in which case they will breed themselves out of the body politic by default: 'a childless wastrel is a terminating evil.'

It's true that *Mankind in the Making* doesn't include any of those perorations to pitilessness and steel-hearted genocide that so blot *Anticipations*; but, by evading this fundamental, the book is, because more evasive, less savoury. At no point in his analysis can Wells conceive of this increasing population as possessing any inherent value. On the contrary: human life is a dangerous inundation. In a truly bizarre image, which Wells nonetheless insists is 'a permissible picture of human life', he invites us to '[imagine] all our statesmen, our philanthropists and public men, our parties and institutions gathered into one great hall, and into this hall a huge spout, that no man can stop, discharges a baby every eight seconds'. Stem the 'unending stream of babies' or drown civilisation. It is a dehumanising image, and leads Wells into some inhumane speculation about child mortality: 'a portion of infant and child mortality represents no doubt the lingering and wasteful removal from this world of beings with inherent defects, beings who, for the most part, ought never to have been born, and need not have been born under conditions of greater foresight' [*Mankind*, 88].

Bibliography

Arendt, Hannah (1951). *Origins of Totalitarianism*. New York, Schocken Books.
Bergonzi, Bernard (1961) *The Early H.G. Wells: A Study of the Scientific Romances*. University of Toronto Press.
Phillips, Adam (2006). *Side Effects*. Harmondsworth, Penguin.

7

Kipps: A Study in Artistry
Kipps (1905)

Kipps, this 'Story of a Simple Soul', is the first bona-fide masterpiece of Wells's comic-pathetic mimetic mode. For that reason, and as indicative of the artistry Wells put into his fiction generally, it merits discussion at greater length.

Kipps is a draper's assistant in Folkestone whose life is going nowhere until it is transformed by an out-of-the-blue inheritance of a house and £26,000. The bulk of the novel explores his various funny and touching fish-out-of-water experiences as he tries to adjust to being so abruptly rich. The funniest and most touching of these involve his hypergamous desires—hypergamy is 'bedding a woman from a class superior to one's own'. When still a draper Kipps took a woodcarving class on Thursday nights and fell deeply and hopelessly in love with the young woman who taught it, the beautiful and refined Helen Walsingham. Now that he is rich, and since Helen happens to be financially distressed, he finds himself in a position to propose marriage. She accepts. Kipps is taken in hand by a small circle of the higher-class Folkestonites, in particular, a man called Mr Coote, although there is little they can do to raise the tone of Kipps's exuberantly lower-middle-class speech, manner and essence. *Kipps* is divided into three books. Book 1 details Kipps's school days and his time as a draper's assistant ending, at Chap. 6 'The Unexpected', with his inheritance. Book 2 follows through into Kipps's new life of wealth and his betrothal to Helen Walsingham; Book 3 is rather disproportionately shorter than the first two, and ties-up the story as Kipps, increasingly malapropos and miserable, jilts Helen and instead marries his childhood sweetheart and social equal Ann. He then loses almost all his money (the solicitor who had been handling his financial affairs, Helen's younger brother, has speculated it all away) and sets up a little bookshop with what's left. The novel ends happily,

© The Author(s) 2019
A. Roberts, *H G Wells*, Literary Lives, https://doi.org/10.1007/978-3-030-26421-5_7

with the Kippses new parents, happier as shopkeepers than they ever were as idle rich people, although there's a sort of double-twist when money Kipps had foolishly put into a theatrical play turns out unexpectedly to have been a golden investment, and he becomes rich again.

But plot-summary really does nothing to convey the flavour of the novel, and it's that flavour that carries the whole: precisely observed, beautifully written, funny, touching and charming. Wells renders not one but two entire social milieux out of a weave of specific detail and incident and has a marvellous eye for the way incongruity parleys embarrassment into a sort of superposition of hilarity and existential agony. Kipps goes through the novel hideously self-conscious, always overwhelmed by the thought of what other people will think of him. At the beginning, he is worried what better-bred people will think. After his inheritance, he worries what his new friends will think, what Helen will think and what servants, waiters and so on will think of him. This is one of the most remarkable things about *Kipps* as a novel. Quite apart from how droll the book is, how effectively illustrative it is of the social mores of Edwardian English life, how vivid is its characterisation—all those 'well-made novel' qualities over which Wells manifests such impressive control—quite apart from all that is the centrality the novel gives to *shyness* and *boredom*. I can't think of a better portrait of shyness and boredom in literature. Indeed, when I think how hugely important both those qualities are in most people's lives I'm frankly astonished by their absence from capital-L Literature. The young Kipps, pre-legacy, is bored by the endless routine of his job in the draper's shop, but even more bored on the days he doesn't have to work.

> On Sundays he was obliged to go to church once, and commonly he went twice, for there was nothing else to do. He sat in the free seats at the back; he was too shy to sing, and not always clever enough to keep his place in the prayer-book, and he rarely listened to the sermon.
>
> In the intervals between services he walked about Folkestone with an air of looking for something. Folkestone was not so interesting on Sundays as on week-days, because the shops were shut ... He would sometimes walk up and down the Leas between twenty and thirty times after supper, desiring much the courage to speak to some other person in the multitude similarly employed. Almost invariably he ended his Sunday footsore. He never read a book; there were none for him to read, and, besides ... he had no taste that way. [*Kipps*, 49–50]

His inheritance ought to alleviate this tedium but in a way only makes it worse. Kipps's agony at having to make social calls and go to parties, as his fiancée insists he does, is beautifully and painfully rendered. Towards the end of book 2 Kipps, now rich, and having booked himself into a luxury hotel, is too shy to get himself lunch. The whole scene is a masterpiece in the painful comedy of social awkwardness.

> He would have liked something to eat very much now, but his inbred terror of the table was very strong. He did at last get by a porter in uniform towards the dining-room, but at the sight of a number of waiters and tables, with remarkable complications of knives and glasses, terror seized him, and he backed out again, with a mumbled remark to the waiter in the doorway about this not being the way. [*Kipps*, 312]

He decides to go to an outside restaurant instead, but that plan goes no better.

> Before all things he didn't want to go into a place and look like a fool … He drifted on to a neat window with champagne bottles, a dish of asparagus and a framed menu of a two shilling lunch. He was about to enter, when fortunately he perceived two waiters looking at him over the back screen of the window with a most ironical expression, and he sheared off at once. There was a wonderful smell of hot food half way down Fleet Street and a nice looking Tavern with several doors, but he could not decide which door. His nerve was going under the strain. [*Kipps*, 313]

Of course, if Kipps were nothing more than this sort of endlessly shrinking violet he would be too passive and irritating to make for a great character. Wells is cannier than that, threading Kipps's acute, sometimes crippling shyness and embarrassment with strands of a more bumptious, thrusting youthful energy. There are just enough glimpses of this assertive Kipps—the last thing he says in the novel is: 'I don't suppose there ever was a chap quite like me before!'—although he does then qualify that with 'Oo! I dunno'—to ratify Jonathan Franzen's later claim that a combination of moral absolutism and a sense of superiority 'is so often the secret heart of shyness'.

Kipps is, manifestly, based on the external events of Wells's young experience as a draper's apprentice, on his youthful social timidity and priggish sexual yearning. Later critics have, by and large, followed Wells in treating 'life' as not only source but structure for this and other Wellsian novels, to their aesthetic disadvantage. For Malcolm Bradbury, Wells contradistinguished himself from his friends James, Conrad and Ford Madox Ford by describing their writing as informed by 'immense artistic preoccupations' whilst declaring his own as interested not in art but life—'before we have done', he boasted, 'we shall have all life within the scope of the novel'.

"Life," from the Naturalists on, obviously meant more than just life, ongoing existence. It meant evolutionary energies, people seen in their environment and history, as representatives of the workings of the world; it was love and death and sex and marriage, plainly and frankly, objectively and critically seen. It was material mass, houses and goods and class relations, detail on detail amassed and considered … One thing was clear; it was not seeking a Flaubertian perfection of art. "Literature is not jewellery, it has quite other aims than perfection, and the more one thinks of 'how it is done' the less one gets it done," said Wells. "What I'm trying to get render is nothing more or less than Life," explains George Ponderevo, the very self-conscious narrator of *Tono-Bungay*.… It was clear that what life required of the writer was not aesthetic wholeness or even Conradian incompleteness but a plain openness. "I fail to see ow I can be otherwise than a lax, undisciplined storyteller," asserts George Ponderevo. "I must sprawl and flounder, comment and theorize." [Bradbury, 105–6]

I quote this at some length as indicative of how many critics have taken *Kipps*, and in order, in as comprehensive a manner as space permits, to contradict it. Though it often suited Wells to characterise what he did as mere journalism, and himself as a simple purveyor of life-drawn récit, the fact remains that not a single novel of his is unmarked by a deeply worked aesthetic proficiency. Bradbury is not exactly saying Wells is a follower of *le Naturalisme* (since he was not), but he is downplaying not only the immanent *irony* that informs the Wellsian mode—irony as comedy in a novel like *Kipps*, irony as the structural fabulation of defamiliarising novums in the science fiction—but the careful attention Wells always paid to literary artistry as such. Wells was not George Ponderevo. John Galsworthy recalled walking on the beach at Sandgate with Wells discussing 'the inner meanings' of *Kipps*, recording his admiration for the 'extreme precision' with which Wells dealt with 'an unimaginably difficult theme'. Extreme precision is much more descriptive of *Kipps* than sprawl and flounder.

On the other hand, evidence for if not sprawl then the compromised artistry of this novel might be thought found in the fact that it took a long time for Wells to pull *Kipps* together. He started writing the first version in 1898 under the working-title *The Wealth of Mr. Waddy*. According to Harris Wilson, who has examined the complicated MSS held in the Wells Archive of the University of Illinois Urbana, 'the six-thousand-odd sheets written intermittently over a period of seven years' contain 'literally scores of false starts, digressions, and abandoned episodes' [Wilson, 63]. In the final published version Part 3 is half the size of Part 1 and one-third of the size of Part 2, a disproportion explained by the fact Wells cut an 11,000-word episode of barely diluted political and utopian speculation from this last section. He was working on the final draft of *Kipps* at the same time as writing *Mankind in the Making* and *A Modern Utopia* and hoped, at one point, to include material germane to the theses of those works in the novel as a discussion between Kipps and a character called Masterman. 'Wells, in this episode,' notes Wilson, 'slips into the discursive and didactic; his characters are almost forgotten as they expound his own social ideas and criticism.' We can be glad he had the sense to cut these passages.

Now we *could* take this protracted and repeatedly revised and cut-about genesis as evidence of Wells's looseness of aesthetic construction: throwing, as it were, stuff at the wall of the novel and seeing what stuck. The *Experiment in Autobiography* says surprisingly little about *Kipps*, although the novel is mentioned briefly in a section titled 'Whether I Am a Novelist' that is mostly given over to a more-or-less self-deprecating account of discussions Wells had with Henry James over the novelist's art. James, says Wells, had high standards for their respective work: 'he thought of [the Novel] as an Art Form and of novelists as artists of a very special and exalted type.' Wells insists that *he* always thought of it on the contrary as a mode of communication, of reaching and teaching people. He reports James's regret that he found himself unable to take Wells's novels 'in any aesthetic or "literary" relation at all' and even concedes the point:

> Tried by Henry James's standards I doubt if any of my novels can be taken in any other fashion. There are flashes and veins of character duly "treated" and living individuals in many of them, but none that satisfy his requirements fully. A lot of *Kipps* may pass, some of *Tono-Bungay*, *Mr. Britling Sees It Through* and *Joan and Peter* and let me add, I have a weakness for Lady Harman and for Theodore Bulpington and—But I will not run on. These are pleas in extenuation. The main indictment is sound, that I sketch out scenes and individuals, often quite crudely, and resort even to conventional types and symbols, in order to get on to a discussion of relationships. [*Experiment in Autobiography*, 414]

The case here for *Kipps* is made on the basis of its characterisation. But in fact, the novel's long gestation indexes, not slapdashness but on the contrary, the length of time it took a conscious literary artist to hone and perfect a very tightly constructed work of literary art. Regardless of what Wells himself might say.

This tightness of construction depends upon the deployment of a network of thematic and symbolic patterns and textual structures that underlie what seems, on the surface, to be a peripatetic set of narrative episodes accumulated around the central character of Arthur Kipps. There are, I would say, five sets of these symbolic-representation nexuses, and I could write a chapter-length account about every one of them. I could, for instance, talk about the *theatrical* trope, in which scenes from the vulgar theatre, and Chitterlow's ridiculous play about a Beetle, are artfully juxtaposed with the concept of well-bred society as an endless quasi-dramatic performance, the script of which is too complex and baffling for Kipps to learn; or I could talk about the way the *bicycle* is used to trope class consciousness, mobility and power throughout; or about the way the novel uses carefully mapped-out *liminal* spaces, from basements and side-doors to the beach itself, from hotels to unbuilt houses, to develop its themes; or on a different level I could talk about the way Wells works with a cleverly understated quasi-Joycean set of *language games*, in which Kipps's non-RP pronunciation is mirrored in, for instance, the middle-class Anagram Tea to which, to Kipps's great terror, he is invited (Fig. 7.1).

This repeated mode of estranging words, of turning them from lucid tokens of communication into baffling blanks, finds its wonderful apotheosis in the novel's conclusion, in which Kipps, who doesn't read books, ends up a bookseller and the narrator of *Kipps* can boast that his novel about Kipps is for sale in Kipps's shop and Kipps doesn't even realise this because Kipps never reads.

In each of these four cases I would argue that Wells very carefully positions references and allusions not only to unify the text longitudinally, as it were (i.e., from the start of the novel to its end), but also to run them in parallel and connect them; such that each nexus of symbolic representation, in its way, combines collectively to adumbrate an overarching theme about, broadly, restraint, obstruction or artificiality on the one hand, and freedom, flow and motion on the other. And in each case, as with the larger texture of the whole novel, there is such a wealth of incidental detail, so many specific qualia invoked in order to create a sense of verisimilitude, of a thickness of

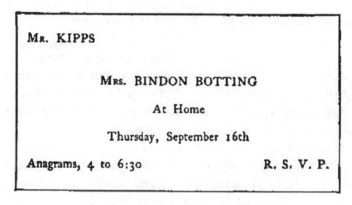

Mr. KIPPS

Mrs. BINDON BOTTING

At Home

Thursday, September 16th

Anagrams, 4 to 6:30   R. S. V. P.

Fig. 7.1 The card inviting Kipps to Mrs Bindon Botting's 'Anagram Tea'

representation in the matter of lived experience, it is striking to think how un-random all these details are. But instead of talking in greater detail about those four I want to spend a little time on a fifth unifying principle: *the cut*. Putting it simply, 'cutting' is the master trope by which the novel provides for its own architectonic wholeness, linking the other four previously mentioned and focussing the main force of what the novel is trying to say. Let me explain what I mean.

In a literal sense *cut* means to sever or slice something, cutting it in half or cutting it open. The word, of course, has other meanings that are relevant to the story of *Kipps*. Most obviously, to 'cut' someone, socially, is pointedly to refuse to engage with them, to snub them, to perform a sort of social exile upon them because they have, in some way, violated the codes of society. These two main meanings of 'cut' are joined by a third, which I'll come to in a little while. Together these three coordinate the symbolic narrative of the novel.

Kipps starts with one of its most iconic moments, as adolescent Kipps and his childhood sweetheart, Ann Pornick plight their mutual troth by cutting a sixpenny-piece in two such that each holds half as keepsake of the other (when David Heneker adapted *Kipps* as hit musical in 1963 he renamed it *Half a Sixpence*, so iconic had this scene become in the book's afterlife). Early in the novel, there are two significant episodes that both involve cuts. First Book 1 Chap. 3, at the Woodworking class where Kipps meets and falls in love with Miss Walsingham and where, clumsily opening a window, he cuts his wrist.

> He turned dolefully. "I'm tremendously sorry," he said in answer to the accusa-tion in Miss Walshingham's eyes. "I didn't think it would break like that,"—as if he had expected it to break in some quite different and entirely more satisfactory manner. ..."You've cut your wrist," said one of the girl friends, standing up and pointing. She was a pleasant-faced, greatly freckled girl, with a helpful disposi-tion, and she said "You've cut your wrist," as brightly as if she had been a trained nurse.
>
> Kipps looked down, and saw a swift line of scarlet rush down his hand. He perceived the other man student regarding this with magnified eyes. "You have cut your wrist," said Miss Walshingham, and Kipps regarded his damage with greater interest. [*Kipps*, 74–75]

This scene extends, drolly, for some time; characters later in the novel refer back to it. The next chapter introduces the actor-dramatist manqué Chitterlow, who, riding his bicycle, literally collides with Kipps, knocking him over and cutting open his trousers: "'Here's the back of my trouser leg all tore down,'" said Kipps, "and I believe I'm bleeding"' [91]. In the second half of the novel, these physical cuts are replaced by emotional ones. Having now acquired enough money to win Miss Walsingham (because of her financially straitened circumstances), Kipps struggles to fit into her higher-class circles: his accent is still too common and his fancy new clothes are indicative only of him trying too hard. Walsingham takes it on herself to 'educate' him on these matters. Kipps calls, wearing a fancy silk hat of which he is particularly proud and the experience is, for him, *cutting*.

> She took him in hand in perfect good faith. She told him things about his accent, she told him things about his bearing, about his costume and his way of looking at things. She thrust the blade of her intelligence into the tenderest corners of Kipps' secret vanity, she slashed his most intimate pride to bleeding tatters. [*Kipps*, 260–61]

Kipps, we might say, is cut to the quick. It's after this, and with a proleptic glimpse of the direction the story is going, that the narrator reverts to the society meaning of the word 'cut', with a finely judged gentle comic irony:

> Charitable as one may be, one must admit there are people who do things, impossible things; people who place themselves 'out of it' in countless ways; people, moreover, who are by a sort of predestination out of it from the beginning, and against these Society has invented a terrible protection for its Cootery, the Cut. The cut is no joke for anyone. It is excommunication. You may be cut by an individual, you may be cut by a set or you may be—and this is so tragic that beautiful romances have been written about it—'Cut by the County.' [*Kipps*, 280–81]

'It never dawned upon Kipps', the narrator adds, deadpan, 'that he would one day have to face this terrible front, to be to Coote not only as one dead but as one gone more than a stage or so in decay, cut and passed, banned and outcast for ever.' And as this inevitable catastrophe approaches, Kipps is cut again physically—'Kipps got up late, cut his chin while shaving, kicked a slipper into his sponge bath and said, "Desh!"' [300]). He realises he doesn't love Helen, does love Ann, and in a panic, he rushes off to London—he *cuts and runs*, we might say.

Then, after the scene in the London hotel where he is too shy to arrange for his own lunch quoted above, he comes to an understanding about his own desires. Instead of tying the knot with Helen he cuts it: jilts her and elopes with Ann. All this cutting reaches a kind of climax in Book 3, after Kipps has married Ann, and just before he discovers he has lost all his money. Kipps goes for a walk and chances upon Coote: his former chaperon into higher society now outraged at Kipps's desertion of Helen—a man whose very name is a variant on the word 'cut'.

> At the sight of him Coote started visibly. Then a sort of *rigor vitae* passed through his frame, his jaw protruded and errant bubbles of air seemed to escape and run about beneath his loose skin. His eyes fixed themselves on the horizon and glazed. As he went by Kipps could hear his even, resolute breathing. He went by, and Kipps staggered on into a universe of dead cats and dust heaps, rind and ashes—*cut*! Cut! [*Kipps*, 429]

This reiterated physical and metaphorical cutting is the novel's way of driving home Kipps's disconnection from the *corpus civile*. That Kipps is, in some existential, if comico-pathetic, way cut-off from his various dreams is the larger logic of the book. It's why working in a draper's is the 'right' way for Wells to start his character's journey. After all: what does a draper's shop do, except cut up cloth to sell?

With remarkable deftness this thematic of 'cutting' is sedulously connected by Wells to the other nexuses of semantic-symbolic unity in the novel—so: Kipps's first encounter with the bicycle is when Chitterlow collides with him, cutting his trouser and leg; so it is that the Anagram Tea consists of 'cutting up' and rearranging words (and the way Kipps himself is cut up by the experience of it); so the landscape is sliced through or cut up in ways that actualise the narrative. Even Chitterlow's theatrical ambitions connect to this: for when he has wealth Kipps invests money in Chitterlow's absurd play (not because he believes it will succeed but because he thinks he owes Chitterlow for alerting him to the fact of his inheritance). The twist is that the play becomes a huge hit, generating enormous amounts of money from which Kipps can then take his *cut*. This also speaks to Wells's decision to change the name of his protagonist from 'Waddy' to 'Kipps'. *Kip, kipp* or *kyppe* (plural *kips*) means 'the untanned hide of a young or small beast, such as a calf, lamb, or young goat', and also 'the leather made from such hide; kip leather'. That is to say, it means a fabric that has been literally cut from the body of a young beast. Kip, the young draper's assistant, is named for an artefact of cutting.

There's more to say here, because, of course, 'cut' has another meaning— an indecent one—a meaning also important to this novel: it is an old English word for 'vagina'. In *Twelfth Night* Malvolio picks up the forged-letter he believes to have been written by his mistress Olivia, and declares: 'by my life, this is my lady's hand: these be her very C's, her U's, and her T's, and thus she makes her great P'. It's not sophisticated humour, although that doesn't mean it isn't funny; and *cut* at least avoids the sheer aggressive unpleasant-ness of the word's modern derivative, cunt.

Kipps, as novel, is about a young man caught between the choice of two beautiful women, and it ends with him choosing one, marrying her and fathering a child. It is, in one unavoidable sense, a novel about sex. But Kipps himself is, as per the code of lower-middle-class respectability into which he was born, enormously inhibited about sexual matters. There is nothing of the bedroom whatsoever in Kipps's yearning after the beautiful Helen. They never kiss; they are rarely even alone together. She is in his eyes more angel than fleshly woman and the longer their engagement goes on, and the closer Kipps comes to his actual wedding night, the more alarmed he becomes at the pros-pect. When, as a prelude to jilting her, he runs off to London and stays in the Royal Grand he is prudishly outraged by the ladies' evening attire in the din-ing room: 'they were scorchers. Jest a bit of black velvet over the shoulders!… wicked-looking women'. Staring at the flesh on display 'he found a waiter regarding him and blushed deeply. He did not look again for some time and became confused about his knife and fork over the fish. His ears became vio-lently red.' This awkwardness, the specifically erotic component of Kipps's vast shyness, is a piece of reportage, reflecting the actual sexual mores of the 'respectable' lower middle classes of 1905. But it is more than that in the pat-tern of the novel. It connects with the mystery of Kipps's mother. We gather, without it ever being spelled out in so many words, that young Kipps was raised by his elderly uncle and aunt because his mother (whom he, and we, never meet) had him illegitimately. Conceivably, connecting to the novel's thematic nexuses, she was an actress, which is to say prostitute; somebody liv-ing in the liminal spaces of polite society. Perhaps the cut that haunts the cut-and-flayed Kipps throughout his life is the primal cut, the one that made him. According to Eric Partridge's *Dictionary of Slang* 'kip' was also slang for a brothel.

Sex, in this novel, is simultaneously surface-unspeakable and a palpable below-the-surface force (as it is in a great many nineteenth- and early-twentieth-century novels, of course). This aspect of the writing is magnified by the fact that Kipps is an unusually sexually immature and shy protagonist. The mere sight of naked shoulders makes his ears burn red. Only in the very last pages, as Kipps holds his new-born son in his trembling arms, does the narrator feel licensed to say: 'the once rabbit-like soul that had been so amazed by the discovery of "chubes" in the human interior and so shocked by the sight of a woman's shoulder-blades … was at last facing the greater realities' [*Kipps*, 464].

We can say of Wells what the critic Christopher Ricks says of Keats: 'Keats as a man and a poet was especially sensitive to and morally intelligent about, embarrassment', which state Ricks defines as 'constrained feeling or manner arising from bashfulness or timidity' [Ricks, 1, 3]. As with Keats, there is something peculiarly English about Wells's apprehension of shyness and embarrassment—Ricks wonders 'is embarrassment not only a nineteenth-century sentiment but a narrowly English one?'; and two of the larger points about Ricks's argument seem to me to apply particularly well to Wells's *Kipps*—that this is art that challenges the reader to experience embarrassment, and that the root of this shyness is less social than sexual. For Ricks it is a great strength of Keats that he is

> one of the very few erotic poets who have come at embarrassment from a different angle of necessity: from the wish to pass directly through—not to bypass (however principled and perceptive the bypassing)—the hotly disconcerting, the potentially ludicrous, distasteful, or blush-inducing. [Ricks, 68]

One of Ricks's key comparisons is the never-embarrassed suavity of Byron. There are plenty of blushes in *Don Juan*, Ricks notes, but 'they never work upon us, as Keats's do, by implicating us in the hot tinglings of sensation; they are always seen from outside. The limpidity and lucidity of Byron's style act as a cordon sanitaire against contagious embarrassment [Ricks, 83]. Mutatis mutandis, we could make a similar distinction between Wells and his friend Henry James. James finds an obliquity and a complexity in human sexual affairs, and in his novels such affairs very rarely run smooth; but we are never embarrassed *on behalf of* James's characters, I think. Like Byron, although in a different manner, the sheer suavity of his style acts as a *cordon sanitaire* against such blushing and cringing. Not so Wells: for him, the path to his novel's core lies right through those embarrassments. He makes the most of them, and he makes his readers feel them, and he does both things brilliantly. Sexual desire is complex, or it is often so; but embarrassment shares the epithet that characterises Kipps's soul in the subtitle Wells chose for his novel: it is simple.

So where are we? Kipps, whose name encodes having been cut. Kipps who is literally repeatedly cut in the novel, and whose whole social trajectory bends towards the metaphorical cut of higher-society exile. Kipps, whose love life stays true to the cut sixpence he shares with his childhood sweetheart. Kipps whose shyness and embarrassment, in this story of love, marriage, sex and childbirth, is haunted by the 'cut' of womanhood. *Kipps* the novel that took 8 years to write, including many reworkings and many passages cut from the

draft—most particularly the cutting out of an 11,000-word 'Masterman' episode from Part 3. Cut to—

Tolstoy. An unsigned article in the *Saturday Review* for 22 April 1905,
almost certainly written by Wells, begins: 'Twenty years ago Tolstoy was
hardly known outside Russia. We remember mentioning his existence to an
American novelist of first rank, a great admirer of Turgenev, who did not seem
inclined to believe that people would soon come to recognise the greater
power of Tolstoy. Who has not heard of Tolstoy now?' [see Philmus (1977)].
The American novelist of first rank must be Henry James, of course. Rosamund
Bartlett notes that:

> a year after this review was published, Wells would write Tolstoy a fan letter,
> telling him he had read everything by him he could find in English, about 18
> volumes, and that, in his opinion, of all the works he had had the fortune to
> read, *War and Peace* and *Anna Karenina* were the "most magnificent and all-
> encompassing". [Bartlett]

I can't prove Wells had Tolstoy on his mind writing *Kipps*, but it seems to
me overwhelmingly likely. What is Kipps, after all, except a lower-class
Pierre? (presumably, it is the very obviousness of this observation that has
kept critics from noticing it). Of course Kipps's inheritance is not wealth on
the same sort of scale as Pierre's, and, of course, Kipps doesn't live through
anything as traumatic as the Napoleonic invasion of Russia. But then again,
Tolstoy's interest in Pierre is less to do with the specific nature of those sorts
of externals and more with—precisely—the simplicity of his soul, which is
delineated via the complex there-and-back-again of his reaction to his personal change in fortunes. It's stating the obvious to note that that's also what
Kipps, as a novel, is about. The notion that there is anything Tolstoyan in
Wells's writing has, I suppose, gone out of fashion; but the fact that it used
to be *in* fashion—that there used to be a time when books like Marinita
Davis's *A Study of Tolstoi and H.G. Wells as Educators* (1929) could be published—suggests that there is at least something in the comparison. At any
rate, and despite the obvious differences in tone between Tolstoyan epic dignity and Wellsian social comedy, it's worth insisting that *Kipps* is, in one
sense, a Tolstoyan novel.

John Bayley talks about the 'dynamic absurdity' of Tolstoy's Pierre—distinguishing this from 'the merely passive absurdity' of the novel's non-Russian
characters, and it's a good way of describing Kipps too. Like Kipps, Pierre
works hard to fit himself into a system which can never be home for him, and
one of the saving graces of his simplicity is that, on some level, he always

knows this (think of the scene where Pierre is inducted into the Freemasons and how awkwardly that goes—at the ceremony 'a childlike smile of embarrassment, doubt and self-derision appeared on Pierre's face against his will'). But there's a larger Tolstoyan point which bears on Kipps as a novel. Bayley asks: 'what are the elements of antagonism, as Tolstoy sees it, between French and Russians?' And he answers:

> The Russians represent a *family*; the French, by contrast, represent a system—the terrible *it* which Pierre becomes aware of when the Frenchmen whom he thinks he has got to know during his captivity are suddenly revealed as automata, controlled by some impersonal force which is pressing him towards destruction, a force which overrides humanity. [Bayley, 136]

This is a powerful insight, I think, and one that opens the whole of *War and Peace* to us; but it shines a light into *Kipps* too. The higher society into which Kipps is thrust is repeatedly characterised by Wells, often hilariously, as a fractal web of abstruse and counter-intuitive rules and conventions. Kipps hopes to navigate it with the help of Mr Coote, and by poring over books with titles like '*Manners and Rules of Good Society, by a Member of the Aristocracy*'—'TWENTY-FIRST EDITION'—and 'that admirable classic, *The Art of Conversing*'. But naturally enough Kipps struggles with these cryptic mazes of systemised behaviour.

> Kipps returned with these to his seat, placed the two before him, opened the latter with a sigh and flattened it under his hand. Then with knitted brows he began to read onward from a mark, his lips moving. … Kipps rubbed his fingers through his hair with an expression of some perplexity and went back to the beginning. [*Kipps*, 209]

The novel's comedy styles its hero's erotic dilemma this way: as the choice between an arbitrary and artificial system of rules and conventions—Helen—and Ann, the quasi-familial closeness of the girl-next-door from Kipps's own social class. Kipps's closest ally, beyond his actual blood relative uncle and aunt, is Sid, the brother of the woman he marries. It is Sid who finds Kipps wandering hungry through the streets of London because he is too shy to dare the rebarbative systemised rituals of expensive restaurants, invites him home and feeds him mutton. The book rewards spontaneity (like Kipps giving Chitterlow £2000) and deprecates unspontaneous, regulated and systemised modes of living. We could say, in Tolstoyan mode, that Kipps is Russian, where the world of Helen, Coote and their ilk is French.

Bibliography

Bartlett, Rosamund (2014) 'Tolstoy Translated', *Financial Times* (8th August 2014). https://on.ft.com/2MjzvWl.

Bayley, John (1966). *Tolstoy and the Novel*. London, Chatto.

Bradbury, Malcolm (1993). *The Modern British Novel*. London: Secker and Warburg.

Philmus, Robert M. (1977). 'H.G. Wells as Literary Critic for the *Saturday Review*', *Science Fiction Studies* 4:2, pp. 166–193.

Ricks, Christopher (1984). *Keats and Embarrassment*. Oxford, Clarendon Press.

Smith, David (1986). *H G Wells: Desperately Mortal. A Biography*. New Haven/London: Yale Univ. Press.

Wilson, Harris (1971). 'The Death of Masterman: A Repressed Episode in H. G. Wells's *Kipps*'. *PMLA* 86:1, pp. 63–69.

8

Sex

The Sea Lady (1902); *The Food of the Gods* (1904)

The Sea Lady was first published in *Pearson's Magazine* (July–December 1901) and in book form the following year. A mermaid comes ashore at Sandgate on the Kent coast and is adopted by a wealthy English family, the Buntings, who have a holiday home there. They cover up her fish-tail with a blanket, put her in a bath chair, recruit a maid to attend to her and name her (since originally she has no name) 'Doris Thalassia Waters'. This Sea Lady, charming, polite and well-spoken, becomes a local star. The novel open with pleasant if lightweight comedy-of-manners stuff, as if Wells is reworking 1895's *The Wonderful Visit*, providing another ingenuous outsider's perspective on the absurdities of human life. Read on a little further, though, and we begin to realise that's not what the novel is doing at all. The Sea Lady already knows all the important things about human life and has neither need nor inclination to explore our world. She has different motive for coming onto the land.

In fact, *The Sea Lady* is a Silver Fork retelling of *Undine* (1811), the fairy tale novella by the German Romantic Friedrich de la Motte, Baron Fouqué. Wells is perfectly up-front about this: '"You know it's most extraordinary and exactly like the German story," said Mrs. Bunting. "Oom—what is it?" "Undine?" "Exactly—yes"' [*Sea Lady*, 2:3]. In Freiherr Fouqué's tale, Undine craves a soul, something a mermaid can obtain only by loving and being loved by a mortal man. She falls in love with a brave and noble knight called Sir Huldbrand. When they marry, Undine relinquishes her native immortality and gains her soul; but at the same time, she warns Huldbrand that should he ever reject her or send her away, her possessive and capricious water-spirit uncle Kühleborn will reclaim her and she would be lost to him forever. For a

© The Author(s) 2019
A. Roberts, *H G Wells*, Literary Lives, https://doi.org/10.1007/978-3-030-26421-5_8

while, the two live happily in Huldbrand's castle keeping the jealous water spirits away by blocking up the castle's fountain. But the Lady Bertalda, who had hoped to marry Huldbrand before he fell in love with Undine, suggests that they all take a boat trip together down the Danube to see Vienna. On this jaunt, Huldbrand flirts with Bertalda and so loses his wife to Kühleborn. Huldbrand returns to his castle broken-hearted, but in time he recovers sufficiently to marry Bertalda. But Undine is not dead, and this wedding is a bad idea. On her wedding night Bertalda, discovering a freckle on her perfectly fair neck, orders the fountain uncovered so she can wash it away, and through this aperture, Undine is able to enter the castle. 'Silently Undine threw back her veil and Huldbrand saw her, fair as on the day he had won her for his bride. As he looked upon her, he knew that he had never loved anyone in all the wide world as he loved Undine.' She kisses him, he dies, and she glides away. At his tomb, a spring starts up.

Wells's retelling replaces the sentimentality of Fouqué's 1811 original with a much sprightlier tone, comic and sharply-observed, although the mood shifts markedly towards the end of the novel into something more opaque and haunted. The Huldbrand figure is Harry Chatteris, a handsome young man, friend of the Buntings and Liberal parliamentary candidate in the upcoming elections, and betrothed to the eminently respectable Adeline Glendower—Wells's Bertalda—beautiful, well-bred and with a strong sense of her political duty. Wells's Sea Lady is a more worldly-wise Undine than Fouqué's; she has been, we might say, stalking Chatteris for some time. This love triangle is the meat of the story. Chatteris is helpless before the immortal seductive powers of the Sea Lady. He breaks the engagement off with Adeline. Mrs Bunting, belatedly realising that the Sea Lady is not so innocent as she pretends, throws her out ('I've been very much deceived in you, Miss Waters—very much indeed'). The mermaid, independently wealthy on account of a casket filled with gold, jewels and treasure she has brought with her from the sea, is in no way incommoded by this and takes a suite for herself and her maid in a nearby hotel. Summoned down from London by Mrs Bunting to try and patch things up, Melville has a long talk with the jilted Adeline. She wants to know what this Sea Lady has that *she* hasn't, and he doesn't spare her feelings: 'you are austere. You are restrained. Life—for a man like Chatteris—is schooling… You are too much—the agent general of his duty.' When she presses him, Melville deploys a metaphor with an interesting authorial-biographical resonance, considering that Wells had very recently built himself a lovely new house and installed his wife in it whilst reserving to himself the option of going off to have sex with other women.

"It is like having built a house in which he is to live. For him, to go to her is like going out of a house, a very fine and dignified house, I admit, into something larger, something adventurous and incalculable.... You—you have the quality—"

He hesitated.

"Go on," she insisted. "Let us get the meaning."

"Of an edifice." [*Sea Lady*, 235–36]

This is, perhaps, a little too obviously nudging us to take the story as allegorising, in the figures of the two women, the security of marriage and the excitement of extramarital sex respectively—from, of course, the point-of-view of the man. The novel does at least prevent its (male) readers from having their erotic-fantasy cake and eating it too. At the story's end Chatteris first resolves to give up the Sea Lady, then abruptly breaks his own resolution, goes to the Sea Lady's hotel at midnight and runs off with her, physically carrying her through the lobby and out the front door. 'And when she see my face,' the night porter later recalls, 'she threw her head back laughing at me. As much as to say, *got 'im!*' They find the Sea Lady's expensive shawl on the beach. Evidently, he carried her into the waters and sank beneath the waves to her world and his death. In sum: Chatteris chooses exotic sexual fantasy over respectable marriage and it kills him.

The incongruity between these later, rather earnest conversations and the earlier chapters' more jovial tone of polite comic incongruity may explain why people have tended not to praise *The Sea Lady*. It wasn't a contemporary success, commercially speaking (although neither was it exactly a flop: there were new UK editions in 1907 and 1910, and a second edition in America 1908) and it isn't much liked by Wellsians today: 'a poor piece of work' according to Norman and Jeanne Mackenzie. Wells's son Anthony West calls it 'his least Wellsian book'. Paul Kincaid says: 'the novel was not a success and it is easy to see why. Despite the mermaid, it is not really a full-blooded work of the fantastic, and as a social novel it is thin compared to the other mainstream novels Wells was writing at this time' [Kincaid, 88]. 'My father', Anthony West suggests, 'wrote the book to get something off his chest that he had not been able to admit to himself, or discuss with Jane.' He means that Wells wrote it during the period when he and his wife were negotiating, in person and by letter, the terms on which Wells was to be permitted, or licensed, to pursue sexual relations with other women. West calls this 'their private treaty', and he thinks *The Sea Lady* records his buried sense that such freedom 'might have hidden costs' [West, 259]. That seems a likely, if rather over-obvious, thing to say. But the peculiar distinctiveness of *The Sea Lady* proceeds on the way it resists simple decoding (this is also part of its unlikableness). It is a fable that has to do with sex, certainly, but in a frustratingly oblique way.

The germ of the tale was an encounter with a teenager called May Nisbet, the illegitimate daughter of Wells's journalist-friend E.F. Nisbet. When Nisbet died unexpectedly Wells (always financially generous to his friends) paid May's school fees, told her to call him 'Uncle Bertie' and invited her to his Sandgate house for holidays. In Wells recalls her as 'a gawky and rather sullen girl' of 'fifteen or sixteen' who did not attract him, until

> … one day upon the beach at Sandgate she came down towards me wearing a close-fitting bathing dress; instantly she seemed the quintessence of sunlit youth to me, and I was overwhelmed with a rush of physical desire. [*H. G. Wells in Love*, 61]

He adds 'I never gratified that physical desire', although he seems to have at least tried it on ('I made love to May Nisbet but quite vaguely and inconclusively' is how he puts it; *made love*, of course, in the old Victorian-Edwardian sense, somewhere between 'courting' and 'propositioning': 'hitting on' may be the nearest contemporary equivalent). The implication is that the force of this thwarted desire lies behind his portrait of the disruptive energies of the Sea Lady herself. A good way of reading the novel is to trace its tonal recalibration in terms of these two modes of apprehending sexual desire. Sex can be simple fun, a straightforward pleasure. Sex can be an unreciprocated or impossible yearning. It might even suddenly transition from one to the other, from comedy to transcendental mooning-about. That's surely what we have in the shape of this novel.

We might say that this novel takes its part in that rich tradition of English sex-comedy from *Twelfth Night* to the *Carry On* movies; the comic tradition that believes it absolutely hilarious that everybody thinks about sex all the time but nobody is allowed actually to talk about it. That same tradition that believes all communication is *double entrendres* and all physical action slapstick because all innocent communication and ordinary behaviour is continually bothered and troubled by bawdy communication and lewd behaviour. Wells's big joke is the old one about mermaids. I mean, isn't it funny? That these iconic representatives of female sexual allure have fish-tails instead of spreadable legs and fish-scales instead of penetrable genitalia? What would a red-blooded male even do with such a being? *Is* that funny? I have to say I'm not sure. It's built, of course, upon an older misogynistic libel that women's vaginas exude an unpleasant fishy odour. Generations of schoolboys have read the footnote explaining Hamlet's joke about Polonius being a 'fishmonger' and sniggered at the reference to prostitution.

Perhaps the big joke of *The Sea Lady* is not that everybody thinks about sex but nobody is allowed to talk openly about it, but the rather different notion that everybody thinks about sex all the time, but nobody is actually allowed to *have* it. All we can ever do is access symbols for sex, stand-ins for sex, with the twist that *actual* sex (as, for example, between handsome Chatteris and beautiful Adeline) becomes itself only a sort of stand-in for sex, a mere symbol, a sex that doesn't satisfy the yearning that wanting-to-have-sex represents. *The Sea Lady* is about that search for the other kind of sex, the sex that isn't actual in-the-world sex. A Lacanian would say that the discomforting revelation around which this novel is structured, and which has unendeared it to so many, is the truth that the *objet petit a* simply doesn't correspond to the *grand a*, which is The Real, and which it supposedly gestures towards representing. We repeatedly apprehend the former and in doing so repeatedly fail to apprehend the latter. Chatteris frets, in his conversation with Melville, over why exactly he is so ready to throw over Adeline and go after the Sea Lady. The latter is beautiful, yes, but then so is the former!

> Why should her smile be so sweet to me, why should her voice move me! Why her's and not Adeline's? Adeline has straight eyes and clear eyes and fine eyes, and all the difference there can be, what is it? An infinitesimal curving of the lid, an infinitesimal difference in the lashes—and it shatters everything—in this way. Who could measure the difference, who could tell the quality that makes me swim in the sound of her voice. [*Sea Lady*, 273]

This is an acute insight into desire as such (after all, why *do* we fall so completely for this one person, when this other person, and so many other people beside them, differ in appearance and personality only by infinitesimals?). It's also another of the book's big jokes. Because all this angels-on-a-pinhead worrying away at infinitesimal curvings of eyelids, and infinitesimal differences in eyelashes, very obviously, dances around the most patent difference between the two women, Adeline and the Sea Lady: that one has a vagina and the other doesn't. One might think that has some bearing on which of the two possessed more sexual allure. Except that *The Sea Lady* in effect advances the counter-intuitive thesis that men find women *without* vaginas more attractive than women with.

That's also part of the British 'Carry-On' tradition of double entendre humour, of course. When Bernard Bresslaw puts on a dress, other men suddenly find him immensely alluring, begin chucking him under his chin and propositioning him and so on. We can take this as funny one way, in that these men are clearly stupid or rather than their lust has made them blind to the reality of things: *ha ha, look what idiots these men are! Can they not see this is not an attractive woman but on the contrary a big ugly man in a dress? Ha ha they must be idiots not to notice such an obvious thing!* But we can take it as funny in a rather different way, too: the joke might be, *look at these Englishmen pretend to desire women but in fact are all homosexuals, and need only the flimsiest and most patent of excuses to reveal their true nature.* This is the big joke behind the Billy Wilder movie *Some Like It Hot* (1959), and especially its lovely final line ('Well, nobody's perfect!'). Indeed, the way that line works, capping-off that whole marvellous final scene in the speedboat, is to reveal that the joke's been on Jack Lemmon's character all along. It is Joe E. Brown's Osgood Fielding III in effect saying: 'has it really taken you this long to understand that I'm gay? Do I really have to spell it out for you so blatantly?' In some ways, *The Sea Lady* is very *Some Like It Hot*-esque. As if to say: 'which of these women would you rather have sex with, Marilyn Monroe or Jack Lemmon? I should warn you that one of them doesn't have a vagina.' Of course, there are differences. *Some Like It Hot* commits to its idea that the stuff it's about is funny stuff throughout. *A Sea Lady* loses its lightness somewhere around the two-thirds mark and grows more portentous the closer it gets to its end. Jack Lemmon heads out to sea on a rousing punchline; Harry Chatteris heads out to sea to drown, and the final paragraphs of the novel manage the same sort of doleful music and use the same sort of imagery as (and conceivably even were an actual inspiration for) the famous final paragraph of Fitzgerald's *The Great Gatsby* (1925):

> Ever and again the darkness east and west of that glory would be lit by a momentary gleam of phosphorescence; and far out the lights of ships were shining bright and yellow. Across its shimmer a black fishing smack was gliding out of mystery into mystery. Dungeness shone from the west a pin-point of red light, and in the east the tireless glare of that great beacon on Gris-nez wheeled athwart the sky and vanished and came again.
>
>   I picture the interrogation of his lantern going out for a little way, a stain of faint pink curiosity upon the mysterious vast serenity of night. [*Sea Lady*, 8:3]

This isn't funny, obviously. It's poignant, with a kind of low-key plangency that aims for a sort of numinousness. It is saying that the incongruity and opacity of sexual desire is a haunting rather than a comical thing. It's also forcing the shape of the novel, formally speaking, into something like the opposite of a joke. A joke tells an ordinary story that, at its end, jolts unexpectedly into a hilarious punch line. This novel spends most of its time being funny, only to jolt at the end into something unfunny.

The Sea Lady herself is quite straightforwardly a *femme fatale*, a seductress whose capricious irruption into the settled circle of the Buntings results in danger, scandal and death. Chatteris proves perfectly helpless in the face of her overwhelming erotic power. Think again about the incident which Wells says prompted the novel: teenage May Nisbet coming out of the sea in her tight-fitting bathing costume. Quite apart from the seediness of this—a 35-year-old father-of-two lusting so brazenly over a 15-year-old girl—there is the question of its psychological mendacity. What I mean by that is the way Wells's autobiographical account deliberately inverts the power dynamic of the encounter when he writes it up. In *The Sea Lady*, the woman is the one who has all the power. I suppose we could say that in order to convey how potent was the effect this 'overwhelming rush of physical desire' was for Wells, he styles the encounter as one where the man is helpless before the overwhelming power of the woman. But we are entitled to doubt that it felt that way to young May Nisbet, still a child, financially dependent on Wells, trying to enjoy a summer holiday in the aftermath of her father's death, having this older man panting all over her.

This fiction by which men in effect blame women for the fact that they (the men) find the women sexually attractive is an ancient one, toxic and still prevalent today. Jacqueline Rose notes that when a sexually alluring female is introduced into a story 'the woman is by definition troubled because the category of female sexuality has already been constituted as disturbance at this level of narrative form'. This, in turn, reflects back upon the (straight male) experience of being shaken by an unexpectedly powerful desire, of the kind Wells was registering with his vision of young May Nisbet. As Rose puts it:

As if desire lights upon its object, finds itself disarmed and then punishes the woman for the upset produced. Only a woman whose charm leaves the onlooker's own identity intact can escape the weight of a condemnation which has been decided almost before the question has been put. [Rose, 116]

The monstrosity of the Sea Lady is physically manifested in her fishy tail, which has to be covered up but on another level, it is, as-it-were existentially, something much more predatory and morbid. And a touch of that 'I blame you for the effect you have on me' pathology, seeping into the structure of this novel, sours much of the humour. If Wells wasn't sure what he was writing, it may have been because what he was writing wasn't actually something he wanted to acknowledge.

Though she comes literally from the depths, the Sea Lady's actual existence is depthless, which is to say, timeless: 'there are no nights and days, you know,' she says. 'No time nor anything of that sort.' This observation puzzles simple-minded Mrs Bunting: 'but how do you tell when it's Sunday?' The merfolk don't, of course, since they don't worship God, and this leads to an embarrassed hiatus in the conversation which Adeline, in an attempt to change the subject, only makes worse:

> Miss Glendower, perceiving that she had been a trifle urgent, tried to cover her error by expressing a general impression.
> "I can't see it," she said, with a gesture that asked for sympathy. "One wants to see it, one wants to be it. One needs to be born a mer-child."
> "A mer-child?" asked the Sea Lady.
> "Yes—Don't you call your little ones—?"
> "What little ones?" asked the Sea Lady. She regarded them for a moment with a frank wonder, the undying wonder of the Immortals at that perpetual decay and death and replacement which is the gist of human life. [*Sea Lady*, 2:5]

There are no children in the timeless undersea, and no sex, since sex is the means by which mortality engages time to overcome itself. The flat opacity of the Sea Lady's impregnable sexual allure is thrown all the more starkly into relief by this fact. But perhaps, we're missing the obvious. Return to Fouqué's original *Undine*: what that mermaid in that story was looking for wasn't sex or even love, but a soul. Wells's Sea Lady has come looking for the same thing. However handsome he is, Chatteris is not her object so much as her means to that end. We're all missing something obvious, and maybe it's not sex, but soul; not 15-year-old girls coming out of the sea in close-fitting bathing suit so much as the oceanic feeling itself.

If sex is something queerly elusive in *The Sea Lady* it becomes, by the end of *The Food of the Gods and How it Came to Earth* (1904) something gigantic and unmissable. Bensington and Redwood, Wells's existentially myopic scientists, creates 'Herakleophorbia' or 'Boomfood', a dietary stimulant that provokes giganticism in the creatures that eat it. The substance escapes into the environment, and the south-east of England is plagued by wasps big as hawks, rats big as cows and other beasts, including eventually giant human beings. Wells's account of these events lacks some of the narrative drive and much of the plangent, tragically-tinged seriousness of *War of the Worlds* or *The Time Machine*. But the novel does contain a superb central conceit, some gripping set-pieces, and it has the memorable and eloquent imagination-haunting quality of the best S.F. Wells's giants are beauties.

Of course, Wells was not the first writer to cover this topic. Giants have been part of fairy tales for millennia and play important roles in Swift's *Gulliver's Travels* (1726) and Lewis Carroll's *Alice in Wonderland* (1865)—two great fantasy novels with which *Food of the Gods* is in obvious dialogue. But

Wells is doing something new. Swift's aim was, broadly, satirical; and his Brobdingnagian giants and Lilliputian miniatures are in part about dramatising a sense of proportion, man's proper place in the cosmos. Alice eats a prototype 'boom food' (her magical mushroom) and grows prodigiously, thereby giving Carroll a metaphor for childhood—that time of life when we literally experience abrupt shootings-up in height. But Wells is doing something else with his central metaphor, besides (that is) using it as a platform for both exciting action and social comedy.

To put it more precisely: by following-through on its concept Wells's short novel does something neither Swift nor Carroll manage. Swift's giants simply are a fixed part of his imagined global landscape. Carroll's Alice experiences childhood's shifts in scale, but she herself doesn't grow up. But growing up is precisely the theme of *The Food of the Gods*, not just in the individual sense, but in the larger, social sense. Wells is anticipating a coming *maturity* of humanity. The young giants at the novel's end are one version of his 'coming race', a frequent feature of his speculative writing: the Samurai or Overmen whom, he hoped, would move mankind as a species out of its bickering infant-stage into the broad sunlit uplands of his imagined utopian future. To put it another way: if the *Alice* books are about the childhood of one girl, then Wells's novel is about the childhood of society as a whole.

This is why the book is structured the way it is, and why so much of it is given over to a slightly bantering comedy-of-class-manners that has, I suppose, not aged particularly well. I don't mean to be too harsh. Some of the comedy still works: the sections about baby Redwood breaking his playroom, having to be wheeled around in a reinforced invalid chair rather than a pram, and booming 'Dadda' and 'Babba' at bus drivers and policemen 'in a sociable democratic way' is still liable to make a reader laugh. But for much of the book, Wells's Dickensian pastiche is only occasionally droll and is more often than not downright clunking. Here, for example, certain rude mechanicals hired to construct a giant chicken coop, express their low opinion of the scientists.

> "I haven't theen much of 'im yet," said Mr. Skinner. "But as far as I can make 'im out 'e theems to be a thtewpid o' fool."
>
> "I thought 'e seemed a bit Dotty," said the carpenter from Hickleybrow.
>
> "'E fanthieth 'imself about poultry," said Mr. Skinner. "O my goodneth! You'd think nobody knew nothin' about poultry thept 'im."
>
> "'E looks like a 'en," said the carpenter from Hickleybrow; "what with them spectacles of 'is." [*Food of the Gods*, 2.1]

This has its place in the whole, though, because *Food of the Gods* is about a world's transition from small to big, from triviality to greatness. The first portion accordingly not only fills us in on Wells's pseudo-scientific 'food', it also paints a portrait of society as bumbling and childish. The littleness of this vision of England parlays naturally into comedy. Even the more able of Wells's adults engage in childish knockabout—clambering down holes, falling into ponds; and his scientists are as messy with their 'boom food' as any toddler. To begin with, there don't seem to be any properly constituted authorities at all, nobody to take charge of the increasingly alarming situation. Even when 'government' gets involved, later on, it takes the form of the pettiness of Caterham, a kind of pigmy demagogue. By contrast, Wells draws the young human giants with a great deal of dignity, and by the end, they achieve a tonal grandeur compatible with their physical dimensions. Their stature is greater than ours in more than simply physical terms.

The crucial thing about these giants is that they are the future. Here's Redwood, at the end, watching his giant son and their giant comrades preparing for war: 'the two giants who were working in the corner began a rhythmic hammering that made a mighty music to the scene ... about him were the young giants, huge and beautiful, glittering in their mail'. By this stage, this Wagnerian tone has entirely replaced the drollery of the earlier sections:

> The voice of the giant children spoke to one another, an undertone to that clangorous melody of the smiths. His tide of doubt ebbed. He heard the giant voices, he heard their movements about him still. It was real, more surely it was real—as real as spiteful acts! More real, for these great things, it may be, are the coming things, and the littleness, bestiality, and infirmity of men are the things that go. [*Food of the Gods*, 5:3]

That fence-sitting 'it may be' aside, this encapsulates the moral of the book. It is why Wells chooses to tell this story via giants. It is not just that their great size correlates to the 'greatness' he anticipates as replacing humanity's pettiness and infirmity—although, obviously, it does. But it is something more. Wells's giants are *unmissable*. They are the very obviousness of the positions that seemed to Wells himself perfectly clear and inevitable, despite the fact that most of his contemporaries couldn't see them—the passing away of the belittling old world and the coming of new greatness. This is why his giants, unschooled outsiders though they are, light naturally upon progressive ideological positions identical with Wells's own—young giant Caddles asking with seeming ingenuity, why the idle rich have all the money and the poor have to do all the work, for instance; or young Redwood and the giant princess together repudiating (as Wells himself did, in his private life) the restrictions of Edwardian conventional sexual morality. His giants are the enormous truth of things that little people contrive, somehow, to overlook; they are, to employ a cliché, the elephant in the room. They, like the novel in which they appear, are not to be missed.

Bibliography

Kincaid, Paul (2013). '(Mis)representing Wells', *Journal of the Fantastic in the Arts* 24:1 (87), pp. 83–96.

Mackenzie, Norman and Jeanne Mackenzie (1973) *The Time Traveller: the Life of H G Wells*. London: Weidenfeld and Nicholson.

Rose, Jacqueline (1986). *Sexuality in the Field of Vision*. London, Verso.

Smith, David ed. (1998).*Correspondence of H G Wells: Volume 1, 1880–1903*, London: Pickering and Chatto.

West, Anthony (1984). *H G Wells: Aspects of a Life*. London: Hutchinson.

9

Socialism and America

The Future in America (1906); *This Misery of Boots* (1907); *Will Socialism Destroy the Home?* (1907); *New Worlds for Old* (1908); *The War in the Air* (1908)

Wells joined the Fabian Society in March 1903 and left it in September 1908. His time as a member makes for a complicated and not terribly edifying story, but there's no avoiding it; the Fabians were the focus of his political thought through the first decade of the 1900s and were the proximate cause for a good deal of his writing at this time.

The Fabian Society was founded in London, 1884, with the aim of promoting socialism via reform and democracy rather than revolution. It still exists today, and its own website boasts of the role it played in some of the major developments in twentieth-century British social and political history:

Against the backdrop of the Match Girls' strike and the 1889 London Dock strike, the landmark *Fabian Essays* was published, containing essays by George Bernard Shaw, Graham Wallas, Sidney Webb, Sydney Olivier and Annie Besant. All the contributors were united by their rejection of violent upheaval as a method of change, preferring to use the power of local government and trade unionism to effect change.

The early Fabians' commitment to non-violent political change was underlined by the role many Fabians played in the foundation of the Labour Party in 1900. None of the early Fabian Society were more significant than Beatrice and Sidney Webb in developing the ideas that would come to characterise Fabian thinking and in developing the thorough research methodology that remains a feature of the Society to the present day. Both prodigious authors, Beatrice and Sidney wrote extensively on a wide range of topics, but it was Beatrice's 1909 Minority Report to the Commission of the Poor Law that was perhaps their most remembered contribution. This landmark report provided the foundation stone for much of the modern welfare state. [http://fabians.org.uk/]

© The Author(s) 2019
A. Roberts, *H G Wells*, Literary Lives, https://doi.org/10.1007/978-3-030-26421-5_9

The Fabians certainly had a place in the developing British socialist movement although Andrew Thorpe's standard *History of the British Labour Party* insists 'the Fabians were not as influential as they like to claim' [Thorpe 13]. Labour historians tend to prioritise the role played by Trades Unionists and the members of the Labour Representation Committee—actual workers like Keir Hardie and Arthur Henderson. The Fabian Society, on the other hand, was in essence, a middle-class organisation. Its most prominent members were affluent bourgeois individuals like the Webbs, Pease, Bland and Nesbit. As Ian Britain notes: 'all membership records and contemporary observations testify to the almost exclusively middle-class origins of the Fabian Society's adherents, from the time of its earliest foundation in 1884 onwards' [Britain, 6]. The question for the moment is how Wells fitted into this world. He was, clearly, not middle class like the Webbs; but neither was he properly working class. We would probably situate him somewhere in between these two strata. Of course, by the 1900s he was a self-made man and very wealthy; but that's not to say he exactly fitted-in with the affluent middle- and upper-middle-class majority of the Fabians. It's not coincidental, I think, that Wells's closest friend in the Fabian Society was George Bernard Shaw, who, by virtue of being Irish, stood rather outside the bindweed complexities of English class identity.

The two things that the Fabians hoped Wells would bring to the Society were a new energy—one of Wells's great talents was his 'go', what he sometimes described as 'whoosh'—and his popular reach, his widely read journalism and fiction, to get the message out. And Wells was initially keen, although what he wanted was a large-scale reform of the organisation. He proposed doing away with the governing committee, establishing a triumvirate of elected leaders, expanding the Society's membership, new and larger headquarters in London, a dedicated newspaper and other things. The Fabians wanted his energy, and they got it: he read papers before the Society, published a pamphlet called *The Faults of the Fabians* in 1906 and followed it up in quick order with another pamphlet containing proposals for reform (*Reconstruction of the Fabian Society*, 1906). He lobbied, travelled the country and moved motions. Looking back in the *Experiment in Autobiography* he describes what he encountered as 'the little Fabian Society, wizened already though not old', and summarises his approach: 'I envisaged that reconditioned Fabian Society as becoming, by means of vigorous propaganda, mainly carried on by young people, the directive element of a reorganized socialist party.' He adds, with characteristic half-self-deprecation:

> The idea was as good as the attempt to realize it was futile. On various occasions in my life it has been borne in on me, in spite of a stout internal defence, that I

can be quite remarkably silly and inept; but no part of my career rankles so acutely in my memory with the conviction of bad judgement, gusty impulse and real inexcusable vanity, as that storm in the Fabian tea-cup. From the first my motives were misunderstood, and it should have been my business to make them understandable. I antagonized Shaw and Beatrice Webb for example, by my ill-aimed aggressiveness… I was fundamentally right and I was wrong-headed and I left the Society, at last, if possible more politically parliamentary and ineffective than I found it. [*Experiment in Autobiography*, 564–65]

The episode is epitomised by the saga of Wells's short book, *This Misery of Boots*. Wells first published this piece, under the title 'The Misery of Boots', in the *Independent Review*, December 1905 and delivered it as a talk to Society on 12 January 1906. It is nicely judged piece of introductory Socialism from, in a literal as well as a metaphorical sense, the ground up—Wells remembers his childhood, looking up from his basement through the grating, to where he could see only the feet of passers-by; and goes on through the various cellars, garrets and apprentice rooms in which he has lodged, dim, closed in, filled with shadows, away from the sun. He points out that boots figure much more largely in the lives of those who can ill afford them than in the lives of the affluent, and for that reason the affluent don't understand how hugely important they are, how profoundly immiserating it is to have to wear ill-fitting or broken-down boots that pinch the toes or expose the heel. Wells neatly captures how these petty miseries restrict and degrade life, and how they aggregate into something monstrous. From this he extrapolates:

Here on the one hand—you can see for yourself in any unfashionable part of Great Britain—are people badly, uncomfortably, painfully shod, in old boots, rotten boots, sham boots; and on the other great stretches of land in the world, with unlimited possibilities of cattle and leather and great numbers of people, who, either through wealth or trade disorder, are doing no work. And our question is: "Why cannot the latter set to work and make and distribute boots?" [*Boots*, 4]

His point is that the problem of boots cannot be solved piecemeal; everything that goes into their making and distribution must be altered, and that means that all the processes of manufacture and distribution must be altered as well. The book's last chapter contains an oblique snipe at the Fabians:

Let us be clear about one thing: that Socialism means revolution, that it means a change in the every-day texture of life. It may be a very gradual change, but it will be a very complete one. You cannot change the world, and at the same time not change the world. You will find Socialists about, or at any rate men calling themselves Socialists, who will pretend that this is not so, who will assure you that some odd little jobbing about municipal gas and water is Socialism, and back-stairs intervention between Conservative and Liberal the way to the millennium. You might as well call a gas jet in the lobby of a meeting-house, the glory of God in Heaven! [*Boots*, 5]

Despite this, the piece went down well, especially with younger Fabians. The proposal was made to publish it as a separate book, but this stalled. Wells, in a hurry to get things moving before he left for America in March 1906, followed up 'The Misery of Boots' by presenting a manifesto for change to a meeting of the Society in February: the Society had 700 members and ought to have 7000 'and everything to scale'. Fabianism 'strikes the observer as being still half a drawing-room society … playing at polito-sociological research'. Their engagement with the world amounted to 'a little dribble of activities'. Wells called for more money, new offices, the opening of the Society freely to new members (up to this point prospective members had to be vetted by the executive) and undertaking large-scale outreach and propaganda work. The executive agreed to set up a committee to look into Wells's proposals, but there were grumblings, and Wells's manner did nothing to smooth them over. Shaw wrote to him on 17 February saying 'we cannot afford to quarrel with you because we want to get tracts out of you' but warning him that 'when we treat your onslaught as onslaught and hold the fort against you, don't suppose we are in a huff'.

Publicly and behind the scenes, debate clattered on through 1906. Webb told Shaw that he thought the 'Boots' piece more or less disposable, and Shaw wrote back: 'do not underrate Wells … you do not appreciate the effect his writing produces on the imagination of the movement.' Shaw knew very well how popular Wells was with younger Fabians. Not that he was any happier with Wells's proposals than was Sidney Webb; and other key Fabians, especially Hubert Bland, had taken very strongly against Wells. According to Anthony West, 'my father found Bland third-rate and incredible and did his best to ignore him' whilst 'Bland's distaste for my father became a positive enmity' [West, 294]. West thinks the hidden key to all the Fabian furore was sexual; that Wells was too popular with the Fabian wives and daughters.

At any rate, the Society held off from publishing the pamphlet, now retitled *This Misery of Boots*. Edward Pease insisted that what he called 'sneers' against Shaw and the Webbs be removed, and Shaw himself wrote to Wells on the 11 September 1906 advising him that 'as a matter of intellectual loyalty' he had better cut the offending passages. Sidney Webb himself wrote to Wells commending his 'very interesting and well put' critique of the Fabians, but saying he did not 'believe the Society will accept your proposals'. Matters came to a head at the end of the year at the society's December meeting. After various speeches, Shaw worked his magic on the assembly, turning accepting or rejecting Wells's ideas into a vote of confidence on the Fabian leadership itself:

> With the audience won as only Shaw knew how to win it, he was able to close the trap. "There is nothing for it now but annihilation of the present executive or unconditional surrender by Mr Wells," he said. Most of his colleagues wanted to press the matter to a vote, but that would have put such members of the special committee [that had investigated Wells's proposals] as Sydney Oliver and Maud Reeves in an ignominious position. H.G. ... had no option but to rise and—with the best grace he could muster—withdraw his amendment. [Mackenzies, 218]

It was a humiliating defeat for Wells. A few days later Shaw tried to conciliate his friend by suggesting he might be able to take a position on the Fabian executive in the Spring, but Wells, say the Mackenzies, 'was never able to adjust himself to the tempo of Fabian affairs' [221]. The whole affair wound slowly down. 'The order of the Fabian Samurai perished unborn,' is how Wells puts it, in the *Experiment in Autobiography*. 'I went, discoursing to undergraduate branches and local branches, to Oxford, Cambridge, Glasgow, Manchester and elsewhere pursuing the lengthening threads of our disputes. The society would neither give itself to me to do what I wished with it, nor cast me out. It liked the entertainment of its lively evenings. And at last I suddenly became aware of the disproportionate waste of my energy in these disputes and abandoned my attack.' He resigned from the Fabians in 1908 and worked his experiences and the workings of politics they revealed to him, into his novel *The New Machiavelli* (1911).

Still: as petty as this drama reads today, it would be a mistake to dismiss it as nothing more than a dusty triviality. That Wells wished subsequently to style it in those terms had more to do with his own wounded *amour propre* than the reality. By 'reality' I mean the ways in which the Fabian society did actual good in the world. Whilst this teacup storm was miniaturely raging, Beatrice Webb had joined the Royal Commission on the Poor Law, something Balfour handed over to the new Liberal government that had ousted him in the General Election of January 1906. This commission eventually published its majority report in 17 February 1908, proposing the abolition of the workhouses and the locally elected Boards of Guardians who oversaw them, along with various other things. Webb published what amounted to a dissenting 'minority report', and this document had a much wider impact. Barbara Wootton summarises her conclusions:

> Beatrice started from the assumption that "the poor" were not a class apart, but a miscellaneous collection of all sorts of people who had been impoverished in various ways—as by illness, old age or unemployment. She therefore sought her remedy in the provision of specialist agencies competent to handle these contingencies before they led to destitution. In effect, this led her to sketch what turned out to be something like a forecast of the social legislation which was subsequently developed. Beatrice wanted free medical treatment, pensions for the aged and a national system of labour exchanges and training centres to minimise unemployment. [Wootton, 23]

As the Fabian Society website quoted above says: 'it was Beatrice's 1909 Minority Report to the Commission of the Poor Law that … provided the foundation stone for much of the modern welfare state.' Adopted in effect wholesale by the Labour Party, and put into practice across the board after the 1945 Labour electoral landslide, it completely altered the social landscape of the UK. Of course, what Wells calls for in *The Misery of Boots* is more than just an ameliorative superstructure of free schools and hospitals, it is the ground-level nationalisation of all collective property: 'the establishment of a new and better order of society by the abolition of private property in land, in natural productions, and in their exploitation'. 'If,' he declares, 'you are not prepared to struggle for that, you are not really a Socialist.' The 1945 Attlee government created a National Health Service and nationalised the railways along with some other industries, but it did not abolish private property. Could it have? There's a practical side to that question, but also an ideological side. Wells proposals for the Fabians were not that it should assume the responsibilities of the Labour Party in toto, but they might have injected precisely this doctrinal rigour into the movement. His failure left the Society as what it now, rather bathetically, calls itself: a think-tank. Things might have been different.

In the middle of this Fabian kerfuffle, Wells left the country to undertake his trips to the USA, armed with letters of introduction to various eminent Americans. He toured New York, Boston, Chicago and Washington, giving lectures and meeting, among many, Theodore Roosevelt, Booker T. Washington and Maxim Gorki (who happened to be visiting the country at the same time). He published bulletins of his travels in *Harper's Weekly* July–October, collecting these together as *The Future in America: a Search After Realities* in

1907. 'I went over there to find whatever consciousness or vague consciousness of a common purpose there may be, what is their Vision, their American Utopia,' he said [*Future in America*, 1:5].

That 'Vision', at least as it emerges from this book, is one of sheer magnitude, with the USA as 'a sort of gigantesque caricature of the existing world, everything swollen to vast proportions and massive beyond measure' [1.1]. Many of the constitutive essays include goggle-eyed panegyrics to size as such, the distinctively American sublime. The New York chapter includes what amounts to a prose-poem in praise of the prodigality of the Brooklyn Bridge:

> Its greatness is not in its design, but in the quality of necessity one perceives in *its inanimate immensity*. One sees parts of Cyclopean stone arches, one gets suggestive glimpses through the jungle growth of business now of the back, now of the flanks, of the monster; then, as one comes out on the river, one discovers far up in one's sky the long sweep of the bridge itself... But the distinctive effect is the mass, the black torrent, rippled with unmeaning faces, the great, the unprecedented multitudinousness of the thing, the inhuman force of it all. [*Future in America*, 3:1]

Promenading New York fills him with a sense of 'an immeasurably powerful forward movement of rapid eager advance, a process of enlargement and increment in every material sense' [3:2]. He visits Ellis Island and finds it 'quietly immense', astonished at the huge crowds patiently waiting: 'this year the [immigrant] total will be 1,200,000 souls, pouring in, finding work at once, producing no fall in wages. They start digging and building and making. Just think of the dimensions of it!' [3:3]. Throughout his life, Wells was vulnerable to this rather facile admiration for scale as such. His advocacy of a World State tacitly valorises it as the apotheosis of the constructed Sublime. At Niagara Wells is less struck by the natural sublime than the technological one: '[the] dynamos and turbines of the Niagara Falls Power Company impressed me far more profoundly' [4:2]. Chicago is 'a wilderness of skyscrapers', where 'growth forced itself upon me again as the dominant American fact, but this time a dark disorder of growth' [4:3].

This bigness is partly a matter of topography and engineering, and partly a matter of raw populousness. And it is this latter that dominates the second half of the book, the country's 'indigestion of immigrants', a circumstance that tempts Wells into Jeremiah-style prophecies of gloom:

> In the "colored" population America has already ten million descendants of unassimilated and perhaps inassimilable labor immigrants.... And I have a fore-

boding that in this mixed flood of workers that pours into America by the million to-day there is to be found the possibility of another dreadful separation of class and kind. [*Future in America*, 9:3]

Morlocks and Eloi. 'The immigrants are being given votes, I know,' Wells says, in one anti-democratic articulation, 'but that does not free them, it only enslaves the country.' Wells's account of his meeting with Booker T. Washington repudiates integral racism without quite giving up racism as such. On the one hand Wells rehearses racial libels ('the uncontrollable violence of a black man's evil passions'; 'stupidity'; 'physical offensiveness, [and] peculiar smell') precisely in order to dismiss them for the lies that they are; and he's clear on the extent to which environment shapes being, praising the higher levels of civilisation and culture amongst West Indian Blacks, and conceding Washington's retort concerning the greater degradation and violence of South African Blacks. 'Think,' Wells exhorts his readers, 'of all that must have happened in wrongful practice and wrongful law and neglected educational possibilities before our Zulus in Natal were goaded to face massacre, spear against rifle!' [12:1]. Washington argues for a mode of enlightened segregation, but Wells disagrees: 'that black and white might live without mingling and without injustice, side by side—that I do not believe. Racial differences seem to me always to exasperate intercourse unless people have been elaborately trained to ignore them.' And though the meeting ends with a heartfelt Wellsian peroration to 'the quality of the resolve, the steadfast effort hundreds of black and colored men are making to-day to live blamelessly, honorably, and patiently', this chapter also contains passages like this:

It is to the tainted whites my sympathies go out. The black or mainly black people seem to be fairly content with their inferiority; one sees them all about the States as waiters, cab-drivers, railway porters, car attendants, laborers of various sorts, a pleasant, smiling, acquiescent folk. But consider the case of a man with a broader brain than such small uses need, conscious, perhaps, of exceptional gifts, capable of wide interests and sustained attempts, who is perhaps as English as you or I, with just a touch of color in his eyes, in his lips, in his fingernails, and in his imagination. Think of the accumulating sense of injustice he must bear with him through life, the perpetual slight and insult he must undergo from all that is vulgar and brutal among the whites! [*Future in America*, 12:2]

It is a little hard to know how to take this, except as a hostage to racist fortune, implying, as it does, that a degraded existence is fine for 'true' Blacks, but would become an existential outrage once degrees of Whiteness is admitted. 'A pleasant, smiling, narrow-brained, acquiescent folk' is a particularly offensive phrase.

This discussion of race inflects the book's earlier celebration of the size of the country with something more pessimistic as if race itself were poisoning the possibilities of American technological sublime. When Wells meets Roosevelt, in the book's final chapter, the President makes reference to *The Time Machine*:

> He mentioned a little book of mine, an early book full of the deliberate pessimism of youth, in which ... the descendants of the workers had become etiolated, sinister, and subterranean monsters, the property-owners had degenerated into a hectic and feebly self-indulgent race, living fitfully amid the ruins of the present time. With one of those sudden movements of his, he knelt forward in a garden chair ... and then thrusting out his familiar gesture, a hand first partly open and then closed. "Suppose after all," he said, slowly, "that should prove to be right, and it all ends in your butterflies and morlocks. That doesn't matter now. The effort's real. It's worth going on with. It's worth it." [*Future in America*, 15:5]

Butterflies and Morlocks is either a Rooseveltian misremembering of the novel's specifics or else an interesting midrash on the Wellsian original text. Who, we might ask, breaks a butterfly upon a Wells?

Returning from the vastness of America to find himself again embroiled in the, as he saw it, miniscule pettiness of the Fabians did nothing to reconcile Wells to his role in the movement. But though his time with the Fabians proved relatively short-lived, Wells approached the end of the first decade of the twentieth century more committed to socialism than ever. He continued his energetic production of journalism and lecturing. Some of the best of these pieces were collected in *New Worlds for Old* (1908), a book subtitled (in later editions) 'A Plain Account of Modern Socialism'. This was a book, in its day, both successful and influential, one that introduced a generation to socialist ideas, converting many. Indeed so successful did it become that its Aladdin-inspired title became a shorthand for socialist ambition as such. Leo Bloom, in the 'Circe' section of Joyce's *Ulysses* (1922) lays out his political beliefs: 'I stand for the reform of municipal morals and the plain ten commandments,' he declares. 'New worlds for old... All parks open to the public day and night. Free money, free rent, free love.' The reference to Wells's book is actually a mild Joycean anachronism—the novel is supposed set in 1904—but otherwise Bloom is being specific: parks open to the public, are in Wells's Chap. 12 'Administrative Socialism'; and 'Free Love' is discussed in chapter 'Would Socialism Destroy the Home?' And in this passage, with what is surely another glance back to *The Time Machine*, Wells speculates about a possible human future:

> The plain answer is that under our present conditions the *Breeding-Getter* wins, the man who can hold and keep and reproduce his kind. Aggressive, intensely acquisitive, reproductive people—the ignoble sort of Jew is the very type of it—are the people who will prevail in a social system based on private property and mercantile competition. No creative power, no nobility, no courage can battle against them. And below—in the slums and factories, what will be going on? The survival of a race of stunted toilers, with great resisting power to infection, contagion and fatigue, omnivorous as rats…. [*New Worlds for Old*, 9:6]

The terminal ellipsis there is Wells's own: one of his stylistic tics, designed to invite the reader to let his/her imagination expand into the darkly Morlockian spaces otherwise only hinted at. It raises one of the book's unavoidable blots—Wells's crudely social-Darwinist racism, embodied here by the above-quoted passage's ignoble Jew, posited as an explicit threat to social health and harmony. We must doubt the progressive bona fides of any book that indulges in such hoogah-boogah racist arm-waving. But Wells says repeatedly in *New Worlds For Old* that there are only two options: *Socialism*, and *Plutocracy*—what later socialists call capitalism. The opposition of 'Plutocracy and Socialism', he insists, 'is the supreme social and political fact in the world at the present time' [8:1]. Personifying this opposition as a Jew taking advantage of a Gentile Worker was one of the ways the struggle was urged upon the broader population, and not only by Wells. It has, alas, remained a persistent, if often subterranean, strand in leftist thinking, right up to the present day. This is, of course, contentious ground and I don't want to misrepresent it by only skating over its surface, any more than I want to suggest that *New Worlds for Old* is primarily anti-Semitic in the thrust of its argument. It isn't. The anti-Semitism is mentioned in passing. But that is precisely the point: because the fact that this only needs a passing mention that reveals the ways in which the society and culture out of which the book was written had internalised so comprehensive an ideological animus against the Semite that it could be invoked with the merest nod. Here's Bryan Cheyette:

> The Phoenicians, as Joyce learnt, were a mercantile Hebrew-speaking people who were commonly perceived as ancient equivalents of the contemporary Jewish bourgeoisie. Such 'parallels between contemporaneity and antiquity', as

Eliot argued in his review of *Ulysses* began to be exploited as early as Gustave Flaubert's *Salammbô* (1850)... Wells's *New Worlds for Old* (1908) and *The Outline of History* (1920) both make a popularly held parallel between the historic Semitic Phoenicians and the contemporary British-Jewish plutocracy. [Cheyette, 259]

Cheyette goes on: 'the destruction of Carthage, a "Semitic" city in Wells's terms, is implicitly referred to throughout *The Waste Land*' and 'is at the heart of Ezra Pound's understanding of the "unity" of Eliot's poem. ... Pound had written that "London has just escaped, from the First World War, but it is certain to be destroyed in the next one, because it is in the hands of international financiers. The very place of it will be sown with salt, as Carthage was, and forgotten by men."' And here is Wells in *New Worlds for Old*:

> Which is the better master—the democratic State or a "combine" of millionaires? Which will give the best social atmosphere for one's children to breathe—a Plutocracy or a Socialism?... There is, it is said, a tendency in Plutocracies either to become unprogressive, unenterprising and stagnantly autocratic, or to develop states of stress and discontent, and so drift towards Cæsarism. The latter was the fate of the Roman Republic, and may perhaps be the destiny of the budding young Plutocracy of America. But the developing British Plutocracy, like the Carthaginian, will be largely Semitic in blood, and like the Carthaginian may resist these insurgent tendencies. [*New Worlds for Old*, 8:1]

In other words—or not other words, but *these actual words*—who is to be master, the democratic State or a 'combine' of Semitic millionaires? This sense that the old Gentile aristocracy was being squeezed out by a more aggressive and fundamentally Jewish plutocracy also crops up in the novels Wells was writing through these years. It's there at the beginning of *Tono-Bungay* (1909), where the narrator recalls growing up in 'Bladesover House', formerly under the command of the elderly English Lady Drew, now 'let furnished to Sir Reuben Lichtenstein ... since old Lady Drew died'.

> To borrow an image from my mineralogical days, these Jews were not so much a new British gentry as "pseudomorphous" after the gentry. They are a very clever people, the Jews, but not clever enough to suppress their cleverness. [*Tono-Bungay*, 1:3]

It starts to look as though putting the title of Wells's book into the mouth of *Ulysses*' Jewish protagonist Leo Bloom was actually an example of sinuous Joycean irony.

Another, fictional consequence of Wells's American trip was the short novel *The War in the Air* (1907), a fantasia on the possibilities of aerial warfare. The hero of this brisk science fiction adventure tale is lower middle class Bert Smallways, a character whose name might perhaps strike us as just a touch too Dickensianly over-determined. The first portion of the novel is a sort of motor-bicycle *Kipps*; Bert and his brother Tom run a motor repair shop in Kent and take their girlfriends out for jaunts on borrowed motorbikes. Meanwhile a bumptious fellow called Butteridge invents a heavier-than-air flying machine ('something in the nature of a bee or wasp … in the middle was a long rounded body like the body of a moth, and on this Mr. Butteridge could be seen sitting astride, much as a man bestrides a horse') which he plans to sell to the highest bidder. But mischance intervenes. Bert happens to be on the beach at Dymchurch when he sees a balloon descend in distress; inside it is the portly Butteridge and his innamorata, a matronly blonde lady who has fainted. Bert is one of several people who rushes to the basket, helps Butteridge pass the unconscious lady out, and accidentally falls into the basket as Butteridge tumbles accidentally out: 'the balloon, released from the twenty-five stone or so of Mr. Butteridge and his lady, was rushing up into the sky at the pace of a racing motor-car. "My crikey!" said Bert; "here's a go!"'

The book then shifts tone from comedy towards something more thoughtfully elegiac, threaded with lyric moments of this kind:

> To be alone in a balloon at a height of fourteen or fifteen thousand feet—and to that height Bert Smallways presently rose—is like nothing else in human experience. It is one of the supreme things possible to man. It is to be still and alone to an unprecedented degree. It is solitude without the suggestion of intervention; it is calm without a single irrelevant murmur. It is to see the sky. No sound reaches one of all the roar and jar of humanity, the air is clear and sweet beyond the thought of defilement. [*War in the Air*, 3:1]

Bert, blown across the channel comes down at a German airfield where he is immediately hustled aboard the flagship of the huge German zeppelin fleet by its hotheaded commander Prince Karl Albert. Karl Albert believes Bert to be Betteridge, whom he has apparently been expecting, and whose blueprints he proposes to buy. The Germans realise their mistake soon enough, but by then the fleet is airborne and on its way to attack New York.

And so Bert watches, an unwilling passenger, as the Germans wreck New York from the skies: 'a great crash and uproar, the breaking down of the Brooklyn Bridge … the bursting of bombs in Wall Street and the City Hall' [6:1]. The city surrenders, but the Germans find that, though a zeppelin fleet is good at destroying things, it is ill-suited to occupying territory. The dirigibles prove vulnerable to small-arm fire from the American resistance and the Germans are forced to retreat to Niagara Falls. Then a large Asian air force arrives, attempting their own invasion of America. Aerial warfare breaks out globally, big cities are all smashed and burned and a plague, the 'Purple Death', sweeps through the population. Bert eventually finds his way back to Britain where his story peters-out into post-apocalyptic quotidiana: 'at times came robbers and thieves, at times came diseases among the beasts and shortness of food, once the country was worried by a pack of boar-hounds he helped to kill; he went through many inconsecutive, irrelevant adventures' [11:5].

The Epilogue is set 30 years later. An old man and a young boy chase a chicken through overgrown Bun Hill towards the ruins of the Crystal Palace. The young lad, baffled as to how humanity could have thrown away the splendours Old Tom has described to him, asks: 'but why didn't they end the War?' Old Tom replies: 'Obstinacy. Everybody was getting 'urt, but everybody was "'urtin" and everybody was 'igh-spirited and patriotic, and so they smeshed up things instead.' What has prevented global destruction hitherto, says the narrator, is partly luck, 'sustained good fortune' [10:1], and partly the relative effectiveness of terrestrial defences against terrestrial attack, a balance built up slowly over millennia. But, *The War in the Air* says, as for the first of these, luck doesn't last forever; and as for the second, aerial warfare completely alters the parameters of conflict. Nowhere is safe from, and no defences can be erected against, destruction raining out of the sky.

Wells was by no means alone in thinking that mass bombing would mean the end of civilisation. Well into the 1930s people predicted any new war would mean the end of the world on those grounds alone. Which is to say, the consensus tended to overestimate how destructive such assault would be. In September 1941 the chief of the air staff, Charles Portal, promised the UK government total victory over Germany by bombing alone in 6 months, if only the war effort could be diverted towards the production of 4000 extra bombers: 43 selected German industrial centres, totalling 15 million inhabitants, were each to be heavily bombed six times in succession, 'in order to exhaust their capacity for recovery'. Churchill rejected Portal's plan, arguing that 'the effects of bombing, both physical and moral, are greatly exaggerated', and warning against the fundamental unreliability of any calculations that did not include the variable of the enemy's reaction. He was right, as subsequent events demonstrated. After their 'success' (if we can use such a word for a manifest crime against a humanity) in obliterating Hamburg, Bomber Command moved on to the attempted annihilation of Berlin. By the time these raids were launched, though, the Germans had reacted to the previous attacks by setting up more and better defences, new searchlights, night fighters with radar, spotters on the ground to guide fighters to their targets, and many more anti-aircraft guns. The result was massive loss of allied aircrew and planes and the survival of Berlin as a city. Only much later in the war, when Germany was exhausted, stretched thin and losing, were Bomber Command able to repeat their earlier 'success' with the total destruction of Dresden (Overy, 2013).

Wells's imagined aerial craft are considerably more vulnerable than were the RAF's real-life bombers. Indeed, the German zeppelins are so flammable that no naked flames are allowed on board, and the crew are forbidden from even carrying matches about their person (one crewmember who has absentmindedly forgotten this rule and brought some matches with him onto the craft, is hanged mid-flight by Prince Albert as an example to the others). Wells's dirigibles are 'absolutely gas tight and filled with hydrogen'. We're reminded 'ultimately that made a highly explosive mixture, but,' the narration adds, a little lamely 'in all these matters risks must be taken and guarded against' [*War in the Air*, 3:5]. In other words, the point of Wells's novels is not the invincibility of these new war-machines—quite the reverse, in fact. It is, on the contrary, the immense fragility of the cities over which they fly. This, in turn, speaks to an assumption about society as such that underlies *War in the Air* as well as other books by Wells. We might recall Jean-François Lyotard's thesis that Modernism involved a shift from 'the idea that society forms an organic whole', to one in which 'the theoretical and even material model is no longer the living organism' but that of the machine, what Lyotard calls a 'cybernetic' logic [Lyotard, 11]. Lyotard's focus is on the way efficiency replaces harmony as the social salient. That's part of Wells's tacit critique too: as for instance with the systematic ruthlessness of the German social order, as he portrays it in this book. But he's more focused in this novel on the comparative *fragility* of a machinic society. The older organic society might absorb shocks which would, Wells says, shatter the newer machinic one.

Bibliography

Britain, Ian (1982). *Fabianism and Culture: A Study in British Socialism and the Arts.* Cambridge Univ. Press.

Cheyette, Bryan (1993). *Constructions of 'the Jew' in English Literature and Society: Racial Representations, 1875–1945.* Cambridge Univ. Press.

Lyotard, Jean-François (1979). *The Postmodern Condition: A Report on Knowledge.* Translated Geoffrey Bennington and Brian Massumi; Manchester University Press, 1984.

Mackenzies, Norman and Jeanne (1973). *The Time Traveller: a Life of H.G. Wells*. London: Weidenfeld.

Overy, Richard (2013). *The Bombing War: Europe 1939–45*. London: Allen Lane.

Thorpe, Andrew (2008). *History of the British Labour Party*. Palgrave, 3rd ed.

West, Anthony (1984). *H G Wells: Aspects of a Life*. London: Hutchinson.

Wootton, Barbara (1984), 'Making Herself Disagreeable', *London Review of Books* 6: 22–23.

10

Amber Reeves

First and Last Things (1908); *Ann Veronica* (1909);
The New Machiavelli (1911)

In addition to a great many less enduring sexual connections, Wells's mature life was structured by five long-term, extramarital love affairs: with Amber Reeves, Elizabeth von Arnim, Rebecca West, Odette Keun and Moura Budberg. The accommodation he reached with Jane in the early 1900s—whatever its precise terms were—freed him to divide his emotional life between on the one hand practical and emotional security with his wife, and, on the other, erotic excitement with his mistresses. And the way he conducted these affairs—or, perhaps it would be more accurate to say, the way these affairs conducted *him*—directly fed his fiction. As his career developed Wells's writing manifested an increasing antipathy not just to conventional ideas and small-c conservative social praxis, but to the idea that sex should not be part of polite discourse. This will-to-unconcealment, as it were, is as central to Wells's aesthetic as it was to his ethos, and if it has a prominent erotic bias, as I think it does, this manifests in the novels not only on the level of content—of the stubborn insistence on including characters having sex inside and outside marriage of the sort that got Wells into trouble with his publishers and critics—but also on the level of *form*. His *Autobiography* is frank on the personal life, and if a portion that was sequestered to be published years after his death, covering his many later affairs, his habit of visiting prostitutes and his other occasional pick-ups, it was not because he wished to conceal these things, but because he did not wish to embroil the other people involved in the controversy his account was bound to attract. When *H. G. Wells in Love* finally appeared (in 1984) it described the brain that wrote it as 'quick and bold' but 'mediocre':

© The Author(s) 2019
A. Roberts, *H G Wells*, Literary Lives, https://doi.org/10.1007/978-3-030-26421-5_10

Its one outstanding quality was a disposition to straightforwardness. I told as fully as I could of the sexual awakening of this brain, of its primary emotional and sentimental reactions, and of the play of its instinctive impulses amidst established conventions of behaviour, up to the establishment of what I called a *modus vivendi* between husband and wife, towards 1900. Thereafter sexual events and personal intimacies had to fall into the background of the story.... But I regretted the dimming of the easy frankness of the beginning. These later personal affairs were of considerable importance; significant sexual and personal intimacies occurred after 1900, and the omission of any particular discussion of them caused, as it were, an effect of partial blankness within the general outline. [*H. G. Wells in Love*, 51–52]

The contrast, aesthetically as well as practically, with Wells's friend Henry James makes for an instructive study in contrasts. *Partial blankness*—in the sense of calculated omission, suggestive ellipses and so on—is the whole Jamesian game, fictionally and autobiographically. Such blankness is intolerable to Wells's aesthetic. 'The main reason for the suppression', Wells explains, 'was, of course, that a number of people who were still living in 1934 were bound to be affected very seriously by a public analysis of the roles they played in my life' [*H. G. Wells in Love*, 52]. Posterity has now dealt with that obstacle.

Of the mature love affairs that meant the most to mature Wells, the first, with Amber Reeves, was the most intense. Anthony West believed his father 'loved Amber Reeves as fully as he was capable of loving anyone' [West, 11]. Since it was a relationship that emerged from Wells's energetic engagement with Fabianism, and since Reeves herself was an intelligent, passionate socialist, the affair articulated a trifecta of erotic, political and literary intensities for Wells.

It's not clear exactly when Wells first met Reeves. She was the eldest of three children of Fabian feminist Maud Pember Reeves and New Zealand politician and social reformer William Pember Reeves, and so it is likely Wells met her at one or other Fabian meeting or lecture early in the first decade of the century. Twenty-year-old Amber went up to Newnham College Cambridge in 1907, to study science. Forty-year-old Wells was certainly her lover there, and conceivably the relationship had been initiated earlier.

The suspicion grew rapidly amongst Wells's fellow Fabians that he was using the organisation as a front to seduce young Fabian women, starstruck and susceptible. It is possible that Wells had already had an affair with Rosamund Bland, the headstrong young daughter of writer Edith Nesbit and her husband the boisterous, licentious founding Fabian Hubert Bland. Rosamund certainly expressed her attraction to Wells, and Wells was a frequent guest at Nesbit's house. He encouraged the pretty young Rosamund in her own literary ambitions. All things considered, it's likely the two *did* become lovers, if only briefly; but the story that Wells tried to run away with Rosamund to Paris, and was prevented by being intercepted by a horsewhip-carrying Hubert Bland at Paddington Station, is most probably apocryphal. Biographers are divided over whether the incident happened at all, and if it did whether it was an actual elopement or something less melodramatic. In her biography of Nesbit, Eleanor Fitzsimons summarises:

> Exactly what happened between Rosamund and Wells remains unclear. Accounts suggest that, sometime during the summer of 1908, Hubert, accompanied by Clifford Sharp, a young Fabian, intercepted them at Paddington Station. They may have been eloping or simply heading to Paris for the weekend. There is some suggestion that Rosamund may have been disguised as a boy, which would indicate it was all a bit of a lark. Various reports suggest that Hubert hauled Wells off a train and punched him. Wells played the whole thing down and denied any genuine interest in Rosamund, but he confided in Violet Hunt, another of his lovers: 'I have a pure flame for Rosamund who is the Most— Quite!' [Fitzsimons, *The Life and Loves of Edith Nesbit*, 123]

The affair marked a breach between Bland, Nesbit and Wells, with Nesbit writing angry letters to Jane rebuking her for permitting her husband's infidelity. 'Rosamund was hastily snatched out of my reach,' Wells recalled later, 'and, in the resulting confusion, married to an ambitious follower of my party in the Fabian Society, Clifford Shar. It was a steamy jungle episode, a phase of coveting and imitative desire, for I never found any great charm in Rosamund.'

Either overlapping with or following immediately after, this tangled episode, Wells's affair with Amber Reeves was a much more substantial matter, although, in the end, it proved even more scandalous. Reeves enjoyed a brilliant academic career at Cambridge, graduating with a double first, and founding the Cambridge University Fabian Society where young women met regularly with men as equals to discuss political and religious questions, and which Wells himself addressed. The sexual connection between Reeves and Wells was, it seemed, based on an intense mutual attraction, Wells's much greater age and unpulchritude notwithstanding. Wells's fictional portrait of Reeves, *Ann Veronica* (1909), became a *succès de scandale*. Amber bore Wells an illegitimate child, named Anna-Jane, a name presumably recording both her mother's fictional identity and Wells's peculiar fondness for the name Jane. But after an abortive attempt at living together, Wells returned to his wife and Amber married a man called Blanco White who was, at least for a time, devoted-enough to her to condone his wife's continuing adultery with Wells. There was a storm of disapproval, from all sides. In a few years, the affair had flared out.

On the one hand, this is the stuff of the merest cliché, one more iteration of that sort of male mid-life-crisis that, by its very commonplaceness, invites ridicule. Norman and Jeanne Mackenzie ('Amber Reeves was now the focus for Wells's dreams and desires') make a hard-to-gainsay point:

> H.G. was now at an age when he could either come to terms with the fact of middle age or defy it by embracing the fantasy of youth. All through his writings he had revealed a profound anxiety about decay and death, and now—in the magic of his relationship with Amber—he hoped to find a means of cheating fate. [Mackenzies, 250]

On the other hand, there *is* something particular about this specific Wellsian dalliance that takes it at least a little out of the ordinary. Anthony West stressed Wells's 'pain of losing her', and to the personal distress which surely Wells suffered must be added the larger quotient of a more *social* humiliation. His affair with Reeves exposed Wells to a range of personal and public shamings: he was blackballed at his London club, shunned by many in the Fabian Society and had to sign an ignominious affidavit drawn up by the lawyers of Blanco White (who adopted Wells's and Reeves's daughter as his own) in which he agreed to cease all contact with Reeves and their child. Beatrice Webb sent poisoned pen-letters to prominent Fabians and others alleging 'that the liaison had been a sordid intrigue in which a lecherous married man had exploited the innocence of an inexperienced and badly brought up girl' and advising people she knew 'as had daughters between fifteen and twenty', to keep their girls out of Wells's way (West, 11). It was all very public and very humiliating.

Reeves's first appearance in Wells's writing occurs in his non-fiction: *First and Last Things* (1908), a short book laying out Wells's 'metaphysics', and his beliefs concerning 'general conduct':

> Recently I set myself to put down what I believe. I did this with no idea of making a book, but at the suggestion of a friend and to interest a number of friends with whom I was associated. We were all, we found, extremely uncertain in our outlook upon life, about our religious feelings and in our ideas of right and wrong. And yet we reckoned ourselves people of the educated class and some of us talk and lecture and write with considerable confidence. We thought it would

be of very great interest to ourselves and each other if we made some sort of frank mutual confession. [*First and Last Things*, 1:1]

The 'friend' mentioned in that second sentence is Reeves, and however much Wells seeks to create the impression of group discussion it was one-on-one intercourse, verbal and sexual, with Reeves that prompted the writing of this book. His discussion of the inadequacy of symbolic logic mentions her by name:

There is another infirmity of the mind to which my attention has been called by an able paper read this spring to the Cambridge Moral Science Club by my friend Miss Amber Reeves. The current syllogistic logic rests on the assumption that either A is B or it is not B. The practical reality, she contends, is that nothing is permanent; A is always becoming more or less B or ceasing to be more or less B. But it would seem the human mind cannot manage with that. [*First and Last Things*, 1:8]

It seems harsh for Wells to blame 'the human mind' for failing to manage the notion that the sun is always more-or-less becoming the moon, or that this real horse in this particular field is always more-or-less becoming that unicorn in that old legend since both propositions are so patently unmanageable. Of course, Nietzsche's *Twilight of the Idols* had repudiated 'Being' in favour of Heraclitan 'Becoming' as far back as 1888, and Henri Bergson was contemporaneously making a whole career out of just that argument. But this passage is nothing so defensible as Bergsonianism. The real giveaway is the mention of Reeves's name. Wells doesn't mean that A and not-A are always blurring into one another; he means that he and Amber Reeves, when they have sex, are always blurring into one another and that he approves of this.

In *First and Last Things* Wells develops a broadly Providential ethics. The book argues, in effect, that we're all part of something larger, all interconnected with one another, and that acceptance of our failures as well as our successes the royal road to happiness. Wells's asserts as a 'primary act of faith' that the Universe not only has a plan but that he, and I, and you, are all crucial to that plan: 'I believe in the scheme, in the Project of all things, in the significance of myself and all life' [2:8]. Discussion of this wavers between more or less interesting, more or less windily digressive; but the moments when Amber Reeves intervenes into Wells's thought are the moments that bring Well back to the tacitly sensual and somatic underpinning of this faith. For example: he downgrades Justice and Mercy from his account of social interaction ('Justice and Mercy are indeed not ultimately different in their nature from such other conventions as the rules of a game, the rules of etiquette, forms of address, cab tariffs and standards of all sorts' [3:24]) preferring to ground social ethics in 'Modesty and self-submission, love and service [as], in the right system of my beliefs, far more fundamental rightnesses and duties'. This bring Reeves back into his account:

> Now here the friend who has read the first draft of this book falls into something like a dispute with me … *love* cannot be felt towards others *as* others. Love is the expression of individual suitability and preference, its positive existence in some cases implies its absolute negation in others. Hence Love can never be the essential and root of social feeling, and hence the necessity for the instinct of abstract justice which takes no account of preferences or aversions. And here I may say that all application of the word *love* to unknown, distant creatures, to mere *others*, is a perversion and a wasting of the word love, which, taking its origin in sexual and parental preference, always implies a preference of one object to the other. To love everybody is simply not to love at all. [*First and Last Things*, 3:25]

Wells agrees with Reeves that talk of loving the whole human race is vapid because impossible. Nonetheless he considers it the ideal to which we should all strive, and a person who loves two people rather than one person is *closer numerically to that ideal*: 'to love two people is surely to love more than to love just one person, and so by way of three and four to a very large number' [3:25]. As if a man should say: yes, I sleep with my wife and also with my mistress, and from time to time with this or that third or fourth other woman, but these are just my stepping stones towards total love for all humanity: surely a less convincing justification for sexual promiscuity than the individual concerned might hope.

There's something markedly *flattening* about the vision of social harmony Wells develops. It's not just the lack of dramatic or novelistic specifics, which perhaps limits the force with which Wells can make his points. It's something more, a valorisation of balanced, loving and serviceable connections that repudiates all verticality. The words 'hierarchy', 'rank' and 'status' nowhere appear in the book. Its ideal world is figured as an equalised collective. Was the relationship between 40 something Wells and Amber Reeves only a few years out of her teenage years really so equal? Could *any* relationship be so, on such terms? Jane Lewis, in a thoughtful account of the affair, notes that 'while contemporaries had no trouble in condemning Wells, Reeves posed greater difficulty' since 'there is no reason to believe that Reeves did not reach out with gusto for Wells. The affair was one of great passion on both sides.' She discusses Beatrice Webb's havering over whether to include Reeves in her condemnation of Wells's actions:

> Beatrice Webb oscillated between condemnation of Reeves—she described her as a 'terrible little pagan—vain, egotistical and careless of other people's happiness' ... 'a little heathen', 'a little liar, superlatively vain', 'unscrupulous'—on the one hand, and pity for a young woman seduced on the other. In the end she settled for Amber-as-victim, blaming Wells for having 'Amber as his demoralized mistress at a time when he was on intimate terms of friendship with her parents.' [Lewis, 84–85]

The problem, of course, is our inability to know how the power dynamic ran *inside* the relationship:

> Reeves was young and H. G. Wells could undoubtedly have stopped the affair if he had chosen to do so; instead he apparently relished Reeves treating him as her mentor and calling him 'Master' (Ann Veronica treats Capes similarly). But this is insufficient to render Reeves a victim.

It's certainly possible to overthink this sort of thing. Doubtless, Wells was simply flattered and excited to have the opportunity of sex with a woman at once beautiful, young, intelligent and prepared to play at this sort of submission. Her calling him 'Master' was presumably only a game. One cannot miss, reading her own writing as well as other contemporaries' accounts of her, how forceful and driven, how un-submissive, Amber Reeves herself actually was. Still: the striking thing is how far Wells pushed the *public* performance of this affair, despite the fact that he must have known this would result in scandal and shame. There was, after all, a traditional template for the conduct of extramarital dalliances, and it stressed secrecy. Wells and Reeves flouted those conventions, presumably telling themselves they refused to collaborate with hypocrisy. 'Their relationship', in the words of the Mackenzies, 'was brazenly indiscreet.' And so it followed, as the night the day, that Wells was shunned, expelled, rebuked, threatened with legal action.

In a letter to his friend Violet Paget Wells gushed: 'I was & am in love with a girl half my age, we have a quite peculiar & intense mental intimacy, which is the finest & best thing we have had or can have in our lives again—& we have loved one another physically and she is going to bear me a child.' The formless on-rush of this piece of impromptu prose rather foregrounds the sense of just how threatened the relationship was by what the letter acknowledges was the 'scandal' it had created. Wells is in a hurry, here: as if he has to get it all out at once before his feelings are interdicted by society or fate. Wells's 'the finest & best thing we have had or can have in our lives again', expresses a sort of *quondam et futurus* sense that what the two lovers cannot have is, precisely, now. Writing to Arnold Bennett in July 1909 Wells said that he had tried to give up Reeves, but that he had 'under estimated the web of affections and memories that held them together'. The account of the relationship he offers Bennett is particularly interesting: 'I am extremely happy' Wells insists, despite 'violent emotional storms'. Might it have been that he was happy not despite but *because of* the violent emotional storms? Might we wonder if the public humiliation the affair brought upon Wells might not have been part of the point of the whole thing? Certainly the publication of *Ann Veronica* in October 1909, and the immediate scandal it created, only intensified the situation.

William Ian Miller argues that humiliation, shame and embarrassment are 'the central emotions of everyday social existence' and that all three are tangled up in complicated ways in our sense of self and of our place in the social nexus and hierarchy. 'I seek', says Miller

> to carve out a domain for humiliation which is distinct from shame on one side and embarrassment on the other.... There is an intimate connection between pretension and humiliation. Humiliation is the emotion we feel when our pretensions are discovered. By taking this view of humiliation I reject masochism or torture as providing the paradigm for humiliation, as some have done. Humiliation inheres in every nook and cranny of the normal. We know it in the myriad little humiliations we frequently suffer or risk suffering in every face-to-face interaction. The humiliation of the perverse, of extremis, of death camps and interrogation rooms, is parasitical on the usual and the familiar, not the other way around. [Miller, 10]

It's not likely Wells was prompted by simple masochism in pushing this scandal into the face of the public in the way he did; but we must wonder if he wasn't aware, on some level, that his pretensions with regard to Amber Reeves, the idea that he was the 'Master', were always already untenable. Say Reeves was using Wells to gain sexual experience, to make her point in the face of the world, to spend time with one of the world's most famous writers and develop her own writerly ambitions, to establish herself as a woman—that at least makes sense. Say, too, that Wells was conscious of his helplessness in the face of her allure. The public shame, then, becomes an everting of the private humiliation. He is, in other words, not so much boasting about something that flatters his esteem, as attempting to get behind the shame of it on a point of 'free love' principle. It's worth noting that his going public, his writing-into-the-world of his private life, is very characteristically Wellsian behaviour (Miller argues that 'how we go about avoiding humiliation is us, is our very character').

It may seem obvious to us that the affair with Amber Reeves was always going to be a short-period passion: an erotically intense flare-up that crashed, inevitably, into the buffers of practicability. But for a while, Wells refused to see this. He rented a room in London, near Eccleston Square, so that Amber, now down from Cambridge, could join him for trysts. Norman and Jeanne Mackenzie, who spoke with Reeves in the 1970s, report that Wells promised to divorce Jane and marry her, but that she rejected this offer, preferring to remain his mistress [Mackenzies, 251]. Wells own account of the affair, inevitably distorted to some degree by hindsight, suggests that it was Reeves who pressured him to divorce his wife, but that 'I could not leave Jane.... I found the idea of divorce from Jane impossible' [*H. G. Wells in Love*, 79, 81]. By April 1909 Reeves was pregnant—at her own instigation, Wells later claimed—and the two of them left the country together. Wells rented a villa in Le Touquet, on the north French coast near Boulogne and set up house. At the same time, he put Spade House on the market and moved Jane and his two sons to a new domicile in Hampstead, north London. Wells even wrote a letter to Amber's furious father insisting that the two planned to make a new life together.

All this *almost*, but not quite, amounted to a definitive break with his old life; but a few weeks later they were back in England, having failed to make a viable go of the Le Touquet life. Rivers Blanco White, who had long been in love with Amber and who was fully aware of the situation with Wells, agreed to marry her and adopt her child as his own. By the summer Wells and Amber agreed mutually to end the relationship, and although Reeves continued sleeping with Wells for a short time after marrying Blanco White, this did not last long. Before the end of the year, Wells had been pressured to sign an undertaking to keep away from Reeves and her new-born child. Wells returned to his wife. 'Jane was wonderful,' he later recalled.

> She betrayed no resentment, no protesting egotism. She had never seen or felt our relationship as being primarily sexual or depending upon sexual preference. She had always regarded my sexual imaginativeness as a sort of constitutional disease; she stood by me patiently, unobtrusively waiting for the fever to subside. [*H. G. Wells in Love*, 82]

The opacity of Jane Wells as a character portrait is one of the odder features of Wells's autobiographical writing, and the above account smacks more than a little of wishful thinking of H.G.'s part—not least since he goes on to, in effect, *blame* his wife for his own philandering ('perhaps is she had not been immune to such fevers I should not have gone astray'), something neither plausible nor very gallant. At any rate, Wells returned to domesticity, in a 'pretty decaying seventeenth-century house in Church Row, Hampstead'. Wells also bought himself a small flat for his own personal use in the centre of town, off Great Portland Street.

The whole episode left Wells feeling miserable and socially exposed. But rather than hide away he instead published a fictional account of his affair with Reeves, opening the whole painful matter to the glare of international publicity. *Ann Veronica* (1909) was, in its day, far and away the most controversial book Wells ever produced. In the preface to the 1924 'Atlantic Edition' of the work, Wells recalls ruefully that 'the book was not so much criticized as attacked with hysterical animosity'. The *Spectator* led the way ('this poisonous book' sets out to destroy 'that sense of continence and self-control which is essential in a sound and healthy state … the muddy world of Mr Wells's imaginings is a community of scuffling stoats and ferrets, unenlightened by a ray of duty or abnegation'). Other reviewers were as outraged. Some lending libraries refused to carry the book, although the scandal also (of course) boosted sales.

The vehemence of this reaction looks, from a twenty-first-century, disproportionate. It is true that Wells had written a novel about a beautiful, spirited 22-year-old who leaves her overbearing father's suburban house to make a go of living on her own in London, and who as part of that new life has sex with a handsome, older, married man, intercourse she initiates. But this was very far from being the first 'New Woman' novel to address such material, and Wells's novel is rather restrained than otherwise in its sexual representation. Indeed, critics of *Ann Veronica* sometimes point to the novel's ending, where the heroine marries her lover and settles down to conventional domesticity and motherhood, as a betrayal of the novel's more radical or feminist potential.

This point is one worth spending a little time on since there is something approaching a critical consensus that *Ann Veronica* is fundamentally a 'political' novel—that is to say, a novel about women's rights, politically conceived. It is often, for instance, taken to be a novel about the suffragettes, whose number Ann Veronica temporarily joins (Chapter 10 dramatises the celebrated 'Rush on the House of Commons' of 13 October 1908, situating Wells's fictional heroine in amongst the actual protesters). Socialists and Fabians also appear, as does Wells himself under the deliberately trivialising pseudonym 'Wilkins':

One evening Ann Veronica went with Miss Miniver into the back seats of the gallery at Essex Hall, and heard and saw the giant leaders of the Fabian Society who are re-making the world: Bernard Shaw and Toomer and Doctor Tumpany and Wilkins the author, all displayed upon a platform ... In the discussion there was the oddest mixture of things that were personal and petty with an idealist devotion that was fine beyond dispute. [*Ann Veronica*, 7:4]

But the novel is as uninterested in political action as it is in the political activists who undertake it. If literary critics, generally speaking, have not proved content to see this, presumably it is because hindsight encourages us to see the political and social emancipation of women as one of the great events of the twentieth century. Judged by that criterion the book does seem to enact a kind of truancy from history. Anne Simpson argues fiercely that Wells's concluding 'presentation of Ann' offered his readers 'a gesture of appeasement' to offset his novel's transgressions against conventional morality, and that this reduction of Ann's femininity to 'utter materiality' amounts to a betrayal of the character, 'robbing the heroine of the individuality she had set out to achieve' [Simpson, 43]. Emelyne Godfrey notes that 'it has been widely asserted that *Ann Veronica*'s credentials as a feminist text are hampered by the ending of the novel' [Godfrey, 9].

It is possible our contemporary sense of the nature of feminism risks overwriting what Wells is actually doing in this book. By 'our' sense I mean something like: a drive towards women's legal, social and cultural equality with men actualised through legislation, education and the public discursive challenging of sexism and misogyny. The way *Ann Veronica* frames its heroine's awakening styles the *public* articulation of female liberation as only a phase through which she passes, part of her extended adolescence, in order to emerge on the other side. That other side is not public, although it is in a sense 'out', a word with some splendid modern resonances where sexual liberation is concerned.

One of the problems modern critical discourse has with a novel like *Ann Veronica* is that contemporary criticism is poorly constituted to talk about fictional character. What I mean is: Wells's own, and his contemporaries', chief praise for the novel was as a *portrait* of a specific individual, the title character. To them, *Ann Veronica*'s success as a novel was a function of the fact that its main character 'lives'. That was the Edwardian idiom, and I'm not sure there's anything quite like it in twenty-first-century literary-critical discourse. 'The author', Wells noted in 1922, after recollecting the scandal and pother the book has occasioned in 1909, 'has at least the consolation of knowing that Ann Veronica was alive to a very high degree.' And so she is.

Anthony West notes that 'there couldn't be any doubt about Ann Veronica herself; she was only too clearly drawn from life. She used turns of phrases familiar to everyone who knew Amber Reeves, spoke in her voice, and behaved as she behaved' [West, 15]. The name Ann Veronica is not only a clear play on 'Amber Reeves', with the same first-initial for the Christian name and with 'Ver' reversing 'Rēv' in the surname, but also references Saint Veronica—she whose handkerchief mopped Christ's brow and came away with the image miraculously printed upon it—whose name believed to reflect her *vera icon*, the truth of her image. In other words, the heroine is called what she is because Wells has set out to produce as true an icon of Amber Reeves as he could.

As an exercise in characterisation, the novel's protagonist is a brilliant success: a compelling combination of attractive self-confidence, wilfulness, idealism and selfishness, combined with a perfectly believable naiveté, almost an active purblindness, about the way the world actually is. Having left her family home with no money Ann Veronica gladly accepts the 'friendship' of one of her father's friends, the tuppishly named Ramage, a man who works in the city and who notoriously cheats on his invalid wife. This bug-eyed old lecher lends her £40, to help with her day-to-day expenses and also to cover her fees at Imperial College where she is studying biology. In the course of her studies, she falls in love with her tutor: the handsome, inconveniently married Godwin Capes. Ann Veronica accepts Ramage's 'loan' unthinkingly, and is equally and blithely unthinking when he starts taking her out for expensive lunches and to the opera. When he tries to kiss her at the opera she is amazed and rebukes him. He apologises and offers to explain himself over dinner; but dinner turns out to be in a 'cabinet particular', a special closed supper room in a high-class brothel. Ramage locks the door and tries to rape her. She resists: 'Ann Veronica had been an ardent hockey player and had had a course of jiu-jitsu in the High School. Her defence ceased rapidly to be in any sense ladylike, and became vigorous and effective … the knuckles of a small but very hardly clinched fist had thrust itself with extreme effectiveness and painfulness under his jawbone and ear' [*Ann Veronica*, 9:2]. He is forced to break off. But though she begs for him to unlock the door, he refuses and instead continues the assault verbally:

"And what on earth," he said, "do you think the world is made of? Why do you think I have been doing things for you? The abstract pleasure of goodness? Are you one of the members of that great white sisterhood that takes and does not give?" …

Ann Veronica was stung to helpless anger.

"Mr. Ramage," she cried, "you are outrageous! You understand nothing. You are—horrible. Will you let me go out of this room?"

"No," cried Ramage; "hear me out! I'll have that satisfaction, anyhow. You women, with your tricks of evasion, you're a sex of swindlers." [*Ann Veronica*, 9:4]

Eventually she does escape and bounces straight into the arms of the Suffragettes. The rapidity of this progression lends the suffragette chapter—the novel's 10th—a supernumerary feel. Not only does it strain credulity (would the Women's Social and Political Union really fast-track a brand new member to the front of the pantechnicon raid on Parliament?) it works structurally only to deliver Ann Veronica into prison where she is forced into the prolonged self-examination she had hitherto neglected. The implication of this plot juxtaposition is that Ann Veronica embraces public, political action *because* she has survived an attempted rape and that when her anger and distress at that assault has cooled she finds herself disinclined to pursue a public form of feminism. After prison, she returns to her father's house full of apology. She continues her studies at Imperial and ends the novel by eloping with her tutor, Capes, and settling to comfortable domesticity.

Ann Veronica is a novel about a fundamentally selfish if attractive young woman who finds her life constricted in a sequence of ways but who ultimately frees herself through sexual ecstasy. That's really the whole of it. Wells takes some pains to externalise Ann Veronica's journey in terms of *buildings*, treating built space both literally and metaphorically. In part, he does this to draw out the way architecture structures humanity's sense of what is 'inside' and what 'outside'. For Wells growing into a properly authentic existence means 'coming out', in both allowing inner desires out into the world, and in literally leaving the stifling domestic spaces of Edwardian bourgeois life. Ann Veronica's early life is located in Morningside Park (Wells's version of Worcester Park, where he and Jane had once lived) 'an estate of little red-and-white rough-cast villas, with meretricious gables and very brassy window-blinds' [1.1]. Life in such houses is both physically and existentially constraining.

All the world about [Ann Veronica] seemed to be—how can one put it?—in wrappers, like a house when people leave it in the summer. The blinds were all drawn, the sunlight kept out, one could not tell what colors these gray swathings hid. She wanted to know. And there was no intimation whatever that the blinds would ever go up or the windows or doors be opened, or the chandeliers, that seemed to promise such a blaze of fire, unveiled and furnished and lit. [*Ann Veronica*, 1.2]

Ann Veronica running-away to London is a deliberate breaking out of these spaces; but instead of exteriority she finds herself in a succession of interiorities: first, the sort of shabby rooms available to unattached women looking to rent, the lower end of the market ('the women who negotiated the rooms looked out through a friendly manner as though it was a mask, with hard, defiant eyes' [5:6]), then 'the biological laboratory of the Central Imperial College' [8.1]. From this collective, rational space the novel moves in its next chapter into the claustrophobic, locked space of potential sexual violence, Ramage's 'cabinet particular' [9.4], and after that the small carceral space of her prison cell, 'at once cold and stuffy'. When she reverts to the paternal-patriarchal interior of Morningside Park in Chap. 12 the novel has made its return to its starting point. This trajectory has been carefully structured by Wells as a series of contrasting pairs. The readily accessible hotel space and the private rented room; the public meetings of the Fabians and the private space of Ramage's cabinet particular; the collective spaces of knowledge and power represented by Imperial College and Parliament and the private space of Ann Veronica's cell. The novel as such advances via this pulse-like logic, and appropriately so, since balancing Ann Veronica's need for a public life and her need for a private (erotic) authenticity of her own defines the larger through-line of the book as a whole. Finally, the story caps off with a climactic pairing of large and small, paying out the novel's games with 'being out' (sexually speaking) and the double-meaning of 'confinement'. First, there is Chap. 16, 'In the Mountains', where Wells self-consciously ratchets-up his prose to convey Ann Veronica's new-discovered sexual bliss. Here all the domestic/collective spaces of the novel's early sections are very deliberately swept aside:

> Instead of English villas and cottages there were chalets and Italian-built houses shining white; there were lakes of emerald and sapphire and clustering castles, and such sweeps of hill and mountain, such shining uplands of snow, as she had never seen before. Everything was fresh and bright … It was too good to be true. She would not sleep for fear of losing a moment of that sense of [Capes's] proximity. [*Ann Veronica*, 16.1]

Wells makes the sexual nature of this exterior space as clear as he can within the broader constraints of mainstream 1909 publishing respectability: 'they loitered along a winding path above the inn, and made love to one another' [16.3]. It's big, and public, and erotic.

After the sexual sublime of this chapter the last chapter, 'In Perspective', reads as a coda: small, private and parturitive. We're back inside a bourgeois interior space, in the dining room of Mr and Mrs Capes's flat, 'a shining dinner-table set for four people, lit by skilfully-shaded electric lights' [17.1]. The couple are hosting a meal of familial reconciliation with Ann Veronica's father and aunt, and looking forward to Ann Veronica's first child. Although the scandal of their elopement has lost Capes his job as a teacher, he has found both fame and fortune writing popular plays. The novel's last passage is Ann Veronica's peroration to the exterior erotic sublimity from which she cannot, now, ever be separated: 'do you remember the mountains? Do you remember how we loved one another? How intensely we loved one another! Do you remember the light on things and the glory of things? I'm greedy, I'm greedy! I want children like the mountains and life like the sky. Oh! and love—love! We've had so splendid a time, and fought our fight and won.' [17.3]

All this stands in important relation to the novel's sexual theme. A twenty-first-century Wells could simply write the sex explicitly, but in 1909 he had to explore Ann Veronica's body through the metaphoricity of all these inner and outer spaces. Because *Ann Veronica* is not really a novel about how a clever and spirited Edwardian girl joins the suffragettes. It is a novel about a girl who wakes up to the sublime jouissance of her own sexuality, a story to which the suffragettes are a side-plot—not because Wells thinks women shouldn't have the vote, but because he sees the Suffragettes as a de-sexed and even anti-sex movement. Miss Miniver, under whose spell Ann Veronica briefly falls, is a frustrated spinster whose erotic energy has been so sublimated by the struggle as to turn her quite against sex ('"Maternity," she said, "has been our undoing"' [2.1])—she persuades Ann Veronica, if only temporarily, that her duty is to sacrifice herself as a martyr to the cause of suffrage. The inverse of this is the quality of attention the novel lavishes on Ann Veronica herself as a sexual body, with an attractive exterior and a secret interior only Capes is permitted to penetrate. Ann Veronica's father calls her 'Little Vee' and cannot bear the thought of her incipient sexual maturity: the 'little' V is her inviolate vagina as well as an abbreviation of her name. Manning, an older man who proposes marriage (a proposal Ann Veronica briefly accepts, although she quickly changes her mind) thinks of her with a stultifying chasteness of imagination: 'Diana—Pallas Athene!' [13.4]. Similarly, the Suffragettes all praise Platonic love as the only true love. Against all this Ann Veronica chafes, waiting only for the right man to open her 'V' and leave the worlds of cold celibacy behind her.

Wells originally planned to write a much longer novel, something with the dimensions of a Victorian triple-decker that would follow-through Ann Veronica's life after her marriage and as she settles into motherhood. In the event, he found there was too much 'monologing' in the later sections and cut them. Had the novel followed the original plan it would, obviously, have had a very different flavour, and a different centre of gravity, to the shorter novel that was actually published. Some sense of how things would have gone is given by Ann Veronica's cameo in Wells's later novel *Marriage* (1912) where she appears, in passing, as

> Mrs. Godwin Capes, the dark-eyed, quiet-mannered wife of the dramatist, a woman of impulsive speech and long silences, who had subsided from an early romance (Capes had been divorced for her while she was still a mere girl) into a markedly correct and exclusive mother of daughters. [*Marriage*, 3.2.7]

Arguably the lack of post-marriage scenes in *Ann Veronica* unbalances the novel. As it stands it builds to an erotic climax and ends there, without post-coital *tristitia*. The advantage in this is how, as the phrase goes, 'sex-positive' it makes the novel: not only how much agency it gives its female protagonist (since she chooses and takes Capes rather than waiting to be asked) but also how much rapture the novel permits her without feeling the need to work in any admixture of guilt, regret or indeed consequence. Kirsten Hertel compares *Ann Veronica* to Bennett's *Man from the North* (1898): two studies in a shared 'Versöhnung mit der Desillusion' ['reconciliation with disillusionment' Hertel, 380]; but such a reading is only possible if we assume the novel is supposed to be a story of a woman's political and social emancipation. If, as I'm suggesting here, we read it as a D.H. Lawrence novel *avant la* Lawrentian *lettre*, a fantasia on female erotic transcendence, then there's no disillusionment with which Ann Veronica needs to reconcile herself. I should add my awkward consciousness that I am a male critic advancing a reading at odds with the consensus of female critics. By contrast, here is Ann Heilmann's withering assessment of the novel:

> Ultimately Ann Veronica is a male fantasy of sexual taming, a self-reflecting mirror that allowed Wells to blank out his gynophobia by overwriting the female consciousness of his heroine with the masculine desire that so neatly frames the text. The novel's circular structure encloses the heroine in two male-dominated homes, those of father and husband, with university—a site of erotic, not academic education—marking the transition from frigid feminism (embodied by man-hating suffragettes) to personal fulfilment through sexual submission. [Heilmann, 60]

To repeat myself, Wells's declared problem is not with votes for women as such, but with what he saw as the sex-negativity of the suffragettes, or more specifically of Pankhurst's Women's Social and Political Union, an organisation arguably hidebound by ideas of middle-class respectability—

especially when compared with some of the other, lesser-known branches of the movement, periodicals like the short-lived weekly *Freewoman*, which advocated radical free love ideas, and more democratic suffragist bodies like the Women's Freedom League and the National Union of Women's Suffrage Societies [see Garner 1984]. Pankhurst, though she certainly played a vital role in winning women the vote, was also an imperialist, a passionate supporter of the war effort post-1914 and a dedicated anti-Bolshevik campaigner, socially and sexually conservative and (after 1926 when she joined the party) politically Conservative too. Her daughter Christine, co-founder of the WSPU and co-campaigner with her mother, was even more anti-sex. To quote Alison Light: 'male power was increasingly denounced by WSPU militants in terms of sexual power, the violence said to be inherent in masculinity itself. There is a direct lineage from Christabel Pankhurst's warnings against the injurious nature of sexual intercourse for women to those radical feminists of the 1970s who saw little to choose between heterosexual penetration and rape' [Light, 20]. A 1913 Christabel Pankhurst pamphlet coined the campaign slogan: *votes for women and chastity for men*. If we read *Ann Veronica* as an attack on nascent feminism then it will, of course, strike us as noisome; but perhaps it's possible to read it as a more focused fictional disagreement with the sexual puritanism of one strand of the suffrage movement—a novel fully aware of the sexually predatory violence of which men are capable, but one which nonetheless affirms its female protagonist's sexual agency and rapture. That's not nothing, I think, from a feminist point of view.

The end of the affair with Reeves, and the breach with the Fabians were synchronous enough to link the two circumstances in Wells's creative imagination, something manifest in *The New Machiavelli* (1911). This large, audacious novel traces the seemingly irresistible rise of an ambitious young politician called Richard Remington, before crashing his career against the inexorable scandal of Remington's affair with the beautiful young Isabel Rivers—Amber Reeves again, under a transparent pseudonym. This novel enabled Wells to work out, in thinly fictionalised form, his residual resentment against the Fabians, and to put some of his political ideas, about a form of state maternity welfare he called 'an endowment for motherhood', before readers. But, mostly, it allowed Wells to continue obsessing over his passion for Reeves.

Indeed, the scandal of the Reeves affair dogged this work on its path to publication. In 1910 Sir Frederick Macmillan, keen to keep one of his firm's bestselling author on his list, made a generous offer for the book on the understanding that it was, in Wells's own words 'a large and outspoken novel about politics'. Actually reading what he had acquired shocked Macmillan. This was, he wrote to Wells, not the political novel he had been promised. It was, on the contrary, a work dealing 'with social questions, and particularly with the question of sex'. Macmillan rejected the work. Wells offered the book to Heinemann, who praised it ('certainly one of the most brilliant books I have read for years') whilst worrying that the transparency of the Reeves material made it too 'dangerous' and 'perhaps libellous' to publish. Wells, starting to worry about finding anybody to publish the work, went back to Macmillan, attempting to reassure him that both Reeves herself and her husband had read the novel in proof form and had no objection to it—in fact, they hadn't, but anyway, this concession failed to mollify Macmillan. Eventually, the novel was published by the firm owned by John Lane, an individual Wells disliked personally and not so respectable a figure in the publishing industry as the other two. The book went on to sell very well and provoked no libel suits but the whole business stung Wells.

New Machiavelli is too large and complex a novel to admit of comprehensive discussion in the space I have here, but its flavour can be illustrated via one episode from late in the story. The book's married narrator-protagonist, Remington has been having an affair with Isabel Rivers. To save his political career the two of them have agreed to separate, with Rivers marrying a complaisant young admirer called Shoesmith (as Reeves had married George Blanco-White). This separation makes Remington miserable. As an ambitious Tory MP, he goes to dinner with a selection of Tory bigwigs: "'A dinner of all sorts,' said Tarvrille, when he invited me; 'everything from Evesham and Gane to Wilkins the author, and Heaven knows what will happen!'" [*New Machiavelli*, 4.3.1]. The party quickly acquires a surreally comic tone as the house in which it is taking place catches fire. A 'penetrating and emphatic smell of burning rubber' grows. Tarvrille sends his butler to investigate and confirmation comes.

> We became aware that Tarvrille's butler had returned. We tried not to seem to listen.
>
> "Beg pardon, m'lord," he said. "The house is on fire, m'lord."
>
> "Upstairs, m'lord."
>
> "Just overhead, m'lord."
>
> "The maids are throwing water, m'lord, and I've telephoned FIRE."
>
> "No, m'lord, no immediate danger."
>
> "It's all right," said Tarvrille to the table generally. "Go on! It's not a general conflagration, and the fire brigade won't be five minutes. Don't see that it's our affair. The stuff's insured." [*The New Machiavelli*, 4.3.1]

And so they go on with their dinner party as the house goes up around them, not unlike the similar scene in that other great critique of British Imperialism, *Carry On Up the Khyber*:

> There was a sudden cascade of water by the fireplace, and then absurdly the ceiling began to rain upon us.... The men nearest would arrange catchment areas of plates and flower bowls. "Draw up!" said Tarvrille, "draw up. That's the bad end of the table!" He turned to the imperturbable butler. "Take round bath towels," he said; and presently the men behind us were offering—with inflexible dignity—"Port wine, Sir. Bath towel, Sir!"

Inside the burning house, the guests discuss of the hypocrisies of imperial power, a debate about the nature of politics as such that critiques the political philosophy of the novel's main character, and therefore of the novel itself. The diners discuss 'the story of the siege of the Legations in China in the year 1900':

> How the reliefs arrived and the plundering began, how section after section of the International Army was drawn into murder and pillage, how the infection spread upward until the wives of Ministers were busy looting, and the very sentinels stripped and crawled like snakes into the Palace they were set to guard. It did not stop at robbery, men were murdered, women, being plundered, were outraged, children were butchered, strong men had found themselves with arms in a lawless, defenceless city, and this had followed.

None of the British were punished for this looting. They all returned to their respectable lives: 'I suppose there's Pekin-stained police officers, Pekin-stained J. P.'s—trying petty pilferers in the severest manner,' says Wilkins. Nowadays, when we tend to take the hypocrisies of imperialism and the corruptions of power as axiomatic, this, of course, doesn't surprise us. But Remington, like his dinner companions, is a believer in the civilising mission of the Empire. The group discusses how such things happen, and Wells drops-in a miniaturised short story in Conradian mode:

> Some man I didn't know began to remember things about Mandalay. "It's queer," he said, "how people break out at times;" and told his story of an army doctor, brave, public-spirited, and, as it happened, deeply religious, who was caught one evening by the excitement of plundering—and stole and hid, twisted the wrist of a boy until it broke, and was afterwards overcome by wild remorse.

Talk then shifts over to the specific grounds of Remington's own politics: his popular slogan 'Love and Fine Thinking' (in effect a twentieth-century renewal of the old Arnoldian call for Sweetness and Light), and his specific policy proposals on 'an Endowment for Motherhood'. But the fact that everybody there knows of his scandalous extramarital affair gives the conversation a mocking spin. The other dinner guests start by baiting the narrator mildly enough: "'ours isn't the Tory party any more,' said Burshort. "Remington has made it the Obstetric Party." "That's good!" said Weston Massinghay, with all his teeth gleaming; "I shall use that against you in the House!"' But then an unnamed Cambridge don ('something in his eyes told me he knew Isabel and hated me for it') attacks his slogan:

> "Love and fine thinking," he began, a little thickly, and knocking over a wine-glass with a too easy gesture. "Love and fine thinking. Two things don't go together. No philosophy worth a damn ever came out of excesses of love. Salt Lake City—Piggott—Ag—Agapemone again—"
>
> Everybody laughed.
>
> "Got to rec'nise these facts," said my assailant. "Love and fine think'n pretty phrase—attractive. Suitable for p'litical dec'rations. Postcard, Christmas, gilt lets, in a wreath of white flow's. Not oth'wise valu'ble." ... Tarvrille glanced at me. I smiled to conceal the loss of my temper.
>
> "Hate," said the little man, emphasising his point with a clumsy fist. "Hate's the driving force. What's m'rality?—hate of rotten goings on. What's patriotism?—hate of int'loping foreigners. What's Radicalism?—hate of lords. What's Toryism?—hate of disturbance. It's all hate—hate from top to bottom. Hate of a mess. Remington owned it the other day, said he hated a mu'll. There you are! If you couldn't get hate into an election, damn it (hic) people wou'n't poll."

This encapsulates *The New Machiavelli* ideological orientation, as fiction: ideals in tension with reactionary pragmatism. What is politics? Is it a set of practical beliefs about how the world can be made better? Or is it a more-or-less cynical programme of power, galvanising support by stoking hatred and xenophobia? Remington goes into politics inspired by the former point of view and is startled to discover how little his attitude is shared. These men at the dinner party regard him and the influential magazine he edits, *The Blue Weekly*, as resources in the political game. More, they think of it *as* a game and don't share Remington's ingenuous belief that it ought to be something more than that. 'It was an extraordinary revelation to me.... They regarded me and the *Blue Weekly* as valuable party assets for Toryism, but it was clear they attached no importance to what were my realities ... their real aim was just every one's aim, the preservation of the class and way of living to which their lives were attuned.' In this, of course, they are genuine Machiavellians. One of the thrusts of Wells's novel is that the utopian of whichever party-political stripe simply cannot make headway against these bedded-in pragmatisms of power. In the aftermath of this dinner party, Remington finds his resolve to stay away from the beautiful Isabel failing, and the novel ends with him abandoning wife and political career and instead decamping to Italy with Rivers and their illegitimate child.

I've quoted this dinner party scene from Book 4 at length in order to touch on a couple of key points, as well as to give a flavour of the novel as a whole— its detailed, penetrating, often funny tone. It is a mannered style, of course: not stilted or reified as yet into the later Wellsian preachiness but clubbish, digressive, recognisable and parody-able; and indeed it dilutes its rhetorical and ideological force, as critique, *by* its discursiveness. The man whose name the narrator doesn't know, who 'began to remember things about Mandalay', and who is presumably Joseph Conrad himself, would make a *Heart of Darkness* or a *Lord Jim* out of the anecdote of the army doctor who loses his head and breaks the boy's wrist. Wells tucks the incident out of the way, into a blink-and-miss-it paragraph, such that the glare of *The New Machiavelli's* big wah-wah love story overwhelms it. And actually, this is about more than, as it were, narrative focus. It's about mode. Conrad mythologises and estranges his material, which gives his *Hearts of Darkness* and *Lords Jim* the calibre of fables, thereby very considerably ramping-up their affect. Wells in mundane novelistic mode familiarises and, to a degree, banalises the material. This is a roundabout way of reiterating that Wells's science fiction, and especially his shorter, more fabulist pieces achieve things, and therefore endure in ways that, his 'realist' fiction simply cannot.

As a whole *The New Machiavelli* is divided, perhaps over neatly, into four sections of four chapters each—although the final section leaves the reader with a sense of deliberate aesthetic incompletion by ending its third chapter *en l'air*, as Remington consoles the weeping Isabel on the train in which they are fleeing respectable life for an uncertain future together. Up to that point, though, Wells builds squarely, with a sense of structural parity. 'Book the First: The Making of a Man' relates Remington's childhood and adolescence in Bromstead; 'Book the Second: Margaret' his courtship and marriage and the beginnings of his political career as a Liberal; 'Book the Third: The Heart of Politics' his developing career, his shift of allegiance to the Conservatives and the reasons for it together with the estrangement that grows between him and his wife; and finally 'Book the Fourth: Isabel' his affair with Rivers, their vacillating attempts to put an end to it and Remington's final sacrifice of his political career and respectability to his love.

Unlike Wells, Remington is the only child of a respectable upper-middle-class family, with a good education, married to a beautiful and wealthy heiress who adores him and who has dedicated her life to helping him achieve his political ambitions. Like Wells, Dick's early political awakening is driven by a sense of the preponderance of muddle in the way the world is disposed, and the lack of any effective collective action to impose social order, efficiency and fairness. And like Wells, Remington first finds his political feet in the London circle of Altiora and Oscar Bailey—cruel but vivid caricatures of Beatrice and Sidney Webb. But the Baileys are Liberals not Fabians, and where Wells's Fabian episode was dominated by his (doomed) attempt to reform and expand the group Remington does not quarrel with the Baileys until the very end of the story, when they take the high moral ground over his affair with Isabel Rivers and spread the scandal. More, the novel contains no equivalent to Shaw, Wells's key Fabian friend and central figure in his political life of the early 1900s. Remington stands as Liberal candidate for 'Kinghamstead' and so enters Parliament, which Wells never did. He then comes to despise the ineffectual posturing of his fellow Liberals and rethinks his political principles—comes, in fact, to believe that society must be organised not only with systemic efficiency but with a guiding ethos of 'the best', an ideology of *aristos*. This, in turn, swings him in the direction of the aristocracy, amongst the duffers and dead-wood of which he discerns some figures of genuine value. He joins the Conservative party, resigns his seat and sets up a weekly magazine called *The Blue Weekly*. All of this, of course, is very far from anything that Wells did or thought.

Beyond his 'Love and Fine Thinking' slogan, Remington's 'big idea' is an endowment for motherhood: state aid to help women with pregnancy and the early years of childcare, to free mothers from economic dependency on men. That looks commendably progressive, even by twenty-first-century standards, although Remington's rationale is rather more eugenicist and race-alarmist than a contemporary progressive would be comfortable endorsing.

> The birth rate falls and falls most among just the most efficient and active and best adapted classes in the community. The species is recruited from among its failures and from among less civilised aliens ... Contemporary civilisations are in effect burning the best of their possible babies in the furnaces that run the machinery. In the United States the native Anglo-American strain has scarcely increased at all since 1830, and in most Western European countries the same is probably true of the ablest and most energetic elements in the community. [*New Machiavelli*, 3.4.5]

It is clearly not coincidental that Remington's fall is tangled up with this question of sexual propagation. He and Margaret have no children, although (as Wells did with Amber Reeves) Remington fathers a child on Isabel Rivers. The final quarter of the book captures very well the messiness and scrappiness of a life in which strong desire is at odds with both public morality and private resolution: Remington and Rivers talking through the hopelessness of their love, trying to be mere friends, failing, resolving on a complete breach, failing there too—all this is very well written. Less effective fictionally speaking is the sheer vehemence of Remington's love rhetoric: the car-alarm insistency and volume of his repeated assertions of his love's intensity ('I love Isabel beyond measure ... I'm not in love with her now; I'm raw with love for her. I feel like a man that's been flayed. I have been flayed') and the speeches he puts into Isabel's mouth: 'our love is the best thing I could ever have had from life. Nothing can ever equal it; nothing could ever equal the beauty and delight you and I have had together. No one could ever know how to love you as I have loved you; no one could ever love me as you have loved me, my king.' This reads as special pleading, of trying too hard to justify the magnitude of the wreck Remington makes of his life by an equal and opposite magnitude of love and desire. It is almost bound to strike us as a false step, dramatically speaking.

There is what Freud would call a manifest and a latent aspect to Remington's desire to impose order on what he sees as the chaos of society: a Superego reaction to a political situation that perpetuates solvable miseries on vast numbers of people, and an Id reaction to do with power and self-aggrandisement. Not that Wells uses the Freudian jargon in this novel, but he is, as a writer, centrally interested in the way desire cuts across rational self-interest: 'I will confess', Remington tells us, 'that deep in my mind there is a belief in a sort of wild rightness about any love that is fraught with beauty, but that eludes me and vanishes again, and is not, I feel, to be put with the real veracities and righteousnesses and virtues in the paddocks and menageries of human reason' [4.1.1.] This is the other salient in the dinner party scene mentioned above: *our house is on fire*. It is on fire as a trope for the clubbish complacency of the ruling elite amongst the dangers of the real world, but it is also on fire with unacknowledged and repressed libidinal drives. St Paul, of course, said it is better to marry than to burn. Remington's dilemma is that he does both.

I'm not suggesting that *The New Machiavelli* fails in terms of setting out its political world. On the contrary: the scenes of party organisation, of the campaign trail and the backstage episodes at the House of Commons are all extremely engagingly and persuasively written. But, really, it's a novel incapable of conceiving of politics as a mass phenomenon. The dramatis personae is a dozen or so influential people in Parliament and journalism, their influence being told rather than shown. For all that Remington leaves the on-fire dinner

party disgusted that his colleagues regard politics as a game, the novel he narrates never goes further than a modular sense of how power actualises itself in
society. The book's second chapter is a splendid account of how the young
Remington's interest in politics were kindled by playing with toy people: 'I
dreamt first of states and cities and political things when I was a little boy in
knickerbockers' he says, adding: 'justice has never been done to bricks and
soldiers by those who write about toys … my bricks and soldiers were my
perpetual drama' [1.1.2]. Perhaps this even touches on something true about
the world. Maybe politics can only ever be a model version of the actual (massive, shifting, chaotic in the strict sense) protocols of the interpersonal net-
works of teeming humanity. But the novel doesn't *want* that to be the case. It
keeps yearning, restlessly, after something more authentic than 'it's all a game'.
The problem is that Wells can't square the personal-political circle. The later
slogan about the personal *being* the political is more than *The New Machiavelli*
can comprehend as a work of art. In its place is a diremption between
Remington's vividly rendered personal passions and his more schematic political ideas and praxis. It leaves the novel feeling, somehow, under-realised.

That's not to say it fails. Indeed I think it is to the book's credit that it makes
no attempt to be a Trollopian exercise à la *Pallisers*—that it wrestles boldly
with the need to constellate the rational and the irrational as political realities
in a way that almost approaches genuine self-criticism. Wells himself, from
Food of the Gods onwards, is prone to a kind of exasperated insistence that his
socialist alternative is gigantically and *obviously* better than the status quo.
Remington deploys exactly that image with regard to his eugenicism:

> Every improvement is provisional except the improvement of the race, and it
> became more and more doubtful to me if we were improving the race at all!
> Splendid and beautiful and courageous people must come together and have
> children, women with their fine senses and glorious devotion must be freed
> from the net that compels them to be celibate, compels them to be childless and
> useless, or to bear children ignobly to men whom need and ignorance and the
> treacherous pressure of circumstances have forced upon them. We all know that,
> and so few dare even to whisper it for fear that they should seem, in seeking to
> save the family, to threaten its existence. It is as if a party of pigmies in a not too
> capacious room had been joined by a carnivorous giant—and decided to go on
> living happily by cutting him dead. [*New Machiavelli*, 3.4.5.]

The real giant in the room is the inevitability that Remington's illicit love
affair would destroy him. The unnamed Cambridge don is right. Love and
fine thinking serve a politician less effectively than hate and no thinking at all.

Remington is living in a burning house, but he is himself the fire: 'You know that physical passion that burns like a fire,' he concludes; the same fire that had scorched through Wells's potential as a Fabian politician.

Bibliography

Garner, Les (1984). *Stepping Stones to Women's Liberty: Feminist Ideas in the Women's Movement 1900–1918*. Farnham. Gower/Ashgate.

Godfrey, Emelyne (2012). *Femininity, Crime and Self-Defence in Victorian Literature and Society From Dagger-Fans to Suffragettes Authors*. London: Palgrave.

Heilmann, Ann (2003). 'Revolting Men? Sexual Fears and Fantasies in Writings by Old Men, 1880–1910' *Critical Survey* 15:3, pp. 56–73.

Hertel, Kirsten (1997). *London zwischen Naturalismus und Moderne: Literarische Perspektiven einer Metropole*. Heidelberg: Universitätsverlag.

Lewis, Jane (1994) 'Intimate Relations between Men and Women: The Case of H. G. Wells and Amber Pember Reeves', *History Workshop* 37, 84–85.

Light, Alison (2007). 'Regular Terrors' *London Review of Books* 29:2, pp. 19–21.

Miller, William Ian (1993) *Humiliation and Other Essays on Honour, Social Discomfort and Violence*. Cornell University Press.

Simpson, Anne (1996). 'Architects of the Erotic: H.G. Wells's "New Women"', in Cora M.Kaplan and Anne B.Simpson, eds., *Seeing Double: Revisioning Edwardian and Modernist Literature*. New York: St Martin's Press.

West, Anthony (1984). *H G Wells: Aspects of a Life*. London: Hutchinson.

11

Tono-Bungay (1909)

The population of notable writers on the southern Kentish coast, where Wells lived in the early years of the twentieth century, was surprisingly large. Wells often visited Henry James at nearby Lamb House in Rye, and introduced him to G.K. Chesterton who also lived close. He also spent a good deal of time with Joseph Conrad: *The Secret Agent* (1907) is dedicated to 'the Chronicler of Mr Lewisham's Love, the Biographer of Kipps and the Historian of the Ages to Come'. Behind the scenes, however, relations between Wells and Conrad were not always cordial. 'We never really "got on" together,' was Wells memory in 1934. '[Conrad] found me Philistine, stupid and intensely English … the frequent carelessness of my writing and my indifference to intensity of effect, perplexed and irritated him. Why didn't I *write*? Why had I no care for my reputation?' For his part, Wells claimed to find Conrad's style 'oppressive', 'as overwrought as an Indian tracery' ('his incessant endeavour to keep prose bristling up and have it "vivid" all the time defeats its end') although even here he conceded that 'in chosen passages and some of his short stories' Conrad achieves something sublime. This difference in aesthetics is instructive.

> I remember a dispute we had one day as we lay on the Sandgate beach and looked out to sea. How, he demanded, would I describe how that boat out there, sat or rode or danced or quivered on the water? I said that in nineteen cases out of twenty I would just let the boat be there in the commonest phrases possible. Unless I wanted the boat to be important I would not give it an outstanding phrase and if I wanted to make it important then the phrase to use would depend on the angle at which the boat became significant. But it was all against Conrad's over-sensitized receptivity that a boat could ever be just a boat. He wanted to see it with a definite vividness of his own. But I wanted to see it

© The Author(s) 2019.
A. Roberts, *H G Wells*, Literary Lives, https://doi.org/10.1007/978-3-030-26421-5_11

and to see it only in relation to something else—a story, a thesis. And I suppose if I had been pressed about it I would have betrayed a disposition to link that story or thesis to something still more extensive and that to something still more extensive and so ultimately to link it up to my philosophy and my world outlook. [*Experiment in Autobiography*, 531]

Wells protests too much. His writing is often stylistically very vividly wrought indeed, and his profession of plainness is contradicted by some of his most successful novels. *Tono-Bungay* (1909)—one of his indubitable masterpieces—is very much a case in point. This is a novel that mixes passages of *Kipps*-y plain *récit* with passages of ornate expressiveness and existential insight comparable to Conrad at his best. Indeed, this very combination of approaches is one of the things that makes the novel as good as it is.

Wells certainly thought highly of *Tono-Bungay*. In his preface to a 1924 reprint he wrote: 'the writer is disposed to regard it as the finest and most finished novel upon the accepted lines that he has written or is ever likely to write'. And his disagreement with Conrad over aesthetic practice is part of an ongoing debate about what the novel should be that also included Henry James, with James making the case for the form as something artistically worked that aimed for symmetrical unity, and Wells favouring the looser discursive tradition of Dickens and Thackeray. In the *Experiment in Autobiography* Wells declares 'I shall never come as near to a deliberate attempt upon The Novel again as I did in *Tono-Bungay*', although he does qualify the assertion:

Even *Tono-Bungay* was not much of a concession to Henry James and his conception of an intensified rendering of feeling and characterization as the proper business of the novelist. It was an indisputable Novel, but it was extensive rather than intensive. That is to say it presented characters only as part of a scene. It was planned as a social panorama in the vein of Balzac. [*Experiment in Autobiography*, 424]

Later he calls it a novel 'on Dickens-Thackeray lines' [546]. It's not that this assessment is inaccurate; it's that it is partial. Critics should resist the urge, even with Wells's smiling self-deprecation as prompt, to bracket his fiction with the more-or-less formless, baggily episodic, quasi-journalistic mode of High Victorian writing. *Tono-Bungay* is, remarkably enough, a novel of Balzacian scope and life that is simultaneously a tightly focused matrix of theme and symbol *à la* Henry James or Conrad. In my earlier discussion of *Kipps* I explored what I took to be Wells's mode of reconciling realist emplotment and convincing mimetic sprawl with symbolic aesthetic unity, via a connected series of repeated tropes to do with bicycles, language games, performance and liminal spaces, all linked together under the novel's master trope of 'the cut'. The result, whilst perhaps not exactly an *intuitive* textual pattern, is nonetheless a comprehensible and eloquent one. *Tono-Bungay* does this same thing on a larger scale, with more coherence and even, I think, more aesthetic polish. I say so despite the fact that this polish is both faecal and infernal. But that's the point. That's precisely Wells's point.

One further context for the publication of *Tono-Bungay* is relevant here. Wells had made friends with Ford Madox Ford, a talented but disorganised writer and editor. Ford, Conrad, Edward Garnett and Wells talked about launching a new magazine, to be called *The English Review*, and Wells, of the four the richest, agreed not only to share joint-editorship with Ford but to put up half the money. It seemed to Wells realistic to aim to sell 5000 copies of each issue, which would guarantee significant profits. Ford used his extensive contacts in the literary world to commission high-quality new writing, and when the first issue appeared in December 1908 it included original work by Thomas Hardy, Henry James, Joseph Conrad, John Galsworthy, W.H. Hudson, R.B. Cunninghame Graham—plus Wells himself, who had committed *Tono-Bungay* to serialisation in the magazine. However, even before the first issue appeared, Ford's amiable incompetence with money and his generally slapdash editorial habits became unignorable. Wells resigned from the editorial position and announced he wished to withdraw his financial commitment. In the event Ford persuaded one of his personal friends, a wealthy aristocrat called Arthur Marwood, to underwrite half the cost of the journal, replacing Wells as financial backer. It was agreed that Wells could step away from his prior commitments, but at the cost of agreeing to forego a fee for the serialisation of *Tono-Bungay*. *The English Review* could have the novel, over which Wells had laboured hard, and of which he was proud, in return for one-fifth of the profits the magazine made whilst the novel was being carried. In the event *The English Review* never sold more the 1000 copies an issue, and the enterprise consistently lost money, so Wells got nothing for the serialisation. (After 12 issues Ford was compelled to sell his interest to Sir Alfred Mond, who applied more professional practices to its production and made it into a profitable enterprise. This was too late for Wells, though.)

The whole bungled episode is neatly apposite, though. *Tono-Bungay* is fundamentally about how large and ambitious plans come, in the end, to ruin and disaster, a portrait of a world governed by principles of the purest meretriciousness. The story returns to Wells's own autobiography, as *Love and Mr Lewisham* had done, although with new wrinkles. So: instead of following-through one version of his life story, Wells chops up different episodes, characters and even versions of himself. He is, for example, both of the book's two main Ponderevos, mildly modified in each case by the logic of fictionalisation; as well as several minor characters. There's Wells the housekeeper's son and Wells scholarship boy; then there's Wells at his friend Gissing's deathbed in France; and Wells the divorcée; not to mention Wells the man who woke to find himself rich and famous, on the strength of nothing more than appealing strings of words he'd concocted out of his own brain.

The novel's narrator, George Ponderevo, grows up the son of a housekeeper at a large Kentish stately home, Bladesover House, and experiences many of the things young H.G. did at Uppark (in the autobiography Wells notes that *Tono-Bungay* '[makes] a little picture of Up Park as "Bladesover"' and [gives] a glimpse of its life below stairs' but insists 'the housekeeper there is not in the least like my mother' [*Experiment in Autobiography*, 33–34]). Young George gets into a fight with a boy and is sent away from Bladesover, first of all to his mother's cousin Nicodemus Frapp, a low baker in Chatham, whose grubby family and proselytising evangelical nonconformism Wells satirises. Unable to endure this new existence, George runs away and back to Bladesover, in another lift from Wells own life: 'I have told just how that happened in *Tono-Bungay* and how I waylaid the procession of servants as they were coming up Harting Hill from Harting Church. I appeared among the beeches and bracken on the high bank. "Cooee Mummy," said I, white-faced and tired, but carrying it off gaily' [*Experiment in Autobiography*, 123]—this scene is almost word-for-word in the novel. George is sent away again as apprentice to his uncle Edward Ponderevo, who runs a chemist's shop in 'Wimblehurst', Wells's version of Midhurst.

Uncle Ponderevo is at the heart of the novel: a larger-than-life charlatan and huckster, living a pinched provincial life whilst dreaming big dreams. And he is a splendid, fully Dickensian creation: memorable and vulgar, energetic and entertaining. Narrator George, who occupies the notionally H.G. position in much of the novel's fictionalised autobiography, is in some ways very un-H.G. (he is shy around women, uncaring of society, a plugger-away and nose-to-the-grindstone sort, almost monk-like at times: 'I like bare things,' he says at one point; 'stripped things, plain, austere and continent things, fine lines and cold colours' [*Tono-Bungay*, 3.3.1]). It is into Uncle Ponderevo that Wells decants all the H.G. 'whoosh'; his energy and ambition, his grand and sometimes foolishly overreaching imagination, his sociability, vulgarity and appetite.

Things don't go well for Uncle Ponderevo at the beginning of the novel. Debts compel him to sell his shop, apprentice George included, and to decamp to London, so passing out of George's life. Young George stays on, and his perseverance with his studies leads to him winning a 'Technical Board Scholarship at the Consolidated Technical Schools at South Kensington' [2.1.2]. For a while *Tono-Bungay* moves into *Love and Mr Lewisham* territory, as George, full of promise, slips into bad habits and moons over a girl. But here the pseudo-autobiographies part company: George's re-encounter with his uncle—now peddling a patent medicine called 'Tono-Bungay', 'the secret of vigour'—lead him to riches. It's a scam, of course, though a more-or-less legal one, and sales are booming. Uncle Edward employs George at £300 a year in an organisational capacity, freeing himself up to do the things he is good at: dreaming up new scam products to sell, and writing compelling advertisements to dupe the public.

The narrative picks up pace after the patent medicine Tono-Bungay becomes a hit. Ponderevo expands his business in a variety of directions and he and his nephew become very wealthy. There's an interlude where George, in an ecstasy of frustrated sexual yearning, marries a beautiful but chilly woman called Marion. He sets her up in an expensive house, quickly discovers that he can't stand her, has an affair and divorces her, all within a dozen pages. This brings us to the novel's halfway point where, having traced an upward trajectory, the narrative now turns the other way. Despite obtaining a title and purchasing an elegant Tudor house, Ponderevo frets that he's not living life as large as he should. He has an affair with a famous novelist, starts building a hubristically vast new house called Crest Hill (it is never completed), increasingly identifies with Napoleon, and reads-up on what he calls 'this Overman idee, Nietzsche—all that stuff' [3.2.9]. His commercial expansion and investments become more overreaching and unstable until, inevitably, it all crashes. George has his own unhappy love affair, with a woman called Beatrice. He increasingly distances himself from Tono-Bungay, using his share in the fortune to devote himself to the ultimate rich-man's hobby: designing and flying aeroplanes.

Finally, after much foreshadowing, the novel reaches its hubris-meets-nemesis finale. Wells is riffing on a number of obvious literary antecedents: Dickens's Merdle (in *Little Dorrit*, 1855–57), Charles Lever's Davenport Dunn (in *Davenport Dunn, A Man of Our Day*, 1859) and Trollope's Melmotte (in *The Way We Live Now*, 1875)—three big Victorian novels that are all versions of the same basic story: a plausible confidence trickster from a dubious social and/or racial background creates a bubble in the world of finance to get rich, buys himself a title and hobnobs with aristocrats, all of whom fall over themselves to be associated with what they assume is an endless fountain of wealth. Inevitably the bubble bursts and the speculator dies. Indeed, I'm not aware of any Victorian counter-representations to this narrative—that is, any

nineteenth-century novels in which investment in shares, or financial speculation, is shown as paying off. Without exception, financial speculation is troped
during this period as pride-going-before-a-fall. Oddly, given its importance to
the rise of industrial Britain, there are no mainstream Victorian or Edwardian
celebrations of enterprise capitalism at all.

Having lost their fortune, the Ponderevos make a desperate bid to win it
back by seizing a quantity of an extremely valuable but radioactive mineral
called 'quap' lying loose on an island off the West African Coast. George char-
ters a boat and crew to recover the quap in an episode of hallucinatory horri-
bleness. Rendered increasingly ill by the inhospitable tropical environment,
and latterly by the sheer toxicity of the quap itself, George comes close to
losing his mind. Finally the quap is all loaded into their steamer and they set
sail for England, but the quap rots through the keel and the boat sinks in the
North Atlantic. George and the crew are rescued, but by the time he gets
home again the game is up for Uncle P. The police are hot on his heels and
George flies him out of the country in one of his experimental planes. They
make it across the Channel, but Uncle P. is very poorly, and he dies in a
Burgundy farmhouse. The novel then wraps-up things for George, who loses
Beatrice, and devotes his life to—of all things—designing new models
of warship.

Wells's working title for the novel was *Waste*. He says as much in the book's
final chapter:

> It is, I see now that I have it all before me, a story of activity and urgency and
> sterility. I have called it *Tono-Bungay*, but I had far better have called it *Waste* …
> I think of all the energy I have given to vain things…. It is all one spectacle of
> forces running to waste, of people who use and do not replace, the story of a
> country hectic with a wasting aimless fever of trade and money-making and
> pleasure-seeking. [*Tono-Bungay*, 4.3.1]

Ditching *Waste* was the right call; for that title would have put Wells's novel
too obviously in the shade of *Our Mutual Friend*. This isn't to deny that
Dickens's late masterpiece is an important antecedent for Wells's novel, since
so obviously it is. It is, however, to say that *Tono-Bungay* ends up doing something rather different to Dickens. Patrick Brantlinger and Richard Higgins
have argued that 'polluting or filthy objects' can 'become conceivably productive, the discarded sources in which riches may lie', adding that '"riches" have
often been construed as "waste"' and noting that 'the reversibility of the
poles—wealth and waste, waste and wealth—became especially apparent with
the advent of a so-called consumer society during the latter half of the

nineteenth century' [Brantlinger and Higgins, 453]. The difference between Dickens and Wells here is that the dust heap in *Our Mutual Friend* is ultimately productive—of the novel's various happy endings, John and Bella's coming child, renewed futures, all washed by the rebirthing quasi-baptismal powers of the Thames. Dickens's is a novel with, as it were, through-flow. *Tono-Bungay* very deliberately lacks that quality. Nothing is reborn in this novel, nothing flows through, the two main characters have no offspring. Their waste cannot be recycled.

So what is 'Tono-Bungay'? We're not precisely told. Obviously it is a brand of patent medicine, non-salutary although marketed as a miracle *remedium omnium*. The early 1900s saw a flurry of social kick-back against the centuries-old practice of selling medically inert, or actively harmful, nostrums to a public anxious about their health. Here, for example, is the 3 June 1905 cover of *Collier's* (a magazine for which Wells sometimes wrote) (Fig. 11.1).

The wider campaign of which this issue was a part led to the better regulation of patent medicines: in 1906 the US Congress passed the Pure Food and Drug Act; and in the UK 1908 saw the appointment of the markedly more public-health interventionist Arthur Newsholme as Chief Medical Officer. It was during this period during that Wells was writing *Tono-Bungay*, giving the book a topicality for its original readers it can hardly have for us in the twenty-first century. When it comes to the novel's own patent medicine, Wells is deliberately vague. It is, according to Uncle Ponderevo's adverts, 'SIMPLY A PROPER REGIMEN TO GET YOU IN TONE' ('Are you bored with your Business? Are you bored with your Dinner. Are you bored with your Wife?' [2.3.1]).

"And what is it?" I pressed.

"Well," said my uncle, and then leant forward and spoke softly under cover of his hand, "It's nothing more or less than ..."

(But here an unfortunate scruple intervenes. After all, Tono-Bungay is still a marketable commodity and in the hands of purchasers, who bought it from—among other vendors—me. No! I am afraid I cannot give it away—)

"You see," said my uncle in a slow confidential whisper, with eyes very wide and a creased forehead, "it's nice because of the" (here he mentioned a flavouring matter and an aromatic spirit), "it's stimulating because of" (here he mentioned two very vivid tonics, one with a marked action on the kidney.) "And the" (here he mentioned two other ingredients) "makes it pretty intoxicating. Cocks their tails. Then there's" (but I touch on the essential secret ... the more virulent substance, the one that assails the kidneys), "which is my idea! Modern touch! There you are!" [*Tono-Bungay*, 2.2.1]

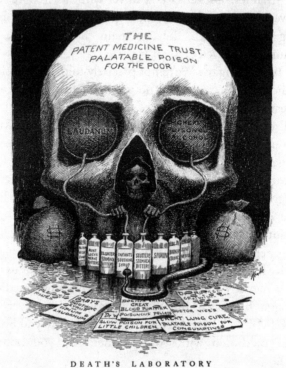

Fig. 11.1 The cover to *Collier's* magazine, 3 June 1905

William Kupinse thinks 'George's refusal to identify the exact formula …
suggests something more than his inability to violate trade secrets. Instead, it
becomes the absent center of Wells's text, in fact a sort of pharmaceutical
mock equivalent to Conrad's "the horror, the horror"' [Kupinse 58]. But
surely the nature of the stuff is less opaque than this. Clearly, Tono-Bungay is
a stimulant, one with certain deleterious consequences for the body, especially
the kidneys. It's pretty clear from this that the 'secret ingredient' is cocaine—
that aggressively stimulating narcotic whose use is nowadays globally pro-
scribed, yet widespread, and which has a markedly deleterious
nephrological effect.

The early 1900s saw health anxieties about cocaine filtering through into the mainstream. Coca-Cola stopped adding cocaine to their drink in 1903. Prior to that date that a glass of Coca-Cola contained about 10 milligrammes of cocaine (for comparison, a typical 'line' of cocaine is 50 mg). In the later nineteenth century there had been a wide range of cocaine-based products on the market. Corsican entrepreneur Angelo Mariani enjoyed tremendous success from the 1860s onwards with his 'Vin Mariani', a mixture of Bordeaux wine and cocaine, 6 mg of cocaine per fluid ounce of wine for the home market, 7.2 mg per ounce for the export market—which, since a medium glass of wine contains 5 fluid ounces, must have delivered quite a hit of the drug. Ulysses S. Grant claimed he was only able to complete his memoirs by drinking this wine; Pope Leo XIII endorsed it, Queen Victoria enjoyed a glass, and 'sculptor Frédéric Auguste Bartholdi declared that if he had used Vin Mariani when designing the Statue of Liberty he would have made it hundreds of metres high rather than forty-six' [Donovan, 51]. John C. Pemberton, the inventor of Coca-Cola, actually started his business with an unlicensed plagiarism of Vin Mariani, 'Pemberton's French Wine Coca', which he advertised as a patent medicine rather than a wine, 'a cure for nerve trouble, dyspepsia, gastroparesis, mental and physical exhaustion, gastric irritability, wasting diseases, constipation, headache, neurasthenia and impotence.' Only when his home state of Georgia banned alcohol did he re-jig the potion to remove the alcohol and so create the brown fizzy drink so globally 'loved' today. There were many other brands, including Magee Marshall's popular 'Health Giving Coca Wine', manufactured in Bolton and Wigan. Products varieties were marketed either as 'Coca Wine', some as 'Tonic Wine', often accompanied by Tono-Bungayish health claims: 'Vibriona Tonic Wine' promised to 'Refresh the Strong, Restore the Weak and Revive the Depressed'. It's to this sub-set of the patent medicine class that Tono-Bungay surely belongs. It is, after all, both intoxicating and stimulating ('cocks their tails').

Cocaine's addictive and toxic properties were well recognised in the later nineteenth century, although it continued to have its advocates as an analgesic and stimulant well into the twentieth. Freud not only used the drug but recommended it to his friends; and Conan Doyle's *Sign of Four* (1890) famously starts with Sherlock Holmes shooting-up with the stuff. But Wells was no fan. In *H. G. Wells in Love*, he recalls his friendship with Sidney Bowkett, the actor and playwright who was prototype for Chitterlow in *Kipps*. Bowkett and Wells both set out on authorial careers at the same time, Bowkett writing plays and Wells novels, but Bowkett never enjoyed his friend's success. 'He had learned to sniff cocaine in America', says Wells sternly, and so 'he fell away from the good resolutions' into 'a life of incoherent lunges and adventures that was to end at last in morpho-mania and insanity' [*H. G. Wells in Love*, 59].

Understanding that Tono-Bungay is, essentially, cocaine opens aspects of the novel to us. Wells's portrait of Uncle Ponderevo, for instance, stresses not only his physical decay, but his weird restlessness and bursts of energy. He never walks or goes, rather he 'jerks' and 'shoots', and though a fat, stocky man he's always fidgeting: 'he fingered his glasses, fretted with things in his waistcoat pockets or put his hands behind him, looked over our heads, and ever and again rose to his toes and dropped back on his heels' [*Tono-Bungay*, 1.2.1]. At the height of his success, Wells's narrator describes him thuswise:

> To the last his movements remained quick and sudden, his short firm legs, as he walked, seemed to twinkle rather than display the scissors-stride of common humanity, and he never seemed to have knees, but instead, a dispersed flexibility of limb. … To make the portrait complete one wants to convey an effect of sudden, quick bursts of movement like the jumps of a Chinese-cracker to indicate that his pose whatever it is, has been preceded and will be followed by a rush. [*Tono-Bungay*, 3.1.1]

That last detail is the tell-tale cocaine-addict flurry. His decline is hastened by the drug, too: back from getting, and losing, the quap George finds his uncle thoroughly doped-up: 'he poured something from a medicine bottle into a sticky little wineglass and drank it. I became aware of the presence of drugs, of three or four small bottles before him among his disorder of papers, of a faint elusively familiar odour in the room' [4.1.1]. No prizes for guessing what the smell is.

This does matter. Many critical accounts of the novel that treat *Tono-Bungay* as a perfectly empty signifier, a mere vacant commodity. But the notion that this 'commodity' has a distinct if deleterious effect on character is central to what the novel is doing. The titular drug is not merely a blank token passed around a system of exchange; it is what poisons the characters out of which the novel construes its narrative. Simon James argues that 'the novel replaces the Bildungsroman of its narrative model with the art of the advertisement. Commodities such as Tono-Bungay are advertised like virtuous conduct in the traditional Bildungsroman, as a remedy that will cure ills and ensure happiness' [James, 109]. It is more than merely advertising, though. The commodity has a direct effect on conduct, which plays into the novel's inverted *Bildung*, turning Uncle P.'s cockney brio and genius into a life of incoherent lunges and adventures that ends at last in morpho-mania and insanity.

So: if cocaine is the ingredient that 'tones' the flabby, exhausted or dispirited patient, the tono portion of this drug, then what of the *bungay*? To be bunged up means to be blocked or constipated (one of the side-effects of cocaine use is severe constipation) and Wells is as interested in the symbolic as the mimetic resonance. This novel is saying: in place of good and healthful food modernity gives us this superficially stimulating but fundamentally toxic pseudo-food, one that pretends to health but is in fact an agent of physical, spiritual and societal blockage. One of the recurring themes of *Tono-Bungay* is that nothing passes naturally through any more; there is neither catharsis nor any inhabitation of the natural cycle whereby life is a process that transfers experience on to posterity. The narrator marries, but has no children ('Marion had acquired a disgust and dread of maternity,' we're told [2.3.5]), because nobody is having children in the world of *Tono-Bungay*:—not the old school English aristocracy, who the novel styles as a mere dead end, like old Lady Drew at Bladesover;—but not the new money men either. Uncle Ponderevo has no children; Crest Hill, the ruinously expensive country house folly that precipitates his end, is described in the novel as 'the empty instinctive building of a childless man' [3.2.10].

This individual childlessness scales to the country as a whole. Old England has died out and left no natural successors. The Jews who buy-up Bladesover when old Lady Drew dies are not presented as the natural succession of a younger generation. On the contrary: 'to borrow an image from my mineralogical days, these Jews were not so much a new British gentry as "pseudomorphous" after the gentry' [1.1.3]. This mineralogical conceit, quite apart from being alarmingly dehumanising, looks forward to the role played by 'quap' in the novel's denouement: something darkly chthonic and radioactive, promising wealth but actually an energetic poison, a malaria or a cancer, that eats through the timbers of the ship of state and sinks it.

'Tono-Bungay' is only a 'food' in a very loose sense of the word, of course, and not a 'food' with any nutritional merit. George's first childhood apprenticeship is to the low baker Nicodemus Frapp, who does produce actual food in bread, but in a very unhygienic fashion ('we had to deal with cockroaches of a smaller, darker variety, and also with bugs of sorts' [3.4.2]. Frapp 'let his nails become disagreeable to the fastidious eye; he had no pride in his business nor any initiative' [1.2.1]). Bread is the Christian staff of life, transformed in worship into the very body of Christ, spiritually as well as physically sustaining; but Frapp's egregious religiosity is as dirty and unsustaining as his bread. Every Sunday the family 'met with twenty or thirty other darkened and unclean people, all dressed in dingy colours that would not show the dirt, in a little brick-built chapel equipped with a spavined roarer of a harmonium'. No transubstantiation here: just ugliness and disease:

> These obscure, undignified people, a fat woman with asthma, an old Welsh milk-seller with a tumour on his bald head, who was the intellectual leader of the sect, a huge-voiced haberdasher with a big black beard, a white-faced, extraordinarily pregnant woman, his wife, a spectacled rate collector with a bent back. [*Tono-Bungay*, 1.2.1]

George stresses the irony of such people invoking 'the strange battered old phrases that were coined ages ago in the seaports of the sun-dry Levant, of balm of Gilead and manna in the desert'. There is no manna in modernity, he is saying; a fact upon which the empty simulacrum of Tono-Bungay capitalises.

In other words, the (cocaine-induced constipation) *bungay* portion of 'Tono-Bungay' is more than just a piece of marketing nomenclature. It is the state of the nation as such, Britain a damned-up, bunged-up, *merde*-impacted land. This is why the final dramatic release of Uncle Ponderevo's apparently endless accumulation is articulated in the novel both in terms of a pseudo-mimetic account of how Ponderevo loses everything—how, that is, the bottom falls out of his world—and with the adventure to the death-named Mordet Island and its vast, literally stinking, poisonous, fundamentally faecal heaps of quap.

> At last I saw with my eyes the heaps my imagination had seen for so long, and felt between my fingers again that half-gritty, half soft texture of quap, like sanded moist-sugar mixed with clay in which there stirs something—
> One must feel it to understand. [*Tono-Bungay*, 3.1.4]

The texture and noisome smell of the quap is a literally sickening thing: 'we were all ill, every one of us, so soon as we got to sea, poisoned, I firmly believe, by quap' [3.4.3]. Later he says 'the malaria of the quap was already in my blood' [3.4.4]. Its very name speaks to its feverishly pathological quality (Hensleigh Wedgwood's *Dictionary of English Etymology* (1865) gives us: '*To Quap, Quave, Quaver*: to quake, pant, tremble; to have a tremulous motion, to shake like a jelly, or lose fat'). Sailing home with a shipful of quap, not just George and his crew but the actual ship itself grow sick, break apart and sink. It's a metaphor of course. In a dozen ways the novel is saying: the whole country is sick, feverish, falling apart. What we need is a cure. We need good medicine, but what we get instead is 'Tono-Bungay'—a fake pill, a mere stimulant that peps people up temporarily but in the longer term makes the feverishness and illness worse. 'Tono-Bungay' is, we might say, the opposite of Derrida's 'pharmakon': not the poison that also cures, but the simulacrum of a cure that actually poisons. Not a philosophically indeterminate concept, but a satirically pointed symbol. 'Tono-Bungay' is one representative example of the ignoble lie on which our modern republic is founded.

Critics talk of Wells adopting the form of a 'traditional' Victorian novel to address the concerns of commercial and technological modernity, but the Victorian novel, in all its variety, and whatever else it was doing, was always a text of through-flow, of story going somewhere, of life passing from older to younger generations. Wells's genius in *Tono-Bungay*, I think, was precisely in repudiating the aesthetics and the ontology of through-flow at every level of the novel's construction. Uncle P. dies anxiously quizzing George as to whether science has proved that there is an afterlife ('You have always been responsible for the science. George. You know better than I do. Is—Is it proved?'). After his death George wanders the streets of the Basque village in which they have ended up, and experiences a sort of anti-revelation—based on Wells's state of mind after Gissing had died in his arms half a decade earlier:

> I slammed the door, and went out into the warm, foggy drizzle of the village street lit by blurred specks of light in great voids of darkness, and never a soul abroad. That warm veil of fog produced an effect of vast seclusion. The very houses by the roadside peered through it as if from another world. The stillness of the night was marked by an occasional remote baying of dogs; all these people kept dogs because of the near neighbourhood of the frontier…
>
> Before and after I have thought and called life a phantasmagoria, but never have I felt its truth as I did that night…. We had parted; we two who had kept company so long had parted. But there was, I knew, no end to him or me. He had died a dream death, and ended a dream; his pain dream was over. It seemed to me almost as though I had died, too. What did it matter, since it was unreality, all of it, the pain and desire, the beginning and the end? There was no reality except this solitary road, this quite solitary road, along which one went rather puzzled, rather tired.
>
> Part of the fog became a big mastiff that came towards me and stopped and slunk round me, growling, barked gruffly, and shortly and presently became fog again. [*Tono-Bungay*, 4.1.8]

This, rather than the opaque recipe for 'Tono-Bungay', is surely the novel's 'the horror! the horror!' moment. There is a road, but it comes from nowhere and it's going nowhere. There is a mist that becomes a dog that becomes mist again. Wells's narrator has set his love life by the impossible star of a Beatrice, and she herself has insisted that they are both dead: 'let's trudge through this blotted-out world together for a time,' she tells him during one of their trysts; 'You see, dear, the whole world is blotted out—it's dead and gone, and we're in this place … We're dead. Or all the world is dead. No! We're dead. No one can see us. We're shadows' [3.4.2]. Wells doesn't overplay his Dante allusions, but there are enough of them for us to piece the intertextual reading together: George has descended, with Uncle P. as his Virgil, into the afterlife. He has worked up the purgatory of his childhood, soared in the paradise of the sky with his aircraft, and explored the depths of hell on the death-named Mordet island, where the stinking quap and intensification of descriptions of actual and metaphorical disease is, I think, in play with the stinking, diseased and bloated sinnerscapes of Dante's Eighth Circle—of Fraud. But George ends, in a Wellsian twist, in Limbo, a place Dante describes as 'oscura e nebulosa' [*Inferno*, 4:10]—dark and misty—never to reach his Beatrice, haunted by the Cerberean mastiffs of the Pyrenean peasantry. Unlike Dante's protagonist he will not pass through and out the other side, but will loiter forever at the ruined mouth of the journey.

Bibliography

Brantlinger, Patrick and Richard Higgins (2006). 'Waste and Value: Thorstein Veblen and H. G. Wells', *Criticism*, 48:4, pp. 453–475.

Donovan, Tristan (2014). *Fizz: How Soda Shook Up the World*. Chicago Review Press.

James, Simon (2012). *Maps of Utopia: H G Wells, Modernity and the End of Culture*. Oxford University Press.

Kemp, Peter (1996) *H.G. Wells and the Culminating Ape: Biological Imperatives and Imaginative Obsessions*. New York: St. Martin's Press.

Kupinse, William (1999). 'Wasted Value: The Serial Logic of H. G. Wells's *Tono-Bungay*', *Novel* 33:1, pp. 51–72.

Newell, Kenneth B. (1968). *Structure in Four Novels by H. G. Wells*. The Hague: Mouton.

Wells, George Philip, ed. (1984). *H. G. Wells in Love: Postscript to an Experiment in Autobiography*. London: Faber and Faber.

12

Mr Polly (1910)

It is little short of astonishing that, overlapping with his work on *Tono-Bungay*'s complex, richly rendered nihilist-elegy for his country, Wells was also working on the lively suffragette adventures of *Ann Veronica* (1909) *and* the superbly judged comic masterpiece of *The History of Mr Polly* (1910). This last book, tonally so radically different to *Tono-Bungay*, is a masterpiece absolutely fit to stand alongside it. And despite their manifold differences there is, I think—to pick up the previous chapter's last point—a Dantean thread that connects both novels. Because *The History of Mr Polly* is a comedy.

This simple observation about the novel unpacks in some quite complicated ways. But to begin with it's worth reiterating it simply: this is a very funny novel indeed, arguably the funniest Wells ever wrote, a beautiful blend of comic character, comic incident and comic appositeness of phrase. *The History of Mr Polly* concerns the life of Alfred Polly, a lower-middle-class man with an imaginative if not high-powered mind. He is a rather feckless individual prone to passivity and gloom, but inventive and, in the final analysis, brave. The novel starts with him as a miserable middle-aged man, keeping a shop in a small Kentish village, based on Sandgate but called Fishbourne: 'Mr. Polly sat on the stile and hated the whole scheme of life—which was at once excessive and inadequate as a solution. He hated Foxbourne, he hated Foxbourne High Street, he hated his shop and his wife and his neighbours—every blessed neighbour—and with indescribable bitterness he hated himself. "Why did I ever get in this silly Hole?" he said. "Why did I ever?"' [1:1]. You will have noted that I said Polly lives in 'Fishbourne' and then quoted text that called the village 'Foxbourne'. There's a reason for that, to which I'll return.

© The Author(s) 2019
A. Roberts, *H G Wells*, Literary Lives, https://doi.org/10.1007/978-3-030-26421-5_12

After this opening, the novel recapitulates Polly's life: the inadequacy of his schooling, the paucity of opportunities, his time working as assistant in a draper's shop. Younger Polly daydreams, does his job poorly, muddles along, gets fired and picks up new jobs here and there. Then his father dies and he inherits £395. This enables him to do nothing for a while except bicycle about Kent, which suits him. He falls in love with a schoolgirl whom he happens to meet sitting on the wall of her school and for 10 days he comes every day at the same time to the same place to declare his love in florid terms derived from the conceit that he is a chivalric knight, his bike his steed and she a damsel imprisoned by a dragon. The girl is more amused than flattered, and when Polly realises that she has invited her school friends to eavesdrop from behind the wall at his ridiculousness he is genuinely heartbroken. It is on this peculiar sort of rebound that Polly marries his cousin Miriam, though he doesn't love her, nor she him; and he ends up sinking his inheritance in a provincial shop that generates neither money nor contentment. Then the novel jumps forward 15 years: Polly is now middle-aged, short, chubby and balding and so miserable that he resolves to commit suicide. We're back at the starting point.

Polly is a man 'whose brain devotes its hinterland to making odd phrases and nicknames out of ill-conceived words, whose conception of life is a lump of auriferous rock to which all the value is given by rare veins of unbusiness-like joy, who reads Boccaccio and Rabelais and Shakespeare with gusto' [*Polly*, 3.2.]. In the early portions of the novel Polly's Joycean or Mrs Gampian or Mrs Malapropian linguistic inventiveness, his way with what Wells call 'epithets', rather gets in the way of his advancement. People don't understand or trust such a speaker: employers fire him or won't hire him. But for the reader Polly's Pollyisms are sheer delight. Polly calls his co-workers 'Stertoraneous Shovers' or 'Smart Juniors', both phrases expressive of disapprobation. In between jobs, he

> went to Canterbury and came under the influence of Gothic architecture. There was a blood affinity between Mr. Polly and the Gothic; in the middle ages he would no doubt have sat upon a scaffolding and carved out penetrating and none too flattering portraits of church dignitaries upon the capitals, and when he strolled, with his hands behind his back, along the cloisters behind the cathedral. "Portly capóns," he used to murmur to himself, under the impression that he was naming a characteristic type of medieval churchman. [*Polly*, 3:2]

'Monuments in the aisles,' Wells tells us, 'got a wreath of epithets: "Metrorious urnfuls," "funererial claims," "dejected angelosity"' [3:2]. Learning to ride his bicycle involves him in what he calls 'little accidentulous misadventures' [5:2]. Kissing is 'oscoolatory exercise' [5:3]. Polly says 'anti-separated' instead of 'anticipated' [5:1] and 'convivial vocificerations' [6:6] instead of 'congratulations'. He contradicts the general belief that Kaiser Wilhelm is about to order a German invasion of Britain by insisting that 'William's not the Zerxiacious sort' [7:6]. He attempts to make the best of his shopkeeper life ('zealacious commerciality!' [7:1]), but trade is slow and he quarrels with all but one of his fellow shopkeepers. The exception is Rusper, who keeps an outfitter's shop and with whom Polly has often heated discussion:

> Rusper's head was the most egg-shaped head he had ever seen; the similarity weighed upon him; and when he found an argument growing warm with Rusper he would say: "Boil it some more, O' Man; boil it harder!" or "Six minutes at least," allusions Rusper could never make head or tail of, and got at last to disregard as a part of Mr. Polly's general eccentricity. [*Polly*, 7:6]

Rusper's wife recognises the allusion to Rusper's bald head, tells her husband and provokes a falling-out between them. After this Polly is perfectly friendless for years.

The crisis of the novel is Polly's attempted suicide. After years of solitary misery and depression he decides to set fire to his shop one Sunday when his wife is at church and afterwards cut his own throat in the cellar. He would thereby put an end to his life and enable Miriam to collect on the insurance. The fire gets started easily enough, but then Polly accidentally drops his shaving razor and, rather than burn to death, runs outside. His shop sets fire to his neighbours' properties and, in a sudden access of heroism, Polly rescues Mr Rumbold's deaf old mother, who lives in the upper storeys of Rumbold's shop. He emerges from the whole episode an unlikely hero: his neighbours are openly glad to have got shot of their unprofitable establishments and able to retrieve their capital via their insurance.

After this the novel shifts gear into its third and final phase: Polly, freed from his suicidal misery by this near-miss, realises he doesn't have merely to endure his life. He can just go off. So Polly takes a small fraction of his insurance pay-out, leaving his wife the lion's share and tramps off through the Kentish and Sussex countryside, enjoying a new sense of existential freedom and happiness. He chances upon a country pub by a river called the Potwell Inn, where he decides to have a bit of food and a pint—or as Wells has him put it: "'Provinder,' he whispered, drawing near to the Inn. 'Cold sirloin for choice. And nut-brown brew and wheaten bread'" [9:3]. Inside is the plumpest woman Mr. Polly had ever seen, seated in an armchair in the midst of all these bottles and glasses and glittering things, peacefully and tranquilly, and without the slightest loss of dignity, asleep. Many people would have called her a fat woman, but Mr. Polly's innate sense of epithet told him from the outset that plump was the word.

"*My* sort," said Mr. Polly, and opened the door very softly, divided between the desire to enter and come nearer and an instinctive indisposition to break slumbers so manifestly sweet and satisfying.

She awoke with a start, and it amazed Mr. Polly to see swift terror flash into her eyes. Instantly it had gone again.

"Law!" she said, her face softening with relief, "I thought you were Jim."

"I'm never Jim," said Mr. Polly.

"You've got his sort of hat."

"Ah!" said Mr. Polly, and leant over the bar. [*Polly*, 9:3]

Polly takes work at the Potwell, doing odd jobs and manning the ferry, a simple barge-and-punt operation. He settles into what proves an idyllic life, with the only cloud on his horizon Jim, who turns out to be the plump lady's nephew. Jim is a violent bully who extorts money from the Inn and warns Polly away from what he considers his territory. Polly considers going, too; but in the end elects, heroically, to stay. The climax to the novel is Polly's serio-comical battle with Jim: first in the Inn and garden, when the two men fight using sticks and broken bottles, which ends when Polly is able to dunk the (stronger and more aggressive) Jim in the river, whereupon we discover that for all his bluster Jim is deeply aquaphobic. They fight twice more, but Jim is chased away at last (having stolen a quantity of Polly's personal possessions, including his clothes). Polly settles into the arcadian pleasures of life at the Potwell, the plump lady cooking delicious food for him, he useful and busy about the Inn, running the punt that serves as ferry and altogether delighted by his surroundings.

The novel's final chapter is a coda: Polly has no regrets about his prior arson, but his conscience bothers him about having abandoned his wife, so he returns to Fishbourne where he discovers her happily running a teashop with her sister, believing herself a widow. It transpires that Jim had drowned in the Medway wearing Polly's clothes, on the evidence of which the authorities had declared the corpse to be Polly's. Miriam recognises Polly of course, but he tells her not to:

"It's you" she said.

"No," said Mr. Polly very earnestly. "It isn't. It just looks like me. That's all."

"I knew that [drowned] man wasn't you—all along. I tried to think it was. I tried to think perhaps the water had altered your wrists and feet and the colour of your hair."

… "Look here, Miriam," said Mr. Polly. "I haven't come back and I'm not coming back. I'm—I'm a Visitant from Another World. You shut up about me and I'll shut up about myself." [*Polly*, 10:2]

The novel ends with Polly, technically dead, perfectly happy in the Potwell, which becomes widely known for the quality of the plump woman's cooking, particularly her omelettes. Indeed so much so that 'a year or so the inn was known both up and down the river by its new name of "Omlets"'. Part of the comedy of this novel is the uncomplicated joy it takes in good food and life's simple, somatic pleasures. Peter Kemp sums up the novel: 'basically, it is the story of a man leaving a boney woman who is a bad cook for a plump woman who is a good cook, and settling down with his new partner to a life of gastronomic bliss in an inn once called "Potwell", now rechristened "Omlets"' [Kemp, 52]. Back, as the phrase goes, to the egg.

The History of Mr Polly is a novel that treats tragic matter in a comic mode. We can agree there's nothing intrinsically funny about social deprivation, isolation, depression, arson and attempted suicide. That Wells contrives to handle this sad stuff as a richly comic resource has more to do with character than with incident or style. Stylistically, *Mr Polly*, though often droll and sometimes laugh aloud, is not notably original, because Wells is so obviously inhabiting a fundamentally Dickensian manner in his prose, which gives the novel a slightly second-hand vibe. Occasionally he even reuses specific Dickensian gags. So for example this, from *Chuzzlewit*:

Mrs Spottletoe … had no refuge but in tears. These she shed so plentifully, and so much to the agitation and grief of Mr Spottletoe, that that gentleman, after holding his clenched fist close to Mr Pecksniff's eyes, as if it were some natural curiosity from the near inspection whereof he was likely to derive high gratification and improvement, and after offering (for no particular reason that anybody could discover) to kick Mr George Chuzzlewit for, and in consideration of, the trifling sum of sixpence, took his wife under his arm and indignantly withdrew. [Dickens, *Martin Chuzzlewit* (1844), 4]

becomes

Mr. Hinks, having displayed a freckled fist of extraordinary size and pudginess in an ostentatiously familiar manner to Mr. Polly's close inspection by sight and smell, turned it about this way and that and, shaking it gently for a moment or so, replaced it carefully in his pocket as if for future use, receded slowly and watchfully for a pace, and then turned away. [*Polly*, 7:5]

If you're going to steal, steal from the best, I suppose. And what really makes *Mr Polly* stand out is also what makes it startlingly original in a manner traceable through a main current of twentieth-century British comedy: the characterisation of Polly himself.

Polly is the first iteration of what went on to become a major English comic 'type' or character: the lower-middle-class man, respectable, in many ways dull (certainly living a dull, unexceptional life) but with an incongruously imaginative and inventive idiom indicative of a left-field imagination uncatered-for by his mundane life. I'm not talking about 'the nerd' here; although that particular stereotype is relevant—but an archetype less specifically tied to a class identity than is the case with a figure like Polly. A much better analogue would be Peter Cook's comic-sublime 'E.L. Wisty', for which role the (in real-life) patrician, public-school-educated Cook would adopt a nasal, lower-middle-class accent, dress in the habiliments of a kind of slightly shabby respectability and deliver deadpan monologues that mixed the quotidian and the surreal. It has to do with class in a way peculiarly English. Cook's influence on the next couple of generations of English comedians means that this 'type' occurs and reoccurs. Its most famous iteration is probably Rowan Atkinson's 'Mr Bean'. It matters for the comedy that Mr Bean dresses smartly: not proper posh (Mr Bean in black tie wouldn't work) but a nice-enough jacket and a modest tie. That's part of his persona, as is his strangulated lower-middle-class voice and his various absurd and holy-fool shenanigans. And it has resonance because, I suppose, many people know people like this: I mean, people who, like Polly, would say not 'I'd like some roast beef and a pint of beer please' but instead 'Provinder, cold sirloin for choice, and nut-brown brew and wheaten bread'. Wikipedia has a whole entry for the phrase 'hail fellow well met'.

What was it that Wells was, so influentially, putting his finger on with this character? Part of the comedy with E.L. Wisty has to do not just with class but with the incongruities of class. When Cook's other great comic creation Sir Arthur Streeb-Greebling witters on about teaching ravens to fly underwater it chimes with our sense that the British aristocracy are all eccentric inbred loons; but when Wisty drones on about bees and world-domination and the 25-shilling meaning of life it hits a note of—what? A strange kind of social aspiration, perhaps. Maybe the larger joke here is simply that a lower-middle-class individual could be so foolish as to aspire to the sort of unhinged eccentricity we associate with the upper classes. It is not the parvenu, a figure with a rather different comic valence. It is that sort of character in which the structures of class as such bend social and therefore personal subjectivity into queer, comical and sometimes oddly dignified shapes. And it finds its formal correlative in the particular school of comic prose that Wells has adapted from Dickens—I mean the way highfalutin vocabulary and Johnsonian elegance of construction are used, with comic incongruity, to describe lowfalutin (as it were) bumptious, ridiculous or daft things. It's the gap between those two qualities, it's that space, that *The History of Mr Polly* so expertly inhabits.

We grow fond of Polly and happy that he ends in a paradisiacal idyll. In the very last chapter of the novel, Polly and the plump woman (now promoted by the novel to the status of 'the fat woman') discuss life and death with an unforced dignity.

> Mr. Polly sat beside the fat woman at one of the little green tables at the back of the Potwell Inn and struggled with the mystery of life. It was one of those evenings, serenely luminous, amply and atmospherically still, when the river bend was at its best. A swan floated against the dark green masses of the further bank, the stream flowed broad and shining to its destiny, with scarce a ripple—except where the reeds came out from the headland—the three poplars rose clear and harmonious against a sky of green and yellow. [*Polly*, 10:3]

Polly confesses his arson to the fat woman, adds that he has abandoned his wife and tells her that the feared Jim is dead. Then he tries to explain to her the intimations of sublimity aroused in him by the sunset. This leads to the novel's final conversational exchange, which is about death:

> A deeper strain had come to the fat woman. "You got to die some day," she said...
> "Whenever there's signs of a good sunset and I'm not too busy," said Mr. Polly, "I'll come and sit out here."
> The fat woman looked at him with eyes in which contentment struggled with some obscure reluctant protest, and at last turned them slowly to the black nettle pagodas against the golden sky.
> "I wish we could," she said.
> "I will."
> The fat woman's voice sank nearly to the inaudible.
> "Not always," she said.
> Mr. Polly was some time before he replied. "Come here always when I'm a ghost," he replied.
> "Spoil the place for others," said the fat woman, abandoning her moral solicitudes for a more congenial point of view.
> "Not my sort of ghost wouldn't," said Mr. Polly, emerging from another long pause. "I'd be a sort of diaphanous feeling—just mellowish and warmish like..."

They said no more, but sat on in the warm twilight until at last they could scarcely distinguish each other's faces. They were not so much thinking as lost in a smooth, still quiet of the mind. A bat flitted by. [*Polly*, 10:3]

One of the strengths of great comedy is that it can so resonantly situate the emotionally touching moment, like this exchange. It picks up on the novel's actual deaths (in particular, the long, mournfully comical account of the funeral of Polly's father in Chap. 4), the prospective death of Polly's planned suicide and the larger theme of spiritual death and waste, the deathly experience of low-grade depression and with a lyric turn manages somehow to repudiate death as such. It's wonderfully done.

This brings me to Dante. The novel starts with Polly *nel mezzo del cammin di sua vita* ('Mr. Polly's age was exactly thirty-five years and a half' [1:2]) contemplating the gigantic hole that lies before him: '"Hole!" said Mr. Polly, and then for a change, and with greatly increased emphasis: "Ole!" He paused, and then broke out with one of his private and peculiar idioms. "Oh! Beastly Silly Wheeze of a Hole!"' Dante opens the *Inferno* also aged 35, also peering into a gigantic hole—Hell. The most obvious difference between Dante's progress through Hell and Polly's through *The History of Mr Polly* is that Polly *ends up* as the ferryman, where Dante encounters the Stygian boatman Charon early on (in canto 3 in fact). We might say that Dante, guided by Virgil, passes deeper and deeper into hell before passing through the other side; where Polly, guided by nobody, slowly emerges out of misery and ends up in a liminal state of blithe death, ferrying people good and evil across the water.

But we can go further. The case can be argued that Wells's novel has nine substantive chapters (and one coda) *because* Dante's hell has nine circles (plus a tenth passage from the centre of the world to the mountain of Purgatory). Wells's Chap. 1 details Polly's youth, neglected in a useless school, more or less friendless and then as a draper's apprentice (sleeping in 'a long bleak room with six beds' [1:3]). It's all waiting for something to happen and very much a limbo state of affairs—Limbo, of course, being Dante's first circle, on the far side of his stygian river. Wells's Chap. 2 tells the story of the dismissal of young Polly's best friend, Parsons, from his position as draper's assistant. He is sacked because he has been blown about by the winds of his passion ('he was blowing excitedly and running his fingers through his hair, and then moving with all the swift eagerness of a man inspired' [2:2]) under the influence of which he dresses the draper's shop window according to his own 'artistic' ideas of red and black, 'an active whirl of gesture, tearing things down and throwing them, and then he went under'. Like a divine wind, as the kamikaze phrase has it; and career-suicidal, a gesture that anticipates Polly's own actual-suicidal plan later in the book and that perhaps mimics Dante's lost souls blown about by the winds of passion in his second circle.

In Chap. 3 Polly himself loses his position and the universe rains and storms upon him, just as Dante's third circle is characterised by hail, rain and black snow: 'the universe became really disagreeable to Mr. Polly. It was brought home to him, not so much vividly as with a harsh and ungainly insistence, that he was a failure in his trade' [3:3]. Dante's fourth circle is where the hoarders are confined'; Chap. 4 is 'Mr Polly an Orphan', and Polly himself torn refusing to invest his small inheritance. Dante's fifth circle contains the wrathful and the sullen. Wells's Chap. 5 includes Polly wrathfully quarrelling with people on his bicycle ('had a bit of an argument. I told him he oughtn't to come out wearing such a dangerous hat—flying at things…. Waw-waw-waw. Infuriacious' [5:2]) and ends with him sullenly miserable after he understands the frivolous way in which the schoolgirl considers him: 'the bottom dropped out of Mr. Polly's world' [5:7]. Dante's sixth circle contains the City of Dis, where heretics are locked in burning stone coffins. Chapter 6 of Wells's novel introduces a step-change in Polly's misery, as he immures himself in the coffin of his marriage to Miriam, and his shop, and settles in the City of Dis-, or Fis-, hbourne.

This brings us to circles seven and eight, and the novel's Chaps. 7 and 8, where Polly is at his most tormented, and Dante's 'Plain of Fire', 'Wood of Suicides' and varieties of Fraud in 'Maleboge' find fictional equivalent in Polly's planned arson, suicide and insurance fraud. Then to what is perhaps the most interesting of Wells's games with Dante: the ninth circle, home in the *Inferno* to those who have betrayed their family, their country, their guests and benefactors and worst of all those who have betrayed their lord, culminating in Satan, trapped in a huge block of ice in the very middle of the Earth. In Wells's Chap. 9, Polly actualises his own happy ending by, in effect, betraying his marriage vows and abdicating all his responsibilities. For him this is a redemptive rather than damnable strategy or so Wells suggests—provided only Polly is prepared to encounter his diabolic alter ego, Jim. There's no question as to Jim's nature. The Plump Woman relates what Jim said to her, after he returned from his first stint in the Reformatory for theft and truancy: 'him like a viper a-looking at me—more like a viper than a human boy. … "They've Reformed me," he says, "and made me a devil, and devil I mean to be to you"' [9:5]. Jim hurts the Plump Woman, steals her money and tries his best to scare Polly away:

Jim was certainly not a handsome person. He was short, shorter than Mr. Polly, with long arms and lean big hands … His almost toothless mouth seemed a cavern in the twilight. Some accident had left him with one small and active and one large and expressionless reddish eye …

He gripped Mr. Polly's wrist with a grip of steel, and in an instant Mr. Polly understood the relative quality of their muscles. He breathed, an uninspiring breath, into Mr. Polly's face.

"What won't I do?" he said. "Once I start in on you." [*Polly*, 9:6]

The serpentine quality, the cavernous mouth (Dante's Satan's mouth is big enough to stuff the whole of Judas's body in), the red eye, even the slobber running down his chin ('… and down each chin/both tears and bloody slobber slowly ran': *Inferno* 34:53–54) are all very reminiscent of Dante's Satan.

The *Inferno* not only puts Satan at the very middle of the world, in the lowest circle of hell, it ensures that Dante and Virgil's path runs right past him. It's the text's way of saying that sin cannot be avoided in this life of ours; we cannot just keep our heads down and hope Satan won't notice us. On the contrary, we have to be brave, to confront Satan, to push on through, go right past him, for only by doing this can we make our way to Purgatory and so to Paradise. Likewise Mr Polly, though he contemplates running away, conscious as he is of Jim's superior strength and pugilistic experience, resolves to face up to the challenge. He defeats his adversary and so emerges in Chap. 10 to contemplate the beauties of the sky, in the passage quoted above, just as Dante emerges at the end of the Inferno, '*e quindi uscimmo a riveder le stelle*'.

I'm not saying *Polly* is a one-to-one mapping of Dante's *Inferno* onto the novel mode, although I appreciate it may appear I have been arguing exactly that case. So let me put it another way. In the first edition (and some later editions too) Wells's Chap. 1 starts with Polly miserable in 'Foxbourne'. Then we get the backstory to his life, before returning to the town, which Wells now calls 'Fishbourne'—I mentioned this earlier. It was, presumably, a simple slip, but I think it an expressive one. The fox, predatory and sly, appearing like a flame in a field, speaks to Polly the arsonist and fraud. The fish, on the other hand, speaks to the river, to water and the baptismal renewal as well as the stygian transition into death which Polly comes to oversee. This is the larger thematic trajectory of *The History of Mr Polly*: from the frozen, prospectless chill of his youth ('he meditated gloomily upon his future and a colder chill invaded Polly's mind' [2:3]), through the blazing fire of his arson attempt that burns down the whole village, finally to the river where he becomes ferryman and finds happiness. This, of course, exactly reverses the passage through Dante's Hell, which goes from Styx to mid-journey fire to deepest circles of frozen gloom. And the other thing about Dante's great, indeed divine, epic?

It's a comedy.

13

Elizabeth von Arnim

Marriage (1912); The Passionate Friends (1913); The Wife of Sir Isaac Harman (1914); The Research Magnificent (1915)

Restless in London, to some extent still suffering emotionally from the end of his affair with Amber Reeves, Wells moved himself, his wife and his two young sons out of the city. In 1911 he bought a house in rural Essex, 20 miles northeast of London at a village called Easton. The house was an eighteenth-century redbrick two-storey cottage and Wells and Jane renovated it and reconstructed the garden, giving it the faux-archaic name of Easton Glebe. Jane was a passionate gardener and increasingly maintained her own life, with her own circle of friends; Wells alternated periods of writerly reclusiveness with periods of sometimes manic sociability. At Easton Glebe he often hosted house parties at which guests would stay over, play games—Wells was especially fond of outdoor games like tennis, badminton and croquet, as well as a roaming game simply called 'ball' that he invented himself. Wells was an energetic maker of friends and had a wide circle: guests at Easton Glebe included Jerome K. Jerome, Liberal politician Charles Masterman (who oversaw the introduction of National Insurance in 1911), Frank Swinnerton, Violet Paget, Arnold Bennett, various Fabian bigwigs, Cynthia Asquith, Charlie Chaplin, Dorothy Richardson, even Wells's first wife Isabel. Accounts of the dinner parties and games, in their letters and elsewhere, bring out the sometimes strenuous quality of Wellsian fun.

By the end of the noughties his two sons with Jane, George Philip (born 1901) and Frank Richard (born 1903) were old enough to be playmates for their father. The three males played elaborate war games, using myriad small lead soldiers, toy houses and trees and elaborate rules—again invented by H.G. Each army had a time-limited period to move their troops and position their toy artillery; cannon would fire little wooden dowels and try to knock

© The Author(s) 2019
A. Roberts, *H G Wells*, Literary Lives, https://doi.org/10.1007/978-3-030-26421-5_13

their enemy. In 1913 Wells published an account of this game, including rules for play and some meditation on wargaming as such. The book, issued under the title *Little Wars: a game for boys from twelve years of age to one hundred and fifty and for that more intelligent sort of girl who likes boys' games and books*—this presumably passed for whimsical charm in 1913 however sexist it strikes us a century later—remains in print and is popular with modern-day wargamers. Wells cannot be given the credit for inventing 'wargaming' (the Prussian army was using *kriegspiels* as training tools as early as the 1820s) but his joys in playing with these models communicates itself to the modern reader very palpably: Michael Paris claims that 'the book sharpened the enthusiasm of many boys and young men for war games' and even 'attracted the attention of some army officers' [Paris, 60]. Real war was just around the corner, of course, but it is the *modular* component to this pastime was surely key. Wells is very often a modular writer, in the sense that he is self-consciously creating smaller-scale models of reality in his art in order to play around with our conceptions—in the sense, in other words, that *A Modern Utopia* (say) is to real-life social engineering as a *kriegspiel* is to actual war. His delight in models and in the manipulation of models, is beautifully expressed in the early chapters of *The New Machiavelli* (1911). Hilaire Belloc, no friend of Wells's, clearly shared this passion:

> Whatever, keeping its proportion and form, is designed upon a scale much greater or much less than that of our general experience, produces upon the mind an effect of phantasy. A little perfect model of an engine or a ship does not only amuse or surprise; it rather casts over the imagination something of that veil through which the world is transfigured … the principal spell of childhood returns as we bend over the astonishing details. We are giants—or there is no secure standard left in our intelligence. It is as though humanity were permitted to break through the vulgar illusion of daily sense, and to learn in a physical experience how unreal are all the absolute standards by which we build. [Belloc, 'The Inn of the Margeride', *Hills and the Sea* (1906)]

This near-metaphysical fascination with the modular, with the miniature and the compact, didn't only inform Wells fiction of the early teens; it also touched his next important love affair.

Little Easton was Wells's home now and where Jane lived; but he still spent much of each week in London working, in his central London flat in Church Row. He later recalled Elizabeth von Arnim, the subject of his next significant *affaire de coeur*, as one among several 'kindly ladies' who visited him in this flat 'helping me get the fever for Amber out of my blood' [*H. G. Wells in Love*,

87]. In fact she was or at least quickly became, much more than a temporary sexual connection. His relationship with her lasted several years, a time during which he wrote a string of thematically related novels. These are sometimes given the denigrating collective name 'the Prig novels', and certainly none of them have the reputation of Wells's earlier masterpieces; but 'prig' is unfair. These are all, in many ways, interesting and powerful novels.

Elizabeth von Arnim, née Mary Annette Beauchamp, was a successful author in her own right: 'Elizabeth' was the name under which she wrote a number of popular novels, beginning with *Elizabeth and her German Garden* (1898) fictionalising her marriage to the German Count from whom she acquired her surname. Wells recalled her as 'a very bright and original little lady'. Indeed, 'little' is the condescending watchword for the whole of Wells's account of the affair: 'The Episode of Little e' he styles it, Elizabeth not even, it seems, meriting a capital letter. 'She was incapable of philosophical thought or political ideas,' he says; although she had her native Irish 'passion for absurdity and laughter' and was 'insincerely sentimental' [*H. G. Wells in Love*, 87].

As a model is usually neater than the thing modelled and so it is in Wells's account of this affair. Indeed, there is something rather offputtingly self-regarding about his narrative. 'I attracted her', he says, laconically, adding that 'she had found love-making with Von Arnim a serious and disagreeable business, but she was aware that it might be far less onerous and more agreeable', thereby creating the self-serving impression that he was the man who gave her the practical experience to confirm that awareness. Not so: von Arnim had had plenty of other lovers before Wells. He goes on: 'we made love very brightly, but I cannot imagine a relationship more free from passion than ours … we carried on the liaison with an impudent impunity. We flitted off abroad and had amusing times in Amsterdam, Bruges, Ypres, Arras, Paris, Locarno, Orta, Florence—and no one was a bit the wiser.' The reality was rather less carefree. After her marriage had irretrievably broken down in the 1890s (the husband himself died in 1910) Von Arnim took a string of lovers, mostly from among her impressive coterie of devoted, younger followers: her children's tutors, Hugh Walpole, even, improbably enough, E.M. Forster. 'She attracted and was attracted to younger men' is how David Smith puts it. Wells met her in 1910 and persisted with his advances despite her initial coolness towards him. At the time he was competing for her affections with the (much younger and better looking) C.S. Stuart and though he did eventually win her round or perhaps did eventually wear her down, it was not plain sailing. 'Eventually (and it is difficult to say how much Elizabeth resisted, as her fiction usually gives her the better of the situations portrayed) the two older people planned a romantic interlude in Ireland' [Smith, 371]. She seems to have changed her mind and gone off instead to Switzerland on her own: 'Wells, now very importunate, followed her to Switzerland, after "reproachful" letters and amid scenes "of quite surprising violence"' (Von Arnim's words in the double-quotation marks). They did become lovers, but, if you believe Von Arnim, it was not the happy-go-lucky fling implied by Wells's account:

> The romantic interlude planned in Ireland finally took place in northern Italy, and although Elizabeth informed her daughter than 'his excessively trying behaviour' broke up the affair, it was an affair conducted at the best of times under difficulty. She liked younger and more adoring men, and did not especially care for the rough and tumble manner in which Wells conducted the early part of his romantic escapades. [Smith, 372]

Wells version reads more like wishful thinking than veracity. He can't keep a kind of unconvincing bragging out of his tone: 'twice we broke a bed—not very strong beds they were but still we broke them—and it was a cheerful thing to hear Little e explaining in pretty but perfect German why her bed had gone to pieces under her in the night.' There's also Wells's anecdote about the two of them reading in the *Times* a disapproving letter by Mrs Humphrey Ward 'denouncing the moral tone of the younger generation' of writers and demonstrating their contempt by stripping naked—outdoors though they were—and '[making] love all over Mrs Humphrey Ward': which might have more point if the two of them actually *were* writers of the younger generation. They weren't, though: Von Arnim, born in 1866, was the same age as Wells, though she looked younger than her years. Indeed, if a detail from Von Arnim's fictionalised version of the affair, *The Pastor's Wife* (1914), is to be believed, when the two of them booked into a continental hotel together the hall porter referred to H.G. as 'Monsieur votre père', which can't have pleased him. In the novel, Von Arnim says of her fictional version of herself at this juncture: 'with the easy tactlessness of one who has not yet learned to be afraid, she looked at him and laughed.' It hardly bodes well. Wells later wanted to characterise the whole thing as a pleasant bit of fun sandwiched between his two much more significant love affairs: Amber Reeves and Rebecca West. In fact it mattered rather more to him in the moment than he later admitted.

Later in life Wells specifically linked the von Arnim relationship to a decline in the quality of the fiction from this time.

> The period in my life between 1910 and 1913 when Little e was my mistress corresponds with several novels that were naturally published a little later than the writing. These are *Marriage*, *The Passionate Friends*, *The Wife of Sir Isaac*

Harman and *The Research Magnificent*. None of them are among my best work
… they have less sincerity and depth than anything else that I have written. [*H. G. Wells in Love*, 93]

It's neither gentlemanly nor, frankly, credible to blame von Arnim for the relative failures of these works.

The first of those titles, *Marriage*, has a particular role to play as a sort of copula between Wells prior deep love for Amber Reeves and his to-come deep connection to Rebecca West. It began life as the unpublished second-half of *Ann Veronica* and in one sense is still a record of Wells's passion for Reeves; at the same time it was Rebecca West's swingeing review of the novel in the feminist magazine *The Freewoman* (19 September 1912) that led to Wells inviting her to lunch, from which eventually developed their affair. West's review denounced Wells's writing as 'clotted' with 'sex mania' that lies on his novels 'like cold white sauce' and dismisses *Marriage* as 'the reaction towards the flesh of a mind too long absorbed in airships and colloids'.

The story follows Marjorie Pope, the daughter of an affluent Edwardian bourgeois family ruled by a crotchety, bumptious father. Wells draws the milieu of upper-middle-class Edwardian summertime life well and when a plane crashes in the middle of the Pope's lawn tennis party it strikes a nice note of romantic disruption. The plane belongs to the super-wealthy Sir Rupert Solomonson ('he was', Wells writes in what might have struck a jaunty note in 1912 but which reads heartsinkingly today, 'manifestly a Jew, a square-rigged Jew—you have remarked of course that there are square-rigged Jews, whose noses are within bounds, and fore-and-aft Jews, whose noses aren't' [*Marriage* 123]). The co-pilot is the not-wealthy but handsome R.A.G. 'Rag' Trafford, a university tutor in science specialising in crystallography. Marjorie falls in love at once and, after some plotty wheelspinning, she and Rag marry. The first-half of the novel hits the same note of happy erotic consummation with which *Ann Veronica* had closed; but in *Marriage* Wells does what he wanted to do with the earlier novel, continuing the story into an as-lengthy account of how 'Mag and Rag' fare as a married couple. Rag works, Mag keeps house and spends his money. They have four children. There are no great traumas or dramas, no infidelities or flaming rows, but as the book goes on there grows an increasing sense of dissatisfaction on both sides. Rag becomes rich thanks to a synthetic rubber he invents (signing an agreement with Solomonson to use the latter's wealth to develop the idea). But Marjorie has bigger plans for him. She wants him to be a great scientist and use that position to go into politics, seeing herself as a great society hostess with the ear of statesmen and eminences. Her insistence that he has 'a sort of power' and 'could make things noble' provokes Rag to throw in his towel: "'I can't go on with my researches," he explained. "I'm sick of this life, Marjorie. I don't want to buy things. I'm sick of buying. I'm at an end. I'm clean at an end"' [*Marriage*, 420–21].

Rag resolves to travel to Labrador. 'He wanted, he felt, to go away alone and face God, and clear things up in his mind' [388]. Persuaded at the last minute by his mother, he takes Marjorie with him, and the two hike off together into the Canadian wilderness. They live alone and talk a great deal. On a hunting trip Rag falls into a rocky crag, breaking his leg. Though he urges Marjorie to leave him, take their supplies and go home, she manages to retrieve him. She lugs him for 3 days on a makeshift sled through the frozen landscape back to their hut where she nurses him back to health. They discuss metaphysics ('we ought to partake of immortality,' Rag argues: 'I mean we're like the little elements in a magnet; ought not to lie higgledy-piggledy, ought to point the same way, be polarized' [479]); and Marjorie comes to a conclusion about her own gender responsibility:

My dear, I've been a fool, selfish, ill-trained and greedy. We've both been floundering about, but I've been the mischief of it. Yes, I've been the trouble. What are we women—half savages, half pets, unemployed things of greed and desire—and suddenly we want all the rights and respect of souls! … A woman has to be steadier than a man and more self-sacrificing than a man, because when she plunges she does more harm than a man. We can't *do* things. [*Marriage*, 488–89]

Mag and Rag resolve return to England, Rag declaring he will give up his research in order to write a book called *From Realism to Reality*, 'a huge criticism and cleaning up of the existing methods of formulation, as a preliminary to the wider and freer discussion of those religious and social issues our generation still shrinks from' [501]. This final portion of the novel and its explicit turn to the classic Sublime (as landscape, but also as a kind of activated theology, a religious kenosis: 'if God chooses to be silent—you must pray to the silence' says Trafford. 'If he chooses to live in darkness, you must pray to the night' [511]) stands in strange relation to the book's first two-thirds, which are pointedly, even over-determinedly, domestic and bourgeois. But *strange* is not dispraise in a properly constituted critical lexicon and, its various sexisms aside, that strangeness parses intriguing novelty out of the traditional lineaments of the novel.

There is a similar deliberate ungainliness in the larger structural form of Wells's next novel, *The Passionate Friends* (1913), a more directly political and polemical work. It's a novel that falls into three discrete storytelling phases, starting as an aristocratic love triangle, digressing from the rather mannered melodrama of this into a much more expansive novel about a tour of India, China and America as a vehicle for the protagonist's awakening political and spiritual consciousness, before, finally, reverting to the original love-story for its tragic denouement.

The Passionate Friends is the life story of Stephen Stratton, from a respectable though not wealthy background (his father is rector of Burnmore). As a child his playmate is Lady Mary Christian, the daughter of local aristocrats and as teenagers these two fall in love. When he turns 19 Stephen proposes marriage, but Lady Mary rejects him. Despite (she says) loving him, she won't marry him for three reasons. Firstly what they have together is too special to be sullied by the material day-to-day of married life; secondly she doesn't want to 'belong' to any man, since she is determined to 'belong to herself' ('"Why should one have to tie oneself always to one other human being?" she asked. "Why must it be like that?"' [*Passionate Friends*, 4:5]) and finally, this last point notwithstanding, she is going to marry somebody else: a wealthy financier called Justin. Her rationale for this last decision is that Justin has lots of money, where Stephen has very little and that she doesn't want to live 'in some dreadful place ... no money ... worried and desperate. One gets ill in such places'. She also reports that Justin has agreed not to trespass on Mary's resolution to 'own herself', even agreeing not to press himself on her, sexually: '"But," I choked. "You! He! He will make love to you, Mary. You will bear him children!" "No. He promises. Stephen,—I am to own myself."' [4, 5] Since Mary later has two daughters with Justin, that is a resolution that manifestly didn't survive contact with reality.

Stephen is heartbroken and takes himself off to South Africa and (it being 1899) the Second Boer War. He proves a naturally gifted officer and distinguishes himself in the fighting. Returning to England he discovers his father has unexpectedly inherited a fortune, freeing him up from the need to get a job. He meets up again with Lady Mary Justin and the two of them become lovers, although this consummation doesn't make him particularly happy. 'From the day', he says,

> that passion carried us and we became in the narrower sense of the word lovers I do not think that we even had the real happiness and beauty and delight of one another. Because, I tell you, there is no light upon kiss or embrace that is not done with pride. I do not know why it should be so, but people of our race and quality are a little ashamed of mere gratification in love. [*Passionate Friends*, 6:9]

His feelings of shabbiness are intensified by the fact that he had, before this secret affair with Mary began, been courting a virtuous young woman called

Rachel More and that she had fallen in love with him. Mary's husband Justin discovers the affair. To public avoid scandal Stephen agrees never to meet with Mary again and promises to leave England altogether for a period of 3 years.

That's the end of the first movement of the novel. Chapter Seven (of twelve) is called 'Beginning Again': Stephen travels and his old Imperialist beliefs crumple under the shock of what he sees. The tenor of the novel shifts too, broadening from its claustrophobic focus on a small group of upper-class English folk into something altogether more panoramic:

> Before my eyes again as I sit here, the great space before the Jumna Musjid at Delhi reappears, as I saw it in the evening stillness against a glowing sky of gold, and the memory of countless worshippers within, praying with a devotion no European displays. And then comes a memory of that long reef of staircases and temples and buildings, the ghats of Benares, in the blazing morning sun, swarming with a vast multitude of multicolored people and the water also swarming with brown bodies.... The sun sinks in the skies of India, the Jumna Musjid flushes again with the glow of sunset, the smoke of evening fires streams heavenward against its subtle lines, and upon those steps at Benares that come down the hillside between the conquering mosque of Aurangzeb and the shining mirror of the Ganges a thousand silent seated figures fall into meditation. [*Passionate Friends*, 8:1]

The mass poverty he encounters convinces him that 'civilization has never yet existed, it has only continually and obstinately attempted to be. Our Civilization is but the indistinct twilight before the dawn.' Stephen travels to China and walks 'the Bruges-like emptinesses of Pekin', where 'the vast pretensions of its Forbidden City' strike him as 'like a cry, long sustained, that at last dies away in a wail' [8:3]. The result of all this is that Stephen dedicates himself to the intrinsically Wellsian project of a utopian World State: 'a new world-city, a new greater State above your legal States, in which all human life becomes a splendid enterprise, free and beautiful'. Stephen concludes his world tour with a trip to America where he makes friends with a US millionaire called Gidding, who shares his beliefs and ambitions: '"Say, Stratton," he said, after a conversation that had seemed to me half fantasy; "Let's *do* it!"' [8:10]—the 'it' in question being: laying the foundations for the coming World State. The two of them set up an international publishing house, 'Alphabet and Mollentrave', employing multiple teams of experts to translate the classics of world literature and science into all the major world languages and making the results cheaply available across the globe. This is one of the most interesting and prescient elements of this novel, I think: 'a huge international organ of information, and of a kind of gigantic modern Bible of world literature' [10:1] anticipating our very own, much later, Wikipedia/Google Books revolution in knowledge. It's in this novel that Wells first uses the phrase that was to become one of his slogans: a call for an 'open conspiracy against potentates and prejudices and all the separating powers of darkness' [9:10].

As this second movement in the story comes to a close, Stephen has put his life in order. He marries Rachel, confessing to her his previous affair with Lady Mary but assuring her all that is behind him now. They start a family (the overall conceit of the novel is that Stephen is addressing the whole narrative to his son for him to read when he comes of age) and slowly builds a reputation as a campaigner for global justice and the amelioration of the human condition. He pushes ahead with the publishing, gets invited to address peace conferences and becomes an important public figure.

All this sets up the final portion of the story. Taking a break from the exhausting whirl of work, Stephen goes on a brief walking holiday in the Alps, *solus*. At a hotel on Engstlen Lake and quite by chance, he meets Mary again. They have promised not to see one another, but since they still love one another they spend the day together. They do not have sex, but the meeting has disastrous consequences nonetheless. Word gets back to London and Mary's husband, the haughty and imperious Justin, announces he will divorce her, with Stephen to be named as co-respondent. Stephen hopes to avert this scandal but his solicitor reveals that Lady Mary deliberately swapped rooms with her own maid in order to occupy the adjacent room to Stephen's: "'You were sleeping with your two heads within a yard of one another anyhow,'" the lawyer notes. "'Thirty-six you had, and she had thirty-seven.' He turned over a paper on his desk. "You didn't know, of course," he said. "But what I want to have"—and his voice grew wrathful—"is *sure evidence* that you didn't know. No jury on earth is going to believe you didn't know. No jury!—Why,"—his mask dropped—"no man on earth is going to believe a yarn like that!'" [11:8].

Things are looking bad for Stephen. His wife Rachel is distraught, struggling and failing to believe Stephen's insistence that he did not have sex with Lady Mary. Stephen himself knows the coming court case will drag down his public reputation and so destroy the good he can accomplish with Alphabet and Mollentrave. But Justin is implacable. So is set-up the novel's *Tale of Two Cities*-style final twist. Lady Mary visits Stephen at his London house one last time, telling him that she has made a deal with her husband: he will not go ahead with the divorce and in return she will agree to be sequestered in some secret fastness, 'a lonely place, my dear—among mountains. High and away. Very beautiful, but lonely' [11:10]. It occurs to Stephen during their conversation that she might be planning suicide, but the real danger of this only really dawns on him after Mary has left. He hurries round to her London house, but she has already killed herself. So Stephen's reputation and his 'great work' are saved, but at the cost of Mary's life. The novel closes with a brief twelfth chapter in which Stephen declares 'I give myself, and if I can I will give you [he's addressing his son], to the destruction of jealousy and of the forms and shelters and instruments of jealousy, both in my own self and in the thought and laws and usage of the world' [12:3].

Speaking broadly, this is a novel attempting to perform the effective transition (by 'effective' I mean: believable, compelling—but also ideologically or politically persuasive) from love as a narrowly personal to love as an effectively global phenomenon. Stephen is somebody with a great capacity for love: he loves Mary deeply and without diminution, through all the vicissitudes of their relationship, from the start to the end of the novel; but he also loves his wife Rachel and his desire to improve the world is motivated by more than just rational calculation. Wells's target in *The Passionate Friends*, 'jealousy', becomes, functionally speaking, the artificial restriction on the whole scope of love as such, the thing that stands in the way of bettering the entire world. And the focus-pull in the novel's middle sections, when Wells opens the narrative convincingly enough to a more global perspective, is a notable achievement, in a writerly technical sense.

Janice Harris may well be right that a key impetus for Wells to write *The Passionate Friends* was 'Wells's growing conception of himself as an ally of the feminists, indeed a feminist himself. Like other social activists during the decade Wells viewed woman suffrage as an obvious necessity but more important was a reconceptualization of men's and women's working, parenting, and sexual lives' [Harris, 406]. But where Wells's next novel, *The Wife of Sir Isaac Harman*, manages at least to situate its female characters in the larger flow, *The Passionate Friends* styles its women as marginal, passive and ultimately sacrificed to a larger project revealed, inadvertently, as patriarchal in both the looser and more precise senses of that word. The novel is a narrative by a father addressed to his son. The first chapters concern the narrator's relationship with his own father. His key working relationship is with his male friend, Gidding; his relationship with Mary, the love of his life, is determined by his antagonism with Mary's husband, Justin, of whom Stephen remarks 'It is a curious thing that in spite of our bitter antagonism and the savage jealousy we were to feel for one another, there has always been, and there remains now in my thought of him, a certain liking, a quality of friendliness' [*Passionate Friends*, 6:9]. The novel's final conclusion is that the only method for cutting the Gordian knot of one man's implacable threat to another man's great work is: the death of a woman they have in common. This sacrifice is needful in order to square, to 'make sense of' the conflicting demands of masculinity: to 'solve' the problem of how male desire for women comes into conflict with male duty to other men. Since the oldest of justifications for male jealousy, the exclusivity of marriage, was masculine fears over paternity it is not coincidental that Wells devotes so much of *The Passionate Friends* to issues of parenthood. *Passionate*, in the title, speaks both to the intensity of Stephen and Mary's feelings and to its fundamental *passivity*; these people are patients, not agents, in their own emotional interactions; and in the larger sense there is a deliberate sense of things happening *to* Stephen, rather than Stephen making things happen.

It leads to a degree of strain, since its claustrophobia (Wells looking back on his hopeless passion for Amber Reeves) cannot be brought into alignment with the spacious forward-looking hope for the coming World State. One symptom of this strain is a new thing in Wells's writing, indicative of a writer struggling, rather, for rhetorical effect. For often this novel's prose falls into roughly approximate blank verse. It doesn't take much to turn this passage, picked more-or-less at random:

> You see, my son, there are two sorts of love; we use one name for very different things. The love that a father bears his children, that a mother feels, that comes sometimes, a strange brightness and tenderness that is half pain, at the revelation of some touching aspect of one long known to one, at the sight of a wife bent with fatigue and unsuspicious of one's presence, at the wretchedness and perplexity of some wrong-doing brother, or at an old servant's unanticipated tears, that is love—like the love God must bear us. That is the love we must spread from those of our marrow until it reaches out to all mankind, that will some day reach out to all mankind. [*Passionate Friends*, 4:8]

into

> You see, my son, there are two sorts of love;
> We use one name for very different things:
> The love a father bears his children, that
> A mother feels, that sometimes comes, a strange
> Brightness and a tenderness half pain,
> Of revelation at some touching aspect
> At the sight of a wife bent with fatigue
> And unsuspicious of one's presence, at
> The wretchedness and the perplexity
> Of some wrong-doing brother, or perhaps
> A servant's unanticipated tears,

All that is love—like [the] love God must bear us.
That is the love that we must spread from those
Of our own marrow til it reaches out
To all mankind, that will some day reach out
To all mankind.

There's quite a lot of this in the novel and it cannot be called a good thing. Wells wrote to Henry James conceding that the book 'is *gawky*' adding 'it has been thrust into the world too soon'. Reviews, though, were respectful and sales healthy and interestingly this was the Wells novel first to be adapted for the screen—the Stoll Film Company mounted an expensive production and released *The Passionate Friends* as a movie in 1922.

Wells's next novel *The Wife of Sir Isaac Harman* (1914) carried through some of these themes. It starts with the novel's version of Wells himself, George Brumley (Wells's middle name yoked to a surname that evokes the town where he was born): a successful novelist, small, energetic, randy, 'one of those very natural-minded men with active imaginations who find women the most interesting things in a full and interesting universe' [*Isaac Harman*, 1:1]. He has been a widower for 3 years and is selling his spacious country house. One potential buyer, Mrs Ellen Harman catches his eye, since she is both very young and very beautiful. Indeed she is so young that he is astonished when he discovers she already has four children. Born Ellen Sawbridge, the daughter of a financially embarrassed middle-class mother, she was courted by the wealthy Sir Isaac Harman, who made his fortune selling sub-par loaves ('Staminal Bread') to the masses and running a chain of cheap, sub-par shops and cafés, the 'International Bread and Cake Stores'. Harman is shallow, acquisitive and gasping, the sort of man who measures his self-worth solely in terms of his possessions. He more-or-less purchases Ellen, installing her in a lavish household and fathering four children in quick succession upon her. Indeed, having so many kids so quickly damages her health: after 'tactful explanation on the part of the elderly and trustworthy family doctor' Harman is persuaded to leave his wife alone for a bit: 'there came a less reproductive phase'.

The bulk of the novel traces Lady Harman's growth from naïf and timid child-bride, living an Ibsenian Dolls-House existence, into self-assured young woman who reads suffragette literature, befriends other women, undertakes her own projects in the world and otherwise 'comes out'. She does all this in the teeth of her husband's implacable opposition. He, furious at her growing independence, leaves a copy of *The Taming of the Shrew* around the house with key passages underlined and explicitly acts the Petruchio to her Katherina—

chapter eight is actually called 'Sir Isaac as Petruchio'. He lectures her, denies her the use of the car to go out and see friends and moves her to a house in the country to keep her away from London society. But instead of taming her, Harman's behaviour only strengthens her resolve to achieve some measure of independence.

Meanwhile Brumley is falling deeper in love with Lady Harman. He tries and fails, to seduce her and resolves instead to style himself as a knight errant dedicated to rescuing her from her misery. Her denial of his sexual advances is polite but firm, determined as she is not simply to pass from one man's ownership to another. They do become friends though, meeting from time to time and exchanging letters in which Brumley says things like 'I would rather kiss the hem of your garment than be the lord of any other woman's life'. And this relationship plays its part, as does Ellen's friendship with a group of suffragette women, in bracing her in her struggle for independence. She founds a number of hostels for the underpaid and homeless waitresses at her husband's cake shops and cafés, some of whom (their wages being so meagre) are driven to prostitution to supplement their income. This angle remains underdeveloped in the novel. Wells's interest in the hostels is that they can act as a piece of plot leverage, with Sir Isaac threatening to defund them if his wife leaves him and so prolonging the conflict and therefore drama in the narrative. Sir Isaac, generally dyspeptic and nervy, falls into rages when his will is thwarted and so grows more ill. His doctor instructs him to take a rest cure on the Continent. He has forbidden his wife from seeing Brumley and in order to keep her hostels financially solvent she has agreed; but the two still correspond. Sir Isaac discovers some of these letters, has an apoplectic fit and dies.

This development frees-up our heroine. Brumley proposes marriage but she turns him down. In part this is for practical reasons: Sir Isaac, like Casaubon in *Middlemarch*, has sought to influence his wife from beyond the grave by a provision in his will that would take the hostels away from her in the event of her remarriage. But her refusal to accept Brumley's suit also reflects her determination not to be owned by another man and Brumley's anguished sense of emasculation in the face of this occupies much of the final section of the novel: 'I am to be your tormented, your emasculated lover to the very end of things,' he whines. 'Emasculated by laws I hate and customs I hate and vile foresights that I despise … I'm going to do what I can. I'm going to be as you wish me to be, to help you, to serve you. If you can't come to meet me, I'll meet you. I can't help but love you, I can't do without you' [12]. It seems they'll carry on as friends and Lady Harman will end the novel a free agent. But then, on the very last page, Wells shuffles his two characters into a fragrant hyacinth garden and closes with a big romantic embrace:

She crouched down upon him and, taking his shoulder in her hand, upset him neatly backwards, and, doing nothing by halves, kissed the astonished Mr. Brumley full upon his mouth. [*Isaac Harman*, 12]

Wells was writing *The Wife of Sir Isaac Harman* at the tail-end of his affair with Elizabeth Von Arnim (he even inserts a reference to Von Arnim's most famous book: Ellen reads *Elizabeth and Her German Garden* and 'was charmed by the book's fresh gaiety, by its gallant resolve to set off all the good things there are in this world, the sunshine and flowers and laughter, against the limitations and thwartings of life' [5:9]). Lady Harman herself, Wells later claimed, was based partly on Agnes Eleanor Williams, a suffragette who married the overbearing W.W. Jacobs (author of 'The Monkey's Paw' and other classics of macabre writing) and partly on Maud Pember Reeves, Amber's mother, who had worked her way slowly out from under the dominance of her husband, William Pember Reeves, to become 'almost before he knew what was happening' a leading suffragette:

The same way of escape was found by the wife of another tyrannous husband, Mrs W. W. Jacobs, and I made a book out of that type of reaction that I think may survive as a fragment of social history, *The Wife of Sir Isaac Harman*. [*H. G. Wells in Love*, 71]

But, despite the surname, W.W. Jacobs wasn't Jewish. And Wells's Isaac Harman is. Which brings us to the elephant in the novel's room: anti-Semitism.

We can presume that Wells decided from the get-go that he wanted to focus his novel's critique on a certain possessive, materialist, jealous and stubbornly destructively mind-set, one he identified as masculine (which is fair enough), plutocratic and—Jewish. There are anti-Semitic gestures all the way through this novel. They are rarely more than gestures, but when one's culture is steeped in anti-Semitic assumptions a gesture is enough. Here is Brumley when, beginning his pursuit of Ellen, he meets her children for the first time.

"Come and be hugged, you dears! Come and be hugged!" Before she knelt down and enveloped their shrinking little persons Mr. Brumley was able to observe that they were pretty little things, but not the beautiful children he could have imagined from Lady Harman. Peeping through their infantile delicacy, hints all too manifest of Sir Isaac's characteristically pointed nose gave Mr. Brumley a peculiar—a eugenic, qualm. [*Isaac Harman*, 3:4]

A *eugenic* qualm.

At school Sir Isaac had not been a particularly prominent figure; his disposition at cricket to block and to bowl "sneaks" and "twisters" under-arm had raised his average rather than his reputation; he had evaded fights and dramatic situations, and protected himself upon occasions of unavoidable violence by punching with his white knuckles held in a peculiar and vicious manner. He had always been a little insensitive to those graces of style, in action if not in art, which appeal so strongly to the commoner sort of English mind; he played first for safety, and that assured, for the uttermost advantage. These tendencies became more marked with maturity. When he took up tennis for his health's sake he developed at once an ungracious service that had to be killed like vermin; he developed an instinct for the deadest ball available, and his returns close up to the net were like assassinations. [*Isaac Harman*, 5:4]

This is quite nasty writing, actually: insinuatingly painting Harman as 'not one of us', not a proper gentleman, as a man naturally (we might say: racially) a sneak, a cheat and a hoarder of wealth. Even blithe young Ellen has her eugenic qualms. Here she is trying to talk herself into sticking with her marriage:

Why, after all, shouldn't she take life as she found it, that is to say, as Sir Isaac was prepared to give it to her? He wasn't really so bad, she told herself. The children—their noses were certainly a little sharp, but there might be worse children. [*Isaac Harman*, 8:5]

Noses crop up more than once:

Just how much she didn't really like her children she presently realized when in the feeble irascibility of their sickness they fell quarrelling. They became—horrid … insisted upon having every single toy they possessed brought in and put upon their beds; Florence was first disingenuous and then surrendered her loot with passionate howlings. The Teddy Bear was rescued from Baby after a violent struggle in which one furry hind leg was nearly twisted off. It jars upon the philoprogenitive sentiment of our time to tell of these things and still more to record that all four, stirred by possessive passion to the profoundest depths of their beings, betrayed to an unprecedented degree in their little sharp noses, their flushed faces, their earnest eyes, their dutiful likeness to Sir Isaac. [*Isaac Harman*, 7:3]

The implication is: Gentile women have sex with Jews, contrary to all the best eugenic ideas and the next thing the world is full of children with sharp noses 'stirred by possessive passion to the profoundest depths of their beings'.

Putting the unmistakeably Jewish name of the heroine's husband right there on the title page of the novel necessarily flags this up. Perhaps the Shakespearian prototype for Wells's novel is not *The Taming of the Shrew* so much as it is *The Merchant of Venice*—a story about how a clever woman bests a wicked Jew by taking on the habiliments of a man, which is in effect what Wells has written here.

To be clear: Wells wasn't an anti-Semite or at least adult Wells wasn't. There are, it is true, some eye-popping passages in 1934s *Experiment in Autobiography* concerning his teenage years: 'I had ideas about Aryans extraordinarily like Mr. Hitler's. The more I hear of him the more I am convinced that his mind is almost the twin of my thirteen-year-old mind in 1879; but heard through a megaphone and—implemented.' Wells goes on to reminisce in a misty-eyed manner: 'I do not know from what books I caught my first glimpse of the Great Aryan People going to and fro in the middle plains of Europe, spreading east, west, north and south … and driving the inferior breeds into the mountains.' *Inferior breeds.* What's worse is the way he concludes with what he presumably believed was mitigation: 'I thought Abraham, Isaac, Moses and David loathsome creatures … but unlike Hitler I had no feelings about the contemporary Jew.' Of course, we might say: that was 13-year-old Wells. Adult Wells had plenty of Jewish friends and repeatedly repudiated Hitlerism. But that doesn't mean he ever escaped the shaping assumptions of the immanent, low-level anti-Semitism that characterised British society at this time. This has, perhaps, something to do with his novelist's impulse not only to diagnose but to personalise and dramatise social problems. Rather than talk about money, greed, unproductive capital acquisition and plutocracy in the abstract, he liked to personify them and such personifications often took on the lineaments of racial libel—as in this novel.

This touches on a larger issue: the extent to which our broader cultural determination retains anti-Semitism as a default even in individuals who are consciously and deliberately not anti-Semitic, even sometimes in people who would consider themselves philo-Semites. Think of Proust. *À la recherche du temps perdu* is amongst other things an extraordinarily sensitive portrait of a Jew, Swann and a potent critique of the reflex anti-Semitism of France during *l'époque de l'affaire Dreyfus*. Marcel loves Swann and writes about him with deep and abiding insight and tenderness. But there are also passages in the novel like the one in *Sodome et Gomorrhe* when Marcel visits the dying Swann and is struck by how repulsively *Jewish* he looks: how 'enormous, tumid, crimson' his nose is, 'fit for a clown or an old Hebrew'. Proust's letters are full of offhand anti-Semitism, even though he was himself half-Jewish. It's complicated.

Wells never explores the Jewish Question in the profound way Proust does. Indeed his jaunty denial that there even *was* such a question is one of the more alarming aspects of his relationship to Jewry more generally. Here he is on his early journalistic days, in the 1890s and his close friendship with Walter Low, another struggling young writer. Low was Jewish, although Wells is over-keen to stress, he didn't *look* Jewish:

> Low was tall and dark, not the Jew of convention and caricature, the ambitious and not the acquisitive sort, mystical and deliberate. He had an extensive knowledge of foreign languages and contemporary literature. He knew vastly more about current political issues than I did. We argued endlessly about the Jewish question, upon which he sought continually to enlighten me. But I have always refused to be enlightened and sympathetic about the Jewish question. From my cosmopolitan standpoint it is a question that ought not to exist. [*Experiment in Autobiography*, 291]

I have always refused to be enlightened and sympathetic about the Jewish question is meant, I suppose, to be offhand and funny, a genial wave of the hand. But it strikes a genuinely catastrophic note in a book published (in 1934) only a few short years before the Final Solution to that very question was put into grisly practice.

With the last of the novels from the 'Von Arnim' years, *The Research Magnificent*, Wells returned to a manuscript he had begun and abandoned a few years earlier. He reworked and completed this as war broke out around him and as his relationship with Von Arnim was superseded by his relationship with Rebecca West (the novel wasn't finally published until 1915). *Research Magnificent* picks up both the explicit World State political polemic of *Passionate Friends* and the adulterous love-yearnings of *Isaac Harman*; and in its Amanda Benham Wells for the last time translates Amber Reeves into fiction. Although the explicit topic of this novel is the future, its approach is backward-looking. Indeed much of the point of *The Research Magnificent* is the way the future becomes become snared by the past. We follow William Porphyry Benham from childhood through adulthood to his (premature) death. Inheriting a fortune, Benham never needs to work. He attends school and university, travels the world, marries and separates from his wife and all the while he is engaged in the novel's titular 'research', which is: how to live a noble and beautiful life.

> This is the story of a man who was led into adventure by an idea. … An idea that can play so large a part in a life must necessarily have something of the compli-

cation and protean quality of life itself. It is not to be stated justly in any formula, it is not to be rendered by an epigram., essentially, Benham's idea was simple. He had an incurable, an almost innate persuasion that he had to live life nobly and thoroughly. His commoner expression for that thorough living is "the aristocratic life." But by "aristocratic" he meant something very different from the quality of a Russian prince, let us say, or an English peer. He meant an intensity, a clearness. [*Research Magnificent*, 'Prelude' 1]

Since Benham's 'research' takes him around the world the novel devolves mostly into travelogue; but although some of these sections are divertingly told—particularly an episode in which Benham and his wife Amanda ingenuously undertake a catastrophic trip through a barbaric Serbia, Montenegro and Albania—they don't add up to a novel in the fullest sense. Much of the text consists of in-text lectures and disquisitions, notionally excerpts from a book Benham was writing 'On the Aristocratic Life', unfinished at his death and being completed by Benham's author-friend White. So we get chunks of familiar Wellsian argumentation: 'preach the only possible peace, which is the peace of the world-state, the open conspiracy of all the sane men in the world against the things that break us up into wars and futilities' [4.7]; 'the Invisible King who is the lord of human destiny, the spirit of nobility, who will one day take the sceptre and rule the earth' [6.4] and

"Prejudice," Benham had written, "is that common incapacity of the human mind to understand that a difference in any respect is not a difference in all respects, reinforced and rendered malignant by an instinctive hostility to what is unlike ourselves. We exaggerate classification and then charge it with mischievous emotion by referring it to ourselves." And under this comprehensive formula he proceeded to study and attack Family Prejudice, National Prejudice, Race Prejudice, War, Class Prejudice, Professional Prejudice, Sex Prejudice, in the most industrious and elaborate manner. [*Research Magnificent*, 6.3]

The novel, though, remains a ragbag. That it's designedly a ragbag hardly redeems it as a work of fiction. It's a single-note roman-à-thèse, arguing that the world as it is presently constituted isn't ready for the sort of beautiful nobility of character and action Wells conceptualised in his *Modern Utopia* Samurai. Benham has all the qualities to make a fine Samurai, but in our world those qualities lead him to alienation, self-questioning, loneliness and eventually to death.

One thing that comes clearly through in *The Research Magnificent* is a sense of Wells chafing against the sheer bovine inertia of all those people of the world living in squalor who still, somehow, resist being redeemed into the gleaming domed cities and hygienic togas of the Wellsian World State. All the people Benham meets are passive, with the single exception of his wife Amanda, who at least has the gumption to have an affair with a less priggish, more attentive man. This universal passivity leads Benham towards the victim-blaming core ideology of fascism itself. A visit to Haiti and the ruined castle of King Henri Christophe ('this black ape of all Emperors' is Wells's appalling description of him), prompts Benham to ponder how tyrants come to power. He concludes:

> Usurpation is a crime to which men are tempted by human dirigibility. It is the orderly peoples who create tyrants, and it is not so much restraint above as stiff insubordination below that has to be taught to men. There are kings and tyrannies and imperialisms, simply because of the unkingliness of men. [*Research Magnificent*, 6.4]

Usurpation is a crime to which men are tempted by human dirigibility is a spectacularly wrongheaded assertion, on a par with *rape is a crime to which men are tempted by human pulchritude* and *arson is a crime to which men are tempted by the flammability of things*. It's that old Übermensch beer, I suppose; a heady brew, the quaffing of which (though Nietzsche is at no point mentioned in this novel) leaves a man drunk with his own sense of clarity of will and liable to blame the oppressed for their own oppression. We can do better than this. More to the point Wells could do better than this and did. And the advent of World War I shook him out of his older habits and led to him writing some of his best work.

Bibliography

Belloc, Hilaire (1906). 'The Inn of the Margeride', *Hills and the Sea*. London Methuen.

Harris, Janice (1994). 'Wifely Silence and Speech in Three Marriage Novels by H. G. Wells', *Studies in the Novel*, 26:4, pp. 404–419.

Paris, Michael (2000). *Warrior Nation: Images of War in British Popular Culture, 1850–2000*. London Reaktion.

Smith, David (1986). *H G Wells: Desperately Mortal. A Biography*. New Haven/London Yale University Press.

14

War

The World Set Free (1914); *An Englishman Looks at the World* (1914); *The War That Will End War* (1914); *The Peace of the World* (1915); *The Elements of Reconstruction* (1916); *War and the Future* (1917)

The start of World War I happened to coincide, for Wells, with a sea change in his personal life. His fame continued to grow, with reputation increasingly accruing more from his non-fiction and journalism than his fiction. Domestically speaking life with Jane continued smoothly: a base from which Wells could range, practically and erotically and a home to which he could return to play games with his two sons and organise lively parties and group-weekends. He was finally past the most intense phase of his infatuation with Amber Reeves, had enjoyed his time with Elizabeth Von Arnim and had started a relationship with Rebecca West—perhaps the most important of Wells's major affairs. War was declared in Britain at 11 pm on 4 August. Later that same day (in fact shortly after midnight), West gave birth to their son, Anthony West.

The war, of course, changed everything, but Wells was already shifting his imaginative centre of gravity. *Anticipations* (1901) had won him a reputation as a prophet of the near future and through 1913 and 1914 he increasingly came to self-identify with this future-seer sense of himself. His novel *The World Set Free* (1914)—written, of course, prior to the war—is the clearest fictional iteration of this new identity. A novel without an individual hero, this book speculates about the creation of nuclear weapons, ordnance for which Wells coined the enduring name 'atom bombs'. The novel sketches their use in 'the Last War': humanity teeters on the brink of utter destruction before managing, after millions of deaths and the annihilation of some of the world's greatest cities, to save itself. The novel ends with a new utopian world state being built on the ruins of the old. As fiction *The World Set Free* (1914) is disquisitional, mostly written in a lecturer's mode that is diversified only

© The Author(s) 2019
A. Roberts, *H G Wells*, Literary Lives, https://doi.org/10.1007/978-3-030-26421-5_14

occasionally by fictioneer's touches, vignettes of individual character disposed into brief narrative arcs. So Wells gives us Holsten (whose scientific breakthrough unleashes the new atomic energy) wandering around London and wondering what the future holds, before reverting to speculative future exposition ('the American Kemp engine, differing widely in principle but equally practicable, and the Krupp-Erlanger came hard upon the heels of this, and by the autumn of 1954 a gigantic replacement of industrial methods and machinery was in progress all about the habitable globe' and much more). There's a second inset story: Frederick Barnet, a rich kid who falls on hard times, is conscripted into the army, fights in northern Europe during the 'Last War' and fades from the novel's view as he takes up post-bellum duties in 'the army of pacification'. After an account of the war the novel moves on to a world-peace conference held in the Alps; into which Wells contrasts good King Egbert, who surrenders his power to the new World State Council, with bad King Ferdinand Charles, 'the "Slavic Fox," the King of the Balkans', who steals a number of atom bombs and tries to use them to leverage his personal power and is shot dead by the Council for his pains. Then: more exposition, describing Wells's future-state utopia. Clean new cities and infrastructure are constructed, currency value is pegged to energy production, English becomes the world language, atomic power frees humans to live as artists and gardeners. Finally storytelling and exposition come together in one last inset life-story: the brilliant, congenitally crippled Marcus Karenin, who has played a large part in reforming the world and who dies in a hospital in the Himalayas, preaching from his deathbed:

> "Man lives in the dawn for ever," said Karenin. "Life is beginning and nothing else but beginning. It begins everlastingly. Each step seems vaster than the last, and does but gather us together for the nest. This Modern State of ours, which would have been a Utopian marvel a hundred years ago, is already the commonplace of life." [*World Set Free*, 5:5]

The broad thesis of this novel is straightforward: soon we will develop weapons capable of utterly destroying civilisation and then we will either extirpate ourselves entirely or, faced with this prospect, mature as a species and put all such foolishness behind us.

Wells's reputation as prophet accrued particular kudos from this novel, something he boasted about in the preface to its 1921 reissue, listing all the things he got 'right' and conceding only that he was wrong to date the coming 'end war' to 1956 rather than 1914–18 ('as a prophet, the author must confess he has always been inclined to be rather a slow prophet'). Contemporaries concurred, as have later critics: 'all this', said *The Advocate of Peace* in their positive review, 'is a vision seen by Mr Wells, but one might imagine it to be the history which will be read a century or more hence' [*The Advocate of Peace*, 76:8 (Aug–Sept 1914), 193]. David Seed talks about the book's 'keen prophetic vision' and David C. Smith praises it for its 'prescience'. And it is true that Wells coined the phrase 'atom bomb', and in doing so named the weapon under whose shadow the second half of the twentieth century and the current portion of the twenty-first, trembles.

But actually Wells gets the central things wrong. For one, he simply misread what Frederick Soddy (the novel's dedicatee) argues in his *Interpretation of Radium* (1909). Soddy's book was Wells's direct inspiration for the novel, and Wells's misprision of it creates atomic weaponry of prodigious oddness. I don't mean to sneer, hindsight-benefitted as I am: and indeed what Wells comes up with here makes for a very striking and memorable SF conceit. But that's not to say it makes sense. His reasoning appears to have gone like this:

1. A conventional bomb explodes instantaneously;
2. But a radioactive element releases half its energy over the course of its *half-life*, which might be many weeks, months, or even years;
3. Therefore an atom bomb would explode *continuously for many weeks, months or even years*.

Of the active ingredient of his bombs, Carolinium (Wells calls this 'Carolinum') we are told that 'what chemists called its half period was seventeen days', and glosses this: 'that is to say, it poured out half of the huge store of energy in its great molecules in the space of seventeen days, the next seventeen days' emission was a half of that first period's outpouring, and so on' [2:4]. Thus his bombs explode with unprecedented force for 17 days and over the following months slowly reduce the intensity of their exploding. There's a kind of genius in the sheer *strangeness* of this conceit, although it's hardly plausible, even by 1914 standards. Wells's bombs are suitcase-sized devices, carried in the open-cockpits of planes, activated by the aviator biting off a fuse with his teeth and dropped over the side. The bombs destroy Paris, Berlin and many other cities and nearly destroy San Francisco ('the Japanese very nearly got San Francisco. The Americans ran the Japanese aeroplane down into the sea and there the bomb got busted … Submarine volcano. The steam is in sight of the Californian coast'). Paris becomes 'a zone of uproar, a zone of perpetual thunderings, lit by a strange purplish-red light, and quivering and swaying with the incessant explosion of the radio-active substance.' [4:3].

In a way a more profound than Wells's version of nuclear weaponry is the compromised social vision of the novel's prophesy. *World Set Free*, like all of

Wells's utopian writings, diagnoses the now as 'a phase of gigantic change in the contours and appearances of human life' [4:11]. He suggests that two generations are enough to separate human beings entirely from ancestral barbarism:

The Highlanders of the seventeenth century, for example, were cruel and bloodthirsty robbers, in the nineteenth their descendants were conspicuously trusty and honourable men. There was not a people in Western Europe in the early twentieth century that seemed capable of hideous massacres, and none that had not been guilty of them within the previous two centuries. [*World Set Free*, 4:11]

Once again, hindsight is easy; but, that said, there's something spectacularly misjudged about standing at the beginning of the twentieth century and declaring *there is not a people in Western Europe capable of hideous massacres now*. It hardly inspires prophetic confidence. Nor has his more fundamental prophecy, the one that structures the whole of *The World Set Free*, proved correct—that once humankind develops weapons with the power literally to destroy the planet, the old ways of global belligerence will be discarded, the weapons unmade and a new utopia of social justice and peace erected in its place. In fact what happened was: humankind, having developed weapons with the power literally to destroy the planet, not only kept them but proliferated them to many different countries and otherwise carried on pretty much as before. Alas.

The true significance of *World Set Free* is not in its hit-and-miss prophesying, but the way it marks a major change in Wells's own broader worldview. Reading those scientists who were, in the early century, investigating radioactivity—'such scientific men as Ramsay, Rutherford, and Soddy'—cured Wells of his attachment to entropy. It's true that this had always been as much an aesthetic as an intellectual attachment; but the general sense that the cosmos was rapidly winding-down, that decay and cosmic death was relatively imminent, was overturned by this new science. 'The world', Soddy argued, 'is no longer slowly dying from exhaustion, but bears within its own means of regeneration so that it may continue to exist in the same physical condition as at present for thousands of millions of years.'

The revelations of radioactivity have removed the physical difficulties connected with the sufficiency of the supply of natural energy, which previously had been supposed to limit the duration of man's existence on this planet. [Soddy, 240–41]

This new 'Radioactivity Wells' is, in crucial ways, a different sort of writer to the older 'Entropy Wells': less imaginatively pessimistic, more spaciously open-ended. It's an important rubicon in his intellectual life and therefore in his career as a writer. It is, perhaps, ironic that the future was opening-up imaginatively for Wells just as the world descended into its most destructive war to date.

During the war Wells's reputation as a journalist and pundit continued to grow and he relied increasingly on the large fees he could command for such work. He was so prolific in this mode that the majority of his newspaper and magazine pieces have never been reprinted. Some were, though: *An Englishman Looks at the World* (1914) is a very varied compendium of Wells's 1909–14 journalism, from Blériot's crossing of the channel and Wells's first experiences in an aeroplane, through pieces on labour unrest, modern warfare to essays on 'The Contemporary Novel' and 'The Possible Collapse Of Civilisation'. Wells comes out against military conscription, opines on the limitations of parliamentary democracy and denies that sociology is a science (since 'counting, classification, measurement, the whole fabric of mathematics, is subjective and deceitful, and that the uniqueness of individuals is the objective truth' [*Englishman*, 14]). The volume also reverts several times to Wells's idea (previously fictionalised as Remington's 'big idea' in *The New Machiavelli*) of 'the Endowment of Motherhood', with Wells mocking the Fabians for not endorsing this notion and praising Teddy Roosevelt for supporting it. It is an idea that combines a more-or-less Feminist commitment to giving women financial security and freedom with an at-root eugenicist agenda that is unavoidably racist. 'The birth-rate, and particularly the good-class birth-rate, falls steadily below the needs of our future' Wells warns [17], where 'good-class' is code for 'white, middle-class, able-bodied'. He admonishes his readership that 'every civilised community' (every white community, that presumably means) 'is drifting towards "race-suicide"'. Speeches alone are not enough: 'I doubt if all the eloquence of Mr. Roosevelt and its myriad echoes has added a thousand babies to the eugenic wealth of the English-speaking world.' So, yes: it's the eve of World War I and—*eugenic wealth*—Wells is still banging on about eugenics:

> The modern State has got to pay for its children if it really wants them—and more particularly it has to pay for the children of good homes. The alternative to that is racial replacement and social decay. That is the essential idea conveyed by this phrase, the Endowment of Motherhood. [*Englishman*, 17]

Here's the very last paragraph in the collection:

> And this Man, this wonderful child of old earth, who is ourselves in the measure of our hearts and minds, does but begin his adventure now. Through all time

henceforth he does but begin his adventure. This planet and its subjugation is but the dawn of his existence. In a little while he will reach out to the other planets, and take that greater fire, the sun, into his service. He will bring his solvent intelligence to bear upon the riddles of his individual interaction, transmute jealousy and every passion, control his own increase, select and breed for his embodiment a continually finer and stronger and wiser race ... Sometimes in the dark sleepless solitudes of night, one ceases to be so-and-so, one ceases to bear a proper name, forgets one's quarrels and vanities, knowing oneself for Man on his planet, flying swiftly to unmeasured destinies through the starry stillnesses of space. [*Englishman*, 26]

Those starry stillnesses are undeniably sublime, but 'mankind must control his own increase, select and breed for his embodiment a continually finer and stronger and wiser race' could hardly be a harder-core eugenicist expression.

Journalism became a central part of Wells's reputation and celebrity during the war years. 'His fame', notes David Smith 'was such that his name sold copies of newspapers and pamphlets', and he took advantage of that fact. The briefest itinerary of his 1914–18 is exhausting to contemplate:

He wrote a half-dozen novels, published four of five collections of his newspaper pieces, which appeared in great numbers. He held a government position for a time, as well as taking a leading part both in the efforts of the British Science Guild to revise the school curriculum and in the various attempts he hoped would bring about a form of the League of Nations. [Smith, 218]

There were also many pamphlets: *The War and Socialism* (1914), which sold for a penny, made the case that winning the war could only be made possible by the reorganisation of the country along socialist lines. The same year saw *The War That Will End War* (1914) compiled out of eleven newspaper and magazine articles and an object lesson in what happens to hostages-to-fortune under the logic of posterity. Wells is certain that Germany will lose and soon—that within 'two or three months' the entire edifice of 'German Imperialism will be shattered'; that 'Prussianism took its mortal wound at the first onset before the trenches of Liège'; that 'the German repulse at Liège was but the beginning of a German disaster as great as that of France in 1871'; that

if you want to see where diplomacy and Weltpolitik have landed Europe after forty years of anxiety and armament, you must go and look into the ditches of Liège. These bloody heaps are the mere first samples of the harvest. [*War That Will End War*, 6]

PUNCH, OR THE LONDON CHARIVARI.—August 12, 1914.

NO THOROUGHFARE

BRAVO, BELGIUM!

Fig. 14.1 Cartoon from *Punch*, 12 August 1914, celebrating Belgian defiance

Wells was not alone in thinking that the defence of Liège, which Germany attacked on 5 August, constituted a war-ending repulse to the Germans. Here's a contemporaneous Punch cartoon (Fig. 14.1):

In fact Liège fell relatively quickly, on 16 August 1914 and the defence it mounted barely delayed the German advance (it also cost some 20,000 Belgian lives, as against 5000 German casualties). So the gate in that cartoon very speedily had the 'No' before its 'Thoroughfare' erased.

Since Wells is certain the Germans are in the process of being defeated, *The War That Will End War* gives a lot of time to the question of how to order the post-war world, proposing inter alia a complete redrawing the map of Europe ('I suggest that France must recover Lorraine, and that Luxemburg must be linked in closer union with Belgium … the break-up of the Austrian Empire has hung over Europe like a curse for forty years. Let us break it up now and have done with it' and so on, for many pages), though he concedes his complete lack of expertise on the matter—'I am a fairly ignorant person and I admit a certain sense of presumptuous absurdity as I sit here before the map of Europe like a carver before a duck.' More worryingly still, the book contains a deal of raw, anti-Semitic blather:

> In the South and East [of the Russian empire] are certain provinces thick with Jews, whom Russia can neither contrive to tolerate nor assimilate, who have no comprehensible projects for the help or reorganisation of the country, and who deafen all the rest of Europe with their bitter, unhelpful tale of grievances, so that it is difficult to realise how local and partial are their wrongs. [*War That Will End War*, 1]

'Thick with Jews' is an especially unpleasant piece of phraseology. Wells is fully aware of the series of anti-Jewish pogroms conducted in Russia between 1881 and the years in which he was writing; but he insists that Jewish prominence 'in the English and still more in the American Press' has had the effect of 'distort[ing] the issue of this', an argument with some very alarming implications indeed. He also engages, once again in victim-blaming: 'the Jews by their particularism invite the resentment of all uncultivated humanity.' Wells asserts the need for Propaganda:

> By means of a propaganda of books, newspaper articles, leaflets, tracts in English, French, German, Dutch, Swedish, Norwegian, Italian, Chinese and Japanese we have to spread this idea, repeat this idea, and impose upon this war the idea that this war must end war. [*War That Will End War*, 8]

This passage comes near the end of the book and contains the main text's only iteration of the titular slogan.

Which brings us *to* that slogan. I'd say that there are four phrases in particular, out of all the many phrases and ideas Wells coined, that have enjoyed the most widespread and enduring afterlife: *time machine*, *League of Nations*, *atom bomb* and *the war to end war*. This latter has a particular pungency, since it went in short order from being a genuine rallying cry to an ironic and bitter reflection on a conflict that killed 17 million, maimed 20 million more and ruined a continent without resulting in any kind of larger benefit for humankind. The surprise is that anybody ever believed it. 'The War That Will End War' is, we can be honest, a blankly self-contradicting phrase. One might as well call a book *The Cholera Bacillus That Will End Dysentery* or *Fucking for Virginity*.

By mid-1915 it was clear that Wells's optimistic predictions of a swift end to the war had been premature. Wells, forced to rethink his position, came more forcefully to believe in the need for a World State as the only permanent solution to the conflict. His article in the *Daily Chronicle*, 'Looking Ahead: After a Year of War' (3 August 1915) insisted that England was 'sweeter spirited and harder working' than it had been at the start of the war. Wells praised what he called the 'democratic army' fighting in France and looked forward hopefully to a 'less submissive' population after the war. His pamphlet *The Peace of the World* (1915) put some flesh on the bones of this possible future with proposals to 'root-out' of the war impulse on a human level. Here Wells is hopeful: 'the people who actually want war', he says, 'are perhaps never at any time very numerous. Most people sometimes want war, and a few people always want war. It is these last who are, so to speak, the living nucleus of the war creature that we want to destroy' [18]. There follows an astute analysis of belligerence as such:

> These war lovers are creatures of a simpler constitution. And they seem capable of an ampler hate. You will discover, if you talk to them skilfully, that they hold that war "ennobles", and that when they say ennobles they mean that it is destructive to the ten thousand things in life that they do not enjoy or understand or tolerate, things that fill them therefore with envy and perplexity—such things as pleasure, beauty, delicacy, leisure. In the cant of modern talk you will find them call everything that is not crude and forcible in life "degenerate." [*Peace of the World*, 19]

But just when you think Wells has said something genuinely penetrating he says something patently ridiculous, as with his claim that 'militarism' is found not amongst professional soldiers, but is rather a feature of 'men overmuch in studies and universities', who

> get ill in their livers and sluggish in their circulations, they suffer from shyness, from a persuasion of excessive and neglected merit, old maid's melancholy, and a detestation of all the levities of life. And their suffering finds this vent in savage thoughts.

—a claim surely untrue, and certainly unevidenced. Wells goes on:

> A vigorous daily bath, mixed society, a complete stoppage of beer, spirits and tobacco, and two hours of hockey in the afternoon would probably make decently tolerant men of all these fermenting professorial militarists. Such a regimen would probably have saved the world from the vituperation of the Hebrew prophets—those models for infinite mischief. [*Peace of the World*, 21]

You'd like to assume a thinker who'd manoeuvred himself into arguing that the Books of Samuel and Joshua are as warlike as they are because their authors didn't bathe enough and didn't play enough hockey would stop, take a step back and have a bit of rethink.

The two pillars of Wells's proposed post-war settlement are 'a World Council organization' and 'propaganda' [37] to inoculate humanity against militarism. Together these will ensure the one thing he considers essential: not disarmament but rather the nationalisation of arms manufacture. 'It is not being suggested that the making of arms should cease in the world, but only that in every country it should become a state monopoly.'

In fact the war went some way towards calcifying certain habits of Wells's thought. Take, for example, *The Elements of Reconstruction* (1916), initially published as by 'D.P.'—short for 'Dominating Personality'. That pseudonym was intended as a piece of whimsy between Wells and his friend Lord Northcliffe. Through 1915 and 1916 Wells and Northcliffe would meet for occasional lunches, during which Northcliffe, acting as Lloyd George's director of propaganda, liked to sound-out Wells to discover what people 'outside the Establishment' were thinking and gauge levels of national negativity towards the war effort. Wells, a man who lacked neither opinions nor the vehemence to express them, argued forcefully that various changes were needful and Northcliffe persuaded him to write his thoughts up as a series of articles for one of this papers, the *Times*. Wells agreed on condition of anonymity—hence 'D.P.'—because he wanted the liberty to express himself without the constraint of his considerable public profile. Since one of the things these articles do is, effectively, to repudiate Socialism, it's conceivable he may also have wanted to protect himself from backlash. Many of friends were still loyal to the movement, after all. At any rate, the articles created considerable buzz, word got out as to their authorship and Wells acknowledged them as his in the volume in which they were collected.

The book argues that Germany had proved better at capitalising on scientific ideas (the example Wells gives is the production of dyes) because it was organised along more centralised and efficient lines. Accordingly Wells proposes a more comprehensive nationalisation: 'replanning of scientific education and research, concurrently with, and as a part of, a systematic amalgamation and co-ordination of industries' [1]. This, however, is not Socialism:

> It is probable that historians will mark the year 1914 as the end of the Socialist movement; it was an ailing movement before that time, and after the war we shall find new oppositions and new formulae replacing the obsolete '-isms' of

the former age. This is not to say that Socialism will be counted to have failed. No movement can be said to have failed which has sat so triumphantly on the grave of its antagonists as Socialism has sat upon the grave of laissez faire. But the movement combined general ideas of the utmost sanity with methods of utter impracticability, and, while the sounder elements of the Socialistic proposal have so passed into the general consciousness as to be no longer distinctive, its rejected factors shrivel and perish as things completely judged, and its name becomes a shelter for 'rebels' and faddists. [*Elements of Reconstruction*, 2]

According to Wells, 'the deadest part of Socialism now is all that centred about the idea of "expropriation".' There will be none of that in his to-be-Reconstructed future: landowners and capitalists, farmers and factory owners can all keep their property, although the Government will buy all their produce from them and distribute it to the population: 'Syndication Without Confiscation' is Wells's slogan here. Other proposals include: an altogether more thorough and focused scientific education will become the norm, the electoral system will change to proportional representation the better to reflect the will of the people and a global Peace League and 'Imperial Parliament' will unify and grow Britain's Empire. There's also a rather wearying amount of detail on tariffs, voting systems and a proposed world court system.

The Elements of Reconstruction is indicative of the stresses that were pulling early twentieth-century Socialism in two different directions. On the one hand there is the line of descent that leads to the present-day democratic socialist movement like the UK Labour Party: a majority genealogy, adapting the Marxian demand for revolution into a democratic ameliorist political programme working to close the gap between rich and poor, building a welfare state and addressing systematic modes of oppression like sexism and racism. But there is another line of descent, comprising those socialists who veered rightward, embracing a tribal nationalism, authoritarianism, the cult of the leader, Imperialism and militarism and in so doing morphed into the fascist movements of the 1930s and 1940s. Oswald Mosley was a committed Fabian in the 1920s and was a minister in Ramsay McDonald's Labour Government before leaving to form his own 'New Party', and thence to the foundation of the British Union of Fascists in 1932. Mussolini was a member of the *Partito Socialista Italiano* for several years, before they kicked him out in 1914 for his repudiation of egalitarianism and his support for the war. He went on to establish the *Partito Nazionale Fascista* in 1921 and we all know what happened after that.

We need to be careful, here. There exists a crudely polemical line of ideological argument, particularly popular in some quarters of the present-day

USA—advanced for instance by Jonah Goldberg's thinly researched and tendentious *Liberal Fascism* (2008)—that socialism and fascism are interchangeable terms. They're not. Claiming they are is a tactic to demonise soft-left politics, to bracket the Democrats with the Nazi party and position the Republican right as the only torchbearer for liberty. There is a real issue, though, in amongst the ideological misdirection. Various fascist parties and groups undeniably started life as socialist parties or groups. It was H.G. Wells himself who coined the phrase 'liberal fascism' in 1932 (though he meant something very different by 'liberal' to Goldberg and his allies). The relevant question for any biography of the man, of course, is how far Wells travelled along this Mosleyan path. And the answer is: not very far. But it's hard to shake the sense, reading *The Elements of Reconstruction*, that the atmosphere of wartime ruthlessness was moving him in that direction. One salient is Empire. Although he doesn't say it in so many words, he was evidently tempted to consider the British Empire (which still at this time covered a third of the globe) as a halfway house to his wished-for World State. So he considers 'the loyalty of our workers under the test of war' to be 'the most hopeful augury for the future of the Empire' [3], hopes that 'Empire is to wax and not wane in the new era' [3], spelling out specific stepping stones to help that happen: 'an Imperial Council' leading to 'an Imperial Parliament' and a widespread programme of high-level education across all British colonial holdings. It's an aspect of Wellsian thought that has been little studied, although one exception is the work of Duncan Bell, who convincingly demonstrates the extent to which, rather than being an anti-imperialist, Wells (especially after World War I) actually wanted to substitute 'inter-imperialism' for 'national-imperialism', conceiving the latter in a noticeably Anglophilic manner. 'Wells insisted that a world state was the only way to bring peace and justice to the world' says Bell, adding that 'despite his firm commitment to universalism, he never lost his admiration for the English-speaking peoples. Throughout his interwar writings, he assigned them a starring role in his assorted projects for world transformation' [Bell, 878].

Wells's public celebrity continued in the ascendant as the war proceeded. In 1916 he was officially invited to tour the Western Front, which journey he wrote up in *War and the Future* (1917). That he was invited at all and given more-or-less unrestricted access to the allied military enterprise including front line trenches, is a mark of his importance as a public figure. He even felt confident enough to ignore government attempts to censor his criticisms of the war's prosecution. Wells told his publisher the white lie (if the potential commission of high treason can be considered a white lie) that the work had been officially approved for publication when it hadn't at all.

The advantage of this freedom is that the book stands today as one of the most vivid first-hand accounts of World War I not written by a serving soldier; full of compelling detail and vivid observations about places and people. Wells is particularly good on the ruined landscapes of the Western front. At Fricourt he's shown round a captured German trench: 'like the work of some horrible badger'. At Dompierre 'the German trenches skirted the cemetery, and they turned the dead out of their vaults and made lurking places of the tombs' ('Dureresque', Wells calls this). He concludes: 'this war is, indeed, a troglodytic propaganda' [3.1]. There are many lovely little turns of phrase: the way 'a weary man is doing the toilet of a machine gun' [3.3]; how, after loading a shell in a big gun, the breech 'closes like a safe door' [4.3]. His account of the situation at Arras has a wonderful Absurdist quality to it: 'the British hold the town, the Germans hold a northern suburb; at one point near the river the trenches are just four metres apart.' 'This state of tension', Wells notes, 'has lasted for long months':

> There is no advantage in an assault; across that narrow interval we should only get into trenches that might be costly or impossible to hold, and so it would be for the Germans on our side. But there is a kind of etiquette observed; loud vulgar talking on either side of the four-metre gap leads at once to bomb throwing. And meanwhile on both sides guns of various calibre keep up an intermittent fire, the German guns register—I think that is the right term—on the cross of Arras cathedral, the British guns search lovingly for the German batteries. As one walks about the silent streets one hears, "Bang—Pheeee—woooo" and then far away "dump." One of ours. Then presently back comes "Pheeee—woooo—Bang!" One of theirs. Amidst these pleasantries, the life of the town goes on. [*War and the Future*, 3.2]

Wells praises the development of the tank, diffidently proud that his story 'The Land Ironclads' (*The Strand Magazine* 1903) had been the direct inspiration to the British government to put money into research and development of this weapon of war: 'they were my grandchildren—I felt a little like King Lear when first I read about them' [3.5]. His descriptions nail the early models' *jolie laide* quality: 'never has any such thing so completely masked its wickedness under an appearance of genial silliness. The five or six I was shown wandering, rooting and climbing over obstacles were as amusing and disarming as a litter of lively young pigs.'

> They are like jokes by Heath Robinson. One forgets that these things have already saved the lives of many hundreds of our soldiers and smashed and defeated thousands of Germans. Said one soldier to me: "In the old attacks you

used to see the British dead lying outside the machine-gun emplacements like birds outside a butt with a good shot inside. Now, these things walk through." [*War and the Future*, 3.5]

He is wise enough not to be distracted by this side of things, though. Most people, Wells, argues, don't think through what the war means, because they are 'swamped by the spectacular side of the business' ('it was very largely my fear of being so swamped myself that made me reluctant to go as a spectator to the front,' he says. 'I knew that my chances of being hit by a bullet were infinitesimal, but I was extremely afraid of being hit by some too vivid impression'). Wells thinks the *real* war is a war of ideas and those ideas are about the future organisation of humankind.

Bibliography

Bell, Duncan (2018). 'Founding the World State: H. G. Wells on Empire and the English-Speaking Peoples', *International Studies Quarterly*. 62:4, 1 December 2018, 867–879.

Soddy, Raymond (1909). *The Interpretation of Radium*. London: John Murray.

Smith, David (1986). *H G Wells: Desperately Mortal*. Yale University Press.

15

Boon and *Bealby*

Boon (1915); *Bealby: A Holiday* (1915)

As a reaction to the war's ongoing grimness, Wells published a couple of comic novels in 1915. The first of these, *Boon*, is known today, if it is known at all, as the book that broke the friendship between Wells and Henry James. Its full title—*Boon, The Mind of the Race, The Wild Asses of the Devil, and The Last Trump; Being a First Selection from the Literary Remains of George Boon, Appropriate to the Times*—identifies the book as being by 'Reginald Bliss', Wells supposedly contributing only an introduction. That Wells wrote the whole lot was pretty much an open secret at the time. James certainly knew and that caused him genuine pain, because the novel contains a sustained and wittily heartless attack upon him. Not to put too fine a point on it Wells eviscerates James in this novel, notwithstanding that the two of them had been friends for decades. Reading James, says Wells, is like watching 'a leviathan retrieving pebbles'; James himself (not, of course, a slim man) is: 'a magnificent but painful hippopotamus resolved at any cost, even at the cost of its dignity, upon picking up a pea which has got into a corner of its den'. The typical Jamesian novel is:

> like a church lit but without a congregation to distract you, with every light and line focused on the high altar. And on the altar, very reverently placed, intensely there, is a dead kitten, an egg-shell, a bit of string… [*Boon*, 4.3]

Just to be sure his target wouldn't miss this attack, Wells left a copy of the novel at James's London club for him to pick up when he was next in town: an act either of deliberate malice, of remarkable thoughtlessness or perhaps of something else.

© The Author(s) 2019
A. Roberts, *H G Wells*, Literary Lives, https://doi.org/10.1007/978-3-030-26421-5_15

At any event, James was deeply hurt and wrote Wells a letter full of wounded dignity: '*Boon* has naturally not filled me with fond elation. It is difficult of course for a writer to put himself fully in the place of another writer who finds him extraordinarily futile.' Wells replied in jocular mode: the novel was 'just a waste-paper basket. Some of it was written before I left my house at Sandgate [in 1909], and it was while I was turning over some old papers that I came upon it, found it expressive and went on with it.' James, unimpressed, wrote back, framing what has become one of his most famous aesthetic assertions:

> Your comparison of the novel to a waste paper basket strikes me as the reverse of felicitous, for what one throws into that receptacle is exactly what one *doesn't* commit to publicity and make the affirmation of one's contemporaries by … It is art that *makes* life, makes interest, makes importance, for our consideration and application of these things, and I know of no substitute whatever for the force and beauty of its process.

Wells's reply to this was chillier: 'when you say "it is art that *makes* life, makes interest, makes importance," I can only read sense into it by assuming that you are using "art" for every conscious human activity. I use the word for a conscious attainment that is technical and special.' And that marked the end of the correspondence and of the James–Wells friendship.

The falling-out has, I think, a greater than merely personal significance. It is symptomatic of two models of what 'the Novel' ought to be doing, battle-lines drawn over the very meaning of Literature in the Modern Age. Simon James has written a good assessment of this, which I'm not inhibited from quoting at length:

> Darko Suvin declares the contest [between Wells and James] 'a draw', but in subsequent versions of specifically literary history, James had tended to have the ascendancy (aided, in no small part, by Wells's undeniable personal insensitiv-ity). Even *Time Magazine*, when putting Wells on its cover in 1926, titled the text that followed 'All Brains, Little Heart', ruling that 'in *Boon*, his wicked attack on Henry James, he may have been assaulting in James what was missing in himself: infinite care and moral responsibility'. James was a theorist crucial both to the New Criticism in the United States and to F R Leavis and *Scrutiny* in the United Kingdom … As university departments of English Literature began to be founded in the 1920s and 30s, James's concern with significant form and moral seriousness exerted a profound influence over the formation of the academic canons of judgement and value, to the detriment of the side of the argument that Wells, still alive was happy to continue, in the *Autobiography* and elsewhere. In the 1920s Wells wrote a caption for a National Gallery Portrait

postcard of James which in draft form reminded that 'he ventured upon the stage and was routed by the gallery'; Wells own copy of this note contains the handwritten addition, 'Keep this, to recall the crime.' As late as 1943, in answer to a letter from Herbert Read, Wells asserted that, 'believe me, Henry James deserved it.' [James (2012), 28–29]

'James deserved it' is an unfeeling and indeed rather cryptic thing to say, and I'll come back to it.

If it's hard for a modern reader to get a handle on *Boon*, that's in part because it is an explicit re-jigging or a modern version, of a book that was once very famous and is now entirely forgotten: William Mallock's *The New Republic* (1877). Wells's alter ego, Boon, organises a 'conference' or literary party in a villa by the sea, inspired by Mallock's book, which itself concerns a literary party in a villa by the sea:

> "Now picture to yourself the immediate setting of my conference. Just hand me that book"
>
> It was Mallock's *New Republic*. He took it, turned a page or so, stuck a finger in it, and resumed … "It's an astonishing thing. Do you know the date of the *New Republic*? The book's nearly forty years old! And since that time there's been nothing like a systematic stocktaking of the English-speaking mind. And I propose a Summer Congress, which is to go into the state of the republic of letters thoroughly."

A venue for the congress is located and rented:

> THIS CLASSICAL VILLA
> with magnificent gardens in the Victorian-Italian style …
> to be
> LET OR SOLD.
> Apply to the owner,
> Mr. W. H. MALLOCK,
> original author of
> "The New Republic."
> Key within.

This novel actually rents the space of another novel in which to erect its text. The party is joined by Edmund Gosse and George Moore, by 'emissaries of Lord Northcliffe and Mr. Hearst, by Mr. Henry James, by Mr. W. B. Yeats, late but keen'. From here we're into Chap. 4, 'Of Art, Of Literature, Of Mr Henry James', which contains several merciless pastiches of the Jamesian manner, with James speaking 'as an indefatigable steam-tug might labour end-lessly against a rolling sea':

> "Owing it as we do," he said, "very, very largely to our friend Gosse, to that peculiar, that honest but restless and, as it were, at times almost malignantly ambitious organizing energy of our friend, I cannot altogether—altogether, even if in any case I should have taken so extreme, so devastatingly isolating a step as, to put it violently, *stand out*; yet I must confess to a considerable anxiety, a kind of distress, an apprehension, the terror, so to speak, of the kerbstone, at all this stream of intellectual trafficking, of going to and fro, in a superb and towering manner enough no doubt, but still essentially going to and fro rather than in any of the completed senses of the word *getting there* ..." [*Boon*, 4.2]

—as well as the cruelly witty description of James as the hippo trying to pick up a pea, quoted earlier.

The book does other things than just attack James. It also surveys the wider literary scene, with little puffs and barbs for and against Shaw, Conrad, Rebecca West, American literature, journalist E B Osborn and various others. Schopenhauer gets discussed at length, as does Houston Stewart Chamberlain, the latter's proto-Nazi Aryan theorising being solidly mocked ('it isn't any sort of truth, it is just a loud lie' [7:2]). And there are some interesting metafic-tional touches: "'All through this book, *Boon*," [Wilkins] began. "What book?" asked Dodd. "This one we are in. All through this book you keep on at the idea of the Mind of the Race....'" [7:1]. That said, it is the Jamesian attack that most stands out.

The book ends with two excerpts, supposedly from Boon's oeuvre. One is 'The Wild Asses of the Devil', in which an author extremely like Wells befriends an old tramp, who turns out to be an actual devil, sent into the world to retrieve 'the asses of Hell' when they happened to escape. The asses transmogrified into human form and, unable to discern them amongst the rest of humanity, the devil has given up. Wells rouses him to go out and give it another go, since these asses 'will do no end of mischief', but the tale ends inconclusively. Finally there's the story of 'The Last Trump', in which the titu-lar magical trumpet is found in a junk shop in Caledonian market and blown by old Briggs to see what would happen. What happens is that the world ends, God and his angels descend; but only a few people even notice and these witnesses are easily dismissed, ridiculed and explained away: 'Men will go on in their own ways', Wells concludes, 'though one rose from the dead to tell them that the Kingdom of Heaven was at hand, though the Kingdom itself and all its glory became visible, blinding their eyes.'

In one sense *Boon* represents Wells trying a new strategy for putting over his familiar agenda: the future of the race, the World State. Much of the book is about helping 'the Mind of the Race' refine itself and facilitate the coming World State. He'd tried this as utopian fiction, as SFnal extrapolation, as preachy interjections into his straight fiction and of course as non-fiction. Here he sees if the material goes over as satiric comedy. It must be said: it doesn't, really. There is too great a mismatch between advocacy and satire. The latter destructively attacks specific targets; the former needs to make a positive, *constructive* case for its imagined future, often in general terms. And though some of the figures targeted in this book figure as examples of what needs to be swept out of the way before the new future can be instantiated, Henry James really doesn't. In what ways exactly, we wonder, does it impede the development of the Mind of the Race if Jamesian prose is a little on the prolix side? The answer, of course, is: it has no bearing at all. Which in turn makes us wonder why Wells gives over so much of *Boon* to roasting his old friend.

As noted above, the elderly Wells later declared: 'believe me, Henry James deserved it.' In what way might he have deserved it? In his account of the affair, Anthony West sides, as we might expect, with his father: James had 'patronised' Wells 'relentlessly' and 'in the most offensive possible way'; 'the older man had written to my father too many times to shower him with oily praise as a preliminary to telling him that his latest book had proved, yet again, that he didn't begin to know what he was doing.' West thinks a letter from James dismissing *The Passionate Friends* ('I find myself absolutely unable [to consider it] in any aesthetic or literary relation at all') and an article James published in the *Times Literary Supplement* criticising various younger writers, Wells included, were the final straws. 'The more my father thought of them, the more intolerable James's papal pretensions seemed to him. The old fat cat could not rest content with his absolute freedom to do his own precious thing—he had to foreclose on all other forms of the novel' [West, 43–44] According to West, Wells was not only entitled to kick back, doing so was profoundly therapeutic for him: 'my father felt that a great load had been lifted from his spirit. His block had been blown away, like a cork from a champagne bottle, and a new novel—*Mr Britling Sees It Through*—was soon absorbing his energies.' There may be some truth in this, partisan though it obviously is. It would certainly explain why the attack on James occupies so disproportionate amount of *Boon*. But there's a tone in West's account of James ('the old fat cat') that chimes with Wells's own mockery and reminds us or ought to, how easily straight men can slip into unconsidered homophobia.

In *Boon*, George Boon, is planning 'rather in the manner of Henry James' a book to be called *The Spoils of Mr. Blandish*, whose protagonist would have no adventures but instead visit places 'consciously taking delicate impressions' of them 'upon the refined wax of his being' [4:4]. The stress is on the passivity as well as the feline decadence and triviality of James's work—on, not to be too over-obvious, the ways in which it is coded as feminine. *Boon* is illustrated throughout with Wells's 'picshuas' and here's the one of Mr Blandish, which is to say, of James himself. Remember that James was by 1915 an elderly and corpulent man, self-conscious about his physical appearance, very sensitive to slight both in terms of his own hyper-refined sensibility and also as (to use today's anachronistic but pertinent terminology) a closeted gay man in a homophobic world. And here's Wells's pained-looking, feminine-lipped, pig-trottered, mincing fatty (Fig. 15.1):

Wells had known James intimately for many years. It's inconceivable he didn't know about James's sexual orientation. And whilst Wells devoted much of his energy to the project of making the world a sexually freer and less repressed place, he is oddly silent on the topic of homosexuality in his writing. It simply doesn't come up in books like *A Modern Utopia*; none of the novels

Fig. 15.1 Wells's 'picshua' of Henry James

contain obviously gay characters; he doesn't address the topic in his journalism. In truth, Wells's view of sex was more than usually egoist. He was a highly sexed individual who projected his own sense of erotic energy outwards, thereby rationalising it back to himself via a basically procreative metanarrative: we must breed the best to enhance the race. This really leaves no room in his model for gay desire. Of course it is true that he had many gay friends (James among them) and there's nothing in his writing we can read as directly homophobic; but that's not to say that he was wholly comfortable with homosexuality. So, for instance, he often teased his friend A.L. Rowse about his gayness (with a nice cattiness, Rowse wrote a marginalium in a biography of Wells he owned, recently sold at auction: 'He was kind enough to send me his books inscribed. I sold them': Peschel, 1). The question is how far *Boon*'s mockery of James is just a rather cruel fun and how far it is the expression of a buried sexual hostility. The novel *might* stand merely as a puckish satire of contemporary literary mores. If it has lost much of its sting, that's because its targets are no longer current (James, ironically enough, aside). But that's not the whole picture here.

In part this because of how much *Boon* owes to its template. As satire, Mallock's *New Republic* has various targets. A main one is Benjamin Jowett who, as Mallock saw it, was dangerously trivialising Christianity by meddling with ecumenicism. But one of its barbs hit home in unexpected ways and that was its attack on Walter Pater ('Mr Rose' in Mallock's book) for being what everybody knew him to be: gay. In Mallock's account Mr Rose is a poseur, an effeminate aesthete whose adoration for Greek literature and culture is only a fig-leaf for his homosexual appetites:

"What but for history should we know," cried Mr. Rose, "of the Χάρις of Greece, of the lust of Rome, of the strange secrets of the Borgias? … Think of the immortal dramas which history sets before us:—Harmodius and Aristogeiton, Achilles and Patroclus, David and Jonathan, our English Edward and the fair Piers Gaveston, ἅμα τ' ὠκύμορος καὶ ὀϊζυρὸς περὶ πάντων, or, above all, those two by the *agnus castus* and the plane-tree where Ilyssus flowed,"—Mr. Rose's voice gradually subsided,—"and where the Attic grasshoppers chirped in shrill summer choir." [Mallock, 3:19]

Χάρις ('grace') is used in the sense that Plato specifies, as that mutual, reciprocal gratification that can only occur between lovers who are equal—as, Plato argues, men and men may be, but men and women cannot. It is, in other words, code, much as talking about 'Greek love' is code (the other bit of Greek quoted is Thetis to her son Achilles in *Iliad* 1:417, 'but now you are doomed to a quick death, weighted with sorrows above all men': Achilles, like Gaveston, is a man as beautiful as he was doomed). There's plenty more like this in Mallock's book and it torpedoed Pater's real-life reputation: put paid, for instance, to his hopes of winning the Oxford Professorship of Poetry. Indeed, Linda Dowling notes that the appearance of Mr Rose came to dominate the way the *New Republic* as a whole was read:

> Mallock's portrait of Mr Rose was to have several unintended consequences of the greatest significance for late-Victorian culture, not the least of which would be its contribution to the constitution of homosexuality as a positive social identity in Oxford and beyond. For with the *reductio ad absurdum* embodied in his portrait of Mr Rose Mallock would implicitly accept the basic premise from which Pater has begun, "that male love has the capacity to initiate powerful cultural change"—and the very brilliance of his satire would unwittingly serve to drive the premise home. [Dowling, 89]

Rehabilitating homosexuality was certainly not Mallock's intention, of course. The point, though, is the ways Wells's *Boon* picks up this tonal agenda of homophobic mockery.

For example: Reginald Bliss, going through Boon's remains, is disappointed to find only the odds-and-ends that constitute the book we are reading. The only thing not in fragmentary form, we're told, is 'a series of sketches of Lord Rosebery, for the most part in a toga and a wreath, engaged in a lettered retirement at his villa at Epsom, and labelled "Patrician Dignity, the Last Phase"—sketches I suppress as of no present interest' [*Boon*, 1:2]. Indeed, Rosebery, the former Prime Minister, crops up several times in the book. Why? Because of the rumours that Rosebery was gay (toga, wreath, decadent 'last phase': you get the drill.) The Marquis of Queensbury—he of Oscar Wilde trial infamy—had pursued Rosebery all the way to Germany with the intention of horse-whipping him for sleeping with his (Queensbury's) son. Edmund Backhouse and George Ives claimed to have had sex with Rosebery and many people, from contemporaries such as Frank Harris to modern-day writers like Neil McKenna, have been sure of his homosexuality.

Consider, too, 'The Wild Asses of the Devil'. What's going on in this strange little fable? Ass means donkey and also means stupid person and the ostensible moral of the story is that Hell has unleashed not malign focused wickedness but a kind of plague of idiocy upon our world. But ass also means arse. (It's a mistake to think the former uniquely US and the latter uniquely UK usage: as the OED makes clear, 'contrary to the widespread belief of [ass] being a euphemism [for arse], it arose as a pronunciation spelling still used in the UK, Australia, New Zealand, etc. that shows the loss of -r- before s increasingly common in all words since the 18th century in both England and its colonies.') The devil Wells's narrator encounters has been working in our world as a seaman. Asked why he hasn't tracked any of the wild asses down, he complains that they look just like regular people; and this leads into the following little exchange:

> "So far as I can see," he said, "they might all be Wild Asses. I tried it once——"
> "Tried what?"
> "The formula. You know."
> "Yes?"
> "On a man named Sir Edward Carson."
> "Well?"
> "Ugh!" said the devil.
> "Punishment?"
> "Don't speak of it. He was just a professional lawyer-politician … How was I to know? …" [*Boon*, 8:5]

To be clear, the notion here is: a sailor has approached Sir Edward Carson and propositioned him as a closet 'wild ass' and in outraged reply Carson has used his legal and political powers to punish the sailor severely. Carson, of course, was the barrister who acted in the trial and therefore the downfall, of Oscar Wilde. Look again at the title of this odd little story. Does it need spelling out? *Wilde. Arses.* Nor does the jocular tone of all this defang its homophobic bite. A certain proportion of the population, though they look just like 'ordinary' human beings, are actually manifestations of a demonic, hellish, impulse, at once bestial and rather absurd? It is hardly a subtle allegory.

This takes us back to the central chapters of the novel, with their portrait of James. What is it that Wells finds so ludicrous and unusual about James, that he also finds threatening enough to merit so elaborate and public a rebuke? 'Believe me, Henry James deserved it.' James joins the party and contributes to the discussion, but is evidently out of place. He falls in with the Irish novelist, George Moore and the two of them go off together. Was George Moore gay? He boasted elaborately of his sexual conquests of women, but he also slept with many men. Moore's biographer Adrian Frazier concludes that he was 'a homosexual man who loved to make love to women' [Frazier, 12]. At any rate, in *Boon* Moore and James hit it off (they weren't even acquaintances in real life). Here they are, walking across the garden together, talking simultaneously, James prolixing on about the symposium, Moore describing an attractively grubby, naked urchin he had spotted in France: 'little exquisite shoulders without a touch of colour and with just that suggestion of rare old ivory'

> With a common impulse the two gentlemen turned back towards the house. Mr. James was the first to break the momentary silence. "And so, my dear Moore, and so—to put it shortly—without any sort of positive engagement or entanglement or pledge or pressure—I *came*." [*Boon*, 4:2. emphasis in original]

Wells adds in a picshua of the odd couple, subtitled: 'Mr. James converses with Mr. George Moore upon matters of vital importance to both of them'. That this 'matter of vital importance to both of them' is never explicitly spelled out in *Boon* is part of the satire on the nebulous emptiness of the Jamesian manner. But on the other hand, it could be a matter the obliquity of which is determined not by literary affectation but by the hefty structures of social disapproval and judicial punishment, the same ones that were brought to bear in the ruining of Oscar Wilde: after seeing an attractive boy 'he *came*'.

I don't want to be too heavy-handed, here. And I'm certainly not suggesting *Boon* is an example of out-and-out queer-bashing. But I do find myself wondering if there is a sniggering, hetero-boys-altogether web of insinuation running through the whole exercise. Art is delight, but Wells thinks it needs to be *more* than delightful: that it needs, in some sense, to be *productive*. James thinks the delight is an end in itself and indeed that it upends the conventional wisdom about the priority of the lived and the aesthetic: 'it is art that makes life, makes interest, makes importance.' Maybe they're not just arguing about art—or perhaps it would be better to say, maybe they're arguing about a wider remit of delight than just the textual. For Wells sex is a pleasure but also a productive engagement with the world, filling it up with new life (with, in point of fact, the eugenically best new life, all the better to bring about the World State). He certainly fathered a good brood of kids himself. Who knows how James personally experienced sex; his writing certainly has eloquent things to say about physical desire and more to the point precisely about such desire as an end in itself, not as the means to a further, worldly end.

Putting it like that will perhaps bring to mind the big debates in Queer Theory from the 1980s to the present. So, for example, a book like Lee Edelman's influential *No Future* (Duke University Press 2004) is a boldly polemical attempt to reclaim ethical as well as aesthetic value in the very specifically childless pleasures of non-future-oriented sex. Read through this kind of a lens Wells's stiff reply—'when you say "it is art that *makes* life" I can only read sense into it by assuming that you are using "art" for every conscious human activity'—looks merely point-missing or perhaps actively disingenuous.

Of course James is talking about more than just the technical business of con-structing a novel when he insists that art makes life. Presumably Wells knew it, too; he'd certainly had enough conversations with James over the years about art, life and everything else. Of course for James aesthetic pleasure is a much wider category than just books and paintings; and of course he thinks aesthetic beauty and aesthetic delight inform life—manners, sex, every-thing—in the fullest sense. The best case I can make, then, is that Wells artic-ulates a sort of refined homophobia in *Boon*: not crude revulsion at gay sex as such, so much as a notionally more considered judgement that gay sex is a dead end, a no-future childless abdication of collection racial responsibility. Perhaps it's in this light that Wells's mockery of the Jamesian aesthetic is best read: not that it is prolixly vapid or empty, but rather that it is a sort of sym-bolic repudiation of fertility, a tacit celebration of Edelman's 'No Future'. That's why it gets described as an 'Altar of the Dead' [4.3], as 'an elaborate, copious emptiness', a 'desert' populated by 'eviscerated people'. It's death in the long-term sense that interested Wells, but which didn't interest James in the least.

If *Boon* is one sort of humorous book, Wells's other 1915 title *Bealby* is quite another. It has something in common with the comic novels of the early Wodehouse—not that Wells is quite capable of Wodehouse's stylistic sublim-ity, comedy-wise: but *Bealby* is certainly a pleasant and amusing read. Its vari-ous comic set-pieces are set in and around a stately home called Shonts, populated by engagingly eccentric set of characters. The title character, Arthur Bealby, is a 13-year-old boy below stairs at Shonts, being raised by his mother, who works in the kitchens. As the novel opens it is deemed time for young Bealby to start working on his own account as a steward's boy. He finds the labour onerous and decides he won't do it. '"Mother," he said, "I'm not going to be a steward's boy at the house anyhow, not if you tell me to, not till you're blue in the face. So that's all about it."' He is marched before the under-butler, Mr. Mergleson ('he was an ample man with a large nose, a vast under lip and mutton-chop side whiskers. His voice would have suited a succulent parrot') who proposes handling the lad's rebellion in the following manner: 'Just smack 'is 'ed. Smack it rather 'ard.' Bealby runs off and so begins his 'holiday'. Meanwhile, Shonts is hosting a weekend party for the great and the good. One of the guests is no less a luminary than the Lord Chancellor of Great Britain, Lord Moggeridge, an individual of austere gruffness, who gets into mildly comic scrapes during his search for a nightcap of whisky. Another guest is the airman Captain Douglas: 'very fair young man … when he was not blushing too brightly he was rather good-looking' [2:3]. To his immense embarrassment, Douglas get unjustly blamed for the Lord Chancellor's whisky misadventure when the real culprit is young Bealby:

> In one hand [Moggeridge] held a cut glass decanter of whisky. In the other a capacious tumbler. Under his arm, with that confidence in the unlimited porta-tive power of his arm that nothing could shake, he had tucked the syphon. His soul rested upon the edge of tranquillity like a bird that has escaped the fowler. … Then something struck him from behind and impelled him forward a couple of paces. He dropped the glass in a hasty attempt to save the syphon.
>   "What in the name of Heavens?" he cried, and found himself alone.
>   "Captain Douglas!" … it seemed to Lord Moggeridge, staggering over his broken glass and circling about defensively, that this fearful indignity could come only from Captain Douglas. [*Bealby*, 2:4]

There is a comical interlude on a golf course and another with a deeply disreputable and dirty old tramp who recruits Bealby to burglary. Wherever he goes Bealby leaves a trail of inadvert destruction behind him. Finally Bealby is apprehended by Douglas, who thinks the lad can exonerate him in the eye of the Lord Chancellor. With some difficulty Douglas arranges an interview with the Lord Chancellor in London, but through a series of mis-understandings this only confirms Moggeridge in his certainty that Douglas was to blame. Humiliated, Douglas leaves in a huff. Young Bealby is delivered back to Shonts where he promises his mother he is willing to "ave another go' at a life of domestic service. And that's where the novel ends.

The whole light-hearted exercise represents a particular sort of fantasy: a fantasy of escape as temporariness. Bealby doesn't manage what Mr Polly does—to get clean away. Indeed, the fort-da there-and-back-again structure of the book is saying something rather different about escape as fantasy than is that earlier (much superior) novel. Like Wodehouse's Blandings, Shonts figures microcosmically, but there's a more pointedly familial or, indeed, oedi-pal drama underlying the escape and return. Bealby leaves his mother for, first, three young women one of whom, Madeleine Philips, is Douglas's mis-tress and upon whom Bealby develops a crush. He then gets to know the father figure of Douglas, who is his competitor for the affections of Madelaine. This little oedipal conflict is styled as playful and it is amusingly written. But ultimately Bealby returns to his mother. Wells, perhaps, was looking for some-thing more than fame and more than sex; the uncertainties of the war years were motivating him into his search for a more fully maternal comfort. He was not destined to find it.

Bibliography

Dowling, Linda (2014). *Hellenism and Homosexuality in Victorian Oxford*. Cornell University Press.

Frazier, Adrian (2000). *George Moore 1852–1933*. Yale University Press.

Funnell, Warwick and Michele Chwastiak (2015). *Accounting at War: The Politics of Military Finance* London. Routledge.

James, Simon (2012). Maps of Utopia: H. G. Wells, Modernity and the End of Culture. Oxford University Press.

Mallock, William Hurrell (1877). *The New Republic; or, Culture, Faith, and Philosophy in an English Country House*. London: Chatto and Windus.

Peschel, Bill (2012). 'The "Tremendous Disliker": A L Rowse'. http://planetpeschel. com/2012/03/the-tremendous-disliker-a-l-rowse/.

West, Anthony (1984). *H G Wells: Aspects of a Life*. London: Hutchinson.

16

Rebecca West
The Secret Places of the Heart (1922)

Wells's affair with Rebecca West, which lasted with ups and downs through the war and into the early 1920s, was perhaps the most important of his life. Upon their first meeting in 1912 Wells was immediately drawn to her. She was exactly what attracted him in a woman: young (19 to his 46) and beautiful, intelligent and outspoken, passionate about the two things that mattered most to Wells—writing and socialism. The attraction appears to have been mutual: Wells was charming, engaged and attentive and not his physical smallness nor his advanced age nor his unpulchritude diminished West's desire. She was a woman who put little store by conventional handsomeness and preferred small men to large—when a journalist came to interview her in later life she met him at the door with a disappointed: 'oh you're *tall*. Small men are so *energetic*' [Clapp, 23]. Not that she was starry-eyed or illusioned about Wells. In 1923, soon after the relationship ended, West wrote a fictionalised version of their affair called *Sunflower* (she elected not to publish this novel during her lifetime; it appeared posthumously in 1986). Even making allowances for the inevitable hostility of any post-break-up reaction, *Sunflower* paints a deeply unflattering portrait of Wells as a lover: she doesn't spare his squeaky voice, his nagging and wheedling manner, his proneness to what we would nowadays call 'mansplaining', his tendency to criticise West in public and to shout at her in private—sometimes, she says, his behaviour 'was so awful that it was raised to a kind of remoteness, like some calamity read of in the newspapers'. At the same time the novel captures something of the sheer forceful vitality of Wells's manner and how beguiling West found this atavistic urgency: 'The first men in the world must have looked like him … For hunting and snaring it would be better if they were little' [West 1986, 123].

© The Author(s) 2019
A. Roberts, *H G Wells*, Literary Lives, https://doi.org/10.1007/978-3-030-26421-5_16

West attempted, in the first instance, to seduce Wells; but he was still engaged in his extramarital relationship with Elizabeth von Arnim and discouraged her—she wrote to him matter-of-factly that this rejection had prompted her to not one but two suicide attempts, although neither seems to have been wholly serious. But the latency period did not last long. By late 1913 they were lovers. The atavistic or bestial element in their mutual attraction informed their pet names for one another: not just in bed but in general conversation and their letters she was 'Panther', he 'Jaguar'. Wells later recalled that the previously virginal West became pregnant on only their second encounter, at Wells's flat in St James's Court: 'it was entirely unpremeditated. Nothing of the sort was in our intention. She wanted to write. It should not have happened and since I was the experienced person, the blame is wholly mine' [*H. G. Wells in Love*, 96]. This pregnancy resulted in the birth of a boy, on 4 August 1914: Anthony West.

Rebecca West was socially adventurous from a young age, manifesting a curious mix of self-assertion, sexual adventurousness and a kind of craving for the stability represented by an older, male partner. These things are not so self-contradictory as they might first appear. Born Cicely Isabel Fairfield in 1892, she grew up with two older sisters and an emotionally frangible mother mostly in Edinburgh—her charismatic father abandoned the family in straitened circumstances and died (alone in a Liverpool boarding-house) when Rebecca was 10. Mrs Fairfield was a talented musician and art and politics were freely discussed in the household, but the strain of being a single parent broke her health both physically and mentally. Though still a teenager Cicely struck out on her own, working in London as a typist and training as an actor. It was from the stage that she took her pseudonym 'Rebecca West', after the emancipated heroine of Ibsen's *Rosmersholm*. Unable to make a go of her theatrical career she took up writing: journalism and reviews for suffragette magazines like *The Freewoman* and other literary criticism—her book-length study of *Henry James* (1916) is still worth reading today as a critical engagement with that novelist. Soon she was also publishing fiction: a novella called 'Indissoluble Matrimony' appeared in the short-lived Vorticist literary magazine *Blast* in 1914 and her first novel *The Return of the Soldier* was published in 1916. Elizabeth Von Arnim had been a commercially successful if rather shallow writer and Amber Reeves had published several novels—*The Reward of Virtue* (1911) is an interesting if uneven fictionalisation of the boredom of married life. But, with West, Wells was the first time involved with a fellow-writer of a calibre close (some critics would insist: superior) to his own. It has taken criticism a while to come to it, but the consensus is now that West is a major twentieth-century writer.

Wells and West's relationship was, as the cliché has it, stormy. Rows alternated with interludes of furious sexual passion. 'We never achieved any adjustment of any sort,' Wells later recalled. 'We came to like each other extremely and to be extremely exasperated with each other and antagonistic.' Wells rented a house in which she and baby Anthony could live in remote Hunstanton in Norfolk, but West was not a natural homemaker. West pressured Wells to divorce Jane and marry her, but he refused, telling her: 'you could never be a wife. You want a wife yourself—you want sanity and care and courage and patience behind you just as much as I do.' When she baited him with 'you've never taken care of me' he retorted, 'nor you of me' [*H. G. Wells in Love*, 99]. This imbalance was aesthetic as well as emotional. West consulted Wells over her writing, but their approaches to their respective arts were incommensurable. She was an intuitive and organic writer, he a much more structured and methodical one. 'She writes like a loom producing her broad rich fabric with hardly a thought of how it will make up into a shape,' is how he later described her creative praxis, consciously or otherwise positioning her as homebound Penelope awaiting the return of her roving lover. 'I,' he added, 'write to cover a frame of ideas.'

I pestered her for three years, "Construct! Construct!"—until she turned on me fiercely and called me a "nagging school-master" [*H. G. Wells in Love*, 102]

The Return of the Soldier is certainly a very unWellsian novel. Jenny, the narrator, nurses an unspoken love for her cousin, handsome, wealthy, honourable Chris Baldry, the soldier of the novel's title. Chris, however, is married to the beautiful Kitty and Jenny helps Kitty keep house in a luxurious Harrow domicile whilst Chris is away fighting at the Western Front. We learn one more important datum: that Kitty and Chris's infant son died, aged "two years earlier. The lad's nursery has been left just as it was. The two women are trapped by their passivity: there is nothing to do but brush one another's hair and wait for Chris to return from the war. Into this airless world comes the lower-middle-class Margaret Grey, née Allington. 15 years earlier she and Chris had had a summer romance, although they have since lost touch with one another. Margaret, now married, has become 'a drab middle-aged woman': her hands are 'seamed' and 'red', her face is 'plain', 'there was something about her of the wholesome, endearing heaviness of the ox or the trusted big dog', 'repulsively furred with neglect and poverty' [West *Return of the Soldier*, 41].

Margaret comes to visit Jenny and Kitty because Chris has written her a letter from France. Concussed by a shell explosion and invalided home, he has lost all memory of his preceding 15 years and thinks himself a young man still

engaged in his affair with Margaret. He understands that he has lost his memory and that Kitty is now his wife; but he does not recognise her. Chris is
living now in his memories of the summer of love her shared with younger
Margaret on 'Monkey Island' on the Thames at Bray.

These three women, all in various ways in love with Chris, recruit a psychiatrist, Dr Gilbert Anderson, to cure him—a quasi-Wells, this character: 'a
little man with winking blue eyes, a flushed and crumpled forehead, a little
gray moustache that gave him the profile of an amiable cat' who is nonetheless
'at once more comical and more suggestive of power than any other doctor I
had ever seen' [West *Return of the Soldier*, 150]. Dr Anderson insists that
Chris must be shocked out of his amnesia by confronting him with the traumatic proof of his infant son Oliver's death. Jenny shows Margaret Oliver's
carefully maintained nursery and we learn that Margaret's own child died
around the same time. Margaret then takes Chris outside where, as Jenny and
Kitty watch through a window, he accepts the truth that his son is dead. Jenny
recognises that Chris is cured when his posture shifts: he comes back up
towards the house 'not loose-limbed like a boy, as he had done that very afternoon, but with the soldier's hard tread upon the heel ... "He's cured!" [Kitty]
whispered slowly. "He's cured!"' Jenny is both gladdened and heartbroken by
this, since she knows it means 'he would go back to that flooded trench in
Flanders, under that sky more full of flying death than clouds, to that
No-Man's-Land where bullets fall like rain on the rotting faces of the dead'.
The double-meaning of the novel's title comes into focus at its end: the soldier
returns from the front and Chris returns from his amnesiac fugue. The first is
a return from war to peace; the second a return from (phantasmic) childhood
to (real) adulthood.

Gordon N. Ray proposes a straightforward biographical reading of *The
Return of the Soldier*: Kitty is West's version of Jane Wells, 'that false goddess,
the Virgin Mother, the nonsexual woman to whom she as the sexual woman
was being sacrificed. She felt that Wells, all unknowingly, was being split and
destroyed by his divided allegiance to two women and two families'—that is
to Jane Wells and her two sons on the one hand and to Rebecca West and her
one on the other [Ray, 86]. In this reading, the story loses specific contact
with the war and the decision taken by its two main female characters 'that
Chris must be cured' becomes a West's resolution about Wells's infantile personality or adolescent attachment to sex as such or perhaps says something
about his writing. Ray scrupulously adds a footnote to his account which he
records Rebecca West herself, whom he interviewed to write his book, pooh-
poohing his theorising:

I should note that Dame Rebecca explicitly disavows [this] interpretation of her novel. She wrote to me on 14 July 1971: ... 'Kitty is not at all my idea of Jane, who was remarkably pretty even in to her middle years, but she was much more of the Establishment. Jane had no look of accustomed luxury, though she had another kind of charm, and she had also a look of determination which was amusing on someone who was so faint in colour and so immobile.' [Ray, 201–02]

Still, something of the emotional cat's-cradle of loving a man who will not disentangle himself from a third party is captured in *The Return of the Soldier*'s richly worked prose.

Wells and West maintained their fiery relationship for almost a decade. 'There was much heat and bad blood between us,' Wells later conceded, since 'we are both impulsive and vividly expressive', but also there was 'a strong strand of personal attachment'. Asked by Ludovic Kennedy, in a BBC television interview broadcast in 1976, about her initial thoughts about Wells, West said: 'I thought he pretended to be a feminist and really wasn't.' An astute judgement. In later life West tended to be either evasive or dismissive of the importance of Wells in her life, but her relationship with her only child, Anthony West, was always fraught. In the words of Lynette Felber:

In Anthony's youth, Rebecca and H.G. quarrelled about Anthony's care and education, but increasingly as their son grew up the argument was displaced into a struggle between Rebecca and Anthony over possession of truth in the form of the authoritative version of Anthony's childhood and upbringing. Rebecca struggled not only against Anthony's charges, but also against those of a society which would accept neither an illegitimate child nor a working mother, concerned with her own needs. In 1961, she bitterly wrote Anthony (now nearly fifty years old): "You have one grievance against me, and one only: that I did not have an abortion and kill you. You can't be so hopelessly stupid that you think that I would have chosen to have an illegitimate child. I had a love-affair with H.G., and I loved him then as I was always to love him, on the understanding that he would not give me a child." [Felber, 40–41]

Wells did not write fictional versions of West with the same assiduous persistence that he wrote fictional versions of Amber Reeves or (later) Odette Keun, but some versions of her do appear in his novels. She comes occasionally into his non-fiction too. 'The War and Women', published in the non-fiction *What Is Coming? A Forecast of Things After the War* (1916) contrasts traditional women 'who wanted to be treated primarily as women' and the unconventional new women types 'irritated and bored by being treated primarily as women':

Compare, say, the dark coquettings of Miss Elizabeth Robins' *Woman's Secret* with the virile common sense of that most brilliant young writer, Miss Rebecca West, in her bitter onslaught on feminine limitations in the opening chapters of *The World's Worse Failure*. The former ... is someone peeping from behind a curtain and inviting men in provocative tones to come and play catch in a darkened harem. The latter is like some gallant soldier cursing his silly accoutrements. [*What Is Coming?*, 171]

But the fact remains that West did not colonise Wells's creative imagination the way some of his other lovers did. He was unfaithful to his wife with West, but he was not faithfully unfaithful with her, since he took various other lovers as well. He had grown much more adept at simply integrating the inconveniences of extramarital sex into his life without disturbing his domestic comfort.

This is exemplified by a novel Wells published soon after the end of the war, *The Secret Places of the Heart* (1922). This novel's protagonist, Sir Richmond Hardy, on the edge of a nervous breakdown, is married to the watery Lady Hardy, to whom he has not been faithful. He comes, with some reluctance, to the offices of a Harley Street doctor, Dr Martineau. 'Face the accepted facts,' admonishes the doctor:

A man's body, his bodily powers, are just the body and powers of an ape, a little improved, a little adapted to novel needs. Can his mind and will be anything better? For a few generations, a few hundreds at most, knowledge and wide thought have flared out on the darknesses of life.... But the substance of man is ape still. He may carry a light in his brain, but his instincts move in the darkness. Out of that darkness he draws his motives. [*Secret Places*, 1.4]

The two men agree to take a 3-week holiday together to get to the bottom of Sir Richmond's problems. They drive first to Maidenhead whilst Hardy talks the doctor through his *vie sexuelle*: his first erotic attachment as a boy to 'Britannia as depicted by Tenniel in the cartoons in *Punch*' [4.2] and to a young girl in a bathing costume seen on the beach at Dymchurch one day and never seen since ('my first human love. And I love that girl still. I doubt sometimes whether I have ever loved anyone else'). Lady Hardy is 'a wonderfully intelligent and understanding woman' who 'has made a home for me—a delightful home ... I owe my home and all the comfort and dignity of my life to her ability'; they have three children and Hardy has built a glittering career. But he has not known sexual satisfaction: 'all the time, I've been—about women—like a thirsty beast looking for water ... I was unfaithful to my wife within four years of my marriage.' Since then he has been a philanderer: 'all the time, hidden away from the public eye, my life has been laced by the thread of these—what can one call them?—love adventures' [4.3]. The rest of the novel is Hardy trying to work out why he is like this.

It's Wells, of course: wife Jane the expert homemaker, Wells himself off philandering like a thirsty beast looking for water. Hardy's specific troubles are connected to the fact that a breach has occurred between him and his current mistress, the novel's Rebecca West, with whom he has a son. This individual is a cartoonist for the newspapers, her art 'a peculiar sort of humorous illustrations' of 'considerable genius' [5.2] who works under the name Martin Leeds (the novel doesn't disclose her actual name). As with Wells and West, Hardy and 'Martin Leeds' are in the grip of mutual sexual fascination despite the fact that 'they jarred upon and annoyed each other extremely' [5.3]. Motoring to Avebury and then Stonehenge, Hardy has a holiday romance with a young American tourist, 'V.V.' Grammont—a character based on the birth-control activist Margaret Sanger, with whom, in real life, Wells had an affair in the summer of 1920—but this is short-lived. Hardy decides that, after all, he really does love Martin Leeds and wants to return to his affair with her. Back in London Hardy discovers a new vigour.

Then, abruptly, Wells kills Hardy off, of pneumonia. His widow thanks Doctor Martineau for the trip the two men had taken ('"That holiday did him a world of good," she said. "He came back to his work like a giant"' [9.1]). The novel's final scene involves Martin Leeds outing herself to Hardy's widow as her late husband's mistress and asking permission to see his body one last time. Lady Hardy permits this: and Leeds, accompanied by Dr Martineau, is let into the drawing room where the coffin is.

> "But all my days now I shall mourn for him and long for him…."
> She turned back to the coffin. Suddenly she lost every vestige of self-control. She sank down on her knees beside the trestle. "Why have you left me!" she cried.
> "Oh! Speak to me, my darling! Speak to me, I tell you! Speak to me!"
> It was a storm of passion, monstrously childish and dreadful. She beat her hands upon the coffin. She wept loudly and fiercely as a child does….
> Dr. Martineau drifted feebly to the window. [*Secret Places*, 9.8; ellipses in original]

Dr Martineau is mostly worried that 'the servants might hear and wonder what it was all about'. The last line of the novel is: 'Always he had feared love for the cruel thing it was, but now it seemed to him for the first time that he realized its monstrous cruelty' [9.8].

Contemporaries weren't quite sure what to make of all this. The characters 'conceal nothing either very sacred, very subtle, or even very interesting' complained the *English Journal*. 'Who cares about the secret places of the heart of Sir Richmond Hardy, the chairman of the fuel commission, the egotistical husband, the libertine?' [*English Journal*, 11:8 (Oct 1922), 522]. This review calls the story 'cold' and thinks Wells 'a cold writer', which touches on something true of this novel. From its moonlight love-making to its relentless intellectualising of erotic desire, even unto the psychiatrist's rather Lovecraftian vision of modern humanity waking from its animal heritage to find itself in 'a great and ancient house high amidst frozen and lifeless mountains in a sunless universe' [1.4] this is a novel about illicit sexual passion that tropes it as, in some core sense, chilly. It's a counter-intuitive move, but an aesthetically interesting one—counter-intuitive not only because actual sex, with its shared body-heat and frottage tends to be actually warm, but because the new-for-the-1920s sexual frankness of writers like D.H. Lawrence tended to talk about sex as heat, a 'hot' liberating escape from intellectual life: 'I believe especially in being warm-hearted in love, in fucking with a warm heart,' is how Mellors puts it in 1928, as he and Lady Chatterley make love before a roaring fire. 'I believe if men could fuck with warm hearts, and the women take it warm-heartedly, everything would come all right. It's all the cold-hearted fucking that is death and idiocy.' There is certainly something strangely cold-hearted about the various sexual infidelities of *The Secret Places of the Heart*. Hardy seduces V.V. with his coolly intellectual conversation, makes love to her outside by moonlight and immediately afterwards freezes her out. It's not coincidental I think that it is a cold that kills him in the end: 'he had worked to the pitch of exhaustion. He neglected a cold that settled on his chest' [9.1].

In other words, Wells in this novel marks the distance between the warm bestial sex-past and the cooler, more intellectual sex-present. Wells, like his avatar Hardy, can't just let himself go, sexually speaking. His kink (as it were) is not just the excitement of extramarital sex, it is extramarital sex with an intellectual equal. *Secret Places* reads like Wells trying to work through, to his own satisfaction, why he is so drawn to this particular sort of erotic interaction. This cold rebellion of his own will against his ageing libido puzzles the mature Wells and he's trying to get to the bottom of it. But the final hot-blooded flare-up of rage and grief by the novel's Rebecca West speaks to a more fundamental mismatch between the two figures than age or outlook.

David Y. Hughes notes that 'the paradigmatic act of Wells's personal life is sexual revolt' and then quotes Robert P. Weeks to the effect that 'Wells's fiction presents us with a unified world that limits its inhabitants, provokes their rebellion, and then frustrates their flight', adding shrewdly: 'illicit sex makes entanglement; the escape becomes the trap; each affair fuels the next … even the ever-patient Amy Catherine [Jane Wells] had complicity not just by tolerating the affairs but by the act of having eloped with Wells from his first wife' [Hughes, 393–94]. Wells's fantasy is a short-circuit, sex as escape from entanglement that is itself entanglement. In *Secret Places* Hardy begins to cool on his ardour for V.V. the very next morning after their moonlit tryst. Wells's previous novels about extramarital sex had largely concerned themselves with practical consequences and with human jealousy. In the *Experiment in Autobiography* (1934) Wells summarises *The Secret Places of the Heart* (1922) as a work in which 'I was thinking not so much of the problem of jealousy, as of love-making considered as a source of waste of energy', so perhaps the way to think of all this is as a realisation of the entropic nature of sexual energy. H.G. wasn't getting any younger, after all.

Bibliography

Clapp, Susanna (1986). 'Little Men', *London Review of Books* 8:14, pp. 23–24.

Felber, Lynette (2002). 'Unfinished Business and Self-Memorialization: Rebecca West's Aborted Novel, *Mild Silver, Furious Gold*' *Journal of Modern Literature*, 25:2, pp. 38–49.

Hughes, David (1987). 'Desperately Mortal', *Science Fiction Studies* 14:3, 392–399.

Ray, Gordon (1974). *H G Wells and Rebecca West*. Yale University Press.

West, Rebecca (1916). *The Return of the Soldier*. London: Century Company.

West, Rebecca (1986). *Sunflower*. London: Virago.

17

Mr Wells Sees Through It

Mr Britling Sees It Through (1916); God the Invisible King (1917); Soul of a Bishop (1917)

Mr Britling Sees It Through (1916), Wells's masterpiece of World War I fiction, remains even a hundred years later little short of astonishing: a vividly realised, involving and by the end genuinely moving work of art. And it was, in its day, an extraordinary success. After a string of books that had managed relatively mediocre sales (Wells's last really successful title, commercially speaking, had been 1910s *Mr Polly*) *Mr Britling* swept all before it. In the UK it was 1916s bestselling novel (released late in the season it nonetheless went through 13 editions before year's end). In the USA, it was the fourth bestselling title of 1916 and, following the USA's entry into the war, it became the number one American bestseller of 1917 [Korda, 16]. Wells earned £20,000 from US sales alone. Reviews were dithyrambic and Maxim Gorky called it 'the finest, most courageous, truthful, and humane book written in Europe in the course of this accursed war'. This was a novel that touched people. It still has that power today, though it is now little read.

Britling is yet another Wellsian character based on Wells himself: an internationally successful writer, living a comfortable life in his Essex home, Matching's Easy; married to his second wife, raising a son (Hugh) alongside two step-children and conducting a discrete affair (his eighth, we're told) with an attractive neighbour. The novel is disposed into three parts. Book the First, entitled 'Matching's Easy at Ease', is a leisurely, immersive and compelling account of the long Edwardian pre-war summer of 1914. A young American, Mr Direck, visits Mr Britling to invite him to go on a talking tour of the USA; but he breaks his wrist (Britling, a terrible driver, crashes the car in which Direck is a passenger), ends up staying for several months and falls in love with Cissie, the sister of the wife of Mr Britling's secretary, a young man called

© The Author(s) 2019
A. Roberts, *H G Wells*, Literary Lives, https://doi.org/10.1007/978-3-030-26421-5_17

Teddy. Also in the company is a German student, the young, hyper-correct ultra-*Deutsch* Herr Heinrich. But even Heinrich has his human side: he takes a squirrel as a pet and sticks loyally by the creature even though it does nothing but bite him; and he falls in love with a local barmaid.

Book the Second, 'Matching's Easy at War', describes the advent of war from the Home-Front perspective. Heinrich, obviously, has to return to Germany and he goes in such a hurry that he leaves many of his possessions in the Britling domicile. Britling's secretary, Teddy, joins up, and though Britling himself is frustrated that he's too old wear a uniform, he is secretly grateful that his beloved son Hugh is too young to conscript. The narrative follows through 1914 and into 1915 with a good deal of specific detail. Teddy is reported missing. Hugh, without consulting his father, lies about his age and joins the army. Britling's elderly Aunt is fatally injured by a bomb dropped by a German Zeppelin—Britling drives to the coast, where she lives and is present at her rather pitiful death. News comes that Teddy is dead (though, later in the novel, this proves mistaken: Teddy comes home again, minus one hand). Hugh writes lengthy, vivid letters home from the trenches. Direck, in an attempt to impress the patriotic Cissie, joins the Canadian army. And finally, in a heart-breaking section of writing, Britling learns that his son Hugh has been killed at the front. This fatality happens on p. 365 of the 433-page novel. It needs the accumulation of those prior 364 pages to build the necessary momentum to make Hugh's death really tell and the result is very moving.

The novel's final section, 'The Testament of Matching's Easy', is its shortest. Learning that Herr Heinrich has also been killed, Britling writes a disconnected but emotionally eloquent letter to the dead boy's parents in Germany. This testament grows as he writes it, until it has traced out an unforced and genuinely touching evolution—out of the deepest despair of grief, towards a religiously tinted acceptance of his personal loss, and of the catastrophe of the war: 'until a man has found God and been found by God, he begins at no beginning, he works to no end ... Only with God. God, who fights through men against Blind Force and Night and Non-Existence; who is the end, who is the meaning' [3.2.11]. After an all-night session writing this testimony, the novel ends with Britling getting up from his desk and looking out through his window:

> Colour had returned to the world, clean pearly colour, clear and definite like the glance of a child or the voice of a girl, and a golden wisp of cloud hung in the sky over the tower of the church. There was a mist upon the pond, a soft grey mist not a yard high. A covey of partridges ran and halted and ran again in the dewy grass outside his garden railings. The partridges were very numerous this

year because there had been so little shooting. Beyond in the meadow a hare sat up as still as a stone. A horse neighed. Wave after wave of warmth and light came sweeping before the sunrise across the world of Matching's Easy. It was as if there was nothing but morning and sunrise in the world. [*Britling*, 3.2.12]

The highest praise I can give the novel is to say it earns this epiphany—that, read in its place, it comes over as neither cheap nor sentimental, but affecting and profound.

Mr Britling, the little Briton, the little representative of a little Britain, 'sees it through' in the sense that he endures, he survives the trauma and disruption the war throws at him (*Look!*, as the title of D.H. Lawrence's end-of-war poetry collection famously exclaimed, *We Have Come Through!*). But in another sense the title means that Britling sees through 'it', the mess and pain of phenomenal existence, to something transcendent. Not everyone has agreed that Wells manages to pull this off. In Hemingway's first-world-war-set *A Farewell to Arms* (1929), the 94-year-old Italian Count Greffi is entertaining the novel's young American protagonist, Frederic Henry, at dinner:

> "Now we will drink the other bottle and you will tell me about the war." He waited for me to sit down.
> "About anything else," I said.
> "You don't want to talk about it? Good. What have you been reading?"
> "What is there written in war-time?"
> "There is *Le Feu* by a Frenchman, Barbusse. There is *Mr. Britling Sees Through It.*"
> "No, he doesn't."
> "What?"
> "He doesn't see through it. Those books were at the hospital."
> "Then you have been reading?"
> "Yes, but nothing any good."
> "I thought *Mr. Britling* a very good study of the English middle-class soul."
> "I don't know about the soul."
> "Poor boy. We none of us know about the soul. Are you *Croyant*?"
> "At night." [Hemingway, 278]

'No he doesn't … he doesn't see through it' is in part Henry's way of saying: you've got that title wrong. Since the novel was not translated into Italian, we can assume Greffi read the 1917 French version, published under the title *Monsieur Britling commence à voir clair*, 'Mr Britling begins to see things clearly', which would explain his error. But it's also Henry's way of saying: Wells's novel doesn't provide the through-vision it pretends to. 'Are you

Croyant?' means 'are you a believer? Do you have religious faith?' and Henry's answer is a deliberate deflection. In Hemingway's fiction there is nothing so comforting as a living God behind the suffering and the death of this world. His characters live by the Hemingway code, an existential stoicism that disdains the spiritual comfort of a pseudo-Christian *deus ex fabula*. Walter Allen intends nothing disrespectful or diminishing when he describes the Hemingway ethos as a *style*: 'the code is as much aesthetic as it is ethical, insisting upon nothingness Hemingway asserts violently man's dignity in the face of nothingness. Man dies: it is intolerable he should die less than well, with a sense of style; and as a man dies so should he live' [Allen, 118]. Allen summarises *A Farewell to Arms* as 'an attempt to get down to some kind of bedrock in a world that has been stripped of all meaning' (adding 'it is Hemingway's triumph that … he learnt a style from despair').

The contrast in the way these two, very different, writers tackle the question of war is instructive. Both are alive to the physical and psychological costs of war, but for Hemingway war is something to be actively engaged, as a test of a specific mode of existential manliness. As against Hemingway's agency, Wells writes about *patience*. For Wells, war is broadly something to be passively endured and it is through this endurance, by observation and then only in a tentative, starting-point way ('commencer à voir clair') that insight is achieved. Wells writes a kind of canny anti-style, concealing a good deal of artistry behind his seeming urbanity and discursiveness; and he avoids anything so stoically forbidding as any Hemingwayian masculinist posturing. He is more interested in humans as compromised and soft, as messy and struggling to get by. I have to say, this seems to me the less mendacious vision of homo sapiens.

This larger Hemingway/Wells contrast is important, I think, not just where this novel is concerned, but in terms of the literature of war as a whole. In the *Iliad* and *Henry V* and *The Red Badge of Courage* war is the arena of individual and collective *action*. Even so sophisticated a representation as *War and Peace* takes it for granted that war is the environment in which the agency of the characters succeeds or is thwarted. Wells's focus on the domestic front enables him to swap that entirely about. There is nothing his characters *can do*: Britling's desire to act is frustrated by his age. The novel's second half expertly details a situation in which there is nothing to be done and everything to be endured and the only way 'through' is patience and spiritual openness. One of the most interesting things about the book is the portrait of the western front it gives us, through Hugh's lengthy letters to his father, in which war itself becomes wholly characterised by the passivity of the soldiers waging it. That reflects the nature of trench warfare itself, of course; and after World War I it became one of the tropes of the representation of war, but Wells gets credit for being the first to write it like this. Wells was also, surely, the first writer to portray PTSD or 'shell shock' in a work of fiction. When Britling's friend Captain Carmine returns home on leave the novel remarks that 'Carmine's face showed nothing of the excitement and patriotic satisfaction that would have seemed natural to Mr. Britling. He was white and jaded, as if he had not slept for many nights':

> It was only when they sat together in the barn court out of the way of Mrs. Britling and the children that Captain Carmine was able to explain his listless bearing and jaded appearance. He was suffering from a bad nervous shock. He had hardly taken over his command before one of his men had been killed—and killed in a manner that had left a scar upon his mind.
>
> The man had been guarding a tunnel, and he had been knocked down by one train when crossing the line behind another. Captain Carmine had found the body. He had found the body in a cloudy moonlight; he had almost fallen over it; and his sensations and emotions had been eminently disagreeable. He had had to drag the body—it was very dreadfully mangled—off the permanent way, the damaged, almost severed head had twisted about very horribly in the uncertain light, and afterwards he had found his sleeves saturated with blood. He had not noted this at the time, and when he had discovered it he had been sick.... Since this had happened he had not had an hour of dreamless sleep. [*Britling*, 2.2.4]

This focus on passivity as the tenor of war runs, I'd argue, through the whole novel. Reaction is prioritised over action, waiting and enduring trump doing and overcoming. The patriotism and *passions* of the war (Britling shocks himself by the unexpected 'strength and passion of his own belligerent opinions' [1.5.13] once war starts) are revealed as iterations of the root of the word passion:—that is, passivity. Wells is especially skilful in the way he inverts the valences of character-in-action. Mr Britling is a writer, but as the war gets going he spends all his time not actively writing but passively reading (reading the newspapers, reading the letters he gets from Hugh). He is engaged in an affair, but rather than actively pursuing Mrs Harrowdean or, as he thinks he ought, actively breaking it off, he just passively lets it fizzle out. More grandly, Britling goes from a person full of self-importance, speaking bombastically about what England 'must' do, the ways in which Germany must be fought and how the continent must be rearranged after England has won its victory, to an individual whose self-importance has been completely hollowed out, struggling to express himself on a purely individual level.

This characterisation of Britling is, of course, central to the project as a whole. John Batchelor argues: 'written with more detachment, this novel would be a study of a figure whose self-centredness verges on the brutal, but by tricking Mr Britling out with comic attributes—his odd clothes and general untidiness, the games he invents, the rather heavily conscious unconventionality of his household's manners, his hair-raising inability to drive his car—Wells works hard to enlist the reader's sympathy.' Batchelor adds, with a rather splendid high-handedness: 'personally, I withhold my sympathy' (he does add an at least: '…until Hugh Britling is killed in the war') [Batchelor, 110]. Whilst this doesn't actively misrepresent the lineaments of the novel, it does seem to me to miss something very important about what Wells is doing.

The petty ludicrousness of Britling is based on an impressively un-self-forgiving, clear-sighting assessment by Wells of his own various petty ludicrousnesses. It is not just a strategy to nudge the reader into liking the character despite his egoism. It's a calculated inversion of the traditional attributes of the warrior. Instead of tragic dignity and nobility Wells stresses how contingent and quotidian and more importantly how silly ordinary life actually is. *Silly* is the quality of existence in war as it is in peace, with the difference that silliness is broadly funny in peacetime and broadly heart-breaking in war. Nobody in this novel dies a heroic warrior's death: Hugh's best friend at the front, known as 'Ortheris', gets his legs blown off by a shell and then sits (of necessity, since he now has no legs) laughing and joking with Hugh about his predicament. He says he's thirsty and as Hugh gets out his water bottle, he dies: '"And I'm done!" And then—then he just looked discontented and miserable and died—right off' (Hugh's letter goes on: 'I couldn't believe he was dead … I began to cry. Like a baby. I kept on with the water-bottle at his teeth long after I was convinced he was dead'). Hugh himself is shot in the head by a freak shot that happens to pass through a tiny 'loop' in the trench defences. Herr Heinrich is taken prisoner on the (German) Eastern front and dies when a fight breaks out between some German and some Croatian prisoners. Captain Carmine's man, as we've seen, is knocked over by a train. It's all deliberately inconsequential and all the more affecting for that. War, Wells is saying, is not a plan or a purpose or any kind of agency. It is randomness and endurance and passivity.

From passivity to passion and back again. *Passion* has a Christian-religious meaning, of course, although it's not one people nowadays necessarily realise. We talk of Christ's passion not because the experience of being crucified was one of intense feelings or strong beliefs, but because it involved God's willing acceptance of an agonising *passivity*. Theologically speaking there is no force in the cosmos capable of compelling God to endure torture and death;

theologically speaking, God is not just an agent, he is *the* agent, he embodies the primary and complete agency that sustains the universe. And yet God accepted the passive agony of being nailed to the cross and the redemption entailed by that sacrifice is the chief mystery of the Christian faith. The willing acceptance of enforced passivity is the wisdom that Britling learns; and the novel's climactic reference—addressed by Britling to Herr Heinrich's parents—to 'Our sons who have shown us God' [3.2.11] is an open-ended gesture towards Christ's filial passion and towards sacrifice as the medium of divine revelation. In his *Autobiography*, Wells describes *Mr Britling Sees It Through* as a novel about 'the passionate desire to find some immediate reassurance amidst that whirlwind of disaster' [Wells, *Experiment in Autobiography*, 573]. That use of 'passionate' is not adventitious.

Conceivably the thoroughness as well as the scope of Wells's anatomy of passivity (of passion) in this novel is one reason why it has fallen off the larger radar. James Campbell discusses the critical culture that has grown up in the wake of Paul Fussell's influential *The Great War and Modern Memory* (1975), a book by which many subsequent 'readings' of World War I literature have oriented themselves. Campbell argues that 'an aesthetic criterion of realism and an ethical criterion of a humanism of passivity' combine in the critical discourse 'to create an ideology' of what he calls 'combat gnosticism'. He thinks that 'such an ideology has served both to limit severely the canon of texts that mainstream First World War criticism has seen as legitimate war writing'.

> The critical tradition that I identify as mainstream and dominant is one that equates the term "war" with the term "combat." As a result, what it legitimates as war literature is produced exclusively by combat experience; the knowledge of combat is a prerequisite for the production of a literary text that adequately deals with war. This is what I mean by combat gnosticism: a construction that gives us war experience as a kind of gnosis, a secret knowledge which only an initiated elite knows. [Campbell, 203–04]

Britling is a work that falls foul of this tacit critical consensus by, very specifically, not being a combat novel or more precisely by extending the definition of combat and combat trauma, bringing it far back behind the front line. It is, we could say, a resolutely non-gnostic novel. Our sons die for us, but the paradox of that passion is that such dying leads back to life, hope and redemption. That quality, in its complexly inwoven senses of fellow-feeling and charity grounded in a shared sense of passivity, is what Mr Britling, ultimately, sees, through the fog of war. It is what ultimately comes clear.

The religious conversion with which *Britling* ends was no mere fictional effect by Wells. At this time he himself abandoned the spiritual agnosticism that had defined his adult life and became, in Greffi's terms, *Croyant*. But this phase did not last long; Wells repudiated it after only a couple of years. In the *Autobiography* he belittled it as 'a falling back of the mind towards immaturity under the stress of dismay and anxiety':

> Everywhere in those first years of disaster men were looking for some lodestar for their loyalty. I thought it was pitiful that they should pin their minds to 'King and Country' and suchlike claptrap, when they might live and die for greater ends, and I did my utmost to personify and animate a greater, remoter objective in *God the Invisible King*. So by a sort of *coup d'état* I turned my New Republic for a time into a divine monarchy ... [Now] I make the most explicit renunciation and apology for this phase of terminological disingenuousness. [*Experiment in Autobiography*, 575–78]

'Disingenuousness' is hardly fair, though. The non-fiction book Wells wrote out of his newfound faith, *God the Invisible King* (1917) is, whatever else it may be, deeply ingenuous. It has not been much loved or even studied. Wells's scholars tend to treat Wells's later recantation as evidence that the whole of this book can be safely ignored. Lovat Dickson styles Wells's life as a passage through a series of governing myths: the myth of evolutionary and scientific advance which informs his early SF, the 'myth of sexual and social revaluation' in *The New Machiavelli*, *Ann Veronica* and other novels of that period and then the 'myth of God the Leader' of *Mr Britling Sees It Through* and *God the Invisible King*:

> The world was passing through a phase when any goal seemed within reach of mankind. But myths dissolve in the face of harsh experience, and the world woke up to reality, leaving the mythmaker frustrated and angry, forced to turn to fresh sources for inspiration. The whole history of man as he saw it had been a series of false starts. Perhaps it was possible for God and man to make a fresh beginning that would not end again in frustration and catastrophe. But the religious myth failed him, as the scientific and sexual ones had done, and he was left unhappy at the end. [Dickson, 307]

There are obvious dangers in reading any author teleologically, like this. We are not obliged to agree with Wells when, in moving from one stage of his life to another, he denies his earlier beliefs. Such denial says more about his desire for an interior sense of developmental consistency than it does about the beliefs themselves. People do not necessarily grow wiser as we grow older. Often, the reverse is true.

What sort of God was Wells worshipping, during this period? One with a personality and not an abstraction ('none of us really pray to that fantastic, unqualified *danse a trois*, the Trinity ... we pray to one single understanding person' [*God the Invisible King*, 1.2]), but not the angry and 'vindictive' God of the Old Testament. Wells is repelled by the radical unknowability of infinitude: 'the veil of the unknown is set with the stars,' he says, 'its outer texture is ether and atom and crystal. The Veiled Being, enigmatical and incomprehensible, broods over the mirror upon which the busy shapes of life are moving. Our lives do not deal with it and cannot deal with it' [1.3]. His God is not this infinity, but rather an inwardness, and therefore something vouched-for by individual experiential encounters with the divine. This doesn't make Him a God of quiet contemplation. On the contrary: 'the true God goes through the world like fifes and drums and flags,' Wells says, 'calling for recruits along the street. We must go out to him. We must accept his discipline and fight his battle' [2.5]. Wells lists a number of attributes of his God: 'God is Courage', 'God is a Person' and 'God is Youth'. On this latter we're told: 'the true God is that God is youth. God, we hold, began and is always beginning. He looks forever into the future' [3.3]. This in turn leads so some rather odd assertions about God's love of humankind.

> The love God bears for man in the individual believer. Now this is not an indulgent, instinctive, and sacrificing love like the love of a woman for her baby. It is the love of the captain for his men; God must love his followers as a great captain loves his men, who are so foolish, so helpless in themselves, so confiding, and yet whose faith alone makes him possible. It is an austere love. The spirit of God will not hesitate to send us to torment and bodily death. [*God the Invisible King*, 4.1]

A very World War I sentiment, we may think. Indeed, towards the end of this book Wells becomes more stridently militarist and aggressive. He's not interested in 'God the son'. His God is 'unfilial': 'the accepted figure of Jesus, instinct with meek submission, is not in the tone of our worship. It is not by suffering that God conquers death, but by fighting ... We cannot accept the Resurrection as though it were an after-thought to a bitterly felt death. Our crucifix, if you must have a crucifix, would show God with a hand or a foot already torn away from its nail, and with eyes not downcast but resolute against the sky' [4.3]. It wouldn't be fair to Wells to call this a fundamental misprision of Christianity, since Wells isn't setting out to interpret Christianity so much as to supersede it. It can, however, be noted that this entirely misses the point of the passion of Christ. Clothing Christ's willing sacrifice in this brittle armour of aggression and domination leads us, in short order, to some very unsavoury political places. 'We of the new faith repudiate the teaching of non-resistance,' brays Wells. 'We are the militant followers of and participators in a militant God … submission is the remotest quality of all from our God.' From here it's a short step to Wells calling for actual theocracy:

> This transfiguration of the world into a theocracy may seem a merely fantastic idea to anyone who comes to it freshly without such general theological preparation as the preceding pages have made. But to anyone who has been at the pains to clear his mind even a little from the obsession of existing but transitory things, it ceases to be a mere suggestion and becomes more and more manifestly the real future of mankind…The kingdom of God on earth is not a metaphor, not a mere spiritual state, not a dream, not an uncertain project; it is the thing before us, it is the close and inevitable destiny of mankind. [*God the Invisible King*, 4.3]

This divinely sanctioned hostility to diversity strikes so illiberal, so caliphatic a note, one almost wonders if Wells is being satirical. But no: his enthusiasm for service to God as the way to leverage diversity into unity and thus achieve his longed-for World State, is perfectly genuine. Every aspect of social praxis and order will be subordinated to this new order: the entire legal system, for instance, will give up petty bickering over torts and rights and become a branch of the church: 'when the world is openly and confessedly the kingdom of God, the law court will exist only to adjust the differing views of men as to the manner of their service to God' [4.9]. All existing priests, vicars, rabbis and mullahs must stand up before their congregations and speak the new truth of his religion, the coming of which 'will impose the renunciation of his temporalities and a complete cessation of services upon every ordained priest and minister as his first act of faith'.

> His course seems plain and clear. It becomes him to stand up before the flock he has led in error, and to proclaim the being and nature of the one true God. He must be explicit to the utmost of his powers. Then he may await his expulsion. [4.10]

The extraordinary unlikeliness of this eventuality may tempt us into thinking Wells is being satirical here, but no: he truly considers his new religion to have so patent a monopoly on truth that no sane person could deny it. Only, he says, the stubbornly base will resist, 'and besides these base people there are the stupid people and the people with minds so poor in texture that they cannot even grasp the few broad and simple ideas that seem necessary to the salvation we experience'. How will Wells ensure that his theocracy doesn't become a mere ecclesiocracy? Frankly, he won't. *God the Invisible King* suggests that there will be no need for churches and priests and the paraphernalia of organised religion in the new dispensation, since everyone will have individual access to God and, collectively speaking, 'the State is God's instrument'. The book closes with the metaphor of Wells's new faith as a gigantic crystal, forming spontaneously:

> This metaphor of crystallisation is perhaps the best symbol of the advent and growth of the new understanding. It has no church, no authorities, no teachers, no orthodoxy. It does not even thrust and struggle among the other things; simply it grows clear. There will be no putting an end to it. It arrives inevitably, and it will continue to separate itself out from confusing ideas. It becomes, as it were the Koh-i-noor; it is a Mountain of Light, growing and increasing. It is an all-pervading lucidity, a brightness and clearness. It has no head to smite, no body you can destroy; it overleaps all barriers; it breaks out in despite of every enclosure. It will compel all things to orient themselves to it. [*God the Invisible King*, 'Envoy']

There will be no putting an end to it. It will compel all things to orient themselves to it. It's an alarming vision.

The Wells of *God the Invisible King* certainly cuts a forbidding and authoritarian figure, but this is not really because he himself believed in the political merits of an authoritarian or spiritually-dirigiste philosophy. It's more likely a kind of category error, a failure of empathy on his part—for this vision of God seems so very undeniable and beneficial to Wells (at this moment in his life) that he simply can't conceive that anybody could disagree with it or at least that any disagreement would soon survive after time spent comprehending the sheer rightness of what Wells is saying. This, I think, explains why Wells's next book is so much less repellent than *God the Invisible King*. Because *The Soul of a Bishop* (1917) is a fictional treatment of the same material, Wells is obliged to engage his empathetic powers, qualities both necessary and sufficient to the creation of fictional characters.

This novel's protagonist is Edward Scrope, a highly-strung and insomniac Bishop, who has become a 'belated doubter' [2.1] after leaving the picturesque old rectory of Ottringham and mounting the episcopal throne at ugly and dispiriting Princhester, a place 'industrial and unashamed', 'a countryside savagely invaded by forges and mine shafts and gaunt black things ... scarred and impeded and discoloured', a landscape in which the human scale is 'jostled and elbowed and overshadowed by horrible iron cylinders belching smoke and flame' [2.2]. In case we miss the point of the cylinders reference, Wells restates the intertextual point: Scrope chats with a local union official:

"There's an incurable misunderstanding between the modern employer and the modern employed," the chief labour spokesman said. "Disraeli called them the Two Nations, but that was long ago. Now it's a case of two species ... We're the Morlocks. Coming up. It isn't our fault that we've differentiated." [*Soul of a Bishop*, 2.5]

Scrope's wife has grown cold, his Votes-for-Women oldest daughter wants, shockingly, to go to university and Scrope himself is losing his faith. Scrope's physician, Dr Dale, diagnoses neurasthenia and suggests treating it with a new kind of hallucinogenic drug. This has an immediate effect: 'his doubts glowed into assurance. Suddenly he perceived that he was sure of God' [5.4]. Scrope meets an Angel who, in effect, summarises *God the Invisible King* for him. Then, in the library of the Athenaeum Club, Scrope encounters God Himself. A second dose of Dr Dale's drug gives him a different vision: the whole world in torment.

Here was India, here was Samarkand, in the light of the late afternoon; and China and the swarming cities upon her silvery rivers sinking through twilight to the night and throwing a spray and tracery of lantern spots upon the dark; here was Russia under the noontide, and so great a battle of artillery raging on the Dunajec as no man had ever seen before; whole lines of trenches dissolved into clouds of dust and heaps of blood-streaked earth. [*Soul of a Bishop*, 7.6]

Scrope resolves to establish a new church on the strength of these visions, but this resolve falters after a third vision, this one unmediated by Dr Dale's peculiar drug, which reveals to him that 'there must be no idea of any pulpit' in the new religion.

Had God any need of organized priests at all? ... the old strand of the priest, the fetishistic element of the blood sacrifice and the obscene rite, the element of ritual and tradition, of the cult, the caste, the consecrated tribe; and interwoven with this so closely as to be scarcely separable in any existing religion was the new strand, the religion of the prophets, the unidolatrous universal worship of the one true God. Priest religion is the antithesis to prophet religion. [*Soul of a Bishop*, 9.2]

The novel ends with the Bishop happy, reconciled to his family and resolved, on his own, to spread the word regarding his new understanding of God. The book's warmth and humour and the modesty of its theological ambitions, do something to leaven the indigestibly authoritarian lump of Wellsian Invisible Kingliness of faith.

Bibliography

Allen, Walter (1964) *Tradition and Dream: the English and American Novel from the Twenties to Our Time*. London: Hogarth Press.

Batchelor, John (1985). *H G Wells*. Cambridge University Press.

Campbell, James (1999). 'Combat Gnosticism: The Ideology of First World War Poetry Criticism', *New Literary History*, 30:1, 203–215.

Dickson, Lovat (1969). *H G Wells: His Turbulent Life and Times*. Macmillan.

Hemingway, Ernest (1929). *A Farewell to Arms*. New York: Scribner.

Korda, Michael (2001). *Making the List: A Cultural History of the American Bestseller*. New York: Barnes & Nobel.

18

League of Nations

In the Fourth Year: Anticipations of a World Peace (1918); The Salvaging of Civilization: The Probable Future of Mankind (1921); Russia in the Shadows (1921); Washington and the Hope of Peace (1922)

Wells did not invent the idea of 'the League of Nations' and his role in the specific discussions and legal framing that lead to the establishment of that organisation proved, in the end, minor. But he did coin the name, and his tireless journalistic advocacy of it—as a stepping stone to his wished-for World State—helped move the collective conceptual centre of gravity (what is something called 'the Overton window') towards a broader acceptance of the idea. Henry Winkler argues that, despite the energetic support not just of Wells, but of influential figures like John A. Hobson and H.N. Brailsford, 'before 1919 no organized group took up the idea of world government' [Winkler 29]. It's not that these individuals lacked an audience—Wells in particular was read by millions. It's that they were commentators and their ideas needed political actors to realise them.

Take for example *In the Fourth Year: Anticipations of a World Peace* (1918), another collection of Wells's wartime journalism, this time arguing the need for a 'League of Free Nations' to resolve all future international disputes in a way that would obviate the need to go to war. Walter Lippmann, who serialised many of the sections of this book in *The New Republic* and who met Wells in person to discuss the larger questions with him, acted as a point of mediation between the book's ideas and the US State Department. Which means that Wells had some influence on the 14th of President Wilson's end-of-war 'Fourteen Points' (1918): 'XIV. A general association of nations must be formed under specific covenants for the purpose of affording mutual guarantees of political independence and territorial integrity to great and small states alike.'

© The Author(s) 2019
A. Roberts, *H G Wells*, Literary Lives, https://doi.org/10.1007/978-3-030-26421-5_18

The actual League of Nations fell far short of Wells's hopes for it. He insisted it should 'possess power and exercise power, powers must be delegated to it' and must 'practically control the army, navy, air forces, and armament industry of every nation in the world' [*In the Fourth Year*, 3]. But the actual League never managed that. It's not that Wells was pie-in-the-sky about his proposals. He has enough of *realpolitik* to see that equal representation of states was a non-starter: 'the preservation of the world-peace rests with the great powers and with the great powers alone' [10]—

There are only four powers certainly capable at the present time of producing the men and materials needed for a modern war in sufficient abundance to go on fighting: Britain, France, Germany, and the United States. There are three others which are very doubtfully capable: Italy, Japan, and Austria. Russia I will mark—it is all that one can do with Russia just now—with a note of interrogation. Some day China may be war capable—I hope never, but it is a possibility. [*In the Fourth Year*, 10]

When America decided not to join the League of Nations it effectively doomed the whole enterprise:—something of which contemporaries were well aware, as per this Punch cartoon from December 1920 (Fig. 18.1):

THE GAP IN THE BRIDGE.

Fig. 18.1 Cartoon from *Punch*, 10 December 1920, satirising the American refusal to join the League of Nations

Lacking this 'keystone', French and British governments of the 1920s and 1930s simply did not engage fully with the League. The advent of a second World War in 1939—the exact thing the League had been instituted to prevent—sounded its death-knell. Hindsight might tempt us to imagine the whole enterprise was doomed from the start. As Paul Kennedy notes 'the League lacked representation for colonial peoples (then half the world's population) and significant participation from several major powers, including the US, USSR, Germany, and Japan; it failed to act against the Japanese invasion of Manchuria in 1931, the Second Italo-Ethiopian War in 1935, the Japanese invasion of China in 1937, and German expansions under Adolf Hitler that culminated in the Second World War' [Kennedy, 10]. But what is sometimes forgotten nowadays is how far it enjoyed enormous popular support, even into the 1930s. The 'League of Nations Union', a British affiliate association, had over 400,000 members 1931–32: with 3000 branches across Britain as well as 'some 4,400 corporate affiliates ranging from trade unions to Boy Scout troops and Women's Institutes, with especially deep penetration in the Protestant churches' [Reynolds, 221]. Whatever else it might be, Wells's enthusiasm for the idea of a League was no eccentric position.

In the Fourth Year makes for a curiously unsatisfying read, nonetheless: full of blind spots, blotted by racism and constantly changing gear between vast, sweeping generalisations and micro-managed tedious detail. On the one hand, Wells booms that humanity 'is facing a choice between the League of Free Nations and a famished race of men looting in search of non-existent food amidst the smouldering ruins of civilization' [8]. On the other, he gets bogged down in pettifogging overanalysis of proposals for election by Proportional Representation and the single transferable vote, the complexities of which system will be ameliorated (he says) by the invention of automatic vote-counting machines that will tally and redistribute votes as necessary ('the Cash Register people', he claims, optimistically, 'will invent machines to do it for you while you wait'). Meanwhile, many of the largest-scale practicalities of running a League of Free Nations are glossed over. In the round, Wells thinks that world peace will be best maintained by 'international' (he means Western) control of a great many mandated territories. The Ottoman Empire should be broken up into 'localised regions' under 'honestly conceived international control of police and transit and trade' [5.2] and Africa, excepting only South Africa and Egypt, must be placed under 'international control' as soon as possible:

What are the ends that must be achieved if Africa is not to continue a festering sore in the body of mankind? The first most obvious danger of Africa is the militarization of the black. General Smuts has pointed this out plainly. The negro makes a good soldier; he is hardy, he stands the sea, and he stands cold. It is absolutely essential to the peace of the world that there should be no arming of the negroes. [*Fourth Year*, 4]

Two centuries of slaver-driven depopulation and a half-century of hugely accelerated imperialist expropriation of valuable resources, accompanied by mass-murder, certainly had something to do with Africa becoming, in Wells's gruesome phrase, 'a festering sore in the body of mankind'; and if the problem was imperialism, it's hard to see how more imperialism could be the answer. Of course, Wells pitches his pan-African mandate as a civilising, not an expropriating, force. But civilisation is really not the focus of *In the Fourth Year*'s African chapter. Instead Wells waxes racist-hysteric: 'the whole negro population of Africa', he declares, 'is now rotten with diseases.' The *whole* population? 'A bacterium that may kill you or me in some novel and disgusting way may even now be developing in some Congo muck-heap.' We can't simply quarantine the Continent because 'Africa is the great source of many of the most necessary raw materials upon which our modern comforts and conveniences depend'. So what Wells calls 'international tutelage' becomes, he believes, absolutely needful. It's hard to overstate the malignancy of this. When Wells frets about bacteria killing 'you or me in disgusting ways' his 'you and me' doesn't include black Africans. He's not talking to them because, in his mind, black Africans are not competent to be part of this discussion of their own political future. Jan Smuts, quoted approvingly here by Wells (the two men were friends) governed South Africa on principles of racial segregation that lead eventually to apartheid and described black Africans as 'children of nature' lacking 'the inner toughness and persistence of the European', men and women without 'those social and moral incentives' to build a civilisation. Such sentiments have not, to put it mildly, aged well.

Wells insists the League of Nations will not simply be Imperialism under a new name (Chapter 5 is titled 'Getting the League Idea Clear in Relation to Imperialism') and he does anticipate—not now but at some unspecified point in the future—a modicum of racial equality in his future: not Black Africans but, according to the structurally racist assumptions of his age, perhaps Indians and maybe Arabs: 'the time is drawing near when the Egyptian and the nations of India will ask us, "Are things going on for ever here as they go on now, or are we to look for the time when we, too, like the [white South] Africander, the Canadian and the Australian, will be your confessed and equal partners?"' Although it doesn't use the term 'mandate', but that's essentially what *In the Fourth Year* advocates. And mandates were the main strategy by which the League of Nations actually operated. But Wells's faith that rule by international mandate would herald a new global dawn proved misguided. As Susan Pedersen comprehensively demonstrates in her history of the movement, mandates were flawed from the beginning.

> The mandate system made imperial governance more burdensome and brought normative statehood nearer. This was not what its architects and officials had intended. To the contrary, they sought at every turn to uphold imperial authority and strengthen the prestige and legitimacy of alien non-consensual rule. The problem was that the internationalization inherent in League oversight worked against those purposes. By offering a platform for wordy humanitarians, belligerent German revisionists and nationalists determined to expose the brutalities of imperial rule, the mandates system not only undermined imperial authority but also—possibly more importantly—led at least some within the European empires to question whether direct rule was desirable anyway. That most local inhabitants had no affection for the mandates system seems apparent. Over time, however, many within the imperial powers lost their sympathy for it as well. [Pedersen 13]

Pederson gives the example of Britain, the (as she puts it) most 'global' of imperial powers, deciding to end mandated rule of Iraq and instead pursue their imperial ambitions through the direct treaty of 1930. It was this, as Pederson convincingly argues, that inspired today's system of global economic imperialism.

The problem with *In the Fourth Year* is more than that its subtitular 'Anticipations of a World Peace' proved so spectacularly wrongheaded—it is not, in other words, that Wells happened to be wrong, in this instance. It's that he was wrong for structural reasons immanent in his thought as such. For example, it is striking that a book proposing a League of Nations at no point involves Wells actually defining what a 'nation' is. He deploys the concept variously, using it sometimes as a racially defined association, sometimes as a geographical or political one, often as a sheer accumulation of individuals and rarely if ever as a historically determined formation. The book's grander slogans suffer by their tendency to elide these, very different, quantities: 'not only is justice to prevail between race and race and nation and nation, but also between man and man; there is to be a universal respect for human life throughout the earth' [9], for instance. It seems elementary to suggest that proposals for a League of Nations must be grounded in a detailed understanding of nationhood as such, prior to determining in what ways those multiple and various quantities can league together, but it is an elementality Wells entirely overlooks.

As early as 1921 Wells was becoming disillusioned with the League. *The Salvaging of Civilization: The Probable Future of Mankind* (1921) still insists on the need for a world state, collective ownership of wealth and resources and a comprehensive drive to educate the whole population of the planet—but it argues the League of Nations 'may be worse' than nothing because 'it may create a feeling of disillusionment about world-unifying efforts'. World unifying is the watchword of *The Salvaging of Civilisation*, and Wells's logic is, in effect: wars happen between nations; do away with nations and there will be no war. We might think that all the creation of a World State would do is convert all wars into civil wars, but Wells won't entertain that notion. 'I do not think we want to get rid of patriotism,' he says 'and I do not think we could, even if we wanted to do so. It seems to be necessary to his moral life, that a man should feel himself part of a community, belonging to it, and it belonging to him.' But he believes that patriotic attachment to the larger unit always trumps patriotic attachment to the smaller. As evidence for this curious belief he instances America, where, he says, Kentuckians are always Americans first and Kentuckians only second.

> Suppose, for instance, there was a serious outbreak of local patriotism in Kentucky. Suppose you found the people of Kentucky starting a flag of their own and objecting to what they would probably call the 'vague international-ism' of the stars and stripes. Suppose you found them wanting to set up tariff barriers to the trade of the states round about them. Suppose you found they were preparing to annex considerable parts of the state of Virginia by force, in order to secure a proper strategic frontier among the mountains to the east, and that they were also talking darkly of their need for an outlet to the sea of their very own. What would an American citizen think of such an outbreak? He would probably think that Kentucky had gone mad. [*Salvaging of Civilisation*, 70–71]

This line of argument, blithely oblivious to the fact that precisely *in America* and within the lifetime of some of Wells's readership, one of the world's most destructive civil wars happened is, shall we say, singular. Wells's desire for World Statehood blinds him to counter-evidence.

The specific legislative lineaments of his proposed World State include 'a Supreme Court determining not International Law, but World Law' a single world currency and global ministries for communications, trade, labour, world health. 'Instead of a War Office and Naval and Military departments, there will be a Peace Ministry studying the belligerent possibilities of every new invention, watching for armed disturbances everywhere, and having complete control of every armed force that remains in the world' [87]. Even a rudimentary understanding of economics tells us that the removal of all borders and the enforcement of a single currency would advantage those portions of the globe already wealthy against those that are poor, tending to bed-in inequalities of opportunity and ownership, to say nothing of the more fundamental risk that whoever controls the 'Peace Ministry' would aggregate into their hands more power than anybody else in the entire history of the globe. Wells is a Nelson putting his telescope to his blank eye and so refusing to see that maxim—the one every schoolchild knows—about power always corrupting. No provision is proposed for checks or balances where this super ministry is concerned. Not for the first time in his career Wells's prophesies are not so much falsified by subsequent events (although, of course, they are) as stymied by their own strange blind spots and limitations. Wells had one of the great speculative imaginations of his age: why did it fail him in this big matter?

Late in 1921 Wells sailed to the USA to write-up the Washington Naval Conference on disarmament as a series of weekly reports for the *New York World* newspaper. The London *Daily Mail* also carried his pieces, or at least it printed the first 14 and then stopped, taking exception to Wells's criticism of the French Prime Minister, Aristide Briand (whom Wells judged a backslider on the question of international disarmament). All 29 of his reports were published in book form as *Washington and the Hope of Peace* (1922) in its British edition and *Washington and the Riddle of Peace in its American*—war-shattered Europe, we presume, hopes, where to the more distantly engaged America peace is a riddle. It is a strange, unsatisfactory book that makes no pretentions to fair or balanced reportage. Wells agitates for global disarmament and his World State and has no interest in even trying to understand contrary view—hence his repeated attacks on Briand. The French premier's disinclination to disband his nation's army and navy are, for Wells, evidence of straightforward geopolitical wickedness. France (a nation only a few short years earlier subjected to an unprovoked invasion that killed 5% of its total and 10% of its adult male, population—some 1.4 million men—leaving many more maimed and invalid) might be forgiven for wanting to retain some degree of defensive military capacity. But for Wells anything short of total disarmament is absolute betrayal. Briand's fears of future aggression are 'alarmist' [13] and 'humbug' [15]. Or, worse, they are deliberate distractions. If France be allowed to keep 'her submarines and Senegalese', Wells says, she would be in a position to 'do as she pleased in Europe' [17]. He accuses France of wanting 'an awful army to over-awe Europe' [12] and calls Briand 'a warlike orator, empty and mischievous, leading France and all Europe to destruction' [16]. Wells refers several times to his evidence-free theory that France is gearing up specifically to attack Britain: 'France is maintaining a vast army in the face of a disarmed world and she is preparing energetically for fresh warlike operations in Europe and for war under sea against Great Britain' [11]. We start to see why the *Daily Mail* asked him to tone it down and why, when he refused, they stopped publishing his reports. It cannot have made Anglo-French diplomatic relations any easier to navigate.

America was not his only destination. In these immediate post-war years, Wells travelled widely. A 2-week trip to Russia in 1920 resulted in *Russia in the Shadows* (1921), the first detailed account by a westerner of the newly Communist state. On this trip Wells's interpreter was his own son George, 'Gip' as he was known, who had just turned 19 and had studied Russian at Oundle School (the first British school ever to teach the language, with Gip's year the first to be given that opportunity). The official invitation for Wells to visit had come from Lev Kamenev, Chair of the ruling Politburo, but the original idea for the visit had likely been Lenin's—Vladimir Ilyich appreciated the propaganda value of having one of the world's most popular and widely read authors write-up the new country. HG and Gip went to Petrograd (not yet renamed Leningrad) and then to Moscow and the climax of this little book is Wells's interview with Lenin himself. Wells was no Marxist and certainly no Leninist (after their conversation Lenin told Trotsky he was 'an unreconstructed bourgeois', a judgement with which it is hard to disagree) but given Wells's socialist/collectivist views and considering the enormous popularity of his war journalism and of *Britling*, it was as much a coup for Lenin to get Wells as it was for Wells to meet Lenin. Gip took photographs, eight pages of which were included in the volume.

Though *Russia in the Shadows* portrays a country desolated by war and on the brink of collapsing into anarchy, Wells says sympathetic things about the aims of the Bolsheviks and is genuinely impressed by Lenin. That fact outraged some in Britain and America. Winston Churchill published an article in the Express under the belligerent title 'This Frightful Catastrophe: Mr Wells and Bolshevism' (5 December 1920) mocking Wells's account as superficial and asking him whether he thought 'cancer could repent?' Wells's reply ('Mr Wells Hits Back—Rejoinder to Mr Churchill's Criticism' *Express*, 12 and 19 December 1920) is worth quoting at length:

> Although I am an older man than Mr Churchill and have spent most of my time watching and thinking about a world in which he has been rushing about vehemently from one superficial excitement to another, he has the impudence to twit me with superficiality.... He believes quite naively that he belongs to a peculiarly gifted and privileged class of beings to whom the lives and affairs of common men are given over, the raw material for brilliant careers. It seems to

him an act of insolence that a common man like myself should form judgments upon matters of statescraft. He is the running sore of waste in our Government.

He could certainly give as good as he got. As for Russia, Wells's dominant impression was 'of a vast irreparable breakdown'.

The great monarchy that was here in 1914, the administrative, social, financial, and commercial systems connected with it have, under the strains of six years of incessant war, fallen down and smashed utterly. Never in all history has there been so great a débâcle before. The fact of the Revolution is, to our minds, altogether dwarfed by the fact of this downfall. The peasant, who was the base of the old pyramid, remains upon the land, living very much as he has always lived. Everything else is broken down, or is breaking down. Amid this vast disorganisation an emergency Government, supported by a disciplined party of perhaps 150,000 adherents—the Communist Party—has taken control. It has—at the price of much shooting—suppressed brigandage, established a sort of order and security in the exhausted towns, and set up a crude rationing system. [*Russia in the Shadows*, 1]

Fascinating though it is as a historical document, it's in this 'poetics of ruin' that Wells's writing really hits home: the rationing, the broken infrastructure, dysfunctional hospitals, people bootless and ragged, the looting of public buildings and art galleries (though not, Wells says, of theatres: Russians respect the theatre too profoundly to loot it). It is all extremely vividly described. 'Ruin; that is the primary Russian fact at the present time,' Wells insists. 'The revolution, the Communist rule is quite secondary to that. It is something that has happened in the ruin and because of the ruin.' Wells believes Russia is about to tumble into the abyss. His refusal to take Marxism seriously means he simply can't see that it will go on to build a superpower out of these ruins. The most he will concede is that the Bolsheviks seem determined: 'albeit numbering less than five per cent, of the population, [they] have been able to seize and retain power in Russia because they were and are the only body of people in this vast spectacle of Russian ruin with a common faith and a common spirit. I disbelieve in their faith, I ridicule Marx, their prophet, but I understand and respect their spirit' [4].

Wells says that Lenin is 'not very like the photographs you see of him because he is one of those people whose change of expression is more important than their features'. The two men, though, talk rather at cross purposes:

Our talk was threaded throughout and held together by two—what shall I call them?—motifs. One was from me to him: 'What do you think you are making of Russia? What is the state you are trying to create?' The other was from him to me: 'Why does not the social revolution begin in England? Why do you not work for the social revolution? Why are you not destroying Capitalism and establishing the Communist State?' These motifs interwove, reacted on each other, illuminated each other. The second brought back the first: 'But what are you making of the social revolution? Are you making a success of it?' And from that we got back to two again with: 'To make it a success the Western world must join in. Why doesn't it?' [*Russia in the Shadows*, 6]

The Lenin Wells meets is the Lenin of his 'Communism is Soviet government plus the electrification of the whole country' phase (that famous slogan dates from 1920) and Wells makes mild fun of him on these grounds: 'Lenin, who like a good orthodox Marxist denounces all "Utopians," has succumbed at last to a Utopia, the Utopia of the electricians.' But the electrification vision also kindles something in Wells's science-fictional imagination:

Can one imagine a more courageous project in a vast flat land of forests and illiterate peasants, with no water power, with no technical skill available, and with trade and industry at the last gasp? Projects for such an electrification are in process of development in Holland and they have been discussed in England, and in those densely-populated and industrially highly-developed centres one can imagine them as successful, economical, and altogether beneficial. But their application to Russia is an altogether greater strain upon the constructive imagination. I cannot see anything of the sort happening in this dark crystal of Russia, but this little man at the Kremlin can. [*Russia in the Shadows*, 6]

Electrification became the first of the USSR's 5-year plans and was completed by 1931. Dark crystal, indeed.

Bibliography

Kennedy, Paul (2007). *The Parliament of Man: The Past, Present, and Future of the United Nations*. New York: Random House.

Pedersen, Susan (2015). *The Guardians: The League of Nations and the Crisis of Empire*. Oxford University Press.

Reynolds, David. (2013). *The Long Shadow: The Great War and the Twentieth Century*. London: Simon and Schuster.

Winkler, Henry (1958). *The League of Nations Movement in Great Britain 1914–1919* (Rutgers University Press.

19

Education

Joan and Peter (1918); *The Undying Fire* (1919); *Socialism and the Scientific Motive* (1923); *The Story of a Great Schoolmaster* (1924)

Wells's disillusionment with the League of Nations did not vanquish his belief in the necessity of working for a World State, but it did redirect his energies. 'How the L of N gatherings bore me', he wrote to Philip Guedalla early in 1919, reporting on his time spent on various committees and governmental bodies engaged in the British contribution to the League. 'I must give up all League of Nations work,' he wrote to his friend the Classical scholar Gilbert Murray: 'I feel physically unable to go on with it. This Committee work fills me with a horror of great darkness.' He resolved to return to his more solitary writerly work, and to focus his energies not on treaties but education. 'For some time,' he told Murray, 'I've thought of writing an Outline of History … I believe the History of Man can be taught as easily as the History of England and that a world educated in such history will be a different and better world altogether' [quoted in Mackenzies, 319–20].

His sons George 'Gip' Philip and Frank Richard were now 18 and 16 respectively and were passing from secondary to tertiary education. The business of finding the best schooling for them, which naturally exercised Wells as a parent, increasingly engaged his prophetic and social-reformist imagination too. A large part of this was down to one man: Frederick William Sanderson, headmaster of Oundle School from 1892 until his death in 1922. Wells and Sanderson became friends when Gip and Frank attended Oundle, and Wells's increasing focus on education reforms through the later teens and 1920s drew largely on Sanderson's ideas. Indeed, Sanderson was the topic of the only biography Wells ever wrote, *The Story of a Great Schoolmaster*, which opens thus:

> Of all the men I have met—and I have now had a fairly long and active life and have met a very great variety of interesting people—one only has stirred me to

© The Author(s) 2019
A. Roberts, *H G Wells*, Literary Lives, https://doi.org/10.1007/978-3-030-26421-5_19

a biographical effort. This one exception is F.W. Sanderson, for many years the headmaster of Oundle School. I think him beyond question the greatest man I have ever known with any degree of intimacy. [*Great Schoolmaster*, 1]

Educational questions very often enter into Wells's journalism of this period, but they also shape several of his fictional works. *Joan and Peter* (1918) is a novel so profoundly engaged with pedagogic questions that it threatens to overwhelm itself with them. It's a lengthy piece of fiction: 750 pages in its first edition, the second longest in Wells's whole oeuvre, and it is a length that becomes wearisome to the reader. The story starts, in the early 1890s, with the marriage of handsome, well-to-do but flibberty Arthur Stubland to beautiful, clever Dolly, followed swiftly by the birth of their son Peter. Dolly, though, has made a mistake. Arthur is nice enough, but she ought to have married her cousin, the vigorous, upright Oswald Sydenham, a man who won the V.C. before he was 20. The problem is that Oswald is disfigured:

It had been quite typical heroism that had won him the V.C. He had thrown a shell overboard, and it had burst in the air as he threw it and pulped one side of his face. But when [Dolly] married, she had temporarily forgotten Cousin Oswald. She was just carried away by Arthur Stubland's profile, and the wave in his hair, and—life. [*Joan and Peter*, 1.3]

Oswald is ten times the man Arthur is, and he loves Dolly, howsoever hopelessly. And she knows she's picked the wrong man, which makes her miserable. But what can she do? She's married now, and has a son. So Oswald takes himself off to pursue British Imperial advantage in central Africa. Meanwhile the Stublands buy a lovely house in the Surrey countryside, and legally adopt a baby girl, the illegitimate daughter of a distant relative—Joan.

What happens next is that Arthur and Dolly, on holiday in Italy, drown when their pleasure-boat overturns. Arthur drowns first, then Dolly. It matters in which order they drown, since they have left conflicting instructions as to what should happen to the children in the event of their death. Dolly has appointed Oswald guardian, but Arthur, who dislikes the fellow, for obvious reasons, has stipulated instead his two suffragette aunts, Phoebe and Phyllis, as guardians, together with another more distant relative, the haughty and elderly Lady Sydenham, only adding Oswald at all as a sort of afterthought concession to his wife's wishes. Initial reports are that Dolly died first, which actualises Arthur's will: Aunts Phoebe and Phyllis assume responsibility for the kids. They believe in a vaguely Rousseauian approach to educating children, letting them run more-or-less wild in the countryside. Lady Sydenham, outraged by the Aunts' atheistical socialism, kidnaps the youngsters, has them forcibly christened and deposited in a conventional prep school in Windsor (Peter) and a private house (Joan). By this time new reports from Italy have revealed that Arthur predeceased his wife, so Dolly's will comes into force, relieving the two socialist aunts and Lady Sydenham of the necessity of caring for the children. Oswald returns from Africa to England to look after the children.

And now we're at page 250 of this 750-page novel, and the story is (bar some wartime Royal Flying Corps adventuring at the very end) pretty much over. The whole tenor of the text slackens and sags as for literally hundreds of pages Oswald treks up and down England to find the best schools for his wards. His search is repeatedly frustrated by the novel's main thesis: that the British education system is not fit for purpose. Oswald repeatedly quizzes pedagogues on why they teach Latin and Greek instead of engineering and maths and German.

A common evasiveness characterized all these head-masters when Oswald demanded the particulars of Peter's curriculum. He wanted to know just the subjects Peter would study and which were to be made the most important, and then when these questions were answered he would demand: "And why do you teach this? What is the particular benefit of that to the boy or the empire?" [*Joan and Peter*, 10.3]

On and on it goes. Once Oswald has located a couple of prep-schools not quite so awful as the others, his search moves on to which public schools will be best for them next. When one headmaster tries to cow Oswald by quoting Greek at him, Oswald returns by reciting a poem in Swahili. Oswald insists on the need for educational reform—science and maths and living languages—and keeps being struck by 'the educational stagnation of England during those crucial years before the Great War' [10.6]. On and on it goes, bludgeoning home Wells's point. Later, with the children placed at the least-worst secondary schools, Oswald undertakes the whole process over again at tertiary level, visiting both Oxford and Cambridge. Eventually, and with reservations, he decides on the light blue rather than the dark. Even here, though, Wells finds only a more elaborate form of education by rote: 'into the Cambridge lecture rooms and laboratories went Joan and Peter, notebook in hand, and back to digestion in their studies, and presently they went into examination rooms where they vindicated their claim to have attended to textbook and lecture … this was their "grind," Joan and Peter considered, a drill they had to go through' [11.13]. Wells drops-in scenes from the later childhood and adolescence of Joan and Peter, their experiences of school and university. They bicker, quarrel, flirt with other boys and girls, but one of the problems the novel has here is that it telegraphs too patently that Joan and Peter are meant to be together, which robs these passages of tension—the various sidebars into possible other relationships are only too evidently going nowhere. Eventually Joan discovers that she and Peter are not blood-relations, such that there is no reason why they couldn't marry. The outbreak of war interrupts this romantic consummation. All the boys from Joan and Peter's circle enlist, including Peter himself. Some of the boys are killed. Peter transfers from the infantry to the Royal Flying Corps. We're now at page 600 of this 750-page novel.

Only at this late stage does the pacing picks up again. The closing stretches of the novel contain vividly written scenes of aerial combat: Peter is posted to an observation balloon on the front line, which is in turn shot down. As he parachutes to safety the plane that punctured his balloon returns to finish him off and strafes his legs in mid-air. He survives though badly hurt and ends the book happy with Joan. The novel's final scene is Oswald reflecting on his experiencing of having raised these kids, and looking forward to working towards a better future for all children: the idea of a World State comes to him 'with the effect of a personal and preferential call' [14.10].

It might be possible to mount a critical defence of *Joan and Peter* not as prolix so much as an embodiment and *therefore* articulation of blockage and inaction as such, as well as a representation and critique of those things on a social and pedagogic level. Oswald has a recurrent nightmare of life as a kind of apotheosis of the Hideous Obstacle:

> A dark forest. He was one of the captains of a vaguely conceived expedition that was lost in an interminable wilderness of shadows; sometimes it was an expedition of limitless millions, and the black trees and creepers about him went up as high as the sky, and sometimes he alone seemed to be the entire expedition, and the darkness rested on his eyes, and the thorns wounded him, and the great ropes of the creepers slashed his face. He was always struggling to get through this forest to some unknown hope, to some place where there was light, where there was air and freedom, where one could look with brotherly security upon the stars; and this forest which was Life, held him back; it held him with its darkness…. He would awaken in a sweating agony. [*Joan and Peter*, 9.3]

In his *Autobiography* Wells is candid in his retrospective assessment: the work 'starts respectably in large novel form and becomes dialogue only towards the end. It is as shamelessly unfinished as a Gothic cathedral. It was to have been a great novel about Education but it grew so large…' [*Experiment*, 420], suggesting that he became pleonastically obstructed in writing a novel about obstruction.

Wells followed the length of *Joan and Peter* with a much shorter, brisker book: *The Undying Fire* (1919) a modern-day version of the *Book of Job*. This novel starts in the cosmic spaces where God and Satan are playing chess. The two immortals re-run their celebrated wager, and select one Job Huss, a character based on Frederick Sanderson, to torment. Like Sanderson with Oundle, Huss is 'the headmaster of the great modern public school at Woldingstanton in Norfolk' [2.2]. Through no delinquency of his, fire kills two pupils at the school and an assistant master is killed 'by an explosion in the chemical laboratory' that sprays him with acid. Worse follows: Huss's lawyer, having embezzled and lost all Huss's money, commits suicide. Huss is diagnosed with cancer and given only a short time to live. Finally Huss learns that his beloved only son, a pilot in the RFC, has been shot down over enemy lines and killed.

His Job's comforters—in the Biblical original, of course, these are Eliphaz the Temanite, Bildad the Shuhite and Zophar the Naamathite—are in Wells's version: Sir Eliphaz Burrows ('the patentee and manufacturer of those Temanite building blocks which have revolutionized the construction of army hutments'), William Dad ('one of the chief contractors for aeroplanes in England') and Joseph Farr, the head of the technical section of Woldingstanton School, who wants to depose Huss and take over as headmaster. Huss knows how sneaky Farr is, but has been unable to replace him because of a shortage of technically skilled teachers. Wells sticks, with varying degrees of ingenuity, to the structure of the Biblical fable. Huss's wife encourages him, though not in so many words, to curse God and die. His comforters needle him in ways paralleling the Tanakhan original. The role of Elihu is played by Huss's physician, Dr Elihu Barrack, who urges Huss to undertake a potentially fatal operation to remove his cancerous lump, and who discusses Huss's existential concerns with him, agreeing and disagreeing by turns. The two of them discuss the high calling of the world's educators.

> What is the task of the teacher in the world? It is the greatest of all human tasks. It is to ensure that Man, Man the Divine, grows in the souls of men. [*Undying Fire*]

Huss is admitted for his operation and under anaesthetic has visions, first of a mocking Satan, and then of God himself who issues a divine promise that mankind shall conquer the stars 'so long as your courage endures' [6.1]:

> It seemed to him that the whole universe began to move inward upon itself, faster and faster, until at last with an incredible haste it rushed together. He

resisted this collapse in vain, and with a sense of overwhelmed effort. The white light of God and the whirling colours of the universe, the spaces between the stars—it was as if an unseen fist gripped them together. They rushed to one point as water in a clepsydra rushes to its hole. The whole universe became small, became a little thing, diminished to the size of a coin, of a spot, of a pinpoint, of one intense black mathematical point, and—vanished. He heard his own voice crying in the void like a little thing blown before the wind: 'But will my courage endure?' [*Undying Fire*, 6.1]

He wakes. The operation is over. The novel's coda is what you'd expect: the removed cancer is revealed to be non-malignant; a distant relative dies leaving Huss a fortune; the boys at Woldingstanton school form a committee to prevent him from being sacked and finally news comes that Huss's son is a prisoner of war, and not dead after all. As a reading of Job, Wells's little fable leans heavily on the final term in the celebrated Biblical verse (quoted several times by Wells): 'who is this that darkeneth counsel by words without knowledge?' [Job 38:2]. Human beings need to *know more*, Wells says, and *know better*. He dedicates the book to 'All Schoolmasters and Schoolmistresses and Every Teacher in the World'. The religious, or perhaps it would be better to say pseudo-religious, frame tacitly elevates the teacher's role into a kind of divinely sanctioned mission, almost a return to Coleridge's ideas of clerisy.

This subject so inspired Wells during the early 1920s that—after being content for decades to influence the political process from behind the scenes and via his journalism—Wells decided to become a Member of Parliament to advocate directly for educational reform. He stood as Labour parliamentary candidate for London University in 1922 (until 1950 London University returned an MP to the Commons, as did Oxford, Cambridge, and nine other universities). He campaigned hard through October and November of that year, but the voters were not persuaded:

Sydney Russell Wells (Conservative/Unionist): 4,037 votes
  Professor Frederick Pollard (Liberal): 2,593
  H G Wells (Labour): 1,420

Wells in 1922 ran on a platform of educational reform: calling this 'the key to the future' and insisting the matter was not being properly addressed by either the Conservatives or Liberals: Lloyd George 'avoids the issue like a sparrow', he said, and 'Bonar Law like an earthworm', which conceivably counted as coruscating political banter in 1922. Still, worm or not, the Conservative Bonar Law was P.M. now; and so he remained until May 1923 when ill health, in the form of an aggressive throat-cancer, forced him to resign (He died a few months later). He was replaced as P.M. by Stanley Baldwin, who decided he needed a mandate from the people and so called a new General Election in 1923. On 21 March 1923 Wells delivered a lecture at a fundraising dinner at the University of London Club—later published as the pamphlet *Socialism and the Scientific Motive* (1923)—announcing that he was standing again, for the same seat and advocating the same cause—the urgency of educational reform on scientific and historical lines: 'We of the Labour Party, as a party, believe in science and in the scientific motive, as a motive altogether superior to profit-seeking.' Come December Wells added precisely seven votes to his 1922 tally:

> Sydney Russell Wells (Conservative/Unionist): 3,833 votes
> Professor Frederick Pollard (Liberal): 2,180
> H G Wells (Labour): 1,427

The 1923 election resulted in a hung parliament, and Ramsay MacDonald formed the UK's first-ever Labour government by negotiating a deal with the Liberals. The Liberal Leader Herbert Asquith only agreed to this deal—indeed, he specifically turned down overtures from the Tories—because he believed MacDonald would prove so incompetent it would destroy Labour support in the country and bring voters back to the Liberals. In the event MacDonald did pretty well, avoiding major strikes, passing Insurance Acts to extend unemployment benefit and getting a Housing Act passed which greatly expanded municipal housing for low paid workers. As a minority government, though, his administration was vulnerable, and in the event it only lasted 10 months. Another general election was held in October 1924. But by then Wells had publicly withdrawn from political campaigning, and did not stand again. In the *Autobiography* he looks back on these 2 years:

> In some manner the new education had to be got into the education office and the syllabuses and the schools, and since no one else seemed to be doing it, I felt under an obligation to try, however ineffectively, to do something about it myself. I turned my reluctant face towards meetings and committee-rooms again. I had had nothing to do with such things since my Fabian withdrawal. I heard with dislike and a sinking heart my straining voice once more beginning speeches. I dislike my voice in a meeting so much that it gives me an exasperated manner and I lose my thread listening to it. I still thought the Labour Party might be the party most responsive to constructive ideas in education, and in order to secure a footing in its councils I stood as Labour candidate for the London University at the 1922 and 1923 elections. I had no prospect of being returned, but I thought that by writing and publishing election addresses and

such leaflets as *The Labour Ideal of Education* (1923) I might impose a modernization of the schools' curriculum, upon the party policy and so get general history at least into its proper place as elementary school history.… But the older men in control of the Labour Party at that time were quite impervious to the idea of changing education. They did not consider education as a matter of primary importance. They had themselves managed very well with very little. [*Experiment in Autobiography* (1934), 630–31]

Bibliography

Mackenzie, Norman and Jeanne Mackenzie (1973) *The Time Traveller: The Life of H G Wells*. London: Weidenfeld and Nicholson.

20

World-Historical

The Outline of History (1920)

Conceived as a comprehensive history of the whole world *The Outline of History* (1920) proved Wells's single most successful book. It had sold a staggering two million copies by the end of the 1920s alone, and, periodically updated, it continued to sell strongly through the century; in 1927, only a few years after publication, Wells told Julian Huxley the book had earned him £60,000—getting on for three million pounds in today's money [Huxley, 151]. Translated into every major language (including Braille) it had an immense impact on mid-century culture and education. There were many subsequent redactions and versions: editions designed for elementary students, large format deluxe editions with many illustrations, some in colour. A cheaper, one-volume condensation, *A Short History*, was followed in 1925 by an edition further condensed and 'adapted for school use', and then another redaction aimed at even younger readers: *The Junior Version of the Outline* (1932). Wells oversaw all the editions, going so far as to entertain the Japanese translator in his home to discuss the book and ensure the best rendering. As well as all these editions Wells also published ancillary volumes: a *Teachers Handbook* and *A Supplement for Practical History*, including ideas for art and crafts, plays and other methods pedagogically to integrate the thesis of the work into school-level work. He really wanted the book to go into schools and colleges. Education, the major theme in both *Joan and Peter* (1918) and *The Undying Fire* (1919), was Wells's chief motivation for writing the *Outline* in the first place. David Smith summarises the situation out of which the book emerged:

> He and his friends on the League of Nations committee had discussed textbooks and methods of education, as a way of preventing future wars, but time did not

© The Author(s) 2019
A. Roberts, *H G Wells*, Literary Lives, https://doi.org/10.1007/978-3-030-26421-5_20

permit them to produce their own. Wells apparently asked members of the committee, especially Alfred Zimmern, Gilbert Murray and Ernest Barker, to work on a new world history to replace the older nationalistic and narrow treatments. They refused on the grounds of lack of time, lack of formal preparation and unwillingness to give the effort. Wells decided he must do it himself. [Smith, 249]

The difficulty was the sheer scale of the task, and the fact that compiling it and writing it would take years of dedicated work which would, in turn, prevent Wells from earning money in his usual way. In the *Experiment in Autobiography* he recalls discussing the project with his wife.

> Before I began it I had a very serious talk with my wife about our financial position. The little parcel of securities we had accumulated before 1914 had been badly damaged by the war. Its value had fallen from about £20,000 to less than half that amount. But the success of *Mr. Britling* had more than repaired that damage and my position as a journalist had improved. We decided that I could afford a year's hard work on this précis of history, although it might bring in very little and even though I risked dropping for a time below the habitual novel reader's horizon. As a matter of fact I dropped below that horizon for good. I lost touch with the reviewers and the libraries, I never regained it, and if I wrote a novel now it would be dealt with by itself by some special critic, as a singular book, and not go into the 'fiction' class. [*Experiment in Autobiography*, 613–14]

Wells is not correct that this project was responsible for eclipsing his work as a novelist; although something of an eclipse *was* evident through the 1920s and 1930s some of these later novels did well, and most of his earlier novels remained in print and sold strongly right through to his death. But there's no denying that the writing the *Outline* entailed genuine risk for Wells. 'I set to work,' Wells says, 'undeterred by my burning boats.'

His process, he later said, involved '"mugging up" the material and writing or rewriting practically all of it myself, and then getting the various parts vetted and revised and, in one part, rewritten by specialists' [*Experiment*, 618]. He relied mostly on a team of six experts: Sir Ray Lankester (director of the Natural History Museum), Sir Harry Johnston (an Africa and Asia expert), Gilbert Murray (the famous classicist), Ernest Barker (political scientist and historian), Sir Denison Ross (Orientalist and Sinophile) and the graphic artist Frank Horrabin, who produced for the work hundreds of beautifully designed maps and charts.

The *Outline* was widely, positively and sometimes dithyrambically reviewed. Not everybody was won over, though. Playwright Henry Jones published a string of hostile articles in the *London Evening Standard* and the *New York*

Sunday Times, attacking Wells as 'a Hater of England' and a 'Bolshevik', someone 'seeking to break in pieces the British Empire and to shake the foundations of civil order throughout the world'. There were more substantive and important critiques, too. Chesterton wrote his own account of human history, *The Everlasting Man* (1925), in explicit rebuttal to Wells's book (he attempted to reaffirm the divinity of Christ, something Wells's history denied) and Hilaire Belloc published a plethora articles in the Catholic journals *Universe*, *Southern Cross* and *Catholic Bulletin* through 1925 and 1926, all attacking Wells in very personal terms as ignorant, childish, biased against Catholics, guilty of 'the very grievous fault of being ignorant that he is ignorant', and possessing 'the strange cocksureness of the man who knows only the old conventional textbook of his schooldays and mistakes it for universal knowledge'. Belloc collected these pieces into a book rather misleadingly called *A Companion to Mr. Wells's 'Outline of History'* (1926). It wasn't a provocation Wells could ignore. He responded to Belloc in a small book entitled *Mr. Belloc Objects to 'The Outline of History'* (1926). Belloc in turn responded with *Mr. Belloc Still Objects* in 1927. 'At the end of the six-year struggle Belloc claimed to have written over 100,000 words in refutation of the central argument of Wells's book' [Pearce, 300]. Ben Lockerd gives a flavour of Belloc's approach:

> Belloc attacks many of Wells's specific points—catching him out on a fairly large number of errors such as stating that … the Immaculate Conception refers to the conception of Jesus. Belloc accuses Wells of 'entertaining unreasoning reactions,' and says that 'these reactions have a common root. They are all provoked by anything traditional'. Belloc notes that the aim of establishing the mechanistic theory of natural selection as the sole cause of speciation is to remove any notion of design from the equation, and thus 'to get rid of the necessity for a Creator'. He attacks with particular vehemence Wells's treatment of priests…. Near the end, Belloc returns with insulting language to what he terms Wells's 'provincialism': 'We are reading in this *Outline of History* the work of a mind closely confined to a particular place and moment—the late Victorian London suburbs. Such a mind has an apparatus quite inferior to the task of historical writing' (227). [Lockerd, 177–78]

Rebutting this ad hominem attack, Wells identified various errors in Belloc's articles and indulged in a spot of ad-hominem-ing of his own (calling Belloc 'rather exceptionally ignorant of modern scientific literature', and 'beautifully absurd' [Wells, *Belloc Objects* 1, 22]). There have been times in the past when religion has, Wells concedes, played an important role in helping human beings to exercise self-control, but 'mankind is now growing out of Christianity;

indeed mankind is growing out of the idea of Deity' [*Belloc Objects*, 54]. Wells's *God the Invisible King* phase is, evidently, far behind him now.

The *Outline of History* as a whole is disposed into forty chapters of varying lengths (though all long), grouped into eight books; with an extra chapter as coda, bracketed solus as 'Book IX: Chapter 41. The Next Stage in History'. The eight books divide into three sections: *prehuman, prehistorical* and *historical*. The first book, 'The Making of Our World', opens with 'the Earth in Space and Time', proceeds through geological long-time and the process of evolution by means of natural selection across the first eons of single-celled and simple organisms, through 'the Age of Reptiles' and into 'the Age of Mammals'. The second ('The Making of Man') speculates about the descent of humankind, through early hominids, Neanderthal Man and on to homo sapiens, and thence through possibilities as to the origin of language, farming, larger-scale social organisation, war and the beginnings of social and cultural civilisation.

The next three books take us into recorded history: Book 3 covers what Wells estimates are 'the first five thousand years' of coherent human historical narrative: from 'Primitive Aryan life', Sumerians, Assyrians, Chaldeans, Egyptians, the early civilisation of India and China, the invention of writing and the coalescence of religious feeling into fixed systems of 'gods and stars, priests and kings' [1:232]. Book 4 concerns 'Judea, Greece and India' from Saul, David and Solomon through to Alexander the Great; and Book 5 'the Rise and Collapse of the Roman Empire'. Book 6 covers 'the beginnings, the rise and the divisions' of Christianity and Islam. Since he is, Wells insists, 'trying to write as if this book was to be read as much by Hindus or Moslems or Buddhists as by Americans and Western Europeans' he declares he will 'hold closely to the apparent facts, and avoid, without any disputation or denial, the theological interpretations that have been imposed upon them' [1:569]. Book 7 is divided equally between the 'Great Empire of Jengis Khan' and the European Renaissance. In Book 8, 'Princes, Parliaments and Powers' Wells rounds-off his narrative by suggesting that the age of monarchic absolutism began to decay in 1700, giving way to a modern political logic of 'new and shapeless forces of freedom in the community' [2.216], manifesting as an upsurge in democratic structures and more integrated polities. He moves briskly through the rise of 'the new Democratic Republics of America and France' and rattles his narrative up to 1920 with a dash through the nineteenth century and World War I. The whole of the nineteenth century (Chapter 39) is summarised as 'the Increase of Knowledge and Clear Thinking: the Nationalist Phase' which leads directly into Chapter 40 'The Close of the Great Power Period'. Wells is arguing that the upsurge in nationalism that marked this epoch—from German and Italian unification to the myriad nationalist movements in British and French imperialist holdings—was a last gasp of the concept, and that the incipient World State was in the process of bringing this 'Great Power' age to a close. It's the wishfullest of Wellsian wishful thinking, and posterity has not endorsed its judgements.

The *Outline* provides a narrative both broad and relatively fine-textured, although it does have its blind spots. Although Wells goes out of his way to create a more global history, the focus is still overwhelmingly European, Asian and Chinese: Africa is hardly mentioned until it becomes a site for European colonial expansion, and the Americas don't appear at all until white settlement. On the plus side Wells's approach is also, mostly, undogmatic. He presents possibilities as possibilities, not probabilities and where scholarly experts disagree he picks a line and mentions alternatives in a footnote. This isn't to say the work is not tendentious. On the contrary, indeed, its *tendenz* is freely acknowledged and on display throughout: that human evolution has been a process of dissemination and diversification that is, through many advances and retreats, working towards a global identity and political unity. It is from this thesis that the work's most dubious subjectivities derive. Wells is not shy of judging this or that historical phenomenon 'a failure', and when he does so it's because it falls short of this particular aim. So, despite achieving much the Roman Empire ultimately failed, says Wells, in that it did not expand to create the World State. Similarly, Christendom is analysed with a fair degree of historical nuance but is ultimately brought to this same severe judicial bar: 'the history of Europe from the fifth century onward to the fifteenth is very largely the history of the failure of this great idea of a divine world government to realize itself in practice' [1:605]. In a way this is fair enough. The advantage with a front-and-centre acknowledged bias is that it's easier for a reader to discount it. And Wells has an unerring sense of when to leaven the drier factual elaboration with an interesting personal anecdote about a historical figure, or an intriguing speculation. There are also what it's tempting to think of as personal touches. Of Alexander's father Philip we're told that 'like many energetic and imaginative men, he was prone to impatient love impulses' [1:373], which sounds like something we can declare with more certainty of Herbert of Wells than Philip of Macedon. Shakespeare, Milton and Dickens are not mentioned, but Plato, Thomas More and Campanella are given respectful nods.

Largely Wells avoids goodies-and-baddies history, but when he slips into that idiom it's generally because the individual involved falls short of Wells's personal and utopian vision of a unified world state. So it is that he attacks Machiavelli ('this morally blind man was living in a little world of morally blind men') because he 'manifestly had no belief in any … Utopian visions of world-wide human order, or attempts to realize the City of God' [2:197]. There's a fairly detailed account of Napoleon's career, but Wells ends up apologising for its length: 'Napoleon bulks disproportionately,' he concedes, but adds: 'he was of little significance to the broad onward movement of human affairs; he was an interruption, a reminder of latent evils, a thing like the bacterium of some pestilence' [2:384]. The *Outline* ends with Wells, in 1920, tabulating what he hopes will be the characteristics of the coming World State:

1. It will be based upon a common world religion, very much simplified and universalized and better understood. This will not be Christianity nor Islam nor Buddhism nor any such specialized form of religion, but religion itself pure and undefiled.
2. And this world state will be sustained by a universal education, organized upon a scale and of a penetration and quality beyond all present experience. The whole race, and not simply classes and peoples, will be educated. …
3. There will be no armies, no navies, and no classes of unemployed people, wealthy or poor.
4. The world-state's organization of scientific research and record compared with that of to-day will be like an ocean liner beside the dug-out canoe of some early heliolithic wanderer.
5. There will be a vast free literature of criticism and discussion.
6. The world's political organization will be democratic, that is to say, the government and direction of affairs will be in immediate touch with and responsive to the general thought of the educated whole population.
7. Its economic organization will be an exploitation of all natural wealth and every fresh possibility science reveals, by the agents and servants of the common government for the common good. Private enterprise will be the servant—a useful, valued, and well-rewarded servant—and no longer the robber master of the commonweal.
8. And this implies two achievements that seem very difficult to us to-day. They are matters of mechanism, but they are as essential to the world's well-being as it is to a soldier's, no matter how brave he may be, that his machine gun should not jam, and to an aeronaut's that his steering-gear should not fail him in mid-air. Political well-being demands that electoral methods shall be used, and economic well-being requires that a currency shall be used, safeguarded or proof against the contrivances and manipulations of clever, dishonest men. [*Outline of History*, 2:586–87]

The first three of these have simply not come to pass, the next three have to some degree and the last two manifestly haven't at all: a strike-rate of three out of eight.

The *Outline* is essentially a political history of mankind, not in the narrow sense of confining itself to actual political institutions, but in the broader sense of exploring the dynamics of human connectivity. In his *Autobiography* Wells calls the *Outline* 'an essay on the growth of association since the dawn of animal communities' [*Experiment in Autobiography*, 614]; and *association* (which is to say: the ways in which and codes by which human beings group themselves together) is a fair thumbnail definition of politics. The whole thing 'planned itself naturally enough', says Wells, 'as a story of communications and increasing interdependence'. As history goes on, tracing the general trend rather than attending to every single up-and-down data point, what we see is: better and better communication between wider dispersed populations of humans that in turn creates greater and greater collective identity. Such, at any rate, is Wells's thesis.

It's a perfectly defensible argument. It may even be true, in the broader sense. But it's a thesis Wells was committed to before he began assembling the specific data that make up the *Outline*, and so a degree of distortion, even of bias, became inevitable. One example of this is found in Wells's concept of nationhood, or rather, in his refusal clearly to define what he means by nation. The *Outline*'s major argument is that the motion of capital-H History is from small tribes to bigger nations and thence from nations to a World State. But Wells nowhere makes clear whether he considers a nation primarily a familial, racial, linguistic, geographical or ideological unit, or merely an entity defined by historical contingency. Any of these cases could be argued, some with more credence than others, but Wells doesn't plump for any of them, preferring to bracket the term as a freer-floating signifier. The first sentence of Chapter 16 ('The First Civilizations') is: 'when the Aryan way of speech and life was beginning to spread … breaking up as it spread into a number of languages and nations, considerable communities of much more civilized men were already in existence in Egypt and in Mesopotamia' [1:183], which leaves it unclear whether we are to take 'nation' as equivalent to 'a considerable community of civilized men' or as a primarily linguistic entity ('languages and nations'), or as something else. Elsewhere Wells says 'the tribe was a big family; the nation a group of tribal families' [1:178] which suggests, without elaborating it, a familial or racial model of nationhood. These are both prehistorical instances. By the time Wells gets into the full swing of his historical grand narrative 'nationhood' is being taken for granted, and always as something to be deplored as an obstacle to the kind of über-national agglomerations that will birth the World State. So: 'China, under the last priest-emperors of the Chow Dynasty, was sinking into a state of great disorder. Each province clung to its separate nationality and traditions, and the Huns spread from province to province' [1:253]. Later he insists 'science knows no nationality' [2:175].

> In the sphere of race or nationality, for example, a "European" will often treat an "Asiatic" almost as if he were a different animal, while he will be disposed to regard another "European" as necessarily as virtuous and charming as himself. He will, as a matter of course, take sides with Europeans against Asiatics. But, as the reader of this history must realize, there is no such difference as the opposition of these names implies. It is a phantom difference created by two names. [*Outline of History*, 2:169]

Identifying with one's nation is 'selfish' [2:257]; nationality 'is really no more than the romantic and emotional exaggeration of the stresses produced by the discord of the natural political map with unsuitable political arrangements' [2:433]. 'Gladstone, in pursuit of his idea of nationality, brought political disaster upon himself' [2:245]. If *Outline of History* is telling a story, then its villain is nationhood. But none of this helps us understand what a nation actually *is*, or explains why people have proved so invested in the notion. In the coda, Wells insists that nationalism 'must follow the tribal gods to limbo'. 'Our true nationality is mankind' [2:614]. His wish hurries this eventuality out the door of world history, and, as we have seen, the *Outline* ends by announcing the coming of the Unified World and the withering away of the nation state.

The problem, here, is not just the judgement of hindsight; although hindsight is not forgiving of Wells's optimism. The problem is that his refusal to theorise nationhood left Wells unable to see how tenacious the nation state was liable to be. The notion, developed in the *Outline*, that the upsurge in nineteenth-century nationalism was a mere blip was never going to be a plausible one, and subsequent history has falsified it pretty comprehensively. Then again, the temptation to pronounce the end of 'the nation state' is one to which plenty of historians have succumbed. Michael Howard thought, in 1978, that 1890–1970 was 'the apotheosis of the nation state' and that the future would be decreasingly nationalist [Howard, 1]. The 'end of history' arguments that swarmed around the end of the last century were not just arguments about the triumph of Capitalism, they were also *globalisation* arguments: arguments that global trade and neoliberalism, eventuating in ever-larger free-trade areas (the EU, NAFTA and the like) would create a Capitalist mirror-image reality of Wells's socialist prediction. Such pseudo-prophetic enthusiasm proved just as premature as Wells's, a century earlier. What with the fragmentation of the USSR in myriad nation-states, resurgent Islamic-inflected nationhood in the middle and near east, Brexit, Trump and others, nationhood is suddenly back in the historical driving seat. Perhaps these ideas will never go away. A couple of years ago David Cannadine quoted Benedict Anderson approvingly, that 'nations should not be seen as eternal and precisely defined units of territorial sovereignty and collective solidarity' but should rather be regarded as 'transient, provisional, ephemeral' [Cannadine, 87]. Cannadine's own book, like Wells's, looks past nationhood to a future human collectivity:

> We need to see beyond our differences, our sectional interests, our identity politics, and our parochial concerns to embrace and to celebrate he common humanity that has always bound us together, that still binds us together today, and that will continue to bind us together in the future. [Cannadine, 264]

This shows that Wells's vision is still alive, and perhaps stands as corrective to my criticisms. I certainly wouldn't deny that nationalism has been the nursery of uncounted evils in human affairs. But I do suggest that Wells underthinks the concept, and is blind to the ways it mediates a whole nest of crucial human identities, passions and interests. He does so because he wants to brush it under the carpet of Deep Time.

Bibliography

Cannadine, David (2013). *The Undivided Past: History Beyond Our Differences* Harmondsworth: Penguin.

Howard, Michael (1978). *War and the Nation State*. Oxford University Press.

Huxley, Julian (1970) *Memories*. George Allen & Unwin.

Lockerd, Ben (2012), '"Superficial Notions of Evolution": Eliot's Critique of Evolutionary Historiography', *Religion & Literature*, 44:1 (2012), 174–180.

Pearce, Joseph (2002). *Old Thunder: A Life of Hilaire Belloc*. London: HarperCollins.

Ross, William (2001) *H G Wells's World Reborn: the* Outline of History *and Its Companions*. Susquehanna University Press.

Smith, David C. (1986). *Wells: Desperately Mortal*. Yale University Press.

21

Futures and Pasts

Men Like Gods (1923); *The Dream* (1924); *A Year of Prophesying* (1924); *Christina Alberta's Father* (1925); *The Way the World Is Going* (1928); *The Shape of Things to Come* (1933)

From 1901s *Anticipations* to 1917s *War and the Future* Wells had parlayed his reputation as a 'prophet' into actual futurology rather than into the longer-term science fiction of his first, great decade. Such speculation has the advantage of more directly engaging an audience's curiosity, perhaps, although it has the disadvantage of being much more fragile to immediate falsifiability. Wells accrued credit for foreseeing the battle tank—less a prediction than a canny technological hypothesis that the world noticed and developed—and for 'predicting' the Great War as a worldwide, high-tech combat (although Wells dated the coming war to c.1950, thought naval power redundant and misunderstood atomic fission). His time on government committees in the final years of the war and his disillusionment first with that process and then with the actuality of the *League of Nations*, left disaffected him with practical future-work; but he never lost his taste for near-future speculation and his 2-year labour delving into the deep past to write the *Outline of History* renewed in him an equal and opposite interest in the deep future. At any rate, the 1920s saw Wells return to something *like* his earlier science-fictional mode, although the books he wrote during this period manifest a significant shift of emphasis from his more enduring, classic SF of the 1890s.

The first of these is *Men Like Gods* (1923), a novel in which various characters slip through an unexplained wormhole in space-time (Einstein is mentioned but the concept is not elaborated) and emerge in a future utopian world. Wells's twist is that, rather than joyfully embracing this vastly better mode of living, the novel's characters dislike it and plot to seize power.

The novel's protagonist, Barnstaple, slides into utopia of the year AD 5000 when driving west out of Slough, just past Windsor. He arrives in the future

© The Author(s) 2019
A. Roberts, *H G Wells*, Literary Lives, https://doi.org/10.1007/978-3-030-26421-5_21

with two other cars who happened to be on the road at the same time, one containing Rupert Catskill, Secretary of State for War (a parodic version of Winston Churchill and portrayed by Wells as a reckless adventurer and dangerous reactionary), with his secretary Freddy Mush, Lady Stella and Mr Cecil Burleigh 'the great Conservative leader', a version of Bonar Law. In the other car is the obnoxious press baron Lord Barralonga (a most unflattering portrait of Lord Beaverbrook) and his low-minded chauffeur Ridley. Most of the novel is a Cook's Tour of Wells's Utopia: a world of two hundred and fifty million well-adjusted individuals living in an advanced mode of political anarchy. Their science is well ahead of our world and the utopians are welcoming to visitors, but the newcomers bring flu and measles with them to which the utopians have no natural immunity. Sickness sweeps the world and the visitors are quarantined away. Here the unscrupulous Catskill persuades the others to plot to overthrow the utopia and take power themselves. Only Barnstaple demurs. The plot doesn't get very far, and the plotters are punished by the utopians—it's not clear in the novel whether they are executed by being atomised, or just shifted into yet another dimension where their wickedness can do less harm. Barnstaple, alone spared, wants to stay in Utopia, but the utopians tell him he needs to return to his own world to help bring about Utopia there, and so he comes home, a changed man: 'he belonged now soul and body to the Revolution, to the Great Revolution that is afoot on Earth; that marches and will never desist nor rest again until old Earth is one city and Utopia set up therein. He knew clearly that this Revolution is life, and that all other living is a trafficking of life with death.'

Men Like Gods is a readable and sometimes even a jolly novel, although underplotted and a little second-hand. This utopia is not a carbon copy of the one in *A Modern Utopia* (1905), but it's close enough. One difference is that Wells felt able to be more sexually explicit: life in 5000 AD is marked by 'much love and laughter and friendship in Utopia and an abundant easy informal social life'. 'They loved no doubt', says Wells: 'subtly and deliciously'. Such loving, it seems, involved neither pity nor tenderness: 'there would be no need for those qualities' [*Men Like Gods*, 2.5.2]. Barnstaple falls for a beautiful young utopian called Lychnis, but the relationship never gets of the ground. At the novel's end he comes to realise that Lychnis 'was one of Utopia's failures'.

> She was a lingering romantic type and she cherished a great sorrow in her heart. She had had two children whom she had loved passionately. They were adorably fearless, and out of foolish pride she had urged them to swim out to sea and they had been taken by a current and drowned. Their father had been drowned in attempting their rescue and Lychnis had very nearly shared their fate. She had

been rescued. But her emotional life had stopped short at that point, had, as it were, struck an attitude and remained in it. Tragedy possessed her. She turned her back on laughter and gladness and looked for distress ... She did not want to talk to Mr. Barnstaple of the brightness of Utopia; she wanted him to talk to her of the miseries of earth and of his own miseries. [*Men Like Gods*, 3.2.7]

She has, in other words, a kind of kink for misery in a world in which nobody is miserable. Wells offers us this as a symptom of the health of his imagined future; but it's hard not to take it, rather, as an index of wider social pathology. You feel that a novel about Lychnis would have been a more interesting proposition than the strangers-in-paradise yarn Wells actually wrote.

Contemporary reviewers noted with approval that Wells was returning to 'utopian' and science-fictional writing: 'after long divagations in strange places', said a review in July 1923's issue of *Advocate of Peace Through Justice*, 'Mr. Wells returns to his early love and unfolds for our benefit another of those pseudo-scientific fairy stories which first brought him recognition', adding a note of regret: 'but Mr. Wells is no longer content to tell an impossible story with an air of conviction. He has a mission and he needs must preach.' That's true, but discursive as *Men Like Gods* is, it does contain science-fictional innovations here too, for this novel is one of the first fictional iterations of something that was to become a staple of science fiction, the many-universes hypothesis. Barnstaple reflects that 'that dear world of honesty and health was ... but one of countless universes that move together in time, that lie against one another, endlessly like the leaves of a book. And all of them are as nothing in the endless multitudes of systems and dimensions that surround them. "Could I but rotate my arm out of the limits set to it," one of the Utopians had said to him; "I could thrust it into a thousand universes"' [3.3.6]. Wells innovates what we would nowadays call 'alt-history', for the historical back-story of his Utopia is similar to, but not identical with, our history—for example, this reality has Christ in its history, but he was killed on a wheel rather than a cross.

On the question of eugenics, though, Wells takes a step backward: this is unambiguously a eugenicist Utopia: 'the Utopians told of eugenic beginnings, of a new and surer decision in the choice of parents, of an increasing certainty in the science of heredity' [1.6.2] The whole is based on the 'deliberate elimination of ugly, malignant, narrow, stupid and gloomy types during the past dozen centuries or so' [2.2.2]. Moreover, Wells imagines a specifically racially segregated eugenic regime: 3000 years had produced no 'general admixture of races': 'the various races mingled socially but did not interbreed very much; rather they purified and intensified their racial gifts and beauties.' *Purifying our racial gifts and beauties* is a slogan unlikely to gladden the progressive's heart.

Aldous Huxley later claimed he began writing *Brave New World* specifically as a satire of and rebuttal to *Men Like Gods* ('gradually it got out of hand', Huxley claimed, 'and turned into something quite different from what I'd originally intended' [Huxley, 198]). And in general Huxley had a remarkably low opinion of Wells, a dislike inflected by some honest-to-goodness *de haute en bas* snobbery: 'a rather horrid, vulgar little man', Huxley called him, whose novels were 'thin, shoddy, uninteresting and written in that dreadful swill-tub style [which was] H. G.'s woodnote'. H.G., for his part, understood very well the snobbery that informed Huxley's animadversion. He himself thought *Brave New World* a betrayal of the future and dismissed it as 'that Bible of the impotent genteel' [Wells, *The New World Order* (1939)]. Though not exactly a reactionary Huxley was an old Etonian and Balliol man, where H G Wells was a lower-middle-class Normal School chap. Class and its immanent toxicity, can never be discounted when considering English cultural or social life. It is as a fugitive from the class into which he was born—a self-made man— that Wells was most disruptive to the un- or underconsidered assumptions of his fellow Britons.

The following year saw another Wellsian future-utopian novel: *The Dream* (1924). The titular dreamer is Sarnac, a citizen of a utopian Earth 2000 years in the future. He has, with his friends, excavated the ruins of an antique town, its railway station and tunnel—all destroyed by nerve-gas in some forgotten war and filled with mummified corpses. After a day's hard digging Sarnac falls asleep and dreams the life, entire, of a certain Harry Mortimer Smith from the end of the nineteenth century. The titular dream, in other words, is Harry's life story. It's a life characterised by the obstacles of poverty, ignorance and the era's pervasive sexual obfuscation, jealousy and possessiveness. Everyman Harry struggles, makes some headway and then dies. In the morning Sarnac relates his dream in detail to his friends and they interject comments upon the (to them) baffling mores, customs and paraphernalia of this vanished time. The contrast is explicitly made between the pinching and immiserating early twentieth century and the bright collective happiness and open possibilities of the utopian future. That's the second meaning of the title, of course: the dream is *our* dream or at least Wells's dream, the one he wishes us to share: the dream of achievable Utopia.

In *Men Like Gods* people from our lapsarian era travel to a far-future Utopia; in *The Dream* a person from that far-future Utopia travels to our era. We get to see the issue from, as it were, both sides. Of course, Sarnac in *The Dream*, 'travels' via dream-vision where Barnstaple and the others in *Men Like Gods* 'actually' travel through a kind of Einsteinian portal in space-time. But in fact both novels are playing intertextual games with Bunyan's *Pilgrim's Progress*. Barnstaple in *Men Like Gods* passes not through Bunyan's Slough of Despond but the actual Slough in Berkshire, then though a magic 'Wicket Gate' into the 'Land which is to come' where he travels, pilgrim-like, through a Valley of Rest, to a place called Quarantine Crag and other such allegorically named locations. Conversely *The Dream* dramatises Bunyan's governing conceit: the ancient tunnel, Sarnac's uneasy sleep, his dream of a pauperised Edwardian past are all, as it were: 'I lighted on a certain place, where was a Denn; And I laid me down in that place to sleep: And as I slept I dreamed a Dream. I dreamed, and behold I saw a Man clothed with Rags.'

Sarnac's man clothed with rags is Harry Mortimer Smith and Sarnac tells Harry's story using the narratorial 'I', as if he lived it himself—born and raised in 'Cherry Gardens' on the South Downs, 'Harry's father is a greengrocer who sinks into drinking and gambling. Harry's sister Fanny is 'a conspicuously lovely girl' runs away from home with is lover—Sarnac's friends think this a brave and wonderful thing, but Victorian social mores ostracise her. Harry gets a job at the publishing firm of Crane & Newberry, where he prospers (some of this section of the novel is based loosely on the career of Wells's friend, Frank Swinnerton) but his courtship of a girl called Hetty is tangled up with the coming of war: 'in 1914 Anno Domini, a magic wand, the wand of political catastrophe, waved to and fro over Europe, and the aspect of that world changed, accumulation gave place to destruction' [2.6.1]. Harry survives the war but returns to find that Hetty is pregnant with another man's child and after some sordid complications this man, Hetty's lover, kills Harry:

> He waylaid me in the passage-way to the yard of Thunderstone House. He had been drinking, and as soon as I saw his flushed face, half-angry and half-scared, I had an intimation of what might befall … The report of the pistol, which sounded very loud to me, came at once, and a feeling as though I'd been kicked in the small of the back. The pistol was one of those that go on firing automatically as long as the trigger is gripped. It fired two other shots, and one got my knee and smashed it. 'Damn the thing!' he screamed and threw it down as though it had stung him. [*The Dream*, 2.7.9]

Harry dies and Sarnac wakes from his dream to see Hetty leaning over him on the utopian hillside, except that 'Hetty had become my dear Sunray who is mistress of my life. And the sunshine was on us and on her face' [2.7.9].

In some senses Wells's life in the 1920s was at a high point: he was more famous, respected and materially well-off than he had ever been. Nonetheless

1922 saw him in a desperate state mentally and emotionally. In the *Experiment in Autobiography* Wells himself identified four such crisis moments in his life story: his youthful period as an apprentice; running away from his first wife; his abortive elopement with Amber Reeves in 1910—and the years 1922–23. It was all down, he thought, to a self-confessed 'fugitive' quality in his makeup: 'At phase after phase I find myself saying in effect: "I must get out of this. I must get clear. I must get away from all this and think and then begin again. These daily routines are wrapping about me, embedding me in a mass of trite and habitual responses. I must have the refreshment of new sights, sounds, colours or I shall die away"' [*Experiment in Autobiography*, 631].

Part of the crisis was a disturbance in the balance that had sustained him emotionally and sexually for a decade—his domestic contentment with Jane at his house in Easton and with Rebecca West in London. West was increasingly dissatisfied with the arrangement. Her young son, Anthony, was not flourishing under the intermittency of his father's visits (for a long time he didn't even realise that Wells was his father) and she was making a significant name for herself as a writer on her own terms. She required a more permanent solution. In late 1922 the two of them arranged to holiday in Spain together, Wells sailing back from the USA and West meeting him at Gibraltar. She later recalled how exhausted the nearly-60-year-old Wells was when he landed, a tiredness that intensified his vanity and irascibility. She found it 'intolerable, then and for a long time afterwards':

> He would go away after a happy time and have to stay away and I would get furious letters alluding to imaginary misfortunes and failures on my part…Or there would be some trouble with the servants and he would then tell me that I was causing all such difficulties by my incompetence and would accuse me of dwelling on these difficulties, if not actually causing them in order that he should leave Jane and marry me. [Mackenzies, 340]

Wells was not sexually exclusive with West and one of his dalliances had uncommon consequences. A 'slight and very pretty woman with a face like the Mona Lisa' called Hedwig Verena had travelled from Vienna to London to translate of some of Wells's writing into German and Wells had initiated an affair with her. 'I excused it to myself', he recalled later, 'on the score of some flirtation of Rebecca with Sinclair Lewis' [*H. G. Wells in Love*, 103–04]. Fräulein Verena responded badly when Wells tried to break things off. She turned up at his London apartment naked except for shoes, stockings and a waterproof overcoat and cut her wrists with a razor in his presence. With the help of the building's hall porter the woman was transferred to Charing Cross Hospital.

Wells, anxious at the scandalous potential of this event, prevailed upon his press-baron friends Lords Beaverbrook and Rothermere to keep the story out of the papers. During his dalliance with her Wells had, thoughtlessly or perhaps with intentional cruelty, sent Verena to Rebecca West for advice on how to get published. West's own account of Verna's suicide attempt implied that Jane Wells was present, but that she fled when the blood started to flow and that a distraught Wells had first called on West herself for support and then later, fearing that he might get caught up in the inquest should Verena die, had attempted to use her as a shield. The precise details cannot be recuperated from the confusion of sources, but one thing is clear: 'at the end of the episode' West was left with feeling that Wells 'was "really insane with selfishness"' and that 'she decided that she had suffered enough and the time had come for her to break every tie linking her to him and to Jane' [West, 99–100]. She presented Wells with an ultimatum: leave Jane and marry her, or agree to pay her an allowance of £3000 a year. In the event they both agreed a third path: Wells paid West a one-off sum of £5000 and agreed to cover all Anthony West's school and university costs. With that they parted. Rebecca West left to tour America in October 1923.

The break-up left Wells in low spirits. In addition to working hard at his writing, he had contested two parliamentary elections in short order (for the University of London seat in 1922 and again in 1923) and campaigning had drained him. He endured a debilitating bout of bronchitis, and was soon to turn 60, a worrying climacteric for a man who had always placed such value on vitality and whoosh, which is to say, on youthfulness. Jane maintained Easton for him as a domestic haven, but they were spending relatively little time together now. She had her grown-up sons, her own circle of friends with whom she visited and took holidays, generally in Switzerland. The bald fact was Wells was lonely. He felt trapped and was looking for a mode of escape. This manifested in his writing as a simultaneous looking backward over his own life, in an attempt to understand his predicament and a renewed focus on imagining the *future*—that future which is necessarily the arena into which escape is possible. The former impulse resulted in a brief first-draft autobiography, named doomily enough 'An Outbreak of Auto-Obituary', dated 20 August 1924 and published in Wells's next book-lengthy collection of journalism, *A Year of Prophesying* (1924). The Auto-Obituary characterised its author as 'a creature trying to find its way out of a prison into which it has fallen' and much of *A Year of Prophesying* strikes a similar tone.

The prophesying exhibits the usual ratio of lucky guess to simple wrongness. Wells predicts small aeroplanes will replace cars as private runabouts (such planes 'need not cost more than a Ford car, even now, and it is almost as easy to fly as it is to drive an automobile' [2]) and that central planning and advances in building technology will result in 'the whole population of industrial London' being 'rehoused in fine and handsome apartment buildings, with night and day lifts, roof-gardens, and ... light, air and conveniences' [50]. But most of the articles are political in nature, with a strong bias towards Wells's big theme: the coming World State, 'that great Confederation of Mankind'. Wells several times regrets that, despite his earlier enthusiasm for the project, 'this League of Nations at Geneva is not even the germ of such a thing' [1]. He reports recent outrage at fascist violence in Italy and decides, alas overoptimistically, this marks 'the beginning of the end of Fascism' [45]. He confidently predicts not only the imminent institution of proportional representation in British politics, but that this change will lead to the 'extinction' of party politics [39]. In his next collection of occasional pieces, *The Way the World Is Going* (1928), the balance is weighted even more notably away from the prophetic and towards the erroneous. Wells sees no future in commercial air-travel and thinks radio broadcasting will never catch-on since gramophone records provide a better quality of sound. He also predicts the introduction of what he calls 'Companionate Marriages', halfway between celibacy and full marriage, to enable people to have sex (with birth control) and then either proceed to full marriage or else, provided there are no children, to dissolve the bond by mutual agreement and no legal complexities. This volume includes many essays on contemporary politics ('What is happening in China? Does it foreshadow a New Sort of Government in the World?') and attacks on 'The Absurdity of British Politics', as well as speculations about how technology will change the world ('The Remarkable Vogue of Broadcasting: will it continue?'; 'Changes in the Arts of War. Are Armies needed any longer?'). Wells, in predictive mode, continues blithely offering multiple hostages to fortune. He thinks a war between Great Britain and the USA is imminent ('such a war is being prepared now. What are intelligent people to do about it?' [14]) and insists democracy is on the way out: 'general elections and municipal elections or any sort of popular elections' will no longer have 'the slightest importance in the affairs of A.D. 2027' [4]. It is too early to say that this latter prophecy has been disproven, but I must say: it's not looking good for Wells's accuracy. More worryingly, Wells repeatedly praises the Kuomintang as the model of what will come to replace the exhausted models of representative democracy: the 'brain and nervous system' of New China, 'the Kuomintang is the most interesting thing by far upon the stage of current events, and the best worth watching and studying' [2]. This occasional authoritarian streak in Wells's is alarming on its own terms and hindsight makes it look foolish as well, but that doesn't mean we should dismiss it. Of course, no political authoritarian likes to think of themselves as tyrannical and Wells's flirtation with circumventing democratic politics combined a sense of frustration at the delay in the arrival of the World State with—importantly for his writing of the 1920s—a more complex dialogue in his own political imagination between understanding the dangers of tyranny and seeing autocracy as in some sense innately regal and ennobling. This was a problematic he explored more eloquently in his fiction than his non-fiction.

So, for example, it was during this turbulent 1924 period that Wells wrote one of his oddest, most striking and most unjustly overlooked novels: *Christina Alberta's Father* (1925). The titular father is Albert Edward Preemby, 'a retired laundryman and widower' who abandons his 'active interest in the Limpid Stream Laundry upon the death of his wife in the year of grace 1920' for more esoteric pursuits [1.1.1] Christina Alberta Preemby is not his biological daughter (she is the result of a holiday affair Mrs Preemby conducted in 1899, before she married Mr Preemby) but nonetheless he dotes on her and she on him. The novel figures, indeed, as a study of these two sharply contrasting character-types. On the one hand we have dreamy, passive, gentle-souled old Albert and his fascination with the supernatural and the occult; on the other fiercely determined, forward-looking Christina Alberta. In his *Autobiography* Wells describes her as 'a much more living figure than Ann Veronica and her morals are far easier' adding with what might be ruefulness, 'but times had changed and not a voice was raised against her' [*Experiment in Autobiography*, 401]. He regrets the lack of scandal to boost sales of this book.

Christina Alberta's activity and energy rolls down the familiar Wellsian groove of social and gender freedom: she takes lovers but repudiates marriage and children in the name of a sort of heroic egoism: 'I have known intelligent girls marry and have children, and when the baby appeared their minds evaporated. They became creatures of instinct, messing about with napkins. I could scream at the thought of it. No, I am an egoist pure and simple. I am Christina Alberta, and her only' [*Christina Alberta's Father*, 3.4.5]. Her many male admirers are drawn by 'her tremendous go. She was always up to something; she preferred standing to sitting, and she kicked her legs about while she talked to you ... he called her the Last Thing, the Van, the Ultimate Modern Girl, and the Life Force.'

Her father is very different. His passive dreaminess becomes, over the course of the novel, stark madness: he loses touch with reality and believes himself the reincarnation of the ancient Sumerian king Sargon the Great. Preemby's delusion is a perfectly harmless one; he threatens nobody and is easily managed by his daughter. He's neatly dressed, polite, coherent, careful with money—in all other respects sane. 'He's not a bit crazy', is how Christina

Alberta puts it to her male admirer Paul Lambone. 'He's just possessed by this one grand impossible idea.' Lambone tends to agree: 'I don't see that a man is insane because he believes he is a King or an Emperor—if some one tells him he is. After all, George V has no other grounds for imagining he is a King. The only difference is that rather more people have told him so' [1.6.3] But the rest of the world doesn't see it this way. Preemby is confined in the Observation Ward of the Gifford Street Infirmary. Here he believes himself in the Underworld and surrounded by demons.

> The strange soulless atmosphere of the place was but the first instant impression of Sargon. It was followed by a far more vivid and terrible realization, that this place was inhabited by beings who were only at the first glance men. Several were in bed; others were dressed in shabby and untidy clothes and either sat on their beds or were seated in chairs about the lower part of the room. One individual only was in motion; a grave-faced young man who was walking with an appearance of concentrated method to and fro in a restricted circle in the far corner of the ward. Another sat and seemed to remove a perpetually recurrent cobweb from his face by a perpetually repeated gesture.... In one of the beds close at hand a young man with a shock of black hair and an expression of fatuous satisfaction, that changed with dramatic suddenness to triumphant fierceness or insinuating lucidity, sat up and gesticulated and composed and recited an interminable poem—something in the manner of Browning. [*Christina Alberta's Father*, 2.3.1]

Very well rendered by Wells (that recurring cobweb is a particularly vivid touch). Another of Christina Alberta's admirers, Bobby Roothby, helps 'Sargon' escape from this grim loony bin, spiriting him away on a motorcycle and installing him in a room in Dymchurch where a reputable physician, Dr Devizes, can visit him. Out of his conversations with Devizes Preemby regains a degree of his sanity. But his health has been broken by his experiences and he dies before he can do anything with this hard-won wisdom.

Christina Alberta's Father is a compelling piece of writing, the best of Wells's 1920s novel by a long way. Wells's friend Carl Jung, speaking at a Viennese press conference in 1928, specifically singled it out for praise:

> My friend the great English writer H. G. Wells has drawn a wonderful picture of this state of affairs in a novel. The hero of his story *Christina Alberta's Father* is a petty businessman, completely imprisoned in his prosaic surroundings and his business. But in his few leisure hours another ego gradually emerges from his subconscious. He fancies he is the re-embodiment of the Babylonian ruler Sargon 1, the reincarnation of king of kings. Some kind of Sargon, in various

disguises, is hiding in every one of us. The fact that he cannot get out of the subconscious and is unable to develop himself is often the case of severe psychic disturbances. [McGuire and Hull, 42]

Indeed, Jung mentions the novel several times in his writing. 'Moral, philosophical and religious problems are, on account of their universal validity, the most likely to call for mythological compensation. In [*Christina Alberta's Father*] by H G Wells we find a classical type of compensation: Mr Preemby, a midget personality, discovers that he is really Sargon, King of Kings.' [Jung, 7: 284]. According to Jung's own account, the genesis of *Christina Alberta's Father* had been a discussion between Wells and Jung about madness and primitivism [Bennet, 93]. It's likely that Jung confided in Wells during one of these conversations about his own youthful mental dissociation and that Wells worked this into his novel:

> The romance of Jung's second self, his 'Personality No. 2', would later dominate his remarkable memoirs, composed in old age ... By Jung's own account, it all began in childhood—while he was being reprimanded by a neighbour for commandeering the fellow's rowing boat. As he took the scolding, Jung began to feel that he was really somebody else, somebody who had lived a long time ago, somebody very important. [Kerr, 4]

The specific lineaments of Preemby's madness do matter, both to the novel and to its effectiveness. *Christina Alberta's Father* would be a completely different novel and a much less interesting one, if Preemby believed himself to be—let's say—Napoleon. The point about Sargon is that, as a deep-historical figure he is as much a mythic as a historical individual; and it is the florescence of *myth* in the mundane pettiness of Preemby's life that is so compelling in Wells's telling. Although we're never in any doubt that Preemby is by conventional standards delusional (even Preemby himself comes to understand this), we also understand that he is finding a way to dignify his life by underpinning and elevating it with ancient myths—exactly, we might say, as Joyce does for Leo Bloom in *Ulysses*. And the point of the superposition of mythic and mundane in this novel, as in *Ulysses*, is transcendent rather than satirical, by way of suggesting the splendour hidden in the ordinary instead of (as it might be) mocking the baseness of the present-day. Though its title character suffers and eventually dies *Christina Alberta's Father* is a novel much more about joy than tragedy. Wells is asserting the fundamental and essentially spiritual dignity of even the most overlooked and neglected of human beings. The point of this novel, in other words, is that Preemby is a king not despite being (in Jung's cruel but accurate phrase) a 'midget personality', but *because of it*: that we are all great-souled and royal no matter how unprepossessing our exteriors. Wells's conversations with Jung about his 'Personality No. 2' are also behind his later *The Bulpington of Blup* (1932) and are discussed in greater detail below (see Chap. 22).

Wells's future-extrapolative novel *The Shape of Things to Come* (1933) is, probably, the last book Wells published that has any kind of currency today. That's a striking thing, since he went on to publish another 30 original titles before his death in 1946 and some of those later works are very good. The reason many people have heard of this book today is less down to its own merits and more to the fact that a famous movie was made of the work: *Things to Come* (1936), produced by Alexander Korda and directed by William Cameron Menzies. Wells collaborated enthusiastically with the filmmakers on this project and wrote the screenplay, visiting the set and offering advice, although the film is a very different beast to the book. Korda focuses on a main character, a businessman John Cabal (played by Raymond Massey) who survives the world's devastating future war and joins a cabal of technocrats called 'Wings Over the World' to outlaw war and build a new utopia.

The film is disposed into three acts: the first opens in the present day, marking the moment when war starts: aerial bombardment, general mobilisation, global conflict. We see Cabal piloting a plane and trying to stop a one-man bomber that is gassing his city. Having shot the plane down, Cabal lands chivalrously to rescues the enemy pilot (played by John Clements) from the wreckage. The two are forced to put on gas masks but the enemy pilot gives-up his gas mask to save the life of a young girl whom they chance upon, and Cabal, impressed at the fellow's sacrifice, takes the girl away with him in his plane. Act Two steps forward to the 1970s. War has dragged on for decades and people have forgotten why they are fighting. A plague called 'the Wandering Sickness' has devastated the population. Civilisation has collapsed and barbaric local warlords rule amongst the ruins. The film concentrates on one such, a warlord known as 'Chief' (played, with rather more campness than one might have thought appropriate for the role, by Ralph Richardson). John Cabal flies into town, landing in a sleekly futuristic plane and announces that he represents an elite band of engineers and mechanics, based in Basra, Iraq, who have formed a group to rebuild civilisation called 'Wings Over the World'. The Wings then fly over, in some impressively art-deco aircraft, easily beat the Chief's antiquated biplanes, drop soporific bombs on the population and take charge. This leads to the movie's final act. A montage shows Everytown (and the rest of the world) being rebuilt as part of the new Wellsian World State utopia. The white and shining monumental architecture of the new

Everytown makes for a visually striking design and proved immensely influential on later cinematic and televisual SF visual stylings of a particular sort of cleanly antiseptic future utopian infrastructure in myriad SF films and TV shows.

We're now in the 2030s. Massey plays his own great-grandson, Oswald Cabal, who is planning a space rocket to advance mankind's domination to the planets. In a poorly prepared-for final drama, an angry mob appears, it seems from nowhere (notionally they have been incited by a reactionary sculptor played by Cedric Hardwicke, who thinks progress has gone too far). The mob swarms towards the rocket's launch-pad intent on wrecking it, but Cabal fires the vessel into space just in time. It's a transparent and unconvincing attempt to wring dramatic tension out of a profoundly undramatic situation. The movie ends with Cabal's pious-pompous speechifying: 'Man … must go on, conquest beyond conquest. First this little planet and its winds and ways. And then all the laws of mind and matter that restrain him. Then the planets about him and at last, out across immensity to the stars. And when he has conquered all the deeps of Space, and all the mysteries of Time, still he will be beginning.'

There are those who think highly of this film, unfazed by its unconvincing characterisation, its stiff acting and its structural awkwardness. It would be rude of me to dismiss such people, but in truth *Things to Come*'s narrative falls between two stools—on the one hand too large-scale and disconnected for us properly to invest emotionally in specific characters (who can care about the aviator who gives us his gas mask to save the girl? What even happens to the latter?)—on the other too bogged-down in its individual stories to create the proper sense-of-wonder *longue durée* of the novel. More, there's a conceptual muddiness at the movie's heart. Is it arguing that the destructive barbarism of its 1940–70 is a necessary period of technological retrenchment in order to wipe the slate of history clean and so enable the gleaming twenty-first-century utopia? Or is the war a regrettable lapse, perfectly avoidable if only the nations of 1940 had listened to figures like Wells and thus a kind of distraction on the path to the broad, sunlit uplands of the film's conclusion? There is also a worrying ideological problematic at play. Not to put too fine a point on it: it's hard to imagine a clearer celebration of technofascism than this motion picture, the gleaming war-machine of the Wings Over the World possessing the highest of high-ground and imposing order on the squabbling barbarism below with shock, awe and superior engineering. This is a movie that says: left to its own devices human society descends into squabbling chaos. That says: only the übermensch focusing his will-to-power through his gleaming aerial machines can save us. The film is a starker fable of fascist victory than the book in part because the appearance of the engineering overlords is so abruptly *deus ex machina*. The compression of filmmaking render the movie's political palate two-tone, which means it only admits of two possibilities: social chaos or rule by the technocratic elite. No other political settlement, says *Things to Come*, is possible or even imaginable.

Fascism was increasingly dominating the Europe political landscape of the 1930s and more than once Wells expressed what might be called pseudo-fascist ideas. In 1932 he delivered a talk entitled 'Liberal Fascism' to the Young Liberals at their Summer School in Oxford in July 1932. It is the belief of the present author that, despite some flirtations with the movement, Wells was no fascist. He repeatedly and clearly repudiated the militarism and nationalism championed by actual fascist movements and his views became more sharply anti-authoritarian in the later 1930s, as events in Nazi Germany showed how illiberal actual fascism, applied efficiently enough, could be. But Wells still felt that there only was one path to a better future—a more or less authoritarian and singular focus of power, the top-down application of which would cut the combined Gordian knots of history, tradition, bureaucracy and petty self-interest. An aggressive commitment to technological and engineering development. Collective will overriding individual selfishness. Wells's son Anthony West waxed wroth at the idea that his father was any kind of fascist fellow-traveller, attacking those who claimed 'it was only my father's vanity that kept him from taking up the totalitarian cause in the early thirties', that 'he would have thrown in his lot [with the fascists] if he hadn't had a swollen-headed feeling that it was their place to come courting him rather than his to go over to them'. West, angrily denying this, attacks those who believed that

> as the author of *The Shape of Things To Come*, my father was one of the creators of the spirit of Munich. According to this thesis the fantasia in question, which first saw the light in 1933 and was very soon afterwards made into a film, with my father's active and enthralled participation, has to be considered as one of the many factors which created public support for the policy of appeasement, because it featured a massive air attack on London, shrewdly previsioned as taking place in 1940. [West, 130]

West is confident that the book and film are actually saying that mass bombing 'is the sort of thing you will more than likely be in for if you don't take a stand against Fascism now' [West, 130]. The real question, I suppose, is the extent to which Wells exhibited culpable naïveté in believing 'fascism' ever could be neatly separated out from its nationalism and militarism. Maintaining a huge fleet of art-deco bombers might be thought strangely inconsistent behaviour for an organisation that had outlawed war, after all.

Wells's screenplay tries to fudge the issue by dropping bombs not of high-explosive but of soporific gas, although this gas does kill Ralph Richardson's 'Chief' character. Massey's Cabal delivers a gloating speech over his body: 'dead, and his world dead with him—and a new world beginning. And now for the rule of the Airman, and a new life for mankind. For now we have to put the world in order'. The point and Wells's Act 2 moral, is that history must be erased, and that a Year Zero inaugurated, with all opposition to the coming top-down technocratic utopia eliminated. There are fewer more terrifying political strategies than insisting upon a Year Zero.

Turning our attention from movie to book we can ask whether it represents a more nuanced, less ideologically poisonous version of this story—from now to a decades-long near future war and out the other side to a World State utopia. The answer is that it does, but only up to a point. Certainly, not only the specifics of the story but its texture or flavour are very different between film and book: the pages are dense with detail, the narrative focus ranges around the world, various individual set-pieces (often vividly realised) intersperse long stretches of expository and explanatory prose. The book has none of the characters of the movie and no clumsily Bunyanesque 'Everytown' touches. Instead it carries-through the stylistic strategies of 1920s *Outline of History* into the future. Indeed, roughly the first quarter of the novel isn't concerned with the 'to-come' at all, instead recapitulating and abbreviating *Outline of History*'s account of the nineteenth century and the first two decades of the twentieth and bringing it up to 1933. And as far as that goes, it still reads pretty well. This, for an account of Hitler (for instance) gets to the nub of the issue:

> He gave vent to the German overstrain. He is the voice of Germany losing control. He denounced foreigners, Jews, Cosmopolitans, Communists, Republicans, owners of property and leaders in finance with raucous impartiality, and nothing is so pleasing to perplexed unhappy people as the denunciation of others. Not their fault, their troubles. They have been betrayed. To Fallada's question, 'Little Man, what now?' his answer was, 'Massacre Jews, expel foreigners, arm and get more arms, be German, utterly German, and increase and multiply.' [*Shape of Things to Come*, 2:7]

But Wells's historico-analytic tone becomes less persuasive as the novel moves further into the future. He does, it's true, imagine World War II breaking out in 1940, but Wells assumes it will be essentially a re-run of 1914–18, a trench-war stalemate dragging-on long into the 1950s. Plague then ravages the shattered remains of civilisation, described in a chapter with some nice zombie-like touches ('nothing would induce [plague victims] to remain in bed or hospital; nothing could keep them from entering towns and houses that were as yet immune. Thousands of these dying wanderers were shot by terror-stricken people whom they approached' [2:9]) but which has nothing to do with meaningful prophecy. Finally, in 1965, the remaining aircraft and shipping companies gather in Basra to consolidate and protect their interests. With the roads ruinous, a monopoly on flight and shipping is effectively a monopoly on all travel and trade and the 'Union of Transport' uses its influence to enforce civilisation and order upon the world. The account of the reconstruction occupies Book 3 ('The World Renaissance: The Birth of the Modern State, 1960–1978') and then we get a Cook's Tour of the World State Utopia in Books 4 and 5: 'The Modern State Militant 1978–2059' and 'The Modern State in Control of Life, 2059 to New Year's Day 2106'. In the novel there's no John or Oswald Cabal, no 'Wings Over the World' and no rocket to outer space, let alone any random mob to disrupt the launch. It's a novel of Stapledonian extrapolation that traces an end to history and a survey of the perfected society. This latter is a remix of many of the old Wellsian props and tropes, from a global currency based on energy rather than precious metals, to the centrality of education, global unity, the eradication of poverty, as well as the latest iteration of Wells's Samurai: a council of 'Air Dictators', who fly around compelling obedience to the new laws. Their credo is 'I shall do nothing worthwhile and nothing worthwhile will be done unless I pull myself together and stiffen up my conduct'. By the end of the novel, humanity has outgrown its need for rule by the Air Dictatorship, which sportingly (and improbably) gives up its power. Homo sapiens is ready for the next phase of human civilisation: radically reshaping the earth ('Geogonic Planning') and a move towards a transcendent group-consciousness of all mankind, to supersede 'our little selves' and become a collective 'Man the Undying who achieves these things through us' [5.9].

Because this whole historical narrative happens much more gradually and with vastly more specific narrative detail, it doesn't feel as wrenching as it does in the movie. But that fine-grained and confident narratorial voice is more than a little misleading. The basic wrench or twist, in historical process is still there, disguised under its great heap of prose. We still go from a species so violent and self-destructive that we all but annihilate ourselves, through the needle's-eye of a dictatorship of technocratic aircraft and ship owners, to a glorious gleaming future Utopia. And we're still entitled to ask: how?

The key, I think, is buried in the middle of the book, and, rather oddly, Wells does not draw attention to it: a short chapter called 'A Note on Hate and Cruelty' that describes human history as mostly dominated by 'systems of hatred' [2:8]. Wells styles hatred as a disease, 'a sort of social dementia' occasioned by 'the absence of a common idea of community'. As communities grow and fill-out more of the world's limited real-estate they press up against other communities and 'civilized motives [give] place to instinctive hostilities and spasmodic impulses' [2:8]. Our problem is that we don't understand that hatred is a disease, which is to say, that it is eradicable in the same way that diseases are eradicable: 'our ancestors did not envisage this as a controllable mental disease. They did not know that it was possible to get through life without hatred, just as they did not know that the coughs and colds that afflicted them and most of the phenomena of senility were avoidable.' This, then, is what enables the transition from our grisly present to Wells's gleaming future. We cure hatred. It's, so far as I can see, the first time Wells, howsoever tentatively, proposes an actual mechanism by which what we might call 'human nature' gets altered far enough to make Utopia practicable. Hatred is not integral to the human animals, he says: it comes about when 'two or more population groups, each with its own special narrow and inadaptable culture and usually with a distinctive language or dialect' finds itself 'by the change of scale in human affairs jammed together or imposed one upon another'. But this hatred is not in any sense a strategic group self-defence, it is rather a kind of group psychosis and literally rather than metaphorically an illness. You may be convinced or not, by this thesis but it suggests one reason why the novel version of this story works more effectively than the film version. The idiom of the movie is melodrama and the currencies of melodrama are hate and its coin-obverse, love. The idiom of the history textbook is necessarily purged of such destabilising emotional intensities. Form matches content rather better that way.

Bibliography

Bennet, Edward Armstrong (1967). *What Jung Really Said*. New York: Schocken Books.

Huxley, Aldous (1963). *Writers at Work: The Paris Review Interviews, Second Series*. New York: Viking.

Jung, Carl (1928) *The Relations Between the Ego and the Unconscious*. in Herbert Read, Michael Fordham and Gerhard Adler, eds. *Collected Works of C G Jung* (translated R. C. Hull) London: Routledge. 20 vols 1957–1970.

Kerr, John (1995). 'Madnesses', *London Review of Books* 17:6 (23 March 1995), pp. 3–6.

Mackenzie, Norman and Jeanne Mackenzie (1973) *The Time Traveller: the Life of H G Wells*. London: Weidenfeld and Nicholson.

McGuire, William and R.F.C. Hull, eds. (1977), *C.G. Jung Speaking: Interviews and Encounters*. Princeton University Press.

Smith, Grover ed. (1969). *Letters of Aldous Huxley*. London: Chatto & Windus.

West, Anthony (1984). *H. G. Wells. Aspects of a Life*. London: Hutchinson.

22

Odette Keun

The World of William Clissold (1926); *Meanwhile: The Picture of a Lady* (1927); *Mr. Blettsworthy on Rampole Island* (1928); *The Autocracy of Mr. Parham* (1930); *The Bulpington of Blup* (1932)

The success of the *Outline of History* added new layers to Wells's public fame, and on the strength of the work's success he travelled widely and continued to meet many famous and influential people through the 1920s and 1930s. His private life, though, was less replete. He still spent time with his wife Jane, although with their two sons now grown-up the Essex house in Easton was less of a home to him. After separating from Rebecca West Wells spent time looking for a new mistress, and, eventually, the mistress found him. A young European admirer called Odette Keun sent Wells a book she had written, an account of her time in post-Revolutionary Russia called *Sous Lenin*. Keun, the half-Italian half-Dutch daughter of a diplomat had, at 36, led a peripatetic and defiantly unconventional life. She declared that she admired the 58-year-old Wells as 'a super-star'. More than his political and futurological work it was Wells's steady insistence on affronting conventional sexual morality that intrigued Keun. The two arranged to meet when Wells visited Geneva in 1924, and became lovers at once. A fortnight later they travelled to France together and Wells rented a farmhouse in the Midi for them both to inhabit— the place was called Lou Bastidon, in a picturesque Provençal valley near the town of Grasse, far enough inland to be pastoral and quiet but close enough to Cannes for easy access to the riviera's socially livelier world. Wells enjoyed this locale so much that at the end of 1926 he bought a nearby house: a spacious Provençal farmhouse which Wells had converted to a luxurious domicile. Keun had the habit of calling her lover 'Lou Pidou', a baby-talk contraction of 'le petit dieu', and this became the name of the house. When the building work was finished Wells instructed the masons to carve 'Two Lovers Built This House' over the fireplace.

© The Author(s) 2019
A. Roberts, *H G Wells*, Literary Lives, https://doi.org/10.1007/978-3-030-26421-5_22

The relationship with Keun lasted through nine increasingly stormy and disruptive years, but, especially at the start, it enabled Wells to settle his life into some kind of balance. Keun stayed out of England—there were difficulties about her acquiring a visa—and she and Wells mostly shared a life in Lou Pidou, enabling Wells neatly to separate out (a neatness practical if not emotional) his lover from his married life at home. He later insisted that this division of his life between England and France was done 'with the connivance and help of my wife, who perceived that I was in grave mental distress and understood how things were with me'. Keun was an enthusiastic lover, grateful (at least at first) for Wells's money after a stretch of impecunious living, and ambitious for her own writing career, something in which she believed Wells would be an asset. And for Wells the stimulation of this new long-term relationship jump-started his fiction once again. Keun shares with Amber Reeves the distinction (if that's what it is) of figuring more directly in more Wellsian novels than any other lover, and although the portrait that emerges of Keun is far from flattering there's no doubting her energy or charisma.

An initial burst of energy produced Wells's longest novel: *The World of William Clissold* (1926). This is a closely autobiographical work, a novel about an old man very like Wells who is trying to make sense of his life. 'Yesterday,' runs the opening sentence, 'I was fifty-nine, and in a year I shall be sixty':

> In the face of these figures I cannot hide from myself that the greater part of my life has been lived. … Maybe I have not so much lost endurance as learnt wisdom. And generally my vigour is unimpaired. It is the dates and figures that will not be denied. They show quite plainly that at most only two decades remain for me, and when they are spent my strongest will be a white-faced, rather shrunken, assisted old man—'wonderful,' they will say. [1:1]

And they will say *how his hair is growing thin*. And how, conversely, his novels are growing fat—*Clissold* was published in three volumes, nearly 900 pages of text. The story the novel tells is so very much like H.G. Wells's life that his literary agent, A.S. Wyatt, prevailed upon him to add a disclaimer in the hope of averting libel suits, The novel's 'preface' disavows autobiographical content, insisting 'this is not a roman à cle' (a typo, perhaps; or else Wells being distracted by the way the French pronounce *clef*). 'It would be a great kindness to a no doubt undeserving author if in this instance William Clissold could be treated as William Clissold, and if Mr Wells could be spared the standard charge … it is a point worth considering in this period of successful personal memoirs that if the author had wanted to write a mental autobiography instead of a novel, there is no conceivable reason why he should not have done so. Clearly he did not want to do so.' This is hardly ingenuous. Despite the fact that Clissold is a wealthy industrialist rather than a writer, and although some of the events of Clissold's life are different to those of Wells's, there's simply no denying that Clissold ventriloquist-dummies all the Wellsian opinions, often at enormous length, all the way through this novel.

The two main components of the novel's construction, tossed salad-like together, are: on the one hand Clissold's memory of his infancy, growth to adulthood, his professional- and love-lives; and on the other Clissold's thoughts on the universe, spun out of conversations he has with famous people, or simply inlaid into the text as a kind of marquetry of myriad lectures. This latter element blurs into a general discursiveness, regrettably characteristic of Wells's later style. And this novel *is* sometimes slackly garrulous, though it is also a much more interesting fictional experiment than it is given credit for being. Its discursive components are often stimulating and pointed, and though its narrative line is a little meagre the portraiture—especially the core characterisation of Clissold and his brother, where Wells manages the technically tricky business of rendering two quite different sorts of people who are still recognisably related to one another—is excellent. In other words the balance in the novel is (deliberately) shifted away from narrative and action and towards character and the discursive elaboration of ideas. This tessellation of fiction and discursive discussion makes for an interesting literary blend.

Interesting isn't necessarily the same as *successful*, of course, and this is not a style that has caught on. To set Wells's experimental text alongside two more famous examples of the life-novel from the same period, Joyce's *Portrait of the Artist as a Young Man* (1916) and Proust's *A la recherche du temps perdu* (1913–27) is to understand the ways in which Wells's manner simply misses the main wave of Modernism. Joyce and Proust were, like Wells, self-consciously experimenting in the literary treatment of semi-autobiographical fiction. Wells subtitles *William Clissold* 'A Novel at a New Angle', and its angular novelty runs through the whole. Colin Wilson—hardly the most level-headed of commentators, of course, but still—thought William Clissold 'as bold an experimental novel as *Ulysses* and, in its own way, as successful' [Tredell, 40]. The larger differences of approach are obvious enough. Joyce in *Portrait* dispenses with the Victorian commentator-narrator altogether, and indeed pares his narrative voice down to basically nothing, which leaves only the vividly isolated epiphanic moments out of which the uncreated Stephen is forged in the smithy of the text. Proust goes, in a sense, to the other extreme, and pares down the constitutive moments-from-a-life to a very few (going to sleep, eating a cake, a grandmother dying, a party here, a trip to the seaside there) in order to foreground *reflection itself*, the multiply-considered and complexly layered self-engagements out of which the Marcel of the novel is construed. Wells steers a middle course between the two approaches. We might think this merely a kind of compromise, but to be fair to him, he manages this middle way in a manner that produces a final result very unlike any conventional novel. Wells's 'new angle' is more than simply the fitting together of equal parts narrative and disquisition to form one complete novel. It's also that this novel includes among its fictional characters a great many real 1920s people, most of them friends of Wells's, whose appearances in the book range from mentions to brief cameos to whole, extended scenes. It is the admixture of the two modes, one fictional and one non-fictional, that had characterised Wells's entire career, here worked more closely than ever before into a lamination. Formally this means fictive narrative and discursive sections woven together, but on the level of representation it means playing quite sophisticated games in the ways fictional characters interact with real people, by way of exploring the solidity, or otherwise, of the ego. And the ego matters to Wells because he apprehends it as one of the obstacles to the people-just-getting-along-ness necessary for his peaceful utopian World State.

Since the novel is so rarely read nowadays, a certain amount of summary is needful. At the start of Book 1 elderly William Clissold is sitting in his London apartment, readying himself to travel to his much more congenial Provençal house, where his lover Clementina is waiting for him. He beguiles the time before his departure by writing the opening chapters of his life story, and summarising the kind of person he is: 'metaphysically I have never been able to get very far beyond Schopenhauer's phrase: *Die Welt als Wille und Vorstellung*. Life to me as to him … is a spectacle, a show, with a drive in it' [1:6]. He chats about the time he met Jung, and about a supper he recently enjoyed with his old friend Sir Rupert York, fossil-expert and director of the Natural History Museum—this latter a portrait of Wells's old friend Sir Ray Lankester. Why Jung gets to appear in the novel in *propria persona* where York is fictionalised under this wars-of-the-roses switchabout moniker Lankester has to do with the larger theme of the novel: the relationship of fiction to history. Clissold takes the train to the south of France and describes his very congenial-sounding set-up there.

Book 2 'The Story of the Clissolds—My Father and the Flow of Things' tells the story of the early youth and upbringing of the two Clissold boys: William and his brother Dickon. Their childhood is overshadowed by the disgrace and suicide of their businessman father, Richard Clissold: 'having been found guilty of falsifying the books of London and Imperial Enterprises and sentenced to seven years' penal servitude' he 'committed suicide and died in the passage behind the court just after he had left the dock. He had swallowed a small capsule containing poison which he had concealed in the lining of his waistcoat.' Mrs Clissold remarries a wealthy London solicitor called Walpole Stent: 'a tall, shy, thoughtful, knickerbockered man with a very large forehead' [2:3]. The boys go to Dulwich College and afterwards to London University to study science, and on reaching adulthood they discard their step-father's surname and become again Clissolds. William trains as a geologist, passes through a socialist phase and out the other side. Indeed Book 2 contains, as an avocado does its indigestible stone, a huge excursus on the inadequacy of Marxism, as Clissold (which is to say, as Wells) understands it. William calls Marx 'the maggot, so to speak, at the core of my decayed socialism' [2:8] and a long stretch of the novel is given over to a purported 'Psycho-Analysis of Karl Marx':

> It is for the psycho-analyst to lay bare the subtler processes in the evolution of this dream of a Proletarian saviour. Everybody nowadays knows that giant, in May-day cartoons and Communist pamphlets and wherever romantic Communism expresses itself by pictures, presenting indeed no known sort of worker, but betraying very clearly in its vast biceps, its colossal proportions, its small head and the hammer of Thor in its mighty grip, the suppressed cravings of the restricted Intellectual for an immense virility. [*Clissold*, 2:8]

Thirty pages of this are followed by a 30-page summary economic history of humankind from 3000 BC to the present, which winds its way back towards the downfall of Clissold senior, caught up (William argues) in the 'credit whirlpool' and global financial 'confusion' that money has become.

Book 3, 'The Story of the Clissolds—Essence of Dickon', carries on the story of William's brother: a man 'canine where I was feline', a 'stout tweed-wearing man'. Forceful, 'Nordic' and large [3:1]. Dickon makes it big in advertising and meets many of the famous names from 1920s retail and media: Harry Gordon Selfridge and Lord Northcliffe have cameos, amongst many others. Dickon innovates in his field, going from 'hoardings and magazine-covers' to 'sky-signs' and 'smoke-writing on the blue' [3:5]. Both men get married: Dickon to Minnie and William to Clara. Since William's marriage is a failure he confesses 'a certain chagrin' that his brother's marriage 'was heartily successful, ostentatiously successful' [3:8]. Both men father children. William separates from his unfaithful wife but is unable, on a technicality, to divorce. He cohabits with a woman called Sirrie Evans. His more socially conventional brother ostracises him for this; but then Sirrie dies and William is accepted back into his brother's bosom. By now it's World War I, and William does important work in the Ministry of Munitions, becoming a public figure of repute and influence. Dickon, despite being 50, joins the army (he becomes what is now called a logistics officer) and ends up with a baronetcy. This book spends some time on the war, and rather more on the missed opportunities of the post-war reconstruction period. Both brothers conclude that a 'new sort of man is wanted' to populate a reformed and harmonious world [3:15], with Dickon believing such a being could be engendered by harnessing the powers of advertising: 'time for the man-midwife … the propagandist, the advertiser, to set about his task, and bring the new order into the world' [3:15]. Book 3 ends with some sharply drawn portraits of the wealthy expats who congregate on the French riviera.

Book 4 'The Story of the Clissolds—Tangle of Desires' occupies itself with William's complicated erotic life: from unhappy marriage to Clara (a woman of 'inevitable unchastity' [4:6]), through his co-habitation with Sirrie Evans until her death of TB in 1905 via some other women to, eventual stability with Clementina Campbell, a pen-portrait of Odette Keun. Clementina's Scotch-Greek pedigree is Wells's version of Keun's half-Dutch and half-Italian/Greek provenance: 'Scotch heredity and Greek heredity do not mix,' says William. 'They make a sort of human Macedonia, a melange of hostile and incompatible districts in the soul. Clementina is in streaks beautifully logical and clear-headed, and in streaks incoherently but all too expressively passionate; she is acutely artistic and rigidly Philistine' [4:14].

The final two books contain much less by way of narrative. Book 5 'The Story of the Clissolds—The Next Phase' is almost exclusively given over to developing Wells's idea of a global 'open conspiracy': eminent men and women (though mostly men), business leaders, politicians, scientists, intellectuals and writers coming together to conspire, in full view, to establish a 'World Republic': 'The world republic is going to be as different from any former state as, let us say, an automobile from a peasant's cart,' promises Clissold [5:4]. Book 6 'The Story of the Clissolds—Venus as Evening Star' is an elongated meditation on the differences between men and women, taking in love and sex and leaning hard on what Clissold sees as the dangerous mendacity of 'romanticism' (in the love affair, rather than the literary movement, sense of the word). It is a peroration to honesty in love and the demystification of sex. 'I know', says Clissold-Wells 'that my insistence in this book upon a completely normal sexual life for an energetic man is a breach of literary decorum. I shall be called over-sexed, when indeed I am merely normally sexed and only abnormally outspoken', which is nicely put. He insists that, of the four major relationships in his life, the one that comes closest to this erotic honesty and companionship is the one he presently enjoys. Clissold's narrative ends with him in Provence, writing, and apparently coming to the decision that he shall propose to Clementina. The last paragraphs are in the future tense:

> In a few moments now she will be standing in my door way, doubtful of her reception. She will look gravely at me for an instant and then smile softly when she sees I have turned my chair away from my table. For that means the morning's writing is over.
>
> There will be a moment of mutual scrutiny, for she will realise immediately that something has changed, and as for me, I shall be diffident, I know not why.
>
> 'Do I interrupt?' she will ask according to our custom.
>
> And I shall say—What shall I say? [*Clissold*, 6:13]

That's the end of *William Clissold*. All that remains of Wells's novel is a coda written by Dickon Clissold: 'and there my brother ceased to write and never wrote again. … He was killed in an automobile accident upon the narrow road leading from the gorge of the Loup to Thorenc on April 24th, 1926. Miss [Clementina] Campbell, who was with him in his car, was killed at the same time. This was perhaps only a day, or a day or two, after the unfinished passage was left.'

William Clissold is a whale of a novel: certainly impressive, surprisingly agile considering its bulk, but also containing a high proportion of blubber. Contemporaries really weren't sure what to make of it. There were some respectful reviews (*The Rotarian*, Dec 1926, said 'this novel is the most important and interesting which the much-productive Mr. Wells has written'), but also some rather more mixed ones. John Maynard Keynes, reviewing the novel for *The New Republic*, called the main character 'a great achievement', but thought the themes 'not all treated equally well' and judged the whole an 'omnium gatherum', not 'a work of art' (*New Republic*, 1 February 1927). In *The English Review* D.H. Lawrence was less conciliatory calling it 'simply not good enough to be called a novel', and A.A.M. Thomson went so far in the direction of mockery as to publish book-length parody *The World of Billiam Wissold* in 1927. Nor was the work a particular commercial success. Still: whatever else is the going on this novel, it showcases some of Wells's very best prose, on a technical level. Here's a rainy day in London from the very beginning, and as sharp, memorable and vivid as piece of descriptive writing as any Wells ever made:

> Outside it is not so much day as a saturated piece of dingy time, a stretch of chewed and damp and dirty fourth dimension between two nights. It rains fitfully, now in fine clouds, now in hysterical downpours, now in phases of

drizzling undecided intermission; and the shops are lit and there are lights in the windows. There is a sort of grey discoloration filtering down from above that I suppose one must admit to be daylight. Wet omnibuses, wet taxicabs and auto-mobiles splash and blunder by. There are a few reluctant foot passengers under wet umbrellas. Everything shines greasily with the rain like the backs of rolling porpoises. [*William Clissold*, 1.1]

There are many like passages to be mined from the experience of reading the novel. The worst we can say of the following, a description of a day in his Provençal house, is that maybe it's a little soft-edged, with just the slightest whiff of sentimentality. It is undeniably vividly rendered, though:

In the early morning the stream-beds and valleys between the crests and ridges are filled with very sharp restricted banks of white mist, and then a conical hill some five or six miles away from here becomes an island of romance. All day long there is a quiet soft change in the features of this scene, hillsides hold the sunlight for a time and then fade away, spurs and summits grow from insignifi-cance to prominence as the sun searches them out on its daily round. Towards sundown Mougins upon its ridge six miles away will at times shine out with such a brightness that I think of Bunyan's Celestial City. Everywhere at this time of year there are rubbish fires burning, and their bright down-feathers of white smoke expand and unroll and dissolve away continually and are continu-ally renewed.

Almost always the sky above this land is a pure clear blue or delicately streaked with filmy cloud, and the sunlight is a benediction. Sundown brings a glow of warm contentment. Then presently the nearer houses lose strength, and faint and die and become white ghosts in the twilight. Amidst the darkling scattered lights appear. [*William Clissold*, 1:15]

But a novel is not made, pointillistically, out of isolated passages of fine writing. It also needs a larger structure, or at least some sort of shape. In *William Clissold* Wells attempts to counter to stolidity of his novel's inset lec-tures with a larger structuring aesthetic of fluidity. Wells's epigraph is Heraclitus's πάντα ρεῖ: and this is a flow that has several valences for the novel. We could say, although Wells doesn't use this specific image, that what his Open Conspiracy is trying to do is find a way of both controlling and harnessing that massive flow after the manner of hydroelectric dam. One main version of the flow is the catastrophe of unregulated capitalism, in which money is so huge and so fluid it washes away human lives and happiness on an epic scale (Clissold's father's suicide is one tangible example of this). Wells describes traders in the City as 'superficial consequences' caught in 'a swirl …

upon a deep flood of changes beyond their understanding' [2:14]. Money flows, as the economists insist it must; but Wells tropes this flow as a kind of catastrophic inundation. The fatuities and hypocrisies of romantic love are, Clissold insists, such another flow, eroding the stability of relationships. Life itself, of course, is the fundamental *res* that ῥεῖ, the thing that flows, finally flowing inevitably away, as the novel's very last paragraph records:

πάντα ῥεῖ. He too has passed. These words, and they are wonderful words and come like a refrain throughout his book, shall be put as his sole epitaph upon his grave! [*Clissold*, 'Epilogue']

That's not to say that the novel is formally shapeless, or fluid. Indeed, quite the reverse. There are two different structuring modes running parallel through this dual project (i.e., the dual project of telling a fictional story about fictional characters and of advancing a real-world discursive account of politics, education and future-planning that includes real-life people). We're likely to think of each of these two elements in linear ways—that is, to think of the metonymic succession of events that make up a linear narrative on the one hand, and the metonymic succession of points that make up a linear argument on the other. Such metonymy is, without question, at play in *William Clissold*. But there's a parallel, nonlinear mode in which the novel advances both its fictional and its argumentative agenda: via metaphorical (rather than metonymic) images and intensities. This in turn is linked to the way childhood 'sets' certain moments for us, moments that then overdetermine certain adult experiences (but not others) as epiphanies, spots of time, transcendences. This is something both Proust and Joyce understood, and their novels simultaneously describe that epiphanic process and embody it. I'd argue that *The World of William Clissold* does something similar, on a larger scale and in perhaps a more intricate way. The sixfold structure of the novel, and a sixfold pattern of repeated images and moments of conceptual intensity, disclose on closer analysis a deliberate, quasi-crystalline design to this only superficially rambling novel. In Book 1 Clissold says: 'things are first seen and heard and felt in childhood, and our minds file these early impressions as key-pictures and refer the later ones to them.' Our childhood images are 'continually refreshed' where 'later experiences are no longer used as new points of reference' [1:3]. To illustrate what he means, he tells us that he has very seen 'autumnal horse-chestnut leaves reflected in brown water and the branches of a horse-chestnut tree coming down close to that still mirror' hundreds of times; but only one memory of this scene really lives in him, and it's the time he first saw it, as a child:

> I was in the old punt on the great pond at Mowbray. The silvery sheet of water had that convex effect one always got there upon a day of absolute calm. It was like a very smooth broad buckler. I think that effect of curvature must have been due to the way the reeds and bushes shaded the edges, or perhaps to some trick in the angle of the reflection of the pines up the slope. Even the ducks and the friendly attendant dab-chick among the lily leaves were silent. Everything was so still that I remember being startled by the sudden 'plop' of a falling husk into the crystalline water behind me. [*William Clissold*, 1:8]

It's a lovely, quasi-Wordsworthian spot-of-time. The way the pond's surface appears slightly convex is an especially vivid touch; not least because it figures as the symbolic emblematisation of the narrator's ego-identity. I'm reminded of the way Golding's *Free Fall* uses its image of the young Sammy in the middle of the park, with a spread of possible paths radiating away before him, any of which he could walk down; except that Golding's purpose it to externalise freedom of choice, where Wells's is to metaphorise the solidity of ego as such, shield-like and poised, yet actually made from a fluid, flowing medium.

Whilst he is on his punt, in the middle of this optical illusion, this Escher curved mirror of the self, everything about young Clissold holds. The silence and stillness become explicitly transcendental ('it is as if the whole world paused. It is as if God was present' [1:8]). But young Clissold is distracted by the beauty of some forget-me-nots amongst the rushes growing at the edge of the pond. He wades into the rushes to seize some of the flowers:

> I waded into the water and mud until my knickerbockers, in spite of all the tucking up I gave them, were soaked. And I picked handfuls of these the loveliest of all English wild-flowers.
>
> Then suddenly came horror, the unqualified horror of childhood. My legs were streaming with blood. The sharp blades of the sedge leaves had cut them in a score of places. Fresh gouts of blood gathered thickly along the cuts, and then darted a bright red ribbon down my wet and muddy skin. 'Oh! Oh!' I cried in profound dismay, struggling and splashing back to the bank and still holding my forget-me-nots with both hands.
>
> Still do I remember most vividly my astonishment at the treachery of that golden, flushed, and sapphire-eyed day. [*William Clissold*, 1:8]

This is not 'narrative' in the traditional sense; it is, rather, an almost imagist rebus for transcendent-stillness followed by the painful impingement of the outside world. As long as he sits in the middle of his magical convex lake of selfhood Clissold is safe, but as soon as he goes searching for beauty outside himself he encounters laceration and trauma. In miniature, this little memory establishes the paradigm for the whole of the novel.

Wells's relationship with Keun was rarely placid, and as the 1920s drew on it became increasingly stormy. The sensuous consolations of Provençal life—food, climate and sex, far from the disagreeable political situation in England, the 1926 general strike and economic recession—inclined him to French living. But Keun's personality was allergic to any kind of settled placidity of life, which registered for her as stagnation and claustrophobia. They had frequent rows. She was uncontrollable, indiscrete, mischievous and anarchic. When Wells's friend Charles Chaplin visited Lou Pidou and remarked the 'Two Lovers Built This House' inscription over the mantle, Wells told him 'we've had it put on and taken off a number of times. Whenever we quarrel I instruct the mason to take it off and when we make up she instructs the mason to put it back.' Wells wanted the spice of sex with Keun; but he also wanted an emotional and sexual settlement that catered for his needs and enabled him to get on with his work. This relationship did not provide the latter.

He was at least able to continue working, restlessly trying different styles and fictional modes. Wells's later 1920s and early 1930s novels are all unalike one another although there is a kind of connecting thread running through them: in various ways they parlay into art the friction between an idea—almost always a political ideal or fantasy—and the uncooperative reality of life into delusion, or dream, or imaginative phantasmagoria. None of these novels are the systematic or logical extrapolation of premises we associate with science fiction, and many of them read like fables or satirical exaggerations. But all of them, in hindsight, record the sense that pressed upon Wells either consciously or unconsciously, that there was something chimerical, something divorced from reality, about the life he was living.

Meanwhile: The Picture of a Lady (1927) is, like *Bealby* (1915), a country house comedy, with rather more political focus, and, alas, rather less funny. The setting is Casa Terragena, a villa on the Italian riviera owned by the super-wealthy Philip Rylands and his wife Cynthia, who is pregnant with the couple's first child. At the Rylands' house-party are present: a famous author called Mr Sempack ('he writes books. Real books … Not books you read. Not novels. Not memoirs. Books that are just books. Like Santayana. Or Lowes Dickinson. Or Bertrand Russell' [*Meanwhile*, 1:1]); an American aesthete, Mr Plantagenet-Buchan and the beautiful Lady Catherine, who has a crush on Sempack, despite the latter's age and ugliness. Indeed, since Sempack is this novel's cipher for Wells himself, it's interesting how unsparing he is of his physical appearance: 'a sprawling person', old and wrinkled 'like Pan half changed into an old olive tree of like some weather-worn Terminus' [1:11].

This, though, doesn't stop several of the female characters adoring him. Also present are Colonel and Mrs Bullace (Bullace is 'a great admirer of Joynson-Hicks. He wants to organise British Fascists. Keep the working man down and save him from agitators and all that. Adores Mussolini' [1.1]), the host's brother, Geoffrey Rylands and Miss Fenimore, who is rather cruelly described by Wells as 'a demi-Stupid, a Stupid in effect, an acquiescent Stupid' [1:6]. She is in awe of Sempack and follows his talk 'from first to last with an enraptured incomprehension' [1:12]. There are various others, including a young woman called 'Puppy' Clarges 'rude, troublesome, occasionally indecent, unchaste' [1:6].

Book 1 describes an evening's dinner party at which Sempack dominates the talk with a series of characteristically Wellsian ideas: that a 'Great Age' is coming, an 'open conspiracy' is needed to bring it about, and so on. Cynthia Rylands, catches her husband Philip *in flagrante* with Puppy Clarges (Puppy flounces back to England, after writing her hostess a note 'of exceptional brevity: "Sorry," wrote Miss Clarges. "I'm gone and I won't worry you again." "Sorry I got caught," Miss Clarges remarked to herself, and licked the envelope' [1:10]). Cynthia Rylands, distraught at her husband's betrayal, asks Sempack's advice. Dubiously enough he in effect instructs her to forgive her husband's infidelity telling her that, of the two available attractive women in the Villa (that is, Lady Catherine and 'Puppy'), Philip did the right thing by choosing to sleep with Puppy. 'He loves nobody but you. If he had wanted to make love—consider! Lady Catherine here … but Lady Catherine is an equal, a personality. He wouldn't look at her, wouldn't dream of her. Because that would be a real infringement of you. That would be a real division of love. But on the other hand there was this Miss Clarges, who disavows all the accessories of sex—and is simply sexual' [1:11]. Sempack assures Cynthia that such infidelity is nothing for her to worry about: it is just 'a consoling and refreshing physical release', 'such a simple thing' 'as healthy a thing physically as breathing mountain air'. Few spouses would be satisfied with this reasoning, I suspect; but it convinces Cynthia. With a murmur of 'my poor little wits!' she agrees with Sempack that her husband's problem is idleness, not wickedness, and persuades him to travel back to England to look after the family coal-mine holdings during the 1926 General Strike.

The novel winds itself to a sort of conclusion. Lady Catherine suddenly breaks off her drawn-out romantic pursuit of Sempack, and hurries to England to join the British Fascists and oppose the General Strike. This happens just as Sempack decides he has fallen in love with her: 'I am in the ridiculous position', is how he puts it to Cynthia, 'of having fallen in love with Lady Catherine; and it isn't any the less disorganising for being utterly absurd. It has made me,

I perceive, absurd' [2:8]. Back in England Catherine knocks over an unemployed man with her car, killing him; but she does not stop at the scene of this
accident. 'She drove on!' Philip reports in one of his letters: 'she drove on,
because she was a patriotic heroine battling against Bolshevism and all that,
for God and King and Fearon-Owen [Wells's fictional British Fascist leader]
and the British Gazette. War is war. Nothing will be done to her' [2:14].
Cynthia gives birth to a son, and her now-penitent husband returns from
England to start their married life over again.

Wells pushed the satire closer to Voltaire for his next novel, *Mr. Blettsworthy
on Rampole Island* (1928), a novel dedicated 'to the immortal memory of
CANDIDE', narrated by Arnold Blettsworthy, scion of a respectable and
ancient English family ('Blettsworthy's Bank is one of the last of the outstanding private banks in these days of amalgamation' [1:1]). Wells aims at a degree
of tonal *Candide*ry in the book's early sections: of Arnold's fictional Oxford
college, we're told 'my life at Lattmeer confirmed my faith in the civilisation
of the universe'; and his assessment of the Boer War, in which conflict his
father dies (not heroically, but via a tragicomical misunderstanding) is
best-of-all-possible-worldsy:

> That Boer War left no scars upon my boyish mind. It was certainly the most
> civilised war in all history, fought with restraint and frequent chivalry, a white
> man's war, which ended in mutual respect and a general shaking of hands. Most
> of us must be orphaned sooner or later, and to have had a father one had long
> forgotten dying, as we supposed, a hero's death in a fair fight, was as satisfactory
> a way of realising that customary bereavement as I can imagine. [*Mr.
> Blettsworthy*, 1:3]

Blettsworthy falls in love with a woman called Olive Slaughter, who 'kissed
with such eagerness and caressed me so tenderly that only my sense of her
perfect innocence restrained the ardour of my responses' [1.4]; and Wells
deftly but cleverly allows us to intuit Olive's perfectly natural appetites and
the obliviousness of Arnold's priggish restraint ('I talked between our kisses of
the high aims to which our passions were to be consecrated, and all my
thoughts surrounded her with protective possessiveness, as though I was a
church dedicated to her and she was the holy altar therein. And so to kissing
again'). Blettsworthy invests £3000 in the business of his friend, Lyulph
Graves; but Lyulph embezzles the money and seduces Olive Slaughter. When
Blettsworthy chances upon the two of them in bed together he goes out of his
mind with jealousy: 'my memories [of this period] are extraordinarily irregu-
lar; now clear and detailed and as sharp as though they came from yesterday

instead of a third of a lifetime ago; now foggy, distorted and uncertain, and now interrupted by gaps of the completest obliteration' [1:5]. In a state of distraction he gets drunk in the Spread Eagle in Thame, cycles off towards Amersham, and is knocked off his bicycle by a tradesman's van. Or perhaps isn't:

> To that point I remember simply and clearly, and then I vanish completely out of my own memory. Probably I went over and was hit by the van. There is no record. Certainly I was stunned. But it is queer I do not remember anything up to the instant of being stunned. [*Mr. Blettsworthy*, 1:6]

Arnold decides a world tour will take his mind off his broken heart, and in Book 2, 'Mr. Blettsworthy put out to Sea', embarks for Rio de Janeiro aboard a tramp steamer called the Golden Lion. But when the ship begins to sink off the South American coast and the crew escape in a lifeboat, the incompetent and disreputable Captain locks Blettsworthy in a cabin to die, acting, it seems from pure malicious animosity. By the time Arnold has broken through the cabin door he is alone on the sinking boat. Then two 'naked men of a dusky buff colour, unpleasantly tattooed' board the ship and take Blettsworthy prisoner, moving him to Rampole Island. The island itself is made of some kind of crystal ('though I have sought it since in museums in order to give it a name, I have never seen anything like it. It resembled a clearish blue purple glass, but with large patches of a more ruddy hue, verging on rosy pink' [3:1]) and its natives worship an unforgiving Mother Deity:

> a jutting mass of rock in the shape of a woman with staring eyes and an open mouth; a splintered pinnacle of rock rose above her like an upraised arm and hand brandishing a club; the eyes had been rimmed with white and the threat of the mouth had been enhanced by white and red paint, suggesting teeth and oozing blood. [3:1]

The tribe are cannibals but as they are about to kill Blettsworthy he begins, without understanding why, to rave and sing ('quite unwittingly I did what was best for myself') and so becomes adopted as the tribe's 'sacred lunatic'. In this capacity he strolls about the island unmolested, wearing the skin of a gigantic ground sloth (which species 'still survives upon Rampole Island') and carrying a phallic staff—'a staff of hard dark wood obscenely carved and decorated' [3:2] (hence, we assume, the island's double entendre name, *ram, pole*): 'when I am fat and well the tribe prospers; do I ail and its fortunes decline'. Years pass; long enough for Blettsworthy to learn the native tongue, although he doesn't really remember the passing of time. The tribe lives in a coastal gorge from which the people are forbidden to leave; above are the uplands, also inhabited; and throughout Blettsworthy's time on the island the war drums beat in prelude to a great battle between the gorge-dwellers and the uplanders.

By this point in the telling, however, something has shifted in the tone of the novel. The drily precise ironic Voltaire voice of Book 1 has become a cruder sarcasm, and the novel engages in some none-too-subtle satire on the mores of early twentieth-century England. Life among the 'savages' is hemmed about with all manner of taboos and rituals, and the getting of wives is a particularly difficult and dangerous business, with the most powerful males reserving all the best women to themselves. Blettsworthy, aware that transgression would lead to his death, lives a celibate life for several years. But when he rescues a young girl called Wena from drowning the two become lovers, sneaking away to a remote cave to have sex. Since Wena belongs to the tribal chief Ardam, this is very dangerous, but Blettsworthy and Wena decide to run away together. As Blettsworthy flees, Ardam shoots him with an arrow in the shoulder, and, staggering onwards, he abruptly … wakes up.

This is the story's twist, and a clashingly unsatisfactory one it proves. Book 4: Blettsworthy regains consciousness in Brooklyn Heights, New York City. He has been experiencing a prolonged feverish hallucination whilst under psychiatrist care. It transpires he is married to a woman called Rowena ('Wena') who rescued him after a taxicab knocked him down. The cave is his apartment he shares with Rowena in New York; the gorge is formed by the skyscrapers of Manhattan. All the various events of Rampole Island map onto the real world: 'for, after all, what was Rampole Island, doctor? It was only the real world looming through the mists of my illusions' [4:2]. That includes the war drums: for World War I has commenced. Blettsworthy enlists in the British Army as a private and Rowena moves to England with him. He survives a gas attack, and advances with his company over No Man's Land ('I fell over a dead body alive with maggots; my knee went into the soft horror') declaring: 'Rampole Island was sanity to this—a mere half-way house to reality' [4:8]. After losing a leg in combat and being invalided home he finds himself on the ward with Lyulph Graves, whose face has been smashed by a shell and whose head is covered all over in bandages except for one eye. Blettsworthy forgives his former friend's trespasses, even going into post-war partnership in Graves's advertising and marketing business. The novel ends with Blettsworthy fitted with a new mechanical leg, 'a middle-aged, outwardly contented figure. Wife and children, this pleasant home we have made at Chislehurst, the business I must attend to if our comforts are to be ample, friends and acquaintances, exercises and amusements' [4:13]. But he is haunted by his memories of Rampole Island: 'I managed to carry on with business and kept touch with practical things throughout. But to fall asleep, to sit alone, to walk with an unoccupied mind, was presently to pass right out of England completely into that familiar gorge of reverie. I would find myself talking aloud to the Islanders and snatch myself back to my real surroundings by a great effort' [4:13]. The last beat of the story is presented as a door out of this torment: Graves persuades Blettsworthy to help him write 'The Prospectus of Mankind—Unlimited' [4:14], and to devote his energies to the coming of the World State.

This twist is quite the disappointment. It's not that its badly handled on its own terms; it's that its incongruity operates not only on the obvious level of content, but, more debilitatingly, on the level of tone. The neatly pastiched Voltairean irony is replaced in the book's latter stages by a deal of earnestness and outrage at the horrors of the world. Of course, it's not that life *isn't* full of horrors. The world through which Candide moved was as horrific as any World War I battlefield. The question is how best to *represent* those horrors, how to make art out of them; not merely to register the fact of them, but to project and tailor them in such a way as to give readers a point of conceptual leverage. To browbeat your audience with miseries will tend in practice to have a politically sedative effect. The genius touch of *Candide* as a novel is the way its galvanically light comedy supplies, as it were, a series of expertly placed electric shocks to our complacency.

In *Mr. Blettsworthy on Rampole Island* Wells attempts to steer a *Candide*-esque story towards a Voltairean moral: *il faut cultiver notre jardin*. But cultivating your garden and agitating for a World State are, really, very different activities. Both are projects to make the world better, it's true; but Voltaire's localised scope is a specific rebuke to the grandiosity that informs things like Wells's World-Statism. This is not a question of scale—you or I might cultivate our gardens with a bit of judicious weeding and pruning; but for Voltaire the phrase meant working his huge estate at Ferney, within sight of Mont Blanc: draining marshes; bringing unused land back under the plough; planting fruit trees and vines; raising livestock and many other things. It's not, to repeat myself, a question of scale but of *focus*. This is where Wells's novel falls so short of the limpid precision of *Candide*. And arguably, outside the confines of this novel, it was the way in which his larger political ambitions fell short of attainment. I'm not arguing, incidentally, that Wells strayed from the Candideian path by mistake or through any failing of artistic control. He knew perfectly well what he was doing. Part 1 and 2 adopt the Voltaire voice, rendering the world as it is accurately enough for the irony to bite; but Part 3, on Rampole Island, quite deliberately abandons this approach, instead rendering our world as grotesque phantasmagoria, exaggerating real-world biases and absurdities into freak-show versions of themselves. The game here is quite different—not the eloquent beauty of innuendoes which is the currency of irony, but the simpler pleasures of preposterousness. The former invites us to engage our interpretive intelligences in the service of a kind of tactfulness of insight, the latter simply projects exaggerations onto the big screen for us to goggle at.

There is also an extra level of textual tricksiness in play; because Blettsworthy's sojourn on Rampole Island has so many commonalities with Wells's unnamed Time Traveller's holiday in 802,701. The obvious difference is that the Traveller spends time in the broad sunny uplands amongst the Eloi where Blettsworthy spends his time trapped down in the gorge with the cannibalistic Morlocks—but that is only to suggest that Wells is telling the same story from two different perspectives. In *The Time Machine* the protagonist has a relationship with a beautiful female aboriginal called Weena whom he rescues from drowning; in *Blettsworthy* the protagonist has a relationship with a beautiful female aboriginal called Wena whom he rescues from drowning. The Eloi in *The Time Machine* live under the baleful gaze of the giant face of the sphinx, which functions as a gateway to the nether realm; the Rampole Islanders of *Blettsworthy*, as we have seen, worship a rock formation that has the form of a merciless goddess's face. More substantively, both novels are commentaries upon the non-teleological nature of evolution, as liable to devolve forms into barbarism as to evolve them into civilisation. Blettsworthy is intrigued by the megatheria, the Giant Sloths, that still survive on the island, and notes how 'so far from Evolution being necessarily a strenuous upward progress to more life and yet more life, it might become, it could and did evidently in this case become, a graceless drift towards a dead end' [3:5]. A fable about how an ordinary person becomes trapped in a hallucinatory phantasmagoria which turns out to be a commentary upon the insanity of a world willing to wage World War I and fit humanity into the cruel procrustean beds of capitalism and sexual prudery is one thing. But a fable about how a writer of celebrated fantasies becomes caught in a feedback loop defined by one of his most famous works is something else entirely.

A different kind of irony animates Wells's next novel, *The Autocracy of Mr. Parham* (1930). The titular protagonist is an unworldly academic historian, conservative and traditionalist, content for much of his life to piddle around in his little Oxford world: 'he had produced several studies—mainly round and about Richelieu and going more deeply into the mind of Richelieu than anyone has ever done before—and given short special courses upon historical themes' [*Parham*, 1:1]. But after 1919 'everything had gone from bad to worse', in Parham's judgement: 'discordance, a disarray of values, invaded the flow of occurrence' [1:1]. For 6 years he has befriended a vulgar but extremely wealthy businessman called Sir Bussy Woodcock (a version of Lord Beaverbrook) in the hope that Woodcock will provide the funding for 'a distinguished and authoritative weekly paper, with double columns and a restrained title heading, of which Mr. Parham would be the editor' [*Parham*, 1:2].

Parham accepts an invitation to join Sir Bussy at a series of séances presided over by 'Mr. Carnac Williams'. At this séance 'the Spirit, which is Will and Power' comes 'like a mighty wind, seeking a way' [2:4] manifesting as phosphorescent ectoplasm that coalesces into a body ('with a shock it came into Mr. Parham's head that he was seeing bones and nerves and blood vessels hurrying to their appointed places in that swimming swirl' [2.5]): a Byronic-looking figure in a white shirt and knee breeches: '"I come from the Red Planet, the planet of blood and virility," said the Visitant ... "I am the spirit of Manhood and Dominion and Order. I have come to England, trembling on the brink of decadence, to raise her and save her"' [*Parham*, 2:5]. The Spirit then 'incorporates' Mr Parham, who finds he is able to command people with a voice they are powerless to resist.

This is the halfway point of the novel: the second half traces how Mr Parham uses his new charisma to seize political power. He orates to huge crowds who palpitate at his every word: 'young men and old men, beautiful women, tall girls like flames and excited elderly persons of every size and shape, all fused in one stupendous enthusiasm' [3:1] and orchestrates a *coup d'état*: 'England fell into his hands like a ripe fruit'. His shock troops 'in uniforms of a Cromwellian cut' [3:2] storm parliament and instal Parham as Lord Paramount. He sweeps away the old order, solves unemployment. ('Young men must be taken in hand and trained for other ends. The women can go into munitions.') He insists 'I am no Individualist, I am no Socialist; these are phrases left over by the Nineteenth Century, and little meaning remains in them now. But I say, of him who does not work for his country, neither shall he eat in it, and that he who will not work generously must be made to work hard' [3:4]. Other policies include luxury taxes: 'lavish entertainments in huge hotels, jazz expenditure, must cease. A special tax on champagne—Yes, a tax on champagne.' Relations with the USA deteriorate, Britain blockades US shipping, and World War II breaks out—between Britain and America.

This conflict occupies the fourth and final book. Parham orders the British navy into action ('a mighty naval crescent within striking distance of New York'

[4:1]) but the American navy's response is 'unexpectedly prompt and in unexpected strength', and Britain does not come out well from the resulting Battle of the North Atlantic. Aerial war breaks out over Europe: 'night after night the air of Europe was filled with the whir of gigantic engines and the expectation of bursting bombs. There was a press agitation in London for "Gas masks for everyone"' [4:3]. Public morale collapses, and defeat seems inevitable. But though things are going badly, Parham is unyielding: '"This is far more than a war between Britain and America," said the Lord Paramount. "Or any war. It is a struggle for the soul of man"' [5:1].

Parham decides the road to victory involves him gassing his enemies on a huge scale, and orders supplies of a new nerve agent, 'Gas L', be readied. This is a gas that kills in an especially tortuous way, that lingers in the air for weeks, and against which the regular gas-mask is useless (only 'a sort of sub-aerial diver's helmet' is any protection): 'Think of the moral effect of it,' Parham's advisers tell him. ('Paris or Berlin, a dead city, dead from men to rats, and nobody daring to go in to clean it up. After such a sample the world would howl for peace at any price whatever.') But Camelford, the industrialist who manufactures Gas L, refuses to play ball. The Lord Protector decides to storm his factory, and flies down to Devon. In a surreal final episode, we discover that the seabed has been raised beyond Land's End to provide a new and well-guarded promontory upon which Camelford's factory is situated, this new territory being given the ancient name Lyonesse. Parham's plan is to gas the factory, killing all inside it, and so seize its supplies. But when Parham moves in with his men, all suited-up, they discover that Camelford has developed an *anti*-gas that renders Gas L perfectly inert, such that Parham's assault is easily overpowered. Camelford subjects the frustrated Parham to a long monologue, telling him his political logic is a thing of the past. A new collective age is coming, 'a new dawn. Men of no nation. Men without traditions. Men who look forward and not back. Men who have realized the will and the intelligence that we obey and possess in common. Our race has to organize the whole world now, a field for this creative energy that flows through and uses and guides us' [5:7]. Camelford has been brewing-up a new gas, of which Gas L was just a preliminary experiment: 'a vapour to enter into blood and nerve and brain and clean the mind of man as it has never been cleaned before. It will allow his brain, so clogged and stifled still by old rubbish, so poisoned and cramped and crippled, to free itself from all that holds it back now from apprehending and willing to the utmost limits of its possibility.' This will lead to 'a new world quite different from the world to which your mind is adapted. A world beyond your dreaming!' [5:7]. It seems the new land of Lyonesse was not artificially raised after all; it just emerged, apparently because the Earth itself had decided it was time to make the 'strange minerals' necessary for this new gas, previously hidden in the seabed, accessible to mankind.

Then—once again, the inevitable, deflating twist: Parham wakes up. He is still at the séance. He and Sir Bussy having both nodded off. Mr Carnac Williams is exposed as a faker, and the evening breaks up. But there's a second twist: it seems that both Parham and Sir Bussy dreamt the same dream, from their respective perspectives, so something uncanny *had* been going on after all. The envoi is that Sir Bussy, startled out of complacency by the vision of war he has just dreamt, declares he will fund the magazine, with the intention of making the world a better place. Parham's hopes leap up, but are immediately crushed: he doesn't want Parham to edit it, or be involved at all: 'a paper—a great paper, financed by Sir Bussy! And not to be his! A paper against him! Six years wasted! Slights! Humiliations! Irritations! Tailors' bills!'

Wells parodic satire on fascism tangles with the pseudo-fascist aspects of his own World State yearnings. Philip Coupland has written about Wells's 'praxis of desire' in this respect:

> While many aspects of Wells's thinking in this area long predated the 1930s, at the same time Wells was additionally and significantly influenced by the new political forces which appeared to be coming to dominance in the early 1930s. Prominent intellectuals of the Labour movement, including Wells's old Fabian colleagues Sydney and Beatrice Webb and Bernard Shaw, and younger Labour figures including Sir Stafford Cripps and G.D.H. Cole, either embraced the authoritarian road to socialism or proposed the radical reform of parliamentary democracy. Labour intellectuals George Catlin and Raymond Postgate saw the need for, respectively, 'a voluntary aristocracy of asceticism' and 'an organization of storm-troopers or ironsides' as essential for their party in the new conditions. [Coupland, 541–2]

In *The Autocracy of Mr. Parham* there is some comedy at the notion that a politely courteous Englishman could ever adopt the preposterous hyper-masculine posturing of Mussolini and the fundamental joke of this novel is the incongruity that so scholarly and effete a figure as Parham should harbour such strongman political aspirations. But it's not the aspirations *as such* that are at fault. Indeed, Wells basically agrees with Parham that the decadence and entangling bureaucracy of democratic process must be swept aside, so that the Will or Collective Vitality of the race can be allowed to realise itself. And Wells still trails varieties of ghastlinesses in his vision's wake ('finance being so largely Jews', says Parham's deputy Gerson, by way of explaining how militarism will reboot and refresh the economy '… and at bottom a Jew is always afraid of a soldier' [3:6]). Even as late as 1936 Wells was praising Fascism for being free of 'democratic taint' and the 'elderly methods of parliamentary democracy'—although to be fair to him, he also criticised it for being infected with the 'poison of nationalism' [*The Anatomy of Frustration*, 275]. Coupland appositely quotes a contemporary, Geoffrey Gorer's *Nobody Talks Politics: A Satire with an Appendix on Our Political Intelligentsia* (1935): 'Mr Wells thinks that he hates fascism; he is horror-struck as any liberal at its brutality, its barbarism, its philistinism, its illogicality and its narrow nationalism; but he puts all the blame on the last quality. If it was only international it wouldn't really be so bad.'

In one sense the problem here is the old Wellsian one: he sees where we are, right now; and he has strong ideas about the version of social and political sanity he wants us all to get to; but the path from here to there is not clear. Indeed, if there is an ironic redemption to the satirical extrapolation of *The Autocracy of Mr. Parham* it is in the contrast between the novel's two modes of bringing about the desired future: Parham, inspired by his Martian spirit, wins power by more-or-less traditional means: campaigning, addressing crowds of followers and seizing Parliament. But Camelford possesses a magic gas which will, when inhaled, cut the Gordian knot altogether and result in an *In the Days of the Comet*-style rewiring of the human brain. This latter strategy is, in effect, a tacit acknowledgement that the obstacle to Wells's World State is *human nature as such*. Absent a reinvention of what it means to be a human being, Wells's flawless World State is stillborn.

Exactly this same diremption between the pettiness of our social lives and the grandeur of our self-conceptions informs the last of these late period Wellsian fables: the peculiarly named *The Bulpington of Blup* (1932). Here Wells returned to the work of his friend Carl Jung. In my discussion of *Christina Alberta's Father*, above, I mentioned the friendship that grew between these two men. From the 1920s onwards Wells and Jung often met, talked and corresponded. Jung's published work several times makes reference to 'my friend H G Wells'; and Wells in turn gave Jung a walk-on part in *The World of William Clissold* (1926). Wells's *Experiment in Autobiography* (1934) frames his entire life story by distinguishing between his actual self and the self he is prone to narrate into existence, 'what Jung would call my *persona*' [*Experiment in Autobiography*, 9].

It seems that Jung confided to Wells something private and personal about his young life in Switzerland, and Wells then used this as the core idea of *The Bulpington of Blup*. The wider world only learnt of Jung's childhood secret in 1962, when Jung collaborated with Aniela Jaffé on his autobiography,

Memories, Dreams, Reflections. Jung recalled his childhood as mostly defined by misery. His mother was a difficult woman, unpredictably alternating remoteness with over-intimate affection. His mild-mannered father was chaplain to a nearby mental hospital and young Jung worried that his own shyness and awkwardness were actually manifestations of 'hereditary taint'. In John Kerr's words, Jung was

> an asocial miscreant, rejected by his peers. Home was no better—the atmosphere was 'unbreathable'—… To relieve periodic choking fits he took to visualising golden angels against a blue background. And there were spaces inside spaces where one might be safe. He carved a tiny mannikin, hid it beneath the attic floorboards, and for a year ritually presented the little man with miniature scrolls written in a secret language. Guilty in his demeanour when challenged, Jung was a natural target at school. [Kerr, 3]

Memories, Dreams, Reflections details the psychological defence mechanism Jung developed to handle this situation. He became convinced that he was two people: 'Personality No. 1' and 'Personality No. 2'. The former was an insecure schoolboy, the individual the world knew; the latter a secret inner identity, a distant, immensely grand and old being, 'close to nature' and above all 'close to the night, to dreams, and to whatever "God" worked directly in him' [Jung, 45]. Jung wasn't always able to maintain an intimate relationship with Personality No. 2, and in later adolescence he actively concentrated on his 'ego' version, No. 1, so as to do as well as possible at school, with No. 2 receding into his background. The two were distinct—for example: when Jung planned to go to college, his Personality No. 1 wanted to study science, No. 2 comparative religion and philosophy—but not schizophrenic, in either the clinical or layman's sense of the term. Jung argued that we all, to one degree or another, carry these two sorts of souls within us. It seems that No. 2 had a name (beyond, i.e., 'Personality No. 2') but Jung didn't disclose it to Jaffé. John Kerr thinks the name was Goethe, and that young Jung might have believed himself Goethe's reincarnation

Turn to Wells. *The Bulpington of Blup* is a novel about shy, troubled youngster called Theodore Bulpington, the only child of a forceful, difficult mother and ineffectual father (a poet with a weak chest). Theodore is conscious of a much grander version of himself within himself. This is how the novel opens:

> There had been a time when he felt that he ought not to call himself The Bulpington of Blup. Though it was only in his own mind that he called himself the Bulpington of Blup. He never called himself the Bulpington of Blup to any

other human being. But to himself he did it continually. For some years he made a great effort not to be The Bulpington of Blup any more, to be simply and really what he was—whatever that might be … He had determined to look facts in the face—squarely in the face. He would go for walks whispering, "I am just Theodore Bulpington, a commonplace youth." Even so he would find himself putting it in phrases that betrayed him. "It ill becomes the Bulpington of Blup to shirk the harsh visage of reality." [*Blup*, 1:1]

Theodore grows up in the English seaside town of Blayport, a version of Folkestone. But his pinching, mundane Edwardian existence there encourages his mind to imagine a more impressive alternative. Since his real life is 'full of boredom, obligation and frustration' [1:3], *his* Personality No. 2 inhabits a grander locale. His history teacher tells the class that Brighton was originally called *Brighthelmstone*, and London *Londinium*. Theodore invents the idea that Blayport's ancient name was 'Blup':

It made itself a tortuous rocky harbour like a Norwegian fiord. It retreated up formidable gorges. And then it went inland and became a strange mountainous country where there were dense very green forests and the white roads wound about like serpents. One saw it usually from very far off and particularly about the time of sunset. It had walls and pinnacles of a creamy sort of rock that glittered micaceously, and there were always very still and watchful sentinels upon its ramparts. And at the sunset gun the great embroidered banner of The Bulpington fell down fold upon fold, fold upon fold, gold thread and shining silk, and gave place to the little storm flag that fluttered through the night. [*Blup*, 1:2]

Jung, in landlocked Switzerland, had also imagined a rocky port and romantic mediaeval castle as the location ('this is my home') of his 'Personality No. 2'.

Theodore goes up to London to study art at the Rowlands School. He stays with his Fabian aunt, sees George Bernard Shaw speak, and disagrees with the socialists he meets: "'Why talk and work for a Social Revolution if it's bound to happen?' That was a great point to make' [3:7]. He decides he is in love with a childhood friend called Margaret, but nonetheless he has an affair with one of his fellow students, Rachel Bernstein ('in some magic fashion sex had lost all touch of obscenity. Rachel had so filled his mind with herself and her lithe vitality' [4:1])—a betrayal he justifies by arguing that though Theodore loves Margaret, it is the Bulpington of Blup 'that great figure, full as ever of the love and appreciation of life' who is dallying with 'the untidy, eager little

Jewess'. It was not really he, but 'the great young man, so reminiscent of the youthful Goethe, [who] toyed with her' [4:2]. Goethe, no less!

War breaks out and Theodore, in an access of patriotism, enlists ('"Dear England," he whispered. "My England"' [6:2]). His socialist-pacifist friends, Margaret amongst them, are both disgusted with him; and in fact Theodore's reflex patriotism is merely a function of the Bulpington of Blup personality overwhelming his other self. At the front line he has a pacifist epiphany: 'Margaret was right. This is the last insanity of mankind. All these men, the men about him and the men against him, these fantastic men in masks, are mad. Before everything else he must get out of this nightmare, away from these maniacs' [7:10]. He deserts, is captured, and is lucky to avoid execution. The young doctor who examines him, disinclined to send another fellow to the firing squad, files the patently absurd report that Theodore was 'leading [his] men splendidly and a shell exploded' which 'blew [him]—about a mile and a half to the rear' [7:10]. Hospitalised with shell shock, Theodore sees out the rest of the war, and afterwards settles in Paris.

Here he carves out a new life for himself under the name 'Captain Blup-Bulpington' ('—he never specified his regiment') as part of the Parisian literary scene, 'the editor and part owner of a brilliantly aggressive little magazine, called *The Feet of the Young Men*' (printed 'entirely without punctuation marks, merely with gaps of varying length, and all the capital B's and P's put backside foremost'). But after a decade of this life he sells his share and returns to England and parochial obscurity, living with his elderly aunt in her Devonshire cottage and becoming a feature of that provincial world, spinning heroic mendacities about his war-service at dinner parties. At one he invents the tale that, during the final advance, he personally captured the Kaiser, but, recognising his royalty and honourableness, let him go again. His audience of old maids and aunts is suitably impressed. Later, as he walks home under starlight, the uneasy half-awareness that he has been lying encroaches upon him: 'this feeling that he had not been telling the truth increased' [9:7].

> Was he a liar? Was he becoming an outrageously careless and preposterous liar? The sort of liar who isn't even believed? [*Blup*, 9:7]

He hovers on the edge of realising the distortion the Bulpington of Blup has wrought on his life, but reels back, haranguing the silent night sky with his self-justification:

> He considered: "I am that I am." That was still not quite correct, not quite his intention, and he wished to state his intention very plainly. And besides—come to think of it—it was a quotation.

"No—not what I am, that's your affair, perhaps. No, I am what I choose to be. See?"

He whispered that over again. "What I choose to be." That was better. That was right. Thereby he asserted precisely the power of his Will. [*Blup*, 9:7]

Back home he pours himself several large whiskies and salutes his grandfather clock as a fellow old-soldier. The last lines of the novel are: 'A most satisfying evening. Refined intelligent women—ladies. All his values sang together within him.'

By 1932 Wells's fiction sales had been sliding for a while. Ernst Benn, who published all Wells's late 1920s fiction, declined to publish *The Autocracy of Mr. Parham* (1930), citing as many as 10,000 unsold returns on previous Wells titles. Heinemann agreed to publish *Parham*, but they lost £900 on it and weren't interested in *The Bulpington of Blup*, which was instead acquired by Macmillan. Yet Wells himself thought highly of this novel, or at least thought that its protagonist Theodore was as good a piece of characterisation as Kipps (he said this in letters as he was writing it and repeats the judgement in his *Experiment in Autobiography*). Contemporaries did not agree. *The Kirkus Review* (20 January 1933) was particularly cutting:

A disappointing endeavour to get back into the stride of *Tono-Bungay* and *Mr. Polly*. The hero is of the stuff of which literary characters are made, but instead of having flesh and blood and bones and sinews, he is a lay figure, which the author exposes successively to the onslaughts of science, adolescence, religion, the new art, sex in the raw, socialism, communism, death, war, the aftermath of war, and the ultimate supremacy of his fantasy self. Artificial, self-conscious, full. We cannot congratulate Macmillan on re-acquiring him.

Robert Bloom argues that in *The Bulpington of Blup* 'Wells has devised an intriguing form—an anti-Bildungsroman'. The failure of Theodore to grow into any constructive social role derives, Bloom argues, from 'such special and dubious forms of the arts as fin de siècle aestheticism, escapist romanticism, and the reactionary poetics of the twenties' (as per the novel's satire on Modernist Little Magazines). According to Bloom, the novel contrasts the forward-looking science-based action of Margaret Broxted with the backward-looking romantic-conservative and mendacious passivity of Theodore himself: 'Wells' whole career is based on the idea that the world can be, must be, changed for the better by the application of science and good will' [Bloom, 57].

Blup is certainly a wrongfooting novel, but Bloom is surely wrong about the specifics of its wrongfootingness. The anti-Bildungsroman aspect here is not that *The Bulpington of Blup* is not a Bildungsroman. Clearly it *is* a Bildungsroman—the main character grows and evolves, changes, such that he is not the same person at the end of the novel as he was at the beginning. A better argument is surely that this novel works against the grain of the Bildungsroman by inverting the assumptions of the mode's traditional trajectory: the classic form of emotional and existential *maturation*, the Emma Woodhouse or David Copperfield line—a trajectory, that is to say, away from a lower (a less aware, a more foolish) subjectivity and towards a higher authenticity of lived experience. Wells instead creates a character who, led by his secret Jungian Personality No.2, grows and changes into a *less* authentic, *less* wise human being. Appropriately enough for the author of *The Time Machine*, it is a novel not of character evolution but of character devolution.

Theodore is, in plain language, a liar. Insofar as he imposes his lies on the people around him, he's a kind of confidence man—posing in Paris as Captain Blup-Bulpington, rather than cowardly Bulpington the deserter, for instance. Wells's originality is in telling the story of a liar from the inside, and in a way that avoids the Scylla-Charybdis of harsh moral judgement on the one hand, or ironic-satiric diabolical celebration on the other. There's no shortage of liars (from Chaucer's Pardoner through Iago to Melmotte and Merdle) in literature, and no shortage either of trickster figures, from Anansi and Loki to Melville's Confidence-Man and Bulgakov's Professor Woland. But in all those cases the trickster *owns* their trickery. They are, we might say, confident in their confidence-man games. By switching his focus about and tracing the way an otherwise unremarkable boy grows into an adult defined by his self-deception, Wells is attempting something unprecedented in fiction.

This is a novel, in other words, about truth and lies in a non-moral sense. We don't despise Bulpington, even at the end: bragging impossible feats to an audience of gullible old women. In a letter of Aug 1932 to Watt, his literary agent, Wells wrote that Theodore was 'an acutely differentiated character' adding that 'there is something of all of us in his mental tangles, and though he is an unfaithful lover, an outrageous liar and narrowly escapes being shot for cowardice, he keeps more of our sympathy to the end than perhaps some of will care to admit'. This is because the novel is a study not in the morality but in the *psychology* of lying. Several times in his writing Jung argued that any lie, howsoever semantically mendacious, cannot help but be psychologically and imaginatively true. It's not that Wells is trying to downplay the socially destructive wickedness that can result from lying. It's that his focus is on the ways we lie to ourselves rather than on the ways we lie to other people. Why, this novel asks, *do* we lie to ourselves? Usually when we lie to other people we are trying specifically to fool them, for reasons that will specifically advantage us. But why do so many of us lie to ourselves? How can we hope to get away with it? Since the person we are lying to is also *the person doing the lying*, the former surely knows the mendacity of the latter? The common-sense answer to that question, I suppose, would be: we do it to align our desiring self with the constraints of social acceptability as such, or perhaps more to the point, with those constraints as we have internalised them.

Wells's book is suggesting that the real point in lying to ourselves is not to make ourselves feel good, but to make ourselves feel grander—more important, more noble, more sublime. This is where the mythic self-elaboration that turns Theodore into the Bulpington of Blup blurs into religious faith. Wells's friend William James's *Varieties of Religious Experience*, is, in Adam Phillips reading, a work exploring the place where truth flows into creativity. 'The truth of your beliefs is what they can do for you, James says,' is how Phillips put it. 'Truth is the name you will give to whatever turns out to have been good to believe' [Phillips, 78]. *The Bulpington of Blup* is a compelling account of the psychological territorial demands such a self-oriented conception of good entails.

Bibliography

Allen, Walter (1964) *Tradition and Dream: The English and American Novel from the Twenties to Our Time*. London: Hogarth Press.

Bloom, Robert (1977). *Anatomies of Egotism: A Reading of the Last Novels of H. G. Wells*. Lincoln: University of Nebraska Press.

Coupland, Philip (2000). 'H. G. Wells's "Liberal Fascism"', *Journal of Contemporary History*, 35:4, 541–558.

Jung, Carl and Aniela Jaffé (1973), *Memories, Dreams, Reflections*. Translated from the German by Richard and Clara Winston. New York: Pantheon Books.

Kerr, John (1995). 'Madnesses', *London Review of Books* 17:6 (23 March 1995), pp. 3–6.

Phillips, Adam (2006). *Side Effects*. Harmondsworth: Penguin.

Smith, David (1986). *H G Wells: Desperately Mortal*. Yale University Press.

Tredell, Nicholas (1982). *The Novels of Colin Wilson*. New York: Vision/Barnes & Noble.

Wagar, W. Warren (1998). 'Letters from Our Father', *Science Fiction Studies*, 25:3, 526–533.

23

Life Stories

The Book of Catherine Wells (1928); *Experiment in Autobiography* (1934)

Real-life caught up with Wells's fictional and non-fictional speculative subjectivities in 1927. In October of that year Amy Catherine Robbins, who in 1895 had become 'Jane', the second Mrs Wells, died. She had been diagnosed with an inoperable cancer in the spring, and her health declined very rapidly. Wells returned from Europe to be with her and was present at her death. Afterwards he gave himself to grief. Charlotte Shaw, Fabian activist and wife of George Bernard, wrote to T.E. Lawrence after the funeral:

> It was dreadful—dreadful—*dreadful!* ... H G began to cry like a child, tried to hide it at first and then let go. It was terrible beyond anything words can describe: a soul in torment—self torture. He drowned us in a sea of misery and as we were gasping began a panegyric of Jane which made her appear a delicate, flower-like, gentle being, surrounding itself with beauty and philanthropy and love. Now Jane was one of the strongest characters I ever met. She managed H.G. and her good curious sons and her circle generally according to her own very definite and very original theories. Then there came a place where the address said "she never resented a slight, she never gave voice to a harsh judgment." At that point the audience, all more or less acquainted with many details of H.G.'s private life, thrilled, like corn under a wet north wind—and H.G.— H.G. positively howled. (Mackenzies, 353)

He didn't howl for long. Within a few days Wells had returned to Lou Pidou in France and the arms of Odette Keun.

Wells decided to curate a memorial volume in Jane's honour. Back in the mid-1890s Catherine had been his sometime collaborator, nosing out ideas for short articles and newspaper pieces and helping him realise them, and

© The Author(s) 2019
A. Roberts, *H G Wells*, Literary Lives, https://doi.org/10.1007/978-3-030-26421-5_23

whilst the bulk of the resulting saleable pieces were written by Wells, she herself sometimes sketched out and wrote up short stories and other pieces herself. It wasn't a career she developed any further than these few sketches, instead devoting herself to being Wells's homemaker and companion, turning a blind eye to his many infidelities as well as often (most notably with 1920's *Outline of History*) acting as secretary, amanuensis and unpaid researcher. *The Book of Catherine Wells* (1928) is a collection of some of her original writing, with a seven-page introduction by Wells himself. The preface gives us an interesting if inevitably partial view of the dynamic that had for three decades sustained marriage between these, on the face of it, rather incompatible human beings.

> What is more difficult to tell is our slow discovery of the profoundest temperamental differences between us and of the problems these differences created for us. Fundamental to my wife's nature was a passion for happiness and lovely things. She was before everything else gentle and sweet. She worshipped beauty. I am a far less stable creature than she was, with a driving quality that hold my instabilities together. I have more drive than strength, and little patience. I am hasty and incompetent about much of the detailed business of life because I put too large a proportion of my available will and energy into issues that dominate me. (*Book of Catherine Wells*, 'Preface')

You notice how a sweet, if rather patronising, compliment to Catherine morphs into a lengthy and slyly self-serving compliment to H.G. *by* H.G., poorly camouflaged as self-criticism. To be fair to Wells, he was sometimes aware of the ways his ego could lead him towards narcissistic self-regard. But this preface really struggles to balance Wellsian self-criticism with its more particular business, praise for his dead wife:

> It was an easy thing for me to keep my faith in her sense of fair play and perfect generosity. She never told a lie. To the end I would have taken her word against all other witnesses in the world. But she managed to sustain her belief that I was worth living for, and that was a harder task, while I made my way through a tangle of moods and impulses that were quite outside her instinctive sympathy. She stuck to me so sturdily that in the end I stuck to myself. I do not know what I should have been without her. She stabilized my life. She gave it a home and dignity. She preserved its continuity. (*Book of Catherine Wells*, 'Preface')

David C. Smith finds this passage genuinely moving: 'his words seem to me to convey better than any others the extraordinary relationship of Bits and Bins—of Bertie and Jane—of H.G. and Amy Catherine,' he gushes, adding:

Their friends who received the book understood its message clearly. It was not an apology, for none was needed. What it was in a manly way is simply a fare-well—Vale, to the dearest person he had ever known. (Smith, 388)

To me Wells's performance of a rather mannered abjection of personality strikes a rather more calculated note than that. He is saying that Catherine was solid, a homemaker and refuge, the dependable plinth upon which the statue to Wells's mercurial genius could be positioned the better for the world to see it. Describing one's wife as 'sturdy' is hardly a flattering thing to do, after all—and Wells's claim that his 'moods and impulses' were 'quite outside' her ability to sympathise borders on the insulting. Smith may think that no apology was required from Wells to Catherine, but one of them was unmis-takeably wronged and the other unmistakably the wronger, and the ethical gradient of that fact makes Wells's 'oh I've been a mad, impetuous, sexy fool, but she loved me!' act more than a little grating.

I daresay I am being unfair. The truth, in fact, is that we don't know. We don't know how Amy Catherine felt about being so often cheated-on by her husband. We know that she was aware of most, if not perhaps all, of Wells's affairs, and she certainly knew about the most significant relationships: Amy Reeves, Rebecca West and Odette Keun. According to Mary Hunter Austin, who was staying with them at the time, Wells announced that West was preg-nant with his child at dinner, before guests; and Jane Wells's response was a calm remark that 'Rebecca would need help dealing with the consequences'. This, if true, is intriguing. Was it Jane tacitly boasting of her own superior organisational competency, as against West's scatty immaturity? Or was it a different sort of boast, before guests, a way of asserting how cool and collected she was, even in the teeth of so startling a pronouncement? Or was it, maybe, exactly what it appears to be: a neutral judgement by a woman who simply doesn't care that her husband has impregnated another woman? Practically, she certainly condoned Wells's adultery; accepted it, perhaps, as the price to be paid for her materially comfortable existence and for being part of her genius spouse's life. What we cannot know is how she felt about it, what emo-tional contortions she put herself to in order to achieve that outward equa-nimity. Indeed, it's hard even to speculate about this without taking sides. Smith certainly does: from his moist-eyed tribute to Wells's 'manly' refusal to apologise quoted above, to blaming Jane for her husband's cheating. If the two had been 'more sexually compatible', he says, or more precisely 'if she had been willing to accept his needs more completely' then perhaps his multiple infidelities ('these events') 'might not have taken place' [Smith, 212–13]. This unbecoming assertion is Smith at his most hypothetical. *Was* this why Wells strayed? Where the sexual incompatibility of H.G. and Jane is concerned, we only have Wells's version, recorded in *H G Wells in Love*. He says the problem manifested early in their marriage, and attributes their incompatibility to the fact that he was still infatuated with his first wife, Isabel. Conceivably Jane was wholly untroubled by her husband sleeping with other women. Maybe she minded but kept it to herself. More probably she minded at first, but got used to it with time (human beings can get used to anything, in time). Maybe she hated it with a passion, and nagged and ranted and wept in private, but maintained the public façade for her own reasons. That last looks less likely to me, although I also don't get the sense that the two of them agreed on a *mutually* open relationship. I presume that 'we had a common detestation not only of falsehood but of falsity' means: *we didn't lie directly to another, but also didn't maintain any of the polite fictions by which some couples paper-over their emotional cracks.* That claim looks more admirable than it is, though. The rationale 'cheating on your partner is fine so long as you don't lie about it' inadvertently tangles itself in its own ethical nets. The reason lying is bad is because it's a kind of infidelity, an unfaithfulness to the truth, an untrustworthiness. The ethical maths of 'this negative thing, cheating on my wife, is cancelled out by this positive thing, telling her the truth about my cheating' is, simply, a misunderstanding of the logic of the human heart. Adulterers who confess do so to make themselves feel better, not to make their partners feel better. If you're going to cheat, you should at least have the courage to lie about it. You've already transgressed; have the residual decency at least to own that fact.

Then again, maybe not. To repeat myself: we just don't know how Catherine felt about H.G.'s sexual incontinence. Maybe she was fine with it so long as she knew about it. There are people in the world who would feel that way about a partner's infidelity. We can say that Wells's advocacy of freeing humanity's erotic energies from Victorian prudery and oppression was a genuine and, in its way, even a noble thing; and the fact that he lived as well as wrote this new sexual ethos—that, as the phrase goes, he walked the walk as well as talking the talk—is at least consistent. But there's something diminishing, it seems to me, in the way it actually panned-out in his life: not a sexual liberation so much as a kind of semi-licensed serial bigamy, in which Wells found the thrill of sexual novelty with a string of younger women whilst also positioning his wife as a kind of mother confessor, to whom he could always return and unburden himself. That rather suggests that his own psyche remained striated by a fundamentally Victorian sexual guilt, that he needed the absolution of a maternal, home-making, dependable woman to clear Wells's conscience, such that he could once again range out into the world of sexual dalliance. To call such an attitude contemptible is probably to overstate matters; but at least we can say: it's not what he's actually preaching from the pulpit.

It is likely that, despite his repeated infidelities, monogamy was actually closer to the truth of Wells. Even when he is performing 'honesty in confession' in *H G Wells in Love*, he opens with the following: 'I was never a great amorist, though I have loved several people very deeply.' Which is as if to say: I may have been a polygamist, but I have, at least in my own sense of myself, been a *monogamous* polygamist. To point to the evidence of his really quite wide-ranging promiscuity (Anthony West thinks he slept with six to eight women a year throughout his adult life, which would mean he was unfaithful to Catherine with hundreds of people)—is to miss the point. Wells's sentiment is a statement of emotional self-perception, not notches on the bedpost. As Adam Phillips says in his book on the subject: 'the opposite of monogamy is not just promiscuity, but the absence or the impossibility of relationship itself. Indeed, one reason monogamy is so important to us is because we are so terrorised by what we imagine are the alternatives to it … in other words, we do not know whether we want monogamy, but we do know that we fear excess: an excess of company, an excess of solitude' [Phillips, 98]. So it is that the real polygamist's boast is always actually *I was never a great amorist*— rather I have loved a few select people very deeply.

The temptation also exists to imagine the question from the other side—to ask, in other words, what it was that drew so many intelligent, beautiful women to sleep with Wells. He was small, ugly, often ill, with a high, reedy voice and a sometimes overbearing or thoughtless manner, and lower-class in an era that tended sexually to fetishize good breeding and aristocracy. By the same token, of course, he was rich and famous, intelligent and creative, as well as being very charming and witty company. The women who fell for his charms spoke of his feline physical qualities, the dazzle of his bright blue eyes and the fact that his skin smelt of honey—this last probably a result of his diabetes (sugar in the sweat and urine being symptomatic of the disease). Moreover we should not underestimate the appeal, in a more sexually restrictive age, of encountering a man at ease with his own sexual availability, neither possessive nor dismissive of women, and with added advantage of having the reputation ('notoriety', if one prefers) precisely *as* a sexually available man. At any rate, women continued sleeping with him throughout the 1920s and 1930s. Indeed, since the fact of the illegitimate children he fathered on Amber Reeves and Rebecca West suggests he was often careless of prophylaxis in sexual matters, it is mildly surprising that he didn't father more children on other women. It's possible that he did: Labour activist and economist Harold

Laski reported that, in the 1930s, his daughter Diana was friends with an illegitimate daughter of Wells, and that she had urged her father to tell the girl the true identity of her father. Laski declined to do so, and Wellsians generally take the whole story with a pinch of salt; but it's certainly possible that Wells fathered other, unacknowledged children. (Diana Laski was born in 1916 which, if we assume her friend was of a similar age, would place the birth of Wellsian daughter to the late nineteen-teens; see Kramnick and Sheerman.)

Whatever quantity, small or large (conceivably even non-existent) of guilt Wells felt with regard to how he had treated Jane, her death certainly threw him back on himself. His writing of the closely autobiographical novel *The World of William Clissold* (1926) had already fed into this autobiographical impulse; the death of his Jane consolidated it. But the proximate impulse behind the composition of Wells's *Experiment in Autobiography* was the drawn-out, painful break-up of his long-term relationship with Odette Keun that stretched (the break-up, I mean) through 1932 and 1933. He was, now, an old man, and his consciousness of senescence was underpinned by a diagnosis of diabetes at the beginning of the 1930s. He was in a mood to take stock of his life by writing it out as a story. This he composed mostly in Bournemouth between 1932 and 1934 (he'd given over his Provençale house, Lou Pidou, to Keun when he ended their 9-year affair). The work quickly sprawled. He wrote to his friend Harold Laski (8 January 1933): 'I have recently been writing an exhaustingly full and intimate account of my early life up to the age of 35. There is a good mass of letters and sketches available.' The 'sketches' are the 'picshuas', the little doodles Wells was constantly drawing, and which liberally illustrate the *Autobiography*, as they do various others of Wells books (Fig. 23.1).

The letter to Laski goes on to describe the autobiography as 'a sort of diary in pen and ink caricature that makes it rather specially interesting. But I have not yet set myself to discuss how a large book of 200,000 words with two or three score pages of facsimile pictures and photographs can be published.' A fifth of a million words only took him to 35; since the published *Autobiography* takes us all the way up to Wells's late 60s, we have to assume the first MS draft was vast indeed. We don't know exactly how vast. Having finished it, Wells took a working holiday in America and left the MS in the hands of his daughter-in-law Marjorie Wells and his old friend (and former lover), the novelist Dorothy Richardson. It seems these two cut the MS down to a more manageable, although still hefty, 290,000 words. When Wells returned to the UK he checked over, and approved, their work. Hutchinson offered £3300 for the book, but Gollancz outbid them with an advance of £4000—roughly half a million pounds in 2019 money—plus a whopping 20% royalty.

Fig. 23.1 One of Wells's many 'picshuas' from *Experiment in Autobiography*

In the event the book was a notable success; a big seller, praised by his friends, widely and positively covered by reviewers. It was hailed by some as one of the great autobiographies of the age. And, although it's little read today, some critics have endorsed this assessment: Michael Sherborne thinks it 'by far the best of his later books' [Sherborne, 299] and David C. Smith calls it 'one of the great autobiographies of this century … one of the best testaments to the human condition and its possibility' [Smith, 418–19].

It's not hard to see why *Experiment in Autobiography* did so well. Despite its length, it is an extremely compelling piece of writing, full of engaging and often hilarious detail, helped by the fact that Wells knew everyone worth knowing. It gives an absorbing portrait of its times, especially of what it was like growing up in late-Victorian England, and what being young and hopeful and randy was like in the 1890s. And the central figure, Wells's Wells, is as vividly rendered and engaging a piece of characterisation as any in his fiction. We can presume this character bears some relationship to the (if you'll pardon the scare-quotes) 'real' H.G., but one thing to which the *Autobiography* is constantly and gratifyingly alert is how much of fiction there is in any self-assessment or retrospective life-narration, published or not.

Most entertaining of all are Wells's accounts of his literary friendships. Joseph Conrad is 'rather short and round-shouldered with his head as it were sunken into his body. He had a dark retreating face with a very carefully trimmed and pointed beard' [*Autobiography*, 525]. From Wells's account we discover Conrad wrote *Heart of Darkness* and *The Secret Agent* on the same desk that Christina Rossetti had written 'Goblin Market' (when Conrad moved to Kent he rented from Ford Madox Ford a farm called the Pent at the foot of the Downs above Hythe, which had previously been Rossetti's dwelling and which still contained much of her old furniture). And Conrad's first encounter with George Bernard Shaw is hilarious:

> When Conrad first met Shaw in my house, Shaw talked with his customary freedoms. 'You know, my dear fellow, your books won't do'—for some Shavian reason I have forgotten—and so forth.
>
> I went out of the room and suddenly found Conrad on my heels, swift and white-faced. 'Does that man want to insult me?' he demanded.
>
> The provocation to say 'Yes' and assist at the subsequent duel was very great, but I overcame it. 'It's humour,' I said, and took Conrad out into the garden to cool. One could always baffle Conrad by saying 'humour.' It was one of our damned English tricks he had never learnt to tackle. (*Autobiography*, 530)

There's a great deal of stuff like this in the *Autobiography*, and it's very often this charming, although not all the humour is kindly. Encountering his neighbour G.K. Chesterton driving a horse and gig in the narrow Kentish lanes, Wells describes how his friend 'seemed to overhang his one-horse fly' ('rather swollen by the sunshine, he descended slowly but firmly; he was moist and steamy but cordial' [453]). Of Henry James, once his close friend, later estranged and by 1934 (of course) long dead, Wells says he was 'a strange unnatural human being, a sensitive man lost in an immensely abundant brain, which had had neither a scientific nor a philosophical training, but which was by education and natural aptitude alike, formal, formally æsthetic, conscientiously fastidious and delicate. Wrapped about in elaborations of gesture and speech, James regarded his fellow creatures with a face of distress and a remote effort at intercourse, like some victim of enchantment placed in the centre of an immense bladder' [450]. *Bladder* is funny, but in a cruel sort of way. What redeems all this is Wells's real gift for self-deprecation. He very often captures his own absurd, pompous, petty and comical nature, and does so with a lightness of touch and ingenuousness that makes those stories where he is the butt of the joke some of the best. And his literary self-assessment is unforgiving: 'tried by Henry James's standards', he says, none of his novels 'can be taken in any other fashion' than failures: 'I sketch out scenes and individuals, often quite crudely, and resort even to conventional types and symbols, in order to get on to a discussion of relationships' [414].

The question that naturally arises is: what specific relation exists between the character at the heart of this book and the human being Herbert George Wells who lived between 1866 and 1946? It's a question as much about auto-biography as such as it is about Wells's memoir, touching on the fundamental structural misprision of writing as such—the priority, that is, of representation over actuality. Certainly Wells is aware of what he is doing: crafting him-self, unveiling not the *vrai* Wells so much the Wellsian persona. That canny self-awareness is one of the great strengths of the *Experiment in Autobiography* precisely because the persona so created does have value as a way of appre-hending what was 'really' going on to and in the Wellsian sensorium. Representation distorts and exaggerates but it doesn't invent out of whole cloth. This is how Wells puts it, theorising his own autobiographical praxis via Jung:

> A persona, as Jung uses the word, is the private conception a man has of himself, his idea of what he wants to be and of how he wants other people to take him … A biography should be a dissection and demonstration of how a particular human being was made and worked; the directive persona system is of leading importance only when it is sufficiently consistent and developed to be the ruling theme of the story. But this is the case with my life. From quite an early age I have been predisposed towards one particular sort of work and one particular system of interests. I have found the attempt to disentangle the possible drift of life in general and of human life in particular from the confused stream of events, and the means of controlling that drift, if such are to be found, more important and interesting by far than anything else. I have had, I believe, an aptitude for it. The study and expression of tendency, has been for me what music is for the musician, or the advancement of his special knowledge is to the scientific investigator. My persona may be an exaggeration of one aspect of my being, but I believe that it is a ruling aspect. (*Autobiography*, 9–11)

What this means, in practical terms, in this book, is that Wells consistently underplays himself—that he produces a *persona* more comically inept than the public record might suggest was 'actually' the case. Wells was, let's not forget, someone who, almost entirely on the strength of his own energy, genius and persistence, turned himself from a nobody into one of the world's most famous, influential, and wealthy authors. He went from being a draper's apprentice with no prospects to a wealthy man friends with Jung, Beaverbrook, Roosevelt, Marie Stopes, George Gissing, Henry James, Joseph Conrad, Dorothy Richardson and Bernard Shaw, with Roger Fry and Charlie Chaplin and Booker T. Washington, a man who took tea with Prime Ministers, Presidents and Archbishops. He was a man who overcame almost wholly impermeable barriers of class and background in a country and at the time when class and background were greater impediments than almost anywhere in the world, the man who took a congeries of futurist and technological-novum tropes and made them a coherent genre called 'science fiction', who made prophecy respectable and helped reconfigure the political landscape of his homeland. But the Wells who writes his *Autobiography* repeatedly stresses his inadequacies. Remarkably this doesn't come across as false modesty. His modesty has the sheen of genuineness, even of a kind of baffled ingenuity. How did all this happen to me? he seems to be saying.

> The brain upon which my experiences have been written is not a particularly good one. If there were brain-shows, as there are cat and dog shows, I doubt if it would get even a third class prize. … I won't even compare it with such cerebra as the full and subtly simple brain of Einstein, the wary, quick and flexible one of Lloyd George, the abundant and rich grey matter of G. B. Shaw, Julian Huxley's store of knowledge or my own eldest son's fine and precise instrument. But in relation to everyday people with no claim to mental distinction I still find it at a disadvantage. (*Autobiography*, 13)

He is disarmingly honest about the limitations of his own writing: *Mankind in the Making* (1902) is 'extremely sketchy' and its component elements 'do not interlock' [213]; *Joan and Peter* (1918) 'is as shamelessly unfinished as a Gothic cathedral' [420]; *What Is Coming* (1916) was assembled 'in a very blind and haphazard fashion' (he says he would prefer to 'let this little volume decay and char and disappear and say nothing about it' [580]). Of his experience with the Fabians, he notes: 'I can be quite remarkably silly and inept' [564] and the reader feels he's being perfectly honest in acknowledging his silliness and ineptitude.

The key to all this (an English person is liable to say *but of course*) is class. Wells lives his own life on his own terms, but that life is also always already overwritten by the social class into which he was born. Another way of expressing the quality of silliness or ineptitude, of comical bumptiousness, of his whole small-stature squeaky-voiced Britling-y nature, would be to describe him as *a bit vulgar*. A thoroughly class-saturated way of putting things. What Wells never had as a person, and what his *Autobiography* never tries to mimic, are breeding, refinement, elevation, suavity. Repudiating these things and insisting on speaking the plain truth as he sees it is the core of Wells's philosophy of life. Indeed, the truth is that he wasn't even a *parvenu*. He was, in the crushingly snobbish English phrase, a *counter-jumper*. The great merit of his *Autobiography* is that he owns that fact, revels in it, and so makes something potent out of it.

When the *Experiment in Autobiography* was published, Odette Keun, fresh from the grazed heart and bruised ego of the ungainly end of her affair with Wells, reviewed it ungenerously:

> When a really objective biography of Wells will be written, instead of the enormous reel of self-justification which he is still producing, where his very cunning art of feinting, his very subtle trick of inaccuracy in confession, have again succeeded in blinding his audience to the nature of his play, it will be discovered that he has wounded and injured often beyond cure. (Keun, 1252)

She means: he has wounded and injured *me* beyond cure; though she can't say so without sacrificing the pretence of reviewerish objectivity. And doubtless she has a point, although it's (surely) a general point rather than one specific to Wells. Then again, the *Experiment in Autobiography* never sets out to be a letter of exculpation addressed to an ex-lover. If it's a reel it's a reel around the fountain of Wellsian genius. His origins were low, and his adult manner kept betraying that lowness. But lowness is a good, indeed a vital, quality in a well; and without wells how would we drink?

Bibliography

Keun, Odette (1934) 'H. G. Wells—The Player', *Time and Tide* (13–27 October), 1251–1252.

Kramnick, Issac and Barry Sheerman (1993). *Harold Laski: a Life on the Left*. London, Hamish Hamilton.

Phillips, Adam (1996). *Monogamy*. London: Faber.

Saunders, Max (2016). '"Fusions and Interrelations": Family Memoirs of Henry James, Edmund Gosse and Others', in Adam Smyth (ed), *A History of English Autobiography*. Cambridge University Press, 255–268.

Sherborne, Michael (2010) *H.G. Wells: Another Kind of Life*. London, Peter Owen.

Smith, David (1986). *H G Wells: Desperately Mortal*. Yale University Press.

24

Later Non-fiction

The Open Conspiracy (1928); The Science of Life (1930); The Work, Wealth and Happiness of Mankind (1931); After Democracy (1932); The New America: The New World (1935); The Anatomy of Frustration (1936); World Brain (1938); The Fate of Homo Sapiens (1939); Travels of a Republican Radical in Search of Hot Water (1939); The New World Order (1940); The Rights of Man (1940); The Common Sense of War and Peace (1940); The Conquest of Time (1942); Crux Ansata: An Indictment of the Roman Catholic Church (1943)

The acid-test for his non-fiction, one Wells himself would surely have respected, is that of actual posterity. Are his ideas still read and discussed? Do people still orient their lives by his writing? How many of his concepts and phrases have entered common currency? Earlier I suggested four of his coinages that have certainly endured ('time machine', 'atom bomb', 'the war to end war' and 'League of Nations'). A fifth phrase, first used by Wells in his 1912 novel *The Passionate Friends* and repeatedly invoked through his nineteen-teens and 1920s writing, is, as we have seen, 'Open Conspiracy'. His book *The Open Conspiracy*, subtitled *Blue Prints for a World Revolution*, was published in 1928. The phrase, and the idea to which it relates, manifestly hasn't had the afterlife of those other four.

What *is* the open conspiracy? 'The world', says Wells, 'is undergoing immense changes', changes that have 'come through men themselves' [*Open Conspiracy*, 1]. The abolition of distance has reconfigured both the actual social landscapes of work; medical art has attained a level where 'the average life is prolonged, and there is a steady, alarming increase in the world's population' and there have been startling advances in military technology.

© The Author(s) 2019
A. Roberts, *H G Wells*, Literary Lives, https://doi.org/10.1007/978-3-030-26421-5_24

These changes threaten collective disaster. What's needed is the titular conspiracy:

> … a sort of unpremeditated and unorganized conspiracy, against the fragmentary and insufficient governments and the wide-spread greed, appropriation, clumsiness, and waste that are now going on. But unlike conspiracies in general this widening protest and conspiracy against established things would, by its very nature, go on in the daylight, and it would be willing to accept participation and help from every quarter. It would, in fact, become an 'Open Conspiracy,' a necessary, naturally evolved conspiracy, to adjust our dislocated world. (*Open Conspiracy*, 2)

By the 1933 second edition of the book Wells was confidently announcing that his 'open conspiracy' was happening all around them: 'hundreds of thousands of people everywhere are now thinking upon the lines foreshadowed by my Open Conspiracy, not because they had ever heard of the book or phrase, but because that was the way thought was going.' The argument is: we must alter human mental attitudes, through persuasion, collective pressure and most of all through education and activism. Gerald Heard, who had set up the H.G. Wells Society in 1934 to promote Wells's ideas, changed the society's name to 'The Open Conspiracy' in 1935. But by 1936 the society's name reverted back, and the phrase is not one with currency nowadays.

Phraseology aside, we need to decide whether we think the idea itself has merit: the notion that governments can't be trusted to take the world in the right direction, that people can and should organise outside conventional political structures in order to steer history. Some critics have defended Wells's manifesto. Michael Sherborne argues that Wells's campaign here provided 'a boost for a civil society realized today by bodies such as Greenpeace and Amnesty International' [Sherborne, 286]. And, indeed, political pressure groups certainly loom large in today's politics. But, surely, the most influential are not the ones that undertake the Wellsian (or Greenpacific, or Amnesty-Internationalist) line of publicity and education—but rather the ones, like the National Rife Association (NRA) in America, pharmaceutical and insurance mega-corporations throughout the West and the Arms Industries globally, who directly channel the largest quantities of cash, often clandestinely, to sitting government officials. That's clearly not what Wells has in mind here, but it's an eventuality a modicum of common sense might have anticipated.

Wells was for a time almost wooed by Oswald Mosley's 'New Party'—
Harold Nicholson, who had followed Mosely in his defection from Labour
records that in August 1931 he encountered Wells in London 'ill and a trifle
tipsy' and persuaded him to write an article 'for us' ('he says he will do so',
Nicholson recorded, 'since he loves me dearly', adding 'what a darling man'
[Nicholson, 85]). As the decade wore on and Mosely went full fascist, Wells
refused to follow, and his vivid caricature of Mosely in *The Holy Terror* (1939)
is as unforgiving as it is lively. But in the early 1930s Wells found himself
crotchety about democracy. *After Democracy* (1932), subtitled 'Addresses and
Papers on the Present World Situation', dismisses the old nineteenth-century
representative democracy and calls for 'the dictatorship of informed and educated common sense' ('The world', he says, 'is sick of parliamentary politics').
Wells is still insisting upon the need for his Samurai order to enforce order
and happiness on the world, and although he doesn't specifically bang the
eugenicist drum here, the unpleasant odour of that belief-set nonetheless
hangs over his thought like a malarial miasma:

> The world and its future is not for feeble folk any more than it is for selfish folk.
> It is not for the multitude but for the best ... I want to make opportunity uni-
> versal and not miss out one single being who is worthwhile. (*After Democracy*, 50)

In 1934 and 1935 Wells undertook two visits to the USA, the second commissioned by *Collier's*, who wanted Wells's view of the Rooseveltian New
Deal. His articles, later collected as *The New America: The New World* (1935),
report his impressions of the country and voice an anxiety that American
democracy was sliding into mere mob rule. He deplores the influence dema-
gogues have upon public opinion: what he calls 'raucous voices', pulling the
country in radically incommensurate directions. 'The great masses of the
American population were ready and eager for a New Deal,' he says; but 'the
actual New Deal has not gone far enough and fast enough for them, and that
is what the shouting is about' [*New America*, 41].

Education remained the Wellsian watchword, through this whole period.
The prodigious success of *The Outline of History* (1920) inspired Wells to
undertake two companion projects of near-as-dammit total knowledge synthesis: *The Science of Life*, a sort of 'Outline of Biology' published 1929–30
and 1931's *The Work, Wealth and Happiness of Mankind*, concerning economics, politics and sociology. The former volume was co-written with Julian
Huxley and Wells's own son Gip, and whilst it didn't achieve the staggering
success of the *Outline of History* it sold well and was frequently updated and
reworked through the century. The 1938 'Popular Edition' ('fully revised and

brought up to date') was a hefty single volume 1599 pages long, richly supplied with diagrams and illustrations. Wells initiated the project and planned the whole thing in discussion with his collaborators; but in the end (according to Huxley's later estimates) only wrote about 5% of the whole, with Huxley himself writing roughly 70% and Gip 25% (the distribution of royalties did not reflect this division of labour: Wells took 40% of profits and his co-authors 30% each).

Huxley has left a detailed account of what it was like working with Wells, and whilst he is clearly proud of what the three of them achieved—he declares that the book's 'effects are still manifest in the increased space allotted to biology in the educational curriculum, and the greater interest of the general public in biological facts and their consequences' [Huxley, 162]—he also recorded how 'hard and determined a taskmaster' Wells was, often 'exasperated', liable to 'bombard' the young Huxley with letters urging him to write more rapidly and turn revisions around more promptly. Huxley had resigned his professorship at King's College to be able to concentrate on this work, and in the expectation that the earnings from the volume would not leave him thereby out of pocket. He records the following pen-portrait of H.G. at this period:

> H.G.'s curious, atonic, thin voice remains physiologically inexplicable. No eunuch was he for sure. Equally uncharacteristic was his small, neat and undemonstrative handwriting. Small and witty drawings often accompanied his notes, like a shorthand comic strip. His figure was not impressive, more in the tubby line, with small hands and feet. Though he had a remarkable brain, his head was several sizes smaller than most of his friends'. (Huxley, 152)

The work first appeared between 1929 and 1920, in 31 fortnightly instalments under the title *The Science of Life: a summary of contemporary knowledge about life and its possibilities* these being bound up in three volumes as the 'first edition'. It was then re-issued in one volume in 1931. Cassell took the unusual step of re-serialising the book, because the stock market crash of 1929 had interfered with the commercial possibilities of the earlier run, reprinting each of its nine constituent 'books' separately 1934–37. It remains even today an informative read, and although the science is getting on for nine decades old now, much of it still stands up. The most noticeable difference is that of style, or tone—the prose, whilst always clear and expressive hits exactly the patrician note that twenty-first-century pop-sci writers tend to avoid. The book intersperses its technical explanations with quotations from Wordsworth and Shelley, and the later sections stray beyond what we would probably think of the proper bailiwick of such a volume—a chapter on the possibility of a World State ('The Possibility of One Collective Human Mind and Will') is presumably part of Wells's 5%, and there is a chapter on eugenics treating the subject positively (since Huxley was a notorious eugenicist, this may have been one of his):

> Negative eugenics is the prevention of undesirable births. Positive eugenics is the promotion of desirable births. Except in so far as the private judgments of young people about to marry are concerned, no attempts at positive eugenics are traceable in the world about us … [but] in several American states surgical sterilization—a very slight operation, the ligaturing of the oviduct or the vas deferens—is performed upon various types of mental defectives incapable of self-control. 6.000 such operations have been performed in California alone and it would be difficult to find fault with the results. There is pressing need for such negative eugenics in the Atlantic communities. (*Science of Life*, 9.3.6)

There are less hideous chapters too: discussion of 'Borderline Science and the Question of Personal Survival', which speculates about souls surviving death, of 'Dream Anticipation and Telepathy' and a long section on morality, which argues we should conduct ourselves with 'candour', 'restraint and poise', should show consideration for others, avoid repression ('repressions accumulate below any line of conduct continually followed' leading to 'lapses' although 'two thirds of their harmfulness vanishes if this is recognised' [8.51.4]) and also that we should strive to overcome our tendencies to 'evasion, indolence and fear'.

Though both *The Outline of History* and the *Science of Life* sold well and found their way into school and university curricula, the third big 'knowledge synthesis' book of Wells's latter years was markedly less successful. This was the enormous *The Work, Wealth and Happiness of Mankind* (1932), an attempt to consolidate everything that was known about economics, money-theory and social philosophy—inherently a less well-defined subject-category than 'History' or 'Biology'. Though Wells laboured long on this volume and had the highest hopes that it would facilitate his 'Open Conspiracy' and effect real social change, it had by far the least impact of all three.

The project had a troubled gestation. Wells had written *The Outline of History* pretty much *solus*, with some assistance from his wife Jane, running his copy past the eyes of various period specialists. For *The Science of Life* he relied much more heavily on collaborators, and he attempted the same strategy for his new book. But his choice of co-workers was not felicitous. Initially, in 1928, he approached an old acquaintance from his Fabian Society days, Hugh Pembroke Vowles, along with another man called Edmund Cressey.

They were offered a flat fee: a generous sum—it seems Vowles was offered £6000—but not the percentage of copyright that Huxley and Gip had received (Wells also seems to have 'advanced', or possibly just lent, Vowles £800 up-front; the sum was disputed when the case when to law). Vowles worked for a year or so, before Wells's growing dissatisfaction with what he was producing reached caused him to put the whole project on hold, effectively firing Vowles. Then Wells went on holiday. When he returned it was to discover that Vowles had taken his grievance to the Society of Authors (of which organisation Wells was also a member, and which he had supported vigorously through the 1920s and 1930s). Wells was sued for breach of contract. Things got messy. The secretary of the Society of Authors, Herbert Thring, had urged Vowles to seek legal redress, and Wells, feeling under attack, privately printed a pamphlet, *The Problem of the Troublesome Collaborator* (1930), for distribution to members of the Society by way of putting his side of the affair. Both Vowles and Thring considered themselves libelled by the document and said a number of disobliging things about Wells. It all made the eventual legal settlement more complex and expensive. In the end Wells paid Vowles not the £6000 he demanded, but a substantial portion of it, and agreed to publish a new pamphlet (*Settlement of the Trouble Between Mr. Thring and Mr. Wells: A Footnote to The Problem of the Troublesome Collaborator*, 1930) correcting some of the things said in the earlier pamphlet. Wells junked Vowles's work and, since he was now physically ill, for a while the writing of this book fell into desuetude. But the project was too important to Wells's sense of self to abandon. He later recalled that 'I was disposed to anxiety; I thought my time was drawing to an end, and I was fussily urgent to get on with the scheme of work' embodied in the book [*H. G. Wells in Love*, 142]. In fact he wasn't dying. He took his exhaustion and ebbing life-force to a doctor and was diagnosed as diabetic in 1931, after which, responding positively to treatment, he discovered a renewed vitality.

Returning to *Work, Wealth and Happiness* Wells recruited new collaborators. Wells's old friend Graham Wallas read the political chapters, although he was himself ill and actually died in 1932. Wells also recruited his old lover, the father of one of his children, Amber Reeves, now Amber Blanco-White, to work on the money chapters, and his current lover Odette Keun worked extensively on the project too (both Reeves and Keun received a one-eighth share of royalties by way of payment). Wells paid various other experts one-off fees (Alexander Carr-Saunders provided data on population growth and demographic change, for instance). David C. Smith is full of praise for the resulting volume:

The book is an astounding work, especially when one considers than nothing like it had ever before been published. It features strong material on banking, economics, the increase in leisure time, and a history of educational ideas. Perhaps its most outstanding feature (for 1932) were histories of leisure time, games, the theatre and entertainment. Short discrete sections on manufacturing discussed plastics, paper, resin, iron and steel, the transmission and generation of power, production of food, the development of architectural ideas, labour unions, legal education and ideas, banking, the gold standard and its recent abandonment. (Smith, 266)

It's possible to react to *Work, Wealth and Happiness* in less ecstatic mode. Indeed, it is likely to strike the modern reader as a mere hodgepodge; a ragbag of interesting snippets gathered together under a loosely encyclopaedic logic. In amongst the chapters on agricultural fertiliser and the gold standard, on cosmetics and 'spy hunting', Wells is still (in 1932!) advocating eugenics ('there is every reason for the temporary or permanent sterilization of … certain types of defectives' [13:3]) and Chap. 11, on women, is rather hamstrung by Wells's belief that raising children and therefore the domestic sphere is the proper arena for womankind. The science in this book has aged less well than is the case either in *Outline of History* or *The Science of Life*. Economics does not admit of objective truth in the way that biology and physics do; and the technological and sociological components of *Work, Wealth and Happiness* often strike an ungainly, or a deflatingly quaint, note. Of course, Wells wasn't to know the colossal importance, say, plastics would come to have. That doesn't stop his account of them reading as drolly musty and old-fashioned ('these artificial products are used in varnishes and as insulating material for electrical apparatus … Bakelite has become popular' [2:7]). And the book is, frankly, marred by a dearth of properly penetrating analysis of the emergent popular culture of the twentieth century. At roughly the time that Adorno and Horkheimer were doing the preliminary work that would bear fruit in *The Dialectic of the Enlightenment* (1947), with its penetrating and influential anatomy of popular culture, Wells here is piddling around with an over-obvious thesis that 'leisure used to be only for the rich, but in the future everybody will have a lot more of it' and penning creaky old pseudo-Victorian lists like the following:

Leisure has spread down from class to class in the last century or so, and new occupations have been found for it … [we] would classify man's leisure activities roughly after this fashion: as (i) exercise and sports, (2) hygienically unprofitable games, (3) sexual dissipation, gluttony and drunkenness, (4) gossip, parading in costumes and loafing about, (5) seeing shows, (6) wandering and travelling to see and leam, (7) making things for pleasure or, as the Victorians called it, "hobbies," passing insensibly into (8) art, (9) philosophy, scientific enquiry and experiment. (14:1)

Reading this enormous book is certainly laborious, but the twenty-first-century reader is liable to accrue neither wealth nor happiness from such work.

After these largenesses of research and such sprawl of production Wells recovered his self-possession to write *The Anatomy of Frustration* (1936)—a short, readable book that purports to be a summary of a ten-volume treatise called *The Anatomy of Frustration* by one William Burroughs Steele. This little metafictional gameplay is a centenary homage to Carlyle's famous 1836 work of philosophical-fiction *Sartor Resartus* (Carlyle's book purports to be a summary of Diogenes Teufelsdröckh's masterwork, *Clothes: Their Origin and Influence*). Wells, or 'Steele', argues that, underlying all the various kinds of frustration in our life, are core existential frustrations we all have in common, identifies these and proposes ways of addressing them. Or not 'frustrations' so much as 'frustration', singular—for Wells thinks it all boils down to one thing: our self-awareness of mortality. All religion is at root about this, he thinks:

> Man alone of all animals looks beyond the lures of nature and becomes aware of death waiting for him at the end. All religions, all philosophies of conduct, stripped down to their bare essentials, express the consequent impulse to escape this inherent final frustration. … Bodily immortality, immortality of the soul, the oversoul, the overman, the superman, the mind of the species, Nirvana, return to the bosom of god, undying fame, progress, service, loyalties, are all expressions at various angles and levels of the same essential resolve—not to live so as to die. (*Anatomy of Frustration*, 1:2)

Humans prefer not to face this dilemma alone. Rather we band together, 'something outside the individual life cycle is brought in, with which the individual motives can be blended and identified. It is a reaching out to greater entities.' Steele's project purports to think systematically through this universal impulse. Existing creeds and religions are, says Steele, 'partial'. What's needed is a new, comprehensive mode of 'merger-immortality': the subsuming of our finite individuality not in family, or community, or caste, or country, or fellow-religionists, or fellow-proletarians, but the identification of ourselves with all humanity. It's achievable: 'Man is the unending Beginner' [1.4]. Our two present desires are for peace and plenty (Steele/Wells considers such 'desires for world unity and sane economics' to be 'conscious and intellectual desires' [1.5]) and our one, as it were, future desire is: not to die.

Socialism was an instinct in the right direction which failed to follow-through, and Steele focuses a typically Wellsian contumely on Marx ('the essential snobbishness of his hatred of the bourgeoisie, the pretentious crudity of his social psychology, the hocus-pocus of his dialectic' [2.3]). From these starting points, Steele thinks we can move on to what he calls the Next Beginning:

> The Next Beginning must be inevitably a world scheme. It must be a scheme for the production and distribution of all staple requirements throughout the whole earth. It must be a planetary economic plan with a universal theory of property and payment. (*Anatomy of Frustration*, 2.5)

The last part of Wells's work (a summary, supposedly, of 'Steele's tenth book') calls for educational reform, and includes some mockery of the present pedagogic system reminiscent of 1918's *Joan and Peter*. Steele asks 'does one teacher in a hundred ever ask himself what he imagines he is doing to the learner and the world?', and Wells glosses: 'this educational survey becomes for a time an onslaught on dons and teachers' [3.3].

These two notes, (as it were) an octave apart from one another—education and the World State—occur and reoccur through Wells's non-fiction of the 1930s, and it is very hard to assess the merit of Wells's ideas about the latter without letting our advantages of hindsight trip us into mere condescension. Take this bit of *The Anatomy of Frustration*:

> Existing governments, [Steele] explains, have been evolved as militant director-ates concerned primarily with the aggressive and defensive application of force. But in a world-pax the employment of force will be largely a reserve resource of the general police, and the main functions to be discharged by world-wide directive organizations will be economic, financial, and informative. (*Anatomy of Frustration*, 2.5)

It's hard to see the advantage, and easy to see the many practical dangers, in this deliberate conflation of civilian police and militia. Or again: Steele proposes to

> set very definite limits to the use of money. Only for very definite kinds of prop-erty should there be 'free sale.' For food, clothing, adornment, transportation, and shelter, Steele would allow practically 'free purchase'; almost every other kind of acquisition from a pet dog to a mountain valley he would make condi-tional on a more or less completely defined 'proper use.' By a reorganization of distribution and a development of public stock-keeping—a colossal extension of the post office, so to speak—he would squeeze deliberate acquisition for

resale, passive non-manufacturing ownership for monetary profit, that is, out of the category of permissible things.

Everybody gets free food, housing, clothing and a bus pass; but their access to literally everything else they might need or want will be controlled by a huge global bureaucracy, a 'colossal extension of the post office' whose officers will get to determine whether citizens' requests meet a criterion of 'proper use'. The potential for massive corruption, expropriation and misuse of powers is so patent in this proposal it is astonishing that Wells could not see it.

He couldn't, though. It baffled Wells as much as it pained him that, despite all his energetic proselytising, the 1930s were so obviously sliding towards another world war. The experience of reading the lectures and occasional articles collected in *World Brain* (1939) is one of Wellsian grievance that things are going so manifestly wrong all around him, when he has, on so many occasions, explained carefully how to make things come right. The problem, he thinks, is not the lack of utopian ambition among his fellow humans but, on the contrary, an *excess* of it, provoking hastiness of execution that in turn leads to failure. He is sure we all agree that 'all men are brothers', but he also notes that 'Spain and China are poor evidence of that fraternity' (he means the bloodshed of the 1936–39 Spanish Civil War and the then ongoing Chinese Communist insurgency). A panicked world is scrabbling desperately for guidance:

> 'Right' dictators there are and 'Left' dictators, and in effect there is hardly a pin to choose between them. The important thing about them from our present point of view, is that fear-saturated impatience for guidance, which renders dictatorships possible. (*World Brain*, 'Preface')

'The missing factor in human affairs', Wells insists, 'is a gigantic and many-sided educational renascence', for which a 'World Brain' is needful. He is pleasantly imprecise about the actual physiology of this global cortex 'something—a new social organ, a new institution—a World Encyclopedia ... for the present it is desirable to leave this project of a World Encyclopedic organisation vague' [2]. The purpose will be to 'bring all the scattered and ineffective mental wealth of our world into something like a common understanding, and into effective reaction upon our vulgar everyday political, social and economic life' [1]. In fact his campaign for a World Encyclopedia is as old as 1913's *The Passionate Friends*, and was variously restated through Wells's writing of the 1920s and 1930s. It is, unusually for Wells, a prophecy that actually came true, long after his death—for our Wikipedia/Google Books/Project

Gutenberg internet has actualised exactly the World Brain. Alas, it has not had the consequences Wells predicted. He insists the World Encyclopedia would function as 'an organ of adjustment and adjudication, a clearing house of misunderstandings' [2] and so banish all human disagreement. Even a short time spent online today will convince you that this wished-for consummation has—to put it mildly—not come to pass.

World Brain includes various appendices. In the first, 'Ruffled Teachers', Wells responds to a complaint occasioned by his '2400 hours' Address to the Education Section of the British Association for the Advancement of Science, just mentioned. In that talk, he says, he observed that teachers 'were going along much as they did in 1900'. This was reported in the press as him saying teachers were 'drooling along much as they did in 1900', which phrase caused offence to actual teachers. He apologises here, though he blames sloppy reporting for the misunderstanding. A second suggests the problem of 'Palestine' could be easily solved by abolishing religion (he says he wants to get 'Abraham, Isaac, Jacob and Moses' and Palestine itself 'out of the way so that our children shall start with a better perspective of the world') a proposal that lacks somewhat of realism.

This question of religious division is discussed in greater length in *The Fate of Homo Sapiens*—a book published on the very brink of war (in August 1939) that found an immediate audience, passing through three editions in its first fortnight. Beatrice Webb, who had long since become reconciled with Wells after their Fabian falling-out, recorded in her diary: 'it is the work of genius in its indictment of western civilisation'. She wrote to Wells that she and her husband Sidney, who was recovering from a stroke, had read the book 'with unlimited admiration'. The titular Fate is, Wells thinks probably grim, although he also thinks it's still not too late to avert catastrophe and build towards a global utopia. Of war he writes that: 'primitive war was a necessity forced upon the human community by biological success through the production of a surplus of young males ... You can write human history in a variety of ways, but one way of writing it would be to consider how, age after age, humanity has met the problem of What To Do With Our Sons' [*Fate of Homo Sapiens*, 4]. History, according to Wells's slogan, is ecology. The future has become a general issue for the world, in a way that didn't use to be the case and the best possibility for the coming collective survival is not the partial democracy currently signified by the word, but the full democracy of the egalitarian World State. The main obstacle to this, Wells argues, is religion, expanding the term to encompass both traditional faiths and political fanaticism. He starts with the Jews, but although declaring himself broadly sympathetic to the difficulties Judaism faces, he can't seem to shake his belief that the

Jews themselves are at root to blame for their own persecution. He quotes Rabbi Lewis Browne to the effect that 'Gentile intolerance makes the Jews and keeps them together' in order to contradict him: 'I argue that the Jews make themselves and that Gentile intolerance is a response to the cult of the Chosen People', adding with a breeziness that has aged very badly indeed, 'the hostile reaction to the cult of the Chosen People is spreading about the entire world today'.

> No country wants them on such conditions. Why should any country want these inassimilable aliens bent on preserving their distinctness? Palestine is an object lesson. Until they are prepared to assimilate and abandon the Chosen People idea altogether, their troubles are bound to intensify. (*Fate of Homo Sapiens*, 12)

Christianity is characterised as a vast higgled-piggled accumulation of incompatible elements ('century by century, the great fabric of the faith goes on accumulating. It has become a sort of Cumberland Market of religious notions') and Wells asks, in exasperated mode: 'why do intelligent people accept this strange heap of mental corruption as a religion and a rule of life?' [13]. From here it's on to Nazism as a quasi-religion, and Wells's analysis becomes, shall we say, spicier:

> It is plain that the Fuehrer is insane; he shows all the symptoms of a recognized form of sex mania, the jealous fear and hate of the great raping black man—who in his case becomes the Jew. Since in his case his obsession endangers the lives of people about him, he should be certified and put under restraint. … He might be shouting, frothing and orating in a madhouse at the present time. But it happened that he supplied just the inflexible spearhead, the inhuman pertinacity, required to give extreme expression to the feelings of a humiliated and outrageously treated people. (*Fate of Homo Sapiens*, 15)

Australian Prime Minister Joseph Lyons took official exception to these Wellsian comments, expressing outrage at such a description of a sitting Head of State. Indeed, to his immense and enduring credit, Wells's comments earned him a prominent place in Hitler's notorious 'Black Book': he was listed to be eliminated, once the invasion of Britain was completed, by not one but *three* branches of the German military machine: Amtsgruppen VIG, IIB4 and IIIA5. Which is quite the achievement.

The reason why the Australian P.M., in particular, felt moved to comment on Wells's Hitlerian sarcasm was that Wells was engaged, from December

1938 to January 1939, in his only antipodean tour. He spoke to the Australian and New Zealand Association for the Advancement of Science conference, and made various public appearances, radio broadcasts (recordings of two of these survive), lectures, dinners and interviews, and his book-length account of this journey was published as *Travels of a Republican Radical in Search of Hot Water* in November 1939. Australia, not to put too fine a point on it, went wild for Wells; and he did not disappoint, shocking what was, in 1939, still a notably conservative Australian establishment not only—as we have seen—by mocking Hitler as insane, but by speaking against censorship and for abortion. Lyons died unexpectedly, of a heart attack, shortly after Wells left the country, although it is a matter of mere speculation as to whether Wells's gadfly presence hastened this untoward end. Wells's own account of the Lyons incident—'Mr Lyons Protects Hitler, the Head of a Great Friendly Power, From My "Insults"'—is pleasantly droll. Wells insists he is still 'Pro-World-Pax', but, not being a fool, understands that appeasement was a bad strategy. Mid-1939 is, I daresay, late in the day to press that point, but it doesn't make it any less valid. 'Should we resist collectively', Wells asks, 'or appease severally?' adding, 'no one has yet discovered where appeasement ends' [7]. He blames the failure of the League of Nations on 'sentimental nationalism' [9] and makes some bold proposals for educational reform: 'I propose the teaching of Greek History, Latin History, Jewish or Bible History, English History, French History, Medieval History, German History, Chinese History, our Island Story, the Empire and so on and so on, as separate subjects, shall be entirely abandoned' [*In Search of Hot Water*, 9]. This is more than pedagogical reform, it is a new ferocity aimed at history as such—everything from the rise of fascism and the 'Jewish problem' and the new war is a consequence of what he, vividly but unhelpfully, calls 'the poison of history'. It is, to say the least, a problematic argument. Wells's fiction very often takes a frankly cavalier attitude to history, sweeping it away as if it were mere chaff and ashes. But history possesses a determining inertia quite beyond human powers to overcome: the more strenuous the effort to dispatch it, as with Pol Pot's 'Year Zero', the more disastrous and criminal the consequences for ordinary human beings. We can only understand present, and so influence the future, by situating it, historically.

Through the later 1930s Wells put most of his creative energy into a series of novels (discussed in the following chapter), but with the outbreak of the war he shifted back over to non-fiction. He published *The New World Order* in 1940 (it was re-issued bound-in as a twofer with *The Fate of Homo Sapiens* as *The Outlook for Homo Sapiens* in 1942). When he was a child, in the 1880s, he says, 'not only I but most of my generation thought that war was dying out'. The consensus was that a balance of power had been achieved, and though Wells realises such optimism looks foolish from the wrong side of the Great War and at the commencement of the Second World War, he defends his former blitheness. The forces that led to war, though prodigious, were subterranean: 'deeper forces at work that were preparing trouble'. To put an end to war, says Wells, means addressing those forces, and that means abolishing the nation state, reorganising the world economy to make war unprofitable and to revolutionise pedagogy on a global footing to give empower not a small elite but the entire globe through education. The hymn Wells has been singing for two decades now is here set out with a useful economy. Modernity had shrunk the world, in terms of travel and communication, and massively increased the power available to humankind for destructive, as well as creative, purposes ('there is more power expended in a modern city like Birmingham in a day than we need to keep the whole of Elizabethan England going for a year; there is more destructive energy in a single tank than sufficed the army of William I for the conquest of England' [3])—but humankind has persisted stubbornly in thinking in dangerously out-of-date ways about both these new facts of global life. Only a comprehensive collective reform of everything can ensure the survival of the species going forward.

Wells is emphatic on the need to preserve free speech. He had given personal and financial support to the creation of the National Council for Civil Liberties in 1934 (he was vice president of the organisation for a while), and in this book he urges citizens to join it, and otherwise fight for freedom of speech: 'before anything else, therefore, in this survey of the way to world peace, I put free speech and vigorous publication. It is the thing best worth fighting for. It is the essence of your personal honour. It is your duty as a world citizen to do what you can for that' [*New World Order*, 2]. *The New World Order* ends with a ten-point proposal for a Declaration of the Rights of Man. Wells in 1940 wasn't the force in international politics he'd been in 1918, but this, together with his energetic contributions to the Sankey Committee and its 'Sankey Declaration of the Rights of Man' (1940) did at least feed into the process by which the 1948 Universal Declaration of Human Rights was drafted. So in that respect, even in his eighth decade, and howsoever obliquely, Wells was influencing world politics.

An agreement with Penguin meant that Wells produced a string of cheap, paperback non-fiction books through the war. *The Common Sense of War and Peace* (1940) marches briskly once more through familiar Wellsian paces: we must reconfigure our whole global way of doing things, or else we will war ourselves into ultimate destruction. Humanity is still infantile, Wells thinks, and will not be fully grown up until it realises, as all adults do, that it has no need of leaders at all: no Hitler- or Mussolini-style figures. 'Grown Men do not need Leaders. But that does not mean that they will not trust a properly accredited equal who has some specific gift or function. You trust your plumber, your doctor, your cook, your automobile scout, your Ordnance Map, conditionally, without either arrogance or subservience' [1]. Only one thing will guarantee peace: 'World Revolution'.

> I ask you not to be afraid of the word 'Revolution'. Speak English. Don't think of Revolution as an affair of street barricades, the heads of beautiful ladies on pikes, and tumbrils going to the guillotine. Our 'Glorious Revolution' in 1688 had none of these ingredients, and the Revolution that established the Hanoverian Succession was practically bloodless. You can have a Revolution without massacre or violence. But anyhow, I submit that organised world peace and welfare mean such a Revolution in human life as will dwarf all previous revolutions to comparative insignificance. (*Common Sense*, 4)

This is a rather selective, not to say cherry-picked, set of examples of bloodless revolutions; and given the scale of the revolution being proposed in this slim book, and the fact that pretty much everyone in the world of 1940 was armed to the teeth, it can't help but look jejune. The book winds up with a reiterated emphasis on the need for a World Declaration of Human Rights, sketches what they might be, and directs the reader to the 'companion Penguin to this—*The Rights of Man*'. This latter volume is Wells's updated version of *The New World Order* volume from earlier that same year, incorporating the revised Declaration, 'as it has emerged from the hands of Lord Sankey's Drafting Committee' [10].

His next Penguin volume was less temperate. *Crux Ansata* (1943) is an anti-Catholic polemic. Indeed the older Wells grew, the more this strain of prejudice came to the surface (as is often the way with prejudice and people getting older). In 1928 James Joyce had written to him asking for financial support for his literary experiment *Finnegans Wake*, then a work in progress. Wells declined to help, writing back:

> Your training has been Catholic, Irish, insurrectionary; mine, such as it was, was scientific, constructive and, I suppose, English. ... I want a language and statement as simple and clear as possible. You began Catholic, that is to say you began with a system of values in stark opposition to reality. Your mental existence is obsessed by a monstrous system of contradictions. (Gilbert: 274)

By 1940 this animadversion to Catholicism had hardened and in *Crux Ansata* it bursts out with startling intensity. Though only 96 pages long, this book is a sustained and poisonous expression of prejudice. The title's Latin means 'cross with handles', which is to say 'crooked cross' (which is to say 'swastika'), and the moral equivalence between Catholicism and Nazism is the case Wells seeks to advance. We get a sense of the tenor with the opening chapter: 'why do we not bomb Rome?'

> On June 1st, 1942, the enemy bombed Canterbury and as near as possible got the Archbishop of Canterbury. But what is a mere Protestant Archbishop against His Holiness the Pope?
> In March 1943 Rome was still unbombed.
> Now consider the following facts.
> We are at war with the Kingdom of Italy, which made a particularly cruel and stupid attack upon our allies Greece and France; which is the homeland of Fascism; and whose 'Duce' Mussolini begged particularly for the privilege of assisting in the bombing of London.
> There are also Italian troops fighting against our allies the Russians. A thorough bombing (a la Berlin) of the Italian capital seems not simply desirable, but necessary. (*Crux Ansata*, 1)

I have visited Rome, as millions of tourists do annually, and pause in my discussion of Wells's writing here to note my gratitude that it wasn't flattened by the RAF in 1943 and rebuilt in concrete as Slough-su-Tevere. But Wells wants blood. He paints a church distracted from the establishment of the City of God on Earth by internal schism and an obsession with heresy, 'morbidly anxious', 'hunting everywhere for heretics' [*Crux Ansata*, 3]. He ends by confidently asserting 'there will be no Roman Catholic Church at all in the fifth millennium A.D.' [18] and, as a kind of afterthought, denies that he is attacking the religious impulse as such:

> I am deriding organised High Church and Catholic Christianity, and I would like to make it plain that in doing so I am not disregarding what I might call the necessity many minds, perhaps most young minds, feel for something one can express by such phrases as "the fatherhood of God" and "the kingdom of heaven within us". That is the need the Roman Catholic Church trades upon and betrays. (*Crux*, 20)

Bibliography

Gilbert, Stuart ed. (1957). *The Letters of James Joyce, Vol. 1*. New York: Viking.
Huxley, Julian (1970) *Memories*. George Allen & Unwin.

MacKenzie, Norman and Jeanne (1973). *The Time Traveller: the life of H.G. Wells*. London: Weidenfeld and Nicholson.

Nicholson, Harold (1966), *Diaries and Letters 1930–39*. London: Collins.

Sherborne, Michael (2010). *H.G. Wells: Another Kind of Life*. London/Chicago Peter Owen.

West, Anthony (1984). *H G Wells: Aspects of a Life*. London: Hutchinson

25

Later Fiction

The Croquet Player (1936); Star Begotten (1937); Brynhild (1937); The Camford Visitation (1937); The Brothers (1938); Apropos of Dolores (1938); The Holy Terror (1939)

After the death of his wife, and his break-up with Odette Keun, Wells settled into a long-term if sometimes dilute partnership with a Russian aristocrat, writer and spy called Moura Budberg. But Wells's later fiction has little to say about this relationship, because Wells's writerly imagination was still in thrall to the hotter and more distressing time he had had with Keun. When Wells wrote his third volume of autobiography in 1933–34—the one detailing his amorous life, published long after his death—he was in the immediate aftermath of a painful and difficult break-up of his 9-year relationship with Keun and the work is, accordingly, markedly less gallant where his memories of his time with her are concerned than is the case with any other of his lovers. To read *H. G. Wells in Love* is to be given the impression that Wells's many years with Keun, sharing the spacious French house Lou Pidou, were a kind of aberration; where the comparative placidity and accommodativeness provided by Moura Budberg receives an ample and generous narrative that praises her humanity, her outstanding physical charm and her bravery. He goes so far as to identify Budberg as one of only three women he has loved 'steadfastly' in his life, along with his first and second wife (although the later sections of the book detail Budberg's own infidelity and the pain it caused him) [*H. G. Wells in Love*, 60]. The fiction, though, tells a different story. Two major novels from Wells's late period, *William Clissold* and *Apropos of Dolores*, are unambiguously about Keun; he never wrote a novel about Budberg. Perhaps this was because Wells was, broadly, content with Budberg in a way that was never true of Keun, and that the grit of discontent is needful for the rolling of novelistic pearls. Or perhaps it is closer to the truth that Wells loved Keun more than he could admit to himself, and that fiction revealed what was in his heart.

© The Author(s) 2019
A. Roberts, *H G Wells*, Literary Lives, https://doi.org/10.1007/978-3-030-26421-5_25

Wells's later fiction has received very little critical attention. It's not for this reason that it has dropped off the popular radar (critics don't have that sort of power) but the two things are not unconnected. From *The Croquet Player* (1936) through to *You Can't Be Too Careful* (1941) Wells wrote a tensome of unusual, hybrid realist-fantasias mostly concerned with the dislocation of ordinary people in an unfitting and unhealthy world. Two of these books are, I would say, significant achievements in fictional terms: *Apropos of Dolores* (1938) and *The Holy Terror* (1939). The rest are, frankly, not. Indeed, the first five, though all different, share a disposable slightness and read more like expanded short stories than anything else.

The first of these short novels is also the best of them: *The Croquet Player* (1936) a mix of several elements into an uneasy, but strangely memorable, fictional emulsion. First there is the frame story, told by our narrator, George Frobisher, an egregiously unmasculine man, who with his aunt has devoted his life to the sport of croquet. They are good at it: 'croquet is our especial gift. If we did not shrink from the publicity and vulgarity of it we could certainly be champions' [1]. As the novel opens, George and his aunt are spending the summer at a luxury hotel on the Normandy coast, at a place called Les Noupets. Here, on the terrace, he strikes up a conversation with an English doctor named Dr Finchatton.

Finchatton tells George how he took up General Practice in a remote East Anglian district called Cainsmarsh. But instead of a quiet life, he found a closed, superstition-haunted, uncommunicative world. There's a weird, sub-conscious throbbing unpleasantness in the air. The kids go to school with bruises on their bodies about which they will not speak. A dog's carcass turns up, beaten savagely to death. 'I drove back home,' Finchatton recalls at one point. 'There was an old man bending down in a ditch doing something to a fallen sheep and he became a hunched, bent, and heavy-jawed savage. I did not dare look to see what he was doing' [*Croquet Player*, 2]. The fogs and remoteness of the place get under Finchatton's skin. He starts having night-mares. The mood of eerie dread is atmospherically rendered by Wells.

Finchatton speaks to the local vicar, who airs his theory that the Biblical Cain is literally buried in the locality. He blames the recent nightmarish atmo-sphere on the activities of archaeologists, digging up gigantic bones. Finchatton insists these are dinosaur-bones, but the vicar isn't having that.

'The doom of Cain!' he shouted. 'The punishment of Cain!'
  'But why Cain?' I managed to insert.
  'He ended his days here,' the old man declared. 'Oh, I know! Is this called Cainsmarsh for nothing? He wandered over the face of the earth and at last he

came here, he and the worst of his sons. They poisoned the earth. Age after age of crime and cruelty, and then the Flood buried them under these marshes—and there they ought to be buried for ever.' (*Croquet Player*, 2)

Ghost stories trade in the idea that we might be haunted by our recent ancestors; Wells's story asks, why not our more geologically distant forebears too? Finchatton dismisses the idea of Cain argument, but comes to believe that the ghosts haunting the area are Neanderthals.

Finchatton, terrified of losing his mind, consults a London psychiatrist called Norbert who accompanies him to his Les Noupets recuperation. In the novella's final passage Norbert asks George what he thinks of his patient's story. The doctor is adamant that 'there is no such district in the world' as Cainsmarsh. 'It is a myth.'

> 'Our friend,' he said, '*was* a doctor near Ely. Everything he told you was true and everything he told you was a lie. He is troubled beyond reason by certain things and the only way in which he can express them even to himself is by a fable.'
> 'But some of these things—really happened?'
> 'Oh yes. There *was* a case of gross cruelty to a dog. There was a poor old drunken parson who beat his wife. Things of that sort are happening all over the world every day. They are in the nature of things. If you cannot accept things like that, sir, *you cannot live*. And the reason why he has made it all up into that story—' Dr Norbert turned upon me, putting his arms akimbo and glaring at my face. He spoke with slow deliberation, as if he was speaking in capital letters, '—is because the realities that are overwhelming him are so monstrous and frightful that he has to transform them into this fairy tale about old skulls and silences.' (*Croquet Player*, 4)

Which realities? The horrors of the contemporary life, the rise of fascism, the Spanish Civil War (these things are not spelled out in the text, but that's the unmissable imputation). As he tells his story Finchatton keeps interpolating little comments: 'And then Finchatton said a queer thing. "Little children killed by air-raids in the street." I made no comment. I remained quietly attentive. It was an "aside", as actors used to say' [3]. And this reality has infected the doctor's wits too. He has his own theory, to set alongside the ghost of Cain and the restless Neanderthal spirits: that we have, by expanding our consciousness of the past and future, through archaeology and speculation, somehow *broken time* and let in monsters. '"Animals," he said, "live wholly in the present.... But we men, we have been probing and piercing into the past and future. We have been multiplying memories, histories, traditions, we have filled ourselves with forebodings and plannings and apprehensions.

And so our worlds have become overwhelmingly vast for us, terrific, appalling"' [4].

Fitfully but unmistakably, this short novel manages to evoke a powerful unsettling eeriness of tone. And there's a genuinely interesting notion structuring the whole: that instead of being scarily haunted by recent history what truly haunts us nowadays are the deep pre-human past and the technologically monstrous future. That these two things, counter-intuitive as it might seem to say, are psycho-symbolically speaking the *same* thing.

The rightness, here, I might say, has to do with a curious illogicality about what it is that scares us, about in other words the underlying affective rationale of 'the ghost story' as such. What is the pleasure we derive from this curious mode? The classic ghost story is saying something about the relationship of the past and the present. Whatever else it does, a ghost story embroiders one central idea: that the past still touches the present. Common sense and intellect tell us that death draws a line beyond which a person can no longer reach, but our emotions and our subconscious tell us that death may drain momentum from, but cannot stop, the past's grasping hand. A Freudian might put it this way: the classic ghost story is the objective correlative to the inevitable return of the repressed. But a Freudian should also say: the way to exorcise the ghost of the returning repressed is to acknowledge it, to talk it to a cure, to shine the light upon it. That process of explanation dissolves away not the ghost as such (since the ghost expresses the truth that we can never really get mentally past the dead) so much as the specific, nightmarish *form* the ghost adopts. And that's where Wells comes in. He writes a ghost story that says: it makes no sense to be scared of what's been and gone. The dead past is outside the circle of what can harm us. Harm lives in the future, not the past. The truly scary ghost is what is still to come, and what makes it scary is its inevitability. In other words, Wells is tacitly saying: the real reason 'we' enjoy in classic ghost stories is that we know, on some level, that the unnerving sensations we experience are safe, because they are linked to something— the past—that can't really hurt us. The future is a different proposition, and by 1936 Wells could see that a war was coming that was going to hurt us all on an unprecedented scale.

Star Begotten (1937) is a companion piece to *The Croquet Players* in the sense that it focuses not on the uncanny of the dead past but the living future, as embodied by our children. The protagonist is Joseph Davis, a writer of bestselling historical novels, who decides to write 'a deliberately romanticized history of mankind. It was to be a great parade—a cavalcade of humanity … The Pageant of Mankind, the Promise and the Struggle' [1.2]. But writing this work unsettles all his comfortable preconceptions about his world and himself.

Researching history properly, rather than to excavate occasional episodes of sentimental heroism for his novels, reveals it to Davis as a parade of randomness, barbarism and horror. Davis's disaffection is bound up with the difficulties in his marriage to his elfin but elusive wife Mary, pregnant with their first child. She is 15 years his junior and comes originally from the Isle of Lewis. Although he loves her, he also finds her opaque and rather unnerving. She is 'fey', distant, strangely self-contained. 'I feel like a stray from another world,' she tells him, adding: 'but then, you know, I felt very much the same when I was at home in the islands where I was born' [1.3].

At his London club, Davis hears about cosmic rays, 'infinitesimal particles flying at an inconceivable velocity' [2.2]. These, he is told, have the capacity to alter human genetic material. From here it's a short step to speculating that the rays might be being specifically directed at Earth. From where? Why not Mars!

> "Yes, Mars, that wizened elder brother of the planet Earth. Mars, where intelligent life has gone far beyond anything this planet has ever known. Mars, the planet which is being frozen out, exhausted, done for. Some of you may have read a book called *The War of the Worlds*—I forget who wrote it—Jules Verne, Conan Doyle, one of those fellows ..." (*Star Begotten*, 2.2)

Davis becomes convinced that 'Martians have been firing away' cosmic rays 'with increasing accuracy and effectiveness at our chromosomes—perhaps for long ages'; and that this fact explains why 'every now and then in history, strange exceptional figures have appeared, Confucius, Buddha; men with strange memories, men with uncanny mathematical gifts, men with unaccountable intuitions' [3.2]. From here it's a short step to believing that his own unborn child has been Mars-influenced, a representative of a new *homo superbus* to supersede *Homo sapiens*: a 'hard' mind; 'like a lens, revealing and scrutinizing one aspect after another, one possibility after another, and this and that necessary correlation' [8.6]. Davis and his friends greet this possibility with equanimity. '[Stedding] paused and pushed the cigar-boxes towards his guests. "A world gone sane," said Davis. "Planetary psycho-therapeutics," said the doctor. "A sane world, my masters—and then?"' [8.6]. The novel ends with Davis suddenly understanding that not only his unborn son, but his wife and even he himself are already Mars-born humans.

This late novella proved, once again, for Wells, immensely influential in the development of science fiction. In it is the germ for many later tales, from Wyndham's *Midwich Cuckoos* (1957) to Kubrick and Clarke's *2001: A Space Odyssey* (1967): not actual aliens among us, like Wells's *The War of the Worlds*, nor alien artefacts (as in Wells's short story, 'The Crystal Egg'), but rather the *remote influence* of aliens. This influence can, obviously, be spun as a positive or a negative thing; and the problem is that that the positive line lacks conflict, and therefore drama. A story like Tiptree's 'The Screwfly Solution' (1977)—another masterpiece whose core idea can be traced back to *Star Begotten*—is considerably less comforting than Wells's version of the idea, and all the better for it.

The more benignant vision of *Star Begotten* is, in one sense, symptomatic of later career Wells. As co-author of *The Science of Life*, he was up-to-date with evolutionary science and understood perfectly well that natural selection is a non-teleological and random process of sifting mutations through the sieve of environmental chance. And yet notions of evolution as a teleological process have proved remarkably difficult to shake off. Plenty of people continue to see evolution as a process shaped by God, or a Bergsonian élan vital, or Hegelian Geist, or somesuch. *2001: A Space Odyssey* is a reading of the evolution of mind in such terms, with space aliens instead of God, and in its debased, Erich von Däniken form this becomes the kind of comprehensive disbelief in the capacity of *Homo sapiens* to achieve anything by its own lights—a position rather insulting to actual *homines sapientes*. In a small way that's a problem with *Star Begotten* too: Wells's 'Martians' are invoked here to do the work that Wells's own human-centred Open Conspiracy had failed to do and midwife a World State utopia out of the seized-up birth canal of the post-World War I settlement. Wells looks sternly at us over his trim-moustache. We have failed him. Perhaps the task was always beyond us. Perhaps only intervention by ineffably wise space-aliens will bring it to fruition.

The comparison with Wyndham's *Midwich Cuckoos*, a novel conceptually epigone but artistically superior, tells against what Wells is doing in this late novel. Stories of alien invasion are necessarily stories about encountering otherness, or alienness, as disruption. What makes *The Midwich Cuckoos* so extraordinary (something also captured by the 1960 movie adaptation, *Village of The Damned*) is the way it styles the alien not only as a child, but as *our* child. There's a profound truth in this imaginative gesture. I'm as susceptible to sentimentality where children and childhood is concerned as anyone. But at the same time, I'm sure any parent would recognise what I'm talking about when I say that there is a radically *uncanny* quality about children. It's the whole logic of having them. Our children will succeed us. And that's as it should be; no parent would want it any other way. But nonetheless, in odd moments, when you catch a glimpse of them slant, it truly dawns on your: *our children will succeed us*. They are the correlatives of our mortality. Kids are life, are the future, and once we have them they supplant us in both those quantities. Because however genuinely we love our kids the fact is they will be living and loving and drinking wine in the sunshine when we are cold and dead in the ground. That this is precisely the consummation we hope for, precisely the existential point of having children in the first place, doesn't stop it being a truly unnerving thought. Wyndham's novel understands that uncanniness, and dramatises it in a manner as artistically satisfying as it is existentially profound. Wells's prior version of what is essentially the same story doesn't, really. Davis's child is sweet rather than uncanny. It represents not Davis's supersession but his magic passport to a shared future.

> The child lay on its side in its cot in a dreamless sleep. It scarcely seemed to breathe. The expression of that flushed little face with its closed eyes was one of veiled determination. One small clenched fist peeped over the coverlet ... Never, [Davis] thought, had anything in the world looked so calmly and steadfastly resolved to assert its right to think and act in its own way in its own time. (*Star Begotten*, 10.3)

If *The Croquet Player* (1936) and *Star Begotten* (1937) are short novels, *The Camford Visitation* (1937) is a mere novella: barely 70 pages long, and something of a squib. In a fictional amalgamation of Oxford and Cambridge the Master of Holy Innocents College is having breakfast with half a dozen fellows when a mysterious Voice (so capitalised in the novel) joins the conversation: 'What do you mean by education?' Since the Voice has no corresponding body, the Master has the porters check for hidden microphones and speakers. There are none. After this, the Voice goes walkabout, or audabout, through the University. It next speaks to a timid English lecturer at Clayfoot College called Trumber, 'a small, slender, downcast man' who is trying to lecture when the Voice heckles him about the irrelevance of poetry as a pedagogic topic. Trumber seeks guidance from Bream, the vicar of St Hippolytus, who writes up his theory as to what is going on ('some sort of space-time dislocation') as a book, *Extra-Terrestrial Disturbances of Human Mentality*. We're told this title 'has not sold very extensively but it has added greatly to the vicar's prestige'.

Word of the Voice spreads about the town. It is denounced by the Camford Communist Party and finally makes a lengthy and explanatory speech to the entire University, on Congregation Day, in the Great Hall of University:

> I have come out of the deeps beyond space and time to look again at this little planet I have visited since its beginning. ... Why am I saying these things here to you in Camford? You who are assembled here today constitute a typical centre of education. And deliberately you ignore the fact that human life is mental.

The essential thing in human life is education, the growth of a common mind and will. If mankind fails it will be through the failure of its teachers, the weakness of its schools, the obstinacy, the wilful obstruction of its universities. Cannot you realize so plain a thing as that? (*Camford Visitation*, 6)

The final chapter details the various ways the people of Camford explain away the apparition: a dream, a legend, a hallucination, an elaborate practical joke and so on. It's a strange little book, and not a terribly good one: the comedy is thin, the characterisation is all caricature, and there is no story to speak off. Nor did it do well. Although *The Croquet Player* had been a modest success, *The Camford Visitation* was a serious flop. Methuen, the publisher, went with an ambitious initial print-run of 10,000 copies, but by the end of 1939 they still had 7800 unsold copies on their hands, 5000 of these unbound. Methuen wanted to remainder the unsold copies, but Wells refused (he wanted them re-issued with new paper covers and sold as a pamphlet at a cut price). In the end the 5000 were pulped and the rest sold off in dribbles. It was barely reviewed, and fell quickly into obscurity.

Brynhild (1937) is full-length novel, in amongst Wells's various essays in the novella form: an attempt at comedy, although one that misfires. The scene is set in the world of 1930s Literary London, with some real and other fictional, *roman-a-clef* literary figures mentioned, or carrying spears in the background, all arrayed around the story's two main figures: Rowland Palace and his wife Brynhild. Rowland is a small, pompous poet, the author of *Bent Oars* ('it excited the American colony in Paris, and percolated thence to New York, Chicago and the intellectual west' [2]) and other works. At Lady Burnish's May Day Festival one year he is persuaded to wear the fancy dress costume of a Bard, complete with artificial bay-wreath and cardboard lyre. But when the photos appear in the newspaper he looks ludicrous and foolish, not at all the dignified Great Author he considers himself. Stung, he hires a literary agent to renovate and dignify his public reputation and ends the novel a contender for the Nobel Prize not despite but *because of* his meretriciousness.

Brynhild is 12 years her husband's junior, 'tall, slender and shapely … a fair-haired young woman with a broad serene face and kind brown eyes' [12]. The incident with the photos, and her husband's over-reaction, takes her the exact opposite way. As Rowland moves to create an elaborate façade, she does the opposite, and resolves to get in touch with her true self. This leads her into the arms of a younger and rather more handsome writer called Alfred Bunter. Bryn returns to her husband pregnant from this assignation, and with a new flush of life, telling Rowland that she has decided her role in life is to be a mother to a great brood of children. Rowland, startled, has no choice but to agree. 'I thought your attentions to me were getting just a trifle trivial,' she tells him:

> 'I wanted something of my own—really my own. I wanted a role of my own'…
>   Silly old Rowly, she thought, gulling and gullible Rowly, and yet in a way tolerable and likeable Rowly. Substantial. Materially substantial. Smelling slightly of soap and tobacco. Married—extraordinarily married to her, about whom he would never know anything at all, about whom he didn't want to know anything at all. Married. And at the same time she was escaping—going away from all that had held her paralysed for seven years—to something profoundly her own. (*Brynhild*, 267–28)

This may not be as straightforwardly reactionary a conclusion as it looks. Wells's point is not that a woman can only find fulfilment in motherhood; it's that what has been lacking in Brynhild's life was, precisely, deceit. She had been inhumanely honest and true. Now she's doing something secret and dishonest, entirely for herself, and that has made into an actual human being. 'She had become real', is her own assessment. 'Her priggishness had been reft from her. She was a cheat now—like everybody. She was a humbug—like everybody. She was a secret behind a façade. And altogether human. She had grown up at last' [269]. It's an interesting notion although, taken in the round, the novel is an underachievement. Wells has done this sort of thing before, better: wittier and more incisive 'You must not harp', the literary agent Cloote tells Rowland Palace, 'too much on one aspect of a writer's quality.'

> Gissing, for instance, was handicapped by his irony; they called him depressing. Chesterton was pigeon-holed as paradoxical even when he was doing his simple utmost to speak plainly; Wells was pinned down by his being always linked with 'The Future of—this or that.' (But Wells at best was a discursive intractable writer with no real sense of dignity. A man is not called 'H.G.' by all his friends for nothing). (*Brynhild*, 79)

Jokily self-deprecating though maybe, it also speaks to a certain Wellsian bitterness at how grudging was the world's affordance of respect for his work.

Within months Wells had returned to the novella form with *The Brothers* (1938), set during the Spanish Civil War. Brilliant general Richard Bolaris is on the verge of taking an important city for the Fascist cause. In the company of his mistress Catherine he interrogates a high-profile enemy soldier, recently captured—the Communist general Ratzel, who has been coordinating the city's defence. The two men, it turns out, are twin brothers, separated at birth. Most of the novella is taken up with the two of them expounding their respective worldviews. It turns out, despite their notionally opposite political creeds, they both believe the same things.

> "I hate greedy incompetence that has to compel and crush because it cannot direct and govern."
> "And so do I. I hate indiscipline."
> "And so do I."
> "I hate that continual congealing of officialism and professionalism and custom, which is like the hardening of arteries in the state."
> "Well!" said Ratzel, meeting a new idea there. "Yes, so do I—And priests."
> "All sane men resent priests," said Bolaris.
> "And where do you differ;" asked Catherine.
> "We don't differ," said Bolaris. "Evidently when we scrap our catch-words, we don't differ." (*Brothers*, 3.2)

There's little subtlety in all this. At the end of the story Bolaris decides that blood is thicker than ideology and decides Ratzel must avoid the firing squad, escape captivity and flee back to his city. The plan backfires, though. The Reds attack the Fascist position unexpectedly, Bolaris releases Ratzel in the hope he'll call the attack off. Handon, Bolaris's second-in-command, on the ramparts organising the defences, sees Ratzel slinking away through the olive groves and shoots him with a rifle. Bolaris is furious ("'Oh, you fool!' cried Bolaris. "You accursed fool!" and leapt upon his right-hand man with murder in his eyes') and in the struggle Bolaris is killed too.

The autumnal fire of Wells's fictional genius flared up for two last major novels before dampening down again for his last half decade of life. One of these, *Apropos of Dolores* (1938) is a mimetic novel that cleaves closely to Wells's own life; the other, *The Holy Terror* (1939) is a political fantasia that extrapolates from Wells's present into a near future. What these two otherwise utterly different novels have in common is an acute apprehension of the scale of the mismatch between human desire and the inertial anti-desire of the practical circumstances in which our lives actualise themselves. One of these novels traces how desire is thwarted; the other follows through on the unexpected ways in which it is gratified. The difference between these two situations can be summed up in one word: sex.

Apropos of Dolores centres on an unflattering fictionalisation of Odette Keun, portrayed by Wells as an individual dangerously unhinged. Methuen initially agreed to publish the novel in England, but they had second thoughts when their editorial director, E.V. Lucas, who knew Keun personally, apprised the board she was exactly the sort of person likely to sue. Methuen solicited from Wells a letter declaring, disingenuously enough, that Dolores had nothing to do with Keun. When Methuen still hesitated Wells withdrew the novel from them and agreed terms with Jonathan Cape, whose British edition emerged at the end of the year.

The novel's narrator-protagonist is Stephen Wilbeck, an English publisher with a failed marriage in his past (his former wife Alice bore him a daughter and then fell in love with 'the brooding presence of a tall stooping spectacled figure, George Hoopler' [72]). Wilbeck's company, Bradfield, Clews and Wilbeck, publishes a series of educational titles under the collective moniker 'The Way of the World'. The novel starts with Wilbeck in a small town in Normandy called Torquèstol looking to rent the sort of house his second wife Dolores would be prepared to occupy.

Then the story flashes back to Wilbeck's first meeting with the beautiful, half-Armenian, half-Scottish Dolores. On the rebound from his divorce Wilbeck sleeps with her. She then hooks him into marriage by telling him she is pregnant. After he has married her, this pregnancy morphs into a cancer and a great deal more melodramatic posturing, before devolving into non-specific pains that come on when convenient for Dolores (the doctor he consults tells Wilbeck: '"Madame is of a highly nervous type." He half closed his eyes and shook his head slowly from side to side' [105]). Wilbeck has made his bed, and must lie in it. The story provides a series of vignettes of Dolores's often hilariously awful behaviour, all drawn from Keun-esque life. She treats everyone with contempt. In a local tea-room, egged on by its mistress, the Pekinese mounts the well-bred lap-dog of an elderly bourgeois matron. Dolores decides, on a whim, that a fellow diner in a restaurant is a leper and loudly refuses to share the space with them. She persecutes the servants for no good reason. She grows increasingly jealous, in increasingly improbable ways. She believes her husband is having an affair with his typist, then with every woman in London, then that he is 'indulg[ing] for a change in homo-sexuality' [158] (Wells's awkward little hyphen, there) and finally that he is having an incestuous affair with his own daughter. She makes scenes. When Wilbeck warns that she 'might go too far with me' she retorts that, if he leaves her, 'I would take such a revenge upon you. You think I am powerless … No jury would convict me when they heard my story. It would be a tremendous trial' [146].

Just as we start to think that Wells's thumb is too obviously in the balance, and his portrait too one-dimensional, he mixes it up. First we are given Dolores's own perspective. 'I wonder why I love you,' she tells her husband:

There you sit, solemn, dull, a bourgeois bookseller, English, male—as stupid as a bull. You are like a heavy unteachable boy. Your only merit is a sort of uncritical sense of obligation. Once I was one of the most brilliant women on the Riviera, accustomed to gentlemen—to men of title, to princes, to men of the world, to unquestioning gallantry. What am I now? What have you done to me? Everyone says that since our marriage I have become almost as dull as you are. (*Apropos of Dolores*, 190–91)

Then we discover Dolores's 'pains' are no mere figments of her imagination; and indeed are so severe that she is incapable of going to sleep without a powerful analgesic called Semondyle. One evening Wilbeck discovers that Dolores has torn-up a photograph of Wilbeck's daughter in a jealous rage. He goes up to her room to confront her over this, but instead she rails at him, rebuking him with his many inadequacies as a husband, lover and man, insisting over and over that she hates him, promising to ruin his life, to make public that he is sleeping with his own daughter and otherwise to destroy his reputation. After many pages of this she stops suddenly, disconcerted by Wilbeck's reaction ('She caught some new quality of menace in my stillness, and suddenly I saw she was afraid').

She changed her expression to one of acute anguish. She clutched her side. '"My pain!" she cried. "My pain! Always you give me pain. I can't bear it. Oo! Oooh! If only you had it. If only I could give you a taste of it. You give me black blood, you poison my blood. Give me some Semondyle, you brute. Don't stand gloating there! You Sadist!" (*Apropos of Dolores*, 242)

He holds the cup containing the drug to her mouth and tips it for her to drink. In the morning she is dead. She has overdosed.

The question, of course, is whether Wilbeck murdered her. The novel has almost a hundred pages to go at this point, and many of those pages are given over to Wilbeck agonising over the situation. He is both immensely relieved his wife has gone, and simultaneously surprised at how heartbroken he is at her absence. Did he poison her? He claims not to know. The official line is that she took an accidental overdose. Lonely in Torquèstol, Wilbeck invites his daughter Lettice to come and stay with him, but although he has romanticised the possibilities of this father-daughter reunion it is mostly an anti-climax. He tries to make conversation, and gets nowhere. He lectures her about the Normandy world, and she is uninterested. It is striking, in a novel published in 1938, to read so modern-sounding an account of what it is like trying to engage with what would not for a couple of decades yet be called a 'teenager'.

Never in my life have I had to do with such a recessive conversationalist as Lettice. At any time when she is not actually being called upon for response, she seems to lapse into reverie. When she is talked to directly, she has a way of look-ing thoughtful and uttering a remarkably useful word, quite new to me, 'Urm'. (*Apropos of Dolores*, 290)

After much effort he manages to extract from her that she has a boyfriend, that said boyfriend works 'in a shipping office', that he 'adores' her and that she 'keeps him in his place' [295]. The book ends when Lettice goes home and Wilbeck heads off to Paris, a lonely widower. The ambiguity about Dolores's death is never resolved.

'This', says Wells in his preface, 'is a story about happiness, and about lone-liness of spirit, told in good faith.' The novel's opening sentence is: 'I find myself happy, and I have an impression I have been quite happy for two days' [1]. This opening is supposedly narrated before Dolores's death, and its English ambiguity (is *quite*, here, a superlative, or a dialling-down qualifier?) expands through the whole novel. Nor should we be surprised a tale about being happy spends so much of its bulk on describing a state of intense, frus-trated unhappiness. Only in dark, the light, as somebody once said. The cor-ollary to that celebrated *all happy families are alike; every unhappy family is unhappy in its own way* apothegm is that stories can only be properly told about the latter group. Nonetheless, it is quite a striking thing just how far Wells goes down this counter-intuitive route of portraying happiness almost wholly in terms of misery. As if we might say all happy families are only imag-inable in art through the lens of each unhappy family. And perhaps that's less counter-intuitive than I'm suggesting. After all, one of the things that tends to make us happy is our sex life, and good sex can be sufficient to keep us in otherwise boring or malignant relations. Wells's novel addresses sex at length and in detail, and it's clear enough that sex was one of the things that tied Wells to Keun, even as she otherwise embarrassed, infuriated and exhausted him. *Apropos of Dolores* handles this topic well, navigating the tricky waters of those restrictive 1930s cultural codes of sexual expression—the Chatterley trial is a quarter of a century in the future, after all—with some aplomb. Indeed, Wells manages to do something Lawrence himself never managed, to express how sexual desire and masculine sexual activity can be both wonder-fully sustaining of one's self-esteem at the same time as laying bare one's fool-ishly preening self-regard. For Lawrence male sexual desire is always an ennobling, darkly heroizing thing. Wells knows better: a man in the grip of a sexual passion is, fundamentally, a ludicrous figure. 'I thought at the time that this affair would be just an exotic version of various other kindred interludes in my bachelor life,' says Wells's Wilbeck, when he first gets together with Dolores:

I perceive a little chap who is still clinging to the assurance that he was something exceptional as a lover. It is nature's way with us. Few men, I suspect, can resist that dear delusion that the commonest of God's gifts is an outstanding distinction. Yet it is lavished upon the ordinary monkey far beyond our human portion. The facts of the case necessarily remain in a decent obscurity, but I think that in that particular respect my head was rather turned by Dolores. I was, I found for the first time in my life, a tremendous dog. I was a great fellow. I was an outstanding specialist. Casanova certainly wasn't in it with me.

These are subtle matters. Even setting them down makes them glare atrociously. But they are a necessary part of the story. Perhaps if one could tint the paper of a book grey, deepening in tone until at last the text quivered on the verge of the absolutely illegible...

A lot better than a line of stars. (*Apropos of Dolores*, 94–95)

That deepening grey tone is quite a clever mode of representing sexual congress by refusing the represent it. Better than waves on a beach or, as he says, than a line of asterisks. What it understands is that sexual explicitness is, in the erotic sense, a contradiction in terms. It can only have meaning in a biological or medical sense. Desire, beyond anything but the most trivial and superficial sense of the word, is always a form of obliquity. Usually, whatever our rationalisations, we don't actually comprehend why we desire so intensely (sometimes we don't even properly grasp *what* we desire intensely—we only understand *that* we desire). Desire is not something that can be illuminated by the light of reason; it is, on the contrary, the sweetly monstrous manifestation of reason's sleep.

The point is not that Wilbeck's miserable life is relieved from time to time with bouts of good sex. It is a more radical, and more unsettling, idea: that genuinely good sex is only really possible with somebody who makes you miserable, or perhaps it would be truer to say: you have the best sex with somebody you hate. Wilbeck's abortive first marriage, to the nice English girl Alice, is doomed even before Alice falls for gloomy-faced George Hoopler. Alice's affair is a symptom, not the cause, of the break-up. Respectable bourgeois she and her respectable bourgeois husband bore one another. The novel doesn't dilate upon Wilbeck's sex life with Alice, but it doesn't have to. It produced Lettice, but was otherwise manifestly inert, passionless, unexciting. The later episode with teenage Lettice coming to stay with her father and proving to be just as bland and 'urm' as her mother shows this unsexiness or anti-eroticism passing into the next generation. That's the English for you. And Dolores's unhinged intensity of living is not the price Wilbeck pays for a spiced-up sex life, it is the very ground of his sexual satisfaction as such. There's something insightful in this, even, perhaps, something that approaches profundity—not least because Wells is prepared to push this animosity all the way to its most extreme iteration, with Wilbeck's 'murder' of Dolores. That a sufficiently titanic sexual desire broaches murderousness is neither a rational not a very comfortable consideration, but perhaps that's the novel's point: happiness in the sense of desire is not correlative to rationality or comfort.

A rather different attitude to sexual desire is manifest in *The Holy Terror* (1939), Wells's last important novel—at once a restatement of Wells's perennial fantasy of the coming World State and a critique *of* that fantasy, an exploration of the violence and intrinsic irrationality of these ideas. This latter element is something quite new in Wells's career. The narrative here is the life story of a petty-minded, aggressive little man without imagination, empathy or depth of intelligence, who manages by sheer force of personal charisma to become dictator of the whole world.

Our anti-hero is Rudolf Whitlow, a physically small man with a large, white and ugly face. Rud comes from nowhere to seize power in Britain, rides the tumultuous international tide of global war to become world-leader and this new world shapes itself into exactly the kind of utopian ideal we're familiar with from *A Modern Utopia* (1905) and In *The Days of the Comet* (1906) through *Men Like Gods* (1923) to *The Shape of Things to Come* (1933). All of these books, and *Days of the Comet* most egregiously, handwave the transition from desperate now to gleaming utopian future; it happens magically, vaguely, by a process hidden under a cloud of unknowing. In *The Holy Terror* Wells traces out in careful detail a worryingly plausible route from Now to Utopia. He shows us, in other words, how the sausage gets made. This novel reflects Wells's awareness that the transition to his longed-for World State must be an ugly business, which is by way of tacitly acknowledging the ugliness inherent in his own ideological fantasy. This 'shape' of this trajectory is the same as *The Shape of Things to Come*'s: in that we must pass through a backward step into barbarism in order to motivate ourselves to improve the world into utopia. The difference, here, is that the step into barbarism is integral to the move to improve the world—not an arbitrary catastrophe, but a structural element in the process of refashioning.

The Holy Terror is a long novel, divided into four books. Book 1 concerns Rudolf's childhood. As a kid he responds to the mockery of his stouter brothers and his fellow kids (they call him 'The Stink') with violence: 'he was a natural born kicker; he went straight for the shins. He was also a wrist-twister'; 'he was a great smasher of the cherished possessions of those who annoyed him, and particularly the possessions of his brothers Samuel and Alf'; 'he wept very little, but when he wept he howled aloud, and jabbered wild abuse, threats and recriminations through the wet torrent of his howling' [1.1.2]. Attempts to reform him fail. At school he is bullied and fights back violently; only the intervention of the head boy, a handsome doctor's son with a sense of fair play called Dick Carstall, does any good. Rud decides he wants to go to university, though his father ridicules this notion ('"Edjicated proletariat— and what good's that?" Rud, regarding his father, looked still capable of knife-throwing' [1.2.1]). He bullies his mother into stumping up the money by cashing-in her insurance policy. At Camford Rud begins haranguing his fellows students, and political meetings, and discovers his demagogue talent. Carstall, who is also there, training to be a doctor, is impressed.

Book Two follows Rud's entry into practical politics. He has no political views of his own, beyond a belief that the most efficient route to his own empowerment is ipso facto the right ideology. But by testing his speechifying before various different audiences, he develops a core platform, and it's one stingingly (and deliberately) close to Wells's own beliefs: the coming of a world in which hierarchies and localisms have been subsumed into a global unity, beginning with a world-conquering alliance of Britain and America. He sets himself against both Communism and Fascism, proclaiming a 'Common Sense' platform. He meets 'middle-class Fabians, those painless permeators' and 'various leftists, Stalinists, Trotskyites and so forth' as well as the 'purple shirts' of the 'Popular Socialist Party', a group led by the suavely aristocratic Lord Horatio Bohun. This preening, sneering individual is the novel's far-from-flattering version of Oswald Mosley, whom Wells knew and did not like. Rud realises it would be more efficient to infiltrate and take-over the 'Popular Socialist Party' than start a new party from scratch. Book 2 details this process, in painstaking detail.

He is helped by the dire economic situation: a 'National Nutrition Emergency Committee' has appropriated all food supplies in order to ration them out, and when war does break out—at the end of the 1940s, in Wells's timeline—it is a much less decisive, and much longer-drawn-out business than the actual 1939–45 proved. In this environment Rud thrives. He purges the Popular Socialist Party of Bohunists, and remakes it in his image, renaming it 'The Common-Sense Movement', advocating the ethos of the Common Man, efficiency and scientific advance towards a global utopia. Soon enough Rud is dominating British politics.

In some respects, Wells's anticipations of world war were well off the mark (he thinks that the navies of the world will simply be rendered null by the air forces, and that naval crews would mutiny rather than go to sea under such a threat). In other ways, though, he is strikingly prescient. One is struck, reading the latter sections of *Holy Terror*, that Orwell must have read this novel, but that he owed much to it. Rud grasps that whilst the world war is being prosecuted he has extraordinary powers to remake things as he chooses. After many years of fighting, with the enemy exhausted, his generals urge him to authorise a final assault, force 'a general capitulation' of the enemy. But Rud doesn't want the war to end:

"We don't want a capitulation," said Rud. "... From our point of view the war to end war can have no formal end. We've got controlled shipping, amalgam-ated air forces, pooled finance, consolidated news-services, a common uniform. We want to keep them common for evermore. But the day we proclaim Victory and Peace the diplomatists and nationalists will come creeping out of their funk-holes again with their flags and claims and bills on each other and all that sort of thing. Versailles all over again." (*Holy Terror*, 3.2.7)

Nineteen Eighty-Four draws on this idea, of course. In *Holy Terror* Rud's main general Reedly, baulked of the military victory he yearns for, stages a coup. Rud crushes it briskly, ordering senior officers shot. 'Every one of them,' he says. 'Now. Once you start shooting—you have to go on' [3.3.8]. So global war continues, for at least another two years, during which time Rud styles himself the Master Director of the World and working 'to secure the absolute dominance of the Common World State' Things start to come together: 'grad-ually things began to fall into place as the idea that the Common World State had come to stay prevailed over the belief that it was merely a provisional arrangement, pending a satisfactory restoration and adjustment of old claims' [3.3.9]. This artificially prolonged, catastrophic war leads to a genuine rena-scence of mankind. 'Without a break the world war passed into world adjust-ment.' Rud's staff pull hard on all the propaganda levers to manufacture a global cult of personality centred on Rud himself, or on a sanitised and deper-sonalised version of Rud. Democracy is entirely a thing of the past ('a crude return to electoral politics would give every mischievous rascal in the world an opportunity' Rud insists [4.1.5]). Governance happens via a scientifically inflected 'Fundamental Law', steered by Rud and his immediate deputies. A world flag is designed: white saltire on blue ground. Other nations are permitted to keep their flags for the time being, but only on condition they have the World State white saltire imposed over their specific design, like a mark of erasure. Education is radically reformed, and so—another idea, evi-dently, that Orwell lifted wholesale for *Nineteen Eighty-Four*—is language. Rud decrees English the world language, although a programmatically revised and simplified English. One of Rud's deputies notes 'it is remarkable how patriotism still lingers in the blood, I like to think that the coming world language will be English' and is rebuked: 'It will be almost as much English as Middle Saxon is the English in use to-day. Less like. It will have dropped a thousand ambiguous and deflated terms' [4.1.7].

Having established the World State Rud grows lonely and isolated, and from there it's a short step to full-blown paranoia. He has never had a sexual partner, having sublimated all his erotic impulses into his political career. When Bodisham, his intellectual deputy, dies unexpectedly of disease, Rud believes that he was poisoned and has all the attending doctors shot. A round of religious persecutions begins. His deputy Chiffan decides it's his responsibility, as Rud's oldest friend and political disciple, to talk sense into him; but the conversation does not go well. Rud bursts out with decades-worth of repressed sexual resentment, focused on the other man's success with women and has Chiffan marched away and shot. Ill and unhappy, but mistrustful of his doctors, Rud remembers his childhood association with Dick Carstall, and, discovering that Carstall is working now in medicine, recruits him as his personal physician.

> Carstall regarded the Master of the World, and behold he was still the Stink and the sickly-faced orator in the Camford Union, exalted but the same. That little tadpole of a boy with the large head had simply grown to cosmic proportions … He affected a stern dignity and it did not suit his fragile smallness. His looks hadn't improved, his eyes were bright with mania and bloodshot, they seemed to have sunken deeper into their sockets, and his voice was harsher. Master of the world! (*Holy Terror*, 4.2.11)

Carstall doesn't hesitate. Rud recites his symptoms of ill health, and Carstall gives him an injection which he promises will cure him. It's strychnine, and Rud is killed.

The last portion of the novel is a post-mortem. The irony, or at least the closest *The Holy Terror* approaches to irony, is that Rud's revolution has worked. The world is a vastly better place now than it was at the novel's beginning. Rud's successors cover up his insanity, embalm his body and place it (the comparison to Lenin is specifically made) in a huge temple to serve as a place of pilgrimage for the faithful. The myth of the wise guardianship of Rud is more important than the truth. That truth is, says Carstall, he was 'just a nasty, frightened kid, greedy but frightened, horribly afraid of violence, always in a panic, living in an age of panic and expanded a million, a billion times. Until in a world of utter cowardice, he filled the sky.' But on the other hand, 'he killed a multitude of people, he destroyed institutions, traditions, boundaries, in his terror'. Which was good, because 'they were institutions that had to be destroyed … social classes, private property, religious cant, patriotism! They had become shelters for every slinking meanness in the human make-up' [4.3.3]. So the posthumous cult of personality is actively encouraged. Once Rud is removed everything in the World State garden is rosy. The last chapter of the novel is literally set in a sunlit garden, as Carstall—inexplicably unpunished for his act of homicide—is spending time with his little kid, Bunny. Bunny is reading a child's *History of the Revolution* that styles Rud as a hero and a secular god. Was it really like that, Daddy? asks Bunny. And Carstall responds: 'This book exaggerates here and there—and it simplifies things. It simplifies a lot … Broadly anyhow it is the truth' [4.3.5]. How malleable truth can become when our eyes are fixed on an unattainable goal!

Bibliography

Barfoot Cedric C and Theo D'haen eds. (1991). *Tropes of Revolution: Writers' Reaction to Real and Imagined Revolutions 1780–1980*. Amsterdam: Rodopi.

Ketterer, David (2009). 'The "Martianized" H. G. Wells?' *Science Fiction Studies*, 36:2, pp. 327–332.

26

Tethersend

Babes in the Darkling Wood (1940); All Aboard for Ararat (1940); You Can't Be Too Careful (1941); '42 to '44: A Contemporary Memoir (1944); The Happy Turning (1945); Mind at the End of Its Tether (1945)

By the 1940s Wells was an old man, the remarkable energy and drive that had sustained him across his long life finally flagging. He spent the war years mostly in London and tried to keep up at least some of rhythms of his old life—publishing pamphlets, giving speeches. But the fire had gone out of his art. When Moura Budberg was in London he would walk over to see her although, she later reported, even this mild exercise sometimes left him too exhausted for sex. By 1944 he was too frail to leave his house in Hanover Terrace, a domicile he had remained in throughout the Blitz, and despite quite extensive bomb damage to the area. 'Public affairs irritate and disgust me,' he wrote to his friend Elizabeth Healy in February 1945. 'I mend clocks and fuss about the decorations of the house to keep my mind off the follies of mankind. Bombs come and go, they hit next door or down the street or out in the park but they never hit me.'

Something was draining out of Wells's imaginative focus too, as evident in the long novel, *Babes in the Darkling Wood*, that appeared in 1940. It is, according to its subtitle 'A Novel of Ideas', which here means a mixture of turgid semi-dramatic novelisation and undramatic ideation. The main characters, the young couple Stella and Gemini, are staying in a friend's cottage, unmarried in defiance of 1940s social convention. Stella's choleric uncle Hubert Polydore Hopkinshire ('he was a Black and Tan and he's never got over it,' says Stella) writes to say he will come the next day to horsewhip Gemini for debauching his niece. This throws the couple into disarray. Gemini proposes marriage but Stella reminds him 'we agreed we didn't believe in marriage'; so it seems they must separate. Gemini worries about the shallowness

© The Author(s) 2019
A. Roberts, *H G Wells*, Literary Lives, https://doi.org/10.1007/978-3-030-26421-5_26

of sex: 'I am head over heels in love with you, I have been making love to you for a week, I am going to make love to you again just as soon as you stop pretending to comb your hair … [but] what's it got to do with anything, Stella? What's it got to do with the rest of life?' [1.3.3]. Stella thinks he's being too compartmentalising:

> 'What has this love-making to do with anything else, you ask. Well—everything. Sex is not irrelevant to the other side of life. Love, love-making, is as important as hunting, shooting, ploughing, making things, and it's nearer to vital reality. See? Nearer. More than the other side of a coin. Of course it is nearer and closer! Society is built upon sex—more than it is built on any economic or practical necessity.' (*Babes*, 1.3.3)

In Book 2 the lovers are living apart. Stella resumes her studies at Cambridge, even though her uncle Robert, who is a don, assures her that universities are all rotten and in need of radical reformation. The sector's only function, he insists, is to 'produce such men, little T.S. Eliots by the hundred, as a rotten carcass produces blowflies. Without an effort. Mental blowflies' [2.3.3]. Gemini, deciding he needs to do something more active with his life, joins the Soviet war-effort and sails for Sweden, hoping to reach the USSR that way. Germany invades Poland on 1 September and actual war breaks out. Stella, anxious for Gemini's well-being, has a vivid dream of wandering in a dark forest, and encountering a Great Unseen that says to her: 'I am the Guide who will never fail you. I am the Friend who will never desert you'. She tries to get closer.

> The ebony darkness about her became positive. It became an intensity of vision that transcended sight. Something immensely wonderful seemed to be pouring into her mind, and at the same moment she realised with dismay that she was dreaming and on the verge of awakening. She felt that something ineffable was slipping from her and she struggled in vain to retain it. (*Babes*, 3.1.2.)

Gemini is profoundly traumatised by his experiences during the invasion of Poland, and returns to England utterly broken—at first he can't even talk. When he sleeps 'unpleasant dreams' assail him and visions of raped and eviscerated bodies have drained all sexual desire from him. The lovers quarrel, are unhappy, but decide on marriage even though, with Gemini's impotence, they both know it will be a sham marriage: 'Did you ever read a book by D.H. Lawrence, *Lady Chatterley's Lover*?' Stella asks him. 'A stinking book if you like, but true. That would be our story' [4.3.2]. They do get married, but 'she never touched him. She never came within three yards of him.' Gradually

Gemini becomes more like his old self, and is able to re-declare his love for Stella: 'I do now understand everything. Stella dearest, you have brought me back to self-respect.' He enlists in the Royal Navy, crewing a mine-sweeper and Stella becomes a nurse, their marriage still sexless but their hope rekindled for the possibilities of the future.

It is a strange, unsatisfactory sort of novel, recording perhaps an old man's failing comprehension of youth, if also his awareness of that lack of comprehension. Anthony West's biography of Wells describes his father's last days first hand. During the 1940s West was in London working for the BBC. Wells occupied a spacious house overlooking Regent's Park, and West was living in a separate mews flat at the bottom of the garden, known, for some reason, as 'Mr. Mumford's'. 'Whilst this arrangement lasted,' says West, 'I would look in to see him almost every day. I would come in and find him sitting with a light rug over his knees, dozing at what had been his worktable, or, on sunny days, basking in the presence of a variety of potted plants in a big armchair that had been put out for him on the glassed-in balcony at the back of the house. We were sharing silences rather than talking by then.' Rumours had reached Wells's ears (untruths, West insists) that Anthony was involved in some kind of pro-Nazi conspiracy at the BBC. I've no idea about the veracity or otherwise of these rumours, or how they started, but West talks about how 'the nightmare cobweb of lies had fallen between me and my father whilst the flying bomb attack on London was at its height'. West says he planned to explain the whole situation to Wells, and put his mind at rest, but that his father was too ill to broach the topic. Then Wells's health rallied, and 'it seemed wrong to break in on his euphoria with all that stuff'. But then his health collapsed again, and he sank towards death.

> Sitting beside him one day, at once close to and utterly remote from him, and thinking him asleep, I fell into a passion of misery and buried my face in my hands. How long my spasm of pain lasted I have no way of knowing, but when its intensity slackened I suddenly felt that I was being watched. I looked up to find my father's blue eyes fixed on me with the light of his full intelligence in them. We stared at each other for an instant, until he said faintly, 'I just don't understand you …' with that light fading from his eyes as he spoke. He had turned himself off, as it were, and had withdrawn into that absence in which he waited for his coming death. The last chance of communication had gone, and there was not to be another. (West, 152–53. Ellipsis in original)

Wells died on 13 August 1946. *I just don't understand you* is an almost breathtakingly thoughtless and cruel last ever thing to say to your son, given the cloud that was between the two of them. But step back half a decade and the older generation's 'I just don't understand you' in the face of the younger's strange energies and baffling enthusiasms is exactly the tenor of *Babes in the Darkling Wood*. One of the things that does work well about his novel is the way it orchestrates that baffled incomprehension both in terms of an in-text rigidity of moral or social-conventional reaction—as with the couples' parents' stiff-necked disapproval—and in terms of an as-it-were out-text structuring, a story about and embodying a Great Unseen, and attempting to dissipate the cloud-of-unknowing that clings about it.

The Great Unseen in this novel is the mystery of the world as such, but it's more than that. This book—written by an old revolutionary about a new generation of young revolutionaries that he doesn't understand—is, as a whole, a hieroglyph of the ways the old misunderstand the young. The shape of the resulting fiction, in the largest sense is: young love, and especially the intensity of young mutual sexual desire, isolates Stella and Gemini into a bubble where the harshness of the world cannot touch them. Their astronomical names point to a kind of romanticised remoteness from things as they are. From Chap. 3 onwards (that chapter's title is 'The World's Harsh Voice Is Heard Off') the mundial intrudes into this astro-erotic remoteness, or more precisely the stars are forced to come down to earth. Parents are hostile, society is ostracising and unhelpful, and when war breaks out the world as such reveals its tooth-and-claw ghastliness. The young lovers are revealed as too existentially and relationally fragile to survive this shock, and though Gemini is brought back to a semblance of normal social function by the end, the sexlessness of his final marriage to Stella leaves the novel hanging in a very strange place. Nazism must be defeated, but we can't say that the Stella-Gemini nexus has survived contact with reality.

Exhaustion also marks the structure of *All Aboard for Ararat* (1942), a book that Wells got halfway through writing before, manifestly, giving up on it. Elderly writer and HG surrogate, Noah Lammock entertains a caller to his house who announces himself as Mr Lord God Almighty. Believing him an elderly escapee from the local insane asylum, Lammock alerts the institution and chats with the fellow until his minders can come and get him. Wells's God quotes Gosse's *Omphalos*, complains about being trapped in time with the cosmos he has constructed, is bad-tempered about what has happened to his formerly pristine universe, and expresses disdain for grovelers. 'My Bible is fairly plain about it. If only people would read intelligently. The people I favour are upright men who walk with God. It says so over and over again. Not crawlers at his feet. Men who stand up' [*Ararat*, 1]. The longer he talks, the less certain Lammock becomes that he is an insane asylum escapee, and the more he starts to wonder if he is actually God. When staff from the asylum come by, God has mysteriously vanished; though He returns to Lammock over the following days, instructing him (the Biblical Lamech reborn, it seems) to build an ark: 'into that Ark we will put reproductive samples of every good thing that is in the world, beasts, birds, arts and crafts, inventions and discoveries, literature' [1]. Lammock becomes inspired by the prospect of hope for the world, 'mankind reunited in one brotherhood, growing in strength and power for ever' [1]. God suggests transferring all human knowledge onto microfiche: '"it is possible and practicable to make these microphotographic films ... one thing I will certainly grant you moderns," said the Lord, "and that is the extraordinary way your gadgets and contrivances facilitate all sorts of things"' [2].

The novella comes to no conclusion. It doesn't even wind down; it simply stops, mid-sentence. The final chapters of *All Aboard for Ararat* see Lammock waking up the cabin of an actual ark, far out at sea, with no memory of how he got there. Things aren't going well. The ark has sprung a leak. Arrival at Ararat has been delayed. Wells literally gives-up on telling the tale, and instead jots down notes towards the story:

> Fish and seagulls become the main articles of diet. The elephants are put on half rations. A stowaway, giving the name of Jonah (which is as much as to say dove in Hebrew) is discovered like a gross devouring maggot among the ship's stores, thrown overboard, and swallowed by a whale. The whale, after circling about the ark for three days in a manifest indigestion, rejects Jonah contumeliously and offensively. He is taken aboard and complains of his rations ... He shoots an albatross, produces a stagnant and festering calm, and is again put off the ark ... and shot by Noah. But continues to float alongside in an unpleasant manner. He swells in his decay. He is towed round to the lee side but attempts to attach lead sinkers to him fail. (*Ararat*, 5)

Noah and God have one last conversation, and then the story just stops. 'Nor will we cease to fight these overwhelming powers…' Noah begins to say, and Wells drops down his authorial guillotine.

We are sliding down the chute towards the cosmic despair of Wells's very last book, *Mind at the End of its Tether*. Prospero enacts the end of Shakespeare's writing career by abjuring his rough magic and drowning his book deeper than did ever plummet sound. Lammock enacts the approaching end of Wells's career by just—giving up. Then again, the ark itself, Wells's allegory for his hopes of a future achievable Utopia, *is* still afloat, though leaky, under-supplied and dragging along with it the unsinkable corpse of false-prophets who have lyingly promised the same thing. Or maybe the corpse of Wells's earlier over-optimism. Who knows? God is still with Noah, at the end, at least.

Wells had enough energy for one more full-length novel: *You Can't Be Too Careful* (1941). Since in its last few pages this novel extends itself 10 years past its publication date (its subtitle is 'A Sample of Life—1901–1951'), we might argue that it is science fiction, if only in some quasi-homoeopathic sense of the term. Most of it, though, is backward-looking, both in terms of content and, unfortunately, aesthetic ambition, rehashing to *Kipps* and *Polly* without managing their eloquence, gliding comedy or structural complexity. It is, I'm sorry to say, a dreary read—1924's *The Dream* reworked, but with only the pinched and horrible early twentieth century part, the hopeful bright future having been entirely excised. Such a novel might perhaps have worked as a bracing but effective counterweight to the standard Wellsian schtick; but *You Can't Be Too Careful* is a grind, a book that tries too hard to make its point that sexual repression and undereducation have dire consequences.

It is the story of lower-middle-class Edward Albert Tewler, unlikely recipient of the George Cross. Tewler's parents, having brought him into the world in Camden Town in 1901 wonder about having further children, but worry about the cost and the chances of them dying, and (Wells strikes his titular keynote early and often) since 'you can't be too careful' Edward Albert remains an only child. When he is four his father is killed: crossing the road too timidly, he freezes in front of a bus. Edward Albert's widowed mother raises him with an almost pathological solicitude and caution, especially in the matter of his sexual education. Then (in 1914) she too dies, overdosing on patent medicines she has bought for myriad non-existent illnesses. Fourteen-year-old Edward Albert passes into Myame's Commercial Academy. He is an indifferent student, but thanks to a lucky couple of balls at a school cricket match, he acquires an undeserved reputation as a sportsman, a reputation he is canny enough not to endanger by ever actually playing any subsequent sport of any kind. Wells moves, in no hurry, through Edward's adolescence, which period is dominated by 'that complex of impulses, taboos, terrors and repressions, that onset of sex and sex education, which his mother had apprehended so anxiously, gathered about him and closed in upon him' [2.3].

Edward Albert aspires to the Imperial College of Commercial Science's Course of Training in Business Methods, but this requires him to be proficient in French, a language Myame's schooling has not provided him with. In the end this doesn't matter, since he happens to inherit £10,000 from a distant relative. This *Kipps*-y development is a mere plot-point, and is not utilised by Wells as a fully psychodramatic opportunity, as he did in his earlier masterpiece. Rich now, Tewler idles his time in London. He lurks unpleasantly, observing the house opposite ('a young woman who, with a certain disregard of her possible visibility, undressed completely in front of a small mirror. By putting out his own light and standing in the dark, he could see her bright pink illuminated body gradually emerging from her clothes' [3.3]). When he registers that he is sexually attracted to an old friend from his lodging days, Miss Pooley, his reaction is the following: 'he wanted to kill Miss Pooley, he wanted to leap upon her and beat her about and kill her.' Tewler eventually marries respectable Evangeline Birkenhead, but, through mutual ignorance, their first sexual experience does not go well:

> He hardly waited to kiss her. There was a rapid struggle. She felt herself gripped and assailed with insane energy.
>
> 'Oh! oh! oh!' she groaned in crescendo. 'Stop! Ow-woo-woohoo. Oooh!' The climax of the unendurable passed. Her body went limp.
>
> Then Edward Albert was sitting up with an expression of horror on his face. 'Gaw!' he was saying. 'You got some disease? It's blood!'
>
> He dashed for the bathroom.
>
> He came back to discover Evangeline sitting up in a storm of pain, disappointment and fear.
>
> 'You pig,' she said. 'You fool. You selfish young fool. You ignoramus! ... Get out of my way.' ... She dressed swiftly, going to and fro and flinging insults at him. He sat on the soiled and devastated bed considering the situation. (*Careful*, 3.11)

Through the new bride's mind runs 'a pageant of beautiful women down the ages who had had to give their bodies to dwarfed kings and ugly feudal lords' [3.15]. After the birth of their only child, Henry Tewler, she refuses all further sexual activity. At first her husband is disbelieving ('you got to do your juty by me ... you're flying in the face of the laws of Gord and man' [3.18]) but when she insists that 'my body belongs to me and I do what I like with it' he grows wrathful and blames the suffragettes. Soon enough Tewler is kicking at his wife's locked bedroom door ('"Let me in, you bitch," he was shouting. "I want my rights."' [3.19]) and she moves out. Tewler consults a solicitor concerning divorce proceedings, and vents his rage and despair. In reply the lawyer tells him '"the-e-e"—he prolonged the word into a neigh—"prostitute is the safety-valve of the respectable Christian life. That is all I can tell you"' [3.20]. Instead of this, though, Tewler finds carnal comfort with his housekeeper, a widow called Mrs Butter, whom he afterwards marries.

Tewler senior becomes increasingly right wing: expatiating about the Soviet menace and telling his neighbours 'these here Jews seem to be doing a lot of mischief in the world, one way and another' [5.1]. He commends the rise of

Hitler to his golfing partners, and he listens to these latter as they warn him that the French army, by recruiting Black soldiers, is risking the mass rape of white women. As he tees off he fantasises about 'himself as Sir Galahad clearing Soudanese niggers off the links and comforting their victims by a kind word or so before starting his round' [5.2]. World War II breaks out, and Germany comes close to winning in 1940, before 'striking hysterically at Russia', and for the first time encountering a people unencumbered by the sheet-anchor of respectability: a people 'united in their dislike to the German Herrenvolk' who 'fought with an undivided mind. They had discovered that in warfare you cannot be too careless. "Safety last!" said the Russians' [5.2]. Tewler senior is initially shocked into complete inaction by the advent of war, but eventually he joins the Brighthampton Home Guard.

The novel now moves into a speculative near-future. The Germans raid the southern English coast, and Tewler, who happens to be on duty, and in an access of startled recklessness, bayonet-charges a patrol, killing four men, until Polish volunteers come up and complete the rout. For this he is given the G.C. 'That', says Wells, in the novel's coda, 'completes all that is essential in the life of Edward Albert Tewler, his Deeds and Significant Sayings.' The novel ends on a lengthy Wellsian lecture, in which, among sideswipes at Communism and Catholicism ('to-day the most evil thing in the whole world is the Roman Catholic Church. The Communist Party is the identical twin of Catholicism' [6.1]) he concedes that his hero is horrible: 'my loyal but anxious publishers', Wells confides, 'protested that Tewler is detestable', and 'there is not really a nice human being in the book. Couldn't you put in some flash of real nobility in him?' [6.3]. But Wells insists he feels only pity.

> I have told his poor sordid story and that of the people whose lives he helped to spoil; I have mocked at his absurdities and misfortunes and invincible conceit; but all the way along as I wrote it something has protested, 'This is not fair. Given a broader education, given air, light and opportunity, would he have been anything like this?' He is what our civilisation made of him, and this is all it made of him. I have told the complete truth about a contemporary specimen man. (*Careful*, 6.3)

It is, certainly, a bracing novel, often startlingly in its relatively explicit portrayal of sex. In fact one of the most interesting things about this novel is the way it shifts tonally from the scenes of quasi-Dickensian comedy through to a sort of Lawrentian passionate fury of sexual blockage, Edward Albert screaming bitch at his wife, fantasising about sexual violence and ultimately achieving a grisly kind of ecstatic-erotic consummation when his phallic bayonet penetrates and kills four Germans on the beach. Society being so constituted, Wells is saying, he of course receives the George Cross for this action. Why the George Cross for this? That medal is specifically awarded for 'acts of the greatest heroism or for most conspicuous courage in circumstance of extreme danger, not in the presence of the enemy': Tewler a member of the Home Guard, is indeed engaging the enemy when he stabs those Germans—a Military Cross would be much more likely—except that George is the more fitting rebus for Tewler's actions: that old Turkish knight, stabbing his phallic lance into the plump body of that dragon, whilst a toothsome maiden languishes nearby. Revulsion has finally replaced Wellsian optimism about the perfectibility of humankind.

Wells last years alternated phases of exhausted illness with periods in which he was capable of more energy. His last collection of journalism and nonfiction was *'42 to '44: A Contemporary Memoir Upon Human Behaviour* (1944): 35 essays disposed into two sections, 'the Heritage of the Past' and 'How We Face the Future'. Wells didn't intend this volume for general distribution, and instructed his publisher to limit the print-run to 2000 copies. In the preface Wells says: 'there will be no cheaper edition issued at any time and I doubt if second hand copies will ever become abundant.' Wells hurried his publishers into print because his doctors had told him he had only months to live, although in fact he lived for almost another 2 years. In addition to its journalism this volume includes, as an appendix, the dissertation elderly Wells wrote and submitted to the Royal Society. It had become one of the *ideés fixes* of Wells's dotage that he ought to be elected a fellow of this august institution. Many of his friends agreed and blamed political bias amongst those fellows voting 'no' on his election, although it's just as likely that the Society's disinclination to elect him had to do with Wells's lack of significant scientific discovery or invention. At any rate, the elderly Wells forced the issue by submitting a D.Sci dissertation to the extra-mural department of the University of London. Its title was 'A thesis on the quality of illusion in the continuity of the individual life in the higher metazoa, with particular reference to the species Homo sapiens … accepted by the University of London for the doctorate of science'. Julian Huxley gave him feedback on the work, the University awarded him the degree, and he published it in this volume. The Royal Society, however, remained unimpressed. Wells never was elected a fellow.

Hearing that the old man's health was failing, Bertrand Russell came for tea in June 1945. He later recalled how distressed he was to see H.G. so clearly dying. Two more short books remained in him. *The Happy Turning* (1945) describes his daily walk from his home in Hanover Terrace, beside Regent's

Park, round the corner to his club in Mayfair. Not the real walk, a physical exertion of which Wells had been incapable for a while. The book relates how Wells takes that walk in his dreams: 'I am dreaming', is how the story opens, 'far more than I did before this chaotic war invaded my waking hours.' In his dreams, he says he can turn off at hitherto unnoticed 'happy turnings' into a pleasant, cheering dimension where he can stroll, explore and chat with—for instance—Jesus; and also 'leap gulfs unerringly, scale precipices, shin up trees'. It is a book aware how tricky dream-wishes and dream-fulfilment can be. Wells brings in a little Freud ('the subliminal self is never straightforward' [2]) and reflects on his own dreams.

> In the past I do not recall dreams as a frequent factor in my existence, though some affected me very importantly. As a child I used to have a sort of geometrical nightmare as if a mad kaleidoscope charged down upon me, and this was accompanied by intense distress. I may have been very young then, because I cannot remember now how I awakened or whether I conveyed my distress to anyone. Nor have I ever come upon a description of that dream as happening to any other child. (*Happy Turning*, 2)

That striking nightmare says something, perhaps, about the angular inhospitability of the reality principle as it imposes itself on the desires of the id. *The Happy Turning*'s iteration of utopia, the last in Wells's extensive body of utopian writing, is largely rural—Edenic gardens and beautiful landscapes—for 'the architects of Dreamland lay out a whole new world' [6] every time they build. Which is as if to say, geometry is not imposed onto the pliable material of the world, like a mad kaleidoscope, but is instead coeval with it, integral in its eutopic disposition. But it's also to say that such architecture is a matter of wish rather than labour, of plenitude rather than lack. Christ takes the central role in two chapters 'Jesus of Nazareth discusses his failure' and 'Miracles, Devils and the Gadarene Swine', and the proximity of dreams to religion, or more precisely the tension between the dream-fulfilment of faith and the kaleidoscopic horrors of dogma and creed, are part of the point of the book. 'Religions are such stuff as dreams are made of' says Wells, adding:

> The Athanasian Creed is severely logical in dreamland, Isis is transfigured into Hathor, a cow, Quannon, the crescent moon and Murillo's Queen of Heaven, and still the dream flows on. Osiris becomes his own son Horus, who becomes again Osiris and the Virgin Mother, in incessant rotation. (*Happy Turning*, 2)

Young Wells was, of course, very close to his devout mother, a woman who believed absolutely in the Athanasian Creed. Lay out your imaginary H.G. on your imaginary psychiatrist's couch, and it won't take you long to unearth a core reason for his constant sexual promiscuity in his relationship with the mother he adored and who was so hard to please, that *objet a*, here populating the religion of Dreamland with metamorphosing female deities. We don't have any photographs of Sarah Wells as a young woman, but it's certainly possible to use one's imagination to smooth the wrinkles from the photographs of her in old age, extrapolate backwards towards her brunette, fine-faced youth, and so note how very like the fine-faced brunette Mary of Murillo's painting 'Queen of Heaven' (1660) she looks: the shape of their faces and eyes and balance of their features are identical.

Of course, the problem with this level of 'explanation' for Wells's (or any man's) sexual promiscuity is not that it isn't convincing, but rather the opposite: that it's too facile, too obvious. Too much an absolute horizon within which a series of much more particularised and localised behaviours and misbehaviours, fetishes and loves and griefs, flourish and wither. Its explanatory power is too broad-brush. On the other hand, that Wells's Dreamland also contains Osiris becoming Horus becoming again Osiris, this brief glimpse of a son who begets himself bypassing the maternal altogether, is interesting. Wells was a self-made man in the material and financial sense of the phrase, but his real desire (this dream suggests) is to be what nobody can be, self-made in an ontological sense.

Wells began writing *The Happy Turning* in 1943, but dropped it, along with various other unfinished projects as the year went on and his health deteriorated. He took it up again in the summer of 1944, when he experienced a final burst of productivity: finishing this short book, writing *Mind at the End of Its Tether*, and 15 newspaper and journal articles, together with a quantity of other unpublished bits and pieces which, for a while, he was thinking of pulling together into one volume under the title *Exasperations*. Exasperation always, in the end, informs what the artist does, of course: the writer's life is always about not art but the obstacles to art. Wells's entire career involved him moving from fiction to reality and finding in the latter an exasperating refusal to bend to his will. And it is to the real world Wells finally addresses himself in *Happy Turning*, with something like defiance: 'you have no existence apart from mind, and so I shall make an end to you now.'

Julian Huxley had collaborated closely with Wells on *The Science of Life* (1930), and had remained friends with him through the early 1930s; but the two had a falling-out in 1941. 'I was chairing a meeting of the British Association', Huxley recalled in his autobiography, 'and had been instructed to allow only twenty minutes to each speaker, so providing time for general discussion at the end.' H.G. submitted a paper that would take 40 minutes to read, and when Huxley told him this wasn't fair to the other speakers 'an angry correspondence and protest followed'. 'When the time came, I had to ask him to cut short his discourse. He never forgave me.' His wife Juliette, however, remained friends with the old man:

> I never saw him again—but during the last years of his life, when he became too ill to do more than sit in his armchair, Juliette often dropped in to visit. He looked shrunk, she said, his face curiously altered, concentrated around an elongated and pensive nose. Visitors were not encouraged, as they tired him out, and he seemed very lonely. His tea was carefully measured and a piece of cake weighed, to balance his diabetes. A tall Buddha, extending his blessing, stood on the mantlepiece. 'He knows a thing or two,' murmured H.G. (Huxley, 166)

Which brings us, at last, to *Mind at the End of Its Tether* (1945). 'This little book', Wells declares in its preface, 'brings to a conclusive end the series of essays, memoranda, pamphlets, through which the writer has experimented, challenged discussion, and assembled material bearing upon the fundamental nature of life and time. So far as fundamentals go, he has nothing more and never will have anything more to say'. So it proved. *Mind at the End of Its Tether*, a mere slip of a book: 34 pages, in eight short chapters, was the very last thing Wells published.

With such a title we expect pessimism, and Wells does not disappoint. Indeed, pessimism is piled on pessimism, to the point where this short work starts to feel endless, a TARDIS-book longer on the inside than its external page-count can accommodate. On and on it goes, repeating the same obscure and doom-clanging point over and over. Wells has had, he says, an intimation that things are approaching an end 'within a period to be estimated by weeks and months rather than by aeons'. Something profound has changed about the cosmos: 'there has been a fundamental change in the conditions under which life, not simply human life but all self-conscious existence, has been going on since its beginning.' Wells explains, referring to himself in a distancing third-person: 'If his thinking has been sound, then this world is at the end of its tether. The end of everything we call life is close at hand and cannot be evaded [*Mind*, 1].

For Wells to write this some months ahead of the atom bomb being dropped on Hiroshima looks prescient indeed; but Wells is not talking about nuclear weapons. He's talking about something else. Not a super-weapon invented *in* the world, but something existentially prior *to* the world. He insists that 'the cosmic movement of events is increasingly adverse to the mental make-up of our everyday life'; that 'the secular process loses its accustomed appearance of a mental order' [1]. By 'secular process' he means the physical world outside humanity, something he here calls, a little confusingly, 'Eternity'. Wells used to believe that human consciousness and the external world ran together, in intertwined ways, but now he believes 'that congruence with mind, which man has attributed to the secular process, is not really there at all. The secular process … is entirely at one with such non-mental rhythms as the accumulation of crystalline matter in a mineral vein or with the flight of a shower of meteors. The two processes have run parallel for what we call Eternity, and now abruptly they swing off at a tangent from one another' [1]. In other words, it's not, or not just, *Wells's* mind that's at its tether's-end here; it's consciousness as such. Exactly how is not explained.

It's not just the how of this coming apocalypse that remains unexplicated; it's the *what*. The book is surprisingly elusive of exactly what is going on. It is 'the Pattern of Things to Come fading away'; it is 'extinction coming to man like a brutal thunderclap of Halt!' (although Wells immediately contradicts this assertion: 'it never comes like a thunderclap. That Halt! comes to this one to-day and that one next week. To the remnant, there is always, "What next?"' [1]). 'Chaos' and 'a harsh queerness come over things'. It is a kind of cinematic illusion:

> We pass into the harsh glare of hitherto incredible novelty … The cinema sheet stares us in the face. That sheet is the actual fabric of Being. Our loves, our hates, our wars and battles, are no more than a phantasmagoria dancing on that fabric, themselves as unsubstantial as a dream. (*Mind*, 1)

There is some kind of menace out there, lurking in the darkness, in the supracosmic spaces. Wells calls it 'Power', although he isn't happy with the nomenclature ('"Power" is unsatisfactory. We need to express something entirely outside our "universe", and "Power" suggests something within that universe and fighting against us. But we cannot deny this menace of the darkness'). His alternatives won't serve though: '"Cosmic process", "the Beyond", "the Unknown", "the Unknowable", all carry unsound implications'.

This is all in Chap. 1, which comprises almost half the whole book. Subsequent chapters ring changes upon this theme without, really, elucidating it. 'Our universe is not merely bankrupt', he says; 'it has not simply liquidated; it is going clean out of existence, leaving not a wrack behind. The attempt to trace a pattern of any sort is absolutely futile' [3]; Homo sapiens is 'played out', 'the stars in their courses have turned against him and he has to give place to some other animal' [4]. Wells ends the book as gloomy as he started it, 'doubt[ing] that there will not be that small minority which will succeed in seeing life out to its inevitable end'.

It's hard to avoid the sense that Wells is here merely projecting his imminent individual extinction onto the cosmos as a whole. Indeed, there's something ironic in a book that insists the old existential repetitions are coming to an end being, in itself, so very repetitious. But perhaps that's not irony. Perhaps that's the point. This is Wells's cope-stone work, slender though it is. It self-consciously repudiates the very fact of 'the future' as such, as if denying the very grounds on which Wells's fame as a writer rests: an anti-prophetic work that denies there will even be a future to be prophetic about. Or perhaps what Wells is confronting here is not the death of the future, but the death of uncertainty, that quantity which enacts not only the distinction between fact and fiction, but precisely the prophet's distinction between past and future. Wells at the end of his life has lost faith in uncertainty. Without uncertainty into which to expand, Being simply butts its head on the inevitable, over and over, until the particular iteration of Being doing the butting finally stops, as happened with Wells on 13 August 1946, at some time between 4 pm and 5 pm, during his usual afternoon nap.

Still: I'm not sure this is the best context in which to read Wells's final published work. The book contains, for example, nothing of the personal in it. Rather we can contextualise it amongst the large number of books generated by the war and its immediate aftermath that discussed the end of history, or of time itself. Wells was certainly not alone. Lutz Niethammer has identified a whole group of thinkers and writers who were moved by the end of World War II to theorise the end of history as such—he doesn't discuss Wells, but easily could have done—as a reaction to a broader sense of intellectual exhaustion. Malcolm Bull summarises Niethammer's argument:

> European theorists of *posthistoire* [consisted] most notably of Kojève on the Left, Arnold Gehlen (who first deployed the term) and the novelist Ernst Jünger on the Right and (moving between the two extremes) the political theorist Bertrand de Jouvenel and the Belgian politician Hendrik de Man. By finding the connections between the ideas of this seemingly heterogeneous group of (mostly) mid-century writers, Niethammer evokes the mood of historical exhaustion that enveloped radical intellectuals at the end of the Second World War when their political expectations were disappointed and American-style capitalism became dominant in the Western world. (Bull, 23)

Niethammer diagnoses in these diverse thinkers 'the fantasy of a meaningless, but ever continuing course of events' [Niethammer, xi], which is exactly what Wells is complaining of in *Mind at the End of Its Tether*. Niethammer also notes what he calls 'this characteristic mixture of ideas' which 'equates bourgeois society with history, defines the contemporary world in terms of systemic dangers, and maintains hope in the future mainly at the level of individuality'. The ending of history, in this case, means the collapse of bourgeois individualism, which is quite a fruitful way of reading late Wells. He worries about species death as a 'systemic' transference of the ego-individuality of Wells's own mind, and he cannot imaginatively body-forth a new species to supersede the exhausted strain of Homo Sapiens.

It's hard to resist the temptation (although succumbing to it exposes me to the charge of imposing an egregious neatness of pattern on a book that specifically repudiates meaningful pattern) to link this last publication of H.G. Wells back to his first, and thread the needle that links *Mind at the End of Its Tether* to 1893's *The Time Machine*. That earlier fable is also a book about the end of all things, the terminal beach to which the nameless traveller ventures and from which he flinches back in horror, or despair. That story, of course, is presided over by the Sphinx who poses the riddle *what is this monster?* to which the answer is: *us, it is we ourselves*. The monster is man. We are the ones who violate the incest taboo, who murder our fathers and sleep with our mothers, who are compelled to blind ourselves in self-disgust, who range out as far as we can only to feel the tether fastened around our necks go taut. *Mind at the End of Its Tether* discusses the fossil record; but *The Time Machine* actually dramatises those petrific sheaves of deep time. The human traveller encounters Morlocks eating Eloi, and both are his descendants, as are the strange crab creatures and the black eyeball-like blobs under the dying sun. Futurity and the past are the same, inescapable path, and it leads only to death and blindness. The curse cannot be escaped-from, because the curse is us, we are the monster. Wells's *Time Traveller* has no name in this story because what we are, as humans, is nameless.

It's a repetition, rather than a pattern, I think, this parallel between Wells's first and last work; a psychopathological going over and over the same ground, like Lady Macbeth endlessly washing her hands. *Mind at the End of Its Tether* offers neither evidence for Wells's strange presentiment that everything was coming to an end, and develops nothing that looks like a conventional argument. Instead it simply states and restates that the nameless something ('Power', 'Cosmic process', 'the Beyond', 'the Unknown', 'the Unknowable') is bringing doom. That, it seems to me, is the final twist in Wells's twisted final book. He is not *predicting* an apocalypse, because, as Frank Kermode so eloquently shows in *The Sense of an Ending*, it has always been the role of apocalypse to shape the story of our collective existence, to transform the tick-tick of chronological time into the gleaming wonder of *kairos*, the right time, the special time. Rather *Mind at the End of Its Tether* is predicting the radical *absence* of apocalypse, the trapped tick-tick of an endlessly existential cul de sac, the impossibility of shape or meaning as such. Pessimism had never been so pessimistic before. Credit, at least, to Wells for that.

Bibliography

Bull, Malcolm, 'The End', *London Review of Books* 15:5 (11 March 1993), 23–24.
Huxley, Julian (1970) *Memories*. George Allen & Unwin.
Niethammer Lutz (1993). *Posthistoire: Has History Come to an End?* Translated by Patrick Camiller. London, Verso.
West, Anthony (1984). *H G Wells: Aspects of a Life*. London: Hutchinson.

Coda

In 1946 Penguin books issued paperback editions of ten of Wells's titles: *The New Machiavelli*, *War of the Worlds*, *The Island of Doctor Moreau*, *A Short History of the World*, *The Time Machine and Other Stories*, *Love and Mr Lewisham*, *The History of Mr Polly*, *Tono-Bungay*, *The Invisible Man* and *Kipps*. Each volume included this note opposite the title page:

> This edition is one of a uniform set of ten volumes of Mr Wells' works specifically published in commemoration of his eightieth birthday, September 21st 1946. Of each volume a hundred thousand copies have been printed.

In the event, Wells never made it to 80. He died 5 weeks before that anniversary. Still, printing a million copies of an author's backlist is, quite apart from anything else, a hefty vote of confidence in that author's continuing commercial viability a full 50 years after his first novel.

Fifty years later matters were different. The only titles from Wells's enormous back-catalogue still reliably in print at the end of the twentieth century were his early science fiction classics from the 1890s and 1900s, which continued (and have continued) to be enthusiastically consumed by science fiction fans. Otherwise Wells was little read in the 1990s. In 1994 Everyman issued a new edition of 14 Wells titles—the same 10 as Penguin half a century earlier, minus the *Short History*, plus *Ann Veronica* and 4 extra science fiction novels: *First Men in the Moon*, *When the Sleeper Wakes*, *A Modern Utopia* and *Shape of Things to Come*. *Ann Veronica* was then, and still is, often taught when

© The Author(s) 2019
A. Roberts, *H G Wells*, Literary Lives, https://doi.org/10.1007/978-3-030-26421-5

university syllabi cover the New Women or the suffragette movement, but otherwise science fiction had largely swallowed Wells's literary reputation. I do not say so entirely in tones of regret. Wells's SF is extraordinary. But it was, after all, only a small portion of his larger output.

In a broader sense Wells, 50 years after his death, has experienced a simultaneous expansion and diffusion of reputation. His reputation as a writer has survived, even if in attenuated form, but his reputation as a political thinker and theorist has vanished almost without a trace. In the words of Duncan Bell 'Wells's star waned rapidly' after his death: 'even as millions continued to marvel at his "scientific romances" his political writings were largely forgotten. The evolving discipline of International Relations, fighting for credibility in the massive post-war expansion of the social sciences, and shaped by the power dynamics of the Cold War, had little time for such a protean, utopian writer' [Bell, 867].

It's not that Wells's engagements with political theory and praxis have been forgotten, exactly; but they have undergone a process of caricature in popular consciousness. In 1996 the H.G. Wells Society, to mark 50 years since his death, organised a conference under the title 'Reappraising H G Wells'. Takashi Hiraoka, Mayor of Hiroshima, sent a letter commending this conference, and praising Wells for his activism in the cause of world peace.

> This event is held during the 50th year of the promulgation of the Constitution of Japan, which was based on a draft written by H G Wells, who foresaw the invention of the atomic bomb and warned humans against nuclear war. Thus, this event to commemorate his 130th birthday and the 50th anniversary of his death has great significance. [Takashi]

It is indeed remarkable that the post-war Constitution of Japan is based on a draft written by H.G. Wells. Remarkable but untrue: in fact the draft submitted to the Diet of Japan for ratification in 1946 was written by two American army lawyers, Lieutenant Col Milo E. Rowell and Major General Courtney Whitney. Wells was not involved at all. But what's fascinating here is that the mayor of Hiroshima could *think* it true. It's the kind of thing that Wells might have done—he was, after all, part of the Sankey Commission, and his short book *The Rights of Man* (1940) proposed the kind of democratic and pacifist constitutional legal statements upon which a country transitioning, as Japan was, from autocracy to democracy might have utilised.

Wells as 'Mr Future' in *Real Fact Comics* (July 1946)

In other words, Wells's reputation has expanded beyond the Wellsian actuality in various, often surprising ways. A complete survey of the adaptations of Wells's fiction into stage, film and TV is beyond the scope of the present volume—although such adaptation is legion, and weighted very heavily towards the science-fictional—but it is worth noting that Wells has in himself become something of a signifier for 'Edwardian-ness' (along with a very select group of real and fictional figures such as Lloyd George and Sherlock Holmes) and more specifically for a kind of retro-fitted science-fictional or 'steampunk' Edwardian-ness. In the movie *Time After Time* (1979), directed by Nicholas Meyer from his own screenplay, Wells, played by Malcolm McDowell, uses 'his' time machine to pursue Jack the Ripper into 1970s America. The movie is enjoyable hokum—Wells's second wife is revealed as being a twentieth-century woman who agrees to travel back in time with HG and change her name to Jane—construing a version of Wells that says interesting things about our attitudes today to the period, to science fiction and indeed to Wells himself. McDowell, handsome in a boyish way, researched Wells for the role intending to model his performance on reality; but after discovering recordings of Wells's actual speech he declared himself 'absolutely horrified' at the 'squeaky voice and pronounced south-east London accent' he heard: 'it would have resulted in unintentional humour if I had tried to mimic it' McDowell insisted, opting instead for more mellifluous actorly iteration. The result is a better-looking, better-sounding version of Wells, a man whose 'whoosh' is put at the service of rescuing humanity from a serial killer and who mediates a clean-cut sexual allure. Even handsomer is Michael Sheen's portrayal of Wells in the 2006 BBC TV film *H. G. Wells: War with the World,* which centres on a sexed-up dramatisation of Wells's relationship with Rebecca West. David Lodge's novelisation of Wells's life, *A Man of Parts* (2011) lingers over H.G.'s erotic adventures. Lodge mostly cleaves to Wells's own autobiographical descriptions, but when he invents it is often to peculiarly male-ego ends (the prostitute to whom Wells loses his virginity gasps 'my, you've got a big one for a little chap'). Fay Weldon's 1985 account of Rebecca West for the *Lives of Modern Women* series falls back on a pulp idiom to capture the energy of Wells's relationship with her: 'Wells and West! The encounter of giants— Godzilla meets King Kong!' A rather more sophisticated utilisation of pulp idioms is Christopher Priest's novel *The Space Machine* (1976), which treats *Time Machine* and *War of the Worlds* as true and extrapolates a wittily inventive scientific romance that gives Wells himself a cameo. Priest's novel helped kick-start a vogue in steampunk Wellsiana, often featuring Wells himself in heroically exaggerated action-hero mode.

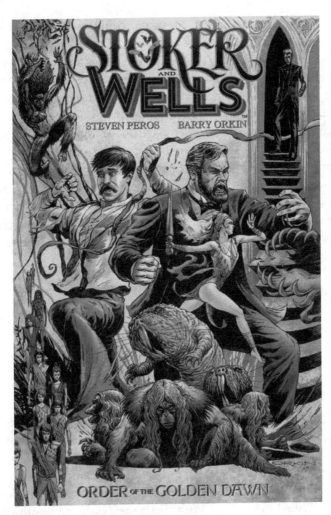

Stoker and Wells (2018). (Art by Barry Orkin)

What is the kernel of the continuing appeal of this iteration of Wells? As the world has grown bigger and more complex, as well as more complexly interconnected, a kind of socio-technological sublime increasingly threatens to overwhelm our individual subjectivities like Hokusai's great wave. Steampunk is, inter alia, an attempt to dress technological advance in the habiliments of a more elegant and refined age, and Wells is one of the ways of focalising that. More, this cultural representation—the boyishly mobile and inventive Wells, the Wells of diverting scientific romances and sexual liberation—speaks, in part, to an ill-focused desire to assert 'the little man' (less so 'the little woman') in the teeth of this intimidating vastness. There is enough of Wells actual life-trajectory in this to give it bite: the physically small individual from small-scale roots who created himself as a world-class writer and thinker. He takes his place alongside other pervasive cultural myths of the small-man who effects great things in a baffling and alarming world—heroic hobbits, magical schoolboys: contemporary iterations of a fundamentally infantalising legendarium of underdoggishness. One need not deprecate these contemporary myths, any more than one need look down on Wells's extraordinary achievements in the field of science fiction, to think this sells his larger achievement short. If there has been one through-line in the present work it has been that Wells was a literary artist of immense, underappreciated talent, a writer whose literary genius, whilst it must of course be central to a literary biography, deserves to be resurrected in a much broader cultural context too.

Earlier I quoted Lovat Dickson's thesis that Wells's life can be construed as having passed through phases governed by distinct myths: the myth of evolutionary and scientific advance which informs his early science fiction, then the 'myth of sexual and social revaluation' in *The New Machiavelli*, *Ann Veronica* and other novels of that period, and then the 'myth of God the Leader' of *Mr Britling Sees It Through* and *God the Invisible King*. Dickson's conclusion ('but the religious myth failed him, as the scientific and sexual ones had done, and he was left unhappy at the end' Dickson, 307) rather underplays the last quarter-century of Wells's life, which was full of extraordinary writing. After the 'failure' of his turn to religion Wells embraced a turn to history and the factual with the *Outline of History* and *The Science of Life*, a phase which overlapped with a fundamentally Jungian period that attempted to reconcile fantasy and reality (*Christina Alberta's Father*, *The Autocracy of Mr. Parham*, *The Bulpington of Blup*) that in turn both overlapped with and informed an autobiographical, self-reflexive phase: *William Clissold*, *The Book of Catherine Wells* and *Experiment in Autobiography*. The final phase in his long and productive existence saw Wells shaken out of creative introspection by the rise of fascism and the return of world war: the last 10 years of his life were dominated by an attempt to re-engage the world on Wellsian terms in order to avoid catastrophe. The world wasn't listening though, and there is something poignant in the dying fall of Wells's last years. That shouldn't distract us, though, from how major and sustained was the bulk of his literary life; and it seems to me the duty of any critic to at least attempt to respect the whole gamut of Wellsian achievement.

Bibliography

Bell, Duncan (2018). 'Founding the World State: H. G. Wells on Empire and the English-Speaking Peoples', *International Studies Quarterly*. 62:4, 1 December 2018, 867–879.

Dickson, Lovat (1969). H G Wells: His Turbulent Life and Times. Macmillan.

McDowell, Malcolm (2002). 'Audio Commentary', *Time After Time* (directed Nicholas Meyer) DVD. Warner Home Video.

Takashi Hiraoka (1996). 'Message', *The H G Wells Newsletter*, 3.11 (August 1996).

Chronology

1866. Born in Bromley, Kent, 21 Sept.

1880 (age 14): apprenticed to Windsor Draper's shop.

1881 (age 15): works as pupil-teacher at 'Uncle' Alfred Williams' school, Wookey, Somerset. Pupil Midhurst School. Apprenticed to Southsea Draper's shop.

1883–84 (age 17–18). Teaches at Midhurst Grammar School.

1884–87 (age 18–20) Studies at Normal School of Science, South Kensington.

1887 (age 20–21) Teaches at Holt Academy, Wrexham, Wales.

1888 (age 21–22) Teaching in London. Publishes 'The Chronic Argonauts' in *Science Schools Journal*.

1890 (age 24) Graduates from London University BSc.

1891 (age 24–25) Teaching biology for Briggs's on the Strand. Marries Isabel Wells, his cousin.

1893 (age 26–27) Separates from Isabel; elopes with Amy Catherine Robbins ('Jane'). Published *Text-Book of Biology*.

1895 (age 28–29). Divorce finalised with Isabel; HG marries Janes. Moves to Woking, Surrey. *Select Conversations with an Uncle*, *The Time Machine* and *The Wonderful Visit* (1895).

1896 (age 29–30). *The Island of Doctor Moreau* and *The Wheels of Chance*.

1897 (age 30–31). *The Plattner Story and Others*; *The Invisible Man*; *Certain Personal Matters*.

1898 (age 31–32). *The War of the Worlds*. Visits Gissing in Italy, his first trip abroad.

1899 (age 32–33). Deterioration of health. *When the Sleeper Wakes*; *Tales of Space and Time*.

© The Author(s) 2019
A. Roberts, *H G Wells*, Literary Lives, https://doi.org/10.1007/978-3-030-26421-5

1900 (age 33–34). *Love and Mr Lewisham*. Moves to Sandgate on the South Kent Coast. Health improves.

1901 (age 34–35). Birth of first son, George 'Gip' Wells. *The First Men in the Moon; Anticipations*.

1902 (age 35–36). *The Sea Lady*.

1903 (age 36–37). Birth of second son, Frank Wells. Joins Fabians. *Mankind in the Making*.

1904 (age 37–38). *The Food of the Gods*.

1905 (age 38–39). *A Modern Utopia; Kipps*.

1906 (age 39–40). Travels to the USA. *In the Days of the Comet. The Future in America*.

1907 (age 40–41). Active in Fabians. *This Misery of Boots*.

1908 (age 41–42). Leaves Fabians. *The War in the Air; New Worlds for Old; First and Last Things*.

1909 (aged 42–43). Affair with Amber Reeves, and birth of Wells and Reeves's daughter Anna. Wells and Jane move to Hampstead. *Tono-Bungay; Ann Veronica*.

1910 (age 43–44). *The History of Mr Polly*.

1911 (age 44–45). Moves to Easton Glebe, Essex. *The New Machiavelli; The Country of the Blind and Other Stories; Floor Games*.

1912 (age 45–46). Meets Rebecca West. *The Great State; Marriage*.

1913 (age 46–47). *The Passionate Friends*.

1914 (age 47–48). Birth of Anthony West, Wells's son with Rebecca West. World War I breaks out. *An Englishman Looks at the World; The World Set Free; The Wife of Sir Isaac Harman; The War and Socialism; The War That Will End War*.

1915 (age 49–49). *Boon; Bealby: A Holiday; The Research Magnificent; The Peace of the World*.

1916 (age 49–50). *What is Coming?; Mr Britling Sees It Through; The Elements of Reconstruction*.

1917 (age 50–51). Wells briefly embraces religion. *God the Invisible King; The Soul of a Bishop; War and the Future*.

1918 (age 51–52). *In the Fourth Year; Joan and Peter: The Story of an Education*. End of World War I.

1919 (age 52–53). *The Undying Fire*.

1920 (age 53–54). *The Outline of History*. Visits the USSR, meets Lenin.

1921 (age 54–55). Attends Washington Conference in the USA. *Russia in the Shadows; The Salvaging of Civilization*.

1922 (age 55–56). Stands, unsuccessfully, as Labour Party parliamentary candidate. *The Secret Places of the Heart; Washington and the Hope of Peace*.

1923 (age 56–57). Relationship with Rebecca West ends. *Men Like Gods. Socialism and the Scientific Motive.*

1924 (age 57–58). Begins relationship with Odette Keun. *The Dream; A Year of Prophesying; The Story of a Great Schoolmaster.*

1925 (age 58–59). *Christina Alberta's Father.*

1926 (age 59–60). Buys and renovates Provençal house, Lou Pidou. *The World of William Clissold.*

1927 (age 60–61). Death of Jane Wells. *Meanwhile.*

1928 (age 62–63). *Mr. Blettsworthy on Rampole Island; The Way the World is Going; The Book of Catherine Wells; The Open Conspiracy.*

1930 (age 63–64). Moves to London. *The Autocracy of Mr. Parham; The Science of Life* (with Julian S. Huxley and G. P. Wells).

1931 (age 64–65). Diagnosed as diabetic. *The Work, Wealth and Happiness of Mankind.*

1932 (age 65–66). *The Bulpington of Blup; After Democracy.*

1933 (age 66–67). *The Shape of Things to Come.*

1934 (age 67–68). *Experiment in Autobiography.*

1935 (age 68–69). *The New America: The New World.*

1936 (age 69–70). Awarded D.Litt by London University. *The Croquet Player; The Anatomy of Frustration.*

1937 (age 70–71). *Star Begotten; Brynhild; The Camford Visitation.*

1938 (age 71–72). *The Brothers; Apropos of Dolores; World Brain.*

1939 (age 72–73). *The Holy Terror; The Fate of Homo Sapiens; Travels of a Republican Radical in Search of Hot Water.*

1940 (age 73–74). *The New World Order; Babes in the Darkling Wood; All Aboard for Ararat; The Rights of Man; The Common Sense of War and Peace.*

1941 (age 74–75). *You Can't Be Too Careful.*

1942 (age 75–76). *The Conquest of Time; Modern Russian and English Revolutionaries* (with Lev Uspensky).

1943 (age 76–77). *Crux Ansata: An Indictment of the Roman Catholic Church.*

1944 (age 77–78). *'42 to '44: A Contemporary Memoir.*

1945 (age 78–79). *The Happy Turning; Mind at the End of Its Tether.*

1946 (age 79). 13 August, dies.

Bibliography

Works by H.G. Wells

1: Wells's Works

Select Conversations with an Uncle (1895)
The Time Machine (1895)
The Wonderful Visit (1895)
The Stolen Bacillus and Other Incidents (1895) [short stories]
The Island of Doctor Moreau (1896)
The Wheels of Chance (1896)
The Plattner Story and Others (1897) [short stories]
The Invisible Man (1897)
Certain Personal Matters (1897)
The War of the Worlds (1898)
When the Sleeper Wakes (1899)
Tales of Space and Time (1899) [short stories]
Love and Mr Lewisham (1900)
The First Men in the Moon (1901)
Anticipations (1901) [non-fiction]
The Sea Lady (1902)
Mankind in the Making (1903) [non-fiction]
The Food of the Gods and How It Came to Earth (1904)
A Modern Utopia (1905)
Kipps (1905)
In the Days of the Comet (1906)

© The Author(s) 2019
A. Roberts, *H G Wells*, Literary Lives, https://doi.org/10.1007/978-3-030-26421-5

The Future in America (1906) [non-fiction]
This Misery of Boots (1907) [non-fiction]
Will Socialism Destroy the Home? (1907) [non-fiction]
The War in the Air (1908)
New Worlds for Old (1908) [non-fiction]
First and Last Things (1908) [non-fiction]
Tono-Bungay (1909)
Ann Veronica (1909)
The History of Mr Polly (1910)
The Sleeper Awakes (1910) [revised edition of *When the Sleeper Wakes* (1899)]
The New Machiavelli (1911)
The Country of the Blind and Other Stories (1911)
Floor Games (1911) [non-fiction]
The Great State (1912) [non-fiction]
Marriage (1912)
Little Wars (1913) [non-fiction]
The Passionate Friends (1913)
An Englishman Looks at the World (1914) [non-fiction]
The World Set Free (1914)
The Wife of Sir Isaac Harman (1914)
The War and Socialism (1914) [non-fiction]
The War That Will End War (1914) [non-fiction]
Boon (1915)
Bealby: A Holiday (1915)
The Research Magnificent (1915)
The Peace of the World (1915) [non-fiction]
What is Coming? (1916) [non-fiction]
Mr Britling Sees It Through (1916)
The Elements of Reconstruction (1916) [non-fiction]
God the Invisible King (1917) [non-fiction]
The Soul of a Bishop (1917)
War and the Future (1917) [non-fiction]
In the Fourth Year (1918) [non-fiction]
Joan and Peter: The Story of an Education (1918)
The Undying Fire (1919)
The Outline of History (1920) [non-fiction]
Russia in the Shadows (1921) [non-fiction]
The Salvaging of Civilization (1921) [non-fiction]
The Secret Places of the Heart (1922)
Washington and the Hope of Peace (1922) [non-fiction]
Men Like Gods (1923)
Tales of Wonder (1923) [short stories]
Tales of Life and Adventure (1923) [short stories]

Socialism and the Scientific Motive (1923) [non-fiction]

The Dream (1924)

A Year of Prophesying (1925) [non-fiction]

The Story of a Great Schoolmaster: Being a Plain Account of the Life and Ideas of Sanderson of Oundle (1924) [non-fiction]

Christina Alberta's Father (1925)

The World of William Clissold (1926)

Meanwhile (1927)

Mr. Blettsworthy on Rampole Island (1928)

The Way the World is Going (1928) [non-fiction]

The Book of Catherine Wells (1928)

The Open Conspiracy (1928) [non-fiction]

The Autocracy of Mr. Parham (1930)

The Science of Life (1930) – with Julian S. Huxley and G. P. Wells [non-fiction]

The Work, Wealth and Happiness of Mankind (1931) [non-fiction]

The Bulpington of Blup (1932)

After Democracy (1932) [non-fiction]

The Shape of Things to Come (1933)

Experiment in Autobiography (1934) [non-fiction]

The New America: The New World (1935) [non-fiction]

The Croquet Player (1936)

The Anatomy of Frustration (1936) [non-fiction]

Star Begotten (1937)

Brynhild (1937)

The Camford Visitation (1937)

The Brothers (1938)

Apropos of Dolores (1938)

World Brain (1938) [non-fiction]

The Holy Terror (1939)

The Fate of Homo Sapiens (1939) [non-fiction]

Travels of a Republican Radical in Search of Hot Water (1939) [non-fiction]

The New World Order (1940) [non-fiction]

Babes in the Darkling Wood (1940)

All Aboard for Ararat (1940)

The Rights of Man (1940) [non-fiction]

The Common Sense of War and Peace (1940) [non-fiction]

You Can't Be Too Careful (1941)

The Conquest of Time (1942) [non-fiction]

Modern Russian and English Revolutionaries (1942)—with Lev Uspensky [non-fiction]

Crux Ansata: An Indictment of the Roman Catholic Church (1943) [non-fiction]

'42 to '44: A Contemporary Memoir (1944) [non-fiction]

Reshaping Man's Heritage (1944)—with J.B.S. Haldane, Julian S. Huxley [non-fiction]
The Happy Turning (1945) [non-fiction]
Mind at the End of Its Tether (1945) [non-fiction]

2. Other Works Cited

Adorno, Theodor (1951), *Minima Moralia*. Translated by E F N Jephcott; Verso, 1974.

Allen, Walter (1964) *Tradition and Dream: the English and American Novel from the Twenties to Our Time*. London: Hogarth Press.

Allen, Walter (1981). *The Short Story in English*. Oxford, Clarendon.

Arendt, Hannah (1951). *Origins of Totalitarianism*. New York, Schocken Books.

Barfoot Cedric, C. and Theo D'haen eds (1991). *Tropes of Revolution: Writers' Reaction to Real and Imagined Revolutions 1780–1980*. Amsterdam: Rodopi.

Batchelor, J.B. (1972), 'Kenneth B. Newell, Structure in Four Novels by H. G. Wells', *Modern Language Review* 67:2, 407–408.

Batchelor, John (1985). *H G Wells*. Cambridge University Press.

Bell, Duncan (2018). 'Founding the World State: H. G. Wells on Empire and the English-Speaking Peoples', *International Studies Quarterly*. 62:4, 1 December 2018, 867–879.

Belloc, Hilaire (1906). 'The Inn of the Margeride', *Hills and the Sea*. London: Methuen.

Bennet, Edward Armstrong (1967). *What Jung Really Said*. New York: Schocken Books.

Bergonzi, Bernard (1961) *The Early H.G. Wells: A Study of the Scientific Romances*. University of Toronto Press.

Bloom, Robert (1977). *Anatomies of Egotism: A Reading of the Last Novels of H. G. Wells*. Lincoln: University of Nebraska Press.

Brantlinger, Patrick and Richard Higgins (2006). 'Waste and Value: Thorstein Veblen and H. G. Wells', *Criticism*, 48:4, pp. 453–475.

Britain, Ian (1982). *Fabianism and Culture: A Study in British Socialism and the Arts*. Cambridge Univ. Press.

Bull, Malcolm, 'The End', *London Review of Books* 15:5 (11 March 1993), 23–24.

Campbell, James (1999). 'Combat Gnosticism: The Ideology of First World War Poetry Criticism', *New Literary History*, 30:1, 203–215.

Cannadine, David (2013). *The Undivided Past: History Beyond Our Differences*. Harmondsworth: Penguin.

Cheyette, Bryan (1993). *Constructions of 'the Jew' in English Literature and Society: Racial Representations, 1875–1945*. Cambridge Univ. Press.

Clapp, Susanna (1986). 'Little Men', *London Review of Books* 8:14, pp. 23–24.

Clark, Timothy (2004). 'Not Seeing the Short Story' *Oxford Literary Review* 26:8, pp. 5–30.

Clute, John and David Langford (2015). 'Sleeper Awakes', *The Encyclopedia of Science Fiction*, 3rd edition. http://www.sf-encyclopedia.com/entry/sleeper_awakes.

Coupland, Philip (2000). 'H. G. Wells's "Liberal Fascism"', *Journal of Contemporary History*, 35:4, 541–558.

Delany, Paul (2008). *George Gissing: a Life*. London: Weidenfeld and Nicholson.

Dickson, Lovat (1969). *H G Wells: His Turbulent Life and Times*. Macmillan.

Donovan, Tristan (2014). *Fizz: How Soda Shook Up the World*. Chicago Review Press.

Dowling, Linda (2014). *Hellenism and Homosexuality in Victorian Oxford*. Cornell University Press.

Ervine, St John G. (1923). *Some Impressions of My Elders*. London, Allen & Unwin.

Felber, Lynette (2002). 'Unfinished Business and Self-Memorialization: Rebecca West's Aborted Novel, *Mild Silver, Furious Gold*' *Journal of Modern Literature*, 25:2, pp. 38–49.

Foot, Michael (1995). *H G: the History of Mr Wells*. London, Doubleday.

Ford, Ford Madox (1937), *Portraits from Life: Memories and Criticism of Henry James, Joseph Conrad, Thomas Hardy, H.G. Wells, Stephen Crane, D.H. Lawrence, John Galsworthy, Ivan Turgenev, W.H. Hudson, Theodore Dreiser, A.C. Swinburne*. Boston: Houghton Mifflin Company.

Frazier, Adrian (2000). *George Moore 1852–1933*. Yale University Press.

Funnell, Warwick and Michele Chwastiak (2015). *Accounting at War: The Politics of Military Finance*. London. Routledge.

Garner, Les (1984). *Stepping Stones to Women's Liberty: Feminist Ideas in the Women's Movement 1900–1918*. Farnham. Gower/Ashgate.

Gilbert, Stuart ed. (1957). *The Letters of James Joyce, Vol. 1*. New York: Viking.

Godfrey, Emelyne (2012). *Femininity, Crime and Self-Defence in Victorian Literature and Society From Dagger-Fans to Suffragettes Authors*. Palgrave.

Hammond, John R. (1984) *The Man With a Nose and the Other Uncollected Short Stories of H G Wells*. London: Athlone Press.

Harris, Janice (1994). 'Wifely Silence and Speech in Three Marriage Novels by H. G. Wells', *Studies in the Novel*, 26:4, pp. 404–419.

Heilmann, Ann (2003). 'Revolting Men? Sexual Fears and Fantasies in Writings by Old Men, 1880–1910' *Critical Survey* 15:3, pp 56–73.

Hemingway, Ernest (1929). *A Farewell to Arms*. New York: Scribner.

Hertel, Kirsten (1997). *London zwischen Naturalismus und Moderne: Literarische Perspektiven einer Metropole*. Heidelberg, Universitätsverlag.

Higgins, Richard (2008) 'Feeling like a Clerk in H. G. Wells', *Victorian Studies* 50: 3, pp. 457–475.

Hillegas, Mark (1967). *The Future as Nightmare: H. G. Wells and the Anti-Utopians*. Oxford: Oxford University Press.

Howard, Michael (1978). *War and the Nation State*. Oxford University Press.

Hughes, David (1987). 'Desperately Mortal', *Science Fiction Studies* 14:3, 392–399.

Huxley, Aldous (1963). *Writers at Work: The Paris Review Interviews, Second Series.* New York: Viking.

Huxley, Julian (1970) *Memories.* George Allen & Unwin.

James, Simon (2012). *Maps of Utopia: H G Wells, Modernity and the End of Culture.* Oxford University Press.

Jung, Carl (1928) *The Relations Between the Ego and the Unconscious.* in Herbert Read, Michael Fordham and Gerhard Adler, eds. *Collected Works of C G Jung* (translated R. C. Hull). London: Routledge. 20 vols. 1957–1970.

Jung, Carl and Aniela Jaffé (1973), *Memories, Dreams, Reflections.* Translated from the German by Richard and Clara Winston. New York: Pantheon Books.

Kemp, Peter (1996) *H.G. Wells and the Culminating Ape: Biological Imperatives and Imaginative Obsessions.* New York: St. Martin's Press.

Kennedy, Paul (2007). *The Parliament of Man: The Past, Present, and Future of the United Nations.* New York: Random House.

Kermode, Frank (1967). *The Sense of an Ending.* Oxford: Oxford University Press.

Kerr, John (1995). 'Madnesses', *London Review of Books* 17:6 (23 March 1995), pp. 3–6.

Ketterer, David (2009). 'The "Martianized" H. G. Wells?' *Science Fiction Studies*, 36:2, pp. 327–332.

Keun, Odette (1934) 'H. G. Wells—The Player', *Time and Tide* (13–27 October), 1251–1252.

Korda, Michael (2001). *Making the List: A Cultural History of the American Bestseller.* New York Barnes & Nobel.

Kramnick, Issac and Barry Sheerman (1993). *Harold Laski: a Life on the Left.* London, Hamish Hamilton.

Kupinse, William (1999). 'Wasted Value: The Serial Logic of H. G. Wells's *Tono-Bungay*', *Novel* 33:1, pp. 51–72.

Lewis, Jane (1994) 'Intimate Relations between Men and Women: The Case of H. G. Wells and Amber Pember Reeves', *History Workshop* 37, 84–85.

Light, Alison (2007). 'Regular Terrors' *London Review of Books* 29:2, pp. 19–21.

Lockerd, Ben (2012), '"Superficial Notions of Evolution": Eliot's Critique of Evolutionary Historiography', *Religion & Literature*, 44:1 (2012), 174–180.

Lyotard, Jean-François (1979). *The Postmodern Condition: A Report on Knowledge.* Translated Geoffrey Bennington and Brian Massumi; Manchester University Press, 1984.

Mackenzie, Norman and Jean Mackenzie (1973). *The Time Traveller: the Life of H G Wells.* London: Weidenfeld.

Mallock, William Hurrell (1877). *The New Republic; or, Culture, Faith, and Philosophy in an English Country House.* London: Chatto and Windus.

McGuire, William and R.F.C. Hull, eds. (1977), *C.G. Jung Speaking: Interviews and Encounters.* Princeton University Press.

McLean, Stephen (2009). *Early Fiction of H G Wells: Fantasies of Science.* Houndmills: Palgrave.

Miller, William Ian (1993) *Humiliation and Other Essays on Honour, Social Discomfort and Violence*. Cornell University Press.

Newell, Kenneth B. (1968). *Structure in Four Novels by H. G. Wells*. The Hague: Mouton.

Nicholson, Harold (1966), *Diaries and Letters 1930–39*. London: Collins.

Niethammer Lutz (1993). *Posthistoire: Has History Come to an End?* Translated by Patrick Camiller. London, Verso.

Overy, Richard (2013). *The Bombing War: Europe 1939–45*. London: Allen Lane.

Paris, Michael (2000). *Warrior Nation: Images of War in British Popular Culture, 1850–2000*. London: Reaktion.

Parrinder, Patrick (1970). *H. G. Wells*. Edinburgh: Oliver & Boyd.

Parrinder, Patrick (1990). 'Wells's Cancelled Endings for "The Country of the Blind"', *Science Fiction Studies* 17:1, pp. 71–76.

Parrinder, Patrick (1995). *Shadows of the Future: H.G. Wells, Science Fiction and Prophecy*. Liverpool, Liverpool University Press.

Pearce, Joseph (2002). *Old Thunder: A Life of Hilaire Belloc*. London: HarperCollins.

Pedersen, Susan (2015). *The Guardians: The League of Nations and the Crisis of Empire*. Oxford University Press.

Peschel, Bill (2012). 'The "Tremendous Disliker": A L Rowse'. http://planetpeschel.com/2012/03/the-tremendous-disliker-a-l-rowse/

Phillips, Adam (1996). *Monogamy*. London: Faber.

Phillips, Adam (2006). *Side Effects*. Harmondsworth, Penguin.

Philmus, Robert and David Hughes (1975) *H. G. Wells: Early Writings in Science and Science Fiction*. Univ of California Press.

Priest, Christopher (2008). *"It" Came From Outer Space: Occasional Pieces 1973–2008*. Hastings East Sussex, Grimgrin Studio.

Ray, Gordon (1974). *H G Wells and Rebecca West*. Yale University Press.

Reynolds, David. (2013). *The Long Shadow: The Great War and the Twentieth Century*. London: Simon and Schuster.

Richardson, Dorothy (1919). *The Tunnel*, London: Duckworth.

Roemer, Kenneth M. (1976). *The Obsolete Necessity: America in Utopian Writings, 1888–1900*. Kent, OH, Kent State University Press.

Ross, William (2001) *H G Wells's World Reborn: the* Outline of History *and Its Companions*. Susquehanna University Press.

Saunders, Max (2016). '"Fusions and Interrelations": Family Memoirs of Henry James, Edmund Gosse and Others', in Adam Smyth (ed.), *A History of English Autobiography*. Cambridge University Press, 255–268.

Schlenker, Charles F. (1861) *A Collection of Temne Traditions, Fables and Proverbs*. London, Church Missionary Society.

Sherborne, Michael (2010). *H.G. Wells: Another Kind of Life*. London/Chicago Peter Owen.

Simpson, Anne (1996). 'Architects of the Erotic: H.G. Wells's "New Women"', in Cora M. Kaplan and Anne B. Simpson, eds., *Seeing Double: Revisioning Edwardian and Modernist Literature* (New York: St Martin's Press).

Smethurst, Paul (2015). *The Bicycle: Towards a Global History*. Palgrave Macmillan.

Smith, David C. (1986). *H.G. Wells: Desperately Mortal: A Biography*. New Haven: Yale University Press.

Smith, Grover ed. (1969). *Letters of Aldous Huxley*. London: Chatto & Windus.

Soddy, Raymond (1909). *The Interpretation of Radium*. London: John Murray.

Stover, Leo ed. (1996), *The Time Machine: A Critical Text of the 1895 London First Edition, with an Introduction and Appendices*. McFarland.

Stover, Leon (2000) *When the Sleeper Wakes: A Critical Text of the 1899 New York and London First Edition*. McFarland.

Suvin, Darko (1979). *Metamorphoses of Science Fiction: On the Poetics and History of a Literary Genre*. New Haven: Yale University Press.

Thorpe, Andrew (2008). *History of the British Labour Party*. Palgrave, 3rd ed.

Tredell, Nicholas (1982). *The Novels of Colin Wilson*. New York, Vision/Barnes & Noble.

Wagar, W. Warren (1998). 'Letters from Our Father', *Science Fiction Studies*, 25:3, 526–533.

Wells, George Philip ed. (1984). *H. G. Wells in Love: Postscript to an Experiment in Autobiography*. London: Faber and Faber.

West, Anthony (1984). *H G Wells: Aspects of a Life*. London: Hutchinson.

West, Rebecca (1916). *The Return of the Soldier*. London: Century Company.

West, Rebecca (1986). *Sunflower*. London: Virago.

Williams, Raymond (1970) *The English Novel from Dickens to Lawrence*. London: Hogarth Press.

Winkler, Henry (1958). *The League of Nations Movement in Great Britain 1914–1919* (Rutgers University Press).

Withers, Jeremy (2017). *The War of the Wheels, H. G. Wells and the Bicycle*, Syracuse University Press.

Wootton, Barbara (1984), 'Making Herself Disagreeable', *London Review of Books* 6: 22/23, 6 December 1984, 22–23.

Index

© The Author(s) 2019
A. Roberts, *H G Wells*, Literary Lives, https://doi.org/10.1007/978-3-030-26421-5